T0237917

Lecture Notes
in Business Information Processing   18

Series Editors

Wil van der Aalst
  Eindhoven Technical University, The Netherlands
John Mylopoulos
  University of Trento, Italy
Norman M. Sadeh
  Carnegie Mellon University, Pittsburgh, PA, USA
Michael J. Shaw
  University of Illinois, Urbana-Champaign, IL, USA
Clemens Szyperski
  Microsoft Research, Redmond, WA, USA

José Cordeiro   Slimane Hammoudi
Joaquim Filipe (Eds.)

Web Information Systems and Technologies

4th International Conference, WEBIST 2008
Funchal, Madeira, Portugal, May 4-7, 2008
Revised Selected Papers

 Springer

Volume Editors

José Cordeiro
Joaquim Filipe
Institute for Systems and Technologies of Information,
Control and Communication (INSTICC) and
Instituto Politécnico de Setúbal (IPS)
Department of Systems and Informatics
Rua do Vale de Chaves, Estefanilha, 2910-761 Setúbal, Portugal
E-mail: {jcordeir,j.filipe}@est.ips.pt

Slimane Hammoudi
ESEO
4 rue Merlet de la Boulaye - BP 30926
49009 Angers cedex 01, France
E-mail: slimane.hammoudi@eseo.fr

Library of Congress Control Number: Applied for

ACM Computing Classification (1998): H.3.5, J.1, K.3.1

ISSN   1865-1348
ISBN-10   3-642-01343-0 Springer Berlin Heidelberg New York
ISBN-13   978-3-642-01343-0 Springer Berlin Heidelberg New York

springer.com

© Springer-Verlag Berlin Heidelberg 2009
Printed in Germany

Typesetting: Camera-ready by author, data conversion by Scientific Publishing Services, Chennai, India
Printed on acid-free paper   SPIN: 12664306   06/3180   5 4 3 2 1 0

Preface

This book contains a selection of the best papers from WEBIST 2008 (the Fourth International Conference on Web Information Systems and Technologies), held in Funchal, Madeira, in 2008, organized by the Institute for Systems and Technologies of Information, Control and Communication (INSTICC), and co-sponsored by the Workflow Management Coalition (WfMC).

The purpose of the WEBIST series of conferences is to bring together researchers, engineers and practitioners interested in the technological advances and business applications of web-based information systems. The series focuses on four main topic areas, covering different aspects of web information systems, including internet technology; web interfaces and applications; society, e-business, and e-government; and e-learning.

WEBIST 2008 received 238 paper submissions from more than 40 countries on all continents. A double-blind review process was enforced, with the help of more than 200 experts from the international Program Committee, each of them specialized in one of the main conference topic areas. After reviewing, 32 papers were selected to be published and presented as full papers and 64 additional papers, describing work-in-progress, as short papers for oral presentation only. Furthermore, 58 papers were presented as posters. The full-paper acceptance ratio was 13%, and the total oral paper acceptance ratio was 40%.

Therefore, we hope that you find the papers included in this book interesting, and we trust they may represent a helpful reference in the future for all those who need to address any of the research areas mentioned above.

March 2009

José Cordeiro
Slimane Hammoudi
Joaquim Filipe

Organization

Conference Chair

Joaquim Filipe   Polytechnic Institute of Setúbal/INSTICC, Portugal

Program Co-chairs

José Cordeiro   Polytechnic Institute of Setúbal/INSTICC, Portugal

Slimane Hammoudi   E.S.E.O., France

Organizing Committee

Paulo Brito   INSTICC, Portugal
Marina Carvalho   INSTICC, Portugal
Helder Coelhas   INSTICC, Portugal
Vera Coelho   INSTICC, Portugal
Andreia Costa   INSTICC, Portugal
Bruno Encarnação   INSTICC, Portugal
Vitor Pedrosa   INSTICC, Portugal
Vera Rosário   INSTICC, Portugal

Program Committee

A.Y. Al-Zoubi, Jordan
Ajith Abraham, Norway
Jacky Akoka, France
Abdullah Alghamdi, Saudi Arabia
Rachid Anane, UK
Margherita Antona, Greece
Grigoris Antoniou, Greece
Elarbi Badidi, UAE
Matteo Baldoni, Italy
Denilson Barbosa, Canada
Cristina Baroglio, Italy
Bernhard Bauer, Germany
David Bell, UK
Orlando Belo, Portugal
Bharat Bhargava, USA

Stefan Böttcher, Germany
Paolo Bouquet, Italy
Christos Bouras, Greece
Stephane Bressan, Singapore
Amy Bruckman, USA
Maria Claudia Buzzi, Italy
Elena Calude, New Zealand
Nunzio Casalino, Italy
Maiga Chang, Canada
Evangelos Christou, Greece
Christophe Claramunt, France
Isabelle Comyn-Wattiau, France
Michel Crampes, France
Alexandra Cristea, UK
Daniel Cunliffe, UK

Pierluigi Plebani, Italy
Bhanu Prasad, USA
Joshua C.C. Pun, Hong Kong
Mimi Recker, USA
Frank Reichert, Norway
Werner Retschitzegger, Austria
Yacine Rezgui, UK
Thomas Risse, Germany
Marco Roccetti, Italy
Dumitru Roman, Austria
Danguole Rutkauskiene, Lithuania
Sourav S. Bhowmick, Singapore
Maytham Safar, Kuwait
Eduardo Sanchez, Spain
Abdolhossein Sarrafzadeh,
    New Zealand
Anthony Savidis, Greece
Vittorio Scarano, Italy
Alexander Schatten, Austria
Alexander Schill, Germany
Jochen Seitz, Germany
Tony Shan, USA
Jamshid Shanbehzadeh, Iran
Quan Z. Sheng, Australia
Keng Siau, USA
Miguel-Angel Sicilia, Spain
Marianna Sigala, Greece
Eva Söderström, Sweden
Pedro Soto-Acosta, Spain
J. Michael Spector, USA

Martin Sperka, Slovakia
Kathleen Stewart Hornsby, USA
Frank Stowell, UK
Carlo Strapparava, Italy
Eleni Stroulia, Canada
Hussein Suleman, South Africa
Aixin Sun, Singapore
Junichi Suzuki, USA
Ramayah T., Malaysia
Taro Tezuka, Japan
Dirk Thissen, Germany
Ivan Tomek, Canada
Bettina Törpel, Denmark
Arun Kumar Tripathi, Germany
Thrasyvoulos Tsiatsos, Greece
Klaus Turowski, Germany
Michail Vaitis, Greece
Christelle Vangenot, Switzerland
Athanasios Vasilakos, Greece
Jari Veijalainen, Finland
Juan D. Velasquez, Chile
Maria Esther Vidal, Venezuela
Maurizio Vincini, Italy
Viacheslav Wolfengagen, Russian Federation
Martin Wolpers, Belgium
Huahui Wu, USA
Lu Yan, UK
Sung-Ming Yen, Taiwan
Janette Young, UK
Weihua Zhuang, Canada

Auxiliary Reviewers

Solomon Behre, USA
Stephan Bloehdorn, Germany
Sebastian Blohm, Germany
Duygy Çelik, Turkey
Frank Fitzek, Norway
Andrea Forte, USA
Vittorio Fuccella, Italy
Carmine Gravino, Italy
Carlos Guerrero, Spain
Larisa Ismailova, Russia
Jan Kolter, Germany
Sergey Kosikov, Russia
Riccardo Martoglia, Italy

Jaime A. Pavlich-Mariscal, USA
Mir Mohsen Pedram, Iran
Octavian Popescu, Italy
Andreas Prinz, Norway
Claudio Schifanella, Italy
Rolf Schillinger, Germany
Francesc Sebé, Spain
Daniel Serrano, Spain
Mikael Snaprud, Norway
Agusti Solanas, Spain
George Spathoulsa, Greece
Sarita Yardi, USA
Jose Zagal, USA

Invited Speakers

Tony Shan	Bank of America, USA
Leszek Maciaszek	Macquarie University, Australia
Claudia Medeiros	UNICAMP, Brazil
Marcin Paprzycki	Systems Research Institute of the Polish Academy of Science, Poland
Rainer Unland	University of Duisburg-Essen, Germany
Klaus Pohl	University Duisburg-Essen, Germany

Table of Contents

Invited Papers

Part I: Internet Technology

Part II: Web Interfaces and Applications

Part III: Society, e-Business and e-Government

Part IV: e-Learning

Invited Papers

The Tao of SOA

Tony C. Shan

IBM, 10712 Hellebore Road, Charlotte, North Carolina 28213, U.S.A.
tonycshan@yahoo.com

Abstract. This paper describes a comprehensive framework aiming to facilitate the effective adoption and operationalization of SOA in large enterprise computing environments, which consists of the Strategy, Automation, Methodology, Patterns, Lifecycle, and Engineering (SAMPLE) aspects. The major pain points in SOA are analyzed, such as the increasing dynamics, growing integration, proliferation of techniques, more heterogeneous platforms, disparate visual notations, intricate processes, disjointed operating models, and fragmented activities of WS-* specifications. The overarching SAMPLE model is designed to provide a sophisticated integration of appropriate capabilities and knowledge to filter the inessential from the essential. In the *Strategy* aspect, a metamodel, technology architecture planning, and strategy roadmapping are presented. The *Automation* aspect deals with tools, service lifecycle, and COTS mapping. The *Methodology* aspect covers a hybrid method, SOA principles, and a methodical process. The prominent elements of the *Patterns* aspect include data caching patterns, a reference model, and open source reference implementation. The *Lifecycle* aspect contains a methodical means to mature IT systems: review, refactoring, reengineering, and rearchitecting (R4). Finally, the *Engineering* aspect evolves the traditional software engineering and systems engineering practices to the service engineering discipline. Moreover, a 10-point list of SOA guidance is introduced from a practitioner's standpoint, which gives best-practice guidelines to adopt and execute SOA practically in big organizations.

Keywords: Service-oriented, computing, framework, model, architecture, process, integration, environment, technology, development, management, roadmap, infrastructure, standards, practice, pattern, method, taxonomy, maturity, lifecycle, tool, platform, and strategy.

1 Introduction

The uniqueness of Information Technology (IT) sets itself differentiated from other traditional industries like car manufacturing in that it primarily deals with bits rather than atoms. Even though software never wears out, there has been hardly any software-intensive application in production that is 100% bug free to run eternally. What is unique is that components in information technology solutions interact in a nonlinear way. As the inherent complexity has exponentially grown in the IT architecture over the years, it has become more challenging as to how to manage the lifecycle of systems development in an effective fashion. The Standish Group published a Chaos Report [1], which showed some interesting findings about the reality of IT industry: a majority

J. Cordeiro et al. (Eds.): WEBIST 2008, LNBIP 18, pp. 3–10, 2009.

of IT projects are routinely behind schedule, over budget, not meeting user requirements, or completely canceled before being deployed to the field. A good number of
highly visible large-scale projects failed in the past few years, confirming the trouble-
some IT situation. For example, the Virtual Case File System [2] by FBI (U.S. Federal
Bureau of Investigation) had to be canceled with an estimated loss of $170 million in
2005. The U.S. Department of Homeland Security was forced to shut down the
Emerge2 program [3], which cost $229 million due to project failure in September
2006. The defect rate in the rolled-out IT systems mandates a vast amount of money in
corporate IT to be allocated not for new development, but rather for bug fixes and
patch maintenance of released applications. Service-Oriented Architecture (SOA) is
called upon to help solve the problem or at least mitigate the daunting issue.

2 Architecture Pain Points

From a systems development lifecycle (SDLC) standpoint, it becomes commonplace
that most design efforts of software-intensive systems are disjointed in silos, similar
to the phenomenon in the old tale of "The Blind Men and the Elephant." The continuous growth of the architecture complexity will make the shortcomings of the fragmented IT development practices become more visible and devastating. SOA, as a
recent revolutionary discipline, is expected by many people to entirely resolve the
prevailing issues. On the contrary, SOA is not a silver bullet to a large extent. If the
anticipation is set wrongly and the effect of SOA is misunderstood, jumping onto
SOA blindly could lead to a catastrophic failure in large-scale organizations. In the
real-world situations, the activities via SOA without forward-thinking planning, appropriate mindsets, well-defined objectives, rationalized reasoning, fact-based justification criteria, sufficient leadership support, proper organizational structure, skillful
resources, disciplined behavior changes, and effective operating models often result in
even worse outcomes than without SOA.

A complex service-oriented solution is usually constructed using a variety of products, tools, packages, libraries, standards, protocols, patterns, interfaces, and models.
It cannot be fully comprehended from a single point of view. There are generally
three key perspectives as described below:

- Business Perspective
    o   Business process model
    o   Value chain flow
    o   Business strategy priorities
    o   Business architecture

- Technology Perspective
    o   Functionality realized as processes and/or services
    o   Mapping of business process activities to service entities
    o   Modeling, notations, and taxonomy
    o   Industry sector-specific standards, e.g. ACORD, iXRetail,
        eTOM, IFW, IFX, SCOR, HL7, NHI

- Operations Perspective
  - o   Quality of services and monitoring
  - o   Enterprise service bus and integration
  - o   Service platforms and frameworks
  - o   Network and storage
  - o   Virtualization and cloud computing

The evolving complexity in a service-oriented solution magnifies some of the key challenges in the architecting practices, such as the increasing dynamics, growing integration points, disparate visual notations, fragmented WS-* specification activities, and barriers to deploy functional governance, which collectively further widen the gap of communications. As an example, a typical large-size enterprise system today deals with the composition and integration of an array of technical selections – an enterprise mashup or portal server, single sign-on, authorization services, customer applications, shared services, reusable assets, business process management, service registry/repository, service management, enterprise service bus, business activity monitoring, legacy systems, EAI, reporting, application frameworks, enterprise information integration, business intelligence, storage, infrastructure, network, quality of services, non-functional requirements, tools, etc. It has come to a consensus by many practitioners that a critical factor to the success of SOA adoption is the effectiveness of handling the complexity of the large-scale architecture as the size and number of details become hardly controllable or manageable via traditional methods.

Divide-and-conquer is a conventional tactics to cope with complexity, in an attempt to decompose the architecture to the level that is sufficiently simple to adequately address the design concerns and craft solution options in a straightforward manner. The technique of abstraction is also widely employed to construct the simplified models by hiding and filtering details that are irrelevant to the level under consideration. In general, complexity can be categorized into three types: *logical* – proof of correctness becomes very difficult, time-consuming, and impossible, *psychological* – comprehensibility to understand, and *structural* – number of elements. Various complexity metrics are available such as the graph-theoretic measure. Nevertheless, the essential complexity is irreducible as pointed out by Fred Brooks [4]. Grady Booch has a similar observation [5] – the most fruitful path of investigation ties architectural complexity to entropy, i.e., the measure of the disorganization of a system and/or the size of the state space of the system. I can "feel" that one system or implementation is more or less complex than another, but I can't empirically defend that feeling in many cases. To make the matter worse, as a program grows, its complexity increases much more than linearly [6]. In reality, architectural complexity is essentially coped with in an art format to a certain degree. Practical approaches tend to be more realistic for better analyzability in the real-world projects.

3   Comprehensive Approach

As defined in the Merriam-Webster dictionary [7], Tao is an art or skill of doing something in harmony with the essential nature of the thing. In plain English, the Tao of SOA is a methodical approach consisting of a range of better-than-ordinary means of strategizing and operationalizing SOA, making the best use of the knowledge available but with often incomplete information due to various constraints – a trait developed by experience, but not taught. The Tao of SOA is intended to help move from chaos to coherence.

A practical SOA approach is proposed, which is composed of Strategy, Automation, Methodology, Patterns, Lifecycle, and Engineering (SAMPLE). The *Strategy* aspect lays out the plans to run SOA in a controlled mode. The *Automation* aspect deals with repeatable and objective processes. The *Methodology* aspect is with regard to the disciplined ways to execute SOA. The *Patterns* aspect documents the best practices and lessons learned, to avoid reinventing the wheel and stay away from the common pitfalls. The *Lifecycle* aspect handles the end-to-end process management and governance of the SOA evolution. Finally, the *Engineering* aspect applies the science and mathematics to the design and manufacture of service-oriented solutions and products.

Figure 1 illustrates the key characteristics of each aspect in the SAMPLE model.

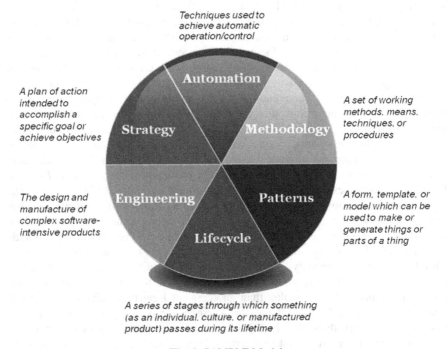

Fig. 1. SAMPLE Model

The *Strategy* aspect lays out a vision blueprint and a mission that is well-aligned with the strategic foresight. As a roadmap of technology strategy, a multi-generation plan is constructed to formulate a variety of work tracks and streams for both future and immediate SOA needs in realization of the technical capabilities. Different stakeholders often possess drastically dissimilar priorities, timelines, funding, restrictions, resources, and drivers in an organization. Techniques like SWOT are employed to analyze the portfolios thoroughly, which builds a foundation to justify the tradeoffs and drive out a balanced approach with minimum risk of failures. A key to the success of the strategic SOA planning is the separation of concerns and responsibilities. The decisions, standards, guidelines and policies must be well-communicated and vetted with appropriate parties. Proper trainings enable the project teams to retool their skillsets in a timely fashion. The strategy contents must be periodically updated as triggered by the changes of the conditions and the advancement of technologies and practices. A detailed breakdown of key activities in a sequence of time spans helps allocate appropriate resources to work on prioritized items for short-term, near-term and long-term goals.

The *Automation* aspect makes use of both commercial and open source products for various development activities in the SOA execution process. The tasks can be categorized into 3 groups: design-time, run-time and change-time, such as service versioning, modeling, testing, build/deploy, management, business activity monitoring, compliance validation, and service repository. A sophisticated service registry/repository catalogs all published services in a central location, with the service metadata specified in a consistent format. It allows for rich search capabilities by the potential service callers and manages the service-level agreements (SLA) for the consumptions at run time. In a heterogeneous environment, the interoperability of services and implementation platforms is critical to maximize the reuse of shared services. Two industry standards by WS-I – Basic Profile (BP) and Basic Security Profile (BSP) – validate the conformance. One may take advantage of advanced computing techniques to enable the transparency of service location in an autonomous on-demand fashion, via workload management, virtualization, cloud computing, self-healing, fault-tolerance, real-time optimization, and so forth. Automatic tools help facilitate the effective control and governance in the change management process.

The *Methodology* aspect addresses the SOA methods that deal with the dimensions of process, people, technology, and information. Standard notations are advocated in modeling and model transformations in round-trip engineering as a discipline in the process. The principles in the agile methods are leveraged for iterative progress in project execution. Common terminology, taxonomy and ontology are defined to facilitate effective communications among the stakeholders of different backgrounds in a semantic fashion. Key indicators and success factors are specified to quantify the progress and growth in terms of the maturity of the SOA program. Service governance practices are enforced to properly manage the changes and issues related to culture, organization, and behavior, with roles and responsibilities clearly identified in a RACI matrix. In addition, streamlined methods in a lightweight format are applied to medium- and small-size projects, to promote the pragmatism and practicality for agility and responsiveness.

The *Patterns* aspect captures and documents the reusable solutions for service, process, asset, and product development. Patterns can be classified into different categories: technical, engineering, solution, implementation, deployment, network, foundation, and infrastructure. Reference models are built as an abstract SOA pattern, which are based upon to create SOA stacks. SOA frameworks are constructed accordingly, where individual capabilities are consequently realized by runtime products to formulate a combination of SOA logical model and physical model, called SOAstructure. Traditional patterns such as GoF design patterns, Java EE patterns, integration patterns, analysis patterns, security patterns, and network patterns are aggregated and adapted to be incorporated in the SOA pattern library. Furthermore, antipatterns are collected to record known pitfalls and lessons learned in the project executions as well.

The *Lifecycle* aspect is about the end-to-end sustainable management in the course of solutions development. A practical process is in use to propel the incremental optimization in maturity. The process comprises review, refactoring, reengineering, and rearchitecting (R4). In the review stage, a comprehensive technical assessment is conducted, which includes the detailed analysis of the business process, systems, applications, data, architecture, technology selections, security, infrastructure, quality of services, testing, integration, systems management, build, deployment, configuration management, operations, and support. Other aspects worth in-depth investigations are tool choices, methodology, process, defect tracking, change control, and code quality metrics. The foremost objective is to identify the pain points and gaps. The outcome of the review activities sets the directions for the next-step course of actions. Refactoring is useful for application internal reorganization, suitable for those systems that do not need a major overhaul, including reorganizing the internal structure, restructuring codes, renaming classes and methods, extracting code segments to become a separate method, consolidating methods, decomposing classes and methods, improving the program design, enhancing the maintainability, eliminating bad-practice codes, moving features between objects, simplifying conditional expressions, dealing with generalization, and maximizing reuse. In reengineering of the business process, software, data, and application, part of a system is reconstituted to a new form, by means of revamping the existing systems and exploiting the most appropriate technologies. Various techniques are utilized to plan, model, integrate and migrate the systems consolidation and decomposition as well as reverse engineering when necessary. In the scenarios where the systems are largely outdated, a fundamental redesign becomes a mandate to rearchitect the solutions. Key facets in the rearchitecting efforts are the business process analysis, conceptual modeling, core services, aggregated services, process workflow, access control, process orchestration, business integration, logical architecture, data architecture, physical architecture, system topology, communications, integration, service interface, application frameworks, and component design.

The *Engineering* aspect evolves the traditional software engineering and systems engineering practices to the service engineering discipline. A service engineering process can be broken down to a series of stages: portfolio assessment, service analysis, service modeling, service realization, service assembly, and service management. Along these stages, three main streams are defined, namely, inputs, activities, and artifacts. This forms a 2-D matrix with each cell detailing the elements for a particular work stage in a specific stream. For example, the key inputs to the service analysis are business use cases, applications suitable for service mining, business trust requirement, business rules, business policies, enterprise taxonomy, business patterns, and service meta-model. The major activities in the service analysis include the domain decomposition, business service identification, mapping of application capabilities to services, impedance rationalization/consolidation, service granularity definition, service classification, service matching, service rationalization, and service consolidation. The core artifacts consists of the deliverables of business services, application services, choreography/orchestration, composition, atomic services, shared services, domain services, portfolio/channel services, infrastructure services, and utility services.

4 Implementation Guide

To efficiently implement the SAMPLE framework in real-life SOA projects, a 10-point list of best practice guidelines is defined as follows.

1. **Start small:** take baby steps for adoption and implementation with low hanging fruits, so the effect and impact can be visible and be promptly evaluated in a short term
2. **Openness:** adopt or create an open structure based on standards, so as to eliminate the product or platform lock-ins
3. **Asynchrony:** promote loose-coupling at different levels and leverage event-driven SOA
4. **Web:** use Web as a platform and migrate to social and collaborative computing with richer user experience via Web X.0, e.g. Wiki, RIA, mashups, and semantic web
5. **Iteration:** enable incremental buildouts via phases in a lifecycle
6. **Simplification:** keep it simple and straightforward (KISS) in the portfolio and infrastructure rationalization
7. **Decisioning:** establish a sophisticated governance model for objective rationale assessment and tradeoff justification without bias
8. **Operationalization:** build a disciplined process for execution and concept localization
9. **Multiplicity:** make full use of multi-dimensional views with multiple metrics and metadata for effective business process monitoring and management
10. **Strategy:** set a winning plan for strategization and develop an overarching SOA framework

As a case study, a pragmatic SOA adoption and execution in a financial institution is articulated in a separate writing [8].

5 Conclusions

As the complexity, size and number of details in IT solutions have been growing at an unprecedented pace, which is keeping going even faster, an adaptive approach is in need to effectively manage the architecting practices in a disciplined manner. The pragmatic approach defined in this paper comprises six aspects – Strategy, Automation, Methodology, Patterns, Lifecycle, and Engineering (SAMPLE). The key challenges in SOA are analyzed, such as the increasing integration, growing dynamics, disparate visual notations, fragmented WS-* specification activities, and barriers to deploy useful governance, collectively resulting in a wider gap of communications. The SAMPLE model is an overarching model aiming to enable a mature integration of proper knowledge and capabilities to filter the inessential from the essential. The *Strategy* aspect addresses the strategy metamodel, technology architecture planning, and strategy roadmapping. The *Automation* aspect covers tools, service lifecycle, and COTS mapping. In the *Methodology* aspect, a hybrid method, SOA philosophy, and a SOA framework are the key components. The prominent elements of the *Patterns* aspect are data caching patterns, reference model, and open source reference implementation. The *Lifecycle* aspect defines a methodical means to mature the systems: review, refactoring, reengineering, and rearchitecting (R4). Last but not least, the *Engineering* aspect deals with the service engineering discipline, which leverages the software engineering and systems engineering practices. Moreover, a 10-point list of SOA guidelines is specified from a practitioner's viewpoint, which provides best-practice guidance to adopt and execute SOA pragmatically in large enterprise computing environments.

References

1. The Standish Group (2006), http://www.standishgroup.com
2. Goldstein, H.: Who Killed the Virtual Case File? IEEE Spectrum (September 2005)
3. Federal Computer Week (2006),
   http://www.fcw.com/online/news/102253-1.html
4. Brooks, F.P.: No Silver Bullet - essence and accident in software Engineering. In: Proceedings of the IFIP Tenth World Computing Conference, pp. 1069–1076 (1986)
5. Booch, G.: Blog (Handbook of Software Architecture) (2007),
   http://booch.com/architecture/blog.jsp?archive=2007-02.html
6. Robinson, J.A.: Software Design for Engineers and Scientists. Newnes, Boston (2004)
7. The Merriam-Webster Online Dictionary (2008),
   http://www.merriam-webster.com
8. Shan, T.C., Hua, W.: A Service-Oriented Solution Framework for Internet Banking. International Journal of Web Services Research 3(1), 29–48 (2006)

Architecture-Centric Software Quality Management

Leszek A. Maciaszek

Macquarie University, Department of Computing, NSW 2109, Sydney, Australia
leszek@ics.mq.edu.au

Abstract. Software quality is a multi-faceted concept defined using different attributes and models. From all various quality requirements, the quality of adaptiveness is by far most critical. Based on this assumption, this paper offers an architecture-centric approach to production of measurably-adaptive systems. The paper uses the PCBMER (Presentation, Controller, Bean, Mediator, Entity, and Resource) meta-architecture to demonstrate how complexity of a software solution can be measured and kept under control in standalone applications. Meta-architectural extensions aimed at managing quality in integration development projects are also introduced. The DSM (Design Structure Matrix) method is used to explain our approach to measure the quality. The discussion is conducted against the background of the holonic approach to science (as the middle-ground between holism and reductionism).

Keywords: Software systems, software quality, software architecture, emergence, complexity, adaptiveness, networks, holarchies, PCBMER, DSM.

1 Introduction

Barry Boehm identifies the main challenges of 21st-century software engineers as: increasingly rapid change, uncertainty and emergence, dependability, diversity, and interdependence [3]. This list of challenges is consistent with observations of other visionaries, such as Rodney Brooks [5]. Jeannette Wing [20] summarizes these challenges in the question: (How) can we build complex systems simply?

Understandably, the answers are not easy. It is obvious, however, that we have to look for answers in software quality management. Quality eludes software engineers. Following other visionaries, such as Grady Booch [4], we argue for the architecture-first approach to software production.

The three main keywords of this paper are: software, quality, and architecture. These three concepts have meanings going beyond computing and information systems. It is therefore important, in the interest of scientific rigor, to define these terms and to structure the paper around them. Accordingly, the paper focuses on these three notions and hopefully provides at least partial answer to Jeannette Wing's question.

2 Software Systems

A *system* is typically defined as "a complex whole the functioning of which depends on its parts and the interactions between those parts." [11, p.3]. This definition is

J. Cordeiro et al. (Eds.): WEBIST 2008, LNBIP 18, pp. 11–26, 2009.
© Springer-Verlag Berlin Heidelberg 2009

unassuming about the scientific methods of studying systems. The following additional characteristic places the system notion in the realm of *holism* as an approach to science – a system is "an integrated whole whose properties cannot be reduced to those of its parts." [7, p.26].

Holism centers on the Aristotelian observation that the whole is greater than the sum of the parts. This observation emphasizes *emergent*, rather than *resultant*, properties in systems. *Emergence* [7] is seen as the arising of quantitative changes and novel structures and behaviors during the process of qualitative changes and self-organization in complex systems. Interestingly enough, *reductionism* (while on the opposite end of scientific investigation) also embraces emergence (albeit in its weaker form) to explain biological evolution and complexity. Reductionists explain arising of new properties in systems in terms of interactions between parts. By contrast, or rather in addition, holists explain new properties (also) as a result of interactions between the whole and its environment.

In this paper and elsewhere [e.g. 16], we follow the middle-ground *holonic* approach to the theory of complex systems. Arthur Koestler's notion of *holon* is an object that is both a whole and a part [12]. It has an integrative tendency to function as part of the larger whole, and a self assertive tendency to preserve its individual autonomy. A complex system is then a stratified (arranged in layers) set of holons (a *holarchy*) able to interact with holons in neighbouring layers and with the environment (or holons in other systems).

While these definitions arise mostly from studies of biological systems, human-made systems need to be subjected to similar studies in order to understand their complexity and evolution. Before we elaborate on this point in later sections, let us categorize the systems of interest to our scientific investigation. Fig. 1 illustrates that software system is part of information system, which in turn is part of enterprise system, and an enterprise system - and therefore also software and information systems - function within an environment.

Software system is understood here as a computerized solution to a business problem. It is a pre-programmed application that executes on a computer or a network of computers. The human user interacts with the software system to perform business processes and tasks.

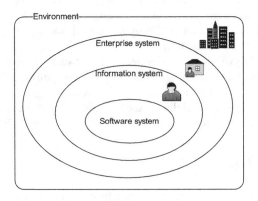

Fig. 1. Kinds of systems

An explicit human icon in Fig. 1 symbolizes that the user interacts with software and that *information system* is a social system in which some information is processed manually and which includes people, procedures, communications, decision making, business rules, internal and external business conditions, etc.

The human icon superimposed on the image of a building symbolizes that *enterprise system* functions within an organization created under relevant laws for a business endeavour. An enterprise is a networked entity and its information systems are typically integrated with its customers, suppliers and other business partners. Such integration involves information systems of the partners and makes use of the Internet and other networks. The image of the city within the *environment* symbolizes integration and interoperability between enterprise systems.

Although the notions of quality and architecture can be, and frequently are, discussed in the context of information and enterprise systems, we take here a more humble viewpoint and relate rather narrowly to software systems. Fig. 2 is a UML class diagram showing categories of software systems relevant to the paper's subject. The classification takes the software development perspective and emphasizes the dominance of integration development in contemporary software production. Most typically, new applications are developed by "value-added" integration of existing applications and data sources.

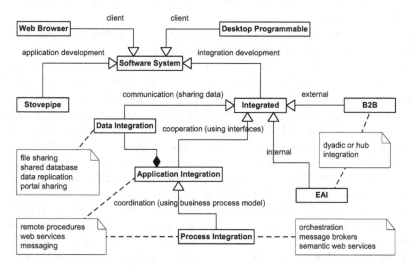

Fig. 2. Classification of software systems

Classification in Fig.2 takes a client/server viewpoint and recognizes pervasiveness of distributed systems. Most modern systems are accessible via a *Web browser* as the client interface. Systems that are programmed and execute exclusively on *desktops* are rare.

From the vantage point of software development, we recognize stovepipe and integrated systems. A *stovepipe* system represents a standalone application, most-likely developed in-house and remaining under the complete control of the development team and IT department.

An *integrated* system may be the result of integrating two or more stovepipe applications. An internal integration is called *EAI* (Enterprise Application Integration). An external integration reaching to business partners is called *B2B* (Business-to-Business). EAI and B2B systems can result from *dyadic* (point-to-point integration) or *hub* integration projects (in which many applications interoperate via a mediating layer of software) [14].

From an organizational standpoint, integration has the "3C" objective – to improve *communication* (via data sharing), *cooperation* (via interoperation at the level of application interfaces), and *coordination* (via orchestration of business processes) [19]. The corresponding categories of integration are called: *data integration*, *application integration* and *process integration*. The comments in UML notes in Fig. 2 identify the main technologies in support of these three kinds of integration [14].

3 Quality and Complexity

Information systems are built to satisfy user *requirements*. We distinguish between functional and non-functional requirements. *Functional requirements* define the desired behavior of a system, i.e. to deliver some output in response to the provided input. *Non-functional requirements* define the desired constraints on the overall characteristics of a system.

Most commonly, *software quality* is defined by a set of attributes related to system's non-functional requirements. Taking another perspective, software quality attributes can be describing a software *product* (e.g. usability) or a software *process* (e.g. productivity) or both (e.g. robustness). This paper concentrates on the product quality, but it defines also a process required to build quality into the product.

Fig.3 is a UML class diagram that classifies product quality requirements. The diagram represents the standard ISO 9126 quality model [2], [10]. The quality requirements placed in the circle refer to the quality of *adaptiveness* (not directly in the ISO standard), which we consider to be the most critical of all requirements.

"An *adaptive system* has the ability to change to suit different conditions; the ability to continue into the future by meeting existing expectations (requirements) and by adjusting to accommodate any new and changing requirements." [16, p.34]. Note that the three constituent sub-qualities of adaptiveness exist as ISO requirements (scalability corresponds to adaptability in the ISO standard). The definitions of quality requirements in Fig. 3 are readily available in software engineering books, manuals or standards.

Systems are complex by their very definition. But what do we really mean by complexity? While there have been many attempts to define complexity in absolute terms, we tend to agree with propositions that '*complex*' is a primitive and relative term, which can only be given a contextual definition. As such, 'complex' can only be understood by its relation to its specific contrary notion of 'simple'. There are many primitive concepts like that, e.g. 'part' as contrary to 'whole', 'same' as the opposite of 'different' [1].

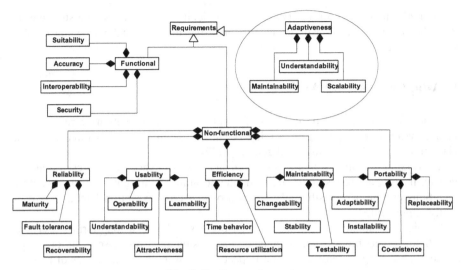

Fig. 3. Quality requirements

The complexity of software systems is *in the wires* – in the linkages and communication paths between software objects. The "wires" create *dependencies* between distributed objects that may be difficult to understand and manage (a software object A depends on an object B, if a change in B necessitates a change in A).

Elsewhere [e.g. 14] we have argued that software complexity can be seen as the other side of the software adaptiveness coin. Furthermore we argue that the task of building quality into software is almost synonymous with the task of making it adaptive. All other software qualities dwarf into insignificance unless the system is adaptive, i.e. it has the ability to change to suit shifting conditions and new requirements.

Software systems need to be viewed as adaptive complex systems. By calling such systems 'adaptive complex', we emphasize that software systems are complex by definition and that our responsibility is to make them adaptive. Building quality into such systems is an undertaking in complexity management.

Quality management is predicated on the expectation that qualities can be measured. It turns out, however, that most *external product qualities* do not have obvious direct metrics. They need to be measured indirectly using criteria that relate to *internal product attributes*. Internal attributes describe the structural properties of software, such as control and data flow structures [9].

Moreover, in the context of quality management, internal attributes are available for measurement early in the lifecycle when the product is being built, and not only when the product is complete. This relates to the known distinction between quality assurance and quality control [17]. *Quality assurance* is about a priori (deductive) building quality into the software, whereas *quality control* is about a posteriori (inductive) verification and validation of quality.

Because internal product attributes describe the structural properties of software, the metrics used to measure them are frequently called *complexity metrics*. Intuitively, the lower the complexity of the software system, the better chance to satisfy non-functional requirements and achieve desired values of external product attributes.

Accordingly, it is sometimes hoped that a complexity metric (if a single such metric could be defined) can constitute a comprehensive measure underlying the overall software quality.

4 Adaptiveness and Architecture

To understand the various dimensions of adaptiveness (or adaptation), a reference to natural systems is proper again. Living organisms seem to possess three levels of adaptation: reversible, somatic, and geno-typic [7].

A *reversible* adaptation is a temporal change due to a short-term stress on an organism. In software terms, any "stress' on the program resulting in error or exception conditions can be a reversible adaptation provided error/exception handling is diligently implemented.

A *somatic* adaptation is a change in an organism due to a long-term stress. Although still reversible, a somatic change is a physiological response of an organism aimed at absorbing the environmental impact. In software terms, all forms of maintenance (including 'perfective maintenance') can be seen as somatic adaptations.

A *geno-typic* adaptation refers to the change in the genetic makeup of an organism. Such a change is irreversible within the lifetime of an organism. It is a change to the lowest levels of a holarchy and to the most 'stable' holons – cells, organelles, molecules. In software terms, a re-design and re-implementation of the system reaching to its smallest components while retaining its architectural backbone can be considered a form of the geno-typic adaptation.

Our notion of adaptiveness is rooted in and emerges from the architectural framework (*meta-architecture*) used to design and implement the system. The architectural design itself must conform to its meta-architecture to ensure the quality of adaptiveness in any compliant complex system. Meta-architecture determines the layers of the (necessary) hierarchical structure in a complex system and specifies allowed dependencies between and inside the layers.

The superimposition of architectural thought on a software system has an important and desirable effect of limiting and controlling emergent properties in the system [16]. While we can accept that in natural systems emergence has elements of mystery and magic [8], we have to acknowledge the deterministic nature of software as well as acknowledge that enterprises operate within the context of prescribed business rules. Notwithstanding claims from scientific quarters dealing with multi-agent systems, semantic web, etc., software cannot adapt by itself to (any major) changes in business rules and environment. However, architecturally-sound software can be adapted through the processes of re-design and re-programming.

There are many meta-architectures that in principle can support the quality of adaptiveness. However, most meta-architectures are undefined for that purpose. To be useful, the meta-architecture must classify possible dependencies according to their ripple effect, i.e. adverse chain reactions on client objects once a supplier object is modified in any way. It must determine metrics to compute cumulative dependencies for particular designs in order to be able to select a design that minimizes dependencies. It must then offer guidelines, principles and patterns, which assist system developers in their quest to adhere to the architectural design while not restricting their intellectual freedom too much [17].

According to the traditional notion of a complex system, the complexity is attributed to the collective interactions between components. Many complex-systems scientists view such systems as *networks* of intercommunicating elements. These are seen as nonlinear dynamical systems [13], [18].

Fig. 4 shows the basic properties of a system understood as a network of intercommunicating elements. It can be easily imagined that the number of communication paths in a network is likely to grow exponentially with the addition of new elements. Moreover, the cycles result in an increased intractability.

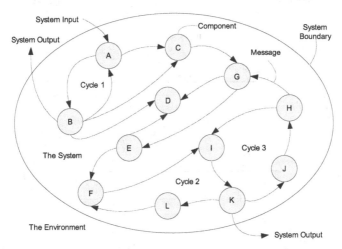

Fig. 4. System as a network

A network is a complex structure that can very quickly grow unmanageable. Like in organizational communications management, we need some form of a hierarchical structure. A *hierarchy* is a system of ranking with some elements superior to others. Also, a hierarchy is a bidirectional communication method that can result in circular dependencies (*cycles*).

It turns out that both these properties of a hierarchy are questionable. Ranking defies the object-oriented paradigm of building systems that assumes a uniform distribution of intelligence among objects. Cycles result in unnecessary complexity and maintenance problems [17].

As discussed earlier, the most complex (and adaptive) systems that we know - biological systems - are neither networks nor strict hierarchies. They can be seen as *holarchies* [12] - special forms of stratified hierarchies without any traces of ranking between elements (holons) and without cycles.

The stratified layers in a holarchy have a degree of autonomy that enables them to adapt to new circumstances and to changes in the environment. The upper layers depend on the lower layers for services but not vice versa. All communication that represents requests for services is downward – typically by means of *message passing* (i.e. messages requesting services).

Lower layers inform of its state changes by publishing new *events* to the subscribers, possibly in the upper layers. Subscribers can then request services (i.e. information that triggered events) from publishers. As a result, upper communication is only by announcing event changes and the nature of these changes is discovered in the downward message passing. This also eliminates cycles of message invocations between layers. The same strategy can be employed to eliminate cycles within layers. The resulting holonic structure (a holarchy) is visualized in Fig. 5.

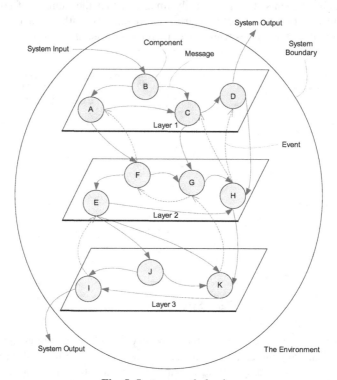

Fig. 5. System as a holarchy

To reiterate, the holonic view of the world forms a middle-ground between reductionism and holism and the holonic structures form a middle-ground between network and hierarchic structures. The stratified order of holonic layers resembles a hierarchy of layers and allows flat networks within layers, but it is different from both. The stratified order is not about rigid transfer of control or about free interconnectedness of nodes, but it is rather about the self-organization of complexity and adaptation.

We believe that a holonic (holarchical) meta-architecture is the sine qua non of any adaptive complex software system. Our holonic *meta-architecture* is known as *PCBMER*. It consists of six layers – Presentation, Controller, Bean, Mediator, Entity, and Resource. Additionally, the PCBMER meta-architecture has always provided (in all its historical forms) a special horizontal layer called Acquaintance [17]. Acquaintance consists exclusively of interfaces. The resulting meta-architecture is called PCBMER-A. Fig. 6 sketches the main properties of PCBMER.

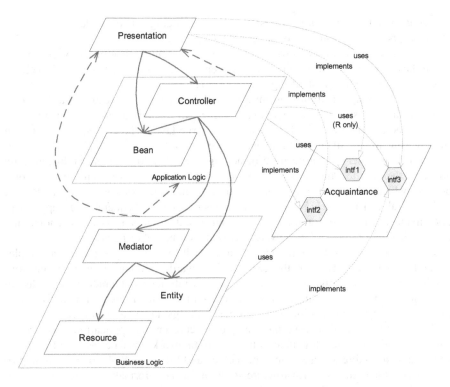

Fig. 6. PCBMER-A meta-architecture

The PCBMER meta-architecture is a structure of architectural layers as normally expected in business information systems. Presentation represents GUI (graphical user interface) in Web browsers. Controller consists of GUI logic drivers and manages Bean value objects rendered in the GUI. Together these two layers represent application logic and are deployed in a Web server.

Mediator takes care of business processes and transactions as well as any constraints expressed in business rules. It manages Entity business objects loaded from data sources or created by the application. The tasks of connecting to data sources and loading/unloading business objects belong to Resource. Together these three layers represent business logic and are deployed in an application server.

The main benefit of the PCBMER meta-architecture lies in the reduction and visibility of object *dependencies*. Upper layers depend only on lower layers. This means that changes in higher layers do not affect lower layers (except for possible changes of observers (subscribers) of events published in lower layers).

Changes in lower layers can be traced back along dependencies to higher layers. However, because downward dependencies are expected to be using *interfaces*, many such changes to concrete objects in lower layers will not propagate up. Moreover, some changes in lower layers will be entirely internal to these layers.

Because of the well-known maintenance and scalability problems of implementation inheritance, *generalization* relationships are not allowed between layers. Moreover, *aggregation* and *association* relationships are not encouraged between layers (except to interfaces) because of a strong coupling that they create.

By contrast, there are no obvious restrictions on communication between objects within layers. Cyclic relationships are an exception. Developers are required to eliminate cycles using appropriate design patterns [17].

Relatively weak constraints on intra-layer dependencies can result in a deterioration of adaptiveness when the layers grow large. An obvious solution to this problem seems to be the creation of sub-layers for any large layer. The consequences of such sub-layering are not all clear and demand more research.

Acquaintance serves the purpose of adding flexibility to the meta-architecture by allowing the architect/developer to establish communication between any two components which otherwise could not directly communicate because of the PCBMER architectural constraints [15]. Two main constraints that Acquaintance supports to circumvent are upward communication when event processing is not a choice and communication (downward or upward) between non-neighboring layers.

In the case of upward communication, a lower layer would use an interface implemented in a higher layer. In the case of downward communication between non-neighboring layers, a higher layer would use an interface implemented in a distant lower layer (in practice this means communication from Presentation to Business Logic layers or communication from Application Logic layers to Resource).

Acquaintance can also serve the purpose of representing application *frameworks*, which provide generic pluggable solutions. Frameworks can be confined to point solutions (addressing a single concern, such as an O/R (object/relational) mapping or can provide the complete infrastructure solution for the information system (e.g. Oracle ADF (Application Development Framework), Spring, Apache Beehive). In the latter case, the framework defines also the meta-architecture and effectively replaces non-framework meta-architectures, such as PCBMER-A.

5 Quantifying Quality

A meta-architecture with the adaptiveness property is a necessary but not sufficient condition for the process of building quality into software systems. A meta-architecture is a *strategic* decision that requires enforcement through tactical and operational undertakings.

On the *tactical* dimension, the meta-architecture has to be reinforced by detailed recommendations based on sound design and implementation patterns and principles. [17]. It also requires quantification by means of metrics that can express the adaptiveness quality of an architectural design and its conformance to the meta-architecture.

On the *operational* dimension, there is a need of constant monitoring to ensure that the implemented system remains adaptive. To this aim, reverse-engineering practices have to be embraced so that any changes to the implementation can be validated against the meta-architecture and measured to ascertain the adaptiveness quality.

In our past work, we have introduced various complexity/adaptiveness metrics. We have attempted to capture the adaptiveness quality in a single measure called *CCD* (Cumulative Class Dependency) or *COD* (Cumulative Object Dependency) [e.g. 16]. We have done so in defiance of suggestions that a single-valued measure of software quality is doomed to failure because of diversity of quality attributes [e.g. 8]. To counteract this problem, our metrics assume an overriding significance of the adaptiveness quality and measure the quality of a solution based with regard to the adherence to the meta-architecture and aimed at minimization of dependencies between software elements.

In this paper, rather than presenting again our formulas for complexity/adaptiveness, we use a systems engineering method of the *DSM* (Design Structure Matrix) [6] to explain our approach to quantifying quality. DSM enables displaying dependencies between software elements in a compact and analytically useful tabular format.

DSM is a square matrix with identical row and column labels denoting software elements. Reading across a row denotes provision of services (method executions, event notifications, etc.) that the element performs on behalf of other elements in that row. Therefore, reading down the column reveals dependencies from the element to other elements in that column.

Fig. 7 and 8 show two DSMs that refer to software elements in Fig. 5. Fig. 7 captures intra-layer dependencies and Fig.8 inter-layer dependencies. The two matrices could be easily combined in one matrix but they are separated here for explanation purposes.

Letters "m" and "e" refer to message and event dependencies, respectively. For example, in Fig. 7, the "m" in row F and column A means that F provides a method execution service to A. Thus A depends on F. The "e" in row A and column F means that A provides a subscription service for events published by F. Thus F depends on A for delivery/placement of events (so that A can subsequently take some action (such as invoking a method on F) or no action at all). Recall from the earlier discussion (but nevertheless arguably) that we do not consider event notifications to subscribers as dependencies that increase complexity or lower adaptiveness of the solution.

Fig. 7 represents *inter-layer dependencies* shown in Fig. 5. All downward dependencies in Fig. 5 signify message passing (calls to methods) to concrete classes – hence letter "m" in Fig. 7 for such dependencies. Because all such dependencies are downward, they appear to the left of the diagonal in the DSM. All upward 'dependencies' in Fig. 5 are events to subscribers – hence the use of letter "e" in Fig. 7. Because all event notifications are upward in Fig. 5 (in general, downward notifications are also allowed), they appear to the right of the diagonal in the DSM.

												P R O V I D E
6	A	B	C	D	E	F	G	H	I	J	K	E
A	1					e						P
B		0										E
C			1					e				N
D				1				e				D
E					2				e			
F	m					0						
G			m				0				e	
H				m				1				
I									0			
J				m						0		
K				m			m				0	

Fig. 7. DSM for inter-layer dependencies

Layer		11	B	A	C	D	F	E	G	H	J	K	I
	B	2											
L1	A	m	1										
	C	m	m	1									
	D			m	0								
	F					2		e					
L2	E					m	1						
	G						m	1					
	H					m		m	0				
	J									2			
L3	K									m	1		
	I									m	m	0	

Fig. 8. DSM for intra-layer dependencies

The numbers in the cells along the diagonal represent the total number of dependencies from a class in the column to all other classes in the neighboring lower layer. The number in the left upper corner of the matrix is the sum of all dependencies on the diagonal. So, the cumulative number of inter-layer dependencies is 6.

Fig. 8 represents *intra-layer dependencies* for all layers shown in Fig. 5. For large systems, a separate DSM could be constructed for each layer. Because dependencies within layers are also acyclic, it should be possible to visualize all message dependencies to the left of the diagonal. To achieve this, the elements within layers have been reordered.

Like in Fig. 7, the numbers in the cells along the diagonal in Fig. 8 represent the total number of dependencies from a class in the column to all other classes in the layer. The number in the left upper corner of the matrix is the sum of all dependencies on the diagonal. So, the cumulative number of intra-layer dependencies is 11. Together the number of dependencies in the system in Fig. 5 is 17.

The DSM model can be used to calculate the COD/CCD in the system. Let the PCBMER layers be l_1, l_2 ... l_n. For any layer l_i, let:

- $s(l_i)$ be the number of objects in l_i
- l_i' be the number of parents of l_i
- $p_j(l_i)$ be the jth parent of l_i

Then, the cumulative object dependency *COD* for a PCBMER holarchy as in Fig. 6 is calculated according to Equation 1 [16]:

$$_{PCBMER}COD = \sum_{i=1}^{n} \frac{s(l_i) * (s(l_i) - 1)}{2} + \sum_{i=1}^{n} \sum_{j=1}^{l_i'} (s(l_i) * s(p_j(l_i))) \tag{1}$$

The COD represents the complexity of the system expressed as the total number of dependencies between objects in the system. The value of the COD metric is in comparing alternative designs for the system. A design with lower COD means lower complexity and higher adaptiveness of the system. Depending on the purpose, the notion of 'object' could mean concrete or abstract class, interface, component, service, package, subsystem, etc.

In general, the DSM model and the COD metric can and should be extended to capture the whole spectrum of dependencies in modern software systems. Apart from message passing and event notifications, dependencies are due to object instantiations, delegation, forwarding, interface inheritance, implementation inheritance, service composition, etc. Different categories of dependencies have different impact on the complexity/adaptiveness quality. The impact should be reflected in the COD calculation by assigning different weights to various dependencies.

The discussion so far has been based on a quite radical assumption that developers of software systems have complete control over applications under development. However, this can only be true when developing internal stovepipe applications with inputs and outputs within the enterprise. This is not the way modern networked enterprises operate. Systems are built by integrating applications and services and *integration* projects link enterprises with customers, suppliers, business partners, and even business competitors.

Building adaptiveness quality into stovepipe applications is hard enough. How to build quality into integrated applications is a huge challenge facing the research community and the industry alike.

In [14] we identified main imperatives for building adaptiveness into solutions resulting from integration projects. We proposed some extensions to the PCBMER meta-architecture and we identified some helpful software engineering practices and technologies. However, the most important question remains unanswered – how to make our applications immune (and therefore adaptive) to changes in services and applications that we integrate with and which are beyond our control?

Answering this question must assume a degree of trust. Integration on any system level, be it enterprise or particular software solution (Fig.1), makes sense only if we trust that the services that we request will be provided. In fact, even the stovepipe applications are integrated with external software, such as code libraries, application frameworks, databases, etc. This integration is trouble-free (most of the time) because we trust (and assume) that any changes to the external software will be upward-compatible with our applications. Similar level of trust, but with regard to software of business partners, must be assumed in B2B integration based on communication or/and cooperation or/and coordination (Fig. 2).

Once we accept that business partners are trustworthy, we need to ensure the quality of adaptiveness on our end of the integrated system. This means, in practical terms, that changes to services we require from our partners and to services we provide to them will be assimilated by our architectural framework. While detailed solutions will differ depending on the integration scope (data, application, or process scope) (Fig. 2), the instrumentation technology will invariably involve encapsulation by means of *provided and required interfaces* [17].

In integration projects, the Acquaintance layer (Fig. 6) represents *required interfaces* (i.e. interfaces to systems or services that our system needs to communicate with) and *provided interfaces* (i.e. implemented by the external systems or services). In general, there may be many containers of Acquaintance interfaces. They could be implemented as, for example, Java packages. A package could contain only required interfaces, or only provided interfaces, or could be connecting just two business partners in dyadic integration, or could represent an integration hub.

Interestingly, but not unexpectedly, the horizontal integration facility provided by Acquaintance interfaces has its corresponding notion in Koestler's holarchies. Koestler used the term *arborization* to emphasize that holarchies are vertical structures. However, these vertical structures are not isolated but entwined with other vertical structures. To emphasize this entwining, Koestler used the term *reticulation* for horizontal network formations between holarchies. Without reticulation, each holarchy would be isolated, and there would be no *integration* of functions. Clearly, any system integration project can be seen as a reticulation process between holarchic structures.

6 Conclusions

The main research results presented in this paper have been successfully validated with regard to *stovepipe* (standalone) systems in numerous experiments, case studies, and (most significantly) on industrial projects (such as referred to in [17]). The ideas with regard to *integration* projects demand further research before they reach the closure sufficient for industrial and other validation.

The difficulty with integrated systems lies not merely in software engineering issues but goes to the core of our architecture-centric approach. The imposition of architectural design on software production makes strong business and technology assumptions. The business assumption is that all partners of an integrated solution are prepared to share data, capacity information, and business processes in the integrated supply chain or vertical market. The technology assumption is that an integrated solution can withstand failures or unexpected changes in the software components and services remaining beyond the control of the enterprise using the solution.

These business and technology factors clearly limit our ability to produce architecture-driven highly adaptive integrated systems. In our research we try to identify these limits and we look for ideas and solutions to overcome them. Fortunately, the ideas abound. Also fortunately (and consistently with our desire to look for solutions in complex natural systems), these ideas aim at creating *self-adaptive systems*. They come from different scientific quarters, but they have the common roots in the AI (Artificial Intelligence) endeavours.

Despite AI spectacular failures of the nineteen eighties, the Internet-driven advancements create new foundations on which AI-inspired ideas of autonomic computing, multi-agent systems or SWS (Semantic Web Services) flourish. SWS is the most technologically advanced of these ideas. The idea of SWS is to be able to dynamically compose applications by discovering and orchestrating Web services (rather than in the process of building applications by manually putting software components together). Semantic Web goes as far as expecting that intelligent software agents can use semantic descriptions of Web services and resources to automate their use to accomplish user goals.

Well, can self-adaptiveness of SWS be the solution to software quality, complexity, change and evolution? Can self-adaptiveness be the replacement for strictly-managed architecture-first software development and integration? As of today, industry adoption of SWS is minimal, success stories are trivial and not coming even close to enterprise-strength solutions, and major research questions are still open.

Notwithstanding the current state of affairs in scientific and industry matters related to SWS, there are other reasons to believe that the ideas and technology of SWS may not provide any radical answer to building quality into software. Firstly, as mentioned in passing, *emergence* is not really the status operandi of contemporary enterprises. Enterprises operate within the context of changing business rules and aim at achieving deterministic business goals. Enterprise systems need to be *designed for change* but they would not normally allow unpredictable patterns and outcomes of service compositions created dynamically by software agents.

Secondly, SWS can be seen as an ultimate form of *outsourcing* in which business information and processes are made available to third parties with all associated risks and business resistance. Thirdly, SWS seem to further complicate already complex systems by abandoning hierarchical architectural structures in favor of introducing a lot of architectural layers just for the sake of mediating and mapping between heterogeneous environments.

To summarize, as researchers we are keen to embrace the notion of self-adaptiveness (and similar concepts such as self-organization, self-healing, self-optimization, etc.) in search for solutions to achieving improved and transparent software quality. As practitioners, we are skeptical and see no evidence that mystery and magic of biological systems can be unraveled to the point that complex artificial systems can be constructed dynamically and can adapt to changes in environment in the way similar to nature. Perhaps the best we can hope for is to use our understanding of structure and behavior of biological systems to offer meta-architectures permitting construction of adaptive software systems. This has been our aim.

Acknowledgements. This research project has been supported by a Marie Curie Transfer of Knowledge Fellowship of the European Community's Sixth Framework Programme under contract number MTKD-CT-2004-509766 (enIRaF).

References

1. Agazzi, E.: What is Complexity? In: Agazzi, E., Montecucco, L. (eds.) Complexity and Emergence. Proceedings of the Annual Meeting of the International Academy of the Philosophy of Science, pp. 3–11. World Scientific, Singapore (2002)
2. Bøegh, J.: A New Standard for Quality Requirements. IEEE Software 25(2), 57–63 (2008)
3. Boehm, B.: Making a Difference in the Software Century. Computer (IEEE), 32–38 (March 2008)
4. Booch, G.: The Economics of Architecture-First. IEEE Software, 18–20 (September/October 2007)
5. Brooks, R.: The Next 50 Years. Comm. of the ACM 51(1), 63–64 (2008)
6. Browning, T.R.: Applying the design structure matrix to system decomposition and integration problems: a review and new directions. IEEE Trans. on Engineering Management 48(3), 292–306 (2001)
7. Capra, F.: The Turning Point. Science, Society, and the Rising Culture. Flamingo, 516 p. (1982)
8. Corning, P.A.: The Re-Emergence of "Emergence": A Venerable Concept in Search of a Theory. Complexity 7(6), 18–30 (2002)

9. Fenton, N.E., Pfleeger, S.L.: Software Metrics. A Rigorous and Practical Approach, 2nd edn., 638 p. PWS Publishing Company (1997)
10. ISO 9126 Software Quality Characteristics (2008), http://www.sqa.net/iso9126.html
11. Jackson, M.: Systems Thinking: Creative Holism for Managers, 352 p. John Wiley & Sons, Ltd., Chichester (2003)
12. Koestler, A.: The Ghost in the Machine, 384 p. Hutchinson (1967)
13. Lansing, J.S.: Complex Adaptive Systems. Annual Rev. Anthropol. 32, 183–204 (2003)
14. Maciaszek, L.A.: Adaptive Integration of Enterprise and B2B Applications. In: Filipe, J., Shishkov, B., Helfert, M. (eds.) ICSOFT 2006, CCIS 10, pp. 3–15. Springer, Heidelberg (2008)
15. Maciaszek, L.A.: Analiza Struktur Zależności w Zarządzaniu Intencją Architektoniczną Systemu (Dependency Structure Analysis for Managing Architectural Intent). In: XV SCR Conference & X KKIO Conference, Szklarska Poreba, Poland, 14 p. (2008) (keynote paper in Polish; to appear)
16. Maciaszek, L.A.: Modeling and Engineering Adaptive Complex Systems. In: Grundy, J., Hartmann, S., Laender, L., Maciaszek, L., Roddick, J. (eds.) Challenges in Conceptual Modelling. Tutorials, Posters, Panels and Industrial Contributions to the 26th International Conference on Conceptual Modeling - ER 2007, CRPIT No. 83, pp. 31–38. ACS (2007)
17. Maciaszek, L.A., Liong, B.L.: Practical Software Engineering. A Case-Study Approach, 864 p. Addison-Wesley, Reading (2005)
18. Mitchell, M.: Complex Systems: Network Thinking. Artificial Intelligence 170, 1194–1212 (2006)
19. Vernadat, F.B.: Interoperable Enterprise Systems: Principles, Concepts, and Methods. Annual Reviews in Control 31, 137–145 (2007)
20. Wing, J.M.: Five Deep Questions in Computing. Comm. of the ACM 51(1), 58–60 (2008)

Adaptability in an Agent-Based Virtual Organization – Towards Implementation

G. Frąckowiak[1], M. Ganzha[1], M. Paprzycki[1], M. Szymczak[1], Y.-S. Han[2], and M.-W. Park[2]

[1] Systems Research Institute Polish Academy of Sciences, Warsaw, Poland
Maria.Ganzha@ibspan.waw.pl
[2] Korea Institute of Science and Technology, Seoul, Korea
myon@kist.re.kr

Abstract. Ability of an organization to adapt to change is one of its important features. When a real-world organization is transformed into a virtual one, with a help of software agents and ontologies, it is important to specify how adaptability can be achieved. In our earlier work we have conceptualized, on a general level, adaptability in an agent-based virtual organization. The aim of this chapter is to discuss how agent adaptability can be implemented.

Keywords: Software agents, virtual organization, agent systems, agent adaptability, ontologies.

1 Introduction

Organizational adaptability to various changes is one of important issues in the world of business (see, for instance [13]. In our recent work ([10,11,14,16]) we have argued that emergent software technologies such as software agents [18] and ontologies [2] could be the base of mapping a real-world organization into a virtual one. We have thus proposed a system in which: (i) organizational structure, consists of specific "roles" and interactions between them, and is represented by software agents and their interactions [10]; while (ii) domain knowledge, resource profiles (representing organizational semantics) and resource matching are ontologically represented and operated on using various forms of semantic reasoning [16]. Second, we have argued that as the real-world organization changes, not only its ontology has to be adjusted, but also "mechanisms of interaction" within its agent-based "representation". Obviously, this concerns not only changes in the the organizational structure itself, but also has to materialize as a response to task changes carried out by the organization (not only changes within specific projects, but also changes in the project portfolio), as well as changing *interests, needs* and *skills* of employees.

In our earlier work ([6,9]) we have discussed in general terms processes involved in both human resource and non-human resource adaptability. One of the important issues was the fact that in addition to changes in the ontology of the organization, software agents that play the key role in supporting workers, have to be adaptable as well. Therefore, the aim of this paper is to extend our earlier results and look in more detail into the question: what will it take for Jade agents (our current platform of choice; [3]) to

J. Cordeiro et al. (Eds.): WEBIST 2008, LNBIP 18, pp. 27–39, 2009.

be adaptable. First is to be able to *generate on demand* agents with needed function-alities to fulfill specified roles. Second is to *modify them* in response to changes in the organization and/or the environment it operates in. To this effect we, first, briefly describe our system. We follow with a discussion how agent adaptability can be actually implemented.

Before proceeding, let us make a few comments. First, note that while our approach to agent adaptability is in part responding to the way that Jade agents operate, results presented here generalize naturally to other FIPA-compliant agent platforms ([1]). Second, work presented here is an extension of results presented in [9,6]. Third, it is assumed that readers possess basic knowledge about software agents and the way they are implemented in modern agent environments, like Jade ([3]).

2   System Overview

The main function of the system under development is to provide users (employees) an infrastructure that will help to fulfill their roles within the organization. Here, the key concepts are utilization of software agents and ontologies. In the proposed system, software agents exist, first, as independent entities, e.g. a *Task Monitoring Agent*, which tracks progress of a specified task, and undertakes appropriate actions in case of any delays. Note that roles that can be fulfilled by software agents alone vary from organi-zation to organization and depend on its specific needs (see, also [14]). Second, every employee has an associated *Personal Agent* (*PA*). This agent has two main functions: (a) it is the interface between the *Employee* and the system (allowing her to utilize all of its functions), and (b) it supports *Employee* in all *roles* that (s)he is to play within the organization. In other words, an agent is integral part of system but also a bridge between the user and the system. It is worthy mentioning, that this notion of a *Personal Agent* follows the general idea put forward by P. Maes [12]. We can easily envision that a "work *PA*" is a part of a "complete *PA*" which supports *User* in all facets of life.

Let us now briefly summarize main features of the proposed system. First, we assume that work carried out within the organization is project-driven (however, the notion of the project is very broad and includes change of a transmission belt in a Ford Mondeo, as well as managing a team of researchers working on a grant-based project). Therefore, it can be stated that all employee activities are focused on tasks leading to completion of a project. After analysis of project-driven real-world organizations, key roles were identified and we represent them in the form of an AML Social Model diagram, in Figure 1.

Here, we can see the general hierarchical management structure that can be applied to almost every standard real-world organization. Structure of the organization consists of *Departments* and *Teams*. Each *Team* has at least one *Team Manager*, while each *Manager* may: (1) manage a team, (2) supervise managers of lower level (in this way a recursive hierarchical structure of the organization is represented), or (3) cooperate with other managers on the same level (e.g. when teams collaborate, or when the CFO and the CIO have to collaborate to introduce a new CRM platform to the organization). Note that: (a) *Organization* is an "environment" for *Departments*, *Managers*, *Teams* and *Workers*; (b) *Organization* cannot exist without at least one *Team*; (c) it is possible for a

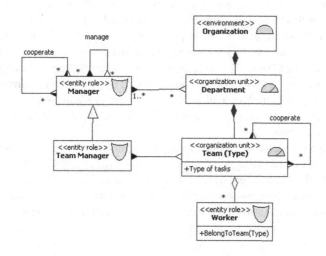

Fig. 1. AML Social Model of an organization

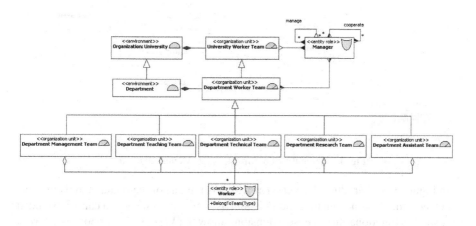

Fig. 2. University; AML Social Model

Team to consist only of a *Manager*—without any *Workers* (e.g. this could represent the case of self-employment). In Figure 1 we also depict the *Worker* who can be a member of any of the teams (obviously at a given stage (s)he is going to be a member of one team).

To illustrate how the proposed conceptualization can be instantiated, in Figure 2 we present example of the real-world organization; a University represented also as an AML Social Diagram.

Here, a number of specific entities have been represented. First, we can see the hierarchical and cooperative structure of University management (entity role *Manager*, right top corner of the figure). The *University Worker Team* organizational unit represents all workers of the *University*. Since the University consists of *Departments*, we can see also the *Department Worker Team* organizational unit, which represents all workers of a *Department*. The *Department* consists of a number of teams. We have considered a large *Department* where we can find the *Management Team* (e.g. consisting of Department Chair and Associate Chairs), *Teaching Team* (comprising all Teaching Faculty), *Technical Team* (consisting of IT support personnel as well as laboratory personnel), *Research Team* (consisting of grant-based all post-graduate and graduate associates), and *Assistant Team* (consisting of one or more Secretaries). Finally, we can see a *Worker*, who belongs to one or more teams.

To complete the picture, in Figure 3 we present an AML Mental Diagram of the *Department*. We present this diagram first, to move from the real-life organization depicted in Figure 2, to the virtual organization, where we talk about specific roles and software agents that support *Employees* in fulfilling them. Second, as it introduces key entities involved in agent adaptability. Finally, as roles identified there will be used in examples across the paper.

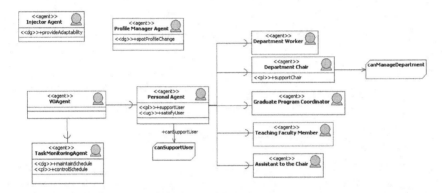

Fig. 3. University Department; AML Mental Diagram

In Figure 3 we introduce the *VOAgent* which is the one of the fundamental concepts of our system. We conceptualize the *VOAgent* as skeleton agent, which can be extended with various functionalities. Those extensions allow the *VOAgent* to support *Employees* in playing specific roles in the organization. The *VOAgent* can be "transformed" into any other agent (see [6] for a similar diagram that presents on a higher/generic level other roles that the *VOAgent* can be transformed into). Here, let us observe first that the *VOAgent* can be transformed into an, above mentioned, *Task Monitoring Agent* (*TMA*). This agent is an independent entity in our system and does not support any *Employee*. Next, we can see that the *VOAgent* can be transformed into a *Personal Agent* (*PA*). The *Personal Agent* provides the basic support of an *Employee*. Note that the *PA* is not associated with any specific role within an organization. As such, it is a generic role that is associated with every worker in the organization. For instance, every *Employee* of the *University* represented as a member of the *University Worker Team* in Figure 2, would have a *Personal Agent* associated with her/him.

In Figure 3 we have identified a few sample roles that exist in a typical large *University Department*: *Department Worker*—a basic role associated with every worker of the *Department, Department Chair, Graduate Program Coordinator, Teaching Faculty Member*, and *Assistant to the Chair*. Note that in smaller *Universities* some teams identified in Figure 2 may not be present, while some roles introduced here may be played by a single person (e.g. the *Department Chair* who is also a *Graduate Program Coordinator*).

Finally, Figure 3 includes auxiliary agents like *Injector Agent* or *Profile Manager Agent* which play crucial role in agent adaptability and will be described later. With this background we can look into processes involved in extending the *VOAgent* to allow it to play required roles.

3   Configuring Generic Agents

3.1   Overview of Agent Adaptability

Before we proceed, let us note that our approach to agent adaptability follows ideas of Tuan Tu and collaborators, from their project *DynamiCS*. For instance, in [17] it was discussed how e-commerce agents can be dynamically assembled from separate components (i.e. communication module, protocol module and strategy module) to address the requirements of the e-commerce environment (to be able to participate in unknown in advance form of price negotiations). While technical details of our approach differ, we follow the same general approach of dynamically (re)assembling agents and adapting their behavior by (re)configuring the set of "modules" that a given agent consists of. In this context let us introduce an initial understanding of the notion of a *module*. Let us thus say that a *module* is an object that encapsulates appropriate knowledge and behaviors required for an agent to instantiate a specific functionality. For instance, a *Department Management Module* will group behaviors and knowledge that allow the *Personal Agent* extended by such module to interact with the system and support a member of the *Department Management Team* in completing *Department Management*-related tasks. Specifically, we that such module will contain all necessary knowledge and behaviors to help the *Department Chair* in managing duty trips of *Department Workers* (see, [7] for a detailed description of duty trip support).

To start discussion of agent adaptability, in Figure 4, we present the use case diagram of processes involved in (re)configuring agents. This Figure should be looked into together with Figure 3.

Here, we can see high-level conceptualization of agent initialization and reconfiguration. Note, that almost every agent in the system (besides some auxiliary agents like the *Injector Agent*) is going to be initialized in the same way. First, the *VOAgent* is going to be created. This agent is able to cooperate with the *Injector Agent* in order to load required modules and knowledge. Subsequent stages of agent initialization include providing it with appropriate modules that allow it to extend itself with functionality required to play (a) specific role(s) (the *Injecting New Modules* function). The process of reconfiguration also involves cooperation between the *IA* and the *VOAgent* (the *Updating Module* function). Note that in the case of agent initialization we can assume that such agent will be able to self-load needed modules. As we will see later, this is not the case when already loaded modules have to be modified/updated.

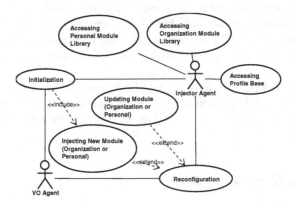

Fig. 4. Functionality of the *Injector Agent*—use case diagram

In order to provide the *VOAgent* with the needed modules the *Injector Agent* has access to:

– *Module Factories,* entities containing factories of every module available in the system (see also the component diagram in Figure 5 for more details). This includes (1) factories of core modules (*Personal Module Library*) which are associated with all functions of a *Personal Agent* (e.g. a *Calendar Managing Module*), (2) specific modules (*Organization Module Library*) created in order to support agent in roles identified in the organization (e.g. *Faculty Evaluation Module* provided to support role of the *Department Chair*), and (3) autonomous agent modules (e.g. *Checking Completion of the Task Module* provided for the *Task Monitoring Agent*).
– *Profile Base,* which stores profiles (i.e. lists of required modules) associated with each role identified within the organization. This information is used to select modules required by a *Personal Agent* supporting a *Department Worker* in fulfilling a specific role.

The *Injector Agent* is involved not only in agent initialization but also in agent reconfiguration. Agent reconfiguration takes place in the following situations:

– One or more profiles in the *Profile Base* have changed and as a result some modules must be added to or removed from an agent supporting functionality specified by such profile(s). Adding a module means that a new functionality is added to the agent (e.g. it will be now able to interface with the new Wiki system installed to manage knowledge in the *University*). Removal of a module means that the agent will no longer support some functionalities (e.g. access to an obsolete *University* blackboard system will be removed).
– The organization modifies some procedures and as a result modules are updated. For instance, a new post of *Associate Chair for Departmental Development* is created and thus selected *Department Workers* will have to report to this new *Associate Chair*. As a result *Personal Agents* of these *Workers* (that support them in their roles) have to have modules involved in communication/dependency structure modified. This process involves removal of the old version of the (*Communication Module*) and loading of new one.

– Agent reconfiguration can also take place in situation when only some part of agent knowledge has to be replaced.

As an example, imagine a *Department Worker* who is a *Professor* in *Department of Biology* (which is a specific instantiation of a role of the *Department Worker*). His *Personal Agent* will have to be loaded with modules that allow it to support her in fulfilling this role; let us name the resulting agent a *Professor Agent*. The organizational profile of the *Department Worker* contains information about unit(s) in the organization to which he belongs (e.g. the *Department of Biology*; see, also [16]). Knowledge about modules required for an agent supporting a *Professor* is stored in the *Profile Base* and can be accessed/extracted by the *Injector Agent*. Therefore, when a new *Professor* is hired by the *University*, first a *PA* is assembled by on the basis of a *VOAgent*. This involves loading it with standard *PA* modules; e.g. module that allows access to the *University* intranet. In the second step of the assembly, *Professor Modules* (e.g. modules that interface with the *Grant Announcement* and the *Duty Trip Support* functionalities; see, [8]) are injected into thus created *PA*, extending its role to support the *Department Worker*. However, when the *Professor* "changes its position within the structure of the organization", some modules are likely going to be added, removed and/or replaced within an already existing *PA*; a case of agent adaptation. For instance, if the *Professor* worked as the *Department Chair*, she had access to personal data of other *Department Workers* in her *Department*. Such access should not longer be allowed to the *Professor* who is not a *Department Chair*, and thus modules supporting it should be removed from her *Personal Agent*.

Note that this example assumed that a specific infrastructure for data/profile change notification exists in the system. However, here we do not intend to discuss this issue, as it is out of scope of this paper.

3.2 General Framework of Agent Adaptability

To discuss how agent creation and adaptation is achieved we have conceptualized it in the form of a component diagram in Figure 5. This diagram combines the generic framework and system artifacts which are specific to the organization in which the system is run. In the context of this chapter we are particularly interested in what is happening within the dash-line rectangle, which delineates the core of the proposed approach.

Let us start our description by recalling from [6] that the *OPM* (*Organization Provisioning Manager*) is an umbrella role that is fulfilled by a number of entities (some of them are agents alone, while some of involve *Employee*(s) supported by their *PA*(s)). For instance, in [10] we have argued that travel recommending functions belong to the *OPM*. Similar claim can be made about the *Grant Announcement* application described in [15]. Finally, searching within the *University* for a classroom available during the Spring 2009 semester every Thursday between 2PM and 4PM is also its role (fulfilled by a different (sub)entity within the *OPM*; see, also [14]). Here, we show that agent adaptability, being the case resource management, is also one of the roles of the *OPM*. Therefore, the above described *Injector Agent* (*IA*), and the *Profile Monitor Agent* (*PMA*) are also "a part" of the *OPM*. The role of the *PMA* is to monitor changes

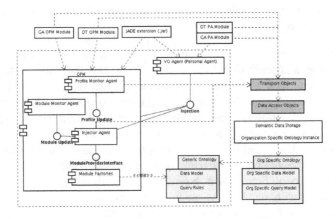

Fig. 5. Component Diagram of agent adaptability

in the data model and to inform the *IA* that a particular profile was updated. Finally, the *Module Monitor Agent* informs the *IA* about new modules or new modules versions introduced into the organization. As a result the *IA* has to reconfigure agents that play a roles connected with those modules. Obviously, any form of (re)configuration is pertinent to both *User*-supporting and autonomous agents, as both of them are created and maintained with the help of the *IA*.

The *IA* communicates also with the *Module Provider Interface*, which associates modules with module factories (stored in the *Module Factories*) and creates instances of modules for the requested resource (e.g. the *Department Worker* fulfilling a given role).

In Figure 5 the *VOAgent* is represented after it has been already transformed into the *PA* (but everything discussed here applies also to cases involving autonomous agents). The *PA* is extended (with functionalities selected according to the specific profile) to support the *Department Worker* in fulfilling a given role. This is achieved by the *IA* through the *Injection Interface*.

In the figure we also represent the *Generic Data Model* and the *Generic Query Model* using ontologies which define concepts universal for any organization in which we could wish to implement the proposed system. These concepts include: human resource, non-human resource, profile, profile access privileges, organization units, module configuration, task, matching types and matching relations (see also [7,16]). Both these generic ontologies can be reused and specified by organization specific data and query models. They are also used to generate classes that implement behaviors of specific modules.

Let us stress, again, that we view all entities and their relations represented within the dashed rectangle as a *generic framework* that will materialize in most organizations (not only the *University*, which is the focus of this paper).

Considering the organization specific elements of the system (elements that will differ between organizations and are represented outside of the generic framework), crucial roles are played by the *Organization Specific Data Model* and the *Organization Specific Query Model*. Both these ontologies reuse the *Generic Ontology*, which is a part of the framework, in order to represent data structures and matching scenarios which are pertinent to the organization. Based on the organization specific ontologies their instances can be created, stored and queried through the *Semantic Data Storage* which is an infrastructure for manipulating and storing semantically demarcated data. For the time being, to support these functionalities, we intend to utilize the Jena ([4]) persistence layer. However, we are well aware of the fact that currently existing semantic data storage and querying software is far from being efficient. As a result, in the future we may select a different persistence technology. Such decision is going to be based mainly on experimental work involving various existing technologies (similar to that described in [5]).

Finally, *Special Function*-related "boxes" represent specific applications that the system is to deal with. Examples of such functions would be the *Duty Trip Support* (see, [16]) and the *Grant Announcement* (see, [8]). Both these functions involve interactions between the *OPM* and the *Personal Agent*. Note that while these functions have been described in the context of a generic *Research Institute*, they fit very well in the *University*-based example presented here.

3.3   Implementing Agent Adaptability

Let us now take a closer look at some crucial, from the point of view of implementing agent adaptability, components of our system. Before proceeding let us note that solutions discussed here are on the basis of our current state of knowledge. It is therefore possible that as we proceed with implementation we may find them lacking in important respects and thus in need of adjusting them.

As mentioned above, from implementation point of view the *VOAgent* is an extension of the `jade.core.Agent` class. The extension must be made in order to provide following functionalities:

- working with modules, in particular, adding, replacing, removing, and registering them
- working with behaviors, monitor them, controlling, adding, removing
- providing access to the *Shared Object Map*, which is an map of objects shared by working behaviors.

Note that module loading, removing and replacing will involve an additional ontology, which we name the *Module Ontology*. When fully developed this ontology will contain terms like *LOAD_MODULE, REMOVE_MODULE, SHOW_MODULE_LIST, UPDATE_MODULE* and will be utilized directly by JADE agents for agent assembly and modifications.

Now we can also define more precisely the concept of a module. Each module is an instance of a single *universal module class*. This class contains:

- Module name and version.
- List of behavior descriptions that should be loaded in order to support a specific functionality. This list is constant for every agent using a specific module. We assume that modules group exactly the same behaviors. Description should contain all data necessary to load the behavior.

- List of objects that should placed in agent's *Shared Object Map*. This list will differ between agents because data used by behaviors will depend on the specific profile utilized by an agent.

We also predict some other properties needed within modules, which however do not belong to this level of abstraction. Such properties could be: date of module creation, sequence number, signature of module creating entity, additional data necessary for module loading, etc.

As an example imagine an instance of the Module class—a *Department Worker Module*—prepared for a *Biology Department Worker*. The name set for this module is *Department_Worker*, the version(let assume that it is not the first one) is 3.0. The list of behavior descriptions contains only one behavior which allows user to interact with other *Department Workers* (specifically, it allows the *PA* that represents a given *Worker* to interact with *PAs* representing other *Workers*). Of course, the real module will contain also other behaviors. Knowledge part of this module contains name of department which is *Biology* and list of other *Department Workers* (again, it is list of *PAs* representing other *Workers*). Now, the instance of the *Department Worker Module* prepared for a different *University Employee*, but from other *Department* (let us say *Chemistry*) will be slightly different. The module name and version won't be different. Also the list of behaviors won't change. The difference will be in the knowledge included in this specific instance. The name of department will be *Chemistry* and because it is a different *Department*, the list of *Workers* will also be different.

An important issue which we have to deal with during agent creation or update is to supply it with definitions of new classes e.g. new behaviors classes, new ontologies, etc. Before loading of any knowledge part or behavior (which are instances of some classes) we have to inform agent about localization of all required classes. Therefore, information about all required classes has to be included into agents' classpath. Currently we assume that each module will contain information about localization of all required classes. However, we acknowledge that class loading is somewhat more complex problem requiring further investigation. For instance, it is also possible that class localization will not be included in the module but there will be some action, performed by the *Injection Agent*, preparing agent for module inclusion.

Note also that behaviors included in modules cannot be default Jade behaviors. We presume that in order to provide agent in full behavior monitoring and control function we have to extend them with names and versions. In other words, agents have to be self-aware as to which versions of which specific behaviors they are build out of.

Now let us extend described thus far concepts and discuss somewhat more complicated issues and some real-life examples of their utility.

4   Examples and Further Considerations

Let as assume that there is a *Department Worker* in the *University* who belongs to *Department Technical Team*. He plays the role of *Technical Support* and his duties include installing software, taking care of hardware problems, preparing auditoriums for lectures, etc. All behaviors supporting this *Department Worker* in fulfilling role of a *Technical Support* will have to be included in his *Personal Agent* in the form of a

Department Technical Support Module. Functionality of this module will help him with incoming requests, reporting his activities, ordering materials (e.g. toner for printers) from university warehouses, etc. This module consists of behaviors supporting, among others, the above mentioned functions, as well as the necessary data, e.g. list of other members of the *Department Technical Team*. Now, let us imagine that we want to create a *VOAgent* and turn it into an extended *PA*, which supports the *Department Worker* in fulfilling the *Technical Support* role.

To achieve this goal, we have to inject the *PA* it with core modules that support the primary role of a *Department Worker* and, of course, include also the *Technical Support Module*. This module is prepared by the *Technical Support Factory* (an instance of a *Module Factory* from Figure 5). In order to inject necessary modules we have to prepare them first. First, the *Injector Agent* obtains names of one or more *Module Factories* that will provide the *VOAgent* with modules that extend it to become a *PA*. When the *Personal Agent* is fully assembled, the *IA* accesses the *Profile Library* and obtains information about role(s) of a given *Department Worker* which is(are) to be supported by its *PA*, as well as a list of modules that have to be associated with each of these roles. In our case this is the *Technical Support* role and a list of modules that constitute the complete support for this role. Next, the *IA* contacts the *Module Provider Interface* and obtains the list of classes implementing particular *Module Factories*. These *Factories* allow the *IA* to create instances of modules for (the) specific role(s).

In our example the *Module Factory* will prepare instance of the module class, which contains all data and behaviors required for the given module. As mentioned before, the *Module Factory* will prepare data that includes, among others, the list of other team members (retrieved from the *Data Model* specifically for the given *Department Worker*). The *Module Factory* will also add descriptions of behaviors (e.g. for dealing with requests, interacting with supply department, etc.) to the module object. Currently, we assume that descriptions of behaviors contain information about behavior's classes and about additional (3'rd party) libraries which should be added to the agent classpath. These Java objects can then be self-injected by the *PA*, turning it into *Technical Support Agent*.

Let us use a different example, and observe what happens when the *Department Worker* (see Figure 3) is promoted to become a *Department Chair* and her *PA* has to be modified to support her in the new role. As a result of the promotion, the organization profile of the *Department Worker* (the *Human Resource Profile*; see [16]) is adjusted. This information becomes known to the *Profile Monitoring Agent*, which in turn informs the *IA* about this fact. The *IA* accesses the *Profile Library* and obtains a complete list of modules that should constitute the *PA* that can support the *Department Worker* in the role of *Department Chair*; and contacts the *Module Provider Interface* to obtain information which classes factory will create modules that need to be injected into the *PA*. On the basis of thus obtained list, the *IA* will modify the *PA*.

Let us now focus on another complex issue. Let us consider, again, the *Technical Support Module*, which provides set of behaviors and knowledge that allow the *PA* to support a *Department Worker* in the role of *Technical Support*. Every change in real-life organization procedure(s) must also affect behaviors of the *Technical Support Agent*. Imagine that before an organizational change members of the *Technical Support* were allowed to exchange requests (as long as they were completed in time) without approval of the *Technical Team Manager*. After the change, members of the *Technical Support Team* are not allowed to exchange requests. All exchanges have to be approved by the *Technical Support Team Manager*. This change affects not only the *Technical Support Team Members* but also several other entities including, for instance, the *Technical Support Team Manager* (and thus their appropriate *Personal Agents*). As a matter of fact, every entity, which takes part in this scenario will have to accommodate the new procedure. This requires reconfiguration of agents representing affected entities. New versions of behaviors and modules must be introduced into the system, and this requires update of appropriate *Module Factories*. New libraries with behavior definitions and module factories have to be stored. Next, the *Injector Agent* must help install new modules with new behaviors to every agent, which role requires using just updated modules.

While injecting new modules is rather easy to achieve (agents can self-inject with additional modules), module updating is a more complex problem. Let us observe that:

- when we introduce new modules we have to be sure that every agent in the system will "instantaneously" start working with the same version of the module; situation in which agents try to communicate with each other while utilizing incompatible procedures/messages/protocols can result in a disaster
- update cannot occur in the middle of a conversation/transaction between any affected agents; as a matter of fact, agents cannot switch behavior version (kill older version and load a new one) if the current one is a part of a still working process.

Combining these two observations makes it easy to see why module update is a very complex issue and may even lead to the need of complete system shutdown. It is only in this case when we can for certain assure that no transaction is in progress and that no agent-version incompatibility will occur. We will investigate this issue in more details, with an attempt at reducing the impact of module updating on the functioning of the system.

5   Concluding Remarks

In this paper we have considered adaptability in an agent-based virtual organization. Specifically, we have concentrated our attention on issues involved in implementation of agent adaptability, while using an example of a *University* to illustrate potential solution and open research questions. We are in the process of implementing the proposed solution and will report on our progress in subsequent publications.

Acknowledgements. Work supported in part by the KIST-SRI PAS "Agent Technology for Adaptive Information Provisioning" grant.

References

1. The foundation of intelligent physical agent (fipa)
2. Semantic web, http://www.w3.org/2001/sw/

3. Jade—java agent development framework. TILab (2008)
4. Jena—a semantic framework for java (2008)
5. Chmiel, K., Tomiak, D., Gawinecki, M., Karczmarek, P., Szymczak, M., Paprzycki, M.: Testing the efficiency of jade agent platform. In: ISPDC 2004, Proceedings of the Third International Symposium on Parallel and Distributed Computing/Third International Workshop on Algorithms, Models and Tools for Parallel Computing on Heterogeneous Networks (ISPDC/HeteroPar 2004), pp. 49–56 (2004)
6. Frąckowiak, G., Ganzha, M., Gawinecki, M., Paprzycki, M., Szymczak, M., Bădică, C., Han, Y.-S., Park, M.-W.: Adaptability in an agent-based virtual organization. In: Internetional Journal Accounting, Auditing and Performance Evaluation (2008) (in press)
7. Frackowiak, G., Ganzha, M., Gawinecki, M., Paprzycki, M., Szymczak, M., Park, M.-W., Han, Y.-S.: Considering Resource Management in Agent-Based Virtual Organization. Springer, Heidelberg (2009)
8. Frackowiak, G., Ganzha, M., Gawinecki, M., Paprzycki, M., Szymczak, M., Park, M.-W., Han, Y.-S.: On resource profiling and matching in an agent-based virtual organization. In: Rutkowski, L., Tadeusiewicz, R., Zadeh, L.A., Zurada, J.M. (eds.) ICAISC 2008. LNCS, vol. 5097, pp. 1210–1221. Springer, Heidelberg (2008)
9. Ganzha, M., Gawinecki, M., Szymczak, M., Frackowiak, G., Paprzycki, M., Park, M.-W., Han, Y.-S., Sohn, Y.: Generic framework for agent adaptability and utilization in a virtual organization—preliminary considerations. In: Cordeiro, J., et al. (eds.) Proceedings of the 2008 WEBIST conference, pp. IS–17–IS–25. INSTICC Press (2008) (to appear)
10. Ganzha, M., Paprzycki, M., Gawinecki, M., Szymczak, M., Frackowiak, G., Badica, C., Popescu, E., Park, M.-W.: Adaptive information provisioning in an agent-based virtual organization—preliminary considerations. In: Nguyen, N. (ed.) Proceedings of the SYNASC Conference, pp. 235–241. IEEE Press, Los Alamitos (2008)
11. Ganzha, M., Paprzycki, M., Popescu, E., Bădică, C., Gawinecki, M.: Agent-based adaptive learning provisioning in a virtual organization. In: Advances in Intelligent Web Mastering. Proc. AWIC 2007, Fontainebleu, France. Advances in Soft Computing, pp. 25–40. Springer, Heidelberg (2007)
12. Maes, P., Guttman, R., Moukas, A.: Agents that buy and sell: Transforming commerce as we know it 42(3), 81–91 (1999)
13. Malhotra, Y.: Role of information technology in managing organizational change and organizational interdependence (1993), http://www.kmbook.com/change/
14. Szymczak, M., Frąckowiak, G., Ganzha, M., Gawinecki, M., Paprzycki, M., Park, M.-W.: Resource management in an agent-based virtual organization—introducing a task into the system. In: Proceedings of the MaSeB Workshop, pp. 458–462. IEEE CS Press, Los Alamitos (2007)
15. Szymczak, M., Frackowiak, G., Ganzha, M., Paprzycki, M., Park, M.-W., Han, Y.-S., Sohn, Y.T., Lee, J., Kim, J.K.: Infrastructure for ontological resource matching in a virtual organization. In: Nguyen, N., Katarzyniak, R. (eds.) Proceedings of the IDC Conference. Studies in Computational Intelligence, vol. 134, pp. 111–120. Springer, Heidelberg (2008)
16. Szymczak, M., Frackowiak, G., Gawinecki, M., Ganzha, M., Paprzycki, M., Park, M.-W., Han, Y.-S., Sohn, Y.T.: Adaptive information provisioning in an agent-based virtual organization—ontologies in the system. In: Nguyen, N.T., Jo, G.S., Howlett, R.J., Jain, L.C. (eds.) KES-AMSTA 2008. LNCS (LNAI), vol. 4953, pp. 271–280. Springer, Heidelberg (2008)
17. Tu, M., Griffel, F., Merz, M., Lamersdorf, W.: A plug-in architecture providing dynamic negotiation capabilities for mobile agents. In: Rothermel, K., Hohl, F. (eds.) MA 1998. LNCS, vol. 1477, pp. 222–236. Springer, Heidelberg (1998)
18. Wooldridge, M.: An Introduction to MultiAgent Systems. John Wiley & Sons, Chichester (2002)

S-Cube: Enabling the Next Generation of Software Services[*]

Andreas Metzger and Klaus Pohl

Software Systems Engineering, University of Duisburg-Essen, 45117 Essen, Germany
{andreas.metzger,klaus.pohl}@sse.uni-due.de

Abstract. The Service Oriented Architecture (SOA) paradigm is increasingly adopted by industry for building distributed software systems. However, when designing, developing and operating innovative software services and service-based systems, several challenges exist. Those challenges include how to manage the complexity of those systems, how to establish, monitor and enforce Quality of Service (QoS) and Service Level Agreements (SLAs), as well as how to build those systems such that they can proactively adapt to dynamically changing requirements and context conditions. Developing foundational solutions for those challenges requires joint efforts of different research communities such as Business Process Management, Grid Computing, Service Oriented Computing and Software Engineering. This paper provides an overview of S-Cube, the European Network of Excellence on Software Services and Systems. S-Cube brings together researchers from leading research institutions across Europe, who join their competences to develop foundations, theories as well as methods and tools for future service-based systems.

Keywords: Service-based Systems, Service Oriented Architectures, Adaptive Systems, Quality of Service, Software Services, Service Infrastructure, Service Composition, Business Process Management.

1 Motivation

The Service Oriented Architecture (SOA) is increasingly adopted by industry as a paradigm for building highly dynamic, distributed and adaptive software systems [1],[2],[3]. Service-based systems are realized by "composing" software services. For the service composer, a software service represents functionality that can be invoked through the service's interface. The actual software that implements this functionality is executed, maintained and owned by the provider of that service. Ideally, the service composer can select from a vast amount of readily available services from a diverse range of service providers. Thus, services take the concept of ownership to the extreme: Not only the development, quality assurance, and maintenance of the software is under the control of third parties, but the software can even be executed and managed by third parties [4].

---

[*] The research leading to these results has received funding from the European Community's Seventh Framework Programme FP7/2007-2013 under grant agreement 215483 (S-Cube). For further information please visit: http://www.s-cube-network.eu/

J. Cordeiro et al. (Eds.): WEBIST 2008, LNBIP 18, pp. 40–47, 2009.
© Springer-Verlag Berlin Heidelberg 2009

1.1 State of the Art: Functional SOA Layers

Currently, the common practice for developing service-based systems following the SOA paradigm distinguishes between three functional layers [4]:

- *Service Infrastructure Layer.* This layer supports describing, publishing and discovering services and provides the run-time environment for the execution of service-based systems. It provides primitives for service communication (e.g., SOAP), mechanisms for connecting heterogeneous services, facilities for service description (e.g., WSDL), as well as capabilities that support the discovery of services (e.g., UDDI).
- *Service Composition and Coordination Layer.* This layer supports the (hierarchical) aggregation of multiple (individual) services into service compositions. Service compositions can – in turn – be offered to service clients, used in further service compositions and eventually be composed to service-based systems. By relying on the service infrastructure layer, the service composition and coordination layer is responsible for specifying (e.g., using BPEL), controlling and coordinating the execution of the aggregated services of a composition and for managing the data flow as well as the control flow between those services.
- *Business Process Management (BPM) Layer.* The BPM layer provides end-to-end visibility and control over all parts of a long-lived, multi-step business process that spans multiple organizations and can involve human actors. The business process management layer provides mechanisms for expressing, understanding, representing and managing an organization in terms of a collection of business processes which are realized in a service-oriented fashion.

1.2 Open Challenges

The current state of the art in SOA is not sufficient to build innovative software services and service-based systems of the future. Although several communities address fundamental issues inherent in the three functional layers, many important challenges are still to be resolved (e.g., see [5] and [6]). Some typical research challenges include:

- *Engineering and Design.* Ideally, the complete behaviour of a service-based system would be described during the design phase. However, service-based systems cannot be specified completely in advance due to the incomplete knowledge about the interacting parties as well as the system's context. As an example, the decision which services from which provider are actually aggregated into the service-based system is often taken during run-time. Due to the fact that many development decisions are taken during run-time, the phase of engineering and design shrinks compared to the run-time (operation) phase. As a consequence, new life cycle models and methods will have to support the agility, flexibility and dynamism required to leverage the potential of service-based systems and to devise innovative, value-added services. As an example, the abundance of available services can help in the requirements analysis phase, since it allows new requirements to emerge because the requirements analyst discovers these services and realizes that they could be beneficial to extending or improving the functionality of the system under development. Thus, service compositions will also be established in a "bottom-up" or even "middle-out" way [4].

- *Adaptation.* Adaptation of a service-based system is typically being triggered through monitoring events, i.e., events that result form the observation of the running systems behaviour. Monitoring however, only observes changes and/or deviations after they have occurred and thus supports reactive adaptations. Reactive adaptations have, among others, the following drawbacks: (1) Executing faulty services or process fragments can have undesirable consequences, such as loss of money and unsatisfied users. (2) Adapting the running system can considerably increase execution time, and therefore reduce the overall performance of the running system. (3) There is typically a time delay between the occurrence of a problem and its detection via monitoring activities which leads to a time delay of executing adaptive actions. Monitoring events might even occur too late for taking adaptive actions. Ideally, proactive adaptation avoids those drawbacks, since the service-based system will adapt itself before the deviation occurs. Proactive adaptation requires novel techniques and methods for diagnosing the system and for observing its context in order to anticipate possible deviations or changes that require an adaptation. Also, the potential consequences of those deviations and changes need to be estimated in order to determine whether it is worth performing the proactive adaptation (e.g., if the consequences are only minor it might be worthwhile not to trigger an adaptation).

- *Quality.* Future service-based systems need to guarantee end-to-end quality and compliance with quality contracts, such as service level agreements (SLAs). End-to-end quality provision implies that the dependency between different quality characteristics (like reliability or performance) must be understood across all layers. For instance, the interrelation between the fulfilment of different QoS characteristics on the infrastructure layer and the achievement of KPIs (key performance indicators) at the business process management layer is still an open issue. As businesses in the future will depend on globally distributed service-based systems, support for the specification, dynamic agreement, and monitoring of service quality will be a critical issue. There is thus a strong need for methods that address the QoS characteristics in a comprehensive and cross-cutting fashion across all layers of a service-based system. Those innovative QoS-techniques and methods have to integrate the phases of SLA conception, negotiation, monitoring and refinement (or re-negotiation). In addition, those approaches need to understand how the context of a service-based system impacts on QoS.

1.3 Need for Interdisciplinary Research

Developing solutions for the research challenges in service-based systems mentioned in the previous section requires the synergy and integration of different research communities.

Those research communities include:

- Business Process Management, which addresses issues at the BPM layer, like agile service networks, business transaction monitoring, or KPIs;

- Service Oriented Computing, which addresses challenges at the service composition and coordination layer (including adaptable, QoS-aware service compositions);
- Grid Computing, which focuses at issues at the service infrastructure layer (e.g., infrastructure mechanisms for run-time adaptation of services);
- Software Engineering, which contributes its huge body of knowledge on engineering and designing software systems, as well as software quality assurance;
- Automated Planning, which provides contributions for contract (and SLA) negotiation as well as automated service composition;
- Information Retrieval, which enables devising advanced service registration and search tools;
- Human Computer Interaction, which addresses issues of context and user modelling.

S-Cube, the European Network of Excellence on Software Services and Systems, brings together leading European research institutes and universities from the above communities. This paper sketches S-Cube's contribution to the next generation of software services and service-based systems. Section 2 provides an overview of S-Cube's objectives and the technical approach followed. Then, Section 3 presents S-Cube's research framework, which introduces a clear separation of concerns between service-related issues. Section 4 concludes the paper and explains how researchers can participate in the S-Cube network.

2   The S-Cube Network of Excellence

The aim of S-Cube is to establish a unified, multidisciplinary, vibrant research community, which intends to achieve world-wide scientific excellence by defining a broader research vision and perspective that will shape the software-service based Internet of the future.

S-Cube is funded for a period of four years by the European Community's Seventh Framework Programme FP7/2007-2013 under Objective 1.2 'Services and Software Architectures, Infrastructures and Engineering'. S-Cube brings together over 70 researchers and over 50 Ph.D. students from 14 institutions. Figure 1 shows the 14 member organizations of S-Cube and their distribution across Europe.

2.1   Objectives

S-Cube pursues the following objectives:

- Re-aligning, re-shaping and integrating research agendas of key European players from diverse research communities. By synthesizing and integrating diversified knowledge, a long-lasting foundation for steering research and for achieving innovation at the highest level will be achieved.
- Inaugurating a Europe-wide common program of education and training for researchers and industry. This will create a common culture that will have a profound impact on the future of the field.
- Establishing a proactive mobility plan to enable cross-fertilisation. This will foster the integration of research communities and the establishment of a common software services research culture.

- Establishing trust relationships with industry. Via European Technology Platforms (specifically NESSI) a catalytic effect in shaping European research, strengthening industrial competitiveness and addressing main societal challenges will be accomplished.
- Defining a broader research vision and perspective. This will shape the software-service based Internet of the future and will accelerate economic growth and improve the living conditions of European citizens.

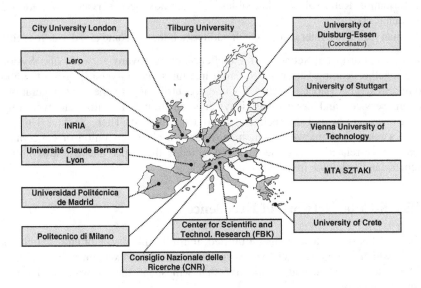

Fig. 1. S-Cube Member Organizations

2.2 Technical Approach

To reach the above objectives, the S-Cube members jointly carry out the following three types of activities:

- *Integration Activities.* Integration activities tackle fragmentation and isolation of research by different means:

  o The S-Cube Knowledge Model will capture terminology and competences of S-Cube members and their research. This will support eliminating the duplication of research efforts, better adjusting research activities of member institutions and restructuring already existing research agendas.
  o The Pan-European Distributed Service Laboratory will be established as a high-quality research infrastructure to provide access to state-of-the-art collaboration facilities (including Grids).
  o S-Cube's diverse and vigorous program of education, training and specialist courses will be provided together with an intensive mobility plan to achieve a cross-fertilisation of knowledge and durable research integration.

- *Joint Research Activities.* Work in S-Cube will be guided by the S-Cube research framework, which will be introduced in Section 3.
- *Spreading of Excellence Activity.* This activity will ensure a broad dissemination of research results, stimulate industrial and commercial interest, and enhance the public visibility of the research results. This includes the S-Cube Web Portal[1], the organisation of international conferences[2], specialised workshops and summer schools[3], as well as a European Ph.D. programme.

3 The S-Cube Research Framework

The S-Cube research framework (see Figure 2) guides the joint research activities carried out in S-Cube. The framework basically distinguishes between principles and methods for engineering and adapting service-based systems and the technology which is used to realize those systems while taking into account issues like QoS and SLA compliance.

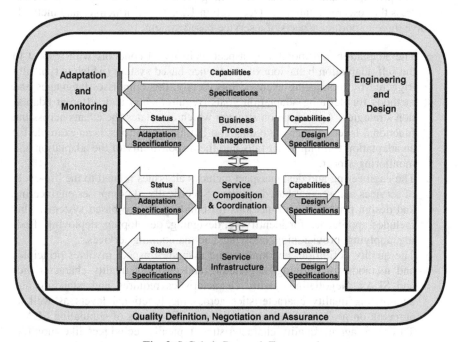

Fig. 2. S-Cube's Research Framework

What makes the S-Cube research framework unique when compared to the traditional "layered" way of developing service-based systems (see Section 1.1) is that it

---

[1] See http://www.s-cube-network.eu/

[2] For example the ServiceWave conference; see http://www.servicewave.eu/

[3] For example the SSME Summer School; see http://www.ssme2008.tsl.gr/

systematically addresses cross-cutting service issues. Further, the framework sets out to make the knowledge of the functional layers (which currently is mostly hidden in languages, standards, etc.) explicit in order to avoid overlaps and to identify gaps in research. Finally, the framework is designed to handle the complexity of developing and adapting service-based systems.

To this end, the elements of the S-Cube research framework are defined by following a clear separation of two concerns:

- *Technologies and Local Principles & Methods.* The three horizontal layers of the framework are – similar to the traditional SOA layers – responsible for techniques and methods which are applicable for the individual layers (in isolation). Also, concrete service technologies fall under the responsibility of the layers; e.g., search engines and virtualization mechanisms on the infrastructure layer, service composition languages (like BPEL), and business process modelling techniques on the BPM layer.

- *Overarching /Cross-cutting Principles, Techniques and Methods.* In addition to the local principles and methods, overarching principles and methods are needed to address the research challenges (see Section 1.2). Those principles and methods involve three important aspects of a service-based system:

  o The adaptation and monitoring aspect includes all concerns with respect to the self-adaptation behaviour of the service-based system (which is typically triggered by monitoring events). Specifically, this comprises languages and methods for defining adaptation goals (requirements) and different adaptation strategies. An adaptation strategy which correlates the events across the functional layers, thereby avoiding conflicting adaptations, is an example for an adaptation technique that falls into the responsibility of the adaptation and monitoring aspect.

  o The engineering and design aspect includes all issues related to the life-cycle of services and service-based systems. Specifically, it comprises engineering and design principles and methods for building service-based systems. This includes approaches for identifying, designing, developing, deploying, finding, applying, provisioning, evolving, and maintaining services.

  o The quality definition, negotiation and assurance aspect involves principles and methods for defining, negotiating and ensuring quality characteristics and SLAs. Negotiating quality characteristics requires understanding and aggregating quality characteristics across the functional layers as well as agreeing on provided levels of quality (e.g., by means of stipulating SLAs). To ensure agreed quality characteristics, typically techniques like monitoring, testing or static analysis (e.g., model checking) are employed.

For each element of the S-Cube research framework, interfaces are defined that describe the capabilities that are provided by one element of the framework to another element, resp., the capabilities required by one element from another. As an example, one interface of the service composition and coordination layer defines which kinds of monitoring events ("status" in Figure 2) are provided for the cross-cutting adaptation strategy defined in the adaptation and monitoring aspect (see above).

4   Conclusions

The innovation that is required to devise the theories, technology and methods needed for making the next generation of services and service-based systems a reality, cannot be delivered by any research group in isolation. It requires the synergy and integration of a variety of research communities including Grid Computing, Service Oriented Computing, Software Engineering, Automated Planning, Information Retrieval, and Human Computer Interaction.

To this end, S-Cube, the European Network of Excellence on Software Services and Systems, brings together major European research institutes and universities to jointly devise the scientific foundations for future service technologies and methods. The results of S-Cube will thus equip the organizations of the future with the capabilities to develop and evolve innovative software services and service-based systems.

In order to strengthen and broaden S-Cube's research efforts, organizations, research groups or researchers are invited to join S-Cube as associate partners. The admission process is published on the S-Cube Web Portal[4].

References

1. Erl, T.: Service-oriented Architecture. Prentice Hall, Englewood Cliffs (2004)
2. Josuttis, N.: SOA in Practice: The Art of Distributed System Design. O'Reilly, Sebastopol (2007)
3. Kaye, D.: Loosely Coupled: The Missing Pieces of Web Services. RDS Press (2003)
4. Di Nitto, E., Ghezzi, C., Metzger, A., Papazoglou, M., Pohl, K.: A Journey to Highly Dynamic, Self-adaptive Service-based Applications. Automated Software Engineering (2008) (to be published)
5. Papazoglou, M., Pohl, K.: S-Cube: The Network of Excellence on Software Services and Systems. In: Di Nitto, E., Traverso, P., Sassen, A., Zwegers, A. (eds.) At Your Service: An Overview of Results of Projects in the Field of Service Engineering of the IST Programme. MIT Press Series on Information Systems, Cambridge (2008)
6. Papazoglou, M., Pohl, K.: Report on Longer Term Research Challenges in Software and Services. Results from two workshops held at the European Commission premises at 8th of November 2007 and 28th and 29th of January 2008, with contributions from Boniface, M., Ceri, S., Hermenegildo, M., Inverardi, P., Leymann, F., Maiden, N., Metzger, A., Priol, T. European Commission (2008), http://www.cordis.lu

---

[4] See http://www.s-cube-network.eu/contact/become-an-associate-partner

Part I

Internet Technology

Web 2.0 OLAP: From Data Cubes to Tag Clouds

Kamel Aouiche, Daniel Lemire, and Robert Godin

Université du Québec à Montréal, 100 Sherbrooke West, Montreal, Canada
kamel.aouiche@gmail.com, lemire@acm.org, godin.robert@uqam.ca

Abstract. Increasingly, business projects are ephemeral. New Business Intelligence tools must support ad-lib data sources and quick perusal. Meanwhile, tag clouds are a popular community-driven visualization technique. Hence, we investigate tag-cloud views with support for OLAP operations such as roll-ups, slices, dices, clustering, and drill-downs. As a case study, we implemented an application where users can upload data and immediately navigate through its ad hoc dimensions. To support social networking, views can be easily shared and embedded in other Web sites. Algorithmically, our tag-cloud views are approximate range top-k queries over spontaneous data cubes. We present experimental evidence that iceberg cuboids provide adequate online approximations. We benchmark several browser-oblivious tag-cloud layout optimizations.

Keywords: OLAP, Data warehouse, Business intelligence, Tag cloud, Social web.

1 Introduction

The Web 2.0, or Social Web, is about making available social software applications on the Web in an unrestricted manner. Enabling a wide range of distributed individuals to collaborate on data analysis tasks may lead to significant productivity gains [1, 2]. Several companies, like SocialText and IBM, are offering Web 2.0 solutions dedicated to enterprise needs. The data visualization Web sites Many Eyes [3] and Swivel [4] have become part of the Web 2.0 landscape: over 1 million data sets were uploaded to Swivel in less than 3 months [5].

These Web 2.0 data visualization sites use traditional pie charts and histograms, but also tag clouds. Tag clouds are a form of histogram which can represent the amplitude of over a hundred items by varying the font size. The use of hyperlinks makes tag clouds naturally interactive. Tag clouds are used by many Web 2.0 sites such as Flickr, del.icio.us and Technorati. Increasingly, e-Commerce sites such as Amazon or O'Reilly Media, are using tag clouds to help their users navigate through aggregated data.

Meanwhile, OLAP (On-Line Analytical Processing) [6] is a dominant paradigm in Business Intelligence (BI). OLAP allows domain experts to navigate through aggregated data in a multidimensional data model. Standard operations include drill-down, roll-up, dice, and slice. The data cube [7] model provides well-defined semantics and performance optimization strategies. However, OLAP requires much effort from database administrators even after the data has been cleaned, tuned and loaded: schemas must be designed in collaboration with users having fast changing needs and requirements [8, 9]. Vendors such as Spotfire, Business Objects and QlikTech have reacted by

J. Cordeiro et al. (Eds.): WEBIST 2008, LNBIP 18, pp. 51–64, 2009.

Table 1. Conventional OLAP versus Web 2.0 OLAP

Conventional OLAP	Web 2.0 OLAP
recurring needs	ephemeral projects
predefined schemas	spontaneous schemas
centralized design	user initiative
histograms	tag clouds
plots and reports	iframes, wikis, blogs
access control	social networking

proposing a new class of tools allowing end-user to customize their applications and to limit the need for centralized schema crafting [10].

OLAP itself has never been formally defined though rules have been proposed to recognize an OLAP application [6]. In a similar manner, we propose rules to recognize Web 2.0 OLAP applications (see also Table 1):

1. Data and schemas are provided autonomously by users.
2. It is available as a Web application.
3. It supports complete online interaction over aggregated multidimensional data.
4. Users are encouraged to collaborate.

Tag clouds are well suited for Web 2.0 OLAP. They are flexible: a tag cloud can represent a dozen or hundred different amplitudes. And they are accessible: the only requirement is a browser that can display different font sizes. They also spark discussion [11].

We describe a tag-cloud formalism, as an instance of Web 2.0 OLAP. Since we implemented a prototype, technical issues will be discussed regarding application design. In particular, we used iceberg cubes [12] to generate tag clouds online when the data and schema are provided extemporaneously. Because tag clouds are meant to convey a general impression, presenting approximate measures and clustering is sufficient: we propose specific metrics to measure the quality of tag-cloud approximations. We conclude the paper with experimental results on real and synthetic data sets.

2   Related Work

There are decentralized models [13] and systems [14] to support collaborative data sharing without a single schema.

According to Wu et al., it is difficult to navigate an OLAP schema without help; they have proposed a keyword-driven OLAP model [15]. There are several OLAP visualization techniques including the Cube Presentation Model (CPM) [16], Multiple Correspondence Analysis (MCA) [17] and other interactive systems [18].

Tag clouds have been popularized by the Web site Flickr launched in 2004. Several optimization opportunities exist: similar tags can be clustered together [19], tags can be pruned automatically [20] or by user intervention [21], tags can be indexed [21], and so on. Tag clouds can be adapted to spatio-temporal data [22, 23].

3   OLAP Formalism

3.1   Conventional OLAP Formalism

Most OLAP engines rely on a data cube [7]. A data cube C contains a non empty set of d dimensions $\mathcal{D} = \{D_i\}_{1 \leq i \leq d}$ and a non empty set of measures $\mathcal{M}$. Data cubes are usually derived from a *fact table* (see Table 2) where each dimension and measure is a column and all rows (or facts) have disjoint dimension tuples. Figure 1(a) gives tridimensional representation of the data cube.

Table 2. Fact table example

Dimensions				Measures	
location	time	salesman	product	cost	profit
Montreal	March	John	shoe	100$	10 $
Montreal	December	Smith	shoe	150$	30 $
Quebec	December	Smith	dress	175$	45 $
Ontario	April	Kate	dress	90$	10 $
Paris	March	John	shoe	100$	20 $
Paris	March	Marc	table	120$	10 $
Paris	June	Martin	shoe	120$	5 $
Lyon	April	Claude	dress	90$	10 $
New York	October	Joe	chair	100$	10 $
New York	May	Joe	chair	90$	10 $
Detroit	April	Jim	dress	90$	10 $

Measures can be aggregated using several operators such as AVERAGE, MAX, MIN, SUM, and COUNT. All of these measures and dimensions are typically prespecified in a database schema. Database administrators preaggregate views to accelerate queries.

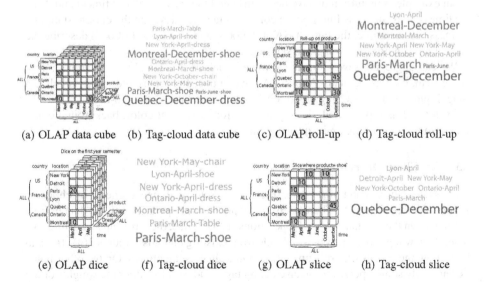

(a) OLAP data cube   (b) Tag-cloud data cube   (c) OLAP roll-up   (d) Tag-cloud roll-up

(e) OLAP dice   (f) Tag-cloud dice   (g) OLAP slice   (h) Tag-cloud slice

Fig. 1. Conventional OLAP operations vs. tag-cloud OLAP operations

The data cube supports the following operations:

- A *slice* specifies that you are only interested in some attribute values of a given dimension. For example, one may want to focus on one specific product (see Figure 1(g)). Similarly, a *dice* selects ranges of attribute values (see Figure 1(e)).
- A *roll-up* aggregates the measures on coarser attribute values. For example, from the sales given for every store, a user may want to see the sales aggregated per country (see Figure 1(c)). A *drill-down* is the reverse operation: from the sales per country, one may want to explore the sales per store in one country.

The various specific multidimensional views in Figure 1 are called *cuboids*.

3.2 Tag-Cloud OLAP Formalism

A Web 2.0 OLAP application should be supported by a flexible formalism that can adapt a wide range of data loaded by users. Processing time must be reasonable and batch processing should be avoided.

Unlike in conventional data cubes, we do not expect that most dimensions have explicit hierarchies when they are loaded: instead, users can specify how the data is laid out (see Section 5). As a related issue, the dimensions are not orthogonal in general: there might be a "City" dimension as a well as "Climate Zone" dimension. It is up to the user to organize the cities per climate zone or per country.

Definition 1 (Tag). *A tag is a term or phrase describing an object with corresponding non-negative weights determining its relative importance. Hence, a tag is made of a triplet (term, object, weight).*

As an example, a picture may have been attributed the tags "dog" (12 times) and "cat" (20 times). In a Business Intelligence context, a tag may describe the current state of a business. For example, the tags "USA" (16,000$) and "Canada" (8,000$) describe the sales of a given product by a given salesman.

We can aggregate several attribute values, such as "Canada" and "March," into a single term, such as "Canada–March." A tag composed of k attribute values is called a k-tag. Figure 1(b) shows a tag cloud representation of Table 2 using 3-tags.

Each tag T is represented visually using a font size, font color, background color, area or motif, depending on its measure values.

3.3 Tag-Cloud Operations

In our system, users can upload data, select a data set, and define a schema by choosing dimensions (see Figure 2). Then, users can apply various operations on the data using a menu bar. On the one hand, OLAP operations such as slice, dice, roll-up and drill-down generate new tag clouds and new cuboids from existing cuboids. Figures 1(d), 1(f) and 1(h), show the results of a roll-up, a dice, and a slice as tag clouds. On the other hand, we can apply some operations on an existing tag cloud: sort by either the weights or the terms of tags, remove some tags, remove lesser weighted tags, and so on. We estimate that a tag cloud should not have more than 150 tags.

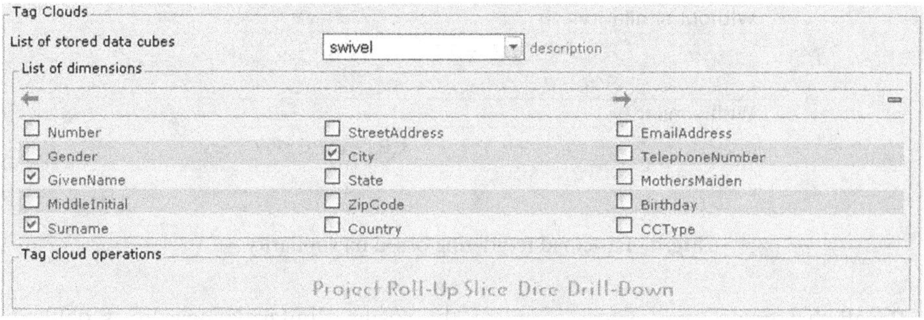

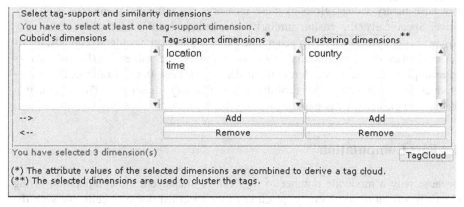

Fig. 2. User-driven schema design

Fig. 3. Choosing similarity dimensions

Tag-cloud layout has measurable benefits when trying to convey a general impression [24]. Hence, we wish to optimize the visual arrangement of tags. Chen et al. propose the computation of similarity measures between cuboids to help users explore data [25]: we apply this idea to define similarities between tags. First of all, users are asked to provide one or several dimensions they want to use to cluster the tags. Choosing the "Country" dimension would mean that the user wants the tags rearranged by countries so that "Montreal–April" and "Toronto–March" are nearby (see Figure 3). The clustering dimensions selected by the user together with the tag-cloud dimensions form a cuboid: in our example, we have the dimensions "Country," "City," and "Time." Since a tag contains a set of attribute values, it has a corresponding *subcuboid* defined by slicing the cuboid.

Several similarity measures can be applied between subcuboids: Jaccard, Euclidean distance, cosine similarity, Tanimoto similarity, Pearson correlation, Hamming distance, and so on. Which similarity measure is best depends on the application at hand, so advanced users should be given a choice. Commonly, similarity measures take up values in the interval $[-1, 1]$. Similarity measures are expected to be reflexive ($f(a, a) = 1$), symmetric ($f(a, b) = f(b, a)$) and transitive: if a is similar to b, and b is similar to c, then a is also similar to c.

Fig. 4. Tag-cloud reordering based on similarity

Recall that given two vectors v and w, the cosine similarity measure is defined as $\cos(v, w) = \sum_i v_i w_i / \sqrt{\sum_i v_i^2 \sum_i w_i^2} = v/|v| \cdot w/|w|$. The Tanimoto similarity is given by $\sum_i v_i w_i / (\sum_i v_i^2 + \sum_i w_i^2 - \sum_i v_i w_i)$; it becomes the Jaccard similarity when the vectors have binary values. Both of these measures are reflexive, symmetric and transitive. Specifically, the cosine similarity is transitive by this inequality: $\cos(v, z) \geq \cos(w, z) - \sqrt{1 - \cos(v, w)^2}$. To generalize the formulas from vectors to cuboids, it suffices to replace the single summation by one summation per dimension. Figure 4 shows an example of tag-cloud reordering to cluster similar tags. In this example, the "City–Product" tags were compared according to the "Country" dimension. The result is that the tags are clustered by countries.

4   Fast Computation

Because only a moderate number of tags can be displayed, the computation of tag clouds is a form of top-k query: given any user-specified range of cells, we seek the top-k cells having the largest measures. There is a little hope of answering such queries in near constant-time with respect to the number of facts without an index or a buffer. Indeed, finding all and only the elements with frequency exceeding a given frequency threshold [26] or merely finding the most frequent element [27] requires $\Omega(m)$ bits where m is the number of distinct items.

Various efficient techniques have been proposed for the related range MAX problem [28, 29], but they do not necessarily generalize. Instead, for the range top-k problem, we can partition sparse data cubes into customized data structures to speed up queries by an order of magnitude [30–32]. We can also answer range top-k queries using RD-trees [33] or R-trees [34]. In tag clouds, precision is not required and accuracy is less important; only the most significant tags are typically needed. Further, if all tags have similar weights, then any subset of tag may form an acceptable tag cloud.

A strategy to speed up top-k queries is to transform them into comparatively easier iceberg queries [12]. For example, in computing the top-10 ($k = 10$) best vendors, one could start by finding all vendors with a rating above 4/5. If there are at least 10 such vendors, then sorting this smaller list is enough. If not, one can restart the query, seeking vendors with a rating above 3/5. Given a histogram or selectivity estimates, we can reduce the number of expected iceberg queries [35]. Unfortunately, this approach is not necessarily applicable to multidimensional data since even computing iceberg aggregates once for each query may be prohibitive. However, iceberg cuboids can still be

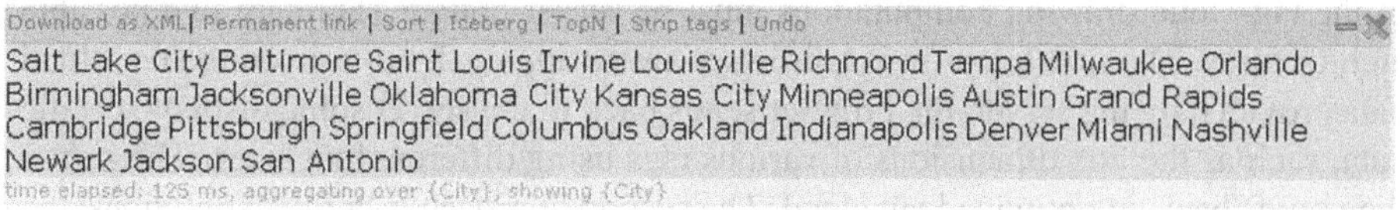

Salt Lake City Baltimore Saint Louis Irvine Louisville Richmond Tampa Milwaukee Orlando
Birmingham Jacksonville Oklahoma City Kansas City Minneapolis Austin Grand Rapids
Cambridge Pittsburgh Springfield Columbus Oakland Indianapolis Denver Miami Nashville
Newark Jackson San Antonio
time elapsed: 125 ms, aggregating over {City}, showing {City}

Fig. 5. Example of non informative tag cloud

put to good use. That is, one materializes the iceberg of a cuboid, small enough to fit
in main memory, from which the tag clouds are computed. Intuitively, a cuboid representing the largest measures is likely to provide reasonable tag clouds. Users mostly
notice tags with large font sizes [24]. A good approximation captures the tags having
significantly larger weights. To determine whether a tag cloud has such significant tags,
we can compute the *entropy*.

Definition 2 (Entropy of a tag cloud). *Let $T \in \mathcal{T}$ be a tag from a tag cloud $\mathcal{T}$, then*
$entropy(\mathcal{T}) = -\sum_{T \in \mathcal{T}} p(T)log(p(T))$ *where* $p(T) = \frac{weight(T)}{\sum_{x \in \mathcal{T}} weight(x)}$.

The entropy quantifies the disparity of weights between tags. The **lower** the entropy,
the **more** interesting the corresponding tag cloud is. Indeed, tag clouds with uniform
tag weights have maximal entropy and are visually not very informative (see Figure 5).

We can measure the quality of a low-entropy tag cloud by measuring false positives
and negatives: false positive happens when a tag has been falsely added to a tag cloud
whereas a false negative occurs when a tag is missing. These measures of error assume
that we limit the number of tags to a moderately small number. We use the following
quality indexes; index values are in $[0, 1]$ and a value of 0 is ideal; they are not applicable
to high-entropy tag clouds.

Definition 3. *Given approximate and exact tag clouds A and E, the false-positive and*
false-negative indexes are $\frac{\max_{t \in A, t \notin E} weight(t)}{\max_{t \in A} weight(t)}$ *and* $\frac{\max_{t \in E, t \notin A} weight(t)}{\max_{t \in E} weight(t)}$.

5 Tag-Cloud Drawing

While we can ensure some level of device-independent displays on the Web, by using images or plugins, text display in HTML may vary substantially from browser to
another. There is no common set of font browsers are required to support, and Web
standards do not dictate line-breaking algorithms or other typographical issues. It is not
practical to simulate the browser on a server. Meanwhile, if we wish to remain accessible and to abide by open standards, producing HTML and ECMAScript is the favorite
option.

Given tag-cloud data, the tag-cloud drawing problem is to optimally display the tags,
generally using HTML, so that some desirable properties are met, including the following: (1) the screen space usage is minimized; (2) when applicable, similar tags are
clustered together. Typically, the width of the tag cloud is fixed, but its height can vary.

For practical reasons, we do not wish for the server to send all of the data to the browser,
including a possibly large number of similarity measures between tags. Hence, some

of the tag-cloud drawing computations must be server-bound. There are two possible architectures. The first scenario is a browser-aware approach [19]: given the tag-cloud data provided by the server, the browser sends back to the server some display-specific data, such as the box dimensions of various tags using different font sizes. The server then sends back an optimized tag cloud. The second approach is browser-oblivious: the server optimizes the display of the tag cloud without any knowledge of the browser by passing simple display hints. The browser can then execute a final and inexpensive display optimization. While browser-oblivious optimization is necessarily limited, it has reduced latency and it is easily cacheable.

Browser-oblivious optimization can take many forms. For example, we could send classes of tags and instruct the browser to display them on separate lines [20]. In our system, tags are sent to the browser as an ordered list, using the convention that successive tags are similar and should appear nearby. Given a similarity measure w between tags, we want to minimize $\sum_{p,q} w(p,q) d(p,q)$ where $d(p,q)$ is a distance function between the two tags in the list and the sum is over all tags. Ideally, $d(p,q)$ should be the physical distance between the tags as they appear in the browser; we model this distance with the index distance: if tag a appears at index i in the list and tag b appears at index j, their distance is the integer $|i - j|$. This optimization problem is an instance of the NP-complete MINIMUM LINEAR ARRANGEMENT (MLA) problem: an optimal linear arrangement of a graph $G = (V, E)$, is a map f from V onto $\{1, 2, \ldots, N\}$ minimizing $\sum_{u,v \in V} |f(u) - f(v)|$.

Proposition 1. *The browser-oblivious tag-cloud optimization problem is NP-Complete.*

There is an $O(\sqrt{\log n} \log \log n)$-approximation for the MLA problem [36] in some instances. However, for our generic purposes, the greedy NEAREST NEIGHBOR (NN) algorithm might suffice: insert any tag in an empty list, then repeatedly append a tag most similar to the latest tag in the list, until all tags have been inserted. It runs in $O(n^2)$ time where n is the number of tags. Another heuristic for the MLA problem is the PAIRWISE EXCHANGE MONTE CARLO (PWMC) method [37]: after applying NN, you repeatedly consider the exchange of two tags chosen at random, permuting them if it reduces the MLA cost. Another MONTE CARLO (MC) heuristic begins with the application of NN [38]: cut the list into two blocks at a random location, test if exchanging the two blocks reduces the MLA cost, if so proceed; repeat.

Additional display hints can be inserted in this list. For example, if two tags must absolutely be very close to each other, a GLUED token could be inserted. Also, if two tags can be permuted freely in the list, then a PERMUTABLE token could be inserted: the list could take the form of a PQ tree [39].

6   Experiments

Throughout these experiments, we used the Java version 1.6.0_02 from Sun Microsystems Inc. on an Apple MacPro machine with 2 Dual-Core Intel Xeon processors running at 2.66 GHz and 2 GiB of RAM.

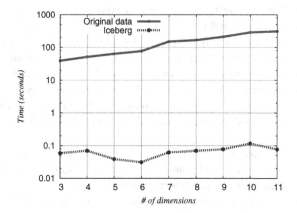

Fig. 6. Computing tag clouds from original data vs. icebergs: iceberg limit value set at 150 and tag-cloud size is 9 (US Income 2000)

6.1 Iceberg-Based Computation

To validate the generation of tag clouds from icebergs, we have run tests over the US Income 2000 data set [40] (42 dimensions and about 2×10^5 facts) as well as a synthetic data set (18 dimensions and 2×10^4 facts) provided by Swivel (http://www.swivel.com/data_sets/show/1002247). Figure 6 shows that while some tag-cloud computations require several minutes, iceberg-based computations can be much faster.

From each data set, we generated a 4-dimensional data cube. We used the COUNT function to aggregate data. Tag clouds were computed from each data cube using the iceberg approximation with different values of *limit*: the number of facts retained. We also implemented exact computations using temporary tables. We specified different values for tag-cloud size, limiting the maximum number of tags. For each iceberg limit value and tag-cloud size, we computed the entropy of the tag cloud, the false-positive and false-negative indexes, and processing time for both of iceberg approximation and exact computation.

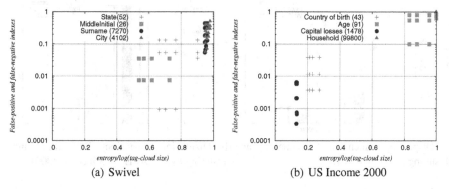

(a) Swivel   (b) US Income 2000

Fig. 7. False-negative and false-positive indexes (0 is best, 1 is worst), values under 0.0001 are not included

We plotted in Figure 7 the false-positive and false-negative indexes as a function of the relative entropy (entropy/log(tag-cloud size)) using various iceberg limit values (150, 600, 1200, 4800, and 19600) and various tag-cloud sizes (50, 100, 150, and 200), for a total of 20 tag clouds per dimension. The Y axis is in a logarithmic scale. Points having their indexes equal to zero are not displayed. As discussed in Section 4, false-positive and false-negative indexes should be low when the entropy is low. We verify that for low-entropy values ($< \frac{3}{4} \log$(tag-cloud size)), the indexes are always close to zero which indicates a good approximation. Meanwhile, small iceberg cuboids can be processed much faster.

Experimentally, we found that the entropy is not sensitive to the iceberg limit, but it grows with the tag-cloud size (see Figures 10(a) and 9(a)). Naturally, the tag-cloud size is bounded by the cardinality of the chosen dimension.

We computed the relative gain in processing time due to the iceberg limit as $(t - t')/t$ where t is the time required for the exact computation whereas t' is the time used by an iceberg computation (see Figures 10(b) and 9(b)). For these tests, the tag-cloud size was set to 150. Generally, the lower the iceberg limit value, the better the gain. High cardinality dimensions benefit less from a small iceberg limit. Also, the ratios of false positive and false negative decrease as the iceberg limit increases. However, for low-cardinality dimensions, these ratios are often close to zero, so only high-cardinality dimensions benefit from higher iceberg limits. Hence, you should choose an iceberg limit small or large depending on whether you have a low or high cardinality dimension.

6.2 Similarity Computation

Using our two data sets, we tested the NN, PWMC, and MC heuristics using both the cosine and the Tanimoto similarity measures. From data cubes made of all available dimensions, we used all possible 1-tag clouds, using successively all other dimensions as clustering dimension for a total of $2 \times (18 \times 17 + 42 \times 41) = 4056$ layout optimizations. The iceberg limit value was set at 150. The MC heuristic never fared better than

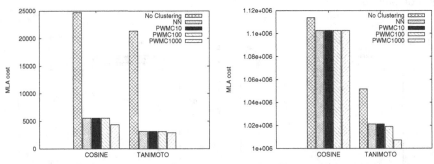

(a) Displaying dimension "Givenname" and clustering by "State" (Swivel)

(b) Displaying dimension "HHDFMX" and clustering by "ARACE" (US Income 2000)

Fig. 8. MLA costs for two examples: the PWMC heuristic was applied using 10, 100 and 1000 random exchanges

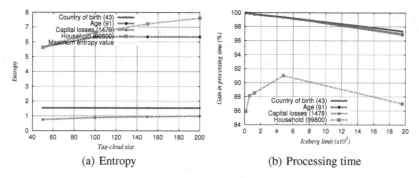

(a) Entropy   (b) Processing time

Fig. 9. Benchmarking iceberg computation over US Income 2000

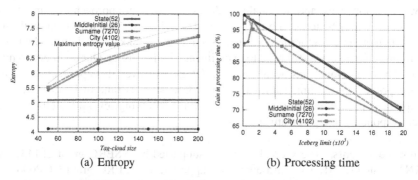

(a) Entropy   (b) Processing time

Fig. 10. Benchmarking iceberg computation over Swivel

Table 3. Comparison of various MLA heuristics over the Swivel data set using the cosine similarity measure (306 tag clouds). The running time is the average of 100 optimizations for tag clouds of size 150. The number of tag clouds (out of 306) having at least a given gain is given.

	NN	PWMC		
		10	100	1000
time (s)	0.003	0.01	0.03	0.2
MLA gain > 0%	154	154	154	154
MLA gain > 30%	143	143	145	148
MLA gain > 70%	112	112	112	116
MLA gain > 90%	97	97	97	99

NN, even when considering a very large number of random block permutations: we rejected this heuristic as ineffective. However, as Figure 8 shows, the PWMC heuristic can sometimes significantly outperform NN when a large number (1000) of tag exchanges are considered, but it only outperforms NN by more than 20% in less than 5% of all layout optimizations. Meanwhile, table 3 shows that if our objective is to reduce the MLA cost by 90%, all heuristics are equivalent. However, it also shows that PWMC can be several order of magnitudes slower than NN: NN is 10 times faster than PWMC with 100 exchanges and 70 times faster than PWMC with 1000 exchanges. Computing the similarity function over an iceberg cuboid was moderately expensive (0.07 s) for a small iceberg cuboid (limit set to 150 cells): the exact computation of the similarity function can dwarf the cost of the heuristics (NN and PWMC) over a moderately large data set. Informal tests suggest that NN computed over a small iceberg cuboid provides significant visual layouts.

7   Conclusions

According to our experimental results, precomputing a single iceberg cuboid per data cube allows to generate adequate approximate tag clouds online. Combined with modern Web technologies such as AJAX and JSON, it provides a responsive application. However, we plan to make more precise the relationship between iceberg cubes, entropy, dimension sizes, and our quality indexes. Yet another approach to compute tag clouds quickly may be to use a bitmap index [41]. While we built a Web 2.0 with support for numerous collaborations features such as permalinks, tag-cloud embeddings with iframe elements, we still need to experiment with live users. Our approach to multidimensional tag clouds has been to rely on k-tags. However, this approach might not be appropriate when a dimension has a linear flow such as time or latitude. A more appropriate approach is to allow the use of a slider [22] tying several tag clouds, each one corresponding to a given attribute value.

Acknowledgements. The second author is supported by NSERC grant 261437 and FQRNT grant 112381. The third author is supported by NSERC grant OGP0009184 and FQRNT grant PR-119731. The authors wish to thank Owen Kaser from UNB for his contributions.

References

1. Heer, J., Viégas, F.B., Wattenberg, M.: Voyagers and voyeurs: supporting asynchronous collaborative information visualization. In: CHI 2007, pp. 1029–1038 (2007)
2. Wattenberg, M., Kriss, J.: Designing for social data analysis. IEEE Transactions on Visualization and Computer Graphics 12(4), 549–557 (2006)
3. IBM: Many Eyes (2007), http://services.alphaworks.ibm.com/manyeyes/ (accessed 7-6-2007)
4. Swivel, Inc.: Swivel (2007), http://www.swivel.com (accessed 7-6-2007)
5. Butler, D.: Data sharing: the next generation. Nature 446(7131), 1–10 (2007)
6. Codd, E.F.: Providing OLAP (on-line analytical processing) to user-analysis: an IT mandate. Technical report, E. F. Codd and Associates (1993)
7. Gray, J., Bosworth, A., Layman, A., Pirahesh, H.: Data cube: A relational aggregation operator generalizing group-by, cross-tab, and sub-total. In: ICDE 1996, pp. 152–159 (1996)
8. Body, M., Miquel, M., Bédard, Y., Tchounikine, A.: A multidimensional and multiversion structure for OLAP applications. In: DOLAP 2002, pp. 1–6 (2002)
9. Morzy, T., Wrembel, R.: On querying versions of multiversion data warehouse. In: DOLAP 2004, pp. 92–101 (2004)
10. Havenstein, H.: BI vendors seek to tap end-user power: New class of tools built to reap user knowledge for customizing analytic applications. InfoWorld 22, 20–21 (2003)

11. Viégas, F., Wattenberg, M., McKeon, M., van Ham, F., Kriss, J.: Harry potter and the meat-filled freezer: A case study of spontaneous usage of visualization tools. In: HICSS 2008, pp. 1–10 (2008)
12. Carey, M.J., Kossmann, D.: On saying "enough already!" in SQL. In: SIGMOD 1997, pp. 219–230 (1997)
13. Taylor, N.E., Ives, Z.G.: Reconciling while tolerating disagreement in collaborative data sharing. In: SIGMOD 2006, pp. 13–24. ACM, New York (2006)
14. Green, T.J., Karvounarakis, G., Taylor, N.E., Biton, O., Ives, Z.G., Tannen, V.: ORCHESTRA: facilitating collaborative data sharing. In: SIGMOD 2007, pp. 1131–1133. ACM, New York (2007)
15. Wu, P., Sismanis, Y., Reinwald, B.: Towards keyword-driven analytical processing. In: SIGMOD 2007, pp. 617–628 (2007)
16. Maniatis, A., Vassiliadis, P., Skiadopoulos, S., Vassiliou, Y., Mavrogonatos, G., Michalarias, I.: A presentation model & non-traditional visualization for OLAP. International Journal of Data Warehousing and Mining 1, 1–36 (2005)
17. Ben Messaoud, R., Boussaid, O., Loudcher Rabaséda, S.: Efficient multidimensional data representations based on multiple correspondence analysis. In: KDD 2006, pp. 662–667 (2006)
18. Techapichetvanich, K., Datta, A.: Interactive visualization for OLAP. In: Gervasi, O., Gavrilova, M.L., Kumar, V., Laganá, A., Lee, H.P., Mun, Y., Taniar, D., Tan, C.J.K. (eds.) ICCSA 2005. LNCS, vol. 3482, pp. 206–214. Springer, Heidelberg (2005)
19. Kaser, O., Lemire, D.: Tag-cloud drawing: Algorithms for cloud visualization. In: WWW 2007 – Tagging and Metadata for Social Information Organization (2007)
20. Hassan-Montero, Y., Herrero-Solana, V.: Improving tag-clouds as visual information retrieval interfaces. In: InSciT 2006 (2006)
21. Millen, D.R., Feinberg, J., Kerr, B.: Dogear: Social bookmarking in the enterprise. In: CHI 2006, pp. 111–120 (2006)
22. Russell, T.: Cloudalicious: folksonomy over time. In: JCDL, p. 364 (2006)
23. Jaffe, A., Naaman, M., Tassa, T., Davis, M.: Generating summaries and visualization for large collections of geo-referenced photographs. In: MIR 2006, pp. 89–98 (2006)
24. Rivadeneira, A.W., Gruen, D.M., Muller, M.J., Millen, D.R.: Getting our head in the clouds: toward evaluation studies of tagclouds. In: CHI 2007, pp. 995–998 (2007)
25. Chen, Q., Dayal, U., Hsu, M.: OLAP-based data mining for business intelligence applications in telecommunications and e-commerce. In: Bhalla, S. (ed.) DNIS 2000. LNCS, vol. 1966, pp. 1–19. Springer, Heidelberg (2000)
26. Cormode, G., Muthukrishnan, S.: What's hot and what's not: tracking most frequent items dynamically. ACM Trans. Database Syst. 30(1), 249–278 (2005)
27. Alon, N., Matias, Y., Szegedy, M.: The space complexity of approximating the frequency moments. In: STOC 1996, pp. 20–29 (1996)
28. Chazelle, B.: A functional approach to data structures and its use in multidimensional searching. SIAM J. Comput. 17(3), 427–462 (1988)
29. Poon, C.K.: Dynamic orthogonal range queries in OLAP. Theoretical Computer Science 296(3), 487–510 (2003)
30. Luo, Z.W., Ling, T.W., Ang, C.H., Lee, S.Y., Cui, B.: Range top/bottom k queries in OLAP sparse data cubes. In: Mayr, H.C., Lazanský, J., Quirchmayr, G., Vogel, P. (eds.) DEXA 2001. LNCS, vol. 2113, pp. 678–687. Springer, Heidelberg (2001)
31. Loh, Z.X., Ling, T.W., Ang, C.H., Lee, S.Y.: Adaptive method for range top-k queries in OLAP data cubes. In: Hameurlain, A., Cicchetti, R., Traunmüller, R. (eds.) DEXA 2002. LNCS, vol. 2453, pp. 648–657. Springer, Heidelberg (2002)
32. Loh, Z.X., Ling, T.W., Ang, C.H., Lee, S.Y.: Analysis of pre-computed partition top method for range top-k queries in OLAP data cubes. In: CIKM 2002, pp. 60–67 (2002)

33. Chung, Y.D., Yang, W.S., Kim, M.H.: An efficient, robust method for processing of partial top-k/bottom-k queries using the RD-tree in OLAP. Decision Support Systems 43(2), 313–321 (2007)

34. Seokjin, H., Moon, B., Sukho, L.: Efficient execution of range top-k queries in aggregate r-trees. IEICE – Transactions on Information and Systems E88-D (11), 2544–2554 (2005)

35. Donjerkovic, D., Ramakrishnan, R.: Probabilistic optimization of top n queries. In: VLDB 1999, pp. 411–422 (1999)

36. Feige, U., Lee, J.R.: An improved approximation ratio for the minimum linear arrangement problem. Inf. Process. Lett. 101(1), 26–29 (2007)

37. Bhasker, J., Sahni, S.: Optimal linear arrangement of circuit components. J. VLSI Comp. Syst. 2(1), 87–109 (1987)

38. Johnson, D., Krishnan, S., Chhugani, J., Kumar, S., Venkatasubramanian, S.: Compressing large boolean matrices using reordering techniques. In: VLDB 2004, pp. 13–23 (2004)

39. Booth, K.S., Lueker, G.S.: Testing for the consecutive ones property, interval graphs, and graph planarity using PQ-tree algorithms. Journal of Computer and System Sciences 13, 335–379 (1976)

40. Hettich, S., Bay, S.D.: The UCI KDD archive (2000), http://kdd.ics.uci.edu (checked 2008-04-28)

41. O'Neil, P., Quass, D.: Improved query performance with variant indexes. In: SIGMOD 1997, pp. 38–49 (1997)

Compressing XML Data Streams with DAG+BSBC

Stefan Böttcher, Rita Hartel, and Christian Heinzemann

University of Paderborn, EIM - Electrical Engineering, Computer Science and Mathematics
Fürstenallee 11, 33102 Paderborn, Germany
{stb,rst,chris227}@uni-paderborn.de

Abstract. Whenever the growing amount of XML data that has to be stored, processed, exchanged, or transmitted becomes a major cost driver or performance bottleneck, XML compression is an important way to reduce these problems. However, many applications, e.g. those exchanging XML data streams, also require efficient path query processing on the structure of compressed XML data streams. We present an XML compression technique called DAG+BSBC, which extends Bit-Stream-Based-Compression (BSBC) [3] by a sparse index to compressed constants that reflects DAG pointers. Furthermore, DAG+BSBC supports XML stream compression, queries on compressed data, and provides a compression ratio that not only significantly outperforms that of other queriable XML compression techniques, like XGrind, but is also very competitive compared to non-queriable compression techniques like gzip and XMill.

1 Introduction

1.1 Motivation

XML is widely used in business applications and is the de facto standard for information exchange in fixed wired networks. Because of the verbose structure of XML, applications operating on continuous XML data streams or requiring very large amounts of XML data and running on platforms such as mobile networks, where storage, bandwidth or energy are limited, will likely benefit from XML compression techniques for the following reason. Applications save energy and processing time not only when loading compressed instead of uncompressed XML data, but also when they execute path queries directly on the compressed data format without decompressing it. We propose an approach to XML compression, called DAG+BSBC, an extension of Bit-Stream-Based-Compression (BSBC) [3]. DAG+BSBC supports path queries on XML data streams while achieving a better compression ratio than other XML compression techniques (e.g. XGrind) which support path queries. Furthermore, DAG+BSBC achieves a better compression ratio than text compression tools like gzip and sometimes even beats the non-queryable format of XMill.

1.2 Contributions

This paper proposes DAG+BSBC which combines the following properties:

- It separates text constants and attribute values of an XML file from the XML tree structure, and removes redundancies in the tree structure by sharing identical sub-trees.

J. Cordeiro et al. (Eds.): WEBIST 2008, LNBIP 18, pp. 65–79, 2009.
© Springer-Verlag Berlin Heidelberg 2009

- It compresses the tree structure to a bit stream and a common sub-tree pointer stream, it collects bit stream positions of element and attribute names in inverted lists, it groups structurally related text constants and attribute values into containers to improve the compression ratio, and it uses sparse pointers referencing constants in these containers.
- It organizes compressed data into packages allowing thus faster access to compressed data and shorter relative addresses in inverted lists and constant containers.
- It provides processing of forward-oriented core XPath queries [19] on compressed data that even outperforms query processing on uncompressed data.
- Beyond our previous paper on Bit-Stream-Based-Compression (BSBC) [3], we
- describe both XML compression strategies, BSBC and DAG+BSBC,
- present the sparse pointer concept for fast access to containers of constants,
- describe navigation on compressed common sub-trees,
- outline how constant access is done on compressed DAG+BSBC data, and
- show that query evaluation can be done faster on BSBC compressed data than on other compressed data formats and even than on uncompressed XML data.

As a result, BSBC and its extension DAG+BSBC have the following advantages. In comparison to other approaches to path queries on XML streams (e.g. AFilter [9]) that support only some axes and that require decompression to process queries, BSBC and DAG+BSBC support the execution of path queries involving all XML axes, and they do not require decompression for the purpose of path query processing. Furthermore, our extensive evaluation demonstrates that the compression ratios achieved by BSBC and by DAG+BSBC outperform those of other XML compression techniques (like XGrind) that support path queries. To the best of our knowledge, there is no other XML compression system that combines the advantages of BSBC or DAG+BSBC.

1.3 Paper Organization

The remainder of this paper is organized as follows. Section 2 describes how a SAX stream is compressed by two compression steps each of which transforms an input data stream into two or three compressed output data streams, and it explains how the document structure is stored in a sub-tree pointer stream and in a bit stream and separated from the elements and attributes which are stored in inverted lists. Section 3 describes how to implement navigation along the XML axes and extended navigation on the bit stream, the sub-tree pointer stream, and the inverted lists. Section 4 compares the compression ratio of BSBC with that of other approaches. Section 5 compares BSBC and DAG+BSBC to related work. Finally, Section 6 summarizes our contributions.

2 The Streams – Key of Our Solution

DAG+BSBC views XML data as an input stream of SAX events that is transformed by two steps into four other streams (c.f. Figure 1).

Step 1 transforms the SAX stream (a) into packages of *constant containers* (b) and an intermediate binary *DAG stream* (c), which is in Step 2 transformed into a *sub-tree pointer stream* (d) representing the backward pointers to shared sub-trees within the

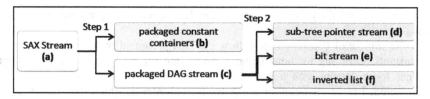

Fig. 1. Compression Steps of the BSBC system

DAG, a *bit stream* (e) capturing the tree structure of the XML data, and an *inverted list* (f), containing a mapping from element and attribute names to positions within the bit stream.

In comparison to DAG+BSBC, BSBC skips Step 1(c), i.e. does not generate a DAG stream and does not share common sub-trees. Instead, BSBC separates the SAX stream (a) into packages of constant containers (b), the bit stream (e) and the inverted lists (f), i.e., packages generated by BSBC do not contain the sub-tree pointer stream of Step 2(d).

2.1 Step 1: Separating XML into DAG Packages and Constant Containers

As we expect a significantly higher repetition ratio for element and attribute names than for constants, we first separate element and attribute names from constants, and we then use a different technique for the compression of element and attribute names than we use for the compression of constants.

Step 1 is done as follows. The input SAX stream is parsed and separated into a stream of two different kinds of packages: packages of constant containers, which contain the *constants*, i.e., the text and attribute values of the SAX stream, and DAG packages which contain the XML structure.

The DAG packages are constructed by a DAG processor like e.g. the one presented in [5] and consist of the following kinds of events: *startElement(id, label)* and *endElement(id, label)*, which are similar to the corresponding SAX events, but which contain an additional, unique node ID id, and the additional event *commonSubtreeFound(id)* which represents a backward pointer to the sub-tree rooted by the node with ID id.

The structure-oriented SAX events, i.e., *startDocument, startElement, endElement,* and *endDocument*, are passed to the DAG compressor. Hereby, the attributes are treated as follows: An attribute definition of the form att="value" is passed as an event sequence *startElement("@att"), endElement("@att")*, which is sent to the DAG compressor, whereas the pair (@att, value) is passed to the constant containers and will be processed later.

Whenever a character-event is received, an event sequence *startElement("=T"), endElement("=T")* is sent to the DAG compressor, and the pair (E,T) is passed to the constant container of E, where E is the label of the parent node of the text node and T is the text value of the character event. However, if an event *startElement("E1")* is directly followed by an event *endElement("E1")* in the SAX stream, i.e., if an empty element tag is found, this is treated like a character-event receiving an empty text node. That is, an event sequence *startElement("=T"), endElement("=T")* is sent to the DAG compressor, and the pair (E1, "") is passed to the constant containers, where "" is the empty constant. This is done to ensure that all leaf nodes are either constants, which are represented by "=T", or attribute nodes, which are represented by a name starting with '@'.

For the storage of constants, we follow the idea presented in XMill [16] and sort the constants according to their parent element into separate data containers. Each container for constants with a parent element or attribute Ei stores the constants' values included in Ei elements or attributes in the order in which they occur in the document. Each container is then compressed using BZip2 which implements Burrows-Wheeler Block-Sorting [7] followed by Huffman-Encoding [15].

In order to support (unbounded) XML streams, we divide both structures (DAG and constants) into packages: Whenever a certain number n of events was received, the DAG that was compressed so far, the path of non-compressed nodes (i.e., the nodes from root to the current node, the next-siblings of which were not yet inserted into the DAG), and the compressed constant containers are passed to Step 2 of DAG+BSBC. This allows a pipelined approach that is capable to compress (unbounded) XML data streams.

2.2   Step 2: Transforming DAG Packages into Multiple Streams

During decompression or query processing, we have to correctly recombine element and attribute names with included constants, i.e., we have to know the correct relative positions of both kinds of data. For this purpose, within Step 2, we use the DAG stream for generating three new streams as follows. We separate element and attribute names from the structure of the DAG stream, i.e., we transfer names to a separate stream, called *inverted lists*. The remaining structure of the DAG stream is stored in the *bit stream* and the *sub-tree pointer stream*. These three streams together enable the traversal of the XML document structure without requiring decompression.

2.2.1   The Bit Stream and the Sub-tree Pointer Stream

The *bit stream* simply contains a "1"-bit for each event *startElement* of the DAG stream, and a "0"-bit for each event *endElement* of the DAG stream.

In an intermediate table, a mapping from node IDs to positions of the corresponding '1'-bit within the bit stream is stored. Whenever a commonSubtreeFound(id)-event is read, the position PID of the node with ID id is looked up, and the pair (P, PID) representing the sub-tree pointer is written to the sub-tree pointer stream, where P is the current position within the bit stream. As one commonSubtreeFound(id)-event may directly follow another commonSubtreeFound(id2)-event in the DAG event stream, there may occur multiple pairs (P,PID), ..., (P,PID2) in the sub-tree pointer stream that refer to the same current bit stream position P. The order of the sub-tree pointers (P,PID), ..., (P,PID2) in the sub-tree pointer stream reflects the document order of the referenced common sub-trees in the original uncompressed XML tree.

2.2.2   The Inverted Lists

In order to store the mapping of element and attribute names to positions within the bit stream, BSBC uses *inverted lists*, where each element or attribute name occurring in the package is associated with a list of relative addresses (N1,N2,...) where the elements or attributes with this name occur. Each element and attribute name is thus stored only once per package within the inverted list, regardless of how often it occurs in the XML data. As furthermore no additional pointers are needed, this succinct representation of elements and attributes and their positions can significantly save space.

While parsing the DAG stream, whenever receiving an event startElement(id, "E1"), a '1'-bit is inserted into the bit stream (as described above), but at the same time, the position P of the new '1'-bit within the bit stream is written to the inverted list of E1.

This will be useful for the typical XPath location steps /E1 and //E1 as outlined in Section 3. In the rare case where the element name of an element at a specific position N, say N=10, is needed, it is still possible to search N in the sorted list of each element E until the position N is found or until a number >N indicates that N will not occur in the sorted list of positions of E elements.

Furthermore, it is possible to sort the inverted lists within each package such that the entries for all attribute names precede the entries for all elements. This makes unnecessary all the "@"-characters used as a prefix for each attribute name. Instead, all the "@"-characters can be replaced by a single pointer per package to the first inverted list of an element.

In order to reach a better compression result, we do not use each element or attribute name in each package. Instead, we use a symbol table and that defines a symbol SE1 for an element or attribute name E1, and we replace each occurrence of E1 by its symbol SE1.

The inverted element list for the constant nodes, i.e., the inverted element list for the element "=T" is not stored in the final compressed data, as each '1'-bit position that is not included in any inverted element list has to be a constant node.

2.3   Optimizing Query Evaluation by Sparse Constant Pointers

Within the evaluation of path queries, we have to find a constant T for a given position P within the bit stream that represents the placeholder "=T" for T. The element label "E1" of the parent of T is being used for identifying the correct constant container CE1, but in order to identify the correct position of T within CE1, we have to know, how many nodes with label "=T" and with a parent node with label "E1" exist up to the current context node. Without any additional information, we would have to count these nodes from the start of the document, i.e., we would not be able to skip parts of the compressed document during query evaluation.

In order to avoid this disadvantage, we provide a sparse index to constants, i.e. we attach to roughly every d-th bit D^1 in the bit stream *constant counters* that count how many nodes with label "=T" and with a parent node with label "E" exist up to D for each element label E that has occurred within the document so far. The value of d can be chosen arbitrarily, where a smaller value supports faster query processing and a larger value results in stronger compression.

---

[1] Here, "roughly every d-th bit D" means that we prefer bits D that correspond to a low depth of the XML tree. Furthermore, we only take D bits that do not belong to a commonly used sub-tree.

3 Navigation on the Streams

As each navigation step on an uncompressed XML document can start at an arbitrarily chosen context node C, each navigation step on the DAG+BSBC-compressed XML document can start at an arbitrary state (P_{start}, S) corresponding to C. Thereby, P_{start} denotes the bit stream position of the start-element tag of C, and S is a stack of continuation pointers. We first explain basic navigation steps on the bit -stream. Then, we use them to compose more complex navigation steps on the bit -stream. Finally, we describe how the stack S of continuation pointers is used for continuing processing after reusing a common sub-tree, and how we find the constant values of a given current context node C.

3.1 Basic Navigation Using the First-Attribute, First-Child and Next-Sibling Axes

Given the bit stream position P_{start} of the current context node C, many navigation steps, e.g., finding C's next–sibling, requires finding the bit stream position P_{end} of C's end-element tag.

3.1.1 Finding the Position P_{end} of the End-Tag

In order to proceed to the bit stream position P_{end} of the "0"-bit in the bit stream that represents the end-tag of the current context node, each start-tag has to be closed by exactly one end-tag, i.e., we search the corresponding "0"-bit for each "1"-bit on the bit stream as follows. The search counts "0"-bits and "1"-bits, starts at the bit stream position P_{start}, and continues counting bits of the bit stream until the number of "1"-bits is equal to the number of "0"-bits, i.e., each start-tag has been closed.

P_{end} may occur in a later package than P_{start}. Note that nevertheless, we can use relative addresses for P_{start} and P_{end} because the operation 'find position P_{end} of the corresponding end tag' operates on the bit streams only, i.e., searching for P_{end} in the bit stream of a later package does not disturb the use of small relative addresses.

3.1.2 Proceeding to the Next-Sibling

In order to find the bit stream Position PNS_{start} of the bit that tells us whether or not the current context node has a next sibling, we first proceed to the position P_{end} of the "0"-bit in the bit stream that represents the end-tag of the current context node. The bit at position $P_{end}+1$, i.e., after the bit representing the end-tag, is a "1"-bit representing the next-sibling if a next-sibling exists, and a "0"-bit otherwise.

3.1.3 Distinguishing Elements and Attributes from Constants

The current context node represented by a "1"-bit at position P_{start} in the bit stream is an element name if the node is an inner node, i.e., if the next bit stream position $P_{start}+1$ also contains a "1"-bit. However, if the next bit stream position $P_{start}+1$ contains a "0"-bit, the current context node represented by the "1"-bit at position P_{start} is a leaf node, i.e., it either is a constant, or it is an attribute name. It is a constant, if and only if P_{start} can not be found in any inverted list of an attribute name.

3.1.4 Determining Element Names and Attribute Names and Distinguishing Elements from Attributes

Which name the element or attribute of the current context node C has, can be distinguished by searching position P_{start} in the inverted lists. C is an attribute or an element, depending on in which kind of an inverted list P_{start} is found. Inverted lists for attributes are distinguished from inverted lists for elements by grouping inverted lists in each package and by providing a pointer to the first inverted list of an element for each package.

3.1.5 Proceeding to the First-Attribute Node

Let P_{start} be the bit stream position of an element node C. C has a first-attribute if and only if bit stream position $P_{start}+1$ contains a "1"-bit and represents an attribute. In this case, $P_{start}+1$ represents C's first-attribute.

3.1.6 Proceeding to the First-Child Node

In order to find the bit stream Position PFC_{start} of the bit that tells us whether the current context node has a first-child, we have to proceed similar as when searching for the first-attribute, except that whenever a "1"-bit represents an attribute instead of the first-child, we use the bit stream to proceed to the attribute's next-sibling.[2] The attribute's next-sibling is either the next attribute, in which case we continue to search for a next-sibling or it is the first-child or it does not exist, which means that there is no first-child.

3.2 Navigation Using the Other Forward Axes

Given a position P_{start} of the start-tag of the current context node, we first determine the position P_{end} of the end-tag of the current context node as explained before. The next step depends on the forward axis to be used.

3.2.1 Proceeding to Descendant-or-Self::E1

When a location step //E1 requires searching a descendant-or-self E1 element, the search is significantly easier than standard path search for a descendant-or-self E1. Only E1 elements with a bit stream position $PE1_{start}$ in the interval of $[P_{start}, P_{end})$ fulfill the descendant-or-self condition. Therefore, in the packages that match these addresses[3], we simply lookup the inverted lists for E1 in order to find the bit stream positions $PE1_{start}$ of E1 descendant nodes with $P_{start} \leq PE1_{start} < P_{end}$.

3.2.2 Proceeding to Child::E1 or to Attribute::A1

When we search a child::E1 or an attribute @A1 respectively, we use the inverted lists of E1 or @A1 in all relevant packages to look for positions $PE1_{start}$ with $P_{start} < PE1_{start} < P_{end}$, and we use the bit streams to check that the depth of $PE1_{start}$ is exactly

---

[2] This is where we find the first-child because further attributes of C are stored as siblings of the first-attribute and the first-child is stored as the 'next-sibling' of the last attribute in our simple element stream.

[3] We use $PE1_{start} < P_{end}$ as a shortcut for 'P_{end} belongs to a later package than $PE1_{start}$ or they belong to the same package and $PE1_{start}$ is less than P_{end}'.

one more than the depth of P_{start}, i.e., the number of "1"-bits is exactly one more than the number of "0"-bits in the bit stream interval from P_{start} to $PE1_{start}$. These positions $PE1_{start}$ represent the element start-tags for the child::E1 elements or the attributes @A1 that we are looking for.

3.2.3 Proceeding to Following-Sibling::E1

When we search a following-sibling::E1, we additionally lookup the bit stream position PP_{end} of the end-tag of the parent of current context node. PP_{end} is the first bit stream position after P_{end} where the number of "0"-bits exceeds the number of "1"-bits by one.

Then, we use the inverted lists of E1 in all relevant packages to look for positions $PE1_{start}$ with $P_{end} < PE1_{start} < PP_{end}$, and we use the bit streams to check that the depth of $PE1_{start}$ is the same as the depth of P_{start}, i.e., the number of "1"-bits is equal to the number of "0"-bits in the bit stream interval from P_{start} to $PE1_{start}$. These positions $PE1_{start}$ represent the element start-tags for the following-sibling::E1 elements that we are looking for.

3.2.4 Proceeding to Following::E1

Finally, when we search a following::E1, we use the inverted lists of E1 to look for positions that are larger than P_{end} or occur in a later package.

3.3 Backward Axes

We do not explicitly consider queries containing backward axes here, as it is possible to rewrite each XPath query using backward axes into an equivalent XPath query using forward axes only. An approach on how to rewrite backward axes is presented in [19].

3.4 Handling Sub-tree Pointers and Finding Constants in DAG+BSBC

So far, we did not mention how to handle the sub-tree pointers stored within the sub-tree pointer stream and how to continue processing when returning from a previously compressed common sub-tree.

Whenever we reach a position P within the bit stream, before we process the bit stream further (e.g. looking for a first-child or for a next-sibling at position P), we process each of the sub-tree pointers (P,PID1), ..., (P,PIDn) stored within the sub-tree pointer stream for position P as follows. We push the pair (P, Depth) to a stack S and continue parsing the bit stream at position PIDk, where k∈{1,...,n}. Here, Depth denotes depth of the current context node in the XML tree, i.e. the difference |"1"-bits| - |"0"-bits| found in the bit stream up to position P. When the end of the sub-tree started at PIDk is reached, i.e., when we read a '0'-bit at the same depth Depth, we pop the pair (P,Depth) from the stack.

3.5 Finding Attribute Values and Text Constant in DAG+BSBC

Now, we can describe how to find the appropriate position of a constant, i.e. a text value or an attribute value, in its constant container, when DAGs or sub-tree pointers are used. When searching a constant V for a given position X within the bit stream,

we also regard the parent element – or parent attribute in the case of attribute values –
E of V in the bit stream. Furthermore, we regard the sparse index to constants attached to roughly every d-th bit stream position, i.e. the constant counters that count
how many constant values V' for a given parent element or parent attribute E' have
been parsed so far (c.f. Section 2.3).

In order to search the constant value for a given bit stream position X, we have to
go back within the bit stream to the last constant pointer, i.e., to the last bit stream position D that contains the constant counters and lookup D's constant counter value O
for the parent element – or parent attribute – E. Afterwards, we start there to count the
number N of constant nodes that have the parent element – or parent attribute – E.
This has to be done in consideration of the sub-tree pointers as described in Section
3.4. As some of the elements might contain mixed mode, we have to consider, that
one element may not only contain a single text node as child, but two or more text
nodes as well.

The constant value V that we are looking for, can then be found as the O+Nth constant value within the constant container of the element – or attribute – E.

4   Evaluation of the Compression

4.1   Compression Ratio

We have implemented BSBC using Java 1.5 and a SAX parser for parsing XML
documents. We have evaluated BSBC on the following datasets:

1. XMark(XM) – an XML document that models auctions [20],
2. hamlet(H) – an XML version of the famous Shakespeare play,
3. catalog-01(C1), catalog-02(C2), dictionary-01 (D1), dictionary-02(D2) – XML
   documents that were generated by the XBench benchmark [22],
4. dblp(DB) – a bibliographic collection of publications.

As can be seen in Table 1, the sizes of the documents reach from a few hundred kilobytes to more than 300 Megabytes.

Table 1. Sizes of documents of our dataset

document	XM	H	C1	C2	DB	D1	D2
Uncompressed size in MB	5.3	0.3	10.6	105.3	308.2	10.8	106.4

We compared BSBC with four other approaches:

– XGrind [21] – a queryable XML compressor,
– gzip – a widely used text compressor,
– XMill [16] – an XML compressor using BZip2 for the compression of constant
  values,

– DTD subtraction [4] – a DTD-conscious XML compressor using bzip2 for the compression of constant values that allows query evaluation and partial decompression.

During our experiments, we have chosen d=100, i.e., approximately each 100th bit contains direct pointers into the constant containers.

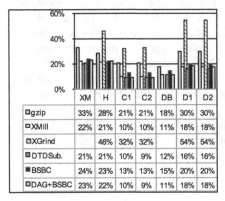

	XM	H	C1	C2	DB	D1	D2
▢gzip	33%	28%	21%	21%	18%	30%	30%
▢XMill	22%	21%	10%	10%	11%	18%	18%
▢XGrind		46%	32%	32%		54%	54%
▤DTDSub.	21%	21%	10%	9%	12%	16%	16%
■BSBC	24%	23%	13%	13%	15%	20%	20%
▢DAG+BSBC	23%	22%	10%	9%	11%	18%	18%

Fig. 2. Compression ratio of the whole XML document

	XM	H	C1	C2	DB	D1	D2
▣Total	24%	22%	9%	9%	12%	18%	18%
▢Structure	6.5%	3.5%	0.3%	0.2%	2.6%	3.3%	3.3%

Fig. 3. Structure compression compared to total compression

The results of our experiments are shown in Figure 2. Using these datasets, XMill performs better for XM, H, DB, D1 and D2 achieving compression ratios that are up to 2% lower than those of BSBC and up to 1% lower than those of DAG+BSBC, whereas DAG+BSBC and BSBC perform better for C1 and DAG+BSBC performs better for C2 achieving compression ratios that are up to 1% lower than those of XMill. However, in contrast to XMill, BSBC and DAG+BSBC allow for evaluating queries on the compressed data and to decompress data only partially.

Our approaches, BSBC and DAG+BSBC, perform significantly better than gzip, and have the additional advantage over gzip that query processing can be performed efficiently directly on the compressed data. The improvements in compression ratios over gzip range from 3% to 12%.

Compared to XGrind – an approach that allows efficient query evaluation and partially decompression – our approaches, BSBC and DAG+BSBC, achieve a higher compression ratio[4]. The difference of the compression ratios (XGrind minus BSBC) range from 19% to 36%.

Compared to DTD subtraction, BSBC and DAG+BSBC achieve a lower compression ratio. The differences of the compression ratios (BSBC minus DTD subtraction) range from 4% up to 2%. In contrast to DTD subtraction, BSBC does not need a DTD and it compresses and decompresses faster.

In a second series of measurements, we have measured the size of the structure compression, i.e., the constant containers were removed from the compressed data.

---

[4] Note that on our test computer, we got access violations when running XGrind on XM and DB and therefore the compression ratios for these two documents are missing.

The results of these experiments, shown in Figure 3, demonstrate that especially the structure compression of DAG+BSBC is extremely high. While DAG+BSBC's total compression achieves a compression ratio of 9% to 24%, the structure compression achieves compression ratios that range from 0.2% to 6.5% of the uncompressed XML structure. The structure compression is up to 40 times stronger than the total compression for C1, in general it is at about 5 times stronger than the total compression.

4.2 Query Processing

In order to evaluate the query performance on compressed data, we have compared the query evaluation on BSBC on packaged XML streams (i.e. without steps 1(c) and 2(d) of section 2) based on the basic navigation as proposed in section 3.1 combined with a generic XPath evaluator with two other approaches. On the one hand, we have compared it with JAXP, the standard XPath evaluator contained in Java 1.6 in order to compare the overall query performance. On the other hand, we have compared it with the generic query evaluation engine used for BSBC but this time working on uncompressed SAX events and using the same elementary navigation operations first-child and next-sibling.

Table 2. XPathMark-A queries used for the evaluation of query performance

ID	Query
Q1	/site/closed_auctions/closed_auction/annotation/description/text/keyword
Q2	/site/closed_auctions/closed_auction//keyword
Q3	/site/closed_auctions/closed_auction[annotation/description/text/keyword]/date
Q4	/site/closed_auctions/closed_auction[descendant::keyword]/date
Q5	/site/people/person[profile/gender and profile/age]/name
Q6	/site/people/person[phone or homepage]/name
Q7	/site/people/person[address and (phone or homepage) and (creditcard or profile)]/name

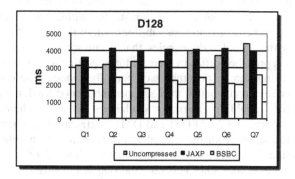

Fig. 4. Query evaluation times for document D128

Our test data set was generated by the XML generator of the XML Benchmark XMark [20] using a scaling factor of 0.001 (116 kB) up to 0.128 (14.5 MB). On our dataset, we have evaluated queries of the XPath benchmark XPathMark-A [13]. The test queries can be seen in Table 2. Figure 4 shows the test results of all queries for the largest document with scaling factor 0.128 and a size of 14.5 MB. For all our test queries, query processing on BSBC performs better than on JAXP. Furthermore, query processing performs better on BSBC compressed data than on uncompressed XML data, as the comparison with our generic query evaluation engine demonstrates.

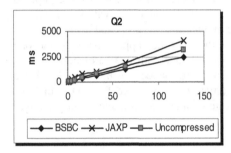
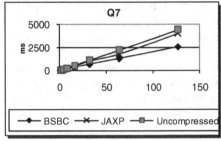

Fig. 5. Query evaluation times for query Q2   **Fig. 6.** Query evaluation times for query Q7

Figures 5 and 6 show the scaling of queries Q2 and Q7. As can be seen in both figures, BSBC's query evaluation time scales linearly depending on the size of the uncompressed XML document. Therefore, it can be used for extremely large documents as well.

5 Related Work

There exist several XML compression approaches, which can be mainly divided into three categories. First, approaches that avoid redundancies within the string values (of element and attribute names as well as of constants) by using dictionaries and tokenization. Second, approaches that avoid redundancies within the structure, i.e., that avoid multiple occurrences of complete sub-trees within the XML document tree. Finally, approaches that avoid redundancies that occur when schema information is known. All these approaches differ in their features, particularly in whether the compressed data structures can be decompressed partially, whether the compressed data structures are queriable, and whether they support unbounded XML data streams.

The last category (avoiding external redundancies given by schema information) includes such approaches as XCQ [18] and DTD subtraction [4]. They both separate the structural information from the textual information and then subtract the given schema information from the structural information. Instead of a complete XML structure stream or tree, they only generate and output information not already contained in the schema information (e.g., the chosen alternative for a choice-operator or the number of repetitions for a *-operator within the DTD). Both approaches, XCQ and DTD subtraction, are queriable and applicable to XML streams, but they can only be used if schema information is available.

XQzip [11] and the approach presented in [6] belong to the second category (avoiding structural redundancies). They compress the data structure of an XML document bottom-up by combining identical sub-trees. Afterwards, the data nodes are attached to the leaf nodes, i.e., one leaf node may point to several data nodes. The data is compressed by an arbitrary compression approach. These approaches allow querying compressed data, but they are not directly applicable to infinite data streams.

An extension of [6] and [11] is the BPLEX algorithm [8]. This approach does not only combine identical sub-trees, but recognizes patterns within the XML tree that may span several levels, and therefore allows a higher degree of compression. In comparison to BSBC, this approach does not explicitly define how to compress text constants and attribute values contained in XML data and how to distinguish both in the compressed XML format.

The first category (avoiding textual redundancies by tokenization) allows for a much faster compression approach than the second one, as only local data has to be considered in the compression as opposed to considering different sub-trees as in the second category.

The XMill algorithm [16] is an example of the first category. It compresses the structural information separately from the data. Data is grouped according to its enclosing element and collected into several containers, and each container is compressed afterwards. The structure is compressed, by assigning each tag name a unique and short ID. Each end-tag is encoded by the symbol '/'. This approach does not allow querying the compressed data.

XGrind [21], XPRESS [17] and XQueC [1] are extensions of the XMill-approach. Each of these approaches compresses the tag information using dictionaries and Huffman-encoding [15] and replaces the end-tags by either a '/'-symbol or by parentheses. All three approaches allow querying the compressed data, and, although not explicitly mentioned, they all seem to be applicable to data streams.

Approaches [2], [10], and [14] are based on tokenization. [10] replaces each attribute and element name by a token, where each token is defined the first time it is used. [2] and [14] use tokenization as well, but they enrich the data by additional information that allows for a fast navigation (e.g., number of children, pointer to next-sibling, existence of content and attributes). All three of them use a reserved byte to encode the end-tag of an element. They are all applicable to data streams and allow querying the compressed data.

The approach in [12] does not belong to any of the three categories. It is based on Burrows-Wheeler Block-Sorting [7], i.e., the XML data is rearranged in such a way that compression techniques such as gzip achieve higher compression ratios. This approach is not applicable to data streams, but allows querying the compressed data if it is enriched with additional index information.

The approach in [23] is another succinct representation of XML. It does not separate the raw data structure that describes the document tree from the tokens representing the elements. Therefore, one byte is required to represent an end-tag, whereas our approach, BSBC, only needs one bit. Furthermore, our separation of structural data from element names does not only allow for a better compression as shown in the evaluation; it also enables a more efficient evaluation of path queries because raw bit data can be compared more efficiently than tokens. A second difference is our use of inverted element lists instead of token-dictionaries, which additionally increases the speed of path query evaluation significantly because the number of possible path hits can be reduced quite fast with a simple lookup within the inverted list.

To the best of our knowledge, the separation of an XML stream into different compressed streams linked by a bit stream that is also used to evaluate path queries is unique to our compression technique, and there is no other XML compression system that combines the advantages of our approach.

6 Summary and Conclusions

We have presented DAG+BSBC, a two-step XML compression approach that is based on DAG compression and supports the compression of XML streams and path queries on compressed data by combining the following advantages. First, both transformation steps can be executed in a pipelined fashion, which avoids storing intermediate data or streams. Second, an XML data stream is separated into its constituent parts: the DAG structure, represented as a bit stream and a sub-tree pointer stream; the sequence of elements and attributes, stored in inverted lists together with their corresponding bit stream positions; and finally, the constants, stored in different containers depending on the element or the attribute embedding the value. This separation allows adapting the compression technique to the node type, i.e., to compress elements and attributes different from constants. Third, the bit stream and the sub-tree pointer stream support fast navigation along all the forward axes. Forth, inverted lists not only provide a better compression of elements and attributes, but, in combination with the bit stream, they also support efficient path queries. Fifth, constants are grouped together according to their embedding element or attribute to achieve better compression.

Our comparative evaluation with other available XML compression approaches shows that DAG+BSBC achieves a better compression ratio within our experiments than the other approaches (e.g. XGrind) that support path queries, that DAG+BSBC beats gzip, and that DAG+BSBC even sometimes beats XMill. Thus, DAG+BSBC is thus a useful technique for applications that require the exchange and querying of large XML data sets or XML streams on platforms with limited bandwidth or energy, as e.g. mobile networks.

References

1. Arion, A., Bonifati, A., Manolescu, I., Pugliese, A.: XQueC: A Query-Conscious Compressed XML Database. ACM Transactions on Internet Technology (to appear)
2. Bayardo, R.J., Gruhl, D., Josifovski, V., Myllymaki, J.: An evaluation of binary XML encoding optimizations for fast stream based XML processing. In: Proc. of the 13th international conference on World Wide Web (2004)
3. Böttcher, S., Hartel, R., Heinzemann, C.: Towards a succinct data format for XML streams. In: International Conference on Web Information Systems (WEBIST) (2008)
4. Böttcher, S., Steinmetz, R., Klein, N.: XML Index Compression by DTD Subtraction. In: International Conference on Enterprise Information Systems (ICEIS) (2007)

5. Böttcher, S., Steinmetz, R.: Data Management for Mobile Ajax Web 2.0 Applications. In: Wagner, R., Revell, N., Pernul, G. (eds.) DEXA 2007. LNCS, vol. 4653, pp. 424–433. Springer, Heidelberg (2007)

6. Buneman, P., Grohe, M., Koch, C.: Path Queries on Compressed XML. In: VLDB (2003)

7. Burrows, M., Wheeler, D.: A block sorting lossless data compression algorithm. Technical Report 124, Digital Equipment Corporation (1994)

8. Busatto, G., Lohrey, M., Maneth, S.: Efficient Memory Representation of XML Documents. In: Bierman, G., Koch, C. (eds.) DBPL 2005. LNCS, vol. 3774, pp. 199–216. Springer, Heidelberg (2005)

9. Candan, K.S., Hsiung, W.-P., Chen, S., Tatemura, J., Agrawal, D.: AFilter: Adaptable XML Filtering with Prefix-Caching and Suffix-Clustering. In: VLDB (2006)

10. Cheney, J.: Compressing XML with multiplexed hierarchical models. In: Proceedings of the 2001 IEEE Data Compression Conference (DCC 2001) (2001)

11. Cheng, J., Ng, W.: XQzip, Querying Compressed XML Using Structural Indexing. In: EDBT (2004)

12. Ferragina, P., Luccio, F., Manzini, G., Muthukrishnan, S.: Compressing and Searching XML Data Via Two Zips. In: Proceedings of the Fifteenth International World Wide Web Conference (2006)

13. Franceschet, M.: XPathMark: an XPath benchmark for XMark generated data. In: Bressan, S., Ceri, S., Hunt, E., Ives, Z.G., Bellahsène, Z., Rys, M., Unland, R. (eds.) XSym 2005. LNCS, vol. 3671, pp. 129–143. Springer, Heidelberg (2005)

14. Girardot, M., Sundaresan, N., Millau: An Encoding Format for Efficient Representation and Exchange of XML over the Web. In: Proceedings of the 9th International WWW Conference (2000)

15. Huffman, D.A.: A method for the construction of minimum-redundancy codes. In: Proc. of the I.R.E. (1952)

16. Liefke, H., Suciu, D.: XMill: An Efficient Compressor for XML Data. In: Proc. of ACM SIGMOD (2000)

17. Min, J.K., Park, M.J., Chung, C.W.: XPRESS: A Queriable Compression for XML Data. In: Proceedings of SIGMOD (2003)

18. Ng, W., Lam, W.Y., Wood, P.T., Levene, M.: XCQ: A queriable XML compression system. Knowledge and Information Systems (2006)

19. Olteanu, D., Meuss, H., Furche, T., Bry, F.: XPath: Looking Forward. In: Chaudhri, A.B., Unland, R., Djeraba, C., Lindner, W. (eds.) EDBT 2002. LNCS, vol. 2490, pp. 109–127. Springer, Heidelberg (2002)

20. Schmidt, A., Waas, F., Kersten, M., Carey, M., Manolescu, I., Busse, R.: XMark: A benchmark for XML data management, Hong Kong, China (2002)

21. Tolani, P.M., Hartisa, J.R.: XGRIND: A query-friendly XML compressor. In: Proc. ICDE (2002)

22. Yao, B.B., Özsu, M.T.: XBench - A family of benchmarks for XML DBMS (2002)

23. Zhang, N., Kacholia, V., Özsu, M.T.: A Succinct Physical Storage Scheme for Efficient Evaluation of Path Queries in XML. In: ICDE (2004)

Shortest Remaining Response Time Scheduling for Improved Web Server Performance

Ahmad AlSa'deh and Adnan H. Yahya

Computer Systems Engineering Department, Birzeit Univeristy, Palestine
{asadeh,yahya}@birzeit.edu

Abstract. The Shortest-Remaining-Response-Time (SRRT) policy has been proposed for scheduling static HTTP requests in web servers to reduce the mean response time. The SRRT prioritizes requests based on a combination of the current round-trip-time (RTT), TCP congestion window size (cwnd) and the size of what remains of the requested file. We compare SRRT to Shortest-Remaining-Processing-Time (SRPT) and Processor-Sharing (PS) policies. The SRRT shows the best improvement in the mean response time. SRRT gives an average improvement of about 7.5% over SRPT. This improvement comes at a negligible expense in response time for long requests. We found that under 100Mbps link, only 1.5% of long requests have longer response times than under PS. The longest request under SRRT has an increase in response time by a factor 1.7 over PS. For 10Mbps link, only 2.4% of requests are penalized, and SRRT increases the longest request time by a factor 2.2 over PS.

Keywords: Web server Performance, Request scheduling policy, Remaining response time scheduling, Comparative scheduling performance.

1 Introduction

Today busy web servers are required to service many clients simultaneously, sometimes up to tens of thousands of concurrent clients [3]. If a busy web server's total request rate increases above the total link capacity or the total server concurrent users, the number of rejected requests increases dramatically and the server offers poor performance and long *response time*, where the *response time* of a client is defined as the duration from when the client makes a request until the entire file is received by the client. The slow response times and difficult navigation are the most common complaints of Internet users [1]. Research shows the need for fast response time. The response time should be around 8 seconds as the limit of people's ability to keep their attention focus while waiting [2]. The question arises, what can we do to improve the response time at busy web servers?

It is possible to reduce the mean response time of requests at a web server by simply changing the order in which we schedule the requests. A traditional scheduling policy in web servers is Processor-Sharing (PS) scheduling. In PS each of *n* competing requests (processes) gets *1/n* of the CPU time, and is given an equal share of the bottleneck link. The PS is fair, and prevents long flows from monopolizing server resources. It has been known from queuing theory that

J. Cordeiro et al. (Eds.): WEBIST 2008, LNBIP 18, pp. 80–92, 2009.

Shortest-Remaining-Processing-Time (SRPT) scheduling policy is an optimal algorithm for minimizing mean response time [10] and [11]. However, the optimal efficiency of SRPT depends on knowing the response time of the requests in advance, and under the assumption that preemption in SRPT implies no additional overhead.

The SRPT scheduling policies on web servers [4], [14], and [15] used the job size, which is well known to the server, to refer to processing time (response time) of the job to implement SRPT for web servers to improve user-perceived performance. In the Internet environment, depending only on the file size for estimating the response time is not enough since it does not take into consideration the client-server interaction parameters over the Internet, like Round-Trip-Time (RTT), bandwidth diversity, and loss rate. Dong Lu et al. [18] have shown that the correlation between the file size and the response time are low, and that the performance of SRPT scheduling on web servers degrade dramatically due to weak correlation between the file size and the response time in many regimes.

To better estimate the user response time we proposed a new scheduling policy in web servers which is called Shortest-Remaining-Response-Time (SRRT) to improve the mean response time of clients [27]. The proposed method estimates the response time for a web client by benefiting from the TCP implementation at the server side only, without introducing extra traffic into the network or even storing historical data on the server. The SRRT estimates the client response time in each visit to a server, and then schedules the requests based on the shortest remaining response time request first. SRRT uses RTT and TCP congestion window size (cwnd) in addition to the size of the requested file for estimating the response time. The *getsockopt()* Linux system call is used by SRRT to get the RTT value and the cwnd "on-the-fly" for each connection. See section 3 for the complete description of SRRT algorithm.

For our experiment, we use a web workload generator to generate requests with certain distribution and focus only on static HTTP requests which form a major percentage of the web traffic [8] and [14]. In 2004, logs from proxy servers show that 67-73% of the requests are for static content [29]. The experiment uses the Linux operating system and Apache web server. Network Emulator represents the WAN environment.

The SRRT is compared to the PS and SRPT scheduling policies in web servers. We find that the SRRT gives the minimum mean response time. We conclude that the client response time is affected by the Internet conditions. So the priority based scheduling policy in web servers should take into consideration the Internet conditions to prioritize the requests.

The rest of the paper is structured as follows. Section 2 discusses relevant previous work in web server requests scheduling. The SRRT scheduling algorithm is presented in section 3. The modifications for Apache web server and Linux operating system to implement SRRT are covered in section 4. The experiment setup and results analysis are given in section 5. Section 6 summarizes the results obtained and discusses possible future work.

2   Literature Review

It is well known from scheduling theory literature [10], [11], [12], and [13] that if the task sizes are known, the SRPT scheduling is optimal for reducing the queuing time and therefore reducing the mean response time. The work based on the SRPT algorithm for web server scheduling can be divided into three categories: web server scheduling theoretical studies, scheduling simulation studies, and scheduling implementation.

The queuing theory is an old area of mathematics that provides the tools needed for analysis of scheduling algorithms in general. N. Bansal and M. Harchol-Balter [7] compare the SRPT policy and the PS policy analytically for an M/G/1 queue with job size distributions that are modeled by a Bounded Pareto distribution. They show that with link utilization 0.9, the large jobs perform better under the M/G/1 SRPT queue than the M/G/1 PS queue. Then they prove that for link utilization 0.5, the SRPT improves performance over PS with respect to mean response time for every job and for every job size distribution. For the largest jobs, the slowdown (response time divided by job size) under SRPT is only slightly worse than under PS [20]. In [19] and [20], interesting results on the mean response in heavy traffic were obtained that show that SRPT performs significantly better than FIFO if the system is under heavy traffic.

In addition to theoretical studies, there are simulation studies of scheduling algorithms for web servers. C. Murta and T. Corlassoli [9] introduce and simulate an extension to SRPT scheduling called Fastest-Connection-First (FCF) that takes into consideration the wide area network (WAN) conditions in addition to request size when making scheduling decisions. This scheduling policy gives higher priority to HTTP requests for smaller files issued through faster connections. This work is done only by simulation without providing a clear idea on how to implement it in real web servers. M. Gong and C. Williamson [16] identify two different types of unfairness: endogenous unfairness that is caused by an inherent property of a job, such as its size. And exogenous unfairness caused by external conditions, such as the number of other jobs in the system, their sizes, and their arrival times. They then continue to evaluate SRPT and other policies with respect to these types of unfairness. E. Friedman et al.[17] propose a new protocol called Fair-Sojourn-Protocol (FSP) for use in web servers. FSP orders the jobs according to the processor sharing (PS) policy and then gives full resources to the job with the earliest PS completion time. The FSP is a modified version of SRPT and it has been proven through analysis and simulation that FSP is always more efficient and fair than PS given any arrival sequence and distribution. Their simulation results show that FSP performs better than SRPT for large requests, while the SRPT is better than FSP for small requests.

The work that implements scheduling for web servers based on the SRPT was done on both the application level, and at the kernel level to prioritize HTTP requests. M. Crovella et al. [4] experimented with the SRPT connection scheduling at the application level. They get an improvement in the mean response times, but at the cost of drop in the throughput by a factor of almost 2. This drop comes as a result of no adequate control over the order in which the operating system services the requests. M. Harchol-Balter et al. [14] implemented SRPT connection scheduling at the kernel level. They get much larger performance improvements than in [4] and the drop in the throughput was eliminated. B. Schroeder et al. [15] show an additional benefit from performing SRPT scheduling for static content web requests. They show that SRPT scheduling can be used to alleviate the response time effects of transient overload conditions without excessively penalizing large requests. SWIFT algorithm[5] extends the work in [14] based on SRPT, but taking into account in addition to the size of the file, the RTT to represent the distance between the client and the server. With this technique, they obtained a response time improvement for large-sized files by 2.5% to 10% additional to the SRPT. In the SWIFT algorithm implementation, they assumed that the HTTP requests are embedded with the RTT in their trace driven experiment. This assumption is not a realistic scenario. Moreover, the implementation of the SWIFT requires additional modifications on the web server to support functions that parse requests to extract the RTT that assumed to be part of client requests. Accordingly, we did not implement the SWIFT to compare it with SRRT. SRRT gets the RTT and congestion window size (cwnd) at the server side for each connection "on-the-fly" by using *getsockopt()* Linux system call to use it with the file size to better estimate the response time in a WAN environment.

3 SRRT Algorithm

The SRRT algorithm benefits from TCP implementation to address most of the client-server interaction on the Internet. TCP has no advance knowledge of network conditions, thus it has to adapt its behavior to network current state by TCP's congestion control mechanism. Due to TCP's congestion control mechanism, TCP window sizes (cwnd) can be bound to the maximum transfer rate $R = $ (cwnd/RTT) bps despite the actual bandwidth capacity of the network path. Also, the TCP congestion control mechanism involves Time-outs that cause retransmissions. Each transmitted packet has a Time-out: an acknowledgment must reach the sender before the Time-out expires; otherwise the packet is assumed lost. RTT is monitored and Time-out is set based on RTT [23] and [24].

After processing an HTTP request, the server code uses the *getsockopt()* to get these useful information about the network condition (cwnd, RTT) that will be used in estimating the remaining response time of the request on the server side. The requested file size is already known by the server. Hence, the remaining response time (RRT) can be approximated as follows (recall that $R = $ (cwnd/RTT)):

$$RRT \approx RTT + \frac{RFS}{R} = RTT\left(1 + \frac{RFS}{cwnd \times MSS}\right) \tag{1}$$

Where *RFS* is remaining length of the requested file(s) in bytes, R is the approximated TCP transfer rate, and *MSS* is the maximum segment size for the connection in bytes.

As seen above, the estimation of RRT depends on three variables; RFS, current RTT, and the current cwnd. Thus we consider almost all aspects that affect data transfer over the Internet since the RTT and the cwnd change dynamically according to network conditions. The estimated RRT is influenced by network conditions. The highest priority is given to the connection that has the best-estimated performance: the connection that needs to transfer small file through an un-congested path, which has short RTT and large cwnd.

4 SRRT Implementation

The experiments have been done using Apache web server since it is the most popular web server [30]. To build SRRT based on Apache running on Linux, basically two things are needed. First, to set up several priority queues at the Ethernet interface. Second, to modify the Apache source code to assign priorities to the corresponding requests.

The data being passed from user space is stored in socket buffers corresponding to each connection. When data streaming passes from the socket buffers to TCP layer and IP layer, the TCP headers and the IP headers are added to form packets. The packet flow corresponding to each socket is kept separate from other flows [14]. After that, packets are sent from IP layer to queuing discipline (qdisc). The default qdisc under Linux is the pfifo_fast qdisc. Figure 1 shows the default data flow in standard Linux. pfifo_fast qdisc is a classless queuing discipline, so it cannot be configured. The packet priorities are determined by the kernel according to the so-called Type-Of- Service (TOS) flag and priority map (priomap) of packets. However, all packets using the default TOS value are queued to the same band (band 1 in the Figure 1). So the three bands appear as a single FIFO queue in which all streams feed in a round-robin service: all requests from processes or threads are given an equal share of CPU time and share the same amount of link capacity, Processor Sharing (PS). Packets leaving this queue drain in a network device (NIC) queue and then out to the physical medium (network link).

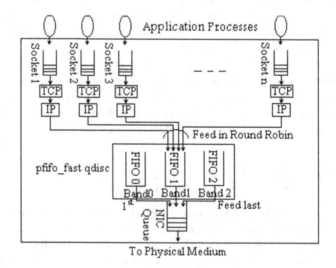

Fig. 1. Data flow in standard Linux

To implement SRRT, we need several configurable priority queues. This can be achieved by Priority (prio) qdisc with 16 priority queues, numbered 0 though 15, which can be configured. The prio qdisc works on a very simple principle. When it is ready to dequeue a packet, the first band (queue) is checked for a packet. If there is one, it gets dequeued. If there is no packet, then the next band is checked, until the queuing mechanism has no more classes to check. Figure 2 shows the prio queuing discipline to implement SRRT.

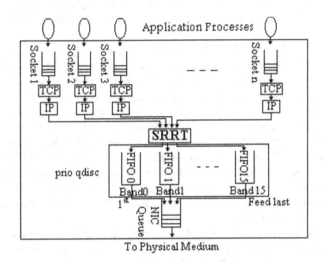

Fig. 2. Data flow in Linux operating system after enabling prio qdisc and adding SRRT algorithm

In the SRRT implementation, the Apache code is responsible for assigning the priorities to the corresponding connection by using *setsockopt()* to determine in which band a packet will be enqueued. Therefore, we made changes to the Apache HTTP Server code to prioritize connections. The modifications are fairly isolated to two specific files: protocol.c and core.c. The installation of the SRRT-modified Apache server is the same as the installation of standard Apache. The only thing that might need to change when experimenting with SRRT server is the priority array values, in the form of response time ranges, to determine the priority class of the socket according to the type of the load.

TCP SYN-ACKs gets by default into the highest priority band (band 0). Here, we will take into consideration the recommendation given by [14]. Because the start up of the connection is an essential part of the total response delay, especially for short requests before the size of the file is known, no sockets are assigned to priority band0, but are assigned to other bands of lower priority, to prevent packets sent during the connection start up waiting in a long queue. The SYN-ACKs constitute a negligible fraction of the total load. Thus assigning them to higher priority does not affect the performance.

5 Setup and Results

5.1 Experiment Setup

The experimental setup consists of seven machines connected by 10Mbps hub in the first experiment and by 100Mbps Fast Ethernet connection switch in the second experiment. Each machine has an Intel Pentium 4 CPU 3.20 GHz, 504 MB of RAM. We used the Linux 2.6.18. One of the machines (the server) runs Apache 2.2.3. The other machines act as web clients. The client machines generate loads using the Scalable URL Request GEnerator (SURGE) [21]. On each client machine, Network Emulator (netem [22]) is used to emulate the properties of a Wide Area Network (WAN).

Request sizes in the World Wide Web are known to follow a heavy-tailed distribution [14] and [28]. We chose SURGE to generate the HTTP 1.1 requests to the server such that they follow the heavy-tailed request size distribution. More than 300,000 requests were generated in each experiment run. We used 2000 different file sizes at the server by running *files* program from SURGE package at the server machine. Most files have a size less than 10KBytes. The requested file sizes ranged from 77B to 3MB. We represent the system load by the number of concurrent users, defined as the number of user's equivalents (UEs) generated by the SURGE workload generator. The web server was run under different UEs. For each number of UEs, the experiment is run for 10 minutes to ensure that all jobs were completed. For each run we measure the mean response time at the client side by using the *pbvalclient* program from the SURGE package.

In our experiments, we assume that clients experience heterogeneous WANs. We have divided our experimental space into six WANs; where each of the six client machines represents a different WAN that shares common WAN parameters by setting the netem parameters. The WAN factors on each client machine are shown in Table 1. We experiment with delays between 50ms and 350ms and loss rates from 0.5% to 3.0%. This range of values was chosen to cover values reported in the Internet Traffic Report [25]. These WAN parameters are applied to incoming (ingress) packets on the network interface of client machines by using *tc* Linux command.

Table 1. Experiment WAN Parameters

WANs	RTT(ms)	Loss (%)
WAN1	50±10	0.5
WAN2	100±20	1.0
WAN3	150±30	1.5
WAN4	200±40	2.0
WAN5	250±40	2.5
WAN6	350±50	3.0

On a web server servicing primarily static files, network bandwidth is the most likely source of bottleneck [14] and [31]. Therefore, our scheduling policy for static contents is applied on the access link out of the web server. We represent the system load (link utilization) by the number of concurrent users UEs generated by SURGE. Neither the CPU utilization nor the memory usage is the bottleneck at the server. For all experiments, the number of concurrent connections did not reach the maximum number of Apache processes (*MaxClients*).

5.2 Results

We compare SRRT with the existing algorithms, namely PS and SRPT. We analyze our observations from the client's point of view in terms of mean response time under the 10Mbps and 100Mbps link capacity. The graphs in Figure 3 show the mean response time for all WANs as a function of server load (number of UEs) for the 10Mbps and 100Mbps link capacities. Since the workload was generated using six client machines; we just merge and sort the log files from the various clients into a single log file and then run the *pbvalclnt* program to find the mean response time of all WANs. SRRT and SRPT show an improvement in the mean response time over PS. Also, the SRRT shows an improvement over SRPT.

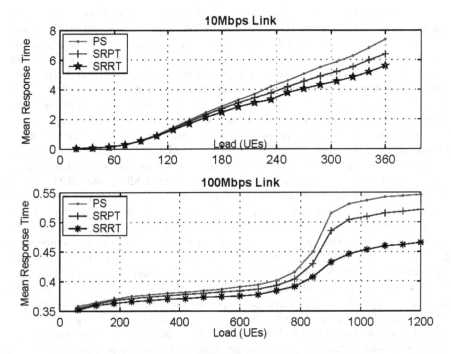

Fig. 3. Mean response time of all WANs under 10Mbps and 100mbps

Table 2 shows the improvement percentage of SRRT over SRPT and PS, in addition to the percentage improvement of SRPT over PS for the two different link capacities; 10Mbps and 100Mbps. This improvement comes from the fact that the bandwidth is shared for all requests under PS. Therefore, all incomplete requests still take fair share of the bandwidth from other requests. Hence, the mean response time of short requests increases. While under the SRRT and SRPT, long requests do not receive any bandwidth and short requests are completely isolated from the long requests. Therefore, completing short requests first and then long requests do not increase the mean response time by giving the chance to the small requests to complete first without competition from long requests. As a result, the PS shows a faster increase in mean response time than under SRRT and SRPT.

Table 2. Percentage improvement of SRRT and SRPT

Link	Algorithms Compared	Improvement	
		Average	Max.
10Mbps	SRRT:SRPT	7.5%	13.2%
	SRRT:PS	13.6%	24.2%
	SRPT: PS	6.8%	13.7%
100Mbps	SRRT:SRPT	7.4%	11.6%
	SRRT:PS	7.1%	16.2%
	SRPT: PS	2.6%	5.8%

SRRT has the best results especially at high loads. This is likely because our approach better estimates the response time by taking into consideration the client-server interaction over the WAN environment. For low loads, the three algorithms show almost similar mean response time. Since for low load the available link capacity is large enough to serve all requests, which in turn results in keeping the number of packets in the transmission queue small so that the effect of scheduling is not noticeable. However, in the low load case the RTT dominates the total communication delay so SRRT shows better behavior over SRPT in this region since SRRT takes into account RTT in estimating response time. For high load but before the link saturates, the improvement of SRRT over SRPT starts to become noticeable. For high load, the SRRT shows a great improvement over the SRPT for all WANs.

The overall requests average percentage improvement of SRRT and SRPT over PS for 10/100Mbps for all WANs is shown in Figure 4. The network WAN1 has the best network conditions (delay and loss) compared to other WANs, so the requests get higher priorities under SRRT and therefore minimize the mean response time. So WAN1 has the best average improvement percentage in SRRT over PS compared to the other WANs. Also, we can see that bad network conditions decrease the improvement of both SRRT and SRPT scheduling techniques over PS. However, SRPT is more affected by bad network conditions than SRRT since it uses only the file size to approximate the expected response time. Server delay dominates the response time for the case of a network with no loss, and in which we ignore RTT. In contrast, under bad condition WANs (large RTT and high loss rate) the transmission and retransmission delays are the dominant parts of the communication delay rather than the delay at the server. The mean response time increases as the RTT and the loss rate increase. Higher RTTs make loss recovery more expensive since the retransmission time-outs (RTO) depend on the estimated RTT. Hence, lost packets cause very long delays based on the RTT and RTO values in TCP. SRRT takes these into consideration indirectly, TCP throughput for a connection being inversely proportional to the square root of the loss [26], by decreasing the cwnd. When losses increase the cwnd decreases. Accordingly, the estimated response time in SRRT increases, so the corresponding connection receives less priority. Therefore, SRRT improvement is slightly decreased by the poor network conditions. As mentioned in[14], "While propagation delay and loss diminish the improvement of SRPT over PS, loss has a much greater effect". SRRT considers the user's network conditions by benefiting from the TCP interaction between the server and the network to take into consideration the realistic WAN factors that can dominate the mean response time.

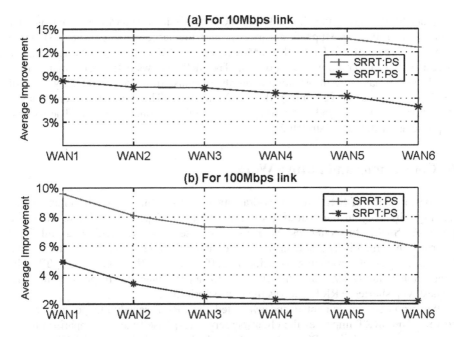

Fig. 4. Average improvement of SRRT and SRPT over PS for 10/100Mbps links

The SRRT/SRPT add an additional overhead compared to PS since they need to assign priorities to the request by invoking *setsockopt()* system call. In addition to *setsockopt()* call, SRRT uses *getsockopt()* system call to get the RTT and the cwnd. However, the additional overhead is not critical under the assumption that the CPU is not the bottleneck. We found about 1% increase in the CPU utilization under SRRT over the PS.

5.3 Starvation Analysis

To see if the improvement in mean response time comes at the expense of starvation for long requests, we look to the response time for each individual request under SRPT and SRRT scheduling algorithms. To quantify the starvation, we use the starvation stretch metric, which is introduced by C. Jechlitschek, and S. Gorinsky in[6]. Starvation stretch $S_x(r)$ of request r under algorithm X is the ratio of response time $RT_x(r)$ under X to response time $RT_{ps}(r)$ under PS:

$$S_x(r) = \frac{RT_x(r)}{RT_{ps}(r)} \qquad (2)$$

The starvation occurs under the algorithm X if $S_x(r) > 1$.

Under SRPT, we found that 2.3% of the requests have starvation stretch greater than 1 under the 100Mbps link capacity, and the largest file (3119822B) has a starvation stretch of 2.1. Under the 10Mps capacity, 2.6% of the requests starved. The largest file has a starvation stretch of 2.4. The SRRT shows better performance than SRPT since it has more information about the response time. For SRRT only 1.5% of the long requests starved under the 100Mbps link. The longest response has a starvation stretch 1.7. Under the 10Mbps, 2.4% of the requests starved. The longest response has a starvation stretch 2.2.

6   Conclusions and Future Work

The performance of SRPT degrades dramatically in the Internet environment which has high diversity in bandwidth, propagation delay and packet loss rate. Thus, we proposed SRRT to better estimate the response time by getting useful TCP information, which is available at web server about the connection, in addition to the file size, without producing additional traffic. The SRRT uses the RTT, the congestion window size, and the file size to approximate the response time. The request with shortest SRRT receives the highest priority.

We proposed, implemented and evaluated the SRRT scheduling policy for web servers. The SRRT improves the client-perceived response time in comparison to the default Linux scheduling (PS) and the SRPT scheduling policies. The SRRT performs better than SRPT and PS at high and moderate uplink load and especially under overload condition. The performance improvement is achieved under different uplink capacities, for a variable range of network parameters (RTTs and loss rate). This improvement does not unduly penalize the long requests and without loss in byte throughput. The implementation of SRRT was done on an Apache web server running Linux to prioritize the order in which the socket buffers are drained within the kernel. The priority of the requests is determined based on the priority array values we have coded in the Apache source code. The choice of these values is based on the experiment trials. After experimenting with different values, we found that the values adopted gave us good results. But we do not claim that this choice is optimal. Also, it is better to make these values configurable by the Apache configuration file to be able to change them as needed or even learn them during experimentation.

Another improvement on SRRT may be done by trying to take other factors that may affect the response time like queue delay approximation and the TCP connection loss rate. To check the validity of this algorithm, it is better to test it on a real web server. Also, it is good to evaluate the SRRT algorithm analytically to examine the validity of the experimental results if possible.

The SRRT is applied to static web requests. Future work can be enhancing it to also schedule dynamic requests where the approximation of the response time is not as easy as for static requests. Also, this work may extend to other operating systems and other web servers. Also, SRRT algorithm may combine with other quality of service measures. For example, if connectivity quality is bad for one client, the server selects a lower quality image to send to the client to improve the response time.

We believe that SRRT scheduling will continue to be applicable in the future, although better link speeds become available and the bandwidth cost decreases. Due to financial constrains, many users will not upgrade their connectivity conditions. Also, the variance in network distance and environment will persist and diversity in delay will continue to exist.

References

1. King, A.: Speed up your site: web site optimization, 1st edn. New Riders, Indiana (2003)
2. Nielsen, J.: The need for speed (1997),
   http://www.useit.com/alertbox/9703a.html
3. Kegel, D.: The C10K problem (2006), http://www.kegel.com/c10k.html
4. Crovella, M., Frangioso, R.: Connection scheduling in web servers. In: USENIX Symposium on Internet Technologies and Systems (1999)
5. Rawat, M., Kshemkayani, A.: SWIFT: Scheduling in web servers for fast response time. In: Second IEEE International Symposium on Network Computing and Applications (2003)
6. Jechlitschek, C., Gorinsky, S.: Fair Efficiency, or Low Average Delay without Starvation. Computer Communications and Networks (2007)
7. Bansal, N., Harchol-Balter, M.: Analysis of SRPT scheduling: investigating unfairness. ACM SIGMETRICS Performance Evaluation Review 29(1), 279–290 (2001)
8. Manley, S., Seltzer, M.: Web facts and fantasy. In: Proceedings of the 1997 USITS 1997 (1997)
9. Murta, C., Corlassoli, T.: Fastest connection first: A new scheduling policy for web servers. In: The 18th International Teletra#c Congress, ITC-18 (2003)
10. Schrage, L., Miller, L.: The queue M/G/1 with the shortest remaining processing time discipline. Operations Research 14(4), 670–684 (1966)
11. Schrage, L.: A proof of the optimality of the shortest remaining processing time discipline. Operations Research 16(3), 678–690 (1968)
12. Smith, D.: A new proof of the optimality of the shortest remaining processing time discipline. Operations Research 26(1), 197–199 (1976)
13. Goerg, C.: Evaluation of the optimal SRPT strategy with overhead. IEEE Transactions on Communications 34, 338–344 (1986)
14. Harchol-Balter, M., Schroeder, B., Agrawal, M., Bansal, N.: Size-based scheduling to improve web performance. ACM Transactions on Computer Systems (TOCS) 21(2), 207–233 (2003)
15. Schroeder, B., Harchol-Balter, M.: Web servers under overload: How schedule can help. ACM TOIT 6(1), 20–52 (2006)
16. Gong, M., Williamson, C.: Quantifying the properties of SRPT scheduling. In: MASCOTS, pp. 126–135 (2003)
17. Friedman, E., Henderson, S.: Fairness and efficiency in web server protocols. In: ACM SIGMETRICS, pp. 229–237 (2003)
18. Lu, D., Sheng, H.: Effects and implications of file size/service time correlation on web server scheduling policies. In: MASCOTS, pp. 258–267 (2005)
19. Bansal, N.: On the average sojourn time under M/M/1 SRPT. ACM SIGMETRICS Performance Evaluation Review 31(2), 34–35 (2003)
20. Bansal, N., Gamarnik, D.: Handling load with less stress. Queueing Systems 54(1), 45–54 (2006)

21. Barford, P., Crovella, M.: Generating representative web workloads for network and server performance evaluation. In: ACM Joint International Conference on Measurement and Modeling of Computer Systems, pp. 151–160 (1998)

22. Linux Foundation.: Network Emulation (Netem) (2007),
http://www.linux-foundation.org/en/Net:Netem

23. Karn, P., Partridge, C.: Improving round-trip time estimates in reliable transport protocols. ACM SIGCOMM Computer Communication Review 25(1), 66–74 (1995)

24. Jacobson, V.: Congestion avoidance and Control. ACM SIGCOMM Computer Communication Review 25(1), 157–187 (1995)

25. Network Services & Consulting Corporation.: Internet Traffic Report (2007),
http://www.internettrafficreport.com

26. Padhye, J., Firoiu, V., Towsley, D., Kurose, J.: Modeling tcp reno performance: A simple model and its empirical validation. IEEE/ACM Transactions on Networking (TON) 8(2), 133–145 (2000)

27. Sa'deh, A., Yahya, A.: Implementation of a new Scheduling Policy in Web Servers. WEBIST (1), 22–29 (2008)

28. Crovella, M., Taqqu, M., Bestavros, A.: Heavy-tailed probability distributions in the World Wide Web. In: A Practical Guide To Heavy Tails, pp. 3–26. Chapman & Hall, New York (1998)

29. IRCache Home.: The trace files (2004), http://www.ircache.net/Traces

30. Netcraft.: Internet monitoring company (2007), http://news.netcraft.com

31. Padmanabhan, V., Sripanidkulchai, K.: The Case for Cooperative Networking. In: Druschel, P., Kaashoek, M.F., Rowstron, A. (eds.) IPTPS 2002. LNCS, vol. 2429, pp. 178–190. Springer, Heidelberg (2002)

Combining Grid, SOA and Web Services for Smaller Computing Environments

Arne Koschel and Carsten Kleiner

University of Applied Sciences and Arts
Ricklinger Stadtweg 120, 30459 Hannover, Germany
ckleiner@acm.org,akoschel@acm.org

Abstract. This paper describes practical experiences from a project to couple Grid and SOA technologies in smaller environments. Web services have been applied in two structurally different case studies to solve tasks with a Grid that is integrated into a SOA and vice versa. The case studies have revealed important insight on how and when to couple SOA and Grid technologies including monitoring aspects. Some interesting general rules are derived on what has to be observed when combining SOA and Grid in smaller environments. Performance and software technical analysis have been used in validating the results. They also clearly showed the benefits gained by employing SOA and Grid concepts form both a performance as well as an architectural perspective.

Keywords: Grid, SOA, Web services, Case studies, SME, Small environments.

1 Introduction

1.1 Motivation

Today's IT systems are often comprised of quite different technical parts. A heterogeneous communication infrastructure is thus used to connect them. To exchange information between such systems XML has established itself as some lingua franca. Based on the XML fundament more specialized languages became popular for service description and communication between systems, A well known example is the combination of service interface description based on WSDL and abstracted service communication with SOAP, in this paper jointly called SOAP/Web Services (SOAP/WS).

No wonder, that SOAP/WS is examined for communication nowadays within enterprise software architectures as well. Especially enterprise IT tries to utilize SOA to become more flexible and to allow for better control. At the same time distributed, parallel problem processing across heterogeneous hardware became more and more popular recently; Grid technology, which couples such systems to become virtual super computers is here the means of choice. Since in both cases (SOA and Grid) communication is required, a common usage of XML-based SOAP/WS ([5], [7], [24]), SOA ([5], [7], [16]) and Grid ([9], [10]) seems interesting for further investigation. Moreover this combination can be seen as an advanced project experience for students.

J. Cordeiro et al. (Eds.): WEBIST 2008, LNBIP 18, pp. 93–106, 2009.

This experience report thus describes two case studies from student projects in the SOA/Grid space and presents experiences gained within them. While the first case study focuses on Grid computing technology for parallel problem solving with some smaller SOA part, the second study uses an SOA combined with a simulated data Grid. Both case studies commonly use SOAP/WS as communication base. Another requirement was the usage of Open Source Software only. For example the Grid technology Globus Toolkit ([11]) was used and the Nagios ([19]) monitoring tool was extended to allow for initial SOA-Grid monitoring. Some performance and software technical analysis was performed as well.

1.2 Related Work

Related work comes from different areas: Coupling of SOA and Grid in very large scale IT landscapes is examined in [14] and [4]. There is even a widely accepted proposed architecture (OGSA; [10]) for these kind of systems. It is however a very general architecture concept (similar in[15]) not focused on a specific problem context.

More specific work just occurs sporadically in some kind of individual solution, e.g. for astronomy ([26]), bioinformatics ([27]), or geosciences ([12], [20]). This paper thus adds more specific work that especially addresses smaller IT environments in the combined GRID/SOA space. The fact that many of the subject related articles are quite recent, supports the claim that there is still much work needed in this area.

For distributed search in Grids a data structure is proposed by [23], not combined with SOA however. Prototypes for easier WS development in Grids are shown in [1], [17], but they assume an SOA to communicate among the Grid nodes only.

2 Concepts and Technologies: SOA, Grid and Web Services

To utilize the benefits of SOA and Grid within one single IT system jointly, a concept is required to couple both technologies. Two options are obvious: Option one utilizes Web services as communication technology between Grid nodes; option two is an SOA, which uses a Grid as some super service for calculation or data storage.

Within option one the nodes of a Grid can be seen as services within an SOA. Each node can typically be used via SOAP/WS and together the services form a Grid. All communication within the Grid is thus based on Web services. Part of the case study for this option is to check, whether the flexibility gained by the usage of Web services help significantly or whether the overall Grid performance is influenced negatively instead. This option is illustrated in figure 1.

Possibly the decision about the practical relevance of this option is even depending on the specific application and the type of Grid (computing Grid, data Grid, etc).

In the second option the whole Grid as one (service) element within an SOA is examined. This option is illustrated in figure 2. The Grid offers its service to other components within the SOA; again SOAP/WS is used, but only to communicate with the node which controls the Grid but not necessarily within the Grid itself. Internally the Grid could instead use any kind of communication protocol. This architectural option seems well suited if an existing computing or data Grid shall be utilized within an

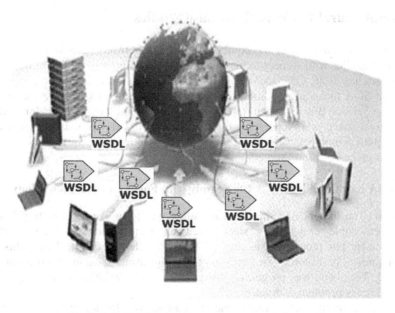

Fig. 1. A Grid using (Web) services protocols internally

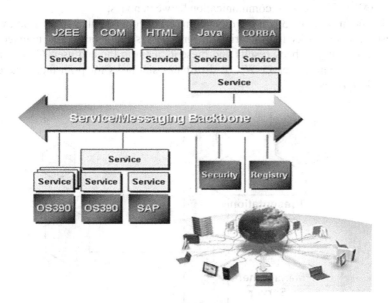

Fig. 2. An SOA utilizes a Grid as a super service

SOA. From an SOA viewpoint the Grid is just another service like other services. Grid specifics are not used.

The following chapter shows a case study for each of those two options. Based on the gained experienced both architecture options are conclusively valued.

3 Architectural Options: Two Case Studies

For a practical evaluation of the combined Grid and SOA concepts in smaller environments (smaller with respect to hardware in use), two prototypes where developed as case studies from Q3/2006 till mid 2007. Both prototypes used open source Grid- and SOA technology (Globus IV-Toolkit [11], Celtix 1.x [3] or Apache CXF Enterprise Service Bus [6]). The development was executed by 11 bachelor students in their final study year, supervised by 2 professors. Effort was 1 day per week per student. Both prototypes were based on medium size Linux PC workstations as well as 2 multi processor Linux servers.

3.1 "RSA Key Challenge" – A Case Study with Focus on Grid Technology

Overview. The idea behind the first case study was to utilize a computing Grid to break (reasonable easy) RSA keys based on factorization of prim numbers. Motivation for this prototype was the "RSA Key Challenge" ([21]). Within this case study a simple "brute force" factorization algorithm using division by prim numbers was used. The focus was on getting started with Grid and SOA technology with a reasonable easy problem domain.

Figure 3 shows the architecture of the first case study. Monitors mean end users, pc symbols mean system components possibly distributed across different computing nodes. SOAP/WS is used for communication between nodes.

Starting point in figure 3 is the presentation server component. It is a servlet, which takes user-initiated tasks for factorization and passes them on to the management server. In return it gets back results and presents them to the end user. Core component is the management server WS. It distributes sub tasks for prim factorization to different Grid nodes.

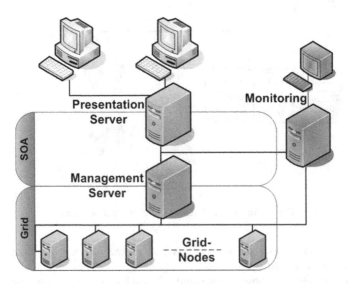

Fig. 3. Architectural elements of case study 1 – "RSA Key Challenge"

For some more technical detail, listing 1 in appendix A shows an excerpt of the management server's WSDL. It contains operations to start and delete (Grid node) jobs, get a list a of current jobs etc. Note the relation to resource descriptions and stateful services, which occasionally occur in Grid service architectures.

Each Grid node is a Web service itself, which takes a number to be factorized and an interval to be tested. If the factorization is successful, the result is returned, otherwise an error. The Grid nodes process their number intervals in parallel. Using the monitoring tool Nagios runtime supervision of the overall SOA-Grid is performed and visualized.

Resulting experiences. Development of the software for this case study was performed just as a typical standard application would have been. No major problems were encountered and the students had no problems to develop software for this specific area. Even the new technologies such as web services and Grid computing did not pose any major challenges apart from the standard setup time required to be familiar with a new technology.

The project team of students was divided into sub teams which were used as domain experts during the course of the project. Domain experts were concerned with tackling the following work packages: project management, detailed specification of the scenario, Grid technology, enterprise service bus (ESB) technology, hardware and system software as well as monitoring.

Some minor problems have been encountered in the Grid software team. These were due to the somewhat unhandy web services layer of the Grid software used (Globus toolkit 4). Consequently this layer has not been used directly in the case study but rather the more basic GridFTP has been used for data transfer on the Globus side. Since the case study's goal was to examine web services in a Grid context the team developed its own web service wrapper for the GridFTP base technology. This wrapper has been based on another open source product, namely the Celtix ESB implementation.

With this case study focusing on using a Grid to solve a computationally complex problem it should also be evaluated how and to what extent a Grid will help to solve the problem faster than a single machine could. Our lab environment for performing this quantitative analysis consisted of up to 4 completely identical Grid nodes. Standard PCs with exactly the same hardware and software components have been used. Since only relative times are relevant in this study the simple hardware is sufficient as long as all nodes use the same.

From our experiments we saw that for very small numbers only the Grid setup time dominates and this using multiple Grid nodes is not reasonable. With a little bit larger numbers we can detect the first significant speedup, but still using a Grid does not gain enough. This situation changes completely with using really large numbers (in our study these numbers consisted of 23 digits, but this is definitely dependent on the hardware used). Here we can observe a significant speedup by using a Grid. Since the setup time of the Grid is negligible here, even two Grid nodes already lead to a near linear speedup. In the case of 4 nodes we even observed super-linear speedup which is due to some specifics of our implementation (and cannot be generalized). In general however, at least relatively linear speedup can be expected. Note, that we did not test speedup which goes widely beyond 4 nodes, e.g. to 100 or 1000 nodes. However, due to the "linear design" of our RSA scenario, we still expect at least very reasonable speedup for larger scale environments as well. This should hold at least as long as we do not hit network speed or latency boundaries significantly.

Figure 4 illustrates that the good performance results by adding more Grid nodes are not dependent on the existence of a solution to the factorization problem (red line) or non-existence (green line). In both cases similar speedup can be achieved. This test has been using large numbers only.

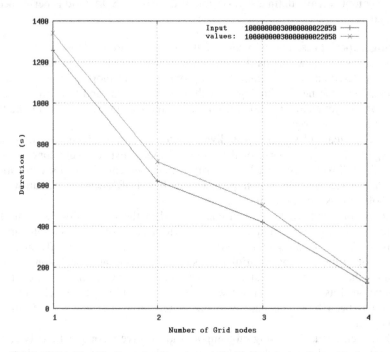

Fig. 4. "RSA Key Challenge" – Speedup with/without solution (large numbers)

In figure 5 the CPU usage during a typical "challenge" run is shown. It can be seen easily, that the management server (red) peaks, whenever new jobs are scheduled. The regular computing nodes (green) show peaks whenever they are working on an assigned block of numbers. After they have finished with a block the CPU usage drops into the depicted values while the node awaits the next block to be assigned by the scheduling node which in turn shows smaller peaks at that time. Other than this, a relatively evenly CPU usage can be observed.

3.2 "IT Web Indexer": A Specialized Web Search Engine with Focus on SOA

Overview. Figure 6 illustrates the second case study. It shows an "IT" specialized Web search engine, an "IT Web Indexer". The components work jointly in a SOA, which uses a simulated data Grid as a storage service. For time reasons, this data Grid was implemented as a distributed, replicated database.

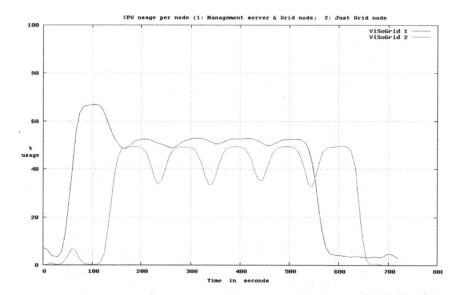

Fig. 5. "RSA Key Challenge" – Typical CPU usage

The IT Web Indexer works as follows: a Web crawler WS manages a list of URLs to be examined in the data Grid. Each loaded Web page is reduced to its text content only and passed to an analysis WS, which examines the page for "IT relevance" by means of a pre-defined IT glossary. If a certain score is exceeded, the page is seen as relevant and stored using the data Grid service. The value is passed to an index server WS, which indexes the word from the Web page, eliminates duplicates etc.

End users access the results by means of a Web page, which interacts with the user (input gathering and validation, result preparation) as well as with the request server WS. The latter separates the user query into IDs, which are prepared as queries for the data Grid storage service. The query result is a list of page IDs, from which the user can pick, like in popular Web search engines.

Experiences. As expected using a SOA with Web Services for communication leads to a system architecture, which is very flexible. On one hand the separation of the whole software system into several functional components induces a very well structured software system. Single components (where a component can be identified by the functionality it provides to the system as a whole) can be replaced by different implementations as desired.

On the other hand the different software components within the case study could be distributed arbitrarily among the available resources. This leads to a well improved usage of resources which can even be adjusted dynamically depending on the current need of the system. Thus it was possible to achieve a pretty good system throughput (measured in terms of web sites scanned and hits found per time unit) even with the very limited resources available in a student project.

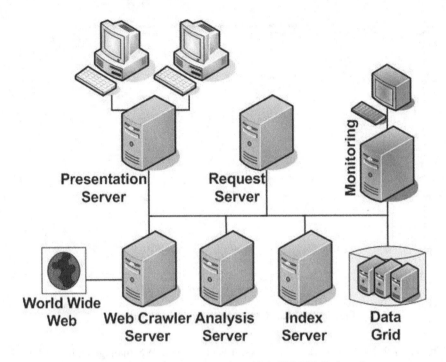

Fig. 6. Case study with focus on SOA: "IT Web Indexer"

As an example for the good flexibility, which the SOA-based design provides, one could exchange the front end easily with a self-developed application, which just calls the appropriate Web service. Other options would be specialized front-ends for mobile devices like PDAs or highly interactive Web GUIs based on Web 2.0 technologies like Ajax. Similarly, the crawler Web service could be implemented in different versions, e.g. to search other data sources like local documents rather than the Web. Figure 7 shows such SOA-based architectural variations of the "IT Web Indexer".

The data Grid providing database storage and access capabilities for the search engine has been included into the SOA as a "super service", meaning that communication with the data Grid is performed just as communication with any service in the system (thus making it a service); on the other hand the data Grid provides much more functionality and its internal complexity is much larger compared to a classical service (making it a super service). Nevertheless viewing the data Grid as a service made it possible to include it smoothly into the system: There was e.g. no need for any specific interaction methods.

In total, the service-based design of the system resulted in a highly flexible architecture, as promised by SOA.

Similar to our study only limited resources will be available in a realistic setting where Grid and SOA are to be employed in smaller environments, e.g. small companies. Our second case study shows that even then a combination of the two technologies can lead to a considerable performance boost due to the flexible architecture and improved resource usage.

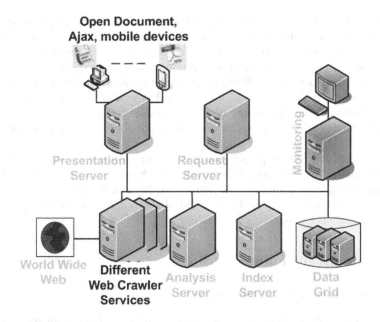

Fig. 7. "IT Web Indexer" – Architectural variations based on an SOA

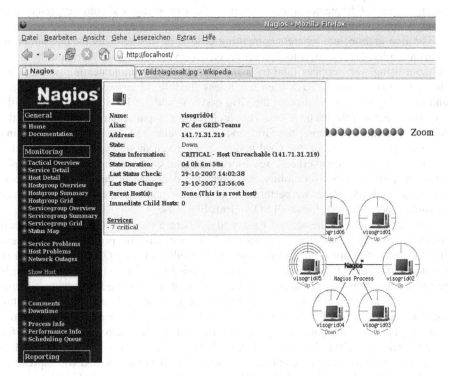

Fig. 8. SOA-Grid-monitoring in action

As in the first case study a specifically extended version of the open source tool Nagios provided integrated monitoring capabilities of both SOA and Grid. Such integrated capabilities proofed to be essential for both the development as well as the operation phase. During the development phase monitoring is important for locating errors originating from the distributed nature of the application. During system operation, monitoring is required for availability control as well as for system tuning issues. Figure 8 shows a screenshot of the running monitoring system, which monitors the SOA-Grid. As can be seen, all nodes run fine except node visogrid04, which is currently down.

In our experience without proper monitoring of the different nodes it is quite difficult to automatically detect available resources which may be employed by a different component for optimized system performance. Without monitoring, the overall SOA-Grid would be much harder to develop and almost impossible to manage even in small environments like ours.

4   Conclusions and Future Work

4.1   Lessons Learned from Case Studies

Both case studies showed that the combination of SOA and Grid technologies is possible without any problems. We can also conclude that both architectural variants may be employed for implementation. Which of the two variants should be preferred is strongly application dependent.

The first architecture where a computing Grid uses web services for internal communication has been proven to provide an easy implementation of a computing Grid. Without using web services (and by using a proprietary communication protocol instead) the system would have been much less flexible. I.e. using different hardware and operating system on some of the Grid nodes would not have been possible without additional development effort. This architecture is particularly beneficial, if the messages exchanged among the Grid nodes are diverse and the hardware, operating system and/or software on the Grid nodes varies. Even though web services incur a certain communication overhead we observed a significant speedup of the Grid application and the improved flexibility outweighs the overhead in this context. The performance analysis, which we performed, showed the significant speedups, which are possible especially even for small SOA-Grids like ours.

The architecture in the second case study, where a database Grid was integrated into a distributed application as a super web service, has also proven to be efficient for this kind of application. In this case the flexibility of the SOA has been used in favor of implementation of the distributed application. The advantage of flexible resource allocation based on a possibly heterogeneous computing infrastructure facilitates an efficient implementation of this complex application. Communication within the data Grid is proprietary in this case, since the messages to be exchanged are fixed and well-known. This holds since they are defined by the database system used for implementing the data Grid. Nevertheless Web services are used to access the data Grid as a whole in order to be able to use the data Grid as flexible and wide spread as possible. The highly increased flexibility shows, that SOA usage makes sense, even for comparable small applications. The easy integration of a Grid as a super-service, as well as flexible exchange or additions of services within the second case study pointed this clearly.

In both studies we observed that a loose coupling of the two concepts Grid and SOA proved beneficial. The Grids have been integrated into the distributed application by means of services in both cases. This makes flexible usage of the Grids possible. Within the Grids services have been used for the computing Grid but not for the data Grid. As a general rule we can state that services within the Grid provide an advantage as long as many diverse services are used within the Grid and a heterogeneous computing infrastructure is used. If that is not the case proprietary communication should be used within the Grid.

Distributed applications running on a heterogeneous infrastructure require advanced monitoring capabilities of the system as a whole. In our studies the tool Nagios with specific extensions developed within the scope of the studies proved to be extremely valuable. It is possible to monitor hardware as well as software status of the system. Monitoring for both Grid and SOA could be nicely integrated and a good overview of the system as a whole is achieved.

All the software developed within the case studies has been based on open source products. The fact that the applications have been successfully implemented based on this kind of software with acceptable effort show that even in such complex application scenarios open source software is an alternative. Especially in the case of SMEs where financial investments in IT have to be quite limited it is important to be able to use open source software. Cheap software complements the potential to use a heterogeneous computing infrastructure and flexible resource allocation very well. Jointly it is possible to implement a complex and highly productive software system at comparable low cost. This is especially important for smaller environments in SMEs.

Eventually, the results showed as well, that such relatively complex integration projects are quite feasible for teaching purposes in (advanced) student courses respectively projects.

4.2 Future Work

The quantitative evaluations of the distributed applications developed in the case studies should be extended further. Especially many more different hardware and software foundations on the Grid nodes should be examined. This could potentially lead to more insight into the influence of heterogeneity for the Grid and SOA applications. Of course interesting as well would be to add significantly more Grid nodes, to validate the scalability results. We plan to explore this in the future. In this case care must be taken however, that our targeted "smaller environments" are still addressed here primarily.

If the customized extensions to Nagios would be extended somewhat further, a tool for general Web Service and Grid management and monitoring could be obtained. Such a tool would be of great benefit to many different SOA-based software systems and has many potential use cases.

The combination of SOA and Grid should also be employed for implementation of real-world applications used within a SME. Practical experiences gained from this kind of applications and from the integration of the different technologies into an actual IT landscape of a SME could reveal further perception of the applicability of the architectural variants. Finally more benefits of the combination of Grid and SOA could be deduced and the necessity for improvements could be detected.

Acknowledgements. We would like to thank our students from the ViSoGrid project team for their highly productive and enthusiastic work in this project. Special thanks goes to the team members E. Friedrich, B. Hellmann, A. Reich, M. Schaaf, and J. Salzwedel.

References

1. Bocchi, L., Ciancarini, P., Moretti, R., Presutti, V., Rossi, D.: An OWL-S based approach to express Grid services coordination. In: Liebrock, L.M. (ed.) Proc. 2005 ACM Symp. on Applied Computing, SAC 2005, Santa Fe, New Mexico, pp. 1661–1667. ACM Press, New York (2005)
2. Bunn, J., van Lingen, F., Newman, H., Steenberg, C., Thomas, M., Ali, A., Anjum, A., Azim, T., Khan, F., Rehman, W.u., McClatchey, R., In, J.U.: JClarens: A Java Framework for Developing and Deploying Web Services for Grid Computing. In: Proc. IEEE Conf. on Web Services (ICWS 2005), pp. 141–148. IEEE CS, Washington (2005)
3. Celtix: Celtix Enterprise Service Bus, 1.x. objectweb.org. Acc. (July 2007)
4. Chen, X., Cai, W., Turner, S.J., Wang, Y.: SOAr-DSGrid: Service-Oriented Architecture for Distributed Simulation on the Grid. In: Proc. 20th Workshop on Principles of Advanced and Distributed Simulation. Workshop on Parallel and Distributed Simulation, pp. 65–73. IEEE CS, Washington (2006)
5. Conrad, S., Hasselbring, W., Koschel, A., Tritsch, R.: Enterprise Application Integration. Spektrum Akademischer Verlag, Germany (2005)
6. Apache CXF Enterprise Service Bus. apache, org. Acc. (July 2007)
7. Erl, T.: SOA: Concepts, Technology, and Design. Prentice-Hall, Englewood Cliffs (2005)
8. Fang, L.: A Scalable Capability-Based Authorization Infrastructure for Web Services in Grids. Doctoral Thesis. UMI Order No. AAI3215173, Indiana University (2006)
9. Foster, I., Kesselman, K.: The Grid 2: Blueprint for a New Computing Infrastructure. Morgan Kaufmann, San Francisco (2003)
10. Foster, I., Kishimoto, H., Savva, A., Berry, D., Djaoui, A., Grimshaw, A., Horn, B., Maciel, F., Siebenlist, F., Subramaniam, R., Treadwell, J., Von Reich, J.: The Open Grid Services Architecture, Version 1.0. Informational Document, Global Grid Forum (GGF) (2005)
11. Foster, I.: Globus Toolkit Version 4: Software for Service-Oriented Systems. In: Jin, H., Reed, D., Jiang, W. (eds.) NPC 2005. LNCS, vol. 3779, pp. 2–13. Springer, Heidelberg (2006)
12. Fraser, R., Rankine, T., Woodcock, R.: Service oriented grid architecture for geosciences community. In: Proc. 5th Australasian symposium on ACSW frontiers (ACSW 2007), pp. 19–23. Australian Computer Society, Inc., Darlinghurst (2007)
13. Friese, T., Smith, M., Freisleben, B.: Hot service deployment in an ad hoc Grid environment. In: Proc. 2nd Intl. Conference on Service Oriented Computing, ICSOC 2004, pp. 75–83. ACM Press, New York (2004)
14. Holmes, V., Johnson, W., Miller, D.: Integrating Web Service and Grid Enabling Technologies to Provide Desktop Access to High-Performance Cluster-Based Components for Large-Scale Data Services. In: Proc. 36th annual symposium on Simulation (ANSS 2003), p. 167. IEEE Computer Society Press, Washington (2003)

15. Huang, Y.: JISGA: A Jini-Based Service-Oriented Grid Architecture. International Journal of High Performance Computing Applications, 317–327 (2003)
16. Krafzig, D., Banke, K., Slama, D.: Enterprise SOA. Prentice Hall, Englewood Cliffs (2005)
17. Kwon, S., Choi, J., Cho, K.: Light-weight service-oriented Grid application toolkit. In: Proc. of the 2006 ACM Symp. on Applied Computing, SAC 2006, Dijon, France, pp. 1482–1486. ACM Press, New York (2006)
18. Lomow, G., Newcomer, E.: Understanding Service-Oriented Architecture (SOA) with Web Services. Addison-Wesley, Reading (2005)
19. Nagios. Nagios Monitoring Toolkit, Nagios.org. Acc. (July 2007)
20. Patra, M., Das, R.: SORIG: A service-oriented framework for rural information grid – an implementation viewpoint. In: Proc. 1st Intl. Conf. on Theory and practice of electronic gov. (ICEGOV 2007), pp. 49–52. ACM Press, New York (2007)
21. RSA. RSA Key Challenge. rsasecurity.com. Acc. (July 2007)
22. Starke, G., Tilkov, S. (eds.): SOA-Expertenwissen. dpunkt, Germany (2007)
23. Tadepalli, P.: Grid-based distributed search structure. In: Proc. of the 44th annual ACM Southeast regional conf., New York, pp. 752–753 (2006)
24. WWW Consortium (W3C). Web Services specifications, W3C.org. Acc. (July 2007)
25. Walker, D.W.: Grid Computing: Infrastructure and Applications. Intl. Journal High Performance Computing, Appl. 17(3), 207–208 (2003)
26. Wang, M., Du, Z., Chen, Y., Cheng, Z.: A SOA Based Pipeline System to Deal with Astronomy Telescope Data. In: Proc. of the 2nd IEEE Intl. Symposium on Service-Oriented System Engineering (Sose 2006), SOSE, pp. 156–166. IEEE Computer Society, Washington (2006)
27. Xu, G., Luo, Y., Yu, H., Xu, Z.: An Approach to SOA-Based Bioinformatics Grid. In: Proc. of the 2006 IEEE Asia-Pacific Conf. on Services Computing, APSCC, pp. 323–328. IEEE Computer Society, Washington (2006)

Appendix A

The following listing 1 shows an excerpt of the WSDL for the management server from the RSA key challenge case study.

Listing 1. WSDL excerpt for RSA key challenge

```xml
<?xml version="1.0" encoding="UTF-8"?>
<wsdl:definitions
  xmlns:soap= "http://schemas.xmlsoap.org/wsdl/soap/"
  xmlns:tns= "http://visogrid ... /Rsakc/"
  <wsdl:types>

    <xsd:element name="addJob">
      <xsd:complexType>  <xsd:sequence>
        <xsd:element name="name" type="string" />
        <xsd:element name="key" type="string" />
      </xsd:sequence>    </xsd:complexType>
    </xsd:element>
    <xsd:element name="addJobResponse">
      <xsd:complexType>  <xsd:sequence>
        <xsd:element name="id" type="int" />
      </xsd:sequence>    </xsd:complexType>
```

```
          </xsd:element>
          <xsd:element name="deleteJob">
            <xsd:complexType>  <xsd:sequence>
                <xsd:element name="id" type="int" />
            </xsd:sequence>      </xsd:complexType>
          </xsd:element>

    </wsdl:types>

    <wsdl:message name="addJobRequest">
      <wsdl:part name="in" element="tns:addJob" />
    </wsdl:message>
    <wsdl:message name="addJobResponse">
        <wsdl:part name="out" element="tns:addJobResponse">
        </wsdl:part>
    </wsdl:message>

    <wsdl:portType name="Rsakc">
      <wsdl:operation name="addJob">
        <wsdl:input message="tns:addJobRequest" />
        <wsdl:output message="tns:addJobResponse" />
      </wsdl:operation>

    </wsdl:portType>

    <wsdl:binding name="RsakcSOAP" type="tns:Rsakc">
      <soap:binding style="document"  transport=
            "http://schemas.xmlsoap.org/soap/http" />
      <wsdl:operation name="addJob">
        <soap:operation soapAction=
              "http://visogrid .../Rsakc/NewOperation" />
        <wsdl:input>
          <soap:body use="literal" />
        </wsdl:input>
          . . .
      </wsdl:operation>

    </wsdl:binding>

    <wsdl:service name="Rsakc">
      <wsdl:port  binding="tns:RsakcSOAP" name="RsakcSOAP">
        <soap:address location=
              "http://visogrid .../SoapContext/SoapPort" />
      </wsdl:port>
    </wsdl:service>
</wsdl:definitions>
```

Towards Dynamic Service Level Agreement Negotiation: An Approach Based on WS-Agreement

Antoine Pichot[1], Oliver Wäldrich[2], Wolfgang Ziegler[2], and Philipp Wieder[3]

[1] Alcatel-Lucent, Route De Villejust
91620 Nozay, France
`antoine.pichot@alcatel-lucent.fr`
[2] Fraunhofer Institute SCAI, Department of Bioinformatics
53754 Sankt Augustin, Germany
`{oliver.waeldrich,wolfgang.ziegler}@scai.fraunhofer.de`
[3] IT & Media Center, TU Dortmund University
44227 Dortmund, Germany
`philipp.wieder@udo.edu`

Abstract. In Grid, e-Science and e-Business environments, Service Level Agreements are often used to establish frameworks for the delivery of services between service providers and the organisations hosting the researchers. While this high level SLAs define the overall quality of the services, it is desirable for the end-user to have dedicated service quality also for individual services like the orchestration of resources necessary for composed services. Grid level scheduling services typically are responsible for the orchestration and co-ordination of resources in the Grid. Co-allocation e.g. requires the Grid level scheduler to co-ordinate resource management systems located in different domains. As the site autonomy has to be respected negotiation is the only way to achieve the intended co-ordination. SLAs emerged as a new way to negotiate and manage usage of resources in the Grid and are already adopted by a number of management systems. Therefore, it is natural to look for ways to adopt SLAs for Grid level scheduling. In order to do this, efficient and flexible protocols are needed, which support dynamic negotiation and creation of SLAs. In this paper we propose and discuss extensions to the WS-Agreement protocol addressing these issues.

Keywords: Commit Protocol, Negotiation, Quality of service, Service level agreement, Web services agreement.

1 Introduction

A Service Level Agreement (SLA) is a contract between a service provider and its customer that describes the service, terms, guarantees, responsibilities and service-level to be provided. In Grids, e-Science and e-Business environments, SLAs are often used to establish service-delivery frameworks between a service provider and a service consumer domain. Such "high-level" SLAs usually define the framework of service provisioning and overall Quality of Service (QoS). However, it is desirable and sometimes even essential for the end-user to have dedicated QoS also for individual services, e.g. in a case of a high-priority service request. In this article we focus on electronic SLAs dynamically negotiated and created by software programs on behalf of end-users. The

J. Cordeiro et al. (Eds.): WEBIST 2008, LNBIP 18, pp. 107–119, 2009.

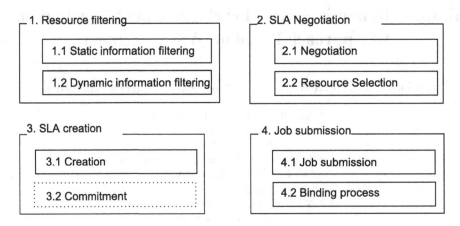

Fig. 1. Resource selection and reservation

use case we consider is resource provisioning, i.e. an SLA-based service provision implies access to various kinds of resources, like computing nodes, network connections, storage areas or any combination of these.

Resource consumption varies over time and is sometimes dependent on the successful completion of previous tasks. An orchestrator communicates on behalf of customers end-users with several local resource managers to negotiate and create dynamic SLAs. In the rest of the document, for reasons of clarity, we will limit the problem scope to use-cases where computing and network resources are needed, and to a Grid scheduler as orchestrator that has to negotiate, select and schedule resources in order to execute a user's job and fulfil its requirements. As we will see, co-ordinating the access to multiple resources at the same time requires specific protocol features that negotiation and agreement protocols do not necessarily have. Fig. 1 describes the different steps to be performed by a Grid scheduler to co-allocate resources: resource filtering, SLA negotiation, SLA creation, and job submission.

Although the WS-Agreement Specication [1] specified by the GRAAP-WG [2] already includes a basic protocol for negotiation of SLAs, a number of use cases and requirements came up which express the need for more sophisticated means of negotiation.The protocol included in the specification was designed to cover the most simple and general case: an offer for an SLA is made by either the service consumer or the service provider and the respective other party may accept or reject the offer. No further negotiation, e.g. in form of a counter offer or request for modication is supported. Since there are situations where an agreement has to be modied at a later state or the process of creating an agreement needs more than the single step, a more sophisticated protocol for negotiation and re-negotiation is needed in addition to the existing one. The group is now working on protocol extensions for the WS-Agreement and one approach for such an extension is presented in this paper.

In the following section we introduce work related to negotiation of SLAs. Section 3 describes SLA negotiation and creation problems, how distributed databases' commit protocol shed light to this problem. Section 4 describes how these problems can be solved using the Web Services Agreement protocol and Section 5 concludes the paper.

2   Related Work

While WS-Agreement, since May 2007 the proposed recommendation of the Open Grid Forum for a language and a protocol to create SLAs, was becoming stable over the last two years, the interest in using SLAs for resource negotiation was growing constantly. One indicator is the number of projects and developments around resource management and scheduling considering or already using SLAs. In the following we briefly discuss the different approaches.

Some of the projects using WS-Agreement, e.g. CATNETS [3], openCCS [4], Agent-Scape [5], the Community Scheduler Framework (CSF) [6] and the VIOLA MetaScheduling Service (MSS) [7], are using WS-Agreement to create the SLAs. Some plan to use WS-Agreement, e.g. the Grid Resource Management System (GRMS) [8] and GridWay [9] are in the planning phase for integrating WS-Agreement. Finally, some have not yet decided which technology to use or are not using a web services stack at all: eNanos [10], Grid superscalar [11] and the Highly-Available Resource Co-allocator (HARC) [12].

CATNETS uses a market oriented mechanism of offers and bids to determine the price of a resource and to create an SLA based on the result, thus no negotiation is used. openCCS, AgentScape and MSS are Grid schedulers and use negotiation to refine offers and requests in order to create SLAs. In case of MSS, this includes negotiation with several resource providers to co-allocate multiple resources or support workflow execution across multiple resources. As WS-Agreement does not include a protocol for negotiating the terms of an SLA (but an "accept/reject" protocol for the whole SLA), the three aforementioned approaches currently use proprietary extensions of WS-Agreement for the negotiation. GRMS and GridWay currently do plan not use WS-Agreement for SLAs between provider and customer, but plan to use WS-Agreement for the communication between multiple co-operating Grid schedulers. This will allow to negotiate usage of resources that are not part of the environment of the the initially accessed Grid scheduler. Scenarios and the corresponding requirements for the protocol are developed in the Grid Scheduling Architecture Research Group (GSA-RG) [13] of the Open Grid Forum. The developers of the eNanos Grid resource broker and the Grid superscalar programming environment are currently evaluating the technology for the integration of SLAs into their tools. In contrast, the HARC developers decided not to use a web services stack and do the negotiation based on plain XML-messages over HTTPS.

Moreover, the GRAAP Working Group has started work on extending WS-Agreement to support negotiation of agreements for use cases where the simple step creation are not sufficient. In this paper we discuss some general problems of negotiation in distributed environments and present first ideas how negotiation could be implemented on top of WS-Agreement.

3   Negotiation, Creation and Commit Protocols

In this section negotiation is briefly discussed followed by a presentation of commit protocols in distributed databases in Section 3.1 and commit protocols for distributed resource management systems in Section 3.2.

To run a job that requires several resources, like networking and computational resources, managed by different resource management systems (RMS), several steps must be performed by a Grid scheduler. Upon receipt of the job request, the scheduler starts the first phase: resource filtering based on static information and dynamic information. Static information does not change over time: number of CPUs, operating system, location, etc. Dynamic information changes over time: availability, load, etc. The second phase is the negotiation process and results in the selection of resources that can satisfy the job request. The third phase is the SLA creation phase concluded by the commitment of all service providers (or local RMS) involved leading to a an reservation of the negotiated resources as described in the SLA. The last phase is the job submission followed by the execution.

Negotiation is a widely studied topic and there are numerous publications addressing different aspects, e.g. [14] is a general purpose negotiation journal, [15] is a survey about negotiation in distributed resource management systems, while [16] and [17] discuss aspects of service negotiation in the Grid. In our context and in the simplest case, a user's job has to be executed and the Grid scheduler has to select between different target systems. If all systems are identical and only one parameter influences the selection, i.e. price, this case is similar to a typical business negotiation between one buyer and several sellers. An auctioning mechanism like the ones described in [18] can be used. Of course, we take the point of view of an end user, if we look at things from a resource provider's point of view, we have several jobs that compete for one resource, i.e. several buyers and one seller. If we look at the scheduler's point of view, we have many jobs that compete for several resources, i.e. many buyers and many sellers. Buyya [18] (page 36) also surveyed several distributed resource management systems based on price.

Automatic negotiation of SLAs is a complex and time consuming process [19,20,21], when even two users have to find an agreement on multiple criteria. Imagine how difficult the problem becomes when multiple entities have to reach an agreement [22]. When at least two resources are needed at the same time to run a job, e.g. a network connection and a processing resource, several steps have to be performed before reaching an agreement between the resource providers and the consumer. Green [21] cites mainly two frameworks for automatic negotiation: ontologies and web services. According to him automated negotiation has three main considerations: The negotiation protocol, the negotiation objects and the decision-making models. He considers two options existing in order to achieve this type of negotiation. One option is for the originating agent to negotiate separately with each Autonomous System (AS) along each potential path to ensure that an end-to-end path is available. The dominant choice however, is to use a cascaded approach where each AS is responsible for the entire path downstream of itself. This approach enhances agent autonomy as it is only responsible for its immediate links. The autonomy of the cascaded approach struggles however with the issue of price. In a cascading scenario an intelligent agent would need to know the utility functions of all the downstream domains if the best price combination is to be determined, which is private information. In contrast, in this paper we limited the scope to protocols that permit the negotiation of agreements between two parties based on WS-Agreement rather than tackling the full complexity of automated negotiation. These bilateral agreements might then be combined into one single agreement.

3.1   Commit Protocols for Distributed Databases

Distributed transactional systems have been widely studied. One of their objectives is to propagate a consistent state across several systems, in a way that at any time all systems can show a consistent state to users. The consistent state or consistent view maintains and propagates between systems a logical coherent state. To provide crash recovery, several operations are logically grouped into transactions. Those transactions permit the change from one consistent view to another. For instance, you do not credit a bank account if you have not debited another bank account. However, these are two independent operations. A bank's distributed database system must group these two operations in one transaction. Thus it permits the change from one consistent state "before the transfer" to another "after the transfer". Database state changes are visible by other users once a transaction is committed to the system. In distributed systems, each transaction can impact several different systems not co-located. Thus distributed database experts have developed commit protocols [23,24,25]. As Skeen described in [26], "The processing of a single transaction is viewed as follows. At some time during its execution, a commit point is reached where the site decides to commit or to abort the transaction. A commit is an unconditional guarantee to execute the transaction to completion, even in the event of multiple failures. Similarly, an abort is an unconditional guarantee to "back out" the transaction so that none of its results persist. If a failure occurs before the commit point is reached, then immediately upon recovering the site will abort the transaction. Commit and abort are irreversible."

When a user needs to make a change in a distributed database, a co-ordinator will propagate this change on all systems. As Skeen explains, upon receipt of a change request the co-ordinator forwards it to all distributed systems. Upon the change request receipt, all slaves go to the wait state. Then they can decide whether or not to accept this change, and send their response. The co-ordinator collects all responses to the change request, if one of them is negative, it goes in the abort state and sends an "abort" to all systems, if all responses are positive, then the co-ordinator goes in the commit state, and sends a "Commit" to all systems. Upon receiving a "Commit" (respectively "Abort") all systems must commit (respectively "Abort") the change request. Fig. 2 (left) represents a slave's two phase commit protocol finite state machine (FSM). This process is the two phase commit process, supported by a two phase commit protocol.

The problem of this process is that in case of system failure. It's impossible to know whether the transaction was committed or aborted. The wait state leads to both commit and abort state. For instance, when the co-ordinator fails after having sent a "commit" to some slaves but not all, the remaining slaves are blocked since they cannot know whether the transaction should be aborted or cancelled.

To provide crash recovery, and avoid blocking problems, Skeen introduced a three phase commit protocol. He added an intermediary state before the commitment as shown in Fig. 2 (middle). This state corresponds to a prepare to commit. It's impossible to jump from this state to an abort state. He proved that if a state transition was possible between the prepare and the abort state, the protocol would be blocking. As a consequence, from any state on the slave's finite state machine it is possible to determine whether the transaction should be committed or aborted in case of failure. In case of failure a slave in the "Wait" state must abort, while a slave in the "Prepare" state must commit.

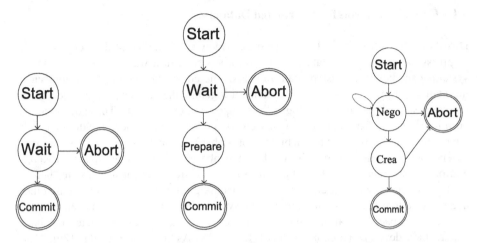

Fig. 2. Two phase commit slave's FSM (left), three phase commit slave's FSM (middle), and SLA negotiation and creation resource provider's FSM (right)

3.2   Commit Protocols for Distributed Resource Management Systems

In an environment with distributed RMS providing guarantees on resource usage, a Grid scheduler may negotiate SLAs with its users. In a co-allocation use case, this SLA takes into account several resources coming from several resource providers. With each independent resource provider a bilateral SLA has to be negotiated and created. A Grid scheduler has to create these bilateral SLAs on behalf of its users. For instance, through the MetaScheduling Service users may request network and computational resources with a dedicated QoS [7]. The Grid scheduler has to orchestrate the individual reservation of network and computational resources. These two reservations are realised as two bilateral SLAs.

The essence of distributed databases' commit protocol is the transaction: a group of individual operations linked logically. In a distributed resource management system, co-allocation requires multiple bilateral SLAs. For a user or a particular service requiring multiple resources, either all of the individual bilateral SLA must be created, or none. The user SLA creation process is a transaction composed of multiple bilateral SLA creation.

Before reaching an agreement, two steps must be performed: negotiation and creation. The negotiation process can involve all resource providers. Its results are input to a resource provider selection process. When two resources are needed, e.g. network and computing, even if the negotiation involves many compute resource providers, only one computational resource will be selected. For many resources offered, the negotiation process does not lead to an SLA creation process. This is the main reason why negotiation must neither obligate the provider nor the consumer of the SLA. However, the SLA negotiation and creation process should minimise the number of discarded agreement creation requests when it has been previously negotiated. This should occur only when there is a race condition: when two or more users are competing simultaneously for the same resource at the same time. The separation of agreement negotiation and agreement creation process and minimising the number of discarded agreement creations after negotiation are conflicting objectives.

One way to observe atomicity of the SLA creation is to use a transaction and to rely on a two phase commit protocol. Once resources have been negotiated, the orchestrator starts the SLA creation process by sending an SLA creation request to the selected resource providers. Then each resource provider responds to the request with yes or a counter offer. If all providers agree, the orchestrator sends a commit reservation to all systems. Upon receipt of this message, the reservation is committed and the SLA created. Fig. 2 (right) shows this process.

When the resource provider receives an SLA negotiation offer, its state changes from "Start" to "Nego". It then answers the negotiation offer by either accepting it or making a counter offer. In case of a counter offer, it stays in the "Nego" state. It can also abort the negotiation and proceed to the "Abort" state. Once the orchestrator decides to start the SLA creation process, upon receipt of the SLA creation request, the resource provider's state changes to the "Crea" state. It stays there if it accepts the reservation otherwise it goes to the "Abort" state. The final "Commit" state is reached when it receives a "Commit" message from the orchestrator and that resources are reserved and made unavailable to the rest of the world. As mentioned above, this simple two phase commit scenario can lead to a race condition during the SLA creation process. While the resource provider is in the "Crea" state, other users see the previous consistent state where resources are still available. To prevent this, the "Crea" state could imply "locking" resources thus providing a pre-reservation for the transaction lifetime. This prevents other users from reserving the same resource at the same time. In case of a lock request, second users' transaction must wait for the lock to be released.

Although the FSMs shown in the middle and on the right-hand side of Fig. 2 look similar, we cannot say that the SLA negotiation and creation process is a three phase commit. It is a blocking protocol as described by Skeen [26]. And it does not provide any guarantees against crashes. One could still imagine a non blocking SLA creation protocol relying on a three phase commit providing crash recovery. It will not be discussed in this article.

4   SLA Negotiation and Creation with WS-Agreement

In order to co-allocate different types of resources and/or resources from different domains, MSS has to negotiate SLAs for the required resources. The easiest way of SLA negotiation is a one step process, where the context, subject and constraints of the negotiation problem are defined. The WS-Agreement protocol natively supports this kind of negotiation by the *getResourceProperties* method. This method returns a set of agreement templates representing acceptable agreement offers for an agreement provider. These agreement templates only provide hints on agreement offers which might be accepted by an agreement provider. They do not guarantee the agreement will be accepted. An agreement template defines one ore more services that are specified by their *Service Description Terms* (SDT), their *Service Property Terms* (SPT), and their *Guarantee Terms* (GT). Additionally an agreement provider can constrain the possible values within the SDTs, SPTs, and GTs by defining appropriate creation constraints within the templates.

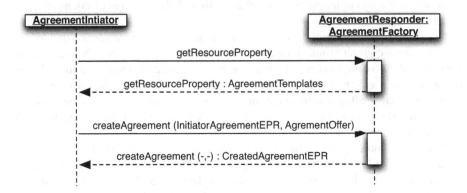

Fig. 3. WS-Agreement one step negotiation

The creation constraints in agreement template can be static or dynamic. Typical examples of a static creation constraints are the minimum and maximum numbers of CPU, nodes, or memory. As these are properties of computing systems that are not likely to change frequently agreement templates that only contain static information usually are not restricted in their lifetime.

Agreement templates can also contain more dynamic information. Such dynamic information can be used to e.g. restrict the guaranteed execution time of a given service based on the current resource availability. Since the availability of resources is likely to change frequently, templates that contain such dynamic components have a short lifetime. A Grid scheduler can use these dynamic templates to efficiently find suitable time slots in order to e.g. co-allocate resources.

However, it is not always desired to expose availability information, or sometimes it is even not possible to do this in a convenient way. A typical example for this is the creation of an SLA in the network domain. Here, it is simply not possible to include the availability information for all possible network paths in a domain within one single SLA template. This would make the templates far to complex and therefore practically unusable. Therefore, the efficient agreement on time constraints in SLAs in only one phase is simply not feasible in this case. More advanced multi-step negotiations are needed to solve this problem.

4.1   Negotiation of Agreement Templates

Negotiation requires an iterative process between the parties involved. To rely on WS-Agreement and minimise the extensions to the proposed standard, we suggest not to negotiate SLAs but to negotiate and refine the templates that can be used to create an SLA. Here, our focus is on the bilateral negotiation of agreement templates.

In the following scenario we describe how an agreement initiator (e.g. the Grid scheduler) negotiates agreement templates with two agreement providers (e.g. a network scheduler and a CPU scheduler). We propose a simple offer/counter offer model. In order to use this model in the WS-Agreement protocol, we propose a new function *negotiateTemplate*. This function takes one template as input (offer), and returns zero or more templates (counter offer). The negotiation itself is an iterative process. In the following scenario we describe a simple negotiation process. During the negotiation process we call the agreement initiator 'negotiation initiator'. Accordingly we refer to the agreement providers as 'negotiation responders'.

1. *Initialisation of the negotiation process*
   First, the negotiation initiator initialises the process by querying a set of SLA templates from agreement providers. To do so, it sends a standard WS-Agreement message, getResourceProperty request, to agreement providers (not shown in Fig. 4). From this templates, the initiator chooses the most suitable one as a starting point for the negotiation process. This template defines the context of the subsequent iterations. All subsequent offers must refer to this agreement template. This is required in order to enable an agreement provider to validate the creation constraints of the original template during the negotiation process, and therefore the validity of an offer.

2. *Negotiation of the template*
   After the negotiation initiator has chosen an agreement template, it will create a new agreement template based on the chosen one. The new created template must contain a reference to the originating template within its context. Furthermore, the agreement initiator may adjust the content of the new created template, namely the content of the service description terms, the service property terms, and the guarantee terms. These changes must be done according to the creation constraints defined in the original template. Additionally, the negotiation initiator may also include creation constraints within the new created template. These

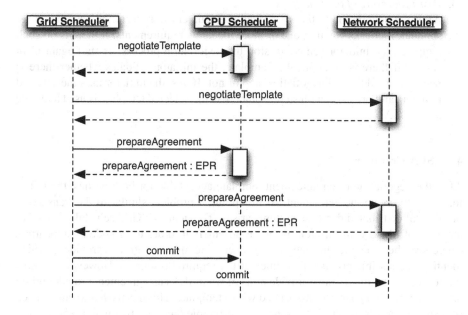

Fig. 4. Extended WS-Agreement SLA negotiation

constraints provide hints for the negotiation responder, within which limits the negotiation initiator is willing to create an agreement. For instance, the initial CPU scheduler template can contain "any number of 2GHz x586 CPU between 5pm to 6pm". And the initiator can request "at least 5 1GHz x586 CPU anytime". After the initiator created the new agreement template according to its requirements, the template is send to responders via a *negotiateTemplate* message (as shown in Fig. 4) When the responder has received a *negotiateTemplate* message, it must first check the validity of the input document (refined template). This step includes (i) retrieving the original agreement template that was used to create the input document, (ii) validating the structure of the input document with respect to the originating template, and (iii) validating the changes of the content in the input document with respect to the creation constraints defined in the originating template.

Once this is done, the agreement provider now checks whether the service defined in the request could be provided or not. In our example, it's only then that the CPU scheduler decides that 5 1GHz x586 CPUs can be provided. If the service can be provided, it just returns the agreement template to the client, indicating that an offer based on that template will potentially be accepted. Otherwise, the provider employs some strategy to create reasonable counter offers. During this process the agreement provider should take into account the constraints of the negotiation initiator. Counter offers are basically a set of new agreement templates that base on the template received from the negotiation initiator. The relationship between dynamic created templates and original ones must be reflected by updating the context of the new templates accordingly. After creating the counter offers the provider sends them back to the negotiation initiator (*negotiateTemplate* response).

3. *Post-processing of the templates*

   After the negotiation initiator received the counter offers from the negotiation responder, it checks whether one or more meets its requirements. If there is no such template, the initiator can either stop the negotiation process, or start again from step 1. If there is an applicable template, the initiator validates whether there is need for an additional negotiation step or not. If yes, the initiator uses the selected template and proceeds with step 2, otherwise the selected template is used to create a new SLA.

4.2 SLA Creation

After the negotiation of an agreement template acceptable for both parties, the initiator needs to create the agreement. At this point, a problem similar to the transaction problem of distributed database systems arises. The goal of a Grid scheduler is to create a set of SLAs with different resource providers in order to provide co-allocation. Therefore, the scheduler first negotiates a set of templates with the providers, which identify the possible provisioning times of the required resources. However, we must not forget that templates only provide hints of what SLAs an agreement provider might accept. There is no guarantee associated with a template. This means that we are in need of a strategy to create all SLAs or none. In principle there are two major strategies to achieve this:

1. *to use transactions to create the SLAs, or*
2. *to create each SLA within one step, applying policies to the SLA.*

The usage of transaction mechanisms to create distributed SLAs, namely the usage of the two phase commit protocol, was already discussed in this paper. Since there is no support for two phase commit in WS-Agreement today, we need to extend the proposed standard to address this problem. This process has been started recently in the OGF working group that created WS-Agreement. A solution consists in adding a type of agreement that must be created in two phases: the first phase is a creation of the agreement triggered by a new *prepareAgreement* message and the second with a new non-standard *Commit* message as shown in Fig. 4.

The other approach is to create an SLA in one step using today's WS-Agreement functions, cancellation mechanisms and incentives. In order to realise this, we need to investigate the content of an SLA. On one hand, an SLA describes the service and its properties. On the other hand, it specifies the guarantees for a specific service. In a co-allocation scenario, where a Grid scheduler uses SLAs to co-ordinate e.g. network and computational resources, it employs execution guarantees in order to assure that the different services are provided at the same time. These guarantees may also include costs that are associated with the service if it is provided successfully, as well as penalties that arise when a guarantee is violated. However, an SLA might be prematurely terminated by the agreement initiator, before the service is actually provided. In fact, this is a cancellation of an SLA. When a service provider guarantees a certain execution time for a service, this normally comprises resource reservations. Therefore, the resource provider wants to prevent the termination of an existing SLA. This can be achieved by including a basic payment within the SLA. The basic payment is potentially a very small amount of money that is even charged if the SLA is terminated by the agreement initiator before the service was actually provided. It is therefore a termination penalty and represents the costs for the overhead produced by the resource reservation. In order to enable the Grid scheduler to efficiently negotiate and create SLAs, there could be a certain time period in which the SLA can be terminated without penalty. The duration of this period can dynamically be specified during the negotiation process. The Agreement provider could use a certain trust index in order to determine the maximum length of this period. This offers a feasible solution for the orchestration of multiple resources using the current one-step SLA creation of WS-Agreement.

5   Conclusions

In this paper we discussed basic functions for resource orchestration in Grids, namely mechanisms to negotiate and create Service Level Agreements using WS-Agreement. SLAs are a basic building block for Grid resource orchestration and distributed resource management. We have shown how a bilateral WS-Agreement based negotiation process is used to dynamically negotiate SLA templates. We proposed an extension of the WS-Agreement protocol, *NegotiateTemplate*, in order to support a simple offer/counter-offer model.

The second relevant part of the resource orchestration process is the creation of distributed SLAs. We have discussed two different strategies to co-allocate SLAs in Grids.

One using a two phase commit with a WS-Agreement *Commit* extension and one using a single phase commit with SLA cancellation and incentives.

Acknowledgements. Some of the work reported in this paper is funded by the German Federal Ministry of Education and Research through the VIOLA project (grant #01AK605L), by the European Commission's IST programme through the CoreGRID Network of Excellence (grant #004265), and by the French Ministry of Industry through the CARRIOCAS project.

References

1. Andrieux, A., Czajkowski, K., Dan, A., Keahey, K., Ludwig, H., Nakata, T., Pruyne, J., Rofrano, J., Tuecke, S., Xu, M.: Web Services Agreement Specification (WS-Agreement). Grid Forum Document, GFD.107, Open Grid Forum (2007)
2. Grid Resource Allocation Agreement Protocol Working Group, https://forge.gridforum.org/projects/graap-wg/
3. Joita, L., Rana, O.: WS-Agreement Use in CATNETS. Technical report, School of Computer Science and Welsh eScience Centre, Cardiff, UK (2006)
4. Keller, A.: openCCS: Computing Center Software. Technical report, Paderborn Center for Parallel Computing (2007)
5. Mobach, D., Overeinder, B., Brazier, F.: A WS-Agreement Based Resource Negotiation Framework for Mobile Agents. Scalable Computing: Practice and Experience 7(1), 23–36 (2006)
6. Community Scheduler Framework, http://sourceforge.net/projects/gcsf/
7. Wieder, P., Wäldrich, O., Ziegler, W.: A Meta-scheduling Service for Co-allocating Arbitrary Types of Resources. In: Wyrzykowski, R., Dongarra, J., Meyer, N., Waśniewski, J. (eds.) PPAM 2005. LNCS, vol. 3911, pp. 782–791. Springer, Heidelberg (2006)
8. Grid Resource Management System, http://www.gridge.org
9. Gridway, http://www.gridway.org/
10. eNanos, http://www.bsc.es/grid/enanos/
11. Badia, R., Sirvent, R., Labarta, J., Perez, J.M.: Programming the GRID: An Imperative Language-based Approach. In: Engineering The Grid: Status and Perspectives, American Scientific Publishers (2006)
12. MacLaren, J.: Co-allocation of Compute and Network resources using HARC. In: Lighting the Blue Touchpaper for UK e-Science: closing conference of ESLEA Project, PoS (ESLEA) 016 (2007)
13. Grid Scheduling Architecture Research Group, https://forge.gridforum.org/projects/gsa-wg/
14. Shakun, M. (ed.): Group Decision and Negotiation. Springer Netherlands (2002)
15. Briquet, C., de Marneffe, P.-A.: Grid resource negotiation: survey with a machine learning perspective. In: PDCN 2006: Proceedings of the 24th IASTED International Conference on Parallel and Distributed Computing and Networks, Anaheim, CA, USA, pp. 17–22. ACTA Press (2006)
16. Kuo, D., Parkin, M., Brooke, J.: Negotiating contracts on the grid. In: Proceedings of the eChallenges 2006 (e-2006) Conference. Exploiting the Knowledge Economy - Issues, Applications, Case Studies, vol. 3. IOS Press, Amsterdam (2006)
17. Kuo, D., Parkin, M., Brooke, J.: A Framework & Negotiation Protocol for Service Contracts. In: 2006 IEEE International Conference on Services Computing (SCC 2006), pp. 253–256 (2006)

18. Buyya, R.: Economic-based Distributed Resource Management and Scheduling for Grid Computing, PhD Thesis. Monash University, Melbourne, Australia (2002)
19. Jennings, N., Faratin, P., Lomuscio, A., Parsons, S., Sierra, C., Wooldridge, M.: Automated negotiation: Prospects, methods and challenges. Group Decision and Negotiation 10(2) (2001)
20. Shen, W., Ghenniwa, H.H., Wang, C.: Adaptive Negotiation for Agent-Based Grid Computing. In: AAMAS 2002 workshop on agentcities: Challenges in Open Agent Environments, Bologna, Italy, pp. 32–36 (2002)
21. Green, L.: Service level negotiation in a heterogeneous telecommunication environment. In: International Conference on Computing, Communications and Control Technologies (CCCT 2004), Austin, TX, USA (2004)
22. Czajkowski, K., Foster, I., Kesselman, C., Sander, V., Tuecke, S.: SNAP: A protocol for negotiation of service level agreements and coordinated resource management in distributed systems. In: Feitelson, D.G., Rudolph, L., Schwiegelshohn, U. (eds.) JSSPP 2002. LNCS, vol. 2537, pp. 153–183. Springer, Heidelberg (2002)
23. Bhargava, B.: Concurrency and Reliability in Distributed Database Systems. Van Nostrand Reinhold (1987)
24. Kohler, W.: A Survey of Techniques for Synchronization and Recovery in Decentralized Computer Systems. ACM Computing Surveys 13(2) (1981)
25. Oszu, M., Valduriez, P.: Principles of Distributed Database Systems. Prentice-Hall, Englewood Cliffs (1991)
26. Skeen, D.: Nonblocking Commit Protocols. In: ACM SIGMOD Int'l. Conf. Management of Data (1981)

Performance Monitoring Enterprise Applications with the BlackBird System

João P. Germano[1], Alberto Rodrigues da Silva[2], and Fernando M. Silva[3]

[1] Vodafone Portugal, AV. D.João II, LT.1.04.01 Parque Nações 1998-017, Lisboa, Portugal
joao.germano@vodafone.com
[2] INESC-ID R. Alves Redol, 9 1000-029, Lisboa, Portugal
alberto.silva@acm.org
[3] INESC-ID R. Alves Redol, 9 1000-029, Lisboa, Portugal
fernando.silva@ist.utl.pt

Abstract. This work describes the BlackBird system, which is an analysis and monitoring service for data-intensive enterprise applications, without restrictions on the targeted architecture or employed technologies. A case study is presented for the monitoring of Billing applications from Vodafone Portugal. Monitoring systems are an essential tool for the effective management of Enterprise Applications and the attainment of the demanding service level agreements imposed to these applications. However, due to the increasing complexity and diversity of these applications, adequate monitoring systems are rarely available. The Black-Bird monitoring system is able to interact with these applications through different technologies employed by the Monitored Application, and is able to produce Metrics regarding the application service level goals. The BlackBird system can be specified using a set of pre-defined Configuration Objects, allowing it to be extensible and adaptable for applications with different architectures.

Keywords: Application monitoring, Systems administration, Application performance, Component, Adaptable.

1 Introduction

As a provider of advanced services and technology, Vodafone is under constant pressure to implement new technologies that will allow the diversification of the provided services and the improvement of existing services. Like in most large scale and technology based business, the Information Technologies (IT) infrastructure has become the main base of support to business processes, and many Enterprise Applications are now considered mission-critical having a direct impact on the performance goals of the entire company.

The complexity and diversity of the business rules and provided services, together with the pressure for fast implementation demand a vast portfolio of different applications. These applications can be extremely diverse, in terms of complexity, architecture, base technologies and application provider. Also, as result of the fierce competition environment, all of these applications are required to constantly evolve in order to implement new business requirements and support new services. In organizations such as

J. Cordeiro et al. (Eds.): WEBIST 2008, LNBIP 18, pp. 120–132, 2009.
© Springer-Verlag Berlin Heidelberg 2009

Vodafone the teams responsible for the operation and management of these applications are faced with the challenge of assuring the best possible quality of service and the attainment of the negotiated Service Level Agrement (SLA). For this task it is essential to have monitoring systems capable of providing a comprehensive view of the application status and the most critical components, in order to anticipate performance problems and act before there is any impact on the quality of service. The currently available monitoring systems can provide efficient monitoring on the network and device level, however, due to the complexity and diversity of the applications, these systems are unable to provide the desired monitoring on the application level.

Most of the available monitoring systems specifically target applications or technologies that have a large user base, are limited to a fixed architecture, and monitor pre-determined system parameters and expected system components. This kind of monitoring ignores all the functionality that is developed over the base application, even though, it is this added functionality that implements the business logic and produces the most relevant contribution to the delivered quality of service. The need for adequate monitoring applications is even more serious for applications developed in house or when the Monitored Application results from an extensive customization of a base application. In this case the only solution is to develop, also in house, the necessary monitoring systems. However, this extra development effort will certainly increase project cost and complexity and risk development delays.

The BlackBird monitoring system is intended for assisting in the effective management of the extremely diversified set of applications from the Information & System Technologies department (DTSI) of Vodafone Portugal. It has two main features: *i)* can monitor an extremely diversified range of applications such as the one found at Vodafone; *ii)* provides complex Metrics that relate to the main application goals. The diagram in fig. 1 represents a general view of the monitoring system, it obtains data from a number of servers using different technologies, calculates metrics and presents the results to the Operators.

1.1 Existing Systems

The need for monitoring systems was born from the need to assure high availability of the first enterprise level systems and networks, and as they matured so did the monitoring systems. Simple Network Management Protocol (SNMP) [9] became the most widely used management protocol and is currently the base to most network and device management systems, HP Openview and Nagios [10]. However, due to the numerous programming languages and the almost infinite number of architectures and purposes, application level monitoring remains an extremely diversified field with no predominant protocols or methodologies.

Application specific systems can provide the best monitoring of any application. However, developing dedicated monitoring systems is a costly process that can only be supported by large companies with a significant application portfolio, and it becomes impossible to combine the monitoring of different applications working together. Examples of such systems are Microsoft Operations Manager. Third party companies will only risk developing application specific systems for applications that can guaranty a large user base. Quest Software provides versions of the Spotlight monitoring system

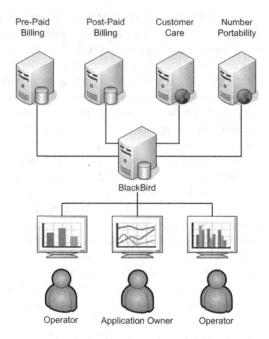

Fig. 1. Monitoring System Overview

for BEA WebLogic Server, Oracle, etc. General purpose monitoring systems aim to provide monitoring services to a range of applications as wide as possible. For this they will implement support for standard monitoring technologies and protocols, and for proprietary protocols used in applications with a large user base. The option taken by most companies for adding monitoring capabilities to their applications is to implement a standard management technology such as SNMP, JMX [11] or WMI [12], for integration with a general purpose monitoring system. One example is ManageEngine from AdventNet.

In terms of architecture, most monitoring systems employ a Manager-Agent architecture, there is usually a central management system and several agents deployed on the monitored system and relay the obtained data to the central management system using a protocol such as SNMP [9]. This is the architecture that emerged from the first network management systems and is currently used by all monitoring systems based on the SNMP protocol. It is especially adequate for monitoring of vast numbers of distributed resources such as computer networks like HP Openview, Nagios [10] or grid computing systems like MonALISA [1].

As more applications evolved from centralized to distributed and from raw processing to providing services, a new monitoring architecture became possible, Agentless Monitoring. In this case there is only a central management system, and all data gathering is accomplished by remote access to the interfaces provided by the Monitored Application. Agentless Monitoring is usually less intrusive, easier to deploy and does not require continuous development, but with limited depth of data gathering. Agentless Monitoring is especially adequate for services based applications and is the only option for proprietary and closed source applications. One example of agentless monitoring system is Longitude from Heroix.

Since the first monitoring systems one key element of the monitoring process has been application instrumentation, which consists in modifying the existing applications in order to collect additional data during run-time. The importance of application instrumentation for the management of complex distributed application resulted in several technology level standards like JMX for Java and Java2 Platform Enterprise Edition (J2EE) and WMI for Products built using the Microsoft .NET framework.

1.2   Related Reserach

Extensive research has been aimed at improving the monitoring support of Enterprise Applications, with the main focus on improving the monitoring extensions provided by the monitored application. Most of this work is focused on the JMX [2] technology which is part of J2SE platform. Although it is only applicable to Java and the J2SE platform, it has a close resemblance to the WMI for the .NET framework, and the main concepts are applicable to other programming languages and architectures, including legacy applications [3]. The use of standard management architectures and instrumentation techniques on enterprise applications opens the way to automated application management and self managed applications [4]. All this research presents a common characteristic, it targets component based applications, and as a result it is possible to obtain a good detail of application monitoring.

Whatever the purpose or technology used the complexity of Enterprise Applications dictates that the full task to be executed must be split between simpler tasks, that will be performed by different program modules. By considering a definition of Component less restrictive than the one usually associated with Component Based Software it should be possible to model any application as component based, where each component may have a number of parameters that can be used as indicators of the general application health and performance. And, by modeling the application, it should be possible to capture a more abstract level of application functionality, which is closer to the business logic and to the main application goals of quality of service.

2   Requirements

The BlackBird monitoring system must provide five key features: *i)* monitor a wide range of applications, being adaptable to the architecture and technologies of the Monitored Application; *ii)* provide component based detailed application level monitoring; *iii)* must be easily adaptable to the evolution of the Monitored Application; *iv)* with low impact on the monitored system, agentless and without additional application instrumentation; *v)* provide a graphic interface for data visualization and configuration.

The Blackbird System aims to provide a monitoring service to an application without imposing any limitations on the target architecture, therefore, the Blackbird System provides a simplified set of Monitoring Operations that allow a user with detailed knowledge of the Monitored Application to specify the required monitoring service: **Commands** to be executed where the result will be stored and used to calculate Metrics; **Metrics** defined by a formula to be executed on the stored data to produce a result

that is related to the application's performance indicators; **Alerts** for evaluating thresholds on Metrics and send notifications; **Graphics** that use the Metric as a data source
and plot the data according to the type and format; **Pages** for containing graphics and
structuring the monitoring interface.

3   Architecture

As proposed in section 1.2, by modeling the Monitored Application as a set of interacting components it should be possible to obtain a more de detailed view of the application status and performance, also, it should be easier to obtain Metrics that relate to the
application performance goals. For the purposes of this work, we consider a simplified
definition of Application Component: *i)* executes a well defined task within the application; *ii)* can be univocally referenced; *iii)* has a set of working parameters which can be
obtained using the application interfaces. Figure 2 represents the Monitored Application
according to this definition.

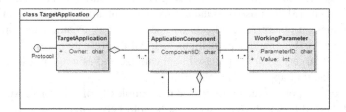

Fig. 2. Application Model

Figure 3 presents the high level Domain Model for the BlackBird System. Each of the
required Monitoring Operations is implemented by a dedicated class, except for **Commands** that is split between the `Module` class and subclasses dedicated to specific
technologies, `DatabaseScript` and `WebserviceRequest`. The `dataStore`
attribute of `Module` stores all data produced by the associated command and provide
support to Metrics calculation.

The `Module` sub classes provide an adaptation layer that isolates the BlackBird architecture from any technology details, they handle all technology specific logic like
establishing a connection, authentication, formatting the command, obtaining and validating the response. Finally, they convert the command result to a normalized Extensible Markup Language (XML) document and deliver that document to the `dataStore`.
For simplifying Metrics definition and calculation, the `dataStore` is designed to be
accessed as a relational entity. The `Metric` class provides the data processing and
aggregation functionalities of the BlackBird System by computing the `formula` specified in the Monitoring Requirement. The `Graphic` class provides the visual presentation to the `Metric` objects, it will use the output of the `Metric` as a data source
and apply the type of graphic and the format request in the Monitoring Requirement. A
`Graphic` may be a table of values or various chart formats. The `Page` class provides
the base for generating the monitoring interface that will be accessed and navigated by
the operators. By combining the information from the `Page` and `Graphic` objects,

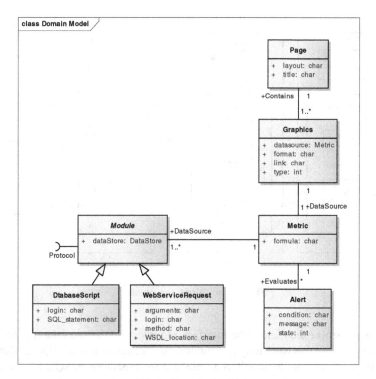

Fig. 3. Domain Model

the BlackBird system generates the required interface as an Web Applicaton containing the requested charts and tables. The `Alert` class provide automatic notification of performance problems.

3.1 BlackBird Components

The Blackbird system uses an agentless architecture, it is composed of an Adaptation Layer itself composed by a variable number local Interface Modules designed for specific protocols, an Aggregation Layer that handles data storage and Metrics calculation, and a Presentation Layer for generating the monitoring pages and graphics. The Component Diagram of the BlackBird System is represented in fig. 4.

The Adaptation Layer provides one of the main features of the BlackBird System, adaptation to the technologies of the Monitored Application. All technology and protocol specific processing is performed by interface modules, where each type of interface module handles a specific technology or protocol, performs all the tasks necessary for executing the requested command, converts the command output to the normalized format and delivers it to the `dataStore`. The Adaptation Layer also performs the first step for providing a monitoring service adapted to the architecture of the monitored system. By allowing multiple `Module` to execute independently it becomes possible to specify as many data sources as required for compiling a complete repository of performance data that will allow the calculation of any relevant Metrics. The ModuleManager

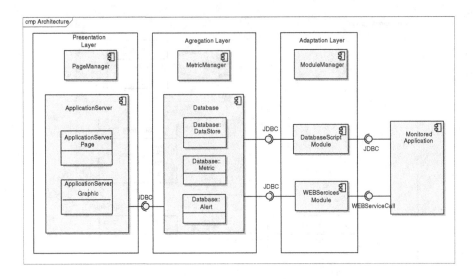

Fig. 4. BlackBird Components

component controls execution of the Interface Modules and manages the `dataStore` of those objects. For this work only two modules where developed, an SQL module that uses JDBC to connect to the monitored Database for executing an SQL statement and an Web Services module that implements the Apache Axis Framework for dynamically invoking Web services. These technologies are base to most of Vodafone applications, and allow the demonstration of the BlackBird capabilities in combining data obtained using different technologies.

The BlackBird architecture is expandable to other types of protocols. Adding support for aditional protocols to the BlackBird system requires no changes to existing components only the development of: *i)* a new interface module to handle the required protocol; *ii)* two new configuration tables and associated views; *iii)* new stored procedures for the edit operations on the new type of module.

The Aggregation Layer stores all performance data in an organized an easily accessible form, performs Metrics calculation and alerts verification. The Aggregation Layer contains the `dataStore` attributes from all existing `Module` objects implemented as database tables and views, the combination of all these objects constitutes a complete repository of all performance data gathered from the Monitored Application. And, since all this data is accessible through relational queries, it should be possible to implement any Metric required by the Application Owner. The Aggregation Layer is responsible for other of the main features of the BlackBird System, Component Based Monitoring. Since all performance data gathered from the application can be used as input for the `Metric` objects, it is possible aggregate the data collected by different Modules using the component identifier to produce Metrics that provide a complete view of all aspects for that Application Component. The MetricManager component is responsible for creating and updating the implementation of `Metric` formulas, and actively evaluating alert conditions.

The Presentation Layer is responsible for the final output of the BlackBird Monitoring System, which are monitoring pages containing visualizations of the status and performance of the Monitored Application. The monitoring pages are generated from the `Graphic` and `Page` objects and deployed on an Application Server as a Web Application. However, the automated generation of the Web Application was considered to be out the scope of this work, so the Webcockpit [13] application is used to generate the monitoring pages based on a configuration file created by the BlackBird System from the existing `Page` and `Graphic` objects. The `PageManager` component is responsible for managing the generation and deployment of the Web Application that provides the monitoring interface.

4 Case Study

The BlackBird System is currently integrated in the production environment of some of the main applications of Vodafone Portugal DTSI, Mediation Device (MD), Pre Paid Billing System (PPB), ARBOR Billing System, Provisioning Agent (PA) and ACTIVIS Number Portability. All are Mission Critical applications that require 24 hour support and monitoring. The previously existing monitoring systems, HP Openview Operations and dedicated monitoring systems, provide complete network and device monitoring and a small degree of application level monitoring. The BlackBird System is used to complement these systems providing detailed application level monitoring.

4.1 Pre Paid Billing System

The PPB application is responsible for lifecycle management and Billing of all pre-paid clients. The PPB application was developed at Vodafone Portugal, it contains an Oracle database and interacts with other systems using WEB Services.

There is already a dedicated monitoring system for PPB which was developed together with the main application, and provides performance information and alerts. Although it delivers extremely valuable information, it implements a static set of Configuration Objects and is not applicable to any other applications. This example will add monitoring of recent functionalities of the PPB application that have not yet been included in the dedicated monitoring system.

One of the tasks performed by the PPB application is credits to the costumer balance. Recent Business Requirements have introduced new types of requests, a database table acts as processing queue and the processing of each request requires a call to a WebService for confirming current balance. The main performance criteria for this task are the average processing time and maximum processing time for these requests. For monitoring this aspect of the PPB application, problems diagnosis and performance tuning, it would be extremely helpful to have a line chart presenting the average request execution time, the average Web Service response time, and the difference between the two times, which represents the contribution of the PPB System to the total processing time.

Once the required output is defined, the Application Owner must elaborate the Monitoring Requirement in order to specify the Configuration Objects necessary for producing the desired monitoring output. The Monitoring Requirement for this example contains the following Configuration Objects: *i)* Login details for the PPB database;

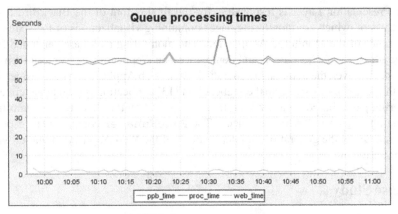

(a) PPB Queue response times

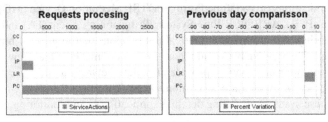

(b) PPB Queue relative performance

Fig. 5. Metrics on the PPB Queues

ii) Login details for Web Service calls; *iii)* SQL command for obtaining the average processing time; *iv)* Web command for obtaining the Web Service response time; *v)* Metric for combining data from both commands; *vi)* A line chart that uses that `Metric`; *vii)* A page for containing the the `Graphic`.

The final output of the PPB monitoring example is shown in fig. 5(a).

This chart in fig. 5(a) shows the evolution of the requests processing time and the contributions of the Web Service call and PPB processing. The output of this graphic is also helpful for performance tuning, since it illustrates the impact of configuration changes on each of the parameters that contribute to the application performance goal.

The BlackBird is able to provide various types of graphics, the barr graphs in fig. 5(b) show the number of pending requests of the various types, and a comparison to the values of the previous day.

In this example the BlackBird System was used for fast implementation of a detailed monitoring service. This incudes a real time comparison to a performance baseline, and a chart on a Metric that aggregates data obtained using different technologies, Database access and Web Services call.

4.2   Mediation Device

The Mediation Device processes billing records of all traffic types, GSM, 3G, GPRS, SMS, etc. It collects billing records from all Network Elements, validates and rates billable records. The Mediation Device was also developed at Vodafone, it contains an Sybase database and was developed using C and Transact SQL. Currently all monitoring and alerts on the Mediation Device Application are provided by scripts and programs integrated in the Openview Operations System.

The Mediation Device processes various types of records refereed to as Data Stream, and for each Data Stream, there are various Network Elements, this architecture can easily be modeled into components. The basic components are the Network Elements that have parameters such as current delay and records processing rate. These elements can be grouped into the main application components the Data Streams. The most critical SLA defined for the Mediation Device are all related to the delay between record generation on the network element and its delivery to the destination billing systems, and the fundamental indicator of performance is the number of records processed per unit of time.

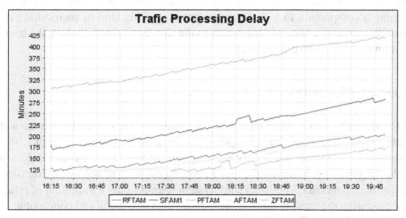

(a) Network Element processing delay

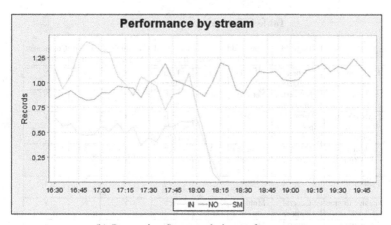

(b) Processing Strems relative performance

Fig. 6. Metrics on the Mediation Device

The chart from fig. 6(a) shows the evolution of the delay in Call Records processing for the Network Element components of the MD application. Because this is batch process the delay tends to evolve in steps. The figure was captured during a peak hour so there is a tendency for an increase in processing delay.

The chart on fig. 6(b) is already an evolution of previous metrics that where adjusted according to the needs of the Application Owners. It shows the evolution of number of Call Records processed per hour for the Stream components of the MD. The values from the previous day are used as a reference, and current values are displayed as percentage of the values for the previous day. This example shows a situation where one of the streams is showing reduced performance, at the same time another stream had a performance peak. This behavior may be the result of resources contention and must be investigated.

In this example the BlackBird System was used to improve the existing monitoring to detail the information on the component level, and provide real time visualization of Metrics directly related to the SLA an performance indicators. This example is also performing a comparison to a performance baseline. This kind of metric has proven very useful as it adds a layer of abstraction to the displayed data, allowing the operator to focus on the main performance trends.

5   Results Discussion

The Monitoring Systems referenced in the Introduction are some of the most widely used and present a representative sample of the existing monitoring solutions. The table 1 summarizes the main features of these systems. Most of these systems allow user defined data gathering, however, the user is usually required to supply an extensive set scripts for obtaining data. The BlackBird System requires only a minimum of information for executing the same command, handles all data validation and conversion. Also, the BlackBird System allows the simultaneous execution of any commands regarded

Table 1. Feature Comparison Table

	Targeted Systems	Supported Protocols	Agent Based	Graphical Interface	Custom Data Gathering	Custom Metrics	Component Based
HP Openview Operations	General Purpose	SNMP	Y	Thin Client	Y	Y	N
Nagios	Network and Host	Network services	Optional	Web	Y	Y	N
Microsoft Operations Manager	Microsoft Applications	WMI	Y	Web and Client and Client	Y	Y	Y
Oracle Enterprise Manager	General Purpose	ODBC and Network services	Y	Web	Y	Y	Y
Spotlight	Dedicated	JMX	Y	Thin Client	N	N	Y
Manage Engine	General Purpose	Multiple	Optional	Web	Y	N	Y
Longitude	General Purpose	Multiple	N	Web	Y	Y	Y
BlackBird	General Purpose	Multiple	N	Web	Y	Y	Y

as necessary. Although most of these system provide some form of support to user defined Metrics, Metrics based on different data sources are usually limited to reporting purposes. The BlackBird System is able to provide real time Metrics based on any combination of data sources. From these systems, the ones that provide a Component Based Monitoring, only support applications developed using the frameworks J2EE or .NET. The BlackBird System introduces a simplified Component definition for extending the concept of component based monitoring to applications that were not developed as Component Base Applications.

The examples from the case study show that the BlackBird System can be used for: *i)* fast implementation of a detailed monitoring service; *ii)* generating Metrics that aggregate data obtained using different technologies; *iii)* improving the existing monitoring to detail the information on the component level; *iv)* providing real time visualization of Metrics directly related to the SLAs an performance indicators; *vi)* real time comparison to a performance baseline.

5.1 Future Work

The BlackBird was designed as an expandable System, therefore some of the main improvements will be new Interface Modules for additional protocols: Remote Shell for access to unix systems, JMX for J2EE applications, WMI for .NET application.

Although the data repository provides an easily accessible source of data, it can become very complex as the number Interface Modules increases. Also, the task of defining Metrics in the BlackBird system requires a good knowledge of the BlackBird architecture and SQL. This task can be greatly simplified by the addition of a graphical query building interface, as an applet on the Configuration Pages or as a separate application.

The daily use of the BlackBird has revealed the need to include controls for selecting the series to display and the data range. Also, in order to comply to the strategy for the DTSI department, a new module for sending information and alerts to HP Openview is under development.

6   Conclusions

The BlackBird System was designed to provide detailed application level monitoring to a range of applications as wide as possible, requiring a minimum of configuration work.

The use of a simplified application model creates a language for describing most applications as a component hierarchy. Also, it allows the definition of common data format for containing performance information independently of any technology details. Data gathering is performed by technology specific Interface Modules, where the Application Owner may specify any number of modules for various protocols. This way, it becomes possible to gather any relevant data independently of the target architecture or the employed technologies. The performance data is stored in DataStore units accessible as relational entities. Data can be referenced by specifying the Module that collected the data and the application component it refers to. Based on this data repository it is possible to create complex metrics that merge data from multiple sources, and metrics that relate to the performance goals for the application.

The BlackBird System application examples on production Enterprise Applications have demonstrated that the BlackBird System can be used for monitoring enterprise applications with non standard complex architectures, and that it can provide valuable metrics close to the main application goals.

References

1. Newman, H.B., Legrand, I.C., Galvez, P., Voicu, R., Cirstoiu, C.: MonALISA: A Distributed Monitoring Service Architecture. In: CHEP 2003, La Jolla, California (2003)
2. Kreger, H.: Java Management Extensions for application management. IBM Systems Journal 40 (2001)
3. Diakov, N.K., van Sinderen, M., Quartel, D.: Monitoring Extensions for Component-Based Distributed Software. In: Fifth International Conference on Protocols for Multimedia Systems (2000)
4. Diaconescu, A., Mos, A., Murphy, J.: Automatic Performance Management in Component Based Software Systems. In: Proceedings of the International Conference on Autonomic Computing (2004)
5. Anley, C.: Advanced SQL Injection In SQL Server Applications. An NGSSoftware Insight Security Research (NISR) Publication (2002)
6. Halfond, W.G.J., Viegas, J., Orso, A.: A Classification of SQL Injection Attacks and Countermeasures. In: IEEE International Symposium on Secure Software Engineering (2006)
7. Mos, A., Murphy, J.: COMPAS: Adaptive Performance Monitoring of Component-Based Systems. In: Proc. of the 2nd ICSE Workshop on Remote Analysis and Measurement of Software Systems (2004)
8. Germano, J.P., Silva, A.R., Silva, F.M.: Blackbird Monitoring System: Performance Analysis and Monitoring in Information Systems. In: Proc. of the WEBIST - International Conference on Web Information Systems and Technologies (2008)
9. Internet Engineering Task Force: Simple Network Management Protocol (SNMP) Applications (October 2008), ftp://ftp.rfc-editor.org/in-notes/rfc3413.txt
10. Ethan Galstad.: Nagios 3.x documentation (October 2008),
    http://nagios.sourceforge.net/docs/nagios-3.pdf
11. Sun Microsystems.: SR-000003 JavaTM Management Extensions (JMXTM) (October 2008), http://jcp.org/aboutJava/communityprocess/final/jsr003/index.html
12. Microsoft Corporation.: Windows Instrumentation: WMI and ACPI (October 2008),
    http://www.microsoft.com/whdc/system/pnppwr/wmi/wmi-acpi.mspx
13. Peter Jonathan Klauser: Webcockpit Open Source Project (October 2008),
    http://webcockpit.sourceforge.net/schema/schema.html
14. Microsoft Corporation.: Performance Optimizations for the XML Data Type in SQL Server 2005 (October 2008),
    http://msdn2.microsoft.com/en-us/library/ms345118.aspx
15. Microsoft Corporation.: XML Best Practices for Microsoft SQL Server 2005 (October 2008),
    http://msdn2.microsoft.com/en-us/library/ms345115.aspx
16. Microsoft Corporation.: XML Support in Microsoft SQL Server 2005 (October 2008),
    http://msdn2.microsoft.com/en-us/library/ms345117.aspx

Developing and Utilizing Ontology of Golf Based on the Open Travel Alliance Golf Messages

Agnieszka Cieślik[1], Maria Ganzha[2] and Marcin Paprzycki[2]

[1] Department of Mathematics and Information Technology
Warsaw University of Technology, Warsaw, Poland
[2] Systems Research Institute Polish Academy of Sciences, Warsaw, Poland
Maria.Ganzha@ibspan.waw.pl

Abstract. While the vision of the Semantic Web is an extremely appealing one, its success depends not only on development of new ontologies that represent various aspects of the world. Pragmatic view suggests that such activities have to go hand-in-hand with facilitating support for existing domain-specific real-world standards. One of such interesting standards that is systematically gaining popularity in the travel industry, is the *Open Travel Alliance* (*OTA*) messaging. Specifically, the *OTA* standardizes the way that businesses in the travel industry can communicate with each other. The aim of this chapter is to outline our efforts leading toward (re)engineering an ontology of golf (understood as a leisurely activity) anchored in the OTA golf messaging specification. Furthermore we discuss how such ontology could be used in a *Travel Support System*. Here, in addition to general scenarios, details concerning implementation of needed translators are presented.

Keywords: Ontology of golf, Open travel alliance, Travel support system, Ontological engineering, Travel ontology utilization.

1 Introduction

Let us start with a simple story. In late February of 2011, professor Hoffman from Stuttgart, Germany has to go to a conference in Florida. Professor Hoffman loves to play golf and would like to combine the conference with a few rounds of golf. Due to the rapid development of agent technology, prof. Hoffman on his laptop has the newest release of MPMG07 Personal Agent—his personal assistant. Furthermore, for some time already, he is using SRIPAS Travel Support System (*TSS*) for all his travel needs. To be able to arrange his trip, he informs his *Personal Agent* (*PA*) about dates of his trip and asks it to arrange all necessary details. The *PA* knows travel preferences of professor Hoffman and uses them to formulate a request to the *TSS*. The *TSS* communicates with various *Travel Service Providers* (e.g. airlines, hotels, golf courses) to make travel arrangements. Furthermore, since prof. Hoffman is one of its regular clients it can utilize this knowledge to (a) filter and sort potential offers, and (b) to make suggestions that go beyond the core of the query (e.g. to suggest a specific restaurant in Orlando that prof. Hoffman is likely to be interested in). In the latter the *TSS* utilizes also knowledge mined from behaviors of its other clients. The proposal is returned to the *PA* of prof.

J. Cordeiro et al. (Eds.): WEBIST 2008, LNBIP 18, pp. 133–156, 2009.

Hoffman, that uses its own knowledge about his preferences to further filter and sort responses (it is the *PA* that may know that, due to the recently increased cholesterol level, prof. Hoffman stopped eating US Diner style food that he was fond off). Some of the decisions may be completed by the *PA*, some may involve prof. Hoffman himself. Some offers can be accepted immediately, while some may require further communication with the *TSS*. All communications between the *PA* and the *TSS* are utilized by the *TSS* to modify its profile of prof. Hoffman to serve him better in the future. As a result of these activities the itinerary is completed and prof. Hoffman can go to Orlando, present his work at the conference and play golf. During and after his trip he may communicate with his *PA* to provide explicit feedback about travel arrangements. This information is used by the *PA* to update prof. Hoffman's profile.

This futuristic story contains a number of issues that we try to address in our ongoing project, in which we are developing an agent-based Travel Support System. Its key features have been summarized in [13,14,16,23] and in references to our earlier work collected there. In this chapter we will focus only on selected new developments, related to communication between various entities involved in making travel arrangements, as well as utilization of ontologies. Work presented here extends and complements material presented in [7,8].

1.1 World of Travel

The story of prof. Hoffman allows us to identify three key groups of key stakeholders of the world of travel.

- *Users*, which may be helped by and represented to the outside world by their *Personal Agents* (for more information about "agents as a personal assistants," see [20]). To check availability of a Marriott Hotel in St Louis, MO, the *PA* may interact with the *Travel Service Provider*, e.g. represented by a Marriott WWW site, or a Marriott Reservation Agent. Obviously, the *PA* may also contact a *Travel Support System* (which is a generalization of the notion of a *Travel Agency* and an example of a infomediary [17]). The *TSS* can provide, for instance, a complete travel package (e.g. airline ticket + car rental + hotel + golf). Obviously, in the first case content personalization will be facilitated solely by the *PA*. Here, we treat various loyalty programs as a part of itinerary preparation, and not as a form of content personalization. In the second case, as suggested above, it is likely that the initial content personalization will take place within the *TSS* (fulfilling its role of the *infomediary*) and the fine tuning (final filtering) will be done by the *PA*.
  Obviously, *Users* may also arrange their travel directly, by communicating via some form of web-interface with entities like the *Travel Support System*, or with *Travel Service Providers* to obtain specific information / reservation. For simplicity of description, from here on we focus our attention only on *Users* represented by their *PAs*.
- Two types of *Travel Service Providers* (*TSP*). The first groups represents, provides information about, and facilitates reservations of specific travel entities (e.g. hotel chains, individual hotels, restaurants, golf course operators). Second, *global reservation systems* (e.g. SABRE) that act as reservation aggregators. While these two

groups differ to a certain extent (e.g. compare reservation system of a non-chain hotel San Max in Catania, Italy with the Amadeus global reservation system), still we can treat them all as end-point providers of reservations. Note also that while global reservation systems are somewhat similar to *Travel Support Systems*, we see the role of *Travel Service Providers* to be limited to activities involved in information provisioning and reservation processing. Finally, existence of loyalty programs, which allows some *TSP*s (e.g. Hilton Hotels) to acquire, store and utilize customer data, matters only as far as internal data processing is concerned (see below).

– *Travel Support Systems*, which in part play the same role as *Travel Service Providers*. Here, we assume that it is unlikely that "anyone" will be able to access global reservation systems directly (e.g. for security reasons). Therefore, *TSS*s will constitute an authorized entry point. They will also provide integrated, and to some extent personalized services (e.g. a vacation package to Milan, consisting of: airline reservation + hotel + opera tickets); see above. As in the case of typical infomediaries, they will not only respond to direct requests of customers, but attempt at selling extra services, selected on the basis of knowledge of habits of all of their customers (e.g. similarly to Amazon.com suggesting additional items based on similarities between customers).

Note that while it is obvious that the role of a *Travel Support System* is changing because of the Internet, still *Users* need to be able to have access to *TSP*s (e.g. to make reservations) while intermediaries (e.g. the *TSS*s) will attempt at earning money by providing value-added services. Therefore, regardless of specific form resulting form the evolution of all of the above identified stakeholders, the general picture presented here should remain valid for some time to come.

1.2 Travel-Related Data Storage and Processing

Let us now discuss how data is likely to be stored and represented by the three groups of stakeholders. While there exist arguments to the contrary, we accept the assumption that utilization of ontologically demarcated data is going to be a crucial part of future development of the Internet, and more generally, computational fabric of the world. Therefore, it is easy to see that the ideal situation would be realization of the vision put forward by the CYC project [21]. Here, a single ontology of "everything" is to be developed and accepted worldwide. If this vision would materialize, all problems related to data interoperability would be gradually solved (by all entities accepting such global ontology). Unfortunately, even casual observation of the way that the Semantic Web is developing suggests that this vision is unlikely to materialize for a very long time, if ever (e.g. due to multilinguality of the world, pragmatic/political needs of individual players, etc.). Instead, we can expect that (a) some entities will move toward ontologies very slowly e.g. large existing players (such as global reservation systems), as well as very small players (such as individual non-chain hotels), (b) some players will utilize domain and business specific ontologies, e.g. hotel chains may use a combination of a "hotel as a tourist entity" ontology and a "hotel as a business entity" ontology, while have no direct use of other travel-related ontologies (e.g. they may want to be able to make a car reservation for their guests, but they will not store or process car rental related data and thus will not need ontology of car rental), (c) *Personal Agents* that reside on computers of their *Users* may utilize simplified ontologies, e.g. ontology of a hotel without concepts related to "hotel as a place for a conference" (including capacity of and equipment available in meeting rooms). Summarizing, we can expect that different entities within the "world of travel" will utilize different data representation (ontologically demarcated, or not). Furthermore, even if data will be stored in an ontologically demarcated fashion, different players are likely to use different ontologies. These ontologies may, but not have to be subsets of a larger, all agreed, comprehensive ontology of travel-related entities.

In our earlier work, we assumed that the *TSS* is going to store information in semantically demarcated form and use it to facilitate personalized information provisioning (see, [14,13,16,23] and references collected there). Moving in this direction we have developed, and later merged, ontologies of a hotel and a restaurant. These two ontologies were created on the basis on the *concept of a hotel* as represented in travel-related WWW sites and *concept of a restaurant* as proposed in the ChefMoz project, respectively [12,15]. Separately we have proceeded to develop a comprehensive ontology of air travel (see, [25,26] for details), which was also merged with ontologies of hotel and restaurant. This ontology is available at [6].

Finally, it should be mentioned, that to represent user profiles and in this way facilitate personalized content delivery, we have adapted, to be used with ontologies, an overlay-based approach proposed originally in [19,10]. In our work, each user is to have his/her preferences represented in a profile incorporated into the ontology of travel (see, [12,13,14,23] for more details).

1.3 Communication in the World of Travel

Thus far, we have argued that the world of travel has, and is likely to have for some time, at least three main groups of stakeholders. Furthermore, we have shown different players within the world of travel are likely to utilize different internal data representations. Thus, one has to ask a question: how will it be possible for them to communicate. One of the more promising answers has been proposed by the Open Travel Alliance (OTA) [2]. OTA was created in 2001 with the aim of developing a standard for communication between various entities represented the world of travel. They have designed message sets defining communication about practically all travel-related activities [4]. Interestingly, as time passes the OTA messaging standards is gaining popularity. For instance, according to the OTA WWW site, its messaging has been adopted, among others, by American and Continental Airlines, Hilton and Marriott Hotels (for a complete list, see [3]). Specific OTA messages concern particular aspects of a travel-related activities and are defined as pairs: a request (RQ) message, and a response (RS) message. Depending on the field of interest, number of such message pairs varies, for instance, from three for a golf course related "conversation," to ten for the air travel.

Let us now assume that OTA messaging becomes a worldwide travel industry standard, which seems to be the case. Then the problem of communication between travel entities becomes solved. It should be clear, that while each of them may use different data representation, storage, and processing, they all will be able to communicate utilizing OTA messages. Obviously, this means that each time messages are to be exchanged, a number of translations needs to take place.

- Within *Travel Service Providers*, incoming OTA requests have to be translated into queries matching their internal data representation. Resulting responses have to be translated "back" into OTA responses and send to requesters.
- For the time being, we assume that travel-related communication between *Users* and their *Personal Agents* does not involve OTA messages. Rather, *Users* fill-in a form (e.g. an HTML template) and the resulting querystring is send to the *PA* (see, [11] for a discussion of how non-agent entities can communicate with software agents). Obviously, we can hope that one day we will be able to use natural language to communicate with the *PA*, but we omit this issue from considerations. The *Personal Agent* takes the *User*-query (expressed in any form) and translates it into an OTA request message, which can be send either to *Travel Service Providers*, and/or to *Travel Support Systems*. Received OTA responses have to be translated into instances of local ontology, as this is the data representation used by the *PA* to process information (e.g. to rank obtained proposals). Obviously, filtered and ordered responses have to be translated into user readable form and communicated to the user (for more details in the case of displaying information on the user device see, [11]).
- The *Travel Support System* receives OTA requests from *Personal Agents* representing *Users*. Some of them can be answered directly by the *TSS*. For instance, since the *TSS* gathers data, and keeps it fresh by systematic updates [16], static elements such as unchangeable characteristics of the golf course can be found by querying the local database of the *TSS*. Specifically, in the current design of the *TSS*, ontologically demarcated travel data is kept in the Jena repository [1]. Therefore, the OTA request message has to be translated into the SPARQL query [5] and executed. The result may then either be translated into an OTA response message and send to the *PA* "as is," or further processed (e.g. to propose other travel related items that a given *User* may be interested in, and in this way to maximize the profit of the *TSS* [16]). The second possibility is that the original request requires access to *Travel Service Providers* (e.g. a request to check availability of a given golf course). Such message can be forwarded to an appropriate *TSP* to obtain the necessary data (see above). The response is then treated as if it was obtained from the local database.

2 OTA Golf Messages

Let us now focus our attention on a specific case of travel-related communication–interactions concerning golf treated as a leisurely activity. Here, the OTA standard identifies three pairs of messages; summarized in Table 1 (see [22] for a complete description). These messages provide the following functionalities: (1) finding a golf course with specific characteristics, (2) checking if a course of interest (e.g. found utilizing the previous message) is available at a specific time and under a specific set of conditions (e.g. maximum price), and (3) making an actual reservation of a selected course.

To illustrate the specific form that OTA messages take, in Figure 1 we present an example on an *OTA_GolfCourseSearchRQ* message (based on [22]). In this message a person who is considered physically challenged under the ADA rules, and requires *Wheelchair Accessibility* (criterion specified as *true*). This person is seeking a course to be played alone (criterion *Singles* specified as *true*) and that has Robert Jones as its *Architect* (criterion is not required—specified as *false*).

Table 1. Summary of OTA golf messages

Message type	List of fields
OTA_GolfCourseSearchRQ—message used to find golf courses that satisfy a given set of criteria; if attribute is specified as *Required* (set to *Yes*) then only courses that meet that criteria will be returned; if *Required* attribute is set to *No*, a course that does not meet that criteria may also be included in the list	Architect, ADAChallenged, Slope, Metal Spikes, Caddies available, Yardage, Personal Carts Permitted, Grass Type, Singles Confirmed
OTA_GolfCourseSearchRS—response lists courses that meet the selected criteria	Golf Course ID, Golf Course address, Contact information—telephone number, List of requested criteria
OTA_GolfCourseAvailRQ—requests information about availability of a specific golf course, satisfying a set of imposed conditions	Golf Course ID, Tee Time—start and end date, Number of golfers, Number of holes, Maximum price for one person
OTA_GolfCourseAvailRS—response provides detailed information about availability	Golf Course ID, Tee Time, Number of golfers, Number of holes, Maximum price for one person, List of fees. Fee has name, information about amount, currency and taxes
OTA_GolfCourseResRQ—message requests reservation of a given golf course	Information about person who makes reservation (first and last name, address, date of birth, telephone number), Mean of payment, Date of game, Number of golfers, Number of carts, List of fees
OTA_GolfCourseResRS—confirms (or denies) reservation of a given golf course	Reservation ID, Information about person who makes reservation (first and last name, address, date of birth, telephone number), Mean of payment (credit cart information), Date of game, Number of golfers, Number of carts, List of fees, Information concerning cancellation penalties and date and time by which a cancellation must be made

In response to the *OTA_GolfCourseSearchRQ* message depicted in Figure 1, the *OTA_GolfCourseSearchRS* message presented in Figure 2 could have been received. This message specifies that two golf courses satisfy the selected criteria. These courses

```
<?xml version="1.0" encoding="UTF-8"?>
<OTA_GolfCourseSearchRQ xmlns=
    "http://www.opentravel.org/OTA/2003/05"
xmlns:xsi="http://www.w3.org/2001/XMLSchema-instance"
xsi:schemaLocation=''http://www.opentravel.org/OTA/
        2003/05 OTA_GolfCourseSearchRQ.xsd"
EchoToken=''54321" TimeStamp="2003-11-12T10:30:00"
Target="Production" Version="1.001"
SequenceNmbr="2432" PrimaryLangID="en"
ID="FL4902" DetailResponse="true">
<Criteria>
  <Criterion Name="Architect" Value="Robert Jones"
                Required="false"/>
  <Criterion Name="Singles Confirmed" Value="Yes"
                Required="true"/>
  <Criterion Name="ADA Challenged" Value="Wheelchair"
                Required="true"/>
</Criteria>
</OTA_GolfCourseSearchRQ>
```

Fig. 1. Example of OTA golf course search request message

have ID's *FL1234* and *FL4321*. Both of them satisfy the required criteria (*Wheelchair Accessibility* and *Singles Confirmed*, while only the first one has been designed by Robert Jones. However, since the *Architect* criteria was not required, also the course designed by Jack Nicklaus can be correctly included in the response.

Assuming that one of these courses has been selected, it is likely that one would like to check its availability at a specific date and time, as well as satisfaction of various additional conditions (e.g. maximum price). This is achieved through the *GolfCourseAvailRQ* and *GolfCourseAvailRS* pair of messages. Finally, if the course is available and conditions are satisfied, a *GolfCourseResRQ* message could be send, requesting a reservation at a specific time. This message would then be followed by a *GolfCourseResRS* message that would confirm the reservation.

3 Designing the Ontology—Preliminary Considerations

Now, we can discuss how *OTA golf messages* can be used as a basis for the development of an *OTA golf course ontology* (to be used, among others, within our *TSS*). Analysis of *OTA golf messages* indicated that two core concepts should be defined. The *Golf Course* concept identifies a golf course and specifies its features. This concept is based directly on the content of the first pair of OTA messages, where golf courses with specific features are sought. It defines an object (golf course) and its *static* features and is represented in Table 2.

The second concept, named *Golf Course Tee Time*, defines information necessary for completing reservation of a golf course. Thus, the *Golf Course Tee Time* concept defines *dynamic* characteristics of a static object specified by the *Golf Course* concept.

```
<?xml version="1.0" encoding="UTF-8"?>
<OTA_GolfCourseSearchRS xmlns=
    "http://www.opentravel.org/OTA/2003/05"
xmlns:xsi="http://www.w3.org/2001/XMLSchema-instance"
xsi:schemaLocation=''http://www.opentravel.org/OTA
        /2003/05 OTA_GolfCourseSearchRS.xsd''
EchoToken="54321" TimeStamp="2003-11-12T10:30:15"
Target="Production" Version="1.002"
SequenceNmbr="2433" PrimaryLangID="en">
<Success/>
<GolfCourses>
  <GolfCourse ID="FL1234" Name=''Sea Grass Golf Resort''>
  <Address>
    <CityName>Jupiter</CityName>
    <PostalCode>21921</PostalCode>
    <County>Palm Beach</County>
    <StateProv StateCode="FL"/>
    <CountryName Code="US"/>
  </Address>
  <Phone AreaCityCode="444" PhoneNumber="423-8954"/>
  <Traits>
    <Trait Name="Architect" Value=''Robert Jones''/>
    <Trait Name=''Singles Confirmed'' Value="Yes"/>
    <Trait Name=''ADA Challenged'' Value="Wheelchair"/>
    <Trait Name="Slope" Value="110"/>
    <Trait Name="Metal Spikes" Value="No"/>
    <Trait Name=''Caddies Available'' Value="No"/>
    <Trait Name="Yardage" Value="6345"/>
    <Trait Name=''Personal Carts Permitted'' Value="No"/>
    <Trait Name="Fivesome" Value="No"/>
    <Trait Name=''Grass Type'' Value="Bermuda"/>
  </Traits>
</GolfCourse>
<GolfCourse ID="FL4321" Name=''Beach Side Golf Resort''>
  <Address>
    <CityName>Palm Beach Gardens</CityName>
    <PostalCode>21932</PostalCode>
    <County>Palm Beach</County>
    <StateProv StateCode="FL"/>
    <CountryName Code="US"/>
  </Address>
  <Phone AreaCityCode="444" PhoneNumber="423-2876"/>
  <Traits>
    <Trait Name="Architect" Value=''Jack Nicklaus''/>
    <Trait Name=''Singles Confirmed'' Value="Yes"/>
    <Trait Name=''ADA Challenged'' Value="Wheelchair"/>
    <Trait Name="Slope" Value="112"/>
    <Trait Name=''Metal Spikes'' Value="Yes"/>
    <Trait Name=''Caddies Available'' Value="Yes"/>
    <Trait Name="Yardage" Value="7102"/>
    <Trait Name="Fivesome" Value="Yes"/>
    <Trait Name=''Grass Type'' Value="Rye"/>
  </Traits>
</GolfCourse>
</GolfCourses>
</OTA_GolfCourseSearchRS>
```

Fig. 2. Example of OTA golf course search response message

In Table 3 we list features that constitute the necessary information to define the *Golf Course Tee Time* concept. Since the "names of features" listed in the table are self-explanatory, we do not define them further.

After identifying two concepts that constitute the core of the *OTA golf ontology*, we have to address the following question: how does this ontology relate to the *TSS*

Table 2. Golf Course concept and its features

Class GolfCourse	
Course ID	ID originates from the OTA_GolfCourseSearchRS message; can be used for getting information about golf course availability and for making reservations
Address	Address of golf course
Contact	Contact information (e.g. telephone number)
Features	List of golf course features

Table 3. Golf Course Tee Time concept and its features

Class GolfCourseTeeTime
Course ID
Start date and time
End date and time
Price
Max price for one person
Number of holes
Number of golfers
Number of games
List if fees

ontology. In other words, we have to establish which already existing / defined concepts can be re-used in the new ontology.

3.1 Common Concepts with the *TSS Ontology*

Ontology re-use is one of important concepts in ontological engineering [9]. Therefore, we have compared the *OTA golf ontology* and the *TSS ontology* and analyzed which concepts can, and should, be re-used. Note that, as seen below, similarity of concepts can sometime be misleading as in actuality their represent different notions. Separately, one should keep in mind that the *OTA golf ontology*, should be made integrable with the *TSS ontology*. To help achieving this goal both ontologies should share as many concepts as possible. Thus, upon analysis of the *TSS* ontology we have identified the following existing concepts that could be re-used.

Outdoor Location—geographical location is associated with most objects populating the *TSS* ontology (i.e. restaurant, hotel, airport). Obviously, this concept is also associated with the golf course. The *OutdoorLocation* class from the *TSS ontology* describes geographical location through a set of geographical properties, such as: street address, country, city/town, region, zip code, reference points or location description (see the *TSS ontology* available at [6] for a complete listing). In the *TSS ontology*, the *Hotel*, the *Restaurant* and the *Airport* classes are sub-classes of the *OutdoorLocation* class. Therefore, the *GolfCourse* class proposed here should also become a subclass of the same *OutdoorLocation* class. This is a natural decision as the *Golf Course* should be an object of the same "nature" as the other objects mentioned here.

Discounts—is the concept that, in general, specifies:

- code of the particular discount,
- amount of reduction of the base-price,
- and contains a short description of the discount policy.

However, when dealing with air travel support we have realized that IATA defined special air travel discount codes [26,25]. Therefore, the question has arisen: how to integrate these with hotel and restaurant discount codes (including both OTA-specific and general discounts—these omitted in the OTA specification). For the purpose of integration of ontologies, "domain-specific" discounts codes were distinguished and defined as subclasses of the general *DiscountTypes* class. Therefore, in the *TSS ontology* there exist three classes defining possible discounts:

- *OTADiscountTypes*—discount types originating from the OTA specification
- *IATADiscountTypes*—discount types originating from the IATA specification
- *DiscountTypes*—general class; all discount types

Obviously, classes *OTADiscountTypes* and *IATADiscountTypes* are subclasses of the *DiscountTypes* class. Note that since the proposed ontology of golf is based on OTA messages, discount concepts used in the *OTA golf ontology* belong to the *OTADiscountTypes* class.

The remaining common parts between the *TSS ontology* and the *OTA golf ontology* are:

- *MeanOfPayment*—concept defining possible mean of payment (e.g cash, credit card, check, etc.),
- *AdressRecord*—class that in the *TSS ontology* describes the address,
- *Currency*—concept that defines what is the currency that the fees are in,
- *FareTax*—concept containing information about taxes,
- *Contacts*—class specifying possible ways of contacting an entity (e.g. the telephone number).

4   The *OTA Golf Ontology*

Based on the above considerations we can now present definitions of the two basic classes of the proposed *OTA golf ontology*. Its remaining features have been described in detail in [7]. First, in Figures 3 we present the class *OutdoorLocation* that the *Golf Course* concept is a subclass of. Next, in Figure 4, we present the RDF representation of the *Golf Course* class.

As discussed above, the *GolfCourse* class is a subclass of the *OutdoorLocation* class and utilizes the *Contacts* concept (from the *TSS ontology*). In its definition we use strings for: *id, courseName, architect*; and an integer for the *slope*.

The second concept that belongs to the core of the *OTA golf course ontology* is the *Golf Course Tee Time*. It is presented in Figure 5 (in the RDF notation) and in Figure 6 in the graphical representation. Finally, in Figure 7 we present the RDF description of the *Price* concept.

```
base : OutdoorLocation  a  rdfs : Class ;
     rdfs : subClassOf  geo : SpatialThing ;
     rdfs : comment  ''Outdoor  location .
            Geographical  and  urban  references .'' .
base : address  a  rdf : Property ;
     rdfs : comment  ''Address  details .'' ;
     rdfs : domain  base : OutdoorLocation ;
     rdfs : range  adrec : AddressRecord .
base : attractionCategory  a  rdf : Property ;
     rdfs : comment  ''Nearby  attractions .'' ;
     rdfs : domain  base : OutdoorLocation ;
     rdfs : range  base : AttractionCategoryCode .
base : indexPoint  a  rdf : Property ;
     rdfs : comment  ''Reference  map  point .'' ;
     rdfs : domain  base : OutdoorLocation ;
     rdfs : range  base : IndexPointCode .
base : indexPointDist  a  rdf : Property ;
     rdfs : comment  ''Distance  from  the  reference  map  point .'' ;
     rdfs : domain  base : OutdoorLocation ;
     rdfs : range  base : IndexPointCode .
base : locationCategory  a  rdf : Property ;
     rdfs : comment  ''Location  category .'' ;
     rdfs : domain  base : OutdoorLocation ;
     rdfs : range  base : LocationCategoryCode .
base : neighbourhood  a  rdf : Property ;
     rdfs : label  ''Neighbourhood '' ;
     rdfs : comment  ''The  neighborhood  of  the  Outdoor  location .'' ;
     rdfs : range  xsd : string ;
r    dfs : domain  base : OutdoorLocation .
base : crossStreet  a  rdf : Property ;
     rdfs : label  ''Cross  street '' ;
     rdfs : comment  ''The  nearest  street  that  crosses  the  street  that
                 the  travel  object  is  on .'' ;
     rdfs : range  xsd : string ;
     rdfs : domain  base : OutdoorLocation .
base : AttractionCategoryCode  a  rdfs : Class ;
     rdfs : comment  ''Possible  categories  of  places  which  might  be
             of  interest  for  visitors / guests  and  can  be
             found  in  the  neighborhood .'' .
base : IndexPointCode  a  rdfs : Class ;
     rdfs : comment  ''Possible  reference  map  points .'' .
base : LocationCategoryCode  a  rdfs : Class ;
     rdfs : comment  ''Possible  location  categories .'' .
```

Fig. 3. OutdoorLocation concept; RDF representation

Observe that while the *GolfCourseTeeTime* class is relatively simple itself (it consists of strings for: *startDate*, *endDate* and *golfCourseID*; float for *maxPrice*; and an integer for *numberOfTimes*), it utilizes also a fairly extensive concept of a *Fee*. This points out to the fact that in addition to the two basic concepts (classes *GolfCourse* and *GolfCourseTeeTime*) we had to define the following additional concepts / classes:

– *Price*—concept of price (includes: amount, taxes, currency, etc.)
– *Fee*—concept of fee (e.g. green fee, cart fee)
– *Description*—contains all additional descriptions that are needed for the traveler to be able to effectively utilize the information provided by the system

Note that the concept of the *Price* is similar to that used in the *TSS ontology*, however in the case of a golf course it is much less complicated than in the case of air travel. Therefore we have decided, for the time being, to leave this concept golf-specific and

```
base : GolfCourse    a  rdfs : Class ;
                       rdfs : subClassOf    loc : OutdoorLocation ;
rdfs : comment  ''Used  for  city  and  geographical  location  description ''.
base : id    a  rdf : Property ;
         rdfs : domain  base : GolfCourse ;
         rdfs : range  xsd : string .
base : name   a  rdf : Property ;
         rdfs : domain  base : GolfCourse ;
         rdfs : range  xsd : string .
base : contactInfo  a  rdf : Property ;
                       rdfs : comment  ''Contact  information .'' ;
                       rdfs : domain  base : GolfCourse ;
                       rdfs : range  phc : Contacts .
base : architect  a       rdf : Property ;
rdfs : comment  ''Golf  course  desiner '' ;
         rdfs : domain  base : GolfCourse ;
         rdfs : range  xsd : string .
base : slope  a       rdf : Property ;
         rdfs : domain  base : GolfCourse ;
         rdfs : range  xsd : integer .
base : availCaddy  a  rdf : Property ;
         rdfs : domain  base : GolfCourse ;
         rdfs : range  xsd : boolean .
base : permCart  a  rdf : Property ;
rdfs : comment  ''Information  if  personal  carts  are  permitted ''
         rdfs : domain  base : GolfCourse ;
         rdfs : range  xsd : boolean .
base : yardage  a    rdf : Property ;
         rdfs : domain  base : GolfCourse ;
         rdfs : range  xsd : float .
base : singlesConfirmed  a  rdf : Property ;
         rdfs : domain  base : GolfCourse ;
         rdfs : range  xsd : boolean .
base : metalSpikes  a  rdf : Property ;
         rdfs : domain  base : GolfCourse ;
         rdfs : range  xsd : boolean .
base : grass  a       rdf : Property ;
         rdfs : domain  base : GolfCourse ;
         rdfs : range  xsd : string ;
```

Fig. 4. *Golf Course* concept; proposed *GolfCourse* class

return to this issue when the *OTA golf ontology* is going to be integrated with the *TSS ontology*.

5   Utilizing OTA Golf Messages and OTA Golf Ontology

In section 1.3 we have summarized translations that need to take place when OTA messages are used to communicate between entities utilizing various forms of internal representation of travel data. In the remaining parts of this chapter we will concentrate our attention on translations involving *Travel Support System* that utilizes the above defined *OTA golf ontology*.

To facilitate the necessary translations, we have designed a *Translation Agent (TA)*. Its actions are summarized in Table 4 (it should be obvious that the *TA*, or its functions could also be used directly by—or within; as a sub-agent of—the *Personal Agent* to fulfill its role in *User* support):

As it can be see in Table 4, in its work the *TA* utilizes two auxiliary structures—the *Conditions* and the *Map*:

```
base : GolfCourseTeeTime  a  rdfs : Class ;

base : golfCourseID  a  rdf : Property ;
      rdfs : domain  base : GolfCourseTeeTime ;
            rdfs : range  xsd : string .
base : amount  a  rdf : Property ;
      rdfs : domain  base : GolfCourseTeeTime ;
      rdfs : range  xsd : float .
base : currencyCode  a  rdf : Property ;
      rdfs : domain  base : GolfCourseTeeTime ;
      rdfs : range  xsd : string .
base : startDate  a  rdf : Property ;
            rdfs : comment  ''Information about date and time in
                  format  yyyy :MM: dd 'T 'HH:mm: ss '' ;
      rdfs : domain  base : GolfCourseTeeTime ;
      rdfs : range  xsd : string .
base : endDate  a  rdf : Property ;
      rdfs : comment  ''Information about date and time in
                  format  yyyy :MM: dd 'T 'HH:mm: ss '' ;
      rdfs : domain  base : GolfCourseTeeTime ;
      rdfs : range  xsd : string .
base : maxPrice  a  rdf : Property ;
      rdfs : domain  base : GolfCourseTeeTime ;
      rdfs : range  xsd : float .
base : numberOfHoles  a  rdf : Property ;
      rdfs : domain  base : GolfCourseTeeTime ;
      rdfs : range  xsd : integer .
base : numberOfTimes  a  rdf : Property ;
      rdfs : domain  base : GolfCourseTeeTime ;
      rdfs : range  xsd : integer .
base : fee  a  rdf : Property ;
      rdfs : domain  base : GolfCourseTeeTime ;
      rdfs : range  fee : Fee .
```

Fig. 5. *Golf Course Tee Time* concept; proposed *GolfCourseTeeTime* class

Table 4. TA actions depending on received messages

Message		TA Actions
message SearchRQ	TA_translate_from_OTAGolfCourse-	TA translates the *OTAGolfCourseSearchRQ* XML message to the structure *Conditions*
message SearchRS	TA_translate_from_OTAGolfCourse-	TA translates the *OTA_GolfCourseSeachRS* XML message to the list of instances of the *GolfCourse* ontology.
message AvailRS	TA_translate_from_OTAGolfCourse-	TA translates the *OTAGolfCourseAvailRS* XML message to the list of instances of the *GolfCourseTeeTime* ontology
message SearchRS	TA_translate_to_OTAGolfCourse-	TA translates the instances of the *GolfCourse* ontology to the *OTAGolfCourseSearchRS* XML message.
message AvailRQ	TA_translate_to_OTAGolfCourse-	TA translates the structure *Map* to the *OTAGolfCourseAvailRQ* XML message
message *Close_system_action*		TA finishes its activity

– The *Conditions* structure contains list of objects of the class *Condition* and has the form:

```
class Condition implements jade . content . Concept
{
    String name_;   /*name of the feature (e.g.  ''Architect '')*/
    boolean required_;  /* is given criterion is required?*/
```

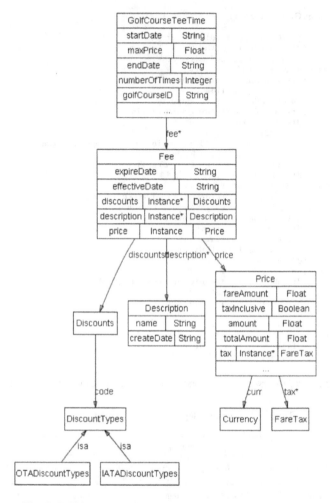

Fig. 6. *Golf Course Tee Time* concept; graphical representation

```
        String valueString; /* value (e.g. ''Jan Kowalski '')*/
        String operation_;  /*operation*/
}
```

Class *Condition* is used to specify criteria of a requested golf course (criteria based on the *OTA_GolfCourseSearchRQ* message). This structure is used to generate the SPARQL query to be executed on the Jena repository.

– The *Map* is a structure from the *TSS*. In the Golf sub-system it is used to specify details of the question regarding golf course availability. *Map* contains the list of objects of the class *MapEntry* and has the form:

```
class MapEntry implements jade.content.Concept
{
    private String key;    /*name of parameter (e.g. "golfCourseId")*/
    private String value;  /*value of parameter(e.g. "AW313")*/
}
```

```
base : Price  a  rdfs : Class ;
      rdfs : comment  ''Description  of  a  price ''.
base : amount  a  rdf : Property ;
      rdfs : domain  base : Price ;
      rdfs : range  xsd : float .
base : taxInclusive  a  rdf : Property ;
      rdfs : domain  base : Price ;
      rdfs : range  xsd : boolean .
base : totalAmount  a  rdf : Property ;
      rdfs : domain  base : Price ;
      rdfs : range  xsd : double ;
      rdfs : comment  ''Total  amount  (taxes  incl.)''
base : fareAmount  a  rdf : Property ;
      rdfs : domain  base : Price ;
      rdfs : range  xsd : double ;
      rdfs : comment  ''Fare  amount  (taxes  excluded)''
base : tax  a  rdf : Property ;
      rdfs : domain  base : Price ;
      rdfs : range  tax : FareTax ;
      rdfs : comment  ''Information  about  taxes ''
base : curr  a  rdf : Property ;
      rdfs : domain  base : Price ;
      rdfs : range  cur : Currency ;
      rdfs : comment  ''The  currency  information .''
```

Fig. 7. *Price* concept; proposed *Price* class

Classes *Conditions*, *Condition*, *Map* and *MapEntry* extend class *jade.content.Concept* and are part of the *GolfCourse* concept.

5.1 Implementing Message Translations

To be able to complete translations summarized in Table 4, the *TA* utilizes classes generated by the *Castor* [24] and the *Jastor* [18] software. Let us look into their utilization in some detail.

Utilization of Castor. Castor is an Open Source data binding framework for Java. Its *Source Code Generator* creates a set of Java classes which represents an object model for an *XMLSchema*, and its input file is an *XSD* file. We used Castor to generate classes for all six OTA messages (see Table 1). Furthermore, Castor generates classes, not only for messages but also for their attributes. For instance let us consider a snippet of the XMLSchema file for the *OTA_GolfCourseSearchRQ* message:

```
<?xml  version=" 1.0 "  encoding ="UTF–8" ?>
<xs:schema  xmlns:xs=" http: //www. w3. org /2001/XMLSchema"
  xmlns=" http: //www. opentravel . org /OTA/2003/05 "
  targetNamespace=" http: //www. opentravel . org /OTA/2003/05 "
<... appropriate  headers  come  here ... >
  <xs:annotation>
      <xs:documentation  xml:lang=" en ">  </ xs:documentation>
  </ xs:annotation>
  <xs:element  name=" OTA_GolfCourseSearchRQ">
    <xs:annotation>
      <xs:documentation  xml:lang=" en ">  </ xs:documentation>
    </ xs:annotation>
  <xs:complexType>
    <xs:sequence>
    <xs:element  name=" Criteria ">
          <xs:complexType>
```

```
<xs:sequence
  <xs:element name="Criterion" maxOccurs="99">
    <xs:complexType>
    <xs:attributeGroup ref="CriteriaGroup"/>
    </xs:complexType>
  </xs:element>
</xs:sequence>
<...>
</xs:schema>
```

Here, within the *OTA_GolfCourseSearchRQ* message there is a list of *Criterion*, which is an attribute that has reference to the *CriteriaGroup*. Now, part of the *XMLSchema* file for the *CriteriaGroup* has the form:

```
<xs:attributeGroup name="CriteriaGroup">
<... appropriate headers come here ...>
<xs:attribute name="Name" type="StringLength1to32" use="required">
</xs:attribute>

<xs:attribute name="Value" type="StringLength1to16" use="required">
</xs:attribute>

<xs:attribute name="Required" type="xs:boolean" use="required">
</xs:attribute>

<xs:attribute name="Operation" type="StringLength1to16" use="optional">
</xs:attribute>
</xs:attributeGroup>
```

Taking this as an input, Castor generates a class for the *Criterion* with methods *get* and *set*. The resulting class would have the following form (fragment):

```
public class Criterion implements java.io.Serializable {
  /** A code representing the criterion on which to filter */
    private java.lang.String _name;
  /** The value of the criterion */
    private java.lang.String _value;
  /** A flag establishing if this criterion
      must be met (value \textit{Yes}) */
    private boolean _required;
  /* keeps track of state for field: _required */
    private boolean _has_required;
  /* Other operations to be used as the filter (e.g. GT, LT, etc.). */
    private java.lang.String _operation;
  //- Constructors -/
  public Criterion() {
      super();
  } //- golfCourse.translations.castor.Criterion()
  //- Methods -/
  /* @return the value of field 'name'. */
    public java.lang.String getName()
      {
          return this._name;
      } //-- java.lang.String getName()
  /* @return the value of field 'operation'. */
    public java.lang.String getOperation()
      {
          return this._operation;
      } //-- java.lang.String getOperation()
  /* @return the value of field 'required'. */
    public boolean getRequired()
      {
          return this._required;
```

```
    } //— boolean getRequired()
 /* @return the value of field 'value'.     */
    public java.lang.String getValue()
       {
           return this._value;
       } //— java.lang.String getValue()
 /*Method hasRequired */
    public boolean hasRequired()
       {
           return this._has_required;
       } //— boolean hasRequired()
private java.lang.String _operation;

//————————————/
//— Constructors —/
//————————————/
public Criterion() {
super();
} //— golfCourse.translations.castor.Criterion()

//————————/
//— Methods —/
//————————/
/**
* @return the value of field 'name'.
*/
public java.lang.String getName()
{
    return this._name;
} //— java.lang.String getName()

/**
* @return the value of field 'operation'.
*/
public java.lang.String getOperation()
{
    return this._operation;
} //— java.lang.String getOperation()

/**
* @return the value of field 'required'.
*/
public boolean getRequired()
{
    return this._required;
} //— boolean getRequired()

/**
* @return the value of field 'value'.
*/
public java.lang.String getValue()
{
    return this._value;
} //— java.lang.String getValue()

/**
* Method hasRequired
*/
public boolean hasRequired()
{
    return this._has_required;
} //— boolean hasRequired()
}
```

In the class generated for the *OTA_GolfCourseSearchRQ* there are methods to *get* and *set* used to obtain and specify list of *Criteria*:

```
public class OTA_GolfCourseSearchRQ implements java.io.Serializable {
...
    /**
     * Field _criteria
     */
    private golfCourse.translations.castor.Criteria _criteria;

...
    /**
     * Returns the value of field 'criteria'.
     *
     * @return the value of field 'criteria'.
     */
    public golfCourse.translations.castor.Criteria getCriteria()
    {
        return this._criteria;
    } //— golfCourse.translations.castor.Criteria getCriteria()
...
    /**
     * Sets the value of field 'criteria'.
     *
     * @param criteria the value of field 'criteria'.
     */
public void setCriteria(golfCourse.translations.castor.Criteria criteria)
    {
        this._criteria = criteria;
    } //— void setCriteria(golfCourse.translations.castor.Criteria)
```

All requested classes generated by Castor have method *marshal* and static method *unmarshal* used to convert Java classes to XML and to transform that XML back into Java code. Specifically, method *marshal* converts an instance of a class to XML. Note that by using the method *marshal* we can transform only instances of a class, not the class itself. In the process we instantiate (or obtain from a factory or from another instance-producing mechanism) that class to give it a specific form. Next, we populate fields of that instance with the actual data. Obviously that instance is unique; it has the same structure as other instances of the same class, but contains distinctive data. For example, when we want to create the XML file from the *OTA_GolfCourseSearchRQ* message, we have two classes: *TA_GolfCourseSearchRQ* and *Criterion*. We must create instances of these classes and insert data into them. Here, we present only an example of utilization of the *marshall* method.

```
\\ create instance of OTA_GolfCourseSearchRQ class
OTA_GolfCourseSearchRQ ota = new OTA_GolfCourseSearchRQ();
\\ set data to this instance
...
\\ create instance of Criteria
Criteria criteria = new Criteria();
\\ put data from list of structure Condtion to Criteria
for(Iterator iter = conditions.getAllConditions(); iter.hasNext();)
{
    Condition condition = (Condition)iter.next();
\\ create instance of class Criterion
    Criterion criterion = new Criterion();
    criterion.setName(condition.getName_());
    criterion.setOperation(condition.getOperation_());
    criterion.setRequired(condition.getRequired_());
    criterion.setValue(condition.getValueString());
    criteria.addCriterion(criterion);
}
\\ put instance of Criteria to instance of class OTA_GolfCourseSearchRQ;
ota.setCriteria(criteria);
}
```

Afterwards, we can convert these instances to XML:

```
/* put values to OTA (object of class OTA_GolfCourseSearchRQ) */
...
Writer writer = new StringWriter();
try {   /* convert object to stream (XML text) */
    ota.marshal(writer);
    }
  catch(MarshalException e) {...}
catch(ValidationException e) {...}
```

And we get the following XML:

```
<?xml version="1.0" encoding="UTF-8"?>
<OTA_GolfCourseSearchRQ xmlns="http://www.opentravel.org/OTA/2003/05"
xmlns:xsi="http://www.w3.org/2001/XMLSchema-instance"
xsi:schemaLocation=
    "http://www.opentravel.org/OTA/2003/05_OTA_GolfCourseSearchRQ.xsd"
    EchoToken="54321"
    TimeStamp="2003-11-12T10:30:00"
    Target="Production" Version="1.001"
    SequenceNmbr="2432"
    PrimaryLangID="en" ID="FL4902"
    DetailResponse="true">
<Criteria>
<Criterion Name="Architect" Value=''Robert Jones'' Required="false"/>
<Criterion Name="Slope" Value="110"
        Required="true" Operation="LessThan"/>
</Criteria>
</OTA_GolfCourseSearchRQ>
```

On the other hand, method *unmarshal* converts XML to an instance of a Java class. For example, let us assume that we want to extract information from the *OTA_GolfCourse SearchRQ* XML message. Then the method that does it has the following general form:

```
Reader reader = new StringReader(text);
try {
    OTA_GolfCourseSearchRQ ota = (OTA_GolfCourseSearchRQ)
            OTA_GolfCourseSearchRQ.unmarshal(reader);
} catch(MarshalException e) {
...
} catch(ValidationException e) {
...
}
```

Here, the *unmarshal* method is invoked with the extracted information as its parameter. As a result, an instance of the *OTA_GolfCourseSearchRQ* class is created. Now, we can use the *get* method to get data from this class (from XML).

Utilization of Jastor. The second generator Jastor is used to generate classes for ontologies (similarly to the way that Castor does for the XMLSchema). Next, we can use Jastor to convert instances of these classes to instances of ontologies and transform back instances of ontologies to objects of generated classes. Jastor generates Java interfaces, implementations, factories and listeners for ontologies. For instance, for the *GolfCourse* concept, Jastor has generated four files:

- interface *GolfCourse* → extends *com.ibm.adtech.jastor.Thing*
- interface *GolfCourseListener* → extends *com.ibm.adtech.jastor.ThingListener*

- class *GolfCourseImpl* → extends *com.ibm.adtech.jastor.ThingImpl*
- class *GolfCourseFactory* → extends *com.ibm.adtech.jastor.ThingFactory*

We used Jastor to generate classes for all ontologies needed in the system: *GolfCourse*, *GolfCourseTeeTime*, *Contacts*, *Description*, *Price*, *Fee*, *AddressRecord*, and *Outdoor-Location*.

For instance, let us consider concept *GolfCourseTeeTime*, which has parameters: *golfCourseId (String)*, *amount (float)*, *currencyCode (String)*, *startDate (String)*, *end-Date (String)*, *maxPrice (float)*, *numberOfHoles (integer)*, *numberOfTimes (integer)*, *list of fees (Fee)*. For this concept, Jastor generates the interface *GolfCourseTeeTime* with methods *get/set* for properties, and the class *GolfCourseTeeTimeImpl* that implements this interface. Let us see a snippet of this interface for the *golfCourseId*

```
public interface GolfCourseTeeTime extends com.ibm.adtech.jastor.Thing {
    ...
    /** Gets the 'golfCourseID' property value
     * @return        {@link java.lang.String}
     * @see           #golfCourseIDProperty    */
    public java.lang.String getGolfCourseID()
        throws com.ibm.adtech.jastor.JastorException;

    /**Sets the 'golfCourseID' property value
     * @param         {@link java.lang.String}
     * @see           #golfCourseIDProperty */
    public void setGolfCourseID(java.lang.String golfCourseID)
        throws com.ibm.adtech.jastor.JastorException;
/**
 * Gets the 'numberOfTimes' property value
 * @return    {@link java.math.BigInteger}
 * @see    #numberOfTimesProperty
 */
public java.math.BigInteger getNumberOfTimes()
    throws com.ibm.adtech.jastor.JastorException;

/**
 * Sets the 'numberOfTimes' property value
 * @param    {@link java.math.BigInteger}
 * @see    #numberOfTimesProperty
 */
public void setNumberOfTimes(java.math.BigInteger numberOfTimes)
    throws com.ibm.adtech.jastor.JastorException;

/**
 * Gets the 'currencyCode' property value
 * @return    {@link java.lang.String}
 * @see    #currencyCodeProperty
 */
public java.lang.String getCurrencyCode()
throws com.ibm.adtech.jastor.JastorException;

/**
 * Sets the 'currencyCode' property value
 * @param    {@link java.lang.String}
 * @see    #currencyCodeProperty
 */
public void setCurrencyCode(java.lang.String currencyCode)
throws com.ibm.adtech.jastor.JastorException;

/**
 * Gets the 'amount' property value
 * @return    {@link java.lang.Float}
 * @see    #amountProperty
```

```java
*/
public java.lang.Float getAmount()
throws com.ibm.adtech.jastor.JastorException;

/**
 * Sets the 'amount' property value
 * @param      {@link java.lang.Float}
 * @see  #amountProperty
 */
public void setAmount(java.lang.Float amount)
throws com.ibm.adtech.jastor.JastorException;

/**
 * Gets the 'numberOfHoles' property value
 * @return     {@link java.math.BigInteger}
 * @see  #numberOfHolesProperty
 */
public java.math.BigInteger getNumberOfHoles()
throws com.ibm.adtech.jastor.JastorException;

/**
 * Sets the 'numberOfHoles' property value
 * @param      {@link java.math.BigInteger}
 * @see  #numberOfHolesProperty
 */
public void setNumberOfHoles(java.math.BigInteger numberOfHoles)
throws com.ibm.adtech.jastor.JastorException;

/**
 * Gets the 'numberOfGolfers' property value
 * @return     {@link java.math.BigInteger}
 * @see  #numberOfGolfersProperty
 */
public java.math.BigInteger getNumberOfGolfers()
throws com.ibm.adtech.jastor.JastorException;

/**
 * Sets the 'numberOfGolfers' property value
 * @param      {@link java.math.BigInteger}
 * @see  #numberOfGolfersProperty
 */
public void setNumberOfGolfers(java.math.BigInteger numberOfGolfers)
throws com.ibm.adtech.jastor.JastorException;

/**
 * Gets the 'maxPrice' property value
 * @return     {@link java.lang.Float}
 * @see  #maxPriceProperty
 */
public java.lang.Float getMaxPrice()
throws com.ibm.adtech.jastor.JastorException;

/**
 * Sets the 'maxPrice' property value
 * @param      {@link java.lang.Float}
 * @see  #maxPriceProperty
 */
public void setMaxPrice(java.lang.Float maxPrice)
throws com.ibm.adtech.jastor.JastorException;

/**
 * Gets the 'startDate' property value
 * @return     {@link java.lang.String}
 * @see  #startDateProperty
 */
public java.lang.String getStartDate()
throws com.ibm.adtech.jastor.JastorException;
```

```
/**
 * Sets the 'startDate' property value
 * @param     {@link java.lang.String}
 * @see  #startDateProperty
 */
public void setStartDate(java.lang.String startDate)
throws com.ibm.adtech.jastor.JastorException;

/**
 * Gets the 'endDate' property value
 * @return    {@link java.lang.String}
 * @see  #endDateProperty
 */
public java.lang.String getEndDate()
throws com.ibm.adtech.jastor.JastorException;

/**
 * Sets the 'endDate' property value
 * @param     {@link java.lang.String}
 * @see  #endDateProperty
 */
public void setEndDate(java.lang.String endDate)
throws com.ibm.adtech.jastor.JastorException;

/**
 * Get an Iterator the 'fee' property values.  This Iteartor
 * may be used to remove all such values.
 * @return    {@link java.util.Iterator} of {@link
 * com.ibm.adtech.jastor.Thing}
 * @see  #feeProperty
 */
public java.util.Iterator getFee()
throws com.ibm.adtech.jastor.JastorException;

/**
 * Adds a value for the 'fee' property
 * @param     The {@link com.ibm.adtech.jastor.Thing} to add
 * @see  #feeProperty
 */
void addFee(com.ibm.adtech.jastor.Thing fee)
throws com.ibm.adtech.jastor.JastorException;

/**
 * Adds an anonymous value for the 'fee' property
 * @return    The anonymous {@link com.ibm.adtech.jastor.Thing} created
 * @see  #feeProperty
 */
public com.ibm.adtech.jastor.Thing addFee()
throws com.ibm.adtech.jastor.JastorException;

/**
 * Adds a value for the 'fee' property.  This
 * method is equivalent constructing a new instance of
 * {@link com.ibm.adtech.jastor.Thing} with the factory
 * and calling addFee(com.ibm.adtech.jastor.Thing fee)
 * The resource argument have rdf:type
 * http://www.w3.org/2000/01/rdf-schema#Resource.
 * That is, this method
 * should not be used as a shortcut for creating new objects in the model.
 * @param     The {@link om.hp.hpl.jena.rdf.model.Resource} to add
 * @see  #feeProperty
 */
public com.ibm.adtech.jastor.Thing addFee(
            com.hp.hpl.jena.rdf.model.Resource resource)
throws com.ibm.adtech.jastor.JastorException;

/**
 * Removes a value for the 'fee' property.  This method should not
```

```
* be invoked while iterator through values.
*In that case, the remove() method of the Iterator
* itself should be used.
* @param     The {@link com.ibm.adtech.jastor.Thing} to remove
* @see  #feeProperty
*/
public void removeFee(com.ibm.adtech.jastor.Thing fee)
throws com.ibm.adtech.jastor.JastorException;
...
}
```

Interfaces generated by Jastor for the ontology extend the interface *com.ibm.adtech.jastor.Thing*. Classes generated by Jastor extend the class *com.ibm.adtech.jastor.ThingImpl* that implements the interface *com.ibm.adtech.jastor.Thing*.

Work with Jastor is very similar to work with Castor. First Jastor generates classes for the ontologies (like Castor does for XMLSchema). Next, we work with instances of these classes. We can convert an instance of a class generated by Jastor to an instance of an ontology (like instances of a class generated by Castor to XML). We can also transform back instances of an ontology to instances of a class generated by Jastor (like converting XML to instances of a class generated by Castor). During translation the *TA* uses classes generated by Castor and Jastor. Thus the *TA* has only to take values from the object of one class and put it to the object of another class.

6   Concluding Remarks

The aim of this chapter was three-fold. First, we have outlined our vision of the future of the world of travel. We have argued, that it will consist of three main groups of stakeholders, that will utilize their own ways of storing and processing data. Therefore, for further development of this area, efforts like the OTA messaging standardization are o particular value. We have used this as a backdrop against which we have shown how we have reverse engineered an *OTA golf ontology* out of *OTA golf messages*. Finally, we have presented an in-depth description of translations that have to take place if a system is to to utilize just proposed *OTA golf ontology* and at the same time utilize *OTA golf messages* to communicate with other travel-related entities. Not only the general approach was discussed, but also implementation details have been presented. We believe that approach like the one presented here is needed also for all remaining OTA-defined standards and we plan to proceed in this direction.

References

1. Jena—RDF persistency engine, http://jena.sourceforge.net/
2. Open travel alliance, http://www.opentravel.org/
3. Ota registration program, http://www.opentravel.org/MembersOnly/RegistrationProgram.aspx
4. Ota specifications, http://www.opentravel.org/Specifications/Default.aspx
5. Sparql—RDF query language, http://www.w3.org/TR/rdf-sparql-query/
6. Travel support system, software repositories, http://www.e-travel.source.forge

7. Cieślik, A., Ganzha, M., Paprzycki, M.: Developing open travel alliance-based ontology of golf. In: Proceedings of the 2008 WEBIST conference (to appear, 2008)
8. Cieslik, A., Ganzha, M., Paprzycki, M.: Utilizing open travel alliance-based ontology of golf in an agent-based travel support system. In: Rutkowski, L., et al. (eds.) ICAISC 2008. LNCS (LNAI), vol. 5097, pp. 1173–1184. Springer, Heidelberg (2008)
9. Fensel, D.: Ontologies: A Silver Bullet for Knowledge Management and Electronic Commerce. Springer, New York (2003)
10. Fink, J., Kobsa, A.: User modeling for personalized city tours. Artificial Intelligence Review (18), 33–74 (2002)
11. Gawinecki, M., Gordon, M., Kaczmarek, P., Paprzycki, M.: The problem of agent-client communication on the internet. Scalable Computing: Practice and Experience 6(1), 111–123 (2005)
12. Gawinecki, M., Gordon, M., Nguyen, N.T., Paprzycki, M., Szymczak, M.: Rdf demarcated resources in an agent based travel support system. In: Golinski, M., et al. (eds.) Informatics and Effectiveness of Systems, Katowice, pp. 303–310. PTI Press (2005)
13. Gawinecki, M., Gordon, M., Nguyen, N.T., Paprzycki, M., Vetulani, Z.: Ontologically Demarcated Resources in an Agent Based Travel Support System, pp. 219–240. Advanced Knowledge International, Adelaide (2005)
14. Gawinecki, M., Kruszyk, M., Paprzycki, M.: Ontology-based stereotyping in a travel support system. In: Proc. of the XXI Fall Meeting of Polish Information Processing Society, pp. 73–85. PTI Press (2005)
15. Gordon, M., Kowalski, A., Paprzycki, M., Pełech, T., Szymczak, M., Wasowicz, T.: Ontologies in a Travel Support System. In: Internet 2005, pp. 285–300. Technical University of Wroclaw Press (2005)
16. Gordon, M., Paprzycki, M.: Designing agent based travel support system. In: ISPDC 2005: Proc. of the ISPDC 2005 Conference, pp. 207–214. IEEE Computer Society Press, Los Alamitos (2005)
17. Hagel III, J., Rayport, J.F.: The coming battle for customer information. Technical report (1997)
18. http://jastor.sourceforge.net/
19. Kobsa, A., Koenemann, J., Pohl, W.: Personalized hypermedia presentation techniques for improving online customer relationships. The Knowledge Engineering Review 16(2), 111–155 (2001)
20. Maes, P.: Agents that reduce work and information overload. Commun. ACM 37(7), 30–40 (1994)
21. http://www.cyc.com/
22. OTA_MessageUserGuide2006V1.0 (2006)
23. Salam, A.F., Stevens, J. (eds.): Utilizing Semantic Web and Software Agents in a Travel Support System, pp. 325–359. Idea Publishing Group, Hershey (2006)
24. http://www.castor.org/
25. Vukmirovic, M., Paprzycki, M., Szymczak, M.: Designing ontology for the open travel alliance airline messaging specification. In: Bohanec, M., et al. (eds.) Proceedings of the 2006 Information Society Multiconference, pp. 101–105. Josef Stefan Institute Press (2006)
26. Vukmirovic, M., Szymczak, M., Ganzha, M., Paprzycki, M.: Utilizing ontologies in an agent-based airline ticket auctioning system. In: Luznar, V., et al (eds.) Proceedings of the 28th ITI Conference, Piscatway, NJ, pp. 385–390. IEEE, Los Alamitos (2006)

Part II

Web Interfaces and Applications

Comparing and Merging Versioned Wiki Pages

Stephan Lukosch[1] and Andrea Leisen[2]

[1] Delft University of Technology, Faculty of Technology Policy and Management
Systems Engineering Department, Jaffalaan 5, 2628BX Delft, The Netherlands
s.g.lukosch@tudelft.nl
[2] Waldlehne 32, 45149 Essen, Germany
andrea@leisen-e.de

Abstract. Collaborative web-based applications support users when creating and sharing information. Wikis are prominent examples for that kind of applications. Wikis, like e.g. *Wikipedia* [1], attract loads of users that modify its content. Normally, wikis do not employ any mechanisms to avoid parallel modification of the same page. As result, conflicting changes can occur. Most wikis record all versions of a page to allow users to review recent changes. However, just recording all versions does not guarantee that conflicting modifications are reflected in the most recent version of a page. In this paper, we identify the requirements for efficiently dealing with conflicting modifications and present a web-based tool which allows to compare and merge different versions of a wiki page.

Keywords: Wiki, Versioning, Page comparison, Page merging.

1 Introduction

Web-based applications become more and more important and are used in different kinds of institutions and organizations. An important category of web-based applications is represented by web-based collaborative systems. Examples are *Google Docs* (http://docs.google.com), *Yahoo Groups* (http://groups.yahoo.com), *YouTube* (http://www.youtube.com), *Google Earth* (http://earth.google.com) or *Wikipedia* (http://www.wikipedia.org).

At Google Earth, users, e.g., tag the map of the earth with points of interest or photography that is shared among all users. At YouTube users tag videos, define categories for videos, and comment videos. Yahoo groups support users in creating places for discussion and exchanging ideas and content. Wikipedia is a web-based encyclopedia that is collaboratively written by many of its readers. For that purpose, Wikipedia uses a wiki that records all changes to the articles and allows to review the history of an article.

Since their introduction by Ward Cunningham in March 1994 [2], wikis achieved sustained success. Wikis are applied in many application domains and many wiki engines have been developed since then [3]. Part of the Wiki success is based on their total freedom, ease of access and lack of structure [4]. Wikis serve as a means for quickly expressing ideas and share information. Their easy way to link pages allows the user to create a hypertext *on-the-fly*.

J. Cordeiro et al. (Eds.): WEBIST 2008, LNBIP 18, pp. 159–173, 2009.

All of the above examples share an important characteristic: They activate users to create and share information instead of only consuming information created by professional site owners. In most of these examples, users are able to create information concurrently. This may lead to conflicting modifications of the same information. To overcome these issues, most wiki engines keep a history of all page versions and allow users to review recent changes by providing a summary. However, when several users edit the same version of a page at the same time, a conflict is reported and it is up to the user to manually include their modifications in the most recent version. Without tool support, this can be tedious and users often omit the merge process. As result not all modifications find their way in the most current version of a wiki page.

In this paper, we describe how we addressed the above issues by extending the standard versioning concept and developing a web-based tool for comparing and merging different wiki pages. For testing and evaluating our approach, we extended the CURE wiki engine [5]. However, our concepts can easily be transferred to other wiki engines. In the following, we first analyze the requirements for a extended versioning concept and a web-based tool that allows to compare and merge different pages. Then, we describe the essential concepts and features of the CURE system, before we present our approach. Finally, we compare our results with the current state of the art, report on first experiences, and conclude our paper with an outlook on future work directions.

2   Requirements Analysis

In this section, we determine the requirements for versioning wiki pages and a tool that allows to compare and merge different versions. For that purpose, we describe a typical use case in which students collaboratively write a paper about Rembrandt using a wiki engine that keeps track of different page versions.

Anja has to write a paper about Rembrandt. Her teacher Mr. Miller has already created a wiki page which all students can access. He also has prepared the structure of the paper as scaffolding in a first version $V1$. Anja starts writing the text in the afternoon and saves her version $V2$. While reading the text she detects a mistake and starts editing the page. When she has finished her changes, she forgets to save the page and leaves the edit view opened.

Next day, Anja is not in school. Mr. Miller asks Beate and Carla to help Anja with the paper. Beate and Carla divide the work. While Beate checks and corrects the part about Rembrandt's life, Carla extends the part about Rembrandt's work. During writing, Beate notices that she also can add content to the other parts of the paper and extends them. When she finishes, she saves the page as version $V3$.

Carla also knows much about Rembrandt and extends first parts of the paper starting from version $V2$. When she saves her work, the wiki reports a conflict as Beate has already modified the version $V2$ and created a new version $V3$. Because she has a date, she ignores the message and leaves her computer. Now, Anja as well as Carla have modified version $V2$ and none of them has integrated the changes in the most recent version $V3$. When their computer or just their web browser would crash now, their changes would get lost. Especially when schedules are tight, loosing intermediate results can make it difficult to meet deadlines. Therefore, the linear versioning concept of standard wiki engines has to be extended and the following requirement has to be met:

R1: Store all page versions in a version tree and make users aware of parallel versions.

When keeping track of all versions, no intermediate results will get lost and the history of a page is completely available. However, when working with text documents merging is time-consuming and difficult. There exist different approaches. Users could copy and paste the differences between different versions. Another approach could be to use an external merge tool. In our opinion, users should not have to switch their work context. Instead users should be able to resolve conflicts in the same application in which the conflicts were created. This leads to the following requirement:

R2: Offer a web-based tool and user interface for comparing and merging different versions of a wiki page.

If there are a lot of differences between two page versions, maintaining the readability of the compared versions becomes difficult. But for merging different versions, readability and thus a semantic understanding is crucial. The readability can be improved when users can decide to suppress differences which are rather unimportant for a semantic understanding, e.g. added empty lines or added white spaces. Therefore, the following requirement has to be fulfilled.

R3: Allow users to define options for the comparison.

When merging different text versions, one often notices typos or comparable small mistakes which require correction. To make such small corrections, it is necessary that the merged version can be edited on-the-fly. Otherwise, the merged version would have to be stored first and changed afterwards which would slow down the merge process. This leads to the following requirement:

R4: Allow users to edit the text of a page while merging two pages.

Continuing in our scenario, Anja continues working on the paper about Rembrandt. Since she was not in school, she does not know that Mr. Miller has involved Beate and Carla in the writing process and Anja saves her changes to version *V2*. Considering R1, Fig. 4 displays the resulting version tree. Starting from version *V1*, Anja has created version *V2*. *V2* has been changed by Anja, Beate, and Carla. Beate has created version *V3*. When Carla stored her changes, she created version *V4*. Finally, Anja now stored her changes and the wiki created version *V6*. Now, three different versions of the same page have to be merged to keep all changes. Obviously, this is much more complicated than merging two different versions. As multiple conflicts can be serialized in conflicts of two different versions, e.g. *V3* and *V4* and the result of this merge with *V6*, the following requirement has to be met:

R5: Support users to solve multiple conflicts by serializing multiple conflicts.

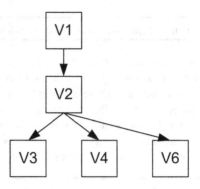

Fig. 1. Version tree

3   CURE in a Nutshell

In this section, we introduce the web-based collaborative system CURE [6]. CURE is used for collaborative work and learning. Typical collaborative learning scenarios are collaborative exercises, tutor-guided groups with collaborative exercises, collaborative exam preparation [7], virtual seminars, and virtual labs [8]. When considering collaborative work typical use cases include group formation, group communication, document sharing, collaborative writing, collaborative task management etc.

From a technical perspective, CURE was built by composing patterns for computer-mediated interaction. We will not go into details of the implementation here, but instead reference to the patterns[1] that were used to create the system and show how they appear in the functional context of user interaction.

Users can structure their interaction in GROUPS that inhabit virtual ROOMS. Fig. 2 shows the abstractions that are offered by CURE. Users enter the web-based collaborative environment via an entry ROOM that is called *Hall*. ROOMS can contain further subrooms, content in the form of so called pages, communication channels (e.g. an EMBEDDED CHAT or a FORUM) and users.

When users enter a ROOM, they can participate in collaborative activities and access the room's communication channels. They can also view the pages that are contained in the ROOM. Users possessing suitable access rights, which are represented as virtual KEYS [10], can freely edit the content of pages [11], with the changes being visible to all members in the room after uploading. Earlier versions of a page remain accessible to allow tracing of recent changes. Pages may either be directly edited using a simple Wiki-like syntax [2], or they may contain binary documents. In particular, the syntax supports links to other pages, other ROOMS, external URLs or mail addresses. The server stores all artifacts to support collaborative access. Thus, when users leave the ROOM, the content stays available, allowing them to come back later and continue their work on the ROOM's pages.

Figure 3 shows a typical ROOM in CURE. The numbers in the figure refer to details explained in the following paragraphs. A ROOM contains documents (①, cf.

---

[1] Pattern names are set in SMALL CAPS and can be found in [9] if no other reference is provided.

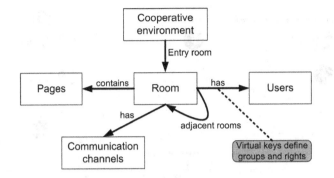

Fig. 2. CURE abstractions

CENTRALIZED OBJECTS) that can be edited by those users, who have sufficient edit rights ②. CURE stores all versions of a page as IMMUTABLE VERSIONS. Users can browse different versions ③ to understand their colleagues' changes (cf. TIMELINE). Communication is supported by two communication channels within a ROOM, i.e. a FORUM ④ and an EMBEDDED CHAT ⑤. Users can send a mail to the ROOM. Users of the ROOM that have sufficient communication rights will receive this message like being a member of a MAILING LIST [12].

By providing a plenary ROOM, sharing and communication in a whole class or organization can be supported. By creating new ROOMS for sub-groups and connecting those to the classes' or organization's ROOM, work and collaboration can be flexibly structured. Starting from the plenary ROOM users can NAVIGATE [10] to the connected subrooms ⑥.

For user coordination, CURE supports various types of awareness information:

1. Users can see in the ROOM'S properties who else has access to this room ⑦.
2. Users can see in a USER LIST ⑧ who else is currently in the same ROOM.
3. If the EMBEDDED CHAT ⑤ is enabled in the ROOM, users can directly start chatting to each other.
4. Users can trace who has previously edited the current page ⑨ (cf. ACTIVE NEIGH-BORS).
5. PERIODIC REPORTS automatically posted to all users of a ROOM include all changes made since the last report was sent.

4   Approach

The following sections will give a detailed description of our approach to address the identified requirements (R1 – R5). To show the feasibility of our approach, we extended the web-based collaborative system CURE that so far does not fulfill any of the identified requirements.

4.1   Version Tree (R1)

To keep a history of all changes, even when users changed the same page version in parallel, we extended the versioning concept in CURE by implementing the pattern

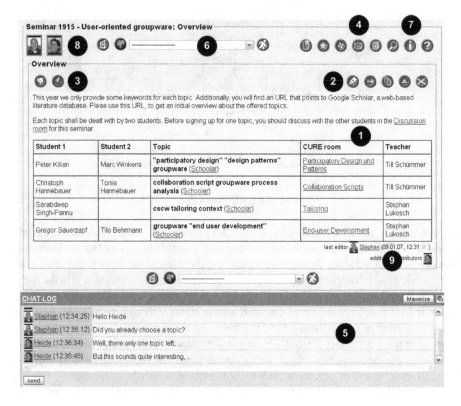

Fig. 3. A room in CURE

IMMUTABLE VERSIONS [9]. In this pattern, versions are immutable as they cannot be changed afterwards. Each modification of a page is stored as new version in a version tree even when two users modified the same page version concurrently. This approach is also used to handle conflicting modifications that result from nomadic interaction with the CURE system [13,14].

Apart from creating a new parallel page version, CURE also creates a so-called *merge-page* which references the parallel versions. After extending the version tree, CURE asks the users to resolve the conflict on the merge-page. CURE thereby prevents users from overwriting changes other users have performed. Fig. 4 shows how the version tree of our scenario is extended with the merge-pages which make users aware of conflicting changes.

4.2   Web-Based Comparison and Merge Tool (R2)

Selecting Different Page Versions.   For comparing and merging, users first have to select two different page versions. We integrated a button, which allows users to directly compare the currently viewed version of a page with its direct predecessor. Apart from that direct access, users can also freely select two different page versions from the version tree of a page in CURE. Fig. 5 shows how CURE displays the version tree. Users

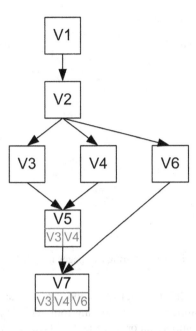

Fig. 4. Version tree in CURE

can select two pages for comparison ① or merging ② by selecting the corresponding radio buttons ③.

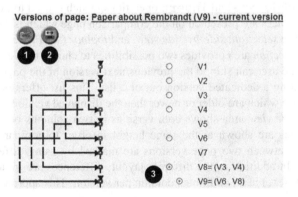

Fig. 5. Selecting pages for comparison or merging in CURE

Since the user must select exactly two versions, two groups of radio buttons were integrated in the page showing version tree (see Fig. 5). In each group, only one version can be selected. All existing versions of a page are available in each group. The selection takes place on the client side in the browser. The number of available radio buttons in each group are adapted to the reasonable ones, once users make their choice. This ensures that users can only select two different versions for comparison or merging.

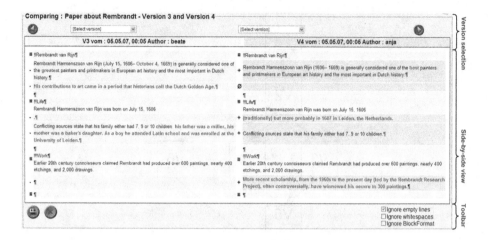

Fig. 6. Comparing two pages in CURE

Additionally, users can alter their selection and can compare or merge different versions, while using the comparison and merging tool. This is possible by using dropdown menus on top the comparison or merging tool (see *Version selection* area in Fig. 6, 7, and 8).

Comparing Different Page Versions.   For the comparison of two pages, we use a standard comparison algorithm [15]. This algorithm first identifies the different lines and then the differences in the different lines. The output of the algorithm is an *edit script*, i.e. a list of `delete` and `insert` operations, which is used to mark the differences. The differences are presented on the comparison page which is divided into the three areas *version selection*, *side-by-side view*, and *toolbar* (see Fig. 6).

The *version selection* area provides two possibilities to choose the versions for comparison. Either the user can skip to the previous/next version of the page by using buttons or by selecting a dedicated version out of a list. This list offers only reasonable versions, i.e. those which are older or newer than the displayed versions.

The *side-by-side view* area shows both versions in two columns beside each other [16]. Similar lines are shown at the same height in order to compare them easily. The differences between two page versions are marked by using different font and color attributes. In addition to the different layout, differences are indicated by suitable symbols (+, -, ≡) in an additional column per version. This approach is also used in Wikipedia [1].

The *toolbar* area offers two buttons for either invoking the merge page or canceling the comparison which means to invoke the version selection page. Additionally, users can choose between three different options which influence the comparison (see Section 4.3).

Merging Different Page Versions.   Apart from the comparison tool, we integrated two different possibilities to merge different page versions in CURE. The first possibility uses the *side-by-side view* (see Fig. 7). The side-by-side view is preferred by,

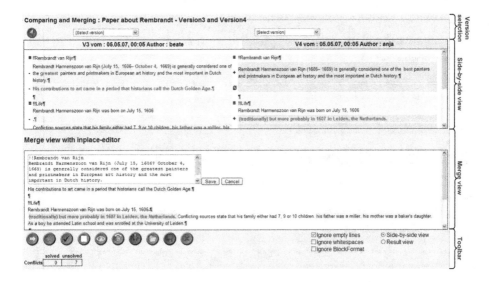

Fig. 7. Merging two pages with the side-by-side view in CURE

e.g., programmers when comparing source code [17]. The second possibility uses only the *merge view* and adds a *result view* (see Fig. 8). Thereby, it offers a more integrated view of the different versions. Experiences have shown that the merge view is preferred for the comparison of literary texts. Since the type of presentation depends on the text type which is compared as well as on the user's personal preferences, we implemented both possibilities.

Both user interface variants support the user while merging. The vertical scrollbars of the side-by-side and merge view in Fig. 7 as well as the merge and result view in Fig. 8 are synchronized. Thereby, users can always see the corresponding parts of the compared and merged versions. In the following, we will describe the merge view, result view, and the toolbar in more detail.

The *merge view* presents both versions in a single integrated view. In contrast to the side-by-side view, identical text-parts are presented only once.

For each difference, users have to decide in the merge view which text should be transferred into the merged version. An automated decision is not possible, because the two versions are not necessarily based on the same version. The differences which have to be solved manually are called conflicts. There are two different types of conflicts:

- *Unary conflict.* Text-parts that appear only in one of the two versions, i.e. difference in one text e.g. inserted or deleted words or lines.
- *Binary conflict.* Text-parts that exist in both versions at the same position, i.e. concurrent difference at the same position in the text.

In case of a *unary conflict*, users have to decide whether this text-part should be transferred into the merged version or not. *Binary conflicts* are positioned directly one after the other. Users have to decide, which of the two possible text-parts should be transferred. It is not possible to transfer both text-parts.

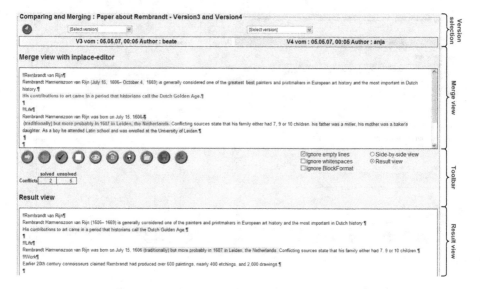

Fig. 8. Merging two pages with the result view in CURE

Users can resolve such conflicts by directly clicking on the conflict. With each click on a conflict, the conflict changes its state. A conflict can be in three different states:

1. *Initial:* Status at the beginning of merge process.
2. *Active:* Text is part of the merged version.
3. *Inactive:* Text is not part of the merged version.

When the conflict state changes, the layout of the conflict is also changed. Table 1 shows the layout of the different conflict states. When all conflicts are solved, i.e. all conflicts have the status active or inactive, the merge process is finished and users can save the merged page as new version.

The *result view* (see Fig. 8) shows users a preview of the merged page. In the beginning of the merge process, only the identical text-parts are shown. With each solved conflict in the merge view the conflict free text-part is added to the result view as well.

Table 1. Layout of the different conflict states

Conflict state	Unary conflict *V1*	Unary conflict *V2*	Binary conflict
Initial	black on light yellow	black on light green	Text *V1*. Text *V2*.
Active	red and fat on light yellow	red and fat on light green	Text *V1*. ~~Text *V2*.~~
Inactive	~~black and crossed out on light yellow~~	~~black and crossed out on light green~~	~~Text *V1*.~~ Text *V2*.

The text-parts are marked with the same background-color as in the merge view such that users can recognize the originating version.

For awareness purposes, the *toolbar* area offers information about the number of solved and unsolved conflicts. Again, users can define the options for comparing to page versions (see Section 4.3). Additionally, the toolbar offers a variety of functions to support users when merging two pages (see Fig. 7 from left to right): transfer remaining differences from the right version, transfer remaining differences from the left version, accept all active and decided conflicts, cancel all modifications, preview the merged page, back to the merge view, save the intermediate merge result, load the last intermediate merge result, save merged page, and return to the version selection.

4.3   Comparison and Merge Options (R3)

Users can choose between three different options which influence the comparison or the merge process (see, e.g., lower right corner of Fig. 6): ignore empty lines, ignore whitespaces, ignore block-format.

Empty lines between text-sections and whitespaces are not relevant for the content of a text. With the options *ignore empty lines* and *ignore whitespaces* users can change the treatment of empty lines and whitespaces as differences. When only textual differences are important, these options help to improve the clearness of a comparison.

Block-formats are formatting instructions in the wiki syntax which mark beginning and end of a character string, e.g. in CURE `~~text~~` is rendered as *italic*. When users choose to *ignore block-formats*, only the formatting instructions are presented as differences and not the formatted text.

4.4   Editing Merged Text (R4)

When merging two pages, users often notice text-parts or words which they would like to correct immediately, e.g. typos, punctuation marks etc. For that purpose, we integrated an editor which allows users to choose the text they want to edit by simply clicking on it. Once the text is chosen, a small edit window appears and allows the users to make spontaneous corrections (see merge view in Fig. 7).

To encourage users to integrate the modifications of other users, only text parts without conflicts can be edited. Thus, users first have to resolve the conflicts before editing can take place. Once all conflicts are resolved, it is possible to edit the entire text. But this is not reasonable. In case of larger modifications, users should save the merged version first and edit the resulting new version afterwards.

4.5   Solving Multiple Conflicts (R5)

When multiple users edit a version of a page simultaneously, conflicting page versions result. By fulfilling R1, no page version gets lost. However, this also results in more than two parallel versions. In case of our example (cf. Section 2), Anja, Beate, and Carla edit the same page which results in three parallel versions. When Carla saves the modified page, CURE now detects the conflict and shows the comparing and merging tool as shown in Fig. 7. However, when Anja saves her page version, three different versions have to be merged.

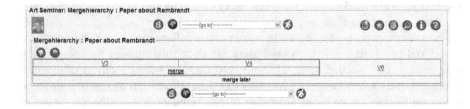

Fig. 9. Merge hierarchy in CURE

Adding an additional column in the side-by-side view (Fig. 7) or integrating another text in the merge view (Fig. 8) is not feasible, as it would be difficult for users to keep an overview. This becomes even more obvious, when considering 4, 5, 6 or even more parallel versions.

In order to simplify the merge process of three or even more pages, we split up the merge process in serially merging two versions. To support the user in serializing the multiple conflicts, CURE shows the merging hierarchy in form of a table (see Fig. 9). The user can start the merging process by clicking on the *"merge"* button and merge the two corresponding page versions. If further versions need to be merged, an updated merging hierarchy is shown again after the user has merged the selected pages. Thereby, the conflicting versions are serially merged and the modifications of all users are taken into account.

5   Related Work

There are several available comparing- and merging tools that run on different platforms and are suitable for different file types like text files, binary files and HTML or XML files. A large part of these tools is based on the *GNU diffutils* [18] and offers a graphical user interface. Some of these tools also support editing and merging of files. In this section, we will analyze some of these tools concerning their functionality. The following list contains some of those tools in alphabetic order: *CharDiff* [19], *DiffDoc* [17], *DiffDog* [20], *CSDiff* [21], *ExamDiff Pro* [22], *Guiffy* [23], *KDiff3* [24], *Meld* [25], *RCS* [26], *TkDiff* [27], *Unix diff* [28], *Wikipedia* [1], and *WinMerge* [29].

Most of these tools work line-based. They try to find common lines and lines that have been inserted or deleted by searching the longest common subsequence between the texts. From the sighted tools *Wikipedia*, *CharDiff*, *DiffDoc*, *WinMerge* and *Guiffy* are analyzed in depth, since they have exemplary character for the different types of comparing and merging tools.

Wikipedia [1] is a wiki that allows visitors to add, remove, edit and change content, typically without the need for registration. If a wiki page is changed, the whole page is stored as new version. In case of a conflict, the new version is not stored and users have to integrate their changes in the most recent version. Otherwise, their changes are lost (violating R1). Within Wikipedia users can compare two versions of a page. The changes between two revisions of a page are displayed side-by-side. However, Wikipedia does not support merging of two different versions (violating R2).

CharDiff 1.2a [19] is a shareware program that detects and presents differences with character precision and overlays files for an integrated display. CharDiff uses standard web browsers for the presentation of the differences. After selecting two files for comparison, the result of the comparison immediately is shown in a single integrated view in the web browser. If the mouse is positioned on the difference, the difference *waggles* in the integrated view. This effect draws the user's attention to the selected difference. A support to merge two files does not exist (violating R2).

Diff Doc 3.50 [17] is a commercial tool for comparing files, e.g. PDF, Word, Excel, RTF, text or HTML files. The two compared files are represented in a *side-by-side* view in the upper part of the user interface in which users can also edit the viewed files. The two compared files can be loaded by opening existing files, by copy and paste of text parts, or by creating new text. In the lower area of the user interface, the differences are either presented in a side-by-side-view or in an integrated view. For the comparison, three options are available: ignore upper and lower case, ignore white spaces, and ignore empty lines. Again, merging is not supported (violating R2).

WinMerge 2.6 [29] is an open source tool for comparing and merging of text files. The two compared texts are shown in a side-by-side view, where identical lines are ordered on the same height and differences within the lines are marked in another color. However, WinMerge does not support to resolve multiple conflicts (violating R5).

Guiffy 7.4 [23] is a Java shareware program for comparing and merging of files. Thus, it can be used with different operating systems. Guiffy supports 3-way merging with its *SureMerge* function and offers an intuitive user interface. But Guiffy is not a web-based tool and does not offer support for solving multiple conflicts (violating R5).

To summarize, none of the above tools fulfills all of the requirements (R1 – R5). Especially, none supports version trees or offers web-based merging support.

6   First Experiences

We split up the evaluation of our support for comparing and merging different wiki page versions in three phases. In the first phase, we have conducted functional tests. These functional tests concentrated on validating the comparing and merging possibilities and checking if our requirements are met. These tests showed that all identified requirements R1 – R5 are fulfilled.

In a second phase, we setup a test environment in our group and let several groups test the system. Feedback from these users with different background, i.e. expert as well as lay users from different departments at our university, indicates that our tools for comparing and merging different wiki pages improve the usability of the system and are highly intuitive for dealing with conflicting modifications in wikis. Furthermore, users have reported that the tools significantly simplify to review recent changes and to resolve conflicts.

CURE is regularly used by our group to conduct seminars as well as lab courses with a blended CSCL approach [30]. In the final evaluation phase, we plan to use CURE together with our tools for comparing and merging in seminars and lab courses which follow the same blended CSCL approach. Based on the gathered interaction data, we plan to evaluate how the tools affect the interaction among the users.

7 Conclusions

Nowadays, web-based applications become more and more important. Especially, collaborative web-based applications activate users to create and share information instead of only consuming it. However, when collaboratively accessing and modifying shared information, parallel modifications can take place. Most wikis record all versions of a page to allow users to review recent changes, but also to ensure that no modifications get lost.

In this paper, we identified five requirements for supporting users when working with different versions in a wiki. We showed how to fulfill these requirements by extending the linear version concept of wikis and integrating a web-based tool for comparing and merging wiki pages in CURE. The overall concepts, like the version tree, the side-by-side view, the result view, the different layouts for highlighting conflicts and differences, and the process for solving multiple conflicts, can easily be transferred to other wiki engines as well.

Up to now, there is no wiki that supports parallel versions and offers a tool for comparing and merging different wiki pages. Thus, our approach which has been integrated in CURE presents a significant step forward. In future, we want to further evaluate the effects of the comparing and merging tools on the usage of CURE. Additionally, we want investigate in how far the merging process can be even more supported by offering more user-defined options for the comparison, by considering the structure of the text, or by enabling automatic merging.

References

1. Wikipedia. Main page — wikipedia, the free encyclopedia (2008) (Online; accessed 10-October-2008)
2. Leuf, B., Cunningham, W.: The WIKI way. Addison-Wesley, Boston (2001)
3. Choicetree, W.: (2008), http://c2.com/cgi/wiki?WikiChoicetree (Online; accessed 10-October-2008)
4. Rick, J., Guzdial, M., Carroll, K., Holloway-Attaway, L., Walker, B.: Collaborative learning at low cost: CoWeb use in english composition. In: Proceedings of CSCL 2002, Boulder, Colorado, USA (2002)
5. Haake, J.M., Schümmer, T., Haake, A., Bourimi, M., Landgraf, B.: Supporting flexible collaborative distance learning in the CURE platform. In: Proceedings of the Hawaii International Conference On System Sciences (HICSS-37), January 2004. IEEE Press, Los Alamitos (2004)
6. Haake, J.M., Schümmer, T., Haake, A., Bourimi, M., Landgraf, B.: Two-level tailoring support for CSCL. In: Favela, J., Decouchant, D. (eds.) CRIWG 2003. LNCS, vol. 2806, pp. 74–82. Springer, Heidelberg (2003)
7. Lukosch, S., Schümmer, T.: Making exam preparation an enjoyable experience. International Journal of Interactive Technology and Smart Education, Special Issue on Computer Game-based Learning 3(4), 259–274 (2006)
8. Schümmer, T., Lukosch, S., Haake, J.M.: Teaching distributed software development with the project method. In: Koschmann, T., Suthers, D.D., Chan, T.-W. (eds.) Computer Supported Collaborative Learning 2005: The Next 10 Years!, pp. 577–586. Lawrence Erlbaum Associates, Mahwah (2005)

9. Schümmer, T., Lukosch, S.: Patterns for Computer-Mediated Interaction. John Wiley & Sons, Ltd., Chichester (2007)
10. Schümmer, T., Fernandéz, A.: Patterns for virtual places, pp. 35–74. UVK Universitätsverlag Konstanz GmbH (2006)
11. Haake, J.M., Haake, A., Schümmer, T., Bourimi, M., Landgraf, B.: End-user controlled group formation and access rights management in a shared workspace system. In: CSCW 2004: Proceedings of the 2004 ACM conference on Computer supported cooperative work, pp. 554–563. ACM Press, New York (2004)
12. Schümmer, T., Lukosch, S.: READ.ME – Talking about computer-mediated communication, pp. 317–342. UVK Universitätsverlag Konstanz GmbH (2007)
13. Lukosch, S., Hellweg, M., Rasel, M.: CSCL, Anywhere and Anytime. In: Dimitriadis, Y.A., Zigurs, I., Gómez-Sánchez, E. (eds.) CRIWG 2006. LNCS, vol. 4154, pp. 326–340. Springer, Heidelberg (2006)
14. Lukosch, S.: Seamless transition between connected and disconnected collaborative interaction. Journal of Universal Computer Science (JUCS), Special Issue on Groupware: Issues and Applications (March 2008)
15. Myers, E.W.: An O(ND) difference algorithm and its variations. Algorithmica 1(2), 251–266 (1986)
16. Yang, W.: Identifying syntactic differences between two programs. Software-Practice and Experience 21(7), 739–755 (1991)
17. DiffDoc (2008), http://www.softinterface.com/Compare-File-Programs/Compare-File-Programs.HTM (Online; accessed October 10, 2008)
18. Diffutils - GNU Project (2008), http://www.gnu.org/software/diffutils/ (Online; accessed October 10, 2008)
19. CharDiff (2007), http://www.tillmann-wegst.de/chardiff/index.htm (Online; accessed March 21, 2007)
20. DiffDog (2008), http://www.altova.com/products/diffdog/diff_merge_tool.html (Online; accessed October 10, 2008)
21. CSDiff (2008), http://www.componentsoftware.com/products/CSDiff/index.htm (Online; accessed October 10, 2008)
22. ExamDiff Pro. (2008), http://www.prestosoft.com/ps.asp?page=edp_examdiffpro (Online; accessed October 10, 2008)
23. Guiffy (2008), http://www.guiffy.com/ (Online; accessed October 10, 2008)
24. KDiff (2008), http://kdiff3.sourceforge.net/ (Online; accessed October 10, 2008)
25. Meld (2008), http://meld.sourceforge.net/ (Online; accessed October 10, 2008)
26. Tichy, W.F.: RCS – a system for version control. Software Practice and Experience 15(7), 637–654 (1985)
27. TkDiff (2008), http://sourceforge.net/projects/tkdiff/ (Online; accessed October 10, 2008)
28. Hunt, J.W., McIlroy, M.D.: An algorithm for differential file comparison. Computing Science Technical Report 41, Bell Laboratories (June 1976)
29. WinMerge (2008), http://winmerge.org/2.6/manual/ (Online; accessed October 10, 2008)
30. Haake, J.M., Haake, A., Schümmer, T., Lukosch, S.: Collaborative learning at a distance with the project method. Educational Technology 45(5), 21–24 (2005)

Are Wikipedia Resources Useful for Discovering Answers to List Questions within Web Snippets?

Alejandro Figueroa

German Centre for Artificial Intelligence - DFKI
Stuhlsatzenhausweg 3, D - 66123, Saarbrücken, Germany
figueroa@dfki.de

Abstract. This paper presents LiSnQA, a list question answering system that extracts answers to list queries from the short descriptions of web-sites returned by search engines, called *web snippets*. LiSnQA mines Wikipedia resources in order to obtain valuable information that assists in the extraction of these answers. The interesting facet of LiSnQA is, that in contrast to current systems, it does not account for lists in Wikipedia, but for its redirections, categories, sandboxes, and first definition sentences. Results show that these resources strengthen the answering process.

Keywords: Web mining, Question answering, List questions, Distinct answers.

1 Introduction

Question Answering Systems (QAS) that discovers answers to list questions have been systematically studied in the Text REtrieval Conference (TREC). List queries, like "*Name books written by C. S. Lewis*", are aimed at finding a set of correct answers that share some sort of relation with each other, and with the question. In TREC, some systems recognise answers in the AQUAINT corpus by looking for answer candidates on lists supplied by online encyclopaedias (e.g., Wikipedia). However, the use of lists as an answer source has achieved modest success, because answers to few list questions can be found on listings.

This work investigates how additional Wikipedia resources can assist in identifying answers to list questions. Contrary to TREC systems, LiSnQA aims at finding answers on the web, in particular within web snippets. The motivation behind extracting answers from web snippets is two-fold: (a) improving the presentation of the outcome to the user, and (b) answers taken from snippets can be useful for determining the most promising documents; more precisely, where most of answers are likely to be. LiSnQA is thus aimed specifically at finding answers on the web.

2 Related Work

In TREC, QAS have explored several strategies in order to find answers to list questions across the AQUAINT corpus. Normally, QAS begin by identifying the *focus* of the query, that is the most descriptive noun phrase of the expected answer type [4]. Hence,

J. Cordeiro et al. (Eds.): WEBIST 2008, LNBIP 18, pp. 174–185, 2009.

the *focus* makes a connection between the question and its answer type. Therefore, some TREC QAS have accounted for pre-defined lists of instances of several *foci*, this way they extract correct answers by matching elements of these lists with a set of fetched passages from the corpus. In particular, [5] made allowances for a list of 7800 famous people taken from biography.com. In addition, they increased their 150 pre-defined and manually compiled lists used in TREC 2003 to 3300 in TREC 2004 [4]. These lists were semi-automatically extracted from WorldBook Encyclopedia articles by searching for hyponomyns. In TREC 2005, [6] generated these lists off-line by means of subtitles and link structures supplied by Wikipedia. This method processed a full Wikipedia page and its related documents. The manual annotation consisted of adding synonymous noun phrases that could be used to ask about the list. One of their findings was that online resources (e.g., Wikipedia) slightly improved the recall for the TREC 2003 and 2004 list questions sets, but not for TREC 2005, despite the wide coverage provided by Wikipedia.

In TREC 2005, [14] obtained patterns for recognising answers to list questions by checking the structure of sentences in the AQUAINT corpus where previously known answers occurred. They discovered that the semantics of the lexico-syntactic constructions of these sentences corresponds to the constructions observed by [3] for detecting hyponomic relations. These constructions, which often occur within natural language texts, are triggered by keywords like *"including"* and *"such as"*. Later, [8] took advantage of the copular pattern *"X is a/an Y"* for acquiring hypernyms and hyponyms for a given lexical term from web snippets.

[10] acquired hyponomic relations from full web documents based on the next three assumptions: (a) hyponyms and their hypernym are semantically similar, (b) the hypernym occurs in many documents along with some of its hyponyms, and (c) expressions in a listing are likely to have a common hypernym. Under these assumptions, [11] acquired hyponyms for a given hypernym from lists in web documents. They showed that finding the precise correspondence between lists elements and the right hypernym is a difficult task. Moreover, many hyponyms or answers to list questions cannot be found in lists or tables, which are not necessarily complete, specially in online encyclopedias. QAS are, therefore, forced to search along the whole text or across several documents in order to discover all answers.

[13] also exploited lists and tables as sources of answers to list questions. They fetched more than 1000 promising web pages by means of a query rewriting strategy that increased the probability of retrieving documents containing answers. This rewriting was based upon the identification of part-of-speech, name entities and a subject-object representation of the prompted question. Documents are thereafter downloaded and clustered. They also noticed that there is usually a list or table on the web page containing several potential answers. They further observed that the title of a page where answers occur, is likely to contain the subject of the relation established by the query. They then extracted answers, and projected them on the AQUAINT corpus.

[2] was guided by the empirical observation of [13]. They made use of the feature *"intitle"* supplied by commercial search engines for boosting the recall of web snippets that contain answers to list questions. More precisely, their system searches for web pages entitled with NNPSs/NNPs discovered during query analysis. Then, [2]

determines the semantic similarity of every snippet to the respective query by making use of a *Latent Semantic Kernel* (LSK) [9]. Hence, answers candidates belonging to snippets semantically closer to the question are more likely to be answers. Another two interesting facets of their answering strategy is that they take advantage of coordinations and bootstrapping in order to infer low frequent answers. This method finished with encouraging results, especially considering that it does **not** make use of any online encyclopedias.

In this paper, LiSnQA is built on top of the system in [2]. We extend this work by mining **Wikipedia** resources for extracting answers to list questions from **web snippets**. Since previous works have shown that lists slightly improve the performance, we investigate how additional resources can contribute to answer list questions.

3   Mining Wikipedia Resources

Wikipedia[1] consists of different sorts of pages including redirection, definition, and categories. In particular, redirection pages contain no definition content, but they link an input string with the respective definition page. We interpret these input strings as rewritings of the main concept. To neatly illustrate, the redirection page of "*Clive S Lewis*" connects this name rewriting to the definition page of "*C. S. Lewis*". Essentially, these mappings are used for building an **off-line** database of name rewritings:

<C. S. Lewis, Clive Staples Lewis>
<C. S. Lewis, C.S. Lewis>

This database is enriched with the alternative name rewritings conveyed in first definition sentences. Consider the following example corresponding to "*C. S. Lewis*":

"Clive Staples 'Jack' Lewis" *(29 November 1898 - 22 November 1963),*
<u>commonly referred to as</u> "**C. S. Lewis**", *was an Irish author and scholar.*

Sentences containing alternative names are discriminated **off-line** on the grounds of pre-defined lexico-syntactic clues. These clues were determined by inspecting high frequent n-grams, occurring in these sentences, that indicate alternative names (e.g., "*also known as*"). Definition pages also provide an additional source of rewritings: translations. For example, the following is a rewriting extracted from the translations of C.S. Lewis's book "*Mere Christianity*":

<Mere Christianity, Mero Cristianismo>

Then, finding out the rewritings of a concept consists of looking for the right entry in this database of rewritings. Additionally, we constructed a second database consisting of all concepts and their respective first definition sentence. In the case of sentences shorter than 150 characters, we consider the first two sentences. All expressions that convey rewritings were removed, along with pieces of text in parentheses. An entry in this database looks as follows:

---

[1] In the scope of this work, we use the snapshot supplied by Wikipedia in January 2008.

Clive Staples 'Jack' Lewis = CONCEPT was an Irish author and scholar.

The entries in this database are enriched **off-line** by its predicate-arguments structure[2]:

be(CONCEPT, Irish author and scholar)

In order to illustrate how these two databases link different concepts, consider the following entry:

The Dark Tower = CONCEPT is a novel written by C.S. Lewis.
be(CONCEPT, novel)
write(novel, by C.S. Lewis)

The equivalence between the different rewritings of "*C. S. Lewis*" is obtained from the first database, and consequently, it can be inferred that both concepts are related to each other, with the type of relationship given by the predicates. Additionally, we built a third **off-line** database consisting of sandboxes, commonly referred to as infoboxes, supplied by Wikipedia. An entry in this database is:

A Grief Observed = {type:book; author:C. S. Lewis; country:United Kingdom; isbn:0553274864; followed_by:Letters to Malcolm; pages:160; preceded_by:An Experiment in Criticism; publisher:Faber and Faber; release_date:1961;}

Lastly, we constructed a fourth **off-line** database consisting of the categories provided by Wikipedia. In the case of *C.S. Lewis*, there are six categories including "*Books by C. S. Lewis*", and "*Novels by C. S. Lewis*".

4   Answering List Questions

LiSnQA makes use of the previous databases for getting reliable answers, extending the query, and improving the recognition of names and answers within web snippets. In particular, these databases are used to empower our system previously presented in [2], this means LiSnQA is built on top of this system. The next sections describe these different improvements in details.

4.1   Discovering Reliable Answers

LiSnQA fetches predicates corresponding to sentences that match entities within the query Q. Here, if LiSnQA cannot find a definition that matches a query entity, it attempts to find sentences that match query entity rewritings taken from the rewritings database. If the question contains no entity, then LiSnQA tries to retrieve sentences containing query plural nouns, excluding the *focus*. If there is no plural noun in the query, LiSnQA fetches sentences, where the *focus* occurs. Here, it is worth remarking

---

[2] We use Montylingua available at http://web.media.mit.edu/~hugo/montylingua/

that words in multi-word *foci* are matched separately, and *foci*, such as "*Name auto-immune diseases*", are matched with and without hyphen. From now on, we refer to this set as $C_W(Q)$, the set of concepts found in Wikipedia that are related to Q.

In order to identify which concept shows strong evidence of being an answer, the corresponding fetched predicates are processed as follows. If the question consists solely of a *focus* (e.g. "*Name auto-immune diseases*"), LiSnQA verifies if any concept in $C_W(Q)$ fulfills the next predicate-arguments structure:

be(CONCEPT, arg_1, arg_2, ..., arg_N)

Where the lemma of *focus* must be aligned with arg_1 or arg_2. This alignment verifies whether or not this lemma is at the end of one of these two arguments, or followed by the conjunction "*or*", or the disjunction "*and*". A deeper alignment is due to *multi-word foci*, like "*auto-immune disease*". In this case, LiSnQA additionally checks if the multi-word *focus* lemma is split across the same argument:

be(CONCEPT,chronic auto-immune skin disease)

If this alignment fails, the lemma of the *focus* is aligned with arg_1 and/or arg_2 of the second predicate. However, the subject of this predicate must be a pronoun. An example is the autoimmune disease "*birdshot retinochoroidopathy*":

be(CONCEPT, form, of uveitis)
be(It, autoimmune disease)

Any concept in $C_W(Q)$ satisfying these constrains is interpreted as a *reliable answer*. However, some queries, such as "*cities with a subway system*", contain additional plural nouns. In these cases, LiSnQA also checks whether the lemma of a plural noun matches an argument of this predicate, but in a position posterior to the lemma of the *focus*. Queries containing entities, like "*songs of The Clash*", are verified if they fulfill one of the next three sets of predicates:

P_1:be(CONCEPT, focus lemma, ..., qentity, ..., arg_N)

P_1:be(CONCEPT, arg_1, arg_2, ..., arg_N)
P_2:vv(*, ..., focus lemma , ..., qentity, ..., arg_N)

P_1:be(CONCEPT, arg_1, arg_2, ..., arg_N)
P_2:vv(*, ..., focus lemma , ..., arg_N)
P_3:vv(*, ..., qentity, ..., arg_N)

The star, the tokens "*vv*" and "*qentity*" stand for anything as subject, anything as verb, and a query entity or a query entity rewriting, respectively. For instance, the following entry in our database satisfies the first set, and hence, "*Groovy Times*" is seen as a *reliable answer*:

Groovy Times = CONCEPT is a song by The Clash, featured on their "The Cost of Living", and released as a promotional single on 1979 in Australia by Epic Records.
be(CONCEPT, song, by The Clash)
feature(, on their "The Cost,of Living")
release(,)

However, some ambiguous concepts, including *"Tommy Gun"*, convey the lemma of the *focus* within the title as a disambiguation feature. In this sort of question, LiSnQA additionally takes into consideration the alignment of the *focus* lemma with this disambiguation feature[3]:

Tommy Gun (song) = CONCEPT was London punk rock band The Clash's 7th single, and the 1st single taken from their 2nd album "Give 'Em Enough Rope".
be(CONCEPT, London punk rock band The Clash)
take(, 1st, from their 2nd album Give 'Em Enough Rope)

This alignment consists in checking whether the *focus* lemma is at the end of the content in parenthesis, and also, it helps to lessen the impact of wrong outputs computed by Montylingua, and for this reason, to distinguish more *reliable answers*. In contrast, in the case of questions with verbs, such as *"novels written by John Updike?"*, the query verb is enforced by matching the verb of the second or third predicate. The matched verb cannot, however, belong to a predicate posterior to the one that matches a query entity or a plural noun lemma. The next example illustrates this:

Terrorist (novel) = CONCEPT is the 22nd novel written by lauded author John Updike.
be(CONCEPT, 22nd novel)
write(novel,)
laud(, author John Updike)

This strategy of inference does not make allowances for questions composed simultaneously of both plural nouns and query entities, because we observed that answering this sort of question requires more than the first definition line. Simply put, this inference procedure assists LiSnQA in determining a set $A_W(Q) \subseteq C_W(Q)$ of *reliable answers*. $A_W(Q)$ is then extended by exploring the database of categories in two ways. Firstly, if the query consists solely of a multi-word *focus*, then LiSnQA adds elements of the category that its label exactly matches the *focus*. If the question additionally has entities, LiSnQA accordingly adds elements of categories that match the *focus*, and an entity within the query or one of its rewritings. For example, the question *"Name Chuck Berry songs"* retrieves the category:

CHUCK BERRY SONGS = {Around and Around; Back in the U.S.A.; Come On; I'm Talking about You; Run Rudolph Run; Johnny B. Goode; Maybellene; Miracles; Memphis, Tennessee; My Ding-a-Ling; Rip It Up; Rock and Roll Music; Roll Over Beethoven; School Days; Sweet Little Sixteen; You Never Can Tell; You Can't Catch Me; Too Much Monkey Business;}

Since the label of the category matches the query *focus* and entity, all its members are added to $A_W(Q)$, and $C_W(Q)$. It is worth remarking here that not all answers in $A_W(Q)$ are included in the matched category. In our example, the *reliable answers* *"No Particular Place To Go"*, and *"Promised Land"* are not members of the category

---

[3] It is worth noting that we show predicates as outputted by Montylingua. This means they are not manually corrected.

"CHUCK BERRY SONGS". Secondly, LiSnQA adds concepts belonging to categories that contain a member in $A_W(Q)$, and their labels match a query entity or a query entity rewriting. It is worth noting that all these new added answers do not necessarily have a definition page in Wikipedia.

Then, LiSnQA searches for entries in the sandbox database corresponding to elements in $A_W(Q)$. In the set of found entries, LiSnQA looks for a common (higher frequent) property that matches an entity (or a rewriting) within the query. In our working category, the higher matching attribute is "**artist**", and has the value "**Chuck Berry**". In addition, LiSnQA obtains the two higher frequent types of sandbox in these entries, in the illustrative category: "**song**" and "**single**". Consequently, LiSnQA adds to $A_W(Q)$ entries in $C_W(Q) - A_W(Q)$ that their type match one of these two last values, and share the same value for the attribute "**artist**". Lastly, if one type of sandbox differs from the *focus* of the query, then it is seen as an *alternative focus*, in our example, the *alternative focus* is "**single**".

4.2 Query Expansion

LiSnQA makes use of $A_W(Q)$ for extending the search queries presented in [2]. This strategy searches for pages predominantly entitled with query entities, NNPSs, NNPs, and documents containing in their body the query *focus*, nouns and verbs. The next search query illustrates this:

intitle:("Chuck Berry")∧inbody:("songs")

A second and a third query are derived from this query by appending hyponomic words to the *focus* as follows:

intitle:("Chuck Berry")∧inbody:("songs like" ∨ "songs including")
intitle:("Chuck Berry")∧inbody:("songs such as" ∨ "songs include")

In addition, a fourth search query is generated, which is aimed at on-line encyclopedias. In [2], each of these four submissions fetched a maximum of 20 snippets. In the present study, since we have our databases taken from Wikipedia, we discard the fourth query, and we split the first submission into four similar submissions that retrieve ten snippets. Answers in $A_W(Q)$ are then allocated in these four queries according to their frequency in Google 5-grams. The following are two 5-grams with their frequencies, and partly/fully aligned Chuck Berry's songs:

213 Chuck/1 Berry/2 's/3 " /4 **Maybellene**/5
138 Chuck/1 Berry/2 's/3 " /4 **Sweet**/5 Little Sixteen

Four aspects are vital in this query expansion method: (a) the frequency estimate of each answer is the higher frequency of its partial or full alignments, when it is appended to the *focus* and to the query entities as shown in the previous illustration, (b) the hierarchy of answers is given by these frequencies, this means answers with high frequencies are allocated in the same search query, so do answers with low frequencies, (c) *reliable answers* with no frequency estimate are allocated alphabetically, and (d) the number of answers added to a query is limited by the length of queries accepted by search engines. In our illustrative example:

1. intitle:("Chuck Berry") $\wedge$ inbody:("singles" $\vee$ "songs") inbody:("You Never Can Tell" $\vee$ "Sweet Little Sixteen" $\vee$ "Roll Over Beethoven" $\vee$ "Maybellene")
2. intitle:("Chuck Berry") $\wedge$ inbody:("singles" $\vee$ "songs") inbody:("No Particular Place To Go" $\vee$ "Rock and Roll Music" $\vee$ "You Can't Catch Me" $\vee$ "Come On")
3. intitle:("Chuck Berry") $\wedge$ inbody:("singles" $\vee$ "songs") inbody:("Back in the U.S.A." $\vee$ "Too Much Monkey Business" $\vee$ "Run Rudolph Run" $\vee$ "Around and Around")
4. intitle:("Chuck Berry") $\wedge$ inbody:("singles" $\vee$ "songs") inbody:("School Days" $\vee$ "Promised Land" $\vee$ "Surfin' USA" $\vee$ "Memphis, Tennessee")

These queries also unveil that an *alternative focus* is concatenated with the query *focus*. In the case of the second and third original queries, if an alternative focus is discovered, these two queries are copied, and the query *focus* is replaced with the *alternative focus*. This generates four queries that are aimed at fetching ten snippets each. If no alternative focus is found, then the two copied queries are extended with *reliable answers*, similar to the previous four queries. If no answers are discovered, and no *alternative focus* is found, then the four original queries are sent [2].

4.3 Name Rewritings Recognition

A main problem of answering list questions is that the type of the *focus* varies widely from query to query. For instance, the query *"countries that produce peanuts"* has countries (locations) as the *focus*, but the question *"Name Chuck Berry songs"* names of songs. This variation plays a crucial role in determining answers, because state-of-the-art NERs do not recognise all types of *foci*. Besides, their performance is affected by truncations in web snippets.

LiSnQA also uses concepts in $C_W(Q)$ for identifying names within web snippets. First, concepts, that are correctly aligned with web snippets, are mapped to a placeholder. Accordingly, their rewritings are also mapped to the respective placeholder. Second, like [2], LiSnQA uses regular expressions for discriminating names on the ground of punctuation and sequences of terms that start with a capital letter. The obtained names, and their respective rewritings, are also replaced with a placeholder. Here, the rewriting database assists LiSnQA in bettering the name recognition by identifying different aliases. For example, *"Maybellene"* and *"Maybelline"* are mapped to the same placeholder.

4.4 Selecting Answers

In [2], answers were selected by inspecting name entities that share syntactic and semantic similarities. This method ranked answers candidates by measuring the semantic similarity to the prompted query of every context where these answers candidates occur. These similarities were computed from the terms-document matrix by means of LSK. In this matrix, the submitted query is seen as a *pseudo-document*, and LiSnQA augments this matrix with the first line definitions respecting concepts in $C_W(Q)$.

Additionally, [2] constructed a set of $R(Q)$ of reliable answers by examining answer candidates that occur in two different coordinations within web snippets. For instance, the next three snippet excerpts add the answers *"The Screwtape Letters"* and *"Mere Christianity"* to $R(Q)$:

*1. C. S. Lewis ... Popular books, **such as The Screwtape Letters**, have...*

*2. ...C. S. Lewis..., of course-books **like Mere Christianity, The Screwtape Letters, The Problem of Pain**, and **Miracles** continue to...*

*3. C. S. Lewis...the author of several apologetics books, **including The Screwtape Letters** and **Mere Christianity**.*

In [2], $R(Q)$ was thereafter extended by discriminating extra reliable answers on the ground of their syntactic bonding with the query by inspecting their frequency given by Google 5-grams, similar to how LiSnQA obtains the frequencies to allocate elements in $A_W(Q)$ within the search queries. They then took advantage of $R(Q)$ for bootstrapping coordinations, and consequently, for inferring some low frequent answers surrounded by *reliable answers*. In the three previous snippets, this boostrapping infers that *"The Problem of Pain"* and *"Miracles"* are also answers. This boostrapping strategy, however, misses answers in coordinations that do not share an answer with another coordination. LiSnQA aims to lessen this drawback by adding answers in $A_W(Q)$, that are in the fetched snippets, to $R(Q)$ and the final output. This way LiSnQA can distinguish extra reliable coordinations, and hence, infer additional answers.

5   Experiments

LiSnQA[4] was assessed by means of the widespread list question sets supplied by TREC from 2001 to 2004. Like [2], we use these standard question sets as reference questions-answers pairs, but contrary to TREC systems, we applied them to the web instead of the AQUAINT corpus.

The reason to left unconsidered questions corresponding to posterior tracks is that it is not possible to unambiguously determine the queries, because these questions are largely dependent upon their context. The manual resolution of this dependence brings about an evaluation that cannot be straightforwardly compared with other systems.

6   Answer Recall

LiSnQA fetches a maximum of 80 web snippets (see section 4.2). Accordingly, a baseline (BASELINE-I) was implemented that also fetches a maximum of 80 snippets by submitting the original query Q to the search engine. In addition, we considered the strategy in [2] as a second baseline (BASELINE-II). Since LiSnQA is built on top of this strategy, it is a good starting point for assessing the improvement of the techniques proposed in the present work. It is worth duly noting here that BASELINE-II does not use encyclopaedia resources.

Table 1 shows the achievements for four TREC datasets. NoS signals the average number of retrieved snippets per query, and NAF the number of questions in which there was no answer in these fetched snippets. This involved a necessary manual inspection of the retrieved snippets, because they do not necessarily contain the same

---

[4] In all our experiments, we used MSN Search: http://www.live.com/

answers supplied by TREC gold standards. Overall, LiSnQA retrieved slightly more snippets than BASELINE-II, and markedly increased the recall of distinct answers for all question sets. This recall was computed as the average ratio of the number of answers retrieved by the system to the number of answers provided by TREC. The reason to use this ratio is two-fold: (a) TREC provides at least one answer to every question, this way undefined ratios are avoided, and (b) additional answers are rewarded according to the size of the reference set, that is one extra answer is rewarded higher if the reference set contains less answers for the respective question. The achieved improvement is due essentially to the fact that answers to list questions tend to co-occur at the sentence or paragraph level. Hence, retrieving pieces of texts containing one answer increases the probability of fetching more answers.

In the light of the results in table 1, we can conclude that the first line database, taken from Wikipedia, supplied a positive way for inferring *reliable answers*, and thus extending the query. On the other hand, it makes the query expansion strategy largely dependant upon the coverage of Wikipedia, which is an undesirable and inescapable consequence. This coverage can be, nevertheless, extended by means of definitions extracted from the web.

LiSnQA: Answer Extraction

Table 2 compares the results obtained by LiSnQA with the top TREC systems and BASELINE-II. First of all, it is worth remarking that, contrary to the AQUAINT corpus, there is uncertainty as to whether or not at least one answer can be found on the web for every question. Second, table 2 shows that LiSnQA ranks between the **top one and two** TREC systems in the first two question sets, while between the **second and the third** in the last two data sets. Although these top TREC approaches are not directly comparable, because they extracted answers from AQUAINT corpus whereas LiSnQA (and BASELINE-II) did it from the Web, the difference in performance is still very fair. Third, LiSnQA betters the performance of BASELINE-II in all question sets, specifically in the case of TREC 2003. In this particular case, LiSnQA obtained a F_1 score 31.81% higher than BASELINE-II, and 10% lower than the score obtained by the **system ranked second**. These results are encouraging, because LiSnQA makes allowances solely for **web snippets**, not for **full documents**. This remarks our highly promising

Table 1. TREC Results (answer recall)

	2001	2002	2003	2004
BASELINE (Recall)	0.43	0.49	0.4	0.65
BASELINE-II(Recall)	0.93	0.90	0.56	1.15
LiSnQA(Recall)	1.14	1.44	0.70	1.45
BASELINE (NoS)	77.72	77.33	80	78.87
BASELINE-II(NoS)	59.83	53.21	51.86	46.41
LiSnQA(NoS)	74.50	59.12	52.59	50.95
BASELINE (NAF)	2	4	8	12
BASELINE-II (NAF)	6	2	8	11
LiSnQA (NAF)	2	2	8	12

Table 2. TREC Final results

	2001	2002	2003	2004
LiSnQA(F_1)	0.40	0.37	0.29	0.32
LiSnQA(Acc.)	0.55	0.48	0.56	0.56
BASELINE-II(F_1)	0.35	0.34	0.22	0.30
BASELINE-II(Acc.)	0.5	0.58	0.43	0.47
Top one(Acc.)	0.76	0.65	-	-
Top two(Acc.)	0.45	0.15	-	-
Top three(Acc.)	0.34	0.11	-	-
Top one(F_1)	-	-	0.396	0.622
Top two(F_1)	-	-	0.319	0.486
Top three(F_1)	-	-	0.134	0.258

results, especially considering other approaches [12,13], which **download and process** more than 1000 full web documents, or submit more than 20 queries to different search engines, finishing with an F_1 score of .464 $\sim$ .469 on TREC 2003. Our strategy can strengthen their strategy, specially their classification and clustering of full documents.

On the whole, LiSnQA fetches snippets containing **more answers** than BASELI-NE-II, but nonetheless, it finishes with a **higher** F_1 score.

7   Conclusions and Future Work

Given our results, we can conclude that short definition descriptions yield a positive way for inferring *reliable answers* to list questions. These answers also showed that can strengthen different steps of the answering process. On the other hand, the methods presented here are largely dependant upon the coverage of Wikipedia. But this coverage can be, nevertheless, extended by means of short definitions extracted from the web (e.g., Google define feature). Here, we envisage that techniques developed in web definition question answering can be used for adding new concepts to this database. These short definitions also help to overcome the drawback that not all answers are conveyed on listings.

The enhancement achieved by LiSnQA is essentially due to two direct causes: (a) the *reliable answers* taken from Wikipedia, which assist LiSnQA in recognising and inferring answers that are hard to extract directly from the retrieved snippets, and (b) the compression of the final output by means of the identification of name rewritings. Certainly, list QAS can enrich the database of rewritings by searching for additional first definition lines on the web that convey alternative names. These rewritings can be found by looking for the target concepts along with some well-known clues that convey alternative names.

Lastly, due to the fact that quantitative evaluations has been a driver of advances in language technologies during the last decades, it is important in the future to account for a test collection of questions and answers extracted from the web. In this way, one can reduce the uncertainty as to whether or not at least one answer can be found on the web for every question, thereby ensuring a fairer, and more reliable as well as stable comparison of systems.

Acknowledgements. This work was partially supported by a research grant from the German Federal Ministry of Education, Science, Research and Technology (BMBF) to the DFKI project HyLaP (FKZ: 01 IW F02).

References

1. Cederberg, S., Windows, D.: Using LSA and Noun Coordination Information to Improve the Precision and Recall of Automatic Hyponymy Extraction. In: Conference on Natural Language Learning (CoNLL 2003), Edmonton, Canada, pp. 111–118 (2003)
2. Figueroa, A., Neumann, G.: Finding Distinct Answers in Web Snippets. In: WEBIST 2008: 4th International Conference on Web Information Systems and Technologies, Funchal, Madeira - Portugal (2008)
3. Hearst, M.: Automatic Acquisition of Hyponomys from Large Text Corpora. In: Fourteenth International Conference on computational Linguistics, Nantes, France, pp. 539–545 (1992)
4. Katz, B., Lin, J., Loreto, D., Hildebrandt, W., Bilotti, M., Felshin, S., Fernandes, A., Marton, G., Mora, F.: Integrating Web-based and Corpus-based Techniques for Question Answering. In: TREC 2003, Gaithersburg, Maryland, pp. 426–435 (2003)
5. Katz, B., Bilotti, M., Felshin, S., Fernandes, A., Hildebrandt, W., Katzir, R., Lin, J., Loreto, D., Marton, G., Mora, F., Uzuner, O.: Answering multiple questions on a topic from heterogeneous resources. In: TREC 2004, Gaithersburg, Maryland (2004)
6. Katz, B., Marton, G., Borchardt, G., Brownell, A., Felshin, S., Loreto, D., Louis-Rosenberg, J., Lu, B., Mora, F., Stiller, S., Uzuner, O., Wilcox, A.: External Knowledge Sources for Question Answering. In: TREC 2005, Gaithersburg, Maryland (2005)
7. Schone, P., Ciany, G., Cutts, R., Mayfield, J., Smith, T.: QACTIS-based Question Answering at TREC 2005. In: TREC 2005, Gaithersburg, Maryland (2005)
8. Sombatsrisomboon, R., Matsuo, P., Ishizuka, M.: Acquisition of Hypernyms and Hyponyms from the WWW. In: 2nd International Workshop on Active Mining, Maebashi, Japan (2003)
9. Shawe-Taylor, J., Cristianini, N.: Kernel methods for pattern analysis, ch. 10, pp. 335–339. Cambridge University Press, Cambridge (2004)
10. Shinzato, K., Torisawa, K.: Acquiring hyponymy relations from web documents. In: HLT-NAACL 2004, Boston, MA, USA, pp. 73–80 (2004)
11. Shinzato, K., Torisawa, K.: Extracting hyponyms of prespecified hypernyms from itemizations and headings in web documents. In: COLING 2004, Geneva, Switzerland, pp. 938–944 (2004)
12. Yang, H., Chua, T.: Effectiveness of Web Page classification on Finding List Answers. In: SIGIR 2004, Sheffield, United Kingdom, pp. 522–523 (2004)
13. Yang, H., Chua, T.: Web-based List Question Answering. In: COLING 2004, Geneva, Switzerland, pp. 1277–1283 (2004)
14. Wu, L., Huang, X., Zhou, Y., Zhang, Z., Lin, F.: FDUQA on TREC 2005 QATrack. In: TREC 2005, Gaithersburg, Maryland (2005)

Personalized Web Search Using Correlation Matrix for Query Expansion

Claudio Biancalana, Antonello Lapolla, and Alessandro Micarelli

Department of Computer Science and Automation
Artificial Intelligence Laboratory
University Roma Tre
Via della Vasca Navale, 79, 00146 Rome, Italy
{biancalana,lapolla,micarel}@dia.uniroma3.it

Abstract. In this work we present a comparing analysis of four Query Expansion (QE) techniques. Sharing the concept of term co-occurrence, we start from a simple system based on bigrams, then we moved onto a system based on term proximity through an approach known in the literature as Hyperspace Analogue to Language (HAL), and eventually developing a solution based on co-occurrence at page level. We have implemented the methods in a system prototype, which has been used to conduct several experiments that have produced interesting results.

Keywords: Personalization, Information retrieval, Query expansion.

1 Introduction

The considerable quantitative increase in the amount of documents on the World Wide Web has led to a scenario in which disorganization gained the upper hand, due to the many different languages composing the documents, typically drafted by a huge number of authors on the Web. This fact leads to the need of supporting the user more efficiently in retrieving information on the web. Users easily find problems in retrieving information by means of a simple Boolean search to check the presence of the searched-for term in the web texts [7]. Indeed, some texts, consisting of terms that are often synonyms, or related to similar topics only, do not allow to conduct a proper search, and only take into consideration a few terms, which could be input by a user who is likely to have no or little experience in on-line searches. The Query Expansion (QE) technique fits in this disordered scenario to support the user in his/her search and allow to widen the search domain, to include sets of words that are somehow linked to the frequency of the term the user specified in his/her query [2]. These may be simple synonyms or terms that are apparently not connected to syntactic meaning, but nevertheless linked to a context that is similar or identical to the one expressed by the original search provided by the user [4]. Such information may be obtained in several ways, the main difference being the source used to obtain further information, which can be retrieved through the preferences explicitly indicated by the user, through the user's interaction with the system [6], through the incremental collection of information that links the query terms to document terms [5](for instance the search session logs [1]) or by means of a simple syntactic analysis of the phrase forms that compose the documents [13],[9].

J. Cordeiro et al. (Eds.): WEBIST 2008, LNBIP 18, pp. 186–198, 2009.

This paper is organized as follows. Section 2 is an overview of the implemented systems. In section 3 we introduce the general architecture of the developed systems. Section 4 presents our experimental setup and gives a detailed description of the results. Finally, in 5 we illustrate our conclusions.

2   The Systems

The systems we present in this work are based on the same approach: the query input by the user into the search engine is expanded through terms linked with the content of the previously visited web pages, hence pertaining to all the user's information needs. Thus, the QE process goes with a mechanism that builds the user model. As for the QE process, it is an approach based on the automatic expansion of the query, based on implicit feedback, formed by the pages previously visited by the user. Besides, the developed systems are referable to global analysis techniques, since nor preliminary search is done through the original query (see figure 1).

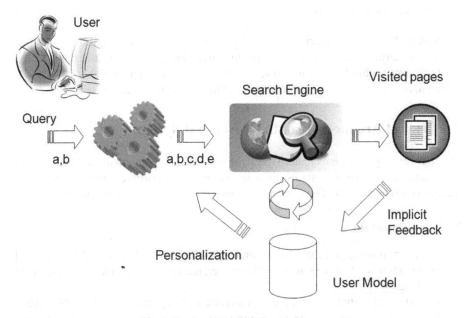

Fig. 1. Personalized Web Search Process

The personalization process and the construction of data structures for the user model are thus incremental, so as to dynamically adapt themselves to the user changing interests. All the developed systems build the user model following the concept of term co-occurrence [12]. By co-occurrence we mean the extent of which two terms tend to appear simultaneously in the same context.

In this research we implemented and rated four systems, each one characterized by two or more different versions. The four systems differ in the way they define the co-occurrence between two terms.

- **System I.** This is the most straightforward system among the implemented ones, both conceptually and computationally. The user model is built around the concept of bigrams, namely a pair consisting of two adjacent terms in the text of a web page. Two terms are considered co-occurring only if adjacent. The context of a term is thus exclusively limited to the term that is directly next to it, either to the left or to the right;

- **System II.** This system is based on the Hyperspace Analogue to Language approach, in which the context of a term is expanded to a window of N adjacent terms. Given a window of N terms, that can be scrolled inside a page text, two terms are considered co-occurring only if they are within such window. The co-occurrence value will be inversely proportional to the distance between the two terms within the window;

- **System III.** Within this system, the context of a term is expanded to the entire page considered. Two terms are then deemed co-occurring only if they are both present, simultaneously, in the same page;

- **System IV.** This is a hybrid system, where the co-occurring of two terms is not just the two terms' frequency in the same document, but also the distance between the two terms within the considered text. It is therefore a system which tries to find a compromise between the approaches used in the previous three systems.

3   General Architecture of the Developed Systems

The four developed systems feature the same architecture to create the user model and to execute the QE. These systems differ in that they adopt different methods to create the co-occurrence matrix. The main architecture elements are the following:

3.1   Creation of the User Model

1. For every training link, the corresponding html page is obtained, and the textual information is taken from it through a parser, the purpose of which is to get rid of html tags;
2. the extracted textual information is analyzed with a part of speech (POS) tagger, MontyLingua [1], which can make a semantic analysis of the text. The text is then broken down into sentences, where nominal and verbal phrases are tracked down; each term is then tagged as adjective, noun, proper noun or preposition;
3. the terms included in the stop word list (a list of words that, owing to their high occurrence within a text document are considered irrelevant for Information Retrieval) are removed from the textual information analyzed by the POS tagger;
4. the textual information previously analyzed by the POS tagger and cleansed of stop words now undergoes stemming, by means of Porter's algorithm [8]. The stemming algorithm allows to trace terms with the same root back to the same word;

---

[1] http://web.media.mit.edu/hugo/montylingua

5. the textual information is analyzed according to the chosen system, taking into consideration or not the extra semantic information gathered by the POS tagger. In all the implemented systems the user model consists of a co-occurrence matrix where, depending on the cases, such co-occurrence is to be seen as a simple bigram for sentences, nominal phrases or documents.

In any case the size of the co-occurrence matrix is given by the number of terms found in the training pages. Each line of the matrix corresponds to a vector representing a term, where each component represents the co-occurrence rate of the considered term with one of the other terms present in the training pages. Bear in mind that the co-occurrence matrix does not refer to the original terms included in the text, rather to their stemmed version.

In all the implemented systems a co-occurrence matrix is taken from each page. The lines of these matrices are normalized so as to obtain comparable values for each line. The matrices of the single pages are added incrementally, in order to form one single matrix of co-occurrences for the entire corpus.

3.2   Execution of the Expansion

1. Given query Q, consisting of n terms q_i, $i = 1, \ldots, n$, for each of the q terms, the corresponding stemmed term q'_i is calculated, hence obtaining the new query Q' to be represented in vectors as $\langle q'_1, \ldots, q'_n \rangle$, $i = 1, \ldots, n$;
2. for each of the terms q'_i, $i = 1, \ldots, n$, belonging to query Q', the vector corresponding to $\vec{cv}_{q'_i} = \langle c_1, \ldots, c_m \rangle$ is taken from the co-occurrence matrix, where m stands for the number of stemmed terms found in the training corpus, a value corresponding to the size of the co-occurrence matrix;
3. given the stemmed term of query $q'_i, i = 1, \ldots, n$, and the corresponding co-occurrence vector $\vec{cv}_{q'_i} = \langle c_1, \ldots, c_m \rangle$, it is possible to calculate the weighting the latter by means of a further co-occurrence measure, indicated as $c - index$. Given the term $q'j, j = 1, \ldots, n$, and the corresponding vector $\vec{cv}_{q'_j} = \langle c_1, \ldots, c_m \rangle$, each component of the latter $c_i, i = 1, \ldots, m$, is replaced by the value $c_i \times c - index(t_i, q'_j)$, with t_i standing for the term corresponding to the co-occurrence measure c_i. The two terms, a and b give:

$$c - index(a, b) = \frac{n_{ab}}{(n_a + n_b - n_{ab})}$$

where n_{ab} stands for the number of documents in the training corpus, in which words a and b are both present, while n_a and n_b indicate the number of documents in the training corpus in which word a and word b are present, respectively. The $c - index$ measure referring to two words therefore increases according to the frequency with which the two words appear together in the document rather than alone. Hence given a term of the query and the corresponding co-occurrence vector, the use of the $c - index$ tends to consolidate co-occurrences with words that usually appear together with the query term, and not much alone;
4. the vectors of co-occurrence with the query terms, to be possibly weighted with the $c - index$, are added up to obtain a single vector representing the terms that mostly co-occur with all the query terms;

5. once obtained the vector $\overrightarrow{cv_Q} = \langle c_1, \ldots, c_m \rangle$, referring to query Q, it is possible to weigh each co-occurrence value c_i, $i = 1, \ldots, m$, with the Inverse Document Frequency (IDF) [11] of the corresponding t_i term. The IDF of each term was calculated beforehand, considering the entire corpus;

6. the components of vector $\overrightarrow{cv_Q} = \langle c_1, \ldots, c_m \rangle$, referring to Q are ordered according to the decreasing co-occurrence values, removing the terms for which the co-occurrence value is 0.0. Starting from vector $\overrightarrow{cv_Q} = \langle c_1, \ldots, c_m \rangle$, we get the vector of ordered pairs $\overrightarrow{cv\_Pair_Q} = \langle (t_1, c_1), \ldots, (t_s, c_s) \rangle$ where s stands for the number of terms co-occurring with the query terms;

7. the stemmed terms present in the vector of ordered pairs are replaced by the original terms through the stemming table, provided that they are not already present in the starting query Q. The original terms are given the co-occurrence value of the corresponding stemmed term;

8. the expansion query relating to query Q is obtained by taking the first n terms of the vector of ordered pairs $\overrightarrow{cv\_Pari\_ex_Q}$. The original query Q terms are then given a co-occurrence value of 1.0 and added to the first n terms. Each query term is weighted according to its co-occurrence value;

9. the obtained query is then input in the search engine, which searches for the pages that mostly pertain to the query. The use of co-occurrence values in the query allows to assign a greater weight to the words with higher co-occurrence values.

It is very interesting to notice that given two terms t_1 and t_2, their similarity value is directly taken from the co-occurrence matrix, considering the element (t_1, t_2) or (t_2, t_1), given the symmetry of the matrix itself.

An approach commonly used - though extremely complicated from a computational viewpoint - in order to determine the similarity between two terms, is to make a comparison between the corresponding vectors within the co-occurrence matrix, for example measures such as cosine distance. This approach can only be used when the QE is made through a global analysis, namely taking into consideration all the documents included in the considered corpus, since the computation in this case can only be done once, off-line, thus generating a new similarity matrix including distance between all the terms present in the collection. We decided to make the similarity matrix equal to the co-occurrence matrix, which can be built in an incremental way. What follows is the description of the main development characteristics of the single systems implemented.

3.3   Bigram-Based System (System I)

This is the simplest QE system among the implemented ones. It is based on a very simple approach, that of limiting the context of a word to its two adjacent words, to the left and to the right. Each word thus forms two pairs, one with the word to the right, and one with the word to the left. Given a document, the terms contained in it are stemmed, and all the pairs of adjacent words, known as bigrams, are searched for. The pair (a, b) was considered to be equal to the pair (b, a), while pairs such as (a, a), where the two terms are identical, were left out. The final co-occurrence value will be equal to the number of times the two words are adjacent in the document.For each document, a co-occurrence matrix is then built, whose lines are normalized. Finally, all the matrices in the training documents are summed up to obtain the co-occurrence matrix.

3.4   HAL-Based System (System II)

Considering the limits of the bigram-based approach, with reference to the small size of a term's context, exclusively associated with the adjacent terms, we decided to expand this context to a window of N terms, using the Hyperspace Analogue to Language approach,[3]. The co-occurrence matrix is generated as follows: once a term is given, its co-occurrence is calculated with the N terms to its right (or to its left). In particular, given a term t and considered the window of N terms to its right (or left) $f_t = \{w_1, \ldots, w_n\}$, we get $co - oc(t, w_i) = \frac{w_i}{i}$, $i = 1, \ldots, N$. During the testing phase, N was given a value of 10. As in the bigram-based approach, pair (a, b) is equal to pair (b, a): hence even in this case the co-occurrence matrix is symmetrical. For each one of the training documents a co-occurrence matrix is generated, whose lines are then normalized. The matrices of the single documents are then summed up, generating one single co-occurrence matrix representing the entire training corpus. The text is broken down into nominal expressions, as before, but instead of gathering all the terms in one single document, the breakdown is maintained intact, in nominal expressions. This is when the HAL algorithm is implemented separately on the single nominal expressions of the document. We want to ascertain if and how much the addition of semantic information, such as the breakdown into nominal expressions, can help enhance performance, still implemented the weighting system of co-occurrences based on the joint use of IDF and $c - index$.

3.5   System Based on Co-occurrence at Page Level (System III)

The systems implemented so far base the construction of the co-occurrence matrix on the proximity of words: in the case of bigrams, co-occurrence is limited to two adjacent words, while co-occurrence in the HAL-based approach is extended to a window of N terms. Both methods take advantage of the concept of word proximity: the more the two words are closer in the text, the higher the probability they will be semantically linked. In the approach we are about to describe, we have decided to pursue a totally different method in building the co-occurrence matrix, which allows to overcome the limit of considering two co-occurring terms only if they are close to each other in the text. Indeed, we tried to implement a system which exploits co-occurrence at a page level, namely trying to track down the pairs of words that usually co-occur within the same training document, regardless of the distance between them; each term in a document is considered co-occurring with all the other terms in that very document. The number of times the term appears in the document is counted, and the vector $\vec{o_v} = \langle (t_1, tf_{t_1}), \ldots, (t_n, tf_{t_n}) \rangle$ is generated, where N stands for the number of different stemmed terms within the training document under discussion. Such vector consists of pairs (t_1, tf_{t_i}), $i = 1, \ldots, N$, where t_i stands for a term present in the document, and tf_{t_i} the number of times it appears in the document. The benefits of this weighting mechanism is evident when the QE is done. As seen before, for each query term, the co-occurrence vector is calculated. These vectors are then summed up. The weighting mechanism makes the contribution of the co-occurrence of the hardly relevant terms of the query in the document corpus less important compared to the co-occurrence of relevant terms. Hence, for each training document, a co-occurrence matrix is generated.

These matrices are then summed up so as to form one single matrix of co-occurrences, which is used for the QE. Once the textual information is obtained from the training links, the POS tagger extracts the nouns, proper nouns and adjectives. Not all these terms are selected, only the first k are used, following an order based on $tf \times idf$. Co-occurrences at a page level are then calculated exclusively using these first k keywords where k is a fixed parameter of the system, which is the same for any page to be analyzed.

3.6   System Based on Co-occurrence at Page Level and Term Proximity (System IV)

System II is exclusively based on the concept of co-occurrence at page level: it attempts to track down the terms that are usually present simultaneously in the same pages, without even considering the distance between the words within the text. Ignoring term proximity within the same document can lead to a considerable loss of information, since two words that are close to each other are more likely to be correlated, from a semantic viewpoint too. That's why we decided to use a hybrid approach, that doesn't use page-level co-occurrence only, but that also considers term proximity, as the bigram-based and HAL-based systems do. Following this idea we implemented and tested a hybrid approach, starting from the extraction of nominal expressions and exclusively considering nouns, proper nouns and adjectives. Moreover, the weighting mechanism based on IDF and $c - index$ is used. In order to carry out the QE, the two vectors of co-occurrence with the query terms are obtained separately, following the HAL-based approach and the approach based on co-occurrence at page level, without extracting the keywords. Such vectors are therefore the same ones obtained from systems I and II respectively. Each vector contains a different type of information: the co-occurrence at page level vector consists of the terms that are usually present in the same documents in which the query terms appear, while the HAL-type co-occurrence vector contains the terms that are usually present in the documents, in proximity of the query terms. The blending of the two types of information is done by introducing a new element which is known as proximity matrix. This matrix is basically an extension of the HAL-based approach. Whilst forming the co-occurrence matrix the HAL-based approach, given a term t, considers t co-occurring with the adjacent N terms, associating a greater co-occurrence value to the terms that are closer to t. The HAL method thus envisages the use of a window of N adjacent terms. We therefore asked ourselves how the use of a preset-size window can entail a loss of information, and we decided to employ a method that allows to consider the proximity of term t with all the other terms in the document. Let us see how the proximity matrix P is built. A matrix P is constructed, having size M, namely the number of stemmed terms present in the training corpus. Each matrix box contains two values, v_1 and v_2, which we initialize at 0.0 and 0, respectively. For each document d of the training documents corpus and for each term t present in d, all terms to the right of t are considered, and distance i from t is measured. Assume that term t' is at distance i from t, we extract from matrix P the pair of values (v_1, v_2) in box (t, t'), and we increase v_1 by $\frac{1.0}{i}$ and v_2 by 1. As for the construction of the query, it is done following the same method adopted in system III. The only difference is to be seen in the proximity measuring when co-occurrence at page level values

---

Algorithm 1. Pseudo-coding algorithm of the co-occurrence-based system at page level (System III)

---

begin
    Δ co-occurrence global matrix initialization, represented by a map of maps
    $M \leftarrow Map([])$
    Δ training documents analysis
    for *doc in D* **do**
        Δ term occurrence map initialization contained in a single document
        $tf \leftarrow Map([])$ Δ term frequency calculation
        for *t in doc* **do**
            if *not t in tf.keys()* **then**
                $tf[t] = 0$
            else
                $tf[t] = tf[t] + 1$
        Δ $tf * idf$ calculation for every terms in the document
        for *t in tf.keys()* **do**
            $tf[t] = tf[t] \times idf(t)$
        Δ get a list ordered by $tf * idf$ of k couples $(t, tf * idf_t)$
        $tfidf\_list = map\_to\_ord\_list(tf)[0 : K]$ Δ normalize $tf * idf$ values
        $tfidf\_list = normalize(tfidf\_list)$ Δ transform the list into map
        $tfidf\_map = Map(tfidf\_list)$ Δ get unique document-terms list
        $term\_list = tfidf\_map.keys()$ Δ update global co-occurence matrix
        for $t_1, tfidf$ *in tfidf_map.items()* **do**
            if *not t_1 in M.keys()* **then**
                $M[t_1] \leftarrow Map([])$
            for t_2 *in term_list* **do**
                if *not t_2 in $M[t_1].keys()$* **then**
                    $M[t_1][t_2] = 0.0$
                else
                    $M[t_1][t_2] = M[t_1][t_2] + tfidf \times tfidf\_map[t_2]$
end

---

of the query terms are extracted. Given term q' belonging to query Q, and having extracted the corresponding co-occurrence at page level vector $\overrightarrow{cv_q}$, the co-occurrence value of each term t' belonging to vector $\overrightarrow{cv_q}$ is multiplied by $\frac{v1}{v2}$, where v_1 and v_2 are the values present in the proximity matrix corresponding to the pair of terms (q', t') based on co-occurrence at page level and term proximity, through which it is possible to understand the assets and weak points of each term, also with reference to the systems based on different approaches.

3.7 Pseudo-coding

In this subsection we show the pseudo-coding of the algorithm which calculates the co-occurrence matrix starting from the set of training documents (see Algorithm 1), and the pseudo-coding of the algorithm for the actual execution of the QE, starting from the data contained in this matrix (see Algorithm 2). With reference to the algorithm calculating co-occurrence at page level with extraction of the first k keywords, we notice that:

- the co-occurrence matrix is represented by a map of maps. In this way, we avoid initializing a square matrix the size of which is the overall number of different terms in the training documents set. Using this matrix would entail a huge waste of memory, since the majority of its elements have a value equal to zero, considering how sparse the matrix is. By using a map of maps on the other hand, it is possible to input the co-occurrence values between the pairs of co-occurring terms in the training documents when such pairs are present;
- the keys() method of a map yields the list of keys;
- the items() method of a map yields the list of pairs (key, value);
- the $IDF(t)$ method yields the inverse document frequency of term t, calculated previously according to the documents belonging to the third level of the DMOZ directory (see section 4.1).

As for the algorithm calculating the QE through the matrix of co-occurrence at page level, we notice that:

Algorithm 2. Pseudo-coding algorithm of the co-occurrence-based system at page level and term proximity (System IV)

---

begin
    Δ co-occurrence global matrix initialization, represented by a map of maps
    $Q \leftarrow [q_1, q_2, ..., q_n]$
    Δ co-occurrence map initialization
    $cooc\_map \leftarrow Map([]) \; \Delta$ stemming
    $Q \leftarrow stemming(Q) \; \Delta$ co-occurrence map update for every terms in the query
    for q in Q **do**
        Δ update co-occurrence map A
        $cooc\_map = sum(cooc\_map, M[q])$
    Δ get an ordered list of couples $(t, cooc\_val)$, sorted by co-occurrence values
    $cooc\_list = map\_to\_ord\_list(cooc\_map) \; \Delta$ transform the list into map
    $cooc\_map = Map(cooc\_list) \; \Delta$ query initialization
    $exp\_query = [] \; \Delta$ query expansion
    for $term, cooc\_val$ in $cooc\_map.items()$ **do**
        Δ get a non-stemmed term list associated to $term$
        $exp\_list = expand(term) \; \Delta$ expand terms
        for $orig\_term$ in exp_list **do**
            $exp\_query.append((orig\_term, cooc\_val))$
    Δ limit query expansion to first k co-occurrence terms
    $exp\_query = exp\_query[0 : K] \; \Delta$ merge original terms
    for q in Q **do**
        $exp\_query.append((q, 1.0))$
    return exp_query
end

- the sum method (`coocMap1, coocMap2`) yields a new map, given from the union of pairs (`key, value`) present in the two maps, `coocMap1` and `coocMap2`; should a key be present in both maps, the corresponding value is given by the sum of values contained in the starting maps;
- the stemming method (Q) yields a new query, obtained by stemming the terms of query Q;
- the expand method (t) yields the list of non-stemmed terms, found in the training documents, whose root is equal to term t.

4 Experimentation

For each of the adopted approaches, the results of the corresponding systems are presented. The comparison between different systems is made by using comparative performance values obtained from the system under examination, on one single topic or the entire benchmark. Such performances are expressed in F1-measures, so as to summarize, in one single measure, precision and recall values. As for the performance measures taken into consideration, we have precision, recall and f1-measure:

$$precision(t) = \frac{n_t}{50} \qquad recall(t) = \frac{n_t}{N_t}$$

$$F1 - measure = \frac{2 \times precision \times recall}{precision + recall}$$

where n_t stands for the number of returned links belonging to topic t, only the first 50 pages are taken in consideration for our tests, and N_t the overall number of test links belonging to topic t present in the index.

4.1 The Employed Benchmark: The Open Directory Project

The Open Directory Project (ODP), also known as DMOZ[2], is a multilanguage directory of links belonging to the World Wide Web, namely a system to collect and classify links. The Open Directory Project has a hierarchic structure: the links are grouped into categories, also known as topics, and subcategories. It is therefore possible to identify a level-based organization within the hierarchy. Given the large quantity of links contained in ODP, we decided to consider only Level III links. The pages corresponding to such links were downloaded from the World Wide Web, by using a parser; the textual information was taken from it, and then it was indexed by means of the Lucene indexing system [3]. Ten topics were then chosen from the Level III topics, five of which corresponding to the user's information needs, and five whose function was exclusively to generate noise in the creation of the user model. Each topic's links were then subdivided in a training set, corresponding to 25% of the links, and set of tests, corresponding to 75% of the links (see table 1).

---

[2] http://dmoz.org
[3] http://lucene.apache.org

Table 1. The employed benchmark: statistics

Topic	Test links	Training links	Information Needs
Sports/Cycling/Human_Powered_Vehicles	15	5	yes
Computers/Home_Automation/Products_and_Manufacturers	27	7	yes
Business/Mining_and_Drilling/Consulting	74	18	yes
Games/Roleplaying/Developers_and_Publishers	52	14	yes
Business/Agriculture_and_Forestry/Fencing	100	27	yes
Shopping/Crafts/Paper	35	7	no
Arts/Performing_Arts/Magic	25	6	no
Science/Publications/Magazines_and_E-zines	26	7	no
Science/Social_Sciences/Linguistics	13	5	no
Recreation/Guns/Reloading	15	5	no
Tot.	382	101	

4.2 Experimentation Methods

Once the user model is generated, it is possible to carry out real tests as follows. A query is built for each topic belonging to the user's information needs. The terms of the query are simply the terms that form the topic name. This query is then expanded according to the user model, and used to search for web pages within the created index, starting from all third-level links. The pages belonging to the training set of the considered topic are removed from the returned pages; only the first fifty are taken into consideration, which include the number of pages belonging to the topic under consideration. The index obtained with Lucene, starting from the third-level link of ODP, consists of 131,394 links belonging to 5,888 topics.

Table 2 compares the performances of the four systems. It is possible to notice that the system based on co-occurrence at page level (system III) clearly achieves better results compared with other systems based on term proximity (system IV), such as bigrams (system I) and HAL (system II).

Indeed, both are based on the concept of term proximity, and more specifically they imply a correlation between two terms when they are close to each other in the text.

Table 2. Comparative F1-Measurement on implemented Systems

Topic	System I	System II	System III	System IV
Computers/Home_Automation/Products_and_Manufacturers	0.00	0.00	0.16	0.16
Sports/Cycling/Human_Powered_Vehicles	0.13	0.06	0.09	0.06
Games/Roleplaying/Developers_and_Publishers	0.14	0.12	0.18	0.16
Business/Mining_and_Drilling/Consulting	0.21	0.27	0.19	0.21
Business/Agriculture_and_Forestry/Fencing	0.34	0.36	0.57	0.48
Average	**F1** 0.16	**F1** 0.16	**F1** **0.24**	**F1** 0.21

Table 3. Comparative F1-Measurement

Topic	no QE	RF	*Nereau*
Computers/Home_Automation/Products_and_Manufacturers	0.05	0.08	0.16
Sports/Cycling/Human_Powered_Vehicles	0.09	0.13	0.09
Games/Roleplaying/Developers_and_Publishers	0.10	0.18	0.18
Business/Mining_and_Drilling/Consulting	0.19	0.14	0.19
Business/Agriculture_and_Forestry/Fencing	0.05	0.14	0.57
Average	**F1**	**F1**	**F1**
	0.10	0.13	**0.24**

This approach, however, entails the loss of information linked to terms that usually co-occur in the documents themselves, but which are not always close to each other in the text. The approach based on co-occurrence at page level hence steers away from the term proximity concept, and tries to track down the terms that are usually simultaneously present in the same documents. The experimentation results show that page-level correlations are stronger than those based exclusively on term proximity within the text: given a page relating to a particular topic, this will feature correlated terms, not because of their proximity, but because they refer to the same topic. We also notice that the system based on keyword extraction is the one that offered the best performance among the presented ones: to calculate the correlation values, this system takes into consideration only the most relevant terms in the text, thus preventing a large quantity of noise from impairing the performance.

Table 3 shows the results obtained by a system based on a traditional content-based user-modeling approach, where documents are represented in the Vector Space Model (VSM) and without Query Expansion, in comparative terms. This system particularly focuses on the update of the user model by means of Relevance Feedback (RF) techniques [10], applied to the training pages content: for each category, the first ten keywords are taken from the corresponding training pages. The keywords are obtained in terms of $tf \times idf$, and are then used to expand the query.

5 Conclusions

In this research we implemented and analyzed an Information Retrieval system, based on QE and Personalization, that may help the user search for information on the Web, with reference to his/her information needs. The four systems implemented are based on the following approaches: bigrams, Hyperspace Analogue to Language (HAL), co-occurrence at page level and co-occurrence at page level with term proximity. Among the developed systems, the one based on co-occurrence at page level and keyword extraction stood out. Indeed, this system, based on an algorithm calculating co-occurrences, obtained the best results, in terms of performance, on the reference benchmark. Experimental results were encouraging and confirmed the correlation with users' interests. In the future we intend to test this approach in comparative terms with other state of the art query expansion techniques using personalization. Moreover, we intend to study ways of integrating NLP knowledge and procedures into our IR system.

References

1. Anick, P.: Using terminological feedback for web search refinement: a log-based study. In: SIGIR 2003: Proceedings of the 26th annual international ACM SIGIR conference on Research and development in informaion retrieval, pp. 88–95. ACM Press, New York (2003)
2. Bai, J., Song, D., Bruza, P., Nie, J.-Y., Cao, G.: Query expansion using term relationships in language models for information retrieval. In: CIKM, pp. 688–695 (2005)
3. Bruza, P.D., Song, D.: Inferring query models by computing information flow. In: CIKM 2002: Proceedings of the eleventh international conference on Information and knowledge management, pp. 260–269. ACM Press, New York (2002)
4. Burgess, C., Livesay, K., Lund, K.: Exploration in Context Space: Words, Sentences, Discourse. Discourse Processes 25(2&3), 211–257 (1999)
5. Gao, J., Nie, J.-Y., Wu, G., Cao, G.: Dependence language model for information retrieval. In: SIGIR 2004: Proceedings of the 27th annual international ACM SIGIR conference on Research and development in information retrieval, pp. 170–177. ACM Press, New York (2004)
6. Gasparetti, F., Micarelli, A.: Personalized search based on a memory retrieval theory. International Journal of Pattern Recognition and Artificial Intelligence (IJPRAI): Special Issue on Personalization Techniques for Recommender Systems and Intelligent User Interfaces 21(2), 207–224 (2007)
7. Jansen, B.J., Spink, A., Saracevic, T.: Real life, real users, and real needs: a study and analysis of user queries on the web. Information Processing and Management 36(2), 207–227 (2000)
8. Porter, M.F.: An algorithm for suffix stripping, pp. 313–316 (1997)
9. Radlinski, F., Joachims, T.: Query chains: Learning to rank from implicit feedback (2005)
10. Salton, G., Buckley, C.: Improving retrieval performance by relevance feedback, pp. 355–364 (1997)
11. Salton, G., Wong, A., Yang, C.S.: A vector space model for automatic indexing. Commun. ACM 18(11), 613–620 (1975)
12. Schütze, H., Pedersen, J.O.: A cooccurrence-based thesaurus and two applications to information retrieval. Inf. Process. Manage. 33(3), 307–318 (1997)
13. Teevan, J., Dumais, S.T., Horvitz, E.: Personalizing search via automated analysis of interests and activities. In: SIGIR 2005: Proceedings of the 28th annual international ACM SIGIR conference on Research and development in information retrieval, pp. 449–456. ACM Press, New York (2005)

Social Semantic Web at Work: Annotating and Grouping Social Media Content

Fabian Abel, Nicola Henze, and Daniel Krause

IVS – Semantic Web Group, Leibniz University Hannover
Appelstr. 4, 30167 Hannover, Germany
{abel,henze,krause}@kbs.uni-hannover.de

Abstract. Common social tagging systems like Flickr, Delicious and others lately became very popular. The key benefits of these systems include that users can easily annotate Web content and benefit from the annotations of other users with improved retrieval support. With GroupMe! we extend the idea of current social tagging systems by enabling users to not only tag Web resources they are interested in, but also to create collections (*groups*) of these Web resources by simple drag & drop operations. The grouping metaphor is intuitive and easy for the users, and our evaluation shows that users appreciate the grouping facility, and use this feature to organize and structure diverse Web content. Technically, the grouping of resources carries valuable information about Web resources and their relations. GroupMe! exploits such information to improve search and retrieval. The RESTful Semantic Web interface of GroupMe! enables also other applications to benefit from the GroupMe! features and makes GroupMe! a Social Semantic Web application.

Keywords: Social media, Semantic web, Tagging, Folksonomy, GroupMe!

1 Introduction

Popular systems like Flickr[1], YouTube[2], Blogger[3] or others, which allow users to share photos, broadcast own videos, or blog about topics they are interested in, are obvious indicators for the success of Web 2.0. These systems have shown that Web users are not satisfied with their role of pure *content consumers*. Instead, Web users want to contribute and collaborate actively by providing their own content, or by annotating (*tagging*) content of other users.

Social media systems like YouTube, BibSonomy[4], and Delicious[5] fulfill these needs perfectly and allow users to create and annotate content collaboratively, hence enable

---

[1] http://www.flickr.com
[2] http://www.youtube.com
[3] http://www.blogger.com
[4] http://www.bibsonomy.org
[5] http://delicious.com

J. Cordeiro et al. (Eds.): WEBIST 2008, LNBIP 18, pp. 199–213, 2009.
© Springer-Verlag Berlin Heidelberg 2009

intercreativity[6]. Furthermore, these systems feature sharing of resources with fellow users, e.g., in YouTube users can share their favorite videos, in BibSonomy their favorite academic papers, and in Delicious their favorite bookmarks. However, all of these systems are more or less limited to a certain media type: Some systems (like YouTube) support only one media type (videos), while other systems, which can handle different kind of media types, lack of an appropriate visualization (in Delicious, e.g., all media types are displayed as normal text links).

In this chapter, we present the GroupMe! system[7], which offers a novel user interface to organize multimedia Web resources. The core idea of the GroupMe! approach is that users can group – via drag & drop – the Web resources they are interested in. Appropriate media wrappers ensure that content of groups is displayed in a concise manner. We report about the evaluation of the GroupMe! system which shows that a) the GroupMe! group concept is very well accepted by the users, b) that users like to combine resources of different media types, and c) that these groups can be used to improve search.

Another disadvantage of today's social media systems is that they are designed for humans and do not comply with the vision of the Semantic Web [7]. Although many of these systems feed back data to the web, interoperability is still not supported sufficiently because application programming interfaces are proprietary and the use of Semantic Web standards is most often avoided. Revyu[8] sets a good example as it adheres to the Linked Data [6] approach. However, it enables software systems just to navigate through its data corpus. GroupMe! goes beyond Linked Data as it also enables applications to create and manipulate data via a RESTful Semantic Web interface. Hence, by combining principles of Social Media and Semantic Web, GroupMe! becomes a Social Semantic Web application.

The chapter is structured as follows: In Section 2 we describe our GroupMe! system, which is evaluated in Section 3, and the RESTful Semantic Web interface of GroupMe!. In Section 4 we compare the GroupMe! system with other state-of-the-art tagging systems. We end with the conclusion in Section 5.

2   GroupMe! System

GroupMe! is a new kind of resource sharing system. It is comparable to social bookmarking systems as it enables users to bookmark Web resources and annotate them with freely chosen keywords (tags). The core idea of GroupMe! is that users build groups of arbitrary multimedia Web resources on a specific topic and tag both, Web resources and groups. Groups can be understood as lightweight wiki pages. But instead of writing own content, users create groups via simple *drag & drop* operations and via visual arrangement of contained resources.

Figure 1 shows a screenshot of the GroupMe! system. It illustrates a typical scenario. Let us assume that user *fabian* plans a trip to the *WEBIST 2008* conference in Funchal, Portugal. Therefore, he wants to build a GroupMe! group containing resources that

---

[6] http://www.w3.org/Talks/9602seybold/slide6.htm

[7] http://groupme.org

[8] http://revyu.com

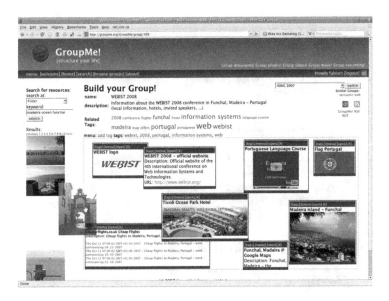

Fig. 1. Screenshot of GroupMe! application: A user drags a photo from the left-hand side Flickr search bar into the GroupMe! group on the right-hand side

are relevant to the trip. Building such a group is simple and requires just three steps. At first fabian specifies the group's name (WEBIST 2008), then he utilizes integrated search engines – like Google or Flickr search engine – in order to search for adequate resources, and finally he adds resources, which are from his point of view relevant, via drag & drop into the group. Figure 1 depicts such a drag & drop operation with a photo gathered from Flickr. Furthermore, it shows the entire group fabian has designed. This group contains images (like a photo of Madeira Island), the official website of the WEBIST 2008, and a shockwave flash movie, which presents several photos of the *Tivoli Ocean Park Hotel* – where the conference was held – and gives the opportunity to book rooms. All elements are visualized according to their media types so that fabian and other users can see relevant information at a glance. For example, the RSS news feed that informs about cheap flights to Madeira (see bottom left) directly presents the latest flight offers to the user. And the video showing a Portuguese language course (see top right) can be played back immediately.

Altogether the arranged group in Figure 2 appears like a *collage of information arti-facts* about *WEBIST 2008 trip*, which is comprehensible for users. Importantly, content of this group is also accessible and understandable for machines. Because, when users create groups, GroupMe! produces RDF:

1. Each user interaction (grouping and tagging) is captured as RDF complying with the lightweight GroupMe! ontology[9], which integrates well known vocabularies

---

[9] http://groupme.org/rdf/groupme.owl

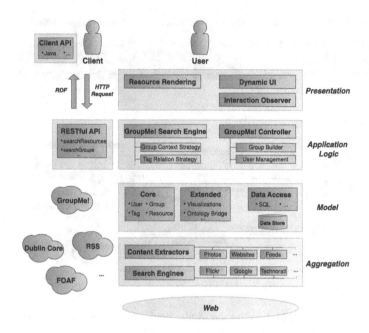

Fig. 2. Technical overview of the GroupMe! application

like $FOAF^{10}$, SKOS[11], or R. Newman's Tag ontology[12]. For a more detailed description of the GroupMe! ontology the reader is referred to [1].

2. Whenever a user drops a new Web resource into a group, domain dependent content extractors gather useful metadata so that resources can be enriched with RDF descriptions, e.g. adding a Flickr photo into a group effects GroupMe! to translate Flickr-specific descriptions into well defined RDF descriptions using *DCMI element set*[13].

RDF created in GroupMe! is made available to other Web applications and can be accessed via RSS feeds or RDF-based RESTful API, which enables other applications to benefit from the GroupMe! features (see Section 2.2).

2.1 GroupMe! Architecture

In technical terms, GroupMe! is a modular Web application that adheres to the Model-View-Controller pattern. It is implemented using the J2EE application framework *Spring*[14]. Figure 2 illustrates the architecture, which consists of four layers:

---

[10] http://xmlns.com/foaf/spec/

[11] http://www.w3.org/TR/skos-reference

[12] http://www.holygoat.co.uk/projects/tags/

[13] http://dublincore.org/documents/dces/

[14] http://springframework.org

Aggregation. The aggregation layer provides functionality to search for resources a user wants to add into GroupMe! groups. Currently, GroupMe! supports Google, Flickr, and of course a GroupMe!-internal search, as well as adding resources by specifying their URL manually. *Content Extractors* allow us to process gathered resources in order to extract useful data and metadata, which is converted to RDF using well-known vocabularies. As mentioned in Section 2, when e.g. adding a Flickr image into a group, a *Photo content extractor* converts Flickr-specific descriptions into RDF descriptions using Dublin Core vocabulary. GroupMe! is furthermore able to query Semantic Web search engines like Sindice[15] and Watson[16] to enrich resource descriptions with additional information gathered from the Semantic Web.

Model. The core GroupMe! model is composed of four main concepts: *User, Tag, Group,* and *Resource*. These concepts constitute the base for the GroupMe! folksonomy (cf. section 2.3). In addition, the model covers concepts regarding the arrangements of groups, etc. The *Data Access* layer cares about storing model objects. The actual data store backend is arbitrarily exchangeable. At the moment we are using a MySQL database.

Application Logic. The logic layer provides various controllers for modifying the model, exporting RDF, etc. The internal GroupMe! search functionality, which is implemented according to the strategy pattern in order to switch between different search and ranking strategies, is made available via a Semantic RESTful API (see Section 2.2). It enables third parties to benefit from the improved search capabilities (cf. Section 3.1), and to retrieve RDF descriptions about resources – even such resources that were not equipped with RDF descriptions before they were added to a GroupMe! group. To simplify usage of exported RDF data, we further provide a lightweight Java *Client API,* which transforms RDF into GroupMe! Java model objects.

Presentation. The GUI of the GroupMe! application is based on AJAX principles. Therefore, we applied frameworks like Scriptaculous[17], DWR[18], or Prototype[19]. Such frameworks provide already functionality to drag & drop elements, resize elements, etc. Visualization of groups and resources is highly modular and extensible. Switching between components that render a specific resource or type of resource can be done dynamically, e.g. visualization of group elements is adapted to their media type (see Fig. 1).

When creating or modifying groups, each user interaction (e.g. moving and resizing resources) is monitored and immediately communicated to the responsible GroupMe! controller so that e.g. the actual size or position of a resource within a group is stored in the database.

By default GroupMe! groups are displayed in the way they were constructed by the creator of the group. However, GroupMe! also provides functionality to visualize groups according to different principles, e.g. resources can be displayed within a timeline, resized according to their popularity, or clustered according to their similarity with

---

[15] http://sindice.com

[16] http://watson.kmi.open.ac.uk

[17] http://script.aculo.us

[18] http://directwebremoting.org

[19] http://prototypejs.org

respect to their tags, media type, etc. Users can therewith easily select a group visualization, which is appropriate for their current requirements.

2.2 RESTful Semantic Web Interface

The RESTful Semantic Web interface of GroupMe! follows the *Resource Oriented Architecture* (ROA) [20], which is an architecture that conforms to the REST approach [9]. The API allows other applications to read, add, modify, and delete data by exploiting the main methods of HTTP [8] (GET, POST, PUT, and DELETE).

GET. The GroupMe! dataset is made available according to the principles of Linked Data [6]. Whenever an application requests RDF – which is done via HTTP GET and HTTP content negotiation (cf. [21]) – then useful information as well as links to related URIs are delivered. In that way the application is enabled to navigate through the whole GroupMe! data corpus. Figure 3 lists an extract of the RDF representation that is provided to applications, which access the group about the WEBIST 2008. The visual representation of that group is displayed in Figure 1.

POST. The HTTP POST method is used to add new content to the GroupMe! system, e.g. to add a new group to the system, to add resources to groups, or to add annotations to resources or groups. To create a new group an application has to post an RDF resource, which is an instance of *groupme:Group* (cf. GroupMe! ontology in [1]), to *http://groupme.org/GroupMe/group*, e.g. the following RDF post would create a new group about WEBIST 2008 with the given title and description.

```
<Group>
 <dc:title>WEBIST 2008</dc:title>
 <dc:description>Information about the WEBIST 2008 conference...
 <dc:description>
</Group>
```

GroupMe! cares about the creation of the URI identifying the group and returns it to the sender of the HTTP request, e.g. *http://groupme.org/GroupMe/group/499*. Groups can be filled with resources by posting resources to the group's URI. Tags and other annotations can be added similarly. Hence, content as listed in Figure 3 can not only be created via the graphical user interface, but also by posting RDF data to the GroupMe! system.

PUT. If a client application sends an HTTP PUT request to an existing resource then GroupMe! modifies the resource that is identified by the URI according to the RDF data that is sent together with the HTTP request, e.g. the following RDF (as part of an HTTP PUT) would change the title and description of the WEBIST group.

```
<Group rdf:about="http://groupme.org/GroupMe/group/499">
 <dc:title>WEBIST 2008 conference </dc:title>
 <dc:description>Interesting stuff about the WEBIST 2008...
 <dc:description>
</Group>
```

a. GroupMe! group:

```
<Group rdf:about="http://groupme.org/GroupMe/group/499">
 <dc:title>WEBIST 2008</dc:title>
 <dc:description>Information about the WEBIST 2008 conference in Funchal,...
 <dc:description>
 <contains rdf:resource="http://groupme.org/GroupMe/resource/503/>
 <contains rdf:resource="http://groupme.org/GroupMe/resource/510"/>
 ...
 <foaf:maker>
  <foaf:Person rdf:about="http://groupme.org/GroupMe/user/fabian">
   <foaf:nick>fabian</foaf:nick>
   <rdfs:seeAlso rdf:resource="http://fabianabel.de/foaf.rdf"/>
  </foaf:Person>
 </foaf:maker>
 <tag:taggedWithTag>
  <tag:Tag rdf:about="http://groupme.org/GroupMe/tag/webist">
   <tag:name>cikm</tags:name>
  </tag:Tag>
 </tags:taggedWithTag>
 ...
</Group>
```

b. Flickr resource:

```
<foaf:Image rdf:about="http://groupme.org/GroupMe/resource/503">
 <dc:title>Madeira Island - Funchal</dc:title>
 <dc:publisher rdf:datatype="&xsd;anyURI">
   http://flickr.com
 </dc:publisher>
 <dc:contributor rdf:datatype="&xsd;anyURI">
   http://flickr.com/user/7677931@N02
 </dc:contributor>
 <rdfs:seeAlso
      rdf:resource="http://static.flickr.com/80/260324314_e2802c50e1.jpg"/>
 ...
 <tag:tag>
  <GroupMeTagAssignment rdf:about="http://groupme.org/GroupMe/tas/734">
   <tag:associatedTag rdf:resource="http://groupme.org/GroupMe/tag/web"/>
   <tag:taggedBy rdf:resource="http://groupme.org/GroupMe/user/fabian"/>
   <tag:taggedOn rdf:datatype="&xsd;date">2007-12-18T11:23:40</tag:taggedOn>
   <moat:meaning rdf:resource="http://dbpedia.org/resource/web/">
  </GroupMeTagAssignment>
 </tag:tag>
 ...
</foaf:Image>
```

c. Google Maps resource:

```
<foaf:Document rdf:about="http://groupme.org/GroupMe/resource/510">
 <dc:title>Napa Valley @ Google Maps</dc:title>
 <wsg84:lat rdf:datatype="&xsd;double">32.6488</wsg84:lat>
 <wsg84:long rdf:datatype="&xsd;double">-16.9063</wsg84:long>
 ...
</foaf:Document>
```

Fig. 3. RDF descriptions of Linked Data in the GroupMe! system

DELETE. Deletion of content is done via HTTP DELETE, e.g. in order to remove the tag assignment shown in Figure 3, an application has to send the HTTP DELETE request to *http://groupme.org/GroupMe/tas/734.*

The HTTP methods are therewith utilized in a way that conforms to HTTP and REST as well. In the current implementation of GroupMe! the POST, PUT, and DELETE operations can only be performed by the owner of a group, which is ensured via an authorization token that has to be included in the header of each corresponding HTTP request.

In general, the Semantic RESTful API of GroupMe! is very easy to use as it just exploits the semantics of HTTP and the semantics defined in the GroupMe! ontology. The API is already used by other applications. For example, [17] presents a GroupMe! client that – among other things – allows to enrich GroupMe! tag assignments with URIs, which describe the semantic meaning of a tag. There are various other possible applications that can be built on top of GroupMe!, e.g. geographical metadata attached to the Google Map in Figure 3 might be adequate for the Flickr image as well and could be utilized by another applications to retrieve photos by locations even if these photos are not directly annotated with geographic coordinates. At the moment we do not specify any rules, which define how the resources can benefit from the metadata of other resources they are grouped with, as we do not understand the *grouping behavior* of the users sufficiently. Applications that exploit GroupMe! data thus have to decide to which extent metadata of a resource is also appropriate for resources of the same group.

2.3   GroupMe! Folksonomy

In social tagging systems data is created by users (the folks), who assign freely chosen tags to resources ($\rightarrow$ *tag assignment*). The evolving collection of such tag assignments is called *folksonomy*[20]. In general, a folksonomy is formally defined using finite sets of users, tags and resources, and a finite set of tag assignments, whereas a tag assignment constitutes a triple of a certain user, tag and resource (cf. [16]). With GroupMe! we introduce a new concept to social tagging systems, namely groups.

Definition 1. *A* group *is a finite set of resources.*

A group is a resource as well. Hence, groups can contain groups, and groups can be tagged by users. With definition 1 we extend the formal definition of a folksonomy introduced in [10] as follows.

Definition 2. *A GroupMe! folksonomy is a 5-tuple* $\mathbb{F} := (U, T, \check{R}, G, \check{Y})$, *where:*

- *U, T, R, G are finite sets that contain instances of users, tags, resources, and groups, respectively,*
- *$\check{R} = R \cup G$ is the union of the set of resources and the set of groups, and*

---

[20] http://vanderwal.net/folksonomy.html

- $\breve{Y}$ *defines a* GroupMe! *tag assignment:* $\breve{Y} \subseteq U \times T \times \breve{R} \times (G \cup \{\varepsilon\})$, *where ε is a reserved symbol for the* empty group context, *i.e. a group that is not contained in another group when it gets tagged by a user.*

Thus, tagging of resources within the GroupMe! system is always done in context of a group, which itself may have tags. In comparison to traditional folksonomies, in which relations between tags mainly rely on their co-occurrences (i.e. two tags are assigned to the same resource), a GroupMe! folksonomy gains new relations between tags:

1. A relation between tags assigned from (possibly) different users to different resources, where the resources are contained in the same group.
2. A relation between tags assigned to a group g and tags assigned to resources that are contained in g.

Relations between resources become in GroupMe! folksonomies more explicit than in traditional folksonomies. In [4] we present ranking algorithms that exploit these new relations and improve the performance of existing folksonomy-based ranking algorithms significantly.

3 Evaluation

This section gives an analysis of the GroupMe! system, in particular on usage and tagging characteristics, and evaluates the effects of the structure given by the groups to search and retrieve resources. The data underlying the analysis was collected during the first three months after the system's launch on July 14, 2007. During the observed period, GroupMe! had a total of 502 resources of which 428 were normal resources and 74 (14.74%) were groups. 929 tag assignments were monitored, with 1.85 tags per resource in average. The overall evolution of resources and groups is given in Figure 4(a).

Interestingly, groups were tagged more extensively than ordinary resources: In average, 2.53 tags were assigned to groups, whereas only 1.73 tags were attached to other resources. Thus, groups were tagged 1.5 times more often than traditional resources.

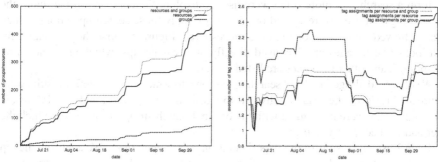

(a) Evolution of number of resources/groups. (b) Average number of tags assigned to resources/groups.

Fig. 4. Evolution of the GroupMe! folksonomy

Table 1. Percentage of resources' media types that are part of GroupMe! groups

Type of Resource	AVG Occurrences
images	41.01%
videos	8.57%
RSS feeds	4.55%
groups	1.87%
other Web resources	43.96%

This effect was present over time, as depicted in Fig. 4(b). Furthermore, at the end of the observed period only 17.57% of the groups were not annotated with any tag in contrast to 32.71% of the resources. These initial observations give support for the hypothesis that users adopt the group idea to organize Web resources, and that they also invest in groups by annotating them.

A typical group in GroupMe! consists of 4 – 8 resources. That we do not observe groups with significantly more members can be explained from the user interface, which gives the users a canvas to place and arrange the Web resources. As the size of this canvas is limited, the on-screen display of the group becomes impractical with too many Web resources. Users collect resources with different media types in their group, as can be seen in table 1. Most popular among the media types are images, followed by videos and RSS feeds. Web sites, academic papers, presentation slides, etc. are denoted as *other Web resources* and are not mentioned separately, because to users they appear as simple bookmarks, i.e. their visualization is not yet adapted to their media type particularly. The possibility to include groups into a group was only seldomly used, we explain this by the small number of available groups during the observation period.

3.1   Analysis of Search Behavior

To examine the effect of groups on search in social tagging systems, we analyzed the search behavior of the users. A *search operation* in our experiment was either a search performed via the search interface, or a search which was initiated whenever a user clicked on a tag in the tag cloud. Obviously, not all clicks on a tag were intended to perform a search, but more often were used to explore the tags, and in particular the popular tags. Hence, we restricted our data set to only those search operations, which were followed by at least one click on a resource. Figure 5 shows how a search result looks like. Images are displayed directly, whereas groups, which are denoted by *"(Group)"*, and other resources are listed textual.

We observed altogether 1747 search operations, to which in average 7.1 results were returned. 11.3% of the results delivered to a search were groups, and 53.11% of the returned results were not tagged with the original search string or the tag on which the user had clicked (*query string*).

Table 2 lists the results of our experiments on search operations. We analyzed the top k search results of each search operation and users' first click on a particular resource within the top k. The average percentage of groups that were part of the top k results was between 10.38% and 15.39%. However, the percentage of search operations, in which users clicked on groups was between 19.40% and 24.51%. For example, when

Fig. 5. Screenshot: typical search result list

Table 2. Analysis of the Top k search results: (1) percentage of groups contained in the top k search results, (2) percentage of users who clicked on groups in the top k search results, (3) percentage of resources and groups in the top k that were not tagged with the given query string, (4) percentage of clicks on untagged resources and untagged groups

Top k	Groups (1)	Group Clicks (2)	Untagged Resources (3)	Untagged Resource Clicks (4)
3	14.70%	19.40%	4.95%	14.93%
5	15.39%	21.69%	17.23%	15.66%
10	12.15%	22.34%	38.14%	21.28%
15	11.89%	22.45%	43.59%	23.47%
20	11.53%	23.00%	46.80%	25.00%
30	10.91%	24.51%	50.73%	25.49%
50	10.38%	24.27%	53.11%	26.21%

considering the top 10 search results, we observed that 12.15% of the results were groups but the percentage of *group clicks* was 1.84 times higher, namely 22.34%. Overall, normalization of resource and group clicks according to the number of resources and groups respectively reveals that groups were selected between 1.39 (Top 3) and 2.76 (Top 50) more frequent than ordinary resources. These observations support the hypothesis that groups itself constitute content users are interested in. The demand for groups is even higher than illustrated in Table 2 because groups can also be accessed using an explorative user interface different from the search interface. However, statistics of the explorative user interface, which has been utilized 271 times, are not considered within our search analysis.

An important benefit of the GroupMe! system is that it provides the ability to increase the recall of queries. For our experiments we implemented search and ranking algorithms that take advantage of the GroupMe! folksonomy model in order to return also resources and groups that are not directly tagged with the given *query string* (cf. Section 2.3). In general, such *untagged resources* are ranked lower than resources which are directly tagged with the given query string. This explains the big increase of the percentage of untagged resources when increasing k (see *Untagged* in Table 2). Table 2 also points out that untagged resources are also well-accepted by users. Considering the top 10, 38.14% of the search results were not tagged with the query string and in 21.28% of the search operations users first clicked on an untagged resource, thus on a resource that would not have been found in a traditional tagging system which just considers direct resource annotations. Consequently, the analysis of users' search operations validates two main hypotheses:

1. Users are interested in the new group concept: Groups are selected about two times more often than they occur within the search result list.
2. GroupMe!'s search and ranking strategies increase recall without reducing proportion of relevant resources remarkably: More than 20% of the clicks in the top 10 are performed on untagged resources and groups.

4   Related Work

GroupMe! is a social tagging system and competes with systems like BibSonomy, Delicious, or Flickr. Table 3 summarizes some characteristics of GroupMe! according to the dimensions in the *tagging system design taxonomy* developed in [14], and compares them with related tagging systems.

Table 3. GroupMe! tagging design in comparison to other social tagging systems. And user incentives in terms of tagging.

Dimension/System	GroupMe!	BibSonomy	Delicious	Flickr
Tagging rights	free-for-all	free-for-all	free-for-all	permission-based
Tagging support	blind/viewable	suggested	suggested	viewable
Aggregation model	bag	bag	bag	set
Object type	multimedia	textual	textual	images
Source of material	global	global	global	user-contributed
Social connectivity	links	links, groups	links	links
Resource connectivity	groups	none	none	groups
User incentives	- future retrieval - contribution - sharing - attract attention - self presentation	- future retrieval - contribution - sharing	- future retrieval - contribution - sharing - attract attention	- future retrieval - contribution - sharing - attract attention - self presentation

Tagging Rights. GroupMe! allows every user to tag everything (*free-for-all*) as this enables us to gather more tags about a resource and also a higher variety of keywords than in constrained systems. However, Flickr restricts tagging e.g. to the resource owner, friends, or contacts.

Tagging Support. When users annotate resources they are not supported with tag suggestions as this would limit the variety of tags. However, they have the ability to list tags that have already been assigned to a resource in context of the actual group. Tags, that have been assigned in context of other groups – and hence are possibly not appropriate in the actual group context – are not visible to the user when tagging (*blind/viewable*).

Aggregation Model. In comparison to Flickr, which does not allow for duplicated tags (*set*), GroupMe! allows different users to assign the same tag to a certain resource (*bag*). This may enable a better evaluation of the importance of the tags.

Object Type. GroupMe! is the only system listed in Table 3 that supports tagging of resources displayed in a multimedia fashion. Although systems like Delicious enable users to bookmark and tag arbitrary Web resources, they just visualize resources in a textual way. Hence, while tagging e.g. an image in Delicious, users usually do not see the image they tag.

Source of Material. Resources that can be annotated and grouped in GroupMe! are globally distributed over the Web, and referenced by their URL. This enables GroupMe! to handle often changing resources like RSS feeds appropriately: Whenever a group is accessed, the most recent versions of the contained resources are displayed.

Social Connectivity. All systems listed in Table 3 allow users to be linked together. GroupMe! does not provide integrated features, but utilizes users' FOAF descriptions in order to identify links between users.

Resource Connectivity. Independent of the users' tags, a few resource sharing systems provide other features to connect resources. There are some systems that allow users to organize themselves into groups, and that provide functionality to retrieve resources, which are related to these groups – e.g. BibSonomy or CiteULike[21]. However, to the best of our knowledge, Flickr and GroupMe! are at the moment the only notable tagging systems that enable users to assign resources to groups explicitly. Such hand-selected groups are highly valued by the users as indicated in our analysis (see Section 3.1).

User Incentives. GroupMe! users have several motivations to annotate resource ranging from simplification of future retrieval to self presentation (e.g. some users tag resources with *holiday* in order to express which locations they have visited).

What makes GroupMe! unique is that groups can be tagged and resources are always tagged in context of a specific group. Thereby, GroupMe! extends the traditional folksonomy model, which has been theorized in [15] or [16], and formalized in [10]. With the GroupMe! folksonomy model (see Section 2.3) new relations between resources, groups and tags emerge that can be exploited by search and ranking algorithms [2]. Search and ranking algorithms that operate on traditional folksonomies have already been successfully applied in order to improve Web search. In [5] the authors introduced *SocialSimRank*, which adapts *SimRank* [13] and computes similarity between tags and resources respectively. Furthermore, Bao et al. presented the *SocialPageRank* algorithm, which ranks Web resources according to how popular they are annotated. *FolkRank* [12] is another folksonomy-based search algorithm, which adapts the famous *PageRank* [18] algorithm and involves user preferences. In [3] we present algorithms, which exploit the GroupMe! folksonomy model, and show that they outperform the mentioned ranking algorithms.

Learning relations between tags is another challenge in social tagging systems that can be utilized to improve retrieval of resources additionally. Hotho et al. presented an

---

[21] http://www.citeulike.org

approach to mine association rules in folksonomies that point to subtag-supertag relations [11]. The GroupMe! folksonomy model provides a foundation to deduce such relations more precisely, e.g. by analyzing tags that have been assigned to a group and tags of group members. At the moment, instead of learning vague semantics, GroupMe! extracts semantic descriptions explicitly when new resources are added to a group. These descriptions can be utilized by other applications offhand via the RESTful Semantic Web interface of GroupMe! (cf. Section 2.2), which ensures higher interoperability than other systems like *CiteULike* or *BibSonomy* that just offer RSS export. GroupMe!'s RESTful Semantic Web interface also goes beyond the principles of Linked Data [6] like implemented in Revyu as it also enables applications to modify existing content or contribute new content to the system.

5   Conclusions

GroupMe! gives users the possibility to *group* Web resources in an easy way – by simple drag & drop operations – and combines this idea with features of social tagging systems. The evaluation of GroupMe! shows that users appreciate the grouping facility to organize Web resources they are interested in. Groups can be seen as *hand selected* collections of Web content for a certain topic or domain. As such, they are also valuable results to search queries, and our investigations have shown that users recognize this and select groups among the search results often.

The structure inherently given by the groups can also be used to infer information about the content of Web resources. The analysis of the search behavior of users revealed that exploitation of that information uncovers relevant content, which – with tagging alone – would not have been found. The RESTful Semantic Web interface transforms GroupMe! into a Social Semantic Web application and enables also other applications to benefit from the advanced GroupMe! features.

References

1. Abel, F.: The Benefit of additional Semantics in Folksonomy Systems. In: Proceedings of the 2nd Ph.D. Workshop in Seventeenth ACM Conference on Information and Knowledge Management (CIKM 2008), October 2008. ACM, New York (2008)
2. Abel, F., Frank, M., Henze, N., Krause, D., Plappert, D., Siehndel, P.: GroupMe! – Where Semantic Web meets Web 2.0. In: Aberer, K., Choi, K.-S., Noy, N., Allemang, D., Lee, K.-I., Nixon, L., Golbeck, J., Mika, P., Maynard, D., Mizoguchi, R., Schreiber, G., Cudré-Mauroux, P. (eds.) ASWC 2007 and ISWC 2007. LNCS, vol. 4825, pp. 871–878. Springer, Heidelberg (2007)
3. Abel, F., Henze, N., Krause, D.: Analyzing Ranking Algorithms in Folksonomy Systems. Technical report, L3S Research Center (2008)
4. Abel, F., Henze, N., Krause, D., Kriesell, M.: On the effect of group structures on ranking strategies in folksonomies. In: Workshop on Social Web Search and Mining at 17th Int. World Wide Web Conference (WWW 2008) (April 2008)
5. Bao, S., Xue, G., Wu, X., Yu, Y., Fei, B., Su, Z.: Optimizing Web Search using Social Annotations. In: Proc. of 16th Int. World Wide Web Conference (WWW 2007), pp. 501–510. ACM Press, New York (2007)

6. Berners-Lee, T.: Linked Data - design issues. Technical report, W3C (May 2007), http://www.w3.org/DesignIssues/LinkedData.html
7. Berners-Lee, T., Hendler, J., Lassila, O.: The Semantic Web. Scientific American 284(5), 34–43 (2001)
8. Fielding, R., Gettys, J., Mogul, J., Frystyk, H., Berners-Lee, T.: Hypertext. Transfer Protocol–HTTP/1.1 (rfc 2616) (June 1999)
9. Fielding, R.T., Taylor, R.N.: Principled design of the modern web architecture. In: Proc. of the 22nd Int. Conf. on Software Engineering (ICSE 2000), pp. 407–416. ACM Press, New York (2000)
10. Hotho, A., Jäschke, R., Schmitz, C., Stumme, G.: BibSonomy: A Social Bookmark and Publication Sharing System. In: Proc. First Conceptual Structures Tool Interoperability Workshop, Aalborg, pp. 87–102 (2006)
11. Hotho, A., Jäschke, R., Schmitz, C., Stumme, G.: Emergent Semantics in BibSonomy. In: Hochberger, C., Liskowsky, R. (eds.) Informatik 2006: Informatik für Menschen, Bonn, October 2006. LNI, vol. 94(2). GI (2006)
12. Hotho, A., Jäschke, R., Schmitz, C., Stumme, G.: FolkRank: A Ranking Algorithm for Folksonomies. In: Proc. of Workshop on Information Retrieval (FGIR), Germany (2006)
13. Jeh, G., Widom, J.: SimRank: A Measure of Structural-Context Similarity. In: Proc. of Int. Conf. on Knowledge Discovery and Data Mining (SIGKDD), Edmonton, Alberta, Canada, July 2002. ACM Press, New York (2002)
14. Marlow, C., Naaman, M., Boyd, D., Davis, M.: HT 2006, tagging paper, taxonomy, flickr, academic article, to read. In: Proc. of the 17th Conf. on Hypertext and Hypermedia, pp. 31–40. ACM Press, New York (2006)
15. Marlow, C., Naaman, M., Boyd, D., Davis, M.: Position Paper, Tagging, Taxonomy, Flickr, Article, ToRead. In: Collaborative Web Tagging Workshop at WWW 2006 (May 2006)
16. Mika, P.: Ontologies Are Us: A unified model of social networks and semantics. In: Gil, Y., Motta, E., Benjamins, V.R., Musen, M.A. (eds.) ISWC 2005. LNCS, vol. 3729, pp. 522–536. Springer, Heidelberg (2005)
17. Okon, E.: Entwurf und Implementierung einer Programmbibliothek zur semantischen Erweiterung von RESTful Web Services. Technical report, L3S Research Center (September 2008)
18. Page, L., Brin, S., Motwani, R., Winograd, T.: The PageRank Citation Ranking: Bringing Order to the Web. Technical report, Stanford Digital Library Technologies Project (1998)
19. Rattenbury, T., Good, N., Naaman, M.: Towards automatic extraction of event and place semantics from flickr tags. In: Proc. of the 30th Int. ACM SIGIR Conf. on Information Retrieval (SIRIR 2007), pp. 103–110. ACM Press, New York (2007)
20. Richardson, L., Ruby, S.: RESTful Web Services. O'Reilly, Sebastopol (2007)
21. Sauermann, L., Cyganiak, R., Völkel, M.: Cool URIs for the Semantic Web. Technical Memo TM-07-01, DFKI GmbH, Kaiserslautern (February 2007)

State-Transition Diagram for
Visual Programming Tool GUEST

Yuka Obu[1], Kazuhiro Maruo[1], Tatsuhiro Yonekura[2]
Masaru Kamada[2], and Shusuke Okamoto[3]

[1] Graduate School of Science and Engineering, Ibaraki University, Ibaraki, Japan
07nd301x@hcs.ibaraki.ac.jp, t44059f@hcs.ibaraki.ac.jp
[2] Department of Computer and Information Sciences, Ibaraki University, Ibaraki Japan
yone@mx.ibaraki.ac.jp, m.kamada@mx.ibaraki.ac.jp
[3] Department of Computer and Information Sciences, Seikei University, Tokyo Japan
okam@st.seikei.ac.jp

Abstract. Many people have been interested in Web 2.0, which is a new concept of Web service. Web sites became sources of information and functionality that enables users to create new content of their own. For this demand, more versatile browsers that enables users to edit and display content based on their creative concepts and preferences are required. Motivated by this demand, we have developed a state-transition diagram-based Web browser programming scheme that supports participatory Web use and enables end-user to interact with Web content. We implemented a prototype of our scheme called GUEST (Graphical User interface Editor by State-transition Diagram). GUEST enables users to define behaviors of a Web browser easily. However, there are some parts of complexity of user interfaces that prevent the users' intuitive understanding in the original version of GUEST. Therefore, in this paper, we focus on user interface, and introduce a new concept of the design.

Keywords: Visual programming, State-transition diagram, Web programming for non-programmers, GUEST (Graphical User interface Editor by State-transition Diagram), New user interface design concept.

1 Introduction

Many people have a great deal of interest over the last few years in the World Wide Web-based services referred to as Web 2.0. Web 2.0 is a new concept of Web services and Web utilization schemes that include a range of Web-related technologies, Web sites and services. One salient feature of Web 2.0 is the concept of the Web as a subjective participation platform. In marked contrast to the earlier Web service, where information was unilaterally delivered to users from isolated sites, Web 2.0 sites are sources of information and functionality that enable users to create new content of their own [1].

New demands have been placed on browsers by widespread use of this capability. They must display the information as it is provided from Web sites and enable users to customize it as they like. Users are now looking for more versatile browsers that will let them edit and display content based on their own creative concepts and preferences.

J. Cordeiro et al. (Eds.): WEBIST 2008, LNBIP 18, pp. 214–227, 2009.

Motivated by this demand, we have developed a state-transition diagram-based Web browser programming scheme that supports participatory Web functions and enables close interaction between the end-user and Web content. Our aim is to customize the content of the Web sites on the user side. Customizing means freely defining the action of the browser so users can browse a site as they like. For example, the user can browse content using mini windows, or, if there are links the user does not want to display, the user can make them disappear. The most important point of our scheme is actualization of these functions on the user side of the Web browser.

To implement this concept, we have developed GUEST (Graphical User interface Editor by State diagram) [2]. GUEST is a Firefox extension that enables users to define the behavior of the browser using a state-transition diagram. Our aim is for users of GUEST to be able to define functions easily even if they have no programming experience. However, there have been some aspects of GUEST that are not easy for beginners. That is, there are some complicated user interfaces that prevent the user from gaining an intuitive understanding of how to use GUEST. Hence we modified and improved some concepts of the design. Here, we introduce a new version of GUEST.

2   Visual Programming

Our objective is to develop Web browser programming capabilities that will enable ordinary non-technically oriented end-users to freely customize the behaviour of the browsers so they can edit and display Web content according to their own preferences.

2.1   State-Transition Diagram Model

To enable users to easily customize the behaviour of browsers, we used the state-transition diagram model. This has been used in object oriented software design and in development as a method of representing the relations between objects.

Basically, state-transition diagrams consist of circles representing states and arrows representing transitions. This model can be applied to many kinds of representations by relating an object to a state and changes under certain conditions to transitions. It is easy to represent something using circles and arrows. Ordinary end-users can comprehend state-transition diagrams more easily than programming languages. Our approach has the advantage of being intuitively easy to understand and easy for end-users to learn [3][4].

Researchers have long been engaged in study of state-transition diagram interfaces [5][6][7], and UML [8] is regarded as one type of state-transition diagram scheme. It is widely used in object oriented software design and development. In the UML-based approach, a line called the link represents the relationship between the objects. The state-transition diagram represents the behavior of each object [9]. UML has been developed for software design. UML has many kinds of diagrams to represent a system, and the state-transition diagram is one of them. The state-transition diagram of the UML is used to generalize and show the method to the event and the state of the object to each event.

Meanwhile, some kinds of state-transition diagram are developed in our project. These diagrams are not for showing generalized image of the relationship between objects. They are adapted for each particular purpose and show the action of the software.

For example, there are the state-transition diagrams for GUI, and interactive animation, and so on. The definition of the state and the transition are different and they are adapted for each purpose. By creating state-transition diagram specialized for each purpose, the best expression for each purpose can be achieved. It can be easy to convert into the source code, and it leads the early understanding of the source code.

2.2 Visual Programming with a State-Transition Diagram

Ordinary language-based programming requires a degree of expertise in a programming language and other specialized knowledge, but the vast majority of users of the Web today do not have these special skills. The programming methods that are available as tools today are poorly suited to enabling ordinary end-users to customize Web browsers that are a kind of application software.

This led us to pursue an alternative visual programming approach that is not based on language. Rather than words and language, visual programming uses a system of diagrams. Compared to language-based programming, this visual approach is far easier to learn (the grammatical rules are more intuitive), involves much less abstract thinking, and requires relatively little use of the keyboard, so it is well suited to the needs of ordinary end-users.

We have exploited these advantages to define a visual language model based on state-transition diagrams. The model defines the action of the content widget, which is a set of widgets for representing Web page content - that is, HTML tags and a style sheet. Using our model both clarifies exactly what is to be customized and helps the end-user understand what is going on. Combining the actions of the widgets in various ways enables a wide range of customization options.

In our programming scheme, the state of widget corresponds to the state of the state-transition diagram, and the action of the user corresponds to the transition. Using this model, a user can define the behaviour of the Web browser.

3   Related Researches

Islay, an interactive animation-authoring tool based on the state-transition diagram, was first proposed in 2005 [3][4]. Islay uses the modern paradigm of object oriented modelling and the classical state-transition diagram to make authoring interactive animation intuitively comprehensible. By using Islay, non-programmers can define the animation of the characters. As a side effect, the user may learn how to define dynamic objects while having fun with animation.

One of Mozilla Firefox's [10] extensions, Greasemonkey [11], is a tool that enables users to gain valuable experiences on the Web. The user writes Greasemonkey scripts, user JavaScripts, to change Web pages. User JavaScripts are executed every time the Web page is loaded and can utilize a full range of functions provided by Greasemonkey. This permits a wide range of customization: changing the layout of a Web page, adding functions to a Web page, and so on. Today, there are many user JavaScripts that have been made available on many Web sites. While these user JavaScripts support advanced customization, they require a high level of programming skill and a specialized knowledge of the Web that are far beyond the abilities of most ordinary end-users.

Platypus [12] is another Mozilla Firefox extension that enables users to modify a Web page from a browser called Platypus GUI and save the changes as a Greasemonkey user JavaScript. GUI enables ordinary end-users to easily customize Web pages. The main drawback of Platypus GUI is that it was designed to customize Web page layouts, so it cannot be used to customize the behavior of Web pages.

Chickenfoot [13] is another extension of this kind. Chickenfoot consists of a library that adds new commands for web automation to the browser's built-in JavaScript language. Chickenfoot has many commands, including pattern matching, form manipulation, and so on. The user inputs these commands and can also use the same variables available to JavaScript to define the behavior of the Web browser. The commands make defining the Web automation easier than the original JavaScript, but the user needs to have knowledge of the commands and JavaScript variables. Therefore, ordinary non-technically oriented end-users may not be able to intuitively comprehend how to use this extension.

Client-side tools and APIs have been developed by the SIMILE project [16]. Appalachian [17] and Piggy Bank [18] are Firefox extensions. Appalachian adds the ability to manage and use several OpenIDs to ease the login parts of a user's browsing experience. Piggy Bank turns a Web browser into a mash-up platform, by enabling a user to extract data from different web sites and mix it together. It also allows the user to store extracted information locally so it can be searched later and to exchange the collected information with others on demand. Timeplot [19], TimeLine [20], and Exhibit [21] are APIs that enable users to create rich content on a Web page. By using these APIs, the user can create interactive widgets on a Web page. The user does not have to know database or complicated web application technologies.

In addition to these programs, we have developed GUEST (Graphical User interface Editor by State diagram). GUEST is a Firefox extension that enables users to define the behavior of the browser using a state-transition diagram. Using GUEST, the user can define behaviors easily even if he or she has no programming experience.

4   GUEST

4.1   Overview

To solve some of the problems that related programs suffer from, we developed a Web visual programming system called GUEST (Graphical User interface Editor by State diagram), which is a Mozilla Firefox browser extension [10].

Mozilla Firefox is a Web browser developed by the Mozilla Foundation that supports plug-in and add-on program packages called extensions. For Firefox extensions, algorithms are written in JavaScript and GUIs are written in XUL[14]. Because the majority of Firefox operations can be controlled from extensions, the process of designing and developing software has been minimized, creating an original Web browser.

Fig. 1 shows a schematic overview of how GUEST works. An overview is also presented in list form below.

1. The user first describes the desired Web browser behavior by editing on the state-transition diagram editor.

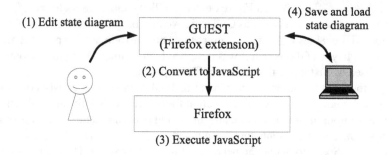

Fig. 1. Schematic overview of how GUEST works

2. The GUEST automatically converts the state-transition diagram to JavaScript
3. The newly defined behavior is executed to the Web content by the Mozilla Firefox Web browser. The defined behaviors are executed every time the page is loaded.
4. The state-transition diagram can be saved and loaded, and the state-transition diagram can be rewritten. The rewritten state-transition diagram is converted to JavaScript, and the user can choose which JavaScript should be executed.

4.2 Functions

GUEST consists of three basic elements: a state-transition diagram editor that generates state-transition diagrams, a conversion function that converts state-transition diagrams to JavaScript, and a file function that saves and reloads the diagrams.

State-transition Diagram Editor.   Fig. 2 shows a typical screenshot of the state-transition diagram editor: widgets (tags) that construct the Web page are listed in the left side bar, the upper right area is the edit window, and the lower right is a browser window.

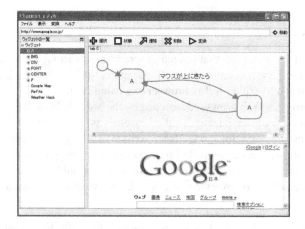

Fig. 2. Screenshot of state-transition diagram editor

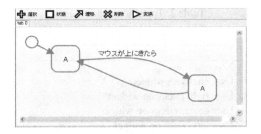

Fig. 3. Screenshot focused on state-transition diagram shown in Fig. 2

A screenshot focused on the state-transition diagram in Fig. 2 is shown in Fig. 3. States are represented by the little squares, and transitions are represented by arrows. The little circle in the upper left corner of the screen in Fig. 3 signifies the initial state of the state-transition diagram. The labels in the state boxes are the state names, and the labels shown alongside transition arrows represent transition conditions. In this figure, the state name is the anchor tag, and the condition of the transition means mouse-over. States include the definition of the action of the label. In Fig. 3, the state on the left has no action, and the state on the right has an action that hides the tag. Consequently, the state-transition diagram in Fig. 3 means that, if the mouse is over the anchor tag, the tag is hidden.

Tables 1 and 2 show the list of action and conditions that can be used in the state-transition diagram editor. By using these actions and conditions in the state-transition diagram, the user can define the behavior as in the following example.

- If the user mouses over the anchor tag, the tag is hidden.
- If the user double clicks the anchor tag, he link opens on a new window.
- If the mouse is over the images, a message box pops up.
- If the mouse is over the anchor tags, mini windows open, displaying the content at the link.

JavaScript Conversion Function. In the conversion from the state-transition diagram to JavaScript program, states are converted to functions (one to one), and the transitions

Table 1. Actions used in states

Actions
No action
Show tag
Hide tag
Show an alert message box
Send message to another edit tab
Load content of link
Open content of link on new browser's tab
Open content of link in mini window
Save image

Table 2. Transition conditions

Conditions
No condition
User clicks on widget
User right clicks on widget
User center clicks on widget
User left clicks on widget
User double clicks on widget
Mouse is over widget
Mouse is moved to side of widget
After several times
After receiving message from another tab
After successful action

are converted to function pointers. This simplifies the automatic conversion of state-transition diagrams to JavaScript.

Part of the script that is converted from the state-transition diagram shown in Fig. 3 is shown below.

```
function gst_dia0(){
    gst_initTag(gAh);
    gst_startDia(ggst_dia0h,gst_st0_0);
}
function gst_st0_0(act){
    if(act){    return;    }
    if(gst_tagObjectList["A"].mouseover) {
        gst_statePointer["gst_dia0"] = gst_st0_1;
        return;    }
}
function gst_st0_1(act) {
    if(act){
        gst_tagObjectList["A"].hideTag(true);
        gst_tagObjectList["A"].setSuccess();
        return;    }
    {    gst_statePointer["gst_dia0"] = gst_st0_0;
        return;    }
}
function gst_startup() {
    gst_dia0();
    gst_startGuestScheduler();
    return;
}
function gst_checkevent() {
    var checklist=new Object();
    checklist['mouseover']='check';
    return checkList;
}
```

GUEST loads and executes the converted JavaScript. GUEST has original libraries to execute actions and conditions. However, the user does not need to consider the JavaScript or the function that controls the behavior of the Web browser. The only thing the user has to do is to edit the state-transition diagram.

State-transition Diagram Save and Load Functions.   GUEST uses Resource Description Framework [15] as the format for state-transition diagram permanent files. RDF is an XML language that describes the metadata of the resources. Therefore, we can describe information such as headlines of articles and other kinds of metadata. RDF has the advantages of reducing the implementation burden and providing a generic permanent file format.

The data stored in the RDF files includes:

1. **State-related data.** State attributes (types of tags, actions, etc.), coordinates of state image in diagrams, names, and so on.
2. **Transition-related data.** Transition attribute (types of events, etc.), coordinates of transition images in diagrams, control points (Bezier curves), names, and so on.
3. **State diagram-related data.** List of state transitions included in state-transition diagrams, URLs of pages for which diagrams have been generated, names, and so on.

By using these RDF files, the user can re-construct the behavior of the Web browser.

5   New Concept of User Interface

5.1   Some GUEST Issues

Because GUEST users do not need to consider the programming language, GUEST's functions may, to some degree, be user-friendly. However, some aspects of the program are not easy for real beginners to use.

1. **The attribute of the state.** In a state-transition diagram edited as in Fig. 3, a state has two attributes. The state name (label of the box) indicates the widget whose action is defined, and the action of the widget is defined simultaneously in a state. However, the user cannot intuitively recognize that the action of the widget is defined. For example even if the action is to hide the tag or to show an alert message box, there are no differences in the appearances. Therefore, we needed to reconsider the attribute of the state.
2. **The meaning of the initial transition.** Fig. 4 shows the initial state of the state-transition editor. As can be seen, there is only a circle indicating an initial transition. The user has to connect the circle with the first state using an arrow. We gave some non-programming users a trial use of GUEST as an experiment. Our observation of the trial showed that users had difficulty understanding the initial transition.
3. **The relation between tag and Web page.** In the state-transition diagram editor, there are lists of the widgets (tags) and the Web browser area. Because the position of the widget is not indicated in the Web browser area, however, the user cannot comprehend the relation between a widget and an appearance on the Web. We had to solve that problem.

Fig. 4. Screenshot of initial state of editor

4. **The function of the tab.** The state-transition diagram editor has the function of a tab. The user can edit the state-transition diagram on some tabs, and then the results are converted into one JavaScript file. And some messages can be sent from one tab to another tab, but this function is rarely used because it is a bit hard to understand, and the concept of the function is not clear.

Considering these issues, we changed some of the user interface design.

5.2 Modification of User Interface

Until now, an object and an action at the same time have always been defined in one state. In our new design concept, we considered an action as a state, and arranged the design as follows:

- A state is redefined as an action of the widget.
- The object whose action is defined by a state-transition diagram is a widget (a tag on a Web page). The action of one widget is defined on one tab. This enables control of the relation between a widget and a state-transition diagram.
- The meaning of the transition condition stays unchanged in the current version of GUEST.
- An initial state that indicates a default status is created instead of a circle and an arrow indicating an initial transition in Fig. 4.
- Tab names are changed from tab0 (tab1, tab2. and so on) to the name of the widget (Image, link, etc.).

Fig. 5 shows an image of these changes. Fig. 6 shows new expression of the state-transition diagram. As can be seen, since each tab handles a widget in a Web page, the relationship between the state-transition diagrams and the object is comprehensible. Moreover, because that relationship will be clearer than in the current version of GUEST, the user is more easily able to intuitively understand.

5.3 Message Passing between Tabs

GUEST has a function that sends messages between tabs. The new user interface design shown in Fig. 5 makes it more useful in passing messages. Using tabs to handle each widget makes message passing between objects more understandable.

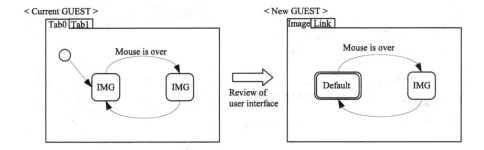

Fig. 5. Image of new user interface

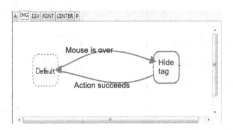

Fig. 6. New expression of the state-transition diagram

A tab, labelled 'A', 'IMG', 'DIV', and so on, indicates an object of actions defined by a state-transition diagram. Messages that relate actions of each object are sent from one tab to another tab. This enables users to comprehend intuitively of the relationship between messages and widgets, or the relationship between each object. Furthermore, in message passing, the timing of the event occurrence is important. This is because the message receiving is a trigger of the next action in a state-transition diagram. In this new user interface, since one object is handled on one tab, the distance and the timing of the message passing is clear. The new tab usage and new expression of state-transition diagram is well adapted to define a state-transition diagram with message passing.

As an advanced usage, this message passing is very useful for definition of a communication between APIs, such as Ajax message.

Fig. 7 shows how messages are passed between tabs. As can be seen for example, when a button is clicked, data is retrieved from the other Web page by Ajax communication. Messages are sent between tabs that indicates the object, such as button, image, page. When the page tab receives the message from the button tab, Ajax message is sent to the other web page. Then, after an image is retrieved by Ajax, a message is sent to the image tab, on the image tab, retrieved image is displayed. By passing messages between tabs, the user can define more interactive behavior.

Fig. 8 shows an example of the state-transition diagram with message passing using Web APIs. In usage of the message passing for Web APIs, each API is set on a tab. In Fig. 8, for example, Web APIs, Google Map, ReFITS Lab, and Weather Hacks, are used. With Google Map API, latitude and longitude can be retrieved. With ReFITS Lab API, the name of the location can be retrieved from latitude and longitude. And with

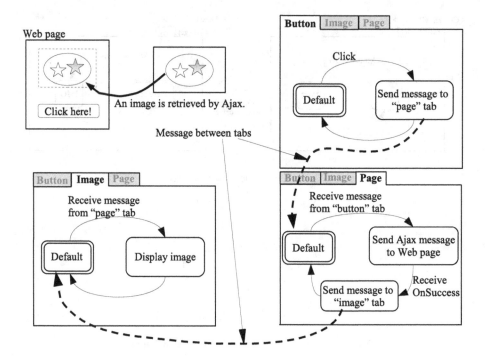

Fig. 7. Behavior of message passing between tabs

Weather Hacks API, weather can be retrieved from the location. The definition of the state-transition diagram with message passing enables to create mash-up behavior of these Web APIs.

As can be seen in Fig. 8, latitude and longitude are retrieved from Google Map, then a message with the latitude and longitude is sent to ReFITS Lab tab. On the ReFITS Lab tab, the name of the location is retrieve from longitude and latitude. And then, a message with the name of location is sent to Weather Hacks tab. On the Weather Hacks tab, the weather is retrieved and a message is sent to the Google Map tab. Then the weather is displayed.

This behavior is that when the user clicks on the map, the weather is displayed on the map. From this definition of the state-transition diagram, user can create the behavior, that the weather is displayed by user's click on the map.

By handling one API as one object, the communication of the data between APIs by the message passing is achieved.

5.4   The Scale of the State-Transition Diagram

GUEST employed a state-transition diagram to define behaviors of Web browser. Here, if the defined behavior becomes complex, there is some degree of concern that the complexity in the state transition chart will increase. Hence, we had set an simple investigation about the scale of the stat-transition diagram that defines the behavior of the browser.

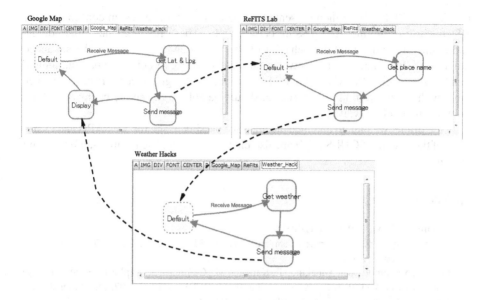

Fig. 8. Example of the state-transition diagram with message passing

For case study of the relationship between the complexity of state-transition diagram and richness of behavior, the number of the state and transition when the following three behavior was defined was counted.

Behavior 1. When the mouse pointer is on an image, the image is hided.
Behavior 2. When the mouse pointer is on links, contents are displayed on the mini window.
Behavior 3. When the map is clicked, the weather of the location is displayed on the mini window. (This is an advanced usage of GUEST using Ajax.)

In the first two cases in above, the number of the state is 2, and the number of the transition is 2. In case of the last one, the advanced usage of Ajax mash-up with message passing, the number of the state is 7, and the number of the transition is 7. In this case, 3 state-transition diagrams are created and for each state-transition diagram has 2 or 3 state and transition respectively.

When the message passing function is used, the state-transition diagram is somewhat complex. But this does not prevent the intuitive comprehension of the state-transition diagram, because the object of the action is clear and the relationship of the message and the object still remains simple.

6   Conclusions

We discussed visual Web browser programming tool, GUEST (Graphical User interface Editor by State diagram), using a state-transition diagram model and presented a proto-type of our scheme. We also discussed difficulties of user interface that the users face in using the GUEST. We then presented the new user interface design concept and the effective use of the message passing between tabs. These functions help users define and intuitively understand the behavior of the Web browser. Moreover, the advanced usage of the message passing between tab enables users to define Ajax communication between Web APIs. Using GUEST with our new design concept, more users, even those with no programming experience, should be able to define the behavior of Web browsers more effectively.

In the future, we plan to enhance the message passing usage for Web APIs and evaluation of the system of GUEST. We are also planning to experiment with usability testing by end-users.

References

1. O'reilly, T.: What Is Web 2.0 (2005),
   `http://www.oreillynet.com/pub/a/oreilly/tim/news/2005/09/30/what-is-web-20.html`
2. Obu, Y., Yamamoto, M., Yonekura, T., Kamada, M., Okamoto, S.: Exploring State-transition diagram-based Web Browser Programming. In: CYBERWORLDS 2007, International Conference on Cyberworlds, Cyberworlds Press (2007)
3. Okamoto, S., Kamada, M., Nakao, T.: Proposal of an Interactive Animation Authoring Tool Based on State-transition diagram. Information Processing Society of Japan. No.SIG 1(PRO24), vol. 46, pp. 19–27 (2005) (in Japanese)
4. Okamoto, S., Shimomura, T., Kamada, M., Yonekura, T.: Programming with Islay. An Interactive Animation Authoring Tool, vol. 47, No.SIG 6(PRO29). Information Processing Society of Japan (2006) (in Japanese)
5. Jacob, R.J.K.: Using Formal Specifications in the Design of a Human-Computer Interface. Communications of the ACM 26(4), 259–264 (1983)
6. Jacob, R.J.K.: A Specification Language for Direct Manipulation User Interfaces. ACM Transactions on Graphics 5(4), 283–317 (1986)
7. Harel, D.: Statecharts: A Visual Formalism for Complex Systems. Sci. Compt. Programming (8), 231–274 (1987)
8. Object Management Group, OMG'S Unified Modeling Language,
   `http://www.omg.org/`
9. Kendall, S.: UML Explained, Pearson Education Japan, 4th edn., Tokyo (2003)
10. Mozilla org., Mozilla Firefox,
    `http://mozilla.jp/firefox/`
11. Greasemonkey, `http://greasemonkey.mozdev.org/`
12. Platypus, `http://platypus.mozdev.org/`
13. Bolin, M., Webber, M., Rha, P., Wilson, T., Miller, R.C.: Automation and Customization of Rendered Web Pages. In: ACM Conference on User Interface Software and Technology, UIST, pp. 163–172 (2005)
14. Mozilla Foundation, XUL, `http://www.mozilla.org/projects/xul/`
15. World Wide Web Consortium, Resource Description Framework,
    `http://www.w3.org/RDF/`
16. SIMILE Project, `http://simile.mit.edu/`
17. Appalachian, `http://simile.mit.edu/wiki/Appalachian`
18. Huynh, D., Mazzocchi, S., Karger, D.: Piggy Bank - Experience the Semantic Web Inside Your Web Browser. In: Gil, Y., Motta, E., Benjamins, V.R., Musen, M.A. (eds.) ISWC 2005. LNCS, vol. 3729, pp. 413–430. Springer, Heidelberg (2005)

19. Timeplot, http://www.simile-widgets.org/timeplot/
20. TimeLine, http://www.simile-widgets.org/timeline/
21. Huynh, D., Karger, D., Miller, R.: Exhibit - Lightweight Structured Data Publishing. In: International World Wide Web Conference. ACM, New York (2007) 978-1-59593-654-7/07/0005

Mashups over the Deep Web

Thomas Hornung, Kai Simon, and Georg Lausen

Institut für Informatik, Universität Freiburg, Georges-Köhler-Allee, Gebäude 51, 79110
Freiburg i.Br., Germany
{hornungt,ksimon,lausen}@informatik.uni-freiburg.de

Abstract. Combining information from different Web sources often results in a
tedious and repetitive process, e.g. even simple information requests might require to iterate over a result list of one Web query and use each single result as
input for a subsequent query. One approach for this chained queries are data-
centric mashups, which allow to visually model the data flow as a graph, where
the nodes represent the data source and the edges the data flow.

In this paper we combine the benefits of such an intuitive graphical modeling
framework for these chained queries with the large class of Web data sources that
are only accessible by filling out forms. These so-called Deep Web sites offer a
wealth of structured, high-quality data but pose also several challenges. We identify and address the main challenges and propose an integrated framework for
answering chained queries.

Keywords: Data-centric mashups, Deep web, Chained queries.

1 Introduction

Aggregating information about a specific topic on the Web can easily result in a frus-
trating and time-consuming task, when the relevant data is spread over multiple Web
sites. Even in a simple scenario, if we try to process the request *"What are the best-
rated movies which are currently in theaters nearby?"* it might be necessary to first
query one Web site for a list of all movies and then iteratively fill out a search form
for each result on another site to find ratings for each movie. For these ad hoc queries
the freshness of the data is of paramount importance, e.g. the user is only interested in
movies that are *currently* shown in theaters.

Answering these queries with traditional search engines is not feasible for several
reasons. First, they do not support the idea of *query chaining*, i.e. using the result set of
a subquery as input for subsequent queries. Second, they (usually) only cover the part
of the Web that is reachable by following links. However, the major part of the Web
consists of dynamically generated result pages of numerous databases, which can only
be queried interactively via Web forms. The amount of data in this *Deep* or *Hidden
Web* [1] is growing exponentially and covers a great subject diversity [2]. To access
this high-quality information in a uniform way, several different proposals have been
made for (meta) search engines that are tailored for these kind of sources, e.g. [3] and
[4] offer a single interface for searching multiple data sources in a specific domain.
Another approach is taken in [5]: here multiple data sources from different domains can
be queried.

J. Cordeiro et al. (Eds.): WEBIST 2008, LNBIP 18, pp. 228–241, 2009.

However, users often may have a clear conception of how to solve the problem in terms of the query order of data sources, but do not want to go through the tedious routine of executing each step in the query process manually. A promising approach for specifying these *query tasks* are mashup tools such as Yahoo Pipes[1], which offer a graphical interface to arrange different machine-accessible data sources in a graph, where nodes represent data sources and arcs model the data flow. This enables users with little or no programming skills to intuitively aggregate information in an ad hoc fashion.

In this paper we take the concept of data mashups to realize chained queries on Deep Web data sources, thus combining the benefits of a graphical query framework with the wealth of existing high-quality data sources. The rest of the paper is structured as follows: Section 2 presents the challenges involved in building such an application and Section 3 presents our running example, which is used throughout the remainder of the paper. Afterwards, we detail the access to Deep Web sources in Section 4 and the combination of these sources into mashup graphs in Section 5. Finally, we introduce our system architecture and present the execution of mashup graphs with special consideration for the limiting factors of an online Web scenario in Section 6, discuss related work in Section 7 and conclude with Section 8.

2   Challenges

Deep Web data sources are essentially databases with a limited, human-oriented query interface. Additionally, the results are not easily accessible in a machine-readable format but the results are only available as plain HTML pages that exhibit some kind of structure and are usually based on a template that is filled with the query answers.

More specifically, we have to consider the following issues for realizing chained queries:

- *Form interaction:* In order to fill out the respective form fields, the user input has to be matched to a legal combination of input element assignments. Here, different constraints can be enforced by the Web form, i.e. some value combinations might not be legal. Another problem is that it might be necessary to navigate through a series of intermediate pages to reach a result page. Due to space limitations we ignore these constraints and assume a single stage interaction, i.e. the form field is filled out with meaningful value combinations and submitted, which directly leads to the result page. For a more detailed discussion of Web form interaction issues and Deep Web navigation we refer the interested reader to [6].
- *Data record extraction and labeling:* Each result page usually contains multiple data records which cluster related information, similar to a row in a labeled table. These data records need to be identified, extracted and labeled correctly. For this purpose we use the fully automated Web data extraction tool ViPER [7,8].
- *Fuzzy result lists:* A formally data-centric Web API always returns exact results, i.e. if more than one result is returned, all results are known to be equally relevant. However Deep Web sources can return a list of results that match the input criteria to some extent, often ranked by relevance.

---

[1] http://pipes.yahoo.com/pipes/

- *Data cleaning:* For each column of a data record the correct data type has to be determined and the data has to be transformed into a canonical representation, e.g. to bridge different representations of numbers. Additionally it might be necessary to convert the data to another reference system, for instance another currency.
- *Assisted mashup generation:* Manually combining different data sources to a mashup graph is only feasible in a small world-scenario, because the user easily looses track of possible and meaningful combinations. Therefore, a ranking criterion for possible input data sources is desirable.
- *Combinatorial explosion:* If we chain data sources, each subsequent data source needs to be queried with all (meaningful) combinations found so far. These query combinations are computed as a combination of the results of the data sources that are connected with an incoming data edge. As we will see in the remainder of this paper, this can lead to a combinatorial explosion in possible value combinations. E.g. let data source Q_3 be the sink in a mashup graph with two incoming data edges from sources Q_1 and Q_2. For an exhaustive search we would have to query Q_3 with $|Q_1| * |Q_2|$ value combinations[2], or in the general case for a data mashup graph with one sink and n incoming data edges $\Pi_{i=1}^{n} |Q_i|$ value combinations need to be considered. Moreover, a typical data mashup graph would more likely have multiple levels as the one shown in Figure 1, which means that the combinations additionally multiply along each path as well.

In the next section we present the running example scenario before we address the abovementioned issues in the following sections.

3   Purchase Decision Support Mashup

When planning to buy an electronic device, it is often desirable to aggregate information from several trustworthy sources considering different aspects. It might for instance not be advisable to buy the device at the store that offers the cheapest price, if the customer service is disappointing. Therefore the user wants to define a mashup graph that assembles the necessary information based on the following Deep Web sources:

- Source Q_1 is the official Web site of a trustworthy magazine, which regularly performs extensive tests of new electronic devices and publishes the results on the Web site,
- Source Q_2 is a searchable, community-driven Web portal with user experience-based ratings and reviews of Web retailers,
- Source Q_3 is an online database of Web retailers and their addresses, searchable by the name of the store,
- Source Q_4 is a route and map service, and
- Source Q_5 is a price comparison service which searches multiple stores for the cheapest price of electronic devices.

Figure 1 shows a mashup graph that yields the desired results. The user is presented with an interface where she can enter the required data that is needed to initialize the

---

[2] Here $|Q_i|$ denotes the number of results of data source Q_i.

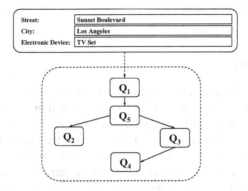

Street:	Sunset Boulevard
City:	Los Angeles
Electronic Device:	TV Set

Fig. 1. Data mashup graph that collects data about TV sets

mashup. First Q_1 is accessed to find the best-rated TV sets and then for each TV set the cheapest stores are determined by Q_5. Afterwards Q_2 and Q_3 are queried in parallel to obtain reviews and addresses for each store and finally Q_4 computes the distance between the initially entered address and each store. As a result the user is presented with a tabular view of the aggregated data and can now decide which TV set meets her desired criteria best.

4   Accessing Deep Web Sources

Generally, Deep Web pages offer a Web form interface with limited query capabilities, where the user has to provide slotted information and gets back an HTML page containing the query results. Because of these limited query interface they are also called *data sources with limited access patterns* [9] and can be compared to basic SQL queries[3]:

```
SELECT out1, ..., outn
FROM database-rel1, ..., database-rell
WHERE in1 =  v1 AND ... AND ink = vk
```

Here, the in1, ..., ink correspond to the attributes of the input form, while v1, ..., vk correspond to the provided values by the user and the out1, ..., outn to the attributes of each result row. Therefore, we can describe each Deep Web data source as the tuple (I, O) where I is the set of input attributes and O is the set of attributes of each result row, e.g. the data source Q_1 could be described as follows: ({Device-Type}, {Device-Name, Picture, Rating, ... }). Unfortunately, this *signature* can often not be derived automatically, especially the attributes of each result row may not be given at all (e.g. in the case of a picture). We call this in the following the *intrinsic signature* of a data source.

   We now introduce the notion of a *user vocabulary* that has been inspired by the idea of social bookmarking. The underlying idea is to match the relevant part of the

---

[3] In a real world scenario, there might also be an ORDER BY clause and more elaborate comparison operators, such as > or ≠.

vocabulary to the intrinsic signature of the data source by labeling the relevant elements in the HTML page.

4.1 User Vocabulary

Social bookmarking is based on the concept of labeling arbitrary things, e.g. Web pages with words, so-called tags. Because we are also interested in the data type of each attribute, we use an ontology of these tags based on an RDFS [10] vocabulary. In this vocabulary each tag is associated with a URI, which is the unique ID of the tag, a label and an XML data type [11]. The user can generate new tags any time during the labeling process and can thereby successively build up her own terminology. The associated data type is used for data cleaning purposes and to check that only meaningful comparison operators are used in the final mashup (cf. Section 5). As a means to organize the vocabulary the user can specify relationships between different tags based on the built-in RDFS predicates rdfs:sameAs (if two tags refer to the same concept) and rdfs:subClassOf (if one tag is more specific than the other).

4.2 Deep Web Query Interfaces

To enable easy and accurate labeling of input attributes the relevant tags can be dragged to the elements of the selected form. The same has to be done for the result page. For this purpose we use the data extraction system ViPER [7], which suggests identified data regions with decreasing importance to the user based on visual information. In general the foremost recommendation meets the content of interest and thus is suggested by default. On the other hand it is also possible to opt for a different region if desired. Regardless of the selection the extraction system always tries to convey the structured data into a tabular representation. This rearrangement enables to automatically clean the data and serves as a comfortable representation for labeling. Again, the user can label the data by dragging tags of her personal vocabulary as depicted in Figure 2[4]; this time to the columns of the resulting table consisting of extracted instances. The picture at the top in Figure 2 shows an excerpt of the original Web page and the tabular representation at the bottom shows the relevant part of the ViPER rendition of this page. The arrows indicate the tags the user has dragged to the column headers. Having in mind that the data originates from a backend database the extraction and cleaning process can be seen as reverse engineering on the basis of materialized database views published in HTML. For the data cleaning process the rule-based approach presented in [8], which allows to fine-tune the extraction and cleaning of data from structured Web pages, is used.

The assigned tags constitute the operational characteristics of a data source. We additionally consider two other properties: the average response time, denoted t_{avg}, and the maximum number of possible parallel invocations of the data source, denoted k.

We can determine t_{avg} by measuring the response time of a source over the last N uses and then taking the geometric mean, i.e. $t_{avg} := \sqrt[N]{\Pi_{i=1}^{N} t_i}$. Here, t_1 is the response time of the last invocation, t_2 the response time of the invocation before that and so

---

[4] The vocabulary is depicted as tag cloud [12] based on the frequency of the used tags.

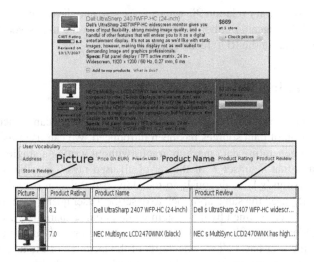

Fig. 2. User-defined vocabulary, depicted as tag cloud

on, and N denotes the size of the considered execution history, e.g. ten. We initially set $t_{avg} := \infty$.

Since each data source is essentially a relational DB with a form-based query interface, which is designed to handle requests in parallel, we can invoke a Deep Web data source multiple times with different input parameters in parallel. Obviously, the number of parallel executions needs to be limited by an upper bound, because otherwise we would perform a Denial of Service attack on the Web source. To assure this, we set $k := 3$ for all data sources for now, but we are working on a heuristic to update k to reflect the capabilities of the underlying data source more faithfully. In the remainder of the paper the following more formal definition of a data source is used:

Definition 1. (Data Source). A data source Q_i is the quintuple $(\mathfrak{I}, \mathfrak{O}, k, t_{avg}, d)$, where $\mathfrak{I}$ is the set of tags that have been dragged to input attributes and $\mathfrak{O}$ is the set of tags that have been dragged to columns in the tabular representation of the result page[5], k is the maximum number of parallel invocations, t_{avg} is the average response time, and d is a short description of the data source.

The provided input arguments of a data source are used to fill out the form, which is then submitted. The data records contained in the result page are then extracted, cleaned and returned as RDF triples [13]. Generally, an RDF graph is defined as a set of triples $\text{stmt}_i := (s_i, p_i, o_i)$, where the subject s_i stands in relation p_i with object o_i. In the following we use $\text{stmts}(s_i) = \{\text{stmt}_1, \ldots, \text{stmt}_n\}$ to denote the set of triples where the subject is identical to s_i, akin to the definition of an individual proposed in [14]. Similarly, $\pi_2(\text{stmts}(s_i)) := \{p_i \mid (s_i, p_i, o_i) \in \text{stmts}(s_i)\}$ is the set of all RDF properties of an individual. In the remainder of the paper, we use the notation $\pi_i(\mathfrak{R})$ to project to

---

[5] For each tag in $\mathfrak{I}$ there is a corresponding label in I of the intrinsic signature of the data source and likewise for $\mathfrak{O}$.

the ith position of an n-ary relation $\mathfrak{R}$, where $1 \leq i \leq n$, and the terms tag and property will be used interchangeably either to identify an item in the user's vocabulary or to denote its counterpart in the RDF result graph.

5   Graphical Modeling of Chained Queries

The previous section has illustrated how Deep Web data sources can be accessed and a more formal notion of data sources has been introduced. We can use this information to assist users in generating data mashup graphs without writing a single line of code. The basic idea is that a subset T of the set of all used tags $\mathfrak{T}$ can be interpreted as properties of $\pi_2(\text{stmts}(s_i))$ analogously to the Universal Relation paradigm presented in [15]. In fact, [5] used the same approach to describe a user query, with the difference that the attributes were defined by the system while in our scenario the user can utilize her own vocabulary. This alleviates the unique role assumption[6] in our case to some extent because the user has a clear conception of the meaning of the tag. Additionally since we assist the user in incrementally building a mashup graph she can incrementally define and further decide on the intended meaning of the query by selecting appropriate sources.

Figure 3 illustrates the mashup generation process. The user first drags the desired tags into the goal tags pane (shown at the bottom). Here she can additionally specify the desired constraints, e.g. that the price should be smaller than 450 EUR. Based on

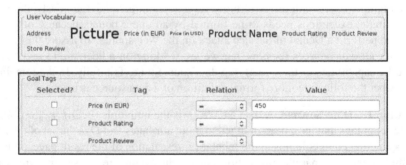

Fig. 3. Excerpt of a result specification for an electronic device

these goal tags, the system assists her in choosing data sources that can contribute to the desired results. By clicking on each start tag the system recommends relevant input data sources. She can select the ones she prefers and then iteratively refine the mashup by invoking the recommendation function for each input data source again. When she is satisfied with the generated data mashup graph, the system collects all missing input attributes. These constitute the global input for the data mashup and are shown in the box above the mashup graph in Figure 1. After finishing the mashup generation, the user can store the generated mashup graph for future use as well.

---

[6] The name of a tag unambiguously determines a concept in the real world.

Each time the user invokes the recommendation system, a ranked list of the best matching data sources is computed and shown based on the coverage of input arguments and the utilization frequency in the past. More formally, let $Q_{selected}$ denote the selected data source. Thereby, the rank of each data source with respect to $Q_{selected}$ can be computed as follows:

Definition 2. (QI Rank). $R(Q_i) := w_1 * \text{coverage}(Q_i) + w_2 * \text{utilization}(Q_i)$, where:

- coverage$(Q_i) := \frac{|\text{ext}(\pi_2(Q_i)) \cap \pi_1(Q_{selected})|}{|\pi_1(Q_{selected})|}$; $\text{ext}(T)$ expands the original set of tags T with all tags that are either equal or more specific with respect to the user's vocabulary,
- utilization$(Q_i) := \frac{f(Q_i)}{f_{total}}$; $f(Q_i)$ is the amount of times Q_i has been used in data mashups before, and f_{total} is the total amount of used data sources. If $f_{total} = 0$, i.e. the first mashup graph is generated, $\frac{f(Q_i)}{f_{total}} := 1$,
- $\Sigma_{i=1}^n w_i = 1$, where n is the number of available data sources. Intuitively, the weights w_i balance the influence of coverage vs. utilization frequency of a data source,
- since coverage$(Q_i) \in [0, 1]$ and utilization$(Q_i) \in [0, 1]$, given the constraints on the weights above, we can assure that $R(Q_i) \in [0, 1]$, where 1.0 indicates a perfect match and 0.0 a total mismatch.

We additionally distinguish between two special cases: If the rank function is computed for a start tag T_i, we define $\pi_1(Q_{selected}) := \{T_i\}$ and if two data sources have the same rank, they are re-ordered with respect to their average response time t_{avg}.

The coverage criterion favors data sources that can provide a large portion of the needed input arguments. The utilization criterion captures the likelihood of a data source to be relevant without regard for the signature. Therefore it is intended to provide an additional hint when choosing between different data sources that match the input signature to some extent. Thus, w_1 should be chosen, such that $w_1 \gg w_2$, e.g $w_1 = 0.8$ and $w_2 = 0.2$.

To assure a meaningful data flow between the data sources, we require that the final mashup graph is weakly connected, i.e. replacing all directed edges with undirected edges results in a connected (undirected) graph.

6   System Architecture and Mashup Execution

The system has been implemented as a plugin for the Firefox browser[7]. Figure 4 depicts a schematic overview of the internal organization. At the heart is a central *blackboard* where all open tasks and results are available to the other components. Assuming that there are already results, *output queue* worker threads process the result messages in parallel (1). Each result message has a reference to the data source that has been queried including the success status. With this result messages, the *workflow automaton* is queried for further tasks (2). The automaton changes its state according to the already accessed data sources and keeps thus track of the current state of the overall mashup

---

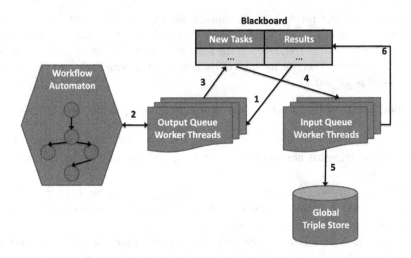

Fig. 4. System Architecture Overview

execution. The output workflow threads then add the new tasks to the blackboard (3). If new tasks are available, the *input queue* worker threads process the query requests in parallel (4) and update the *global triple store* with the results (5). Finally, the new result messages are added to the blackboard (6) and the execution loop continues until the workflow automaton reaches a terminating state. Initially, the workflow automaton adds the initial tasks directly to the blackboard to start the execution. In the remainder of this section we discuss in detail the execution of a single data source access, which consists of two phases: first the valid input combinations are determined and afterwards the results are added to the global triple store[8].

6.1 Computing Query Combinations

As mentioned above it is not advisable to query all possible value combinations. Therefore, we need a way to identify the top m combinations, which are most likely to yield relevant results. [1] presented three different ranking value functions for improving submission efficiency in a Deep Web crawler scenario. They incrementally collected possible value assignments for form elements and assigned weights to them. A weight is increased each time a value assignment is used successfully in a form submission and decreased otherwise.

Deep Web sources usually return a ranked list of results, which we interpret as an assigned weight[9]. Thus, we can similarly compute a rank for each value combination based on those weights. Thus $R_{overall} := \Sigma_{i=1}^{n} R_i$ is the overall ranking, where R_i is the ranking of a value from the ith Deep Web data source. Since the ranks of the input data

---

[8] With respect to the schematic overview in Figure 4, the first phase is carried out by the workflow automaton. Here, the optimal query combinations are computed in combination with the global triple store, which is not depicted in the figure.

[9] If no ranking information is provided, we assign to each value the rank 1.

Input data sources. Results are identified via their rankings:

- $Q_1 = \{1,2,3,4\}$
- $Q_2 = \{1,2,3\}$
- $Q_3 = \{1,2\}$

Resulting combinations:

#	$R_{overall}$	R_1	R_2	R_3
1	3	1	1	1
2	4	1	1	2
3	4	1	2	1
4	4	2	1	1

Fig. 5. Query combination computation for a data source with three different input sources where $m = 4$

sources usually depend on their predecessors as well, the notion of accumulated ranks is introduced in the next section, which considers the access history of each data source. Figure 5 illustrates the computation for three data sources which each return a different number of results[10]. In this example $m = 4$ and therefore we would query the first three combinations in parallel, since we decided to have $k = 3$ in Section 4.2, and afterwards evaluate the fourth combination.

6.2   Data Integration

After a query has been evaluated, we need to integrate the result triples into the global triple store in such a way, that each set $\pi_2(\text{stmts}(s_i))$ contains all required goal tags that were initially specified by the user. If multiple data sources contribute to the overall result, we reconcile the partial results $\text{stmts}(s_i)$ of each graph path in this stage.

Tables 1 and 2 are used to further illustrate this process. Table 1 shows an excerpt of the state of the global triple store after the first source of the mashup (Q_1) depicted in Figure 1 has been accessed and all results have been inserted. Since this was the first data source, nothing has to be done.

Table 1. Triple Store *before* accessing Q_5

#	S	P	O
1	s_1	product-name	"Sharp Aquos"
2	s_1	product-rating	80.0
3	s_1	source	Q_1
4	s_1	rank	1
...	...	...	...

---

[10] Note that in a real-life scenario the accumulated ranks are usually not integers.

Table 2. Triple Store *after* accessing Q_5

#	S	P	O
1	s_1	product-name	"Sharp Aquos"
2	s_1	product-rating	80.0
3	s_1	source	Q_1
4	s_1	rank	1
5	s_1	store-name	"Amazon"
6	s_1	price-eur	1120.00
7	s_1	rank	1
8	s_1	source	Q_5
9	s_3	product-name	"Sharp Aquos"
10	s_3	product-rating	80.0
11	s_3	source	Q_1
12	s_3	rank	1
13	s_3	store-name	"Dell"
14	s_3	price-eur	1420.00
15	s_3	source	Q_5
16	s_3	rank	2
...	...	...	...

Table 2 shows the global store after Q_5 has been accessed. The original triple set stmts(s_1) has been split in two branches: one with the information about the price for the device at the Dell store (the triple set stmts(s_3)) and the other with information about Amazon (the triple set stmts(s_1)) and aggregated with the related pricing data. This split is important, since if all data had been aggregated around s_1 the connection between store and price would have been lost. Another aspect that is shown in Table 2 is that we accumulate the source and ranking information. The source information is used to provide the next data sources with the appropriate input assignments. The ranking information is used to estimate the accumulated ranking of a subject, which is used as input for the query combination computation described in Section 6.1. The accumulated rank is the arithmetic mean over all ranks; $R_{accumulate} := \frac{1}{n}\Sigma_{i=1}^{n}R_i$, where n is the number of rankings.

After all branches have finished executing, all result triples belonging to the same graph path are already reconciled, e.g. in our running example the branches (Q_1, Q_5, Q_2) and (Q_1, Q_5, Q_3, Q_4). To correlate the information between these branches, we join the respective sets stmts(s_i) on their common properties. This is always possible, due to our weakly connected, directed mashup graph assumption. Therefore, each set stmts(s_i) in a different graph path shares at least one property.

Finally, the results are selected with an automatically generated SPARQL [16] query, where all goal tags occur in the SELECT clause and the user-specified constraints are checked in the WHERE clause. The results are then presented in a tabular representation, as if the user had queried an offline RDF graph.

7   Related Work

Data-centric mashup tools are a strong trend at the moment. Representative frameworks to build such mashups based on distributed services or structured data are for instance YahooPipes[11], IBM's QEDwiki[12], and MashMaker [17]. YahooPipes provides an interactive feed aggregator and manipulator to quickly generate its own mashups based on available XML-related services. Additionally, YahooPipes realizes data aggregation and manipulation by assembling data pipes from structured XML feeds by hand. QEDwiki is similar in spirit and is implemented as a Wiki framework, which offers a rich set of commands with a stronger focus on business users. MashMaker supports the notion of finding information by exploring, rather than by writing queries. It allows to enrich the content of the currently visited page with data from other Web sites. Our system differs in the way that we focus on unstructured resources and aim to provide a user with strong automatic mechanisms for data aggregation. As a consequence we concentrate on the problems yielding from Web resource integration, such as form field interaction, automatic content extraction, and data cleaning. Furthermore we assist the user during the assembly of the mashup with our recommendation service, whereas in the above examples the sources have to be manually wired together. In contrast to MashMaker our idea is not to enrich the content of one Web page but to provide an integrated view of multiple sources to aggregate information about a specific topic.

Since our approach is focused on Deep Web sources, we need to solve the problem of extracting and labeling Web data in a robust manner. [18] have shown in a survey the most prominent approaches to Web data extraction. A more recent frameworks fo this task is Dapper[13], which is focused on extraction of content from Web sites to generate structured feeds. It provides a fully visual and interactive web-based wrapper generation framework which works best on collections of pages. Thresher [19], the extraction component of the standalone information management tool Haystack [20], facilitates as well a simple but still semi-supervised and labor-intensive wrapper[14] generation component. Another more complex supervised wrapper generation tool is available from the Lixto company. Here, the generation of the wrapper is also done visually and interactively by the user. [21]. Our framework does not rely on an interactive wrapper generation process which is feasible at a small scale where sources can be manually wrapped. Instead a user only has to label form elements and automatically extracted content with concepts of her own vocabulary. Thus, the integration of new Web resources is totally automated except of the annotation process. This meets the problem of large scale information integration where many tasks have to be automated and wrapper maintenance is an issue.

Another related field are Web search engines, which usually offer a keyword-based or canned interface to Deep Web sources. Recently proposed complete frameworks for querying the Web, especially the Deep Web are [3] and [4] for instance. They cover

---

[11] http://pipes.yahoo.com/pipes/

[12] http://services.alphaworks.ibm.com/qedwiki/

[13] http://www.dapper.net/

[14] A wrapper in this context is only concerned with the extraction of data from Web pages and does not provide any transformation of query capabilities.

tasks like Deep Web resource discovery, schema matching, record linkage and semantic integration tasks. Although there are many similarities between these approaches and our proposed system, they are operating in a bottom-up approach, starting with the Web sources, whereas we model the world from a user-oriented perspective. Additionally we support an ad hoc combination of heterogeneous data sources, which is not supported by these frameworks.

Because our underlying data model is an adapted version of the Universal Relation assumption we share some elements with the architecture proposed in [5]. Especially the idea to bootstrap the mashup generation process with a set of goal tags is similar to the way queries can be specified in their framework. However, in our approach the user can organize his vocabulary without any dependency on domain experts, and the way queries are build on top of the initial specification is different as well. Finally, the Semantic Web application Piggy Bank [22] is also focused on the conversion of Web information into semantically enriched content, but requires as well skilled users to write screen scraper programs as information extraction components. The main idea is that users can share their collected semantically enriched information. In contrast to Piggy Bank, we do not store the information, instead we are interested in querying fresh information on-the-fly with fast and robust extraction and annotation components.

There is also a large body of work in the area of accessing sources with access limitations [9,23]. Here each Deep Web data source is regarded as a Datalog predicate with an access pattern and the idea is to automatically derive optimal Datalog programs that guarantee all accessible answers with minimal accesses. In contrast, our work supports the notion of data level optimization in the way that access paths with the highest average rank are searched first. Additionally, our focus is not on complete coverage but on offering users an intuitive graphical framework to aggregate data to answer ad hoc information needs.

8   Conclusions

Many real-life queries can only be answered by combining data from different Web sources. Especially, Deep Web sources offer a vast amount of high-quality and focused information. In this paper, we described how to make these data sources machine-accessible by tagging the relevant input and output attributes of the underlying intrinsic signature. Afterwards, we introduced our framework for using these data sources in a mashup graph. Currently, we are working on a formal data mashup language with support for loops and recursion.

References

1. Raghavan, S., Garcia-Molina, H.: Crawling the Hidden Web. In: [24], pp. 129–138
2. He, B., Patel, M., Zhang, Z., Chang, K.C.C.: Accessing the Deep Web. Commun. ACM 50, 94–101 (2007)
3. He, H., Meng, W., Yu, C.T., Wu, Z.: WISE-Integrator: A System for Extracting and Integrating Complex Web Search Interfaces of the Deep Web. In: Böhm, K., Jensen, C.S., Haas, L.M., Kersten, M.L., Larson, P.Å., Ooi, B.C. (eds.) VLDB, pp. 1314–1317. ACM, New York (2005)

4. Chang, K.C.C., He, B., Zhang, Z.: Toward Large Scale Integration: Building a MetaQuerier over Databases on the Web. In: CIDR, pp. 44–55 (2005)
5. Davulcu, H., Freire, J., Kifer, M., Ramakrishnan, I.V.: A Layered Architecture for Querying Dynamic Web Content. In: Delis, A., Faloutsos, C., Ghandeharizadeh, S. (eds.) SIGMOD Conference, pp. 491–502. ACM Press, New York (1999)
6. Wang, Y., Hornung, T.: Deep Web Navigation by Example. In: Flejter, D., Grzonkowski, S., Kaczmarek, T., Kowalkiewicz, M., Nagle, T., Parkes, J. (eds.) BIS (Workshops). CEUR Workshop Proceedings, CEUR-WS.org, vol. 333, pp. 131–140 (2008)
7. Simon, K., Lausen, G.: ViPER: Augmenting Automatic Information Extraction with Visual Perceptions. In: Herzog, O., Schek, H.J., Fuhr, N., Chowdhury, A., Teiken, W. (eds.) CIKM, pp. 381–388. ACM, New York (2005)
8. Simon, K., Hornung, T., Lausen, G.: Learning Rules to Pre-process Web Data for Automatic Integration. In: Eiter, T., Franconi, E., Hodgson, R., Stephens, S. (eds.) RuleML, pp. 107–116. IEEE Computer Society, Los Alamitos (2006)
9. Calì, A., Martinenghi, D.: Querying Data under Access Limitations. In: ICDE, pp. 50–59. IEEE, Los Alamitos (2008)
10. Brickley, D., Guha, R.: RDF Vocabulary Description Language 1.0: RDF Schema (2004), http://www.w3.org/TR/rdf-schema/
11. Biron, P.V., Malhotra, A.: XML Schema Part 2: Datatypes Second Edition (2004), http://www.w3.org/TR/xmlschema-2/
12. Hassan-Montero, Y., Herrero-Solana, V.: Improving Tag-Clouds as Visual Information Retrieval Interfaces. In: InScit 2006 (2006)
13. Manola, F., Miller, E.: RDF Primer (2004), http://www.w3.org/TR/rdf-primer
14. Wang, S.Y., Guo, Y., Qasem, A., Heflin, J.: Rapid Benchmarking for Semantic Web Knowledge Base Systems. In: Gil, Y., Motta, E., Benjamins, V.R., Musen, M.A. (eds.) ISWC 2005. LNCS, vol. 3729, pp. 758–772. Springer, Heidelberg (2005)
15. Maier, D., Ullman, J.D., Vardi, M.Y.: On the Foundations of the Universal Relation Model. ACM Trans. Database Syst. 9, 283–308 (1984)
16. Prud'hommeaux, E., Seaborne, A.: SPARQL Query Language for RDF (2007), http://www.w3.org/TR/rdf-sparql-query/
17. Ennals, R., Garofalakis, M.N.: MashMaker: Mashups For the Masses. In: Chan, C.Y., Ooi, B.C., Zhou, A. (eds.) SIGMOD Conference, pp. 1116–1118. ACM, New York (2007)
18. Laender, A.H.F., Ribeiro-Neto, B.A., da Silva, A.S., Teixeira, J.S.: A Brief Survey of Web Data Extraction Tools. SIGMOD Record 31, 84–93 (2002)
19. Hogue, A., Karger, D.R.: Thresher: Automating the Unwrapping of Semantic Content from the World Wide Web. In: Ellis, A., Hagino, T. (eds.) WWW, pp. 86–95. ACM, New York (2005)
20. Karger, D.R., Bakshi, K., Huynh, D., Quan, D., Sinha, V.: Haystack: A General-Purpose Information Management Tool for End Users Based on Semistructured Data. In: CIDR, pp. 13–26 (2005)
21. Baumgartner, R., Flesca, S., Gottlob, G.: Visual Web Information Extraction with Lixto. In: [24], pp. 119–128
22. Huynh, D., Mazzocchi, S., Karger, D.R.: Piggy Bank: Experience the Semantic Web Inside Your Web Browser. J. Web Sem. 5, 16–27 (2007)
23. Nash, A., Ludäscher, B.: Processing Unions of Conjunctive Queries with Negation under Limited Access Patterns. In: Bertino, E., Christodoulakis, S., Plexousakis, D., Christophides, V., Koubarakis, M., Böhm, K., Ferrari, E. (eds.) EDBT 2004. LNCS, vol. 2992, pp. 422–440. Springer, Heidelberg (2004)
24. Apers, P.M.G., Atzeni, P., Ceri, S., Paraboschi, S., Ramamohanarao, K., Snodgrass, R.T. (eds.): VLDB 2001, Proceedings of 27th International Conference on Very Large Data Bases, Roma, Italy, September 11-14, 2001. Morgan Kaufmann, San Francisco (2001)

A Web-Based Version of a Trivial Game to Promote Galician Culture*

Miguel R. Luaces, Oscar Pedreira, Ángeles S. Places, and Diego Seco

Databases Laboratory, University of A Coruña, 15071 A Coruña, Spain
{luaces,opedreira,asplaces,dseco}@udc.es

Abstract. We present in this paper the architecture and some implementation details of a web-based version of a Trivial game. Our implementation achieves such a high degree of interactivity between the players that they perceive the game as being played in real-time. More importantly, no plug-in or applet is used in the architecture of the system. These properties are achieved by means of a carefully designed architecture that uses AJAX (*Asynchronous JavaScript and XML*) for data exchange. Using this approach, it is possible to develop any type of web-based collaborative software with few load on the web server. In the paper, we analyze traditional architectures for web-based applications and we show how our approach overcomes their limitations. Furthermore, we proof the efficiency of our approach by means of an empirical comparison.

Keywords: Web application, User interface, AJAX, Collaborative software, e-Learning.

1 Introduction

The maturity of Internet users and the quality of connections and services available are increasing the demand of interactivity in web applications, not only between the user and the system, but also between the users themselves. However, the characteristics of traditional web applications prevent developers from building collaborative applications or games that require real-time interaction between the users [1]. This is due to two main reasons:

- *Clients cannot exchange information.* Connections in web applications are always established between a client and the server, but never between two clients. Hence, all data exchange must be done through the server.
- *A web server cannot start data transfers.* Web servers can never communicate the information received from one client to the others unless the clients explicitly request it, thus restricting the interaction possibilities between the clients.

As a consequence, applications where users collaborate or interact which each other in real-time to perform a task have to be implemented using *plug-ins* or a similar type

* This work has been partially supported by "Ministerio de Educación y Ciencia" (PGE y FEDER) ref. TIN2006-16071-C03-03, by "Agencia Española de Cooperación Internacional (AECI)" ref. A/8065/07, and by "Xunta de Galicia" ref. 2006/4 and ref. 08SIN009CT.

J. Cordeiro et al. (Eds.): WEBIST 2008, LNBIP 18, pp. 242–252, 2009.

of software for the web browser that controls the exchange of messages between the users. The only alternative without this type of software is that each client requests frequent and periodic updates from the server to retrieve the data that has changed in any other client. However, if data change frequently in the clients or the change has to be perceived as real-time, the load in the web server will be very high because many new pages will have to be created and sent constantly. This results in a limitation in the maximum number of users that can interact. Nevertheless, this approach is better than the previous one in the sense that users do not have to install any plug-in, which is an insuperable restriction in application domains where users do not have the required expertise level.

We have developed a software architecture specifically designed to simulate interactivity between users of a collaborative web application. Users perceive their interaction as real-time, just like if they had a direct connection between them. This architecture has been used to implement a virtual version of the classic board game *Trivial Pursuit* with two important advantages over other applications of this type: it does not require players to download and install any software for the web browser, and a large number of games with many players in each can be played simultaneously in an ordinary web server.

The rest of the paper is organized as follows. In Sect. 2 the rules of *Trivial.gz* are described in order to show the level of interactivity that can be reached with this new approach of web application development. Then, in Sect. 3, we present the differences between the architecture of traditional web applications and the architecture we propose, and we describe AJAX in more detail, showing its advantages for the systematic development of interactive web applications. After that, we present a detailed description of the application architecture in Sect. 4. This development allowed us to evaluate and compare our approach with respect to traditional approaches to web application development, which is presented in in Sect. 5. Finally, Sect. 6 presents our conclusions and some ideas for future work.

2 Trivial.gz

Trivial.gz is an initiative of the Galician Socio-Pedagogic Association (AS-PG, from the Galician name *Asociación Socio-Pedagóxica Galega* [2]) to increase the usage of Galician language on the Internet and among the young people, and it was sponsored by the Galician government. The game was presented during the computer party *XuventudeGaliza.Net*, which took place in Santiago de Compostela in April 2006. The game can currently be played at the web server of the Galician Socio-Pedagogic Association (http://www.as-pg.com/trivial.gz). Figure 1 shows a screenshot of a game being played.

The main objective when the development started was to create a web-based game similar to the Trivial Pursuit board game which could be played on any web browser without having to download any plug-in or applet. Our version of the game has some differences with respect to the original board game in order to get the most out of the virtual environment and to minimize the effects caused by the players not sharing the same physical space during the game. Moreover, a big effort was devoted to simulate

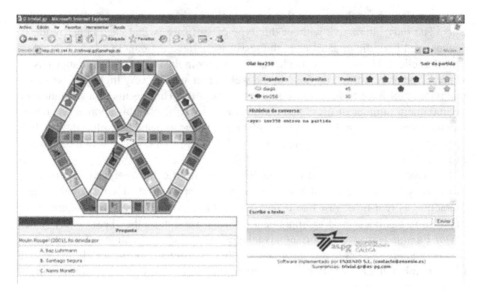

Fig. 1. Screenshot of the game

in a web page the interaction between the players and the actions like rolling the die, moving the tokens, watching the positions and movements of the other players, etc.

In a rough description, the goal of *Trivial.gz* is answering correctly questions of three different difficulty levels and six different subjects: *Culture and Show Business*, *Geography*, *History*, *Language and Literature*, *Science* and *Our World*. All questions have three possible answers of which only one is correct. The board is an hexagon divided into squares of different colors, each representing one of the subjects of the questions. When the game starts, all players start from the central square. The player who has the turn throws the die (by clicking on an animation of the die rolling) and moves on the board in any direction as many squares as the number in the die. When a square is chosen, the same question is showed to all players who can try to answer the question before the time ends. If the question is answered right points are awarded to the player independently of whether the player had the turn or not. If the player with the turn fails the question, the turn passes to the next player. To win the match, the player first has to collect the six *wedges* that are awarded when the question on a vertex of the board is answered right. Then, the player has to proceed to the center square and answer correctly a question from a random subject.

A detailed description of the game rules is outside the scope of this paper. However, we think it is interesting to discuss the modifications that were done to the original rules of the game in order to improve the experience of the players:

- *The game board is updated in real time.* A player can see all the tokens, the die value, who has the turn, and the points of each player. This creates the sensation that the players share the same virtual space.
- *Players can talk.* A chat was added to the game page so that players can communicate. It simulates the verbal interaction between players.

- *Wedges can be lost.* If a player fails the question in one of the squares where wedges are awarded, the player looses the wedge. This makes the game more dynamic and enables players that are losing to recover.
- *It is easier to win wedges.* There is a special square in each side of the board that moves the token to one of the special squares. This makes games faster.
- *Everybody plays.* When the player with the turn chooses a square, the question is presented to all players. Everybody can try to answer the question and points are awarded to everybody that gives the right answer. Furthermore, it can be seen who has already answered the question right or wrong in order to increase the perception of playing with more people.
- *Limited time.* There is a time limit of 30 seconds to answer for the player that has the turn. The time for all the other players is limited to the time required by the player with the turn. This avoids long waits.
- *Player history.* The server keeps track of all the games played, the points achieved by each player, and the statistic of questions answered right for each subject. This gives the game an additional dimension because players can compete not only to win one game, but also to be the one with more games won, with more points, or with better statistics.
- *Solitaire game.* The game can be played by a single player.

The usage statistics of the game are very encouraging. It currently has more than 4400 registered users and more than 6000 questions. The average number of visits is around 50 visits a day. Furthermore, new functionalities are being developed to increase these statistics. The Trivial.gz championships are an example of these functionalities. An administrative tool to configure the championships (i.e. subjects, number of matches that each contestant can play, difficulty, etc.) has been developed and the game engine has been extended. Four championships have been carried out since May 2008 (when this functionality was released) and the average number of contestants is around 36.

3   Differences with Traditional Web Applications

The architecture of traditional web applications follows one of these two philosophies:

- *Server-side applications.* All processing is performed on the web server. Each client request implies a processing time in the server and sending a complete web page to the client. This architecture is not very scalable because the number of pages that the server has to process and send to the clients grows with the interactivity of the application and the number of simultaneous clients.
- *Client-side applications.* In this type of architecture as much processing as possible is performed in the client, thus minimizing the information exchange with the server. This type of applications are usually implemented by means of web browser plug-ins that have to be downloaded, installed and configured. Another approaches use Java applets that require the Java Virtual Machine to be installed and configured. In any case, this philosophy requires some level of expertise from the users, which limits its general use.

An intermediate approach uses scripts in the web pages so that the client-side of the application has a certain amount of processing capabilities without having to install a plug-in or the Java Virtual Machine. AJAX (*Asynchronous JavaScript and XML* [3]) is the name of a new philosophy in the field of web application development. In fact, AJAX is not a new technology but rather a combination of a number of already existing different technologies. The central element is the asynchronous usage of the *XMLHttpRequest* API present in all web browsers of the current generation. This allows a web page that is being visualized at the client-side to use a script language function to request some information from a web server without blocking the user activity. The web server returns the information requested using short XML [4] messages and the web browser invokes a specific script function that can process the response and modify the web page accordingly. Google has been a pioneer in the use of AJAX, as can be seen in Google Suggest, Google Maps or GMail [5].

Figure 2 shows a sequence diagram represented with UML that describes this behaviour. In both figures a user invokes three actions in the user interface of the web application. Figure 2(a) shows the behaviour in the case of traditional web applications. In this case, the user has to wait until the action ends before invoking the following one. Furthermore, the processing time in the server and the amount of information exchanged between the client and the server is usually quite high. Figure 2(b) shows the behaviour in the case of using AJAX. In this case users perceive a higher response speed. They do not have to wait for an action to end before invoking another action because the data exchange is performed asynchronously and long operations do not block the user interface. Moreover, in traditional web applications each content update requires a complete reload of the web page, whereas in a web application using AJAX the information in the XML message is used to redraw the appropriate section of the user interface. Additionally, the processing time in the server and the amount of information exchanged is smaller because the server does not have to create and trasfer complete web pages, but only short XML messages. Furthermore, given that the processing time in the server and the amount of information exchanged between the server and the clients is reduced, AJAX-based web applications can include more interactivity than traditional applications because the remaining processing time and bandwidth can be used to handle a higher number of simultaneous requests.

A number of development tools have appeared around AJAX to make its usage more easy. One of them is *Direct Web Remoting (DWR)* [6]. This open source library has two advantages over the direct use of AJAX. First, it enables the JavaScript code in the client-side to use transparently Java classes in the server-side. That is, it enables the developer to use AJAX in a similar way to CORBA or RPC. This is achieved by dynamically generating JavaScript code that encapsulates AJAX-based calls to the Java classes in the server. The second advantage is that DWR provides the developer with a number of tools to make easier the update of the web page contents in the client-side.

These two technologies are the center of the architecture of our application. However, they do not solve the problem of creating web applications that allow users to interact in real time. Even though it speeds up data exchange between the server and the clients, it does not change the architecture of web applications. That is, data exchange is still performed between the clients and the server and never between clients, and the server

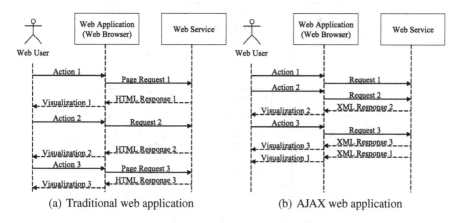

(a) Traditional web application   (b) AJAX web application

Fig. 2. Client-server interaction in different application models

still cannot take the initiative of sending the data it has just received from a client to the other ones.

In order to achieve a high degree of interactivity between the users, in our architecture each client issues frecuent periodical requests to the server and receives the relevant information regarding the state of the game and the other players, which is used to change the user interface accordingly. To keep track of the current state of the game, the server implements a state-machine that is controlled with the information sent by the player that has the turn. Requests to the server can be issued more in response to some actions of the player (such as throwing the dice or answering a question).

This approach cannot be implemented with the traditional architecture of web applications because the amount of information that had to be exchanged between the server and the clients is too high. In order to minimize the processing time in the server and the traffic between the clients and the server, we use AJAX for the communication between the clients and the server. By exchanging information by means of short XML messages, AJAX frees the web server from the creation of complete web pages when the clients requests arrive. Furthermore, the logic of the application is split between the client and the server in such a way that the processing time in the server and the traffic between the server and the clients is minimized. Finally, the functionality in the client-side can be implemented using only JavaScript, thus no special software has to be downloaded or installed.

4   Detailed System Architecture

Figure 3 presents a general view on the architecture of the application. Just like in any web application, one can find two different parts: the server-side module of the application that runs in a web server and it is implemented using *Java Server Pages (JSP)*, and the client-side module that runs in the web browser of the client and it is implemented using JavaScript and dynamic HTML. There is a part of the

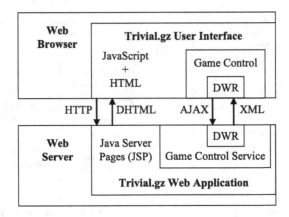

Fig. 3. Application architecture

application that deals with functionality such as user registration, configuration of lists of friends, or querying and browsing statistics of the players, which is implemented as an ordinary web application whose description is out of the scope of this paper. Instead, we will focus on the description of the game control and the simulation of real-time interactivity.

There are two different types of players in the game: the one that currently has the turn, and all the others. The first one has the control of the game and generates events that produce the update of the game state (e.g., rolling the die, choosing the square, or answering the question). The other players only generate an event when they answer the question. The server controls each game being played by means of a state-machine. During the game, the server goes through the states according to the actions invoked by the player that has the turn. The other players do not have any effect on the state-machine, they just query the server periodically to retrieve the current state of the game in order to update their user interface.

The states in the state-machine of the server are the following:

- *Initial state.* Just before the player that has the turn rolls the die. There is no information to be sent to the other players.
- *Dice thrown.* The player with the turn rolls the die and gets a number. The other players receive this number when they request the game state in order to update their user interface.
- *Square chosen.* The player with the turn chooses a square to move and receives a query for that square that is selected randomly by the server. The rest of the players receive the square selected and the question when they request the game state.
- *Answering a question.* Whenever a player without the turn answers a question, the server updates the points of that player and informs the other players of the result. Therefore, all the other players can now whether one player has answered the question right or wrong. When the player with the turn answers the question, the time for answering ends. If the player gave a wrong answer, the turn passes to the following player.

Internally, the server-side module keeps a list of the games that are being played at any given time. Each game consists of a list of players and a list of questions ready to be sent to the players. For each player, the server keeps in memory the points achieved, the wedges won, and the statistic of questions answered right for each subject. The list of questions acts like a memory cache to reduce the frequency of database accesses. Hence, instead of issuing a query to the database each time a question is needed, there is only one database access to retrieve a set of questions that are used during the game. Only when all the questions are used a new database access is performed.

The client-side modules consists of a Dynamic HTML page with JavaScript code. Its operation is based on a JavaScript timer that requests the game state every four seconds and updates the user interface accordingly. When the user invokes actions on the user interface, the JavaScript code informs the server of the event and modifies the user interface with the information retrieved. The time between updates can be easily configured. A longer time reduces the real-time perception of the game but allows for a longer number of simultaneous games in the server. On the other hand, a shorter time improves the real-time perception but requires more computing power on the server side. The time that is currently being used has been empirically chosen to achieve a real-time perception of the game while using an average computer as the web server.

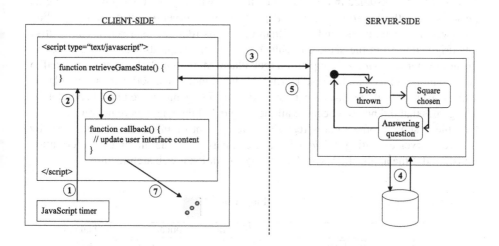

Fig. 4. Communication protocol

Figure 4 shows the development of a game turn. The numbers in the figure match the following enumeration and represent a temporal ordering of the event sequence. First, the JavaScript timer determines the moment to request information from the server (1). After that, a JavaScript function in the client-side module that requests the current game state from the server is invoked (2). The server receives the request and delegates its fulfillment in the business model (3). The business model implements the state-machine that controls the game and computes the information to be answered according to the current state and the current event (4). Then, the server response is encapsulated and sent to the client. An object is built with the information retrieved from the business model and sent to the client (5). The client receives the response, extracts the information from the object, and uses the information to update the user interface content (6). Finally, a new turn starts by showing the animated picture that represents the die (7).

The state-machine that controls the game solves one of the most important drawbacks in applications where clients perform some processing: *to make sure that the messages received in the server are according with the state of the application*. This drawback is especially important in web applications where client-side processing is implemented using JavaScript code. Several applications (e.g. Firebug [7]) can be used to analyze the script code in web applications. Moreover, messages sent to the server can be modified using applications or plug-ins such as Tamper Data [8]. Thus, a user with the required expertise level could cheat easily. For example, a user with the turn could send a message with his favourite *chosen square* without sending the message *throw the dice* if the state-machine had not checked the state of the matches. Therefore, the state-machine must verify all the messages and parameters received by the server.

5   Experimental Evaluation

The *Trivial.gz* is installed in a 3.2 Ghz Pentium IV with one gigabyte RAM. During its presentation at the *XuventudeGaliza.Net* party, the web server received almost a million *hits* (web server requests) and more than 600 visits (defined as a set of consecutive hits originating from the same computer). Most of the requests were concentrated in the hour when a *Trivial.gz* competition took place. More than 200 players competed to achieve more points than the rest. During this hour, more than 800 games were played with an average of three players per game. Exactly 776 games were played completely. The games that did not end because all the players left the board were not registered.

Table 1 shows some figures regarding the amount of information transferred by the web server executing *Trivial.gz* and a comparison to the amount of information transferred if the application were built using a traditional web architecture.

Table 1. Empirical data

	Traditional Application	Trivial.gz
1 message, 1 game, 1 player	35 KBytes	0.31 KBytes
1 game, 1 minute, 3 players	1575 KBytes	14.1 KBytes
100 games, 10 minutes, 3 players	1538.09 MBytes	13.77 MBytes
Network traffic during these 10 minutes	2.56 MBytes/s	23.50 KBytes/s

The HTML code of the web page occupies 35 kilobytes without taking into account neither the images nor the JavaScript code that sends the messages to the server using DWR. On the other hand, the DWR object that the web server sends to each client occupies 313 bytes, i.e. 0.31 kilobytes. As it was explained in Sect. 4, the game information must be updated by each client frequently in order to achieve a real time perception of the game. If we consider an update time of 4 seconds, just like it is currently configured in the application, a traditional web application would require the web server to send the 35 KB of the web page 15 times per minute. This means a total of 525 KB per minute and player, whereas with *Trivial.gz* this amount of information is reduced to 4.7 KB per minute and player.

We can suppose that 100 games with an average of three players were played during 10 minutes in the party where the *Trivial.gz* was presented. In fact, more than 800 games were played in an hour, so our supposition is quite conservative. Considering this activity, 1.5 Gigabytes of information would be transferred through the network in a traditional web application, whereas only 14 Megabytes were sent in *Trivial.gz*. This represents that a traditional web application requires 107 times more space for the same information. As a consequence of this amount of information, a traditional web application would require a bandwidth of 2.56 MBytes/s in the best case (assuming that the traffic distribution is uniform). However, *Trivial.gz* only needed a bandwidth of 23.50 KBytes/s.

6   Conclusions and Future Work

We have presented in this paper the architecture of a web application that implements a trivial-like game where players can follow the game in real time. This was achieved without using any plug-in or applet, which means that the game can be played in almost any computer without the common problems associated to the instalation of these components.

We have described how the AJAX philosophy is used in the implementation for the data exchange between the server and the clients. Moreover, the message exchange protocol designed for *Trivial.gz* and a general architecture for collaborative web applications are also described. These three improvements over traditional web applications minimize the amount of information that has to be transferred between the clients and the server. We believe that this approach can be used to develop any type of collaborative software using a web application with a small load on the web server.

Finally, we have performed an empirical comparison between *Trivial.gz* and a web application based on a traditional web application architecture. This comparison shows the advantages of using our architecture in terms of network bandwith and processing capabilities of the web server.

The application has been a success. The game has a solid player base and it is being used to promote the use of the Galician language among young people. New questions are submitted by player regularly and a board version of the game is being developed. As lines of future work, we are currently working on the improvement of *Trivial.gz* to allow games with a larger number of players. Another improvement that is currently being implemented is the adaptation of the application to make it completely configurable by the final users. When this is achieved, any user will be able to install the application, decide the subjects, and define the questions. A possible field where this application can be used is in education with teachers configuring *Trivial.gz* games with the questions of the lessons they teach in the classroom.

A different line of future work is the study of the requirements of other types of collaborative web applications, such as distance education or collaborative work, and the adaptations that the architecture requires. In this sense, a web-based version of the popular game *Scrabble* [9] is being developed with the same goals in mind.

References

1. Paulson, L.D.: Building rich web applications with ajax. IEEE Computer 38, 14–17 (2005)
2. Galician Socio-Pedagogic Association: Web Site (2007) (retrieved, October 2007), http://www.as-pg.com/
3. Garrett, J.J.: Ajax: A New Approach to Web Applications (2005)(retrieved, October 2007), http://www.adaptivepath.com/publications/essays/archives/000385.php
4. World Wide Web Consortium: Extensible Markup Language (XML) (2006) (retrieved, October 2007), http://www.w3.org/XML/
5. Google: Google Tools Web Site (2007) (retrieved, October 2007), http://www.google.com/intl/en/options/
6. Direct Web Remoting (DWR): Web Site (2007) (retrieved, October 2007), http://getahead.org/dwr
7. Firebug: Web Site (2007) (retrieved, November 2007), http://getfirebug.com
8. Tamper Data: Web Site (2007) (retrieved, November 2007), http://tamperdata.mozdev.org/
9. de Bernardo, G., Cerdeira-Pena, A., Pedreira, O., Places, A.S., Seco, D.: Scrabble.gz: A web-based collaborative game to promote the galician language. IEEE Computer Society Press, Los Alamitos (2008)

Feeling Expression Using Avatars and Its Consistency for Subjective Annotation

Fuyuko Ito[1], Yasunari Sasaki[2], Tomoyuki Hiroyasu[3], and Mitsunori Miki[2]

[1] Graduate School of Engineering, Doshisha University
1-3 Tatara Miyakodani Kyotanabe, Kyoto, Japan
fuyuko@mikilab.doshisha.ac.jp
[2] Department of Science and Engineering, Doshisha University
ysasaki@mail.doshisha.ac.jp, mmiki@mail.doshisha.ac.jp
[3] Department of Life and Medical Sciences, Doshisha University
tomo@is.doshisha.ac.jp

Abstract. Consumer Generated Media(CGM) is growing rapidly and the amount of content is increasing. However, it is often difficult for users to extract important contents and the existence of contents recording their experiences can easily be forgotten. As there are no methods or systems to indicate the subjective value of the contents or ways to reuse them, subjective annotation appending subjectivity, such as feelings and intentions, to contents is needed. Representation of subjectivity depends on not only verbal expression, but also nonverbal expression. Linguistically expressed annotation, typified by collaborative tagging in social bookmarking systems, has come into widespread use, but there is no system of nonverbally expressed annotation on the web. We propose the utilization of controllable avatars as a means of nonverbal expression of subjectivity, and confirmed the consistency of feelings elicited by avatars over time for an individual and in a group. In addition, we compared the expressiveness and ease of subjective annotation between collaborative tagging and controllable avatars. The result indicates that the feelings evoked by avatars are consistent in both cases, and using controllable avatars is easier than collaborative tagging for representing feelings elicited by contents that do not express meaning, such as photos.

1 Introduction

There has been an increase in development and utilization of social software that shares private information, such as photos and diaries, among a community or the general public. As each user publishes their own contents on the web, the amount of web content has increased rapidly. Therefore, it has become difficult to extract necessary information and much of the information that is available is left unused. The current mainstream method of information retrieval is to use keywords for the contents, but searching by subjective information, such as feelings or intention, is expected to allow users to find forgotten information. Therefore, we propose "subjective annotation" in which users annotate contents with subjective information, and construct a content management system to store and browse the contents based on the subjective annotation.

Preliminary experimental results on expressiveness and ease of subjective annotation by collaborative tags used for classification in social bookmarking systems and blogs

J. Cordeiro et al. (Eds.): WEBIST 2008, LNBIP 18, pp. 253–265, 2009.

suggests that it may be difficult to express subjectivity using verbal expressions, such as tags. In this paper, we propose the usage of avatars as a means of nonverbal expression of subjectivity, and report verification of its validity by experiments on the consistency of feelings elicited by avatars over time for an individual or a group of people. We also compare the expressiveness and ease of subjectivity between avatars and tags.

2   Web Content Management and Annotation

Consumer Generated Media (CGM), such as weblogs (commonly referred to as "blogs") and photos, which are published by users, have increased rapidly because the contents previously stored on local terminals are now available on the web. To manage this large amount of web content, social bookmarking services have appeared.

Social bookmarking services manage their contents from the bottom-up by sharing annotations, such as tags or keywords, which are added to the contents by users[1]. This enables the discovery of related contents through tags, and users can reach information that would otherwise be difficult to find.

However, increasing the number of tags makes it difficult for users to keep track of their tags. Social software stores the contents that are important to users, but there are few chances to browse these contents again. Even if tags are added to ease content searching, users will not search the contents without a clear purpose, and many of the contents that may be important for users may be left unused in social software.

3   Subjective Annotation

3.1   What Is Subjective Annotation?

We propose "subjective annotation" which involves adding subjective information, such as feeling or intention, to the contents. Currently, it is common to annotate web contents using a number of tags. Most of these tags explain the contents objectively, and only a few tags indicate subjective information. The social bookmarking service del.icio.us[1] has some tags that indicate subjectivity, such as "to be read," which make it easier for users to determine how to use the contents. At the photo sharing service Flickr[2], some photos are tagged "cute" or "cool," and users can search and classify photos according to their own impressions and values[2]. Therefore, subjective annotation can assist users to make efficient use of web contents.

3.2   Content Management System Based on Subjectivity

Here, we constructed a content management system based on subjective annotation that helps users to discover knowledge from their past experiences. The proposed system recreates their past feelings and excitement by using subjective annotation over a wide variety of contents and reminds users of their behaviors. The system targets the web

---

[1] http://del.icio.us/

[2] http://flickr.com/

contents of social software, such as photo sharing, social bookmarking, and schedule sharing services that are browsed only when users need them. To utilize wasteful accumulated contents, the system accumulates the contents with subjective annotation in social software and provides a content browsing environment based on subjectivity.

3.3 Collaborative Tags for Subjectivity Expression

The expression of subjectivity must be considered to implement subjective annotation. Most annotations describe the contents in some way, and the expressiveness of the current annotation methods regarding subjectivity and user stress must be assessed. First, we adopted collaborative tagging, which is commonly used as a means of annotation of web contents, as an expression of subjectivity and perform an exploratory experiment on the expressiveness of subjectivity and user stress.

In the experiment, 20 participants add tags to 10 photos with subjective information, such as feelings and impressions, and answered a questionnaire survey. A wide variety of subjectivity, such as intention, feelings, and imagery, are used as tags. However, participants report feelings of stress regarding the difficulty of verbalizing subjectivity.

The questionnaire survey indicates that it is difficult to verbalize subjectivity with tags. Therefore, subjectivity must be expressed by a nonverbal method. We adopt an avatar for this purpose, as it seems suitable to express subjectivity such as feelings. It is easy to deal with avatars on computers and users often identify themselves with avatars. Therefore, avatars allow users to express their feelings naturally and they are able to express their feelings with gestures. In addition, recognition of avatars is consistent from person to person, even with different nationalities[3].

4 Avatars as Nonverbal Expression of Subjectivity

4.1 Controllable Avatars for Subjective Annotation

We adopted a controllable avatar to express a wide variety of feelings. The avatar has a variety of patterns of facial expressions, and arm and leg positions. Figure 1 shows examples of avatars and Fig. 2 shows all parts of the avatars. Users combine these face, arm, and leg parts to express their feelings.

The avatar used for nonverbal expression of subjectivity is shown in Fig. 1 as a cartoon character. There are three reasons why we use this type of avatar. First, we feel that Japanese users show a preference for animated illustrations rather than realistic figures like the avatars in Second Life[3]. Second, Takahashi et al.[4] used two different imaginary cartoon characters that are neither humans nor animals. On the other hand, a human character was adopted as an avatar in this research, and enables the users' identities to be expressed by changing hairstyles or hair colors. Thus, the avatar of each user can be recognized visually. However, our avatars do not emphasize the users' identities, such as changing clothes and accessories, because the main focus of our avatars is expression of feeling based on facial expression and body movement. Therefore, our avatars are different from those used by Yahoo[4]. In addition, we will not refer to hairstyles of avatars in this paper.

---

[3] http://secondlife.com/

[4] http://avatars.yahoo.com/

Fig. 1. Avatar examples

Fig. 2. The avatar consists of faces, arms, and legs

4.2 Validity of Avatars for Nonverbal Expression of Subjectivity

The subjective information that is added by subjective annotation will be used as queries to search and classify contents. Furthermore, information filtering based on subjectivity of other users is possible by sharing subjective annotation among communities or the general public, similar to collaborative tags. To achieve this, the following factors must be assessed by experiments.

- Consistency of feelings elicited by avatars for an individual over time.
- Consistency of feelings elicited by avatars in a group of people.
- Comparison of feeling expressiveness between avatars and collaborative tags.

It is necessary to assess whether subjectivity, particularly feelings, elicited by avatars changes significantly over time for an individual, and also within groups of people. Moreover, the comparison of feeling expressiveness, satisfaction level of their own expression, and adaptability of contents must be conducted between avatars and collaborative tags.

5 Consistency of Feelings Elicited by Avatars for an Individual over Time

5.1 Experimental Overview

To facilitate use of avatars for personal information retrieval and experience browsing, the consistency of feelings elicited by the avatars over time was assessed based on a semantic differential method. Moreover, features of feelings over time for each avatar pattern are also discussed.

Avatars. In this experiment, the variety of avatar faces was limited to face parts from (1) to (6) shown in Fig. 2 that are frequently used in a preliminary experiments of feeling expression. Leg parts were fixed to leg parts (1), because participants reported a greater effect of the arms than the legs in the preliminary experiment. A total of 24 avatars (6 face parts × 4 arm parts) were presented to the participants.

Participants. Two men and 2 women ranging in age from 23 to 25 years participated in this experiment. All participants were Japanese undergraduate or graduate students.

Measurement. In this experiment, participants rate the feelings elicited by the avatars using a semantic differential method based on the two-dimensional model of emotion proposed by Lang[5]. Participants rated the arousal and valence from 0 (lowest) to 100 (highest) for each avatar pattern on six continuous scales. A total of 144 stimuli (24 avatar patterns × 6 scales) were presented to the participants.

Each scale was anchored with a pair of antonymous words in Japanese, determined hierarchically. In the preliminary experiment, participants label each avatar pattern with various words indicating feelings. Then, pairs of antonymous words were made from frequently used words. The pairs of words were reduced to the six pairs shown below, which are frequently used in the areas of social psychology and personality psychology, according to the survey results of scale construction of pairs of Japanese antonymous words in a semantic differential method reported by Inoue et al[6]. The approximate translations in English are as follows:

- Arousal
    - scale 1 (intensity): intense - calm
    - scale 2 (activeness): active - passive
    - scale 3 (strength): strong - weak
- Valence
    - scale 4 (joy): joyful - sad
    - scale 5 (amusement): amusing - boring
    - scale 6 (favor): likable - disagreeable

Process

1. After receiving instructions, participants were trained to evaluate feelings.
2. Avatars were presented on the computer screen (see Fig. 3). Moreover, the order of presentation of faces and arms was counterbalanced across the trials.
3. Participants evaluated the feelings elicited by the avatars on each scale. The order of scales was randomized for each avatar. The time limit was set to 40 s for each avatar pattern to induce an intuitive response.
4. Twenty-four avatars were presented by iterating steps 2 and 3. After evaluation, participants answered the questionnaire.
5. From step 1 to 4 was defined as a trial. Six trials were conducted at the following intervals: 1 h, 2 h, 1 day, 2 days, 4 days.
6. More than 2 weeks after step 5, participants were presented with all avatars and means of their evaluated values for each scale. Participants indicated their satisfaction level from 0 to 100.

Fig. 3. Experimental setup

5.2　Results and Discussion

We evaluated the standard deviation of the spread in the evaluated values for feelings elicited by each avatar pattern and defined that as the statistical value. Feelings elicited by the avatar pattern that were more than mean$+1SD$ were particularly inconsistent. Conversely, feelings elicited by the avatar pattern that were less than mean$-1SD$ were particularly consistent. There was an average of 21 avatar patterns that were more than mean$+1SD$ for participants. These patterns correspond to only about 14% of the entire 144 stimuli (24 avatar patterns $\times$ 6 scales). Therefore, feelings elicited by avatars were generally consistent over time for individuals. Moreover, Table 1 shows the amounts of avatar patterns outside the mean$\pm1SD$ range of arousal and valence.

There were more avatar patterns that were more than mean$+1SD$ in scales of arousal (see Table 1). On the other hand, there were more patterns that were less than mean$-1SD$ in the scales of valence (see Table 1). Therefore, valence elicited by avatars is more consistent over time than arousal for an individual.

Figure 4 shows the transition of the total evaluated values for each participant throughout all trials. The figures show that the total evaluated values of arousal change more drastically than valence throughout all trials.

The evaluated values of valence, such as "joy" and "favor," are simply increased and evaluated more positively due to the mere exposure effect[7]. However, the evaluated

Table 1. Avatar patterns outside the mean±1SD range

Participant	>+1SD		<-1SD	
	Arousal	Valence	Arousal	Valence
A	17	2	5	14
B	9	9	7	12
C	17	9	2	14
D	14	8	5	15

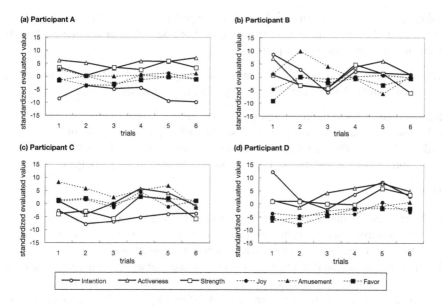

Fig. 4. Total evaluated value of each scale

values of arousal decrease from the first to the third trial, which may have been due to loss of novelty with three trials in one day.

Furthermore, two weeks after the experiment, participants reported the satisfaction level of each avatar pattern and its average evaluation value throughout all trials. The satisfaction level is defined as the statistical value, and we inspected the frequencies of face parts and arm parts in avatar patterns that were less than mean$-1SD$. Face parts (2) (see Fig. 2) appeared frequently in avatar patterns that were less than mean$-1SD$. The satisfaction level of face parts (2) tended to be low, as it is difficult for participants to determine whether the feeling is positive or negative from the surprised face and the evaluation of valence is inconsistent. On the other hand, arm parts (3) (see Fig. 2) appeared frequently in avatar patterns that were more than mean$+1SD$. The satisfaction level of arm parts (3) tended to be high, as waving arms emphasized the feeling expressed by avatars and made a deep impression on the participants.

Taken together, these observations indicate that feelings elicited by avatars are consistent over time for an individual.

6   Consistency of Feelings Elicited by Avatars in a Group of People

6.1   Experimental Overview

We examined use of an avatar as a query for information filtering in a group of people as with collaborative tags. The consistency of feeling elicited by avatars in a group of people was assessed based on a semantic differential method in the same way as in the experiment described in Chapter 5. Features of feelings generated by participants are also discussed.

Design. A 6(faces) × 4(arms) within-subject experiment was performed. The avatar parts used in this experiment were the same as those described in Chapter 5. Overall, 24 avatars were presented to the participants.

Participants. Twenty men and 4 women ranging in age from 21 to 27 years participated in this experiment. All participants were Japanese undergraduate or graduate students.

Measurement. This experiment was performed based on the semantic differential method in the same way as the experiment described in Chapter 5. The pairs of antonymous words anchored on the six scales were also the same as those in Section 5.1. A total of 144 stimuli (24 avatar patterns × 6 scales) were presented to the participants.

Process

1. After receiving instructions, participants were trained to evaluate feelings.
2. Avatars were presented on the computer screen. Moreover, the order of presentation of faces and arms was counterbalanced across the participants.
3. Participants evaluated the feelings elicited by the avatars on each scale. The order of scales was randomized for each avatar. The time limit was set to 40 s.
4. Twenty-four avatars were presented by iterating steps 2 and 3. After evaluation, participants answered the questionnaire.

6.2   Results and Discussion

We evaluated the semi inter-quartile range of standardized evaluated values for each scale, for each avatar to inspect the spread of feelings, and defined that as the statistical value. The feelings elicited by avatar patterns that were more than mean+$2SD$ were particularly inconsistent. Conversely, the avatar patterns that were less than mean−$2SD$ were very consistent. There were 7 avatar patterns that were more than mean+$2SD$. These patterns account for only about 7% of the total of 144 stimuli (24 avatar patterns × 6 scales). Therefore, feelings elicited by avatars are consistent in a group of people as a whole.

Meanwhile, the amounts of patterns outside the mean±$2SD$ range of the semi interquartile range are summarized for arousal and valence (see Table 2). There were more patterns that were more than mean+$2SD$ in scales of arousal. On the other hand, there were more patterns that were less than mean−$2SD$ in the scales of valence. There are two reasons why valence elicited by avatars is more consistent than arousal. First, scales of valence are nominal, and users could recognize feelings from facial expressions. The other reason is that arousal is an interval scale and its degree is inconsistent even within an individual.

Table 2. Avatar patterns outside the mean±2SD range

>+2SD		<-2SD	
Arousal	Valence	Arousal	Valence
7	0	0	2

Avatar patterns and scales that were more than mean$+2SD$ are discussed in detail. Valence shows a much wider spread than arousal when the avatar consists of face parts (3), because it is difficult to determine between pleasure and displeasure from the excited face. Moreover, the evaluation of scale for joy is particularly consistent as compared to the other scales.

Two-way ANOVA of the 6(faces) × 4(arms) patterns was conducted for each of the following scales to inspect the features and effects of feelings elicited by avatars.

Intensity. The interaction between faces and arms was marginally significant ($F(15,345) = 1.58, p < .1$). Fisher's least significant difference (LSD) post hoc test was used to test the differences in pairwise comparisons. The face parts (2), (3), and (5) were different from (1), (4), and (6) ($p < .05$). Therefore, these face parts increase arousal. Meanwhile, arm movement also affects intention, and arm part (3) was significantly different from arm parts (1), (2), and (4) ($p < .05$).

Activeness. The main effects of faces and arms were significant ($F(5,115) = 38.42, p < .01; F(3,69) = 23.53, p < .01$, respectively). However, there was no significant interaction between faces and arms ($F(15,345) = 1.13, n.s.$).

Strength. The interaction between faces and arms was marginally significant ($F(15,345) = 1.74, p < .1$). On LSD post hoc test, face part (4) was significantly different from the other face parts ($p < .05$).

Joy. The interaction between faces and arms was significant ($F(15,345) = 2.18, p < .05$). On LSD post hoc test, the face parts (1) and (3) were significantly different from the other face parts ($p < .05$).

Amusement. The interaction between faces and arms was significant ($F(15,345) = 2.31, p < .01$). On LSD post hoc test, face parts (1) and (3) were significantly different from the other face parts ($p < .05$).

Favor. The interaction between faces and arms was significant ($F(15,345) = 2.25, p < .01$). On LSD post hoc test, arm parts (3) was significantly different from arm parts (1) and (2) when face parts was (3) or (6)($p < .05$).

Taken together, these observations indicate that feelings elicited by avatars were consistent in a group of people and facial expressions affect valence, while arm movements affect arousal, although face parts (2), (3), and (5), which express surprise, excitement, and anger, respectively, increase arousal.

7 Comparison of Feeling Expressiveness between Avatars and Tags

7.1 Experimental Overview

The expressiveness, gap in expression according to the contents, ease, and satisfaction of expression were compared between avatars and collaborative tags representing nonverbal and verbal expression, respectively. In this experiment, participants expressed their feelings elicited by contents consisting of articles as verbal contents and photos as nonverbal contents using avatars or tags.

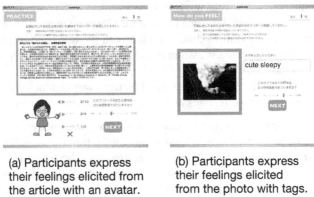

(a) Participants express their feelings elicited from the article with an avatar.

(b) Participants express their feelings elicited from the photo with tags.

Fig. 5. Experimental setups

This experiment was performed using all of the avatar parts shown in Fig. 2. The participants expressed their feelings elicited by contents with a combination of these avatar parts. The format of collaborative tags was open-ended, and participants were permitted to use multiple tags for a single content. Furthermore, participants were allowed to skip the expression if they felt difficulty in expressing their feelings.

The contents were articles and photos on the web. Practically, top 10 bookmarked articles in Yahoo!Japan News[5] as of September 5th, 2007 and top 10 bookmarked photos in Zorg[6] (photo sharing service) as of August 1st, 2007 were chosen for this experiment.

Participants. Twenty men and 4 women ranging in age from 21 to 27 years participated in this experiment. All participants were Japanese undergraduate or graduate students.

Process

1. After instruction, the participants were trained to express their feelings using avatars or tags regarding the sample article and the sample photo. Moreover, the order of using avatars and tags was counterbalanced across the participants.
2. Ten articles and 10 photos were presented on the computer screen (see Fig. 5). The participants expressed their feelings regarding the contents using avatars or tags, respectively. The presentation order of articles and photos was counterbalanced across participants.
3. The participants expressed their feelings regarding the same contents in the same way as in steps 1 and 2 using tags or avatars that have not been used before.
4. After evaluation, the participants answered the questionnaire about their satisfaction.
5. More than 2 weeks after step 4, participants were presented with all of the contents and the avatars or tags expressing their feelings. Participants answered the satisfaction level from 0 to 100.

---

[5] http://headlines.yahoo.co.jp/

[6] http://www.zorg.com/

7.2   Results and Discussion

Figure 6 shows the results of 3 questionnaires on the satisfaction of feelings expression by avatars and tags. The participants responded regarding which of the two expression methods they preferred. Each questionnaire was about the entire contents, articles, and photos. In all questionnaires, none of the participants indicated a preference for tags over avatars.

With regard to all contents, more than 70% of the participants indicated a preference for expressing their feelings using avatars (see Fig. 6(a)). This may have been because an avatar can express feelings that are difficult to verbalize, and an avatar can describe the degree or strength of a feeling.

On the other hand, 58% and 67% of participants indicate a preference for avatars for expression of feelings regarding articles (see Fig. 6(b)) and for photos (see Fig. 6(c)), respectively. Moreover, 38% and 8% of participants indicate that tags are better than avatars for articles and for photos, respectively. Based on the opinions of the participants, it is not difficult to express feelings with tags in the case of articles, as articles themselves are in verbal format. However, the meanings of photos cannot be defined clearly, and it is difficult to verbalize feelings elicited by photos.

In this experiment, participants were allowed to skip expression of feelings if they decided that expression with the suggested method is impossible. The number of skips was 21 times using avatars and 42 times with tags. Thus, it seems easier for users to use avatars than tags.

Furthermore, more than two weeks after the annotation experiment, participants were presented with all of the contents and the avatars or tags expressing their feelings. Participants answered the satisfaction level about the combination of their annotation and the contents. The satisfaction level was standardized for each participant except the contents that were not annotated. The averages of satisfaction level are shown in Table 3.

The results shown in Table 3 confirmed that avatars are preferable over tags when presented with both articles and photos. Some participants also responded that the combination of avatars and contents helps them to remember how they felt about the contents. On the other hand, some participants reported differences in their feelings toward some of the combinations of avatars and contents between the annotation experiment and two weeks later. Overall, avatars may support recall of how users felt when they annotated the content and the influence of the changes in feeling toward the contents must be verified in future studies.

Table 3. Averages of standardized satisfaction level on combination of feeling expression and each content

	Articles	Photos
Avatar	0.073 (0.945)	-0.033 (1.063)
Tag	-0.069 (1.176)	-0.043 (1.258)

Note. A value in parenthesis is standard deviation.

Which expressed your feelings about the contents better, avatars or tags?

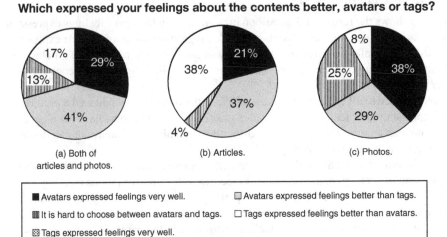

(a) Both of articles and photos.　　　(b) Articles.　　　(c) Photos.

■ Avatars expressed feelings very well.　　　□ Avatars expressed feelings better than tags.

▥ It is hard to choose between avatars and tags.　　　□ Tags expressed feelings better than avatars.

▨ Tags expressed feelings very well.

Fig. 6. Results of questionnaires about satisfaction level of feeling expression

8　Related Work

There have been many studies using avatars: creation of co-presence in online communication[8], interpretation of avatar's facial expressions[9], description language for avatar's multimodal behavior[10], *etc*. However, there have been only a few studies using avatars for feeling extraction. In this section, we will mention representative studies using avatars for feeling extraction.

Takahashi et al.[4] constructed TelMeA, an asynchronous communication support system, that represents the relations among participants and the relations between contents and conversations by the behavior of static avatars. The purpose of TelMeA is similar to ours, because TelMeA was designed to ease interpretation of feelings difficult to express verbally by combining contexts and behaviors of avatars. However, we define feeling expressions by avatars as part of subjective annotation, and plan to use them like collaborative tags for information retrieval and classification in content sharing. Therefore, we verified the consistency of feelings elicited by avatars. Moreover, our avatars can express feeling not only toward contents with clear context but also those with unclear context, such as photos.

Another case, PrEmo[11], is a tool to assess emotional responses toward consumer products. In PrEmo, avatars have 14 behaviors consisting of 7 positive and 7 negative behaviors. Users rate each avatar based on the feelings elicited by the products. This tool enables product impression analysis based on users' feelings. The purpose of PrEmo is similar to ours because it is designed to analyze feelings elicited by targets. However, the results of feeling analysis for each product using PrEmo are mapped together in the emotion space structured by 14 avatar behaviors. Therefore, users cannot easily share their feelings elicited by each product. Moreover, in PrEmo, the rating for each avatar only indicates that the feeling that each avatar represents is present in the users' feeling elicited by products. On the other hand, our avatar can express not only the presence of feelings, but also their degrees.

9   Conclusions

We propose subjective annotation where users add subjective information, such as feelings and intention, to contents. As it is particularly difficult to verbalize a feeling, we adopt avatars to express feelings. To use an avatar as the interface of subjective annotation, the consistency of feelings elicited by avatars over time for an individual, and also the consistency in a group of people were assessed. The results indicate consistency for both cases, although the variation of arousal is wider than that of valence.

In addition, a comparison was conducted regarding feeling expressiveness and satisfaction level between avatars and collaborative tags. The results indicate that avatars are more suitable than tags for expression of feelings, particularly in cases with contents that include no context and no message, such as photos. Overall, avatars can be used for expression of subjective annotation. In future studies, we will improve the control interfaces of avatars to make them more intuitive and continue to verify the practical usefulness of subjective annotation with avatars.

References

1. Mathes, A.: Folksonomy - Cooperative Classification and Communication Through Shared Metadata. Master's thesis, Graduate School of Library and Information Science University of Illinois Urbana-Champaign (2004)
2. Golder, S.A., Huberman, B.A.: Usage patterns of collaborative tagging systems. Journal of Information Science 32(2), 198–208 (2006)
3. Ekman, P., Friesen, W.V.: Constants across cultures in the face and emotion. Personality and Social Psychology 17(2), 124–129 (1971)
4. Takahashi, T., Bartneck, C., Katagiri, Y., Arai, N.: TelMeA - Expressive Avatars In Asynchronous Communications. International Journal of Human-Computer Studies (IJHCS) 62(2), 193–209 (2005)
5. Lang, P.J.: The emotion probe: Studies of motivation and attention. American Psychologist 50(5), 372–385 (1995)
6. Inoue, M., Kobayashi, T.: The Research Domain and Scale Construction of Adjective-pairs in a Semantic Differential Method in Japan. The Japanese Journal of Educational Psychology 33(3), 253–260 (1985)
7. Zajonc, R.B.: Attitudinal effects of mere exposure. Journal of Personality and Social Psychology 9, 1–27 (1968)
8. Ishii, Y., Watanabe, T.: An Embodied Video Communication System in which Self-referentiable Avatar is Superimposed for Virtual Face-to-face Scene. Journal of the Visualization Society of Japan 23(1), 357–360 (2003)
9. Koda, T., Ishida, T.: Cross-cultural Comparison of Interpretation of Avatars' Facial Expressions. Transactions of Information Processing Society of Japan 47(3), 731–738 (2006)
10. Prendinger, H.: MPML: A Markup Language for Controlling the Behavior of Life-like Characters. Journal of Visual Languages and Computing 15(2), 183–203 (2004)
11. Desmet, P.M.: Measuring Emotions. In: Funology: from usability to enjoyment, pp. 111–123. Kluwer Academic Publishers, Dordrecht (2003)

Improving Web Service Discovery
with Personalized Goal

Sanaullah Nazir[1], Brahmananda Sapkota[1], and Tomas Vitvar[2]

[1] Digital Enterprise Research Institute, National University of Ireland-Galway, Galway, Ireland
firstname.lastname@deri.org
[2] Semantic Technology Institute, University of Innsbruck Innsbruck, Austria
firstname.lastname@sti2.at

Abstract. Most of the existing work in web service discovery reflect providers perspective. These discovery techniques improve service descriptions so that the service clearly describes what it offers. This development has led to the use of semantic web technology for web service discovery. A lot of work has gone into improving web service descriptions to support improved web service discovery. In this paper we extend the existing approaches to semantic web service discovery and introduce personalization to it. We also show how personalization affects discovery. We provide a model to represent a user profile, and its usage for improving the accuracy of web service discovery.

1 Introduction

Advancement in web service discovery is mostly centred around the service provider. Use of UDDI [1] has been amongst the initial efforts for improving web service discovery. The inability of web service description language WSDL to describe what the service provides led to the use of semantic technology, involving DAML-S [2], OWL-S [3], WSMO [4] etc. Most of the currently used discovery approaches has been geared towards identifying services which meet the user's requirements. There might be some web services, which provide the same output, but the user of the service could be different.

Context based service discovery [5], [6] is a type of service discovery approaches which concentrate on the user's perspective. But the direction of context based discovery has been dependent on environmental parameters in which the user is searching for a service.

Another discovery approach is QoS based service discovery [7], [8]. In this approach some numeric parameters are set for some characteristics of a service. These values should match with the requirements of the service user, e.g the required shipment time of the product should match with the shipment time provided by the service.

Here it is important to understand that the discovery approaches mostly try to consider what the user requires without considering the profile of the user. In this paper we present a discovery approach involving the user profile as a functional requirement of the service to be matched as well. Answers to the questions such as how a goal can evolve in order to make discovery more accurate, and how the underlying storage architecture supports discovery.

J. Cordeiro et al. (Eds.): WEBIST 2008, LNBIP 18, pp. 266–277, 2009.

The structure of this paper is as follows: Section 2 provides the motivating example, which we use to present our approach of service discovery. Section 3 outlines modeling of web services and goals and Section 4 presents the how the discovery of web services takes place and how goal evolves during the process. This section also describe the peer-to-peer architecture on which the discovery component is relying on. Section 5 describes the tools used to implement the whole architecture, a run through example for the case study is elaborated in section 6. Section 7 presents some of related work done in this direction. Finally, Section 8 draws some conclusions and presents future directions.

2   Motivating Example

In this section we will present a motivating scenario for this research work. In this example different variety of driving licences are issued depending on the person's physical ability and the type of vehicle he drives. The input required from the user is a type of vehicle, whether he holds international/EU-State driving licence, and if he has any disability. The personal profile input would allow the proper discovery of required service(s). If in this case user profile isn't considered then a large amount of services will be discovered from which the selection would have to be done by the user.

3   Service and Goal Modeling

In this section we present language and technique used to model the web services and user goals. For describing web services and user goals WSML-Flight variant of WSML [9] is used. WSML-Flight allows writing simple logical expressions and rules. Web services, goals and ontologies are modeled using WSMO [10].

The reason for modeling and using personalization is to provide different discovery support from user to user, depending on his needs, status and environment, rather than providing crude services. Some work towards personalization for information retrieval has been done in digital libraries [11], where users are modeled in terms of five categories, which are personal data, preferences and restrictions, time and location of delivery, high responsiveness of the service to user's need and privacy of the user data. Moving towards the web, [12], Garrigos has presented reusable models for personalization. In their approach five models are presented. Domain model to defined the structure of domain data, Navigation model to define structure and behavior over the domain data. Presentation model is used to handle the layout of the presentation. The personalization model holds rules for different personalization policies and User model allows to store data needed for the personalization.

In this paper we model the user in terms of his needs and profile. QoS parameters i.e price, delivery time etc are not handled in our model, but are considered to be a non-functional property of the service which the user can negotiate later.

We have modeled the need and profile of the user as a functional property of the service and the goal. Using WSMO for modeling service and user goal, both the profile and the need will be in the funcational description. The profile of the user is defined as a concept in a domain ontology. The reason for having this concept in domain ontology is the varying requirement of profile for the domains. User of the service can be an individual or an organization. A service may be a user of another service, but the profile used will be of the external entity. Some profile inputs may be required for one domain, while those might not be of interest in the other. The service is also dependent on the location of the user, e.g the driving licence service is provided by many countries, but the location input provided by the user will allow providing a more accurate discovery.

A web service W can be modeled in WSMO as follows:

$$W = \{F, B\}$$
$$F = \{W\rho, W\rho'\}$$
$$B = \{\sigma, \sigma'\}$$

F represents functional description of the web service and B represents the behavioral description of the web service. A functional description of web service contains precondition $W\rho$ and postcondition $W\rho'$ of a web service. WSMO provides two more functional descriptions attributes which are assumption and effect. But we are only using precondition and postcondition.

The behavioral description of the service B contains choreography σ and orchestration σ'. The choreography of a web service describes the communication pattern and how the service can be used. Orchestration represents how the overall functionality can be achieved by cooperation of different web service.

The precondition of web service contains rules which allow to verify the user's profile. The profile concept created in the domain ontology is used in the precondition to evaluate the state of the information before service execution. The precondition can be defined as follows:

$$W\rho = \alpha$$

Where

$$\alpha = \{\nu1, \nu2, \nu3, \cdots, \nu n\}$$

Here α is the set of conditions. This set contains individual conditions νi which needs to be fulfilled before the execution of the service. A service can have multiple preconditions; all of them are need to be fulfilled by the user goal. Starting from very generic precondition and moving towards specific precondition for the services. The generic precondition is held by all the services that provide same output. Moving from generic preconditions towards specialized preconditions allows differentiating the profile input required by the various service of the same type.

Service type is basically what a service provides. Web services are said to belong to the same service type if they have a common postcondition, but a varying precondition.

This will allow to repeatedly evolving a goal which can accurately match with a web services or a set of web services.

The postcondition of the web service description defines the state of the information that is reached after the service is executed. The need of the user is modeled in the postcondition of the service. There can be web service which have common postcondition but the precondition they require to be verified are different. Postcondition can be defined as follows:

$$W\rho' = \{\beta\}$$

Here β represents the state of the information after execution of the service.

Benefit of using WSMO for modeling is that it provides support for modeling the user's request. The user's request is divided into two parts, as need of the user and profile of the user.

We follow a similar approach for modeling goal as presented in [13]. We use goal template and goal instance. Goal template can be defined as follows:

$$G' = \{G\rho, G\rho'\}$$

A goal template G' contains precondition $G\rho$ and postcondition $G\rho'$. Precondition of a goal template is the generic precondition which all the services in one service types define.

Following is how goal is defined, Let G represent the WSMO goal:

$$G = \{G\rho'\}$$

Here $G\rho'$ is the postcondition of the goal. User's need is captured by the postcondition of the goal. We are not using precondition in the functional part of the goal. The reason of not using precondition is difficulty for the user to write logical expressions. The user is not interested defining the conditions on the information but rather would like to provide his input as simple data. Thus for supporting the user to define his profile, we use the user's profile concept described in the domain ontology.

The user request then finally comprises of WSMO goal containing postcondition and user data as user's profile concept.

Goal templates are provided by service provider and are created at design time. Transition from goal template to goal takes will be explained in the goal creation section presented later. But for now, goal template is used as a starting point for creating a goal instance.

4   Architecture Overview

4.1   Goal Creation and Service Discovery

This section elaborates the user's perspective of the overall architecture and how a user's request is formalized which is later used for discovery. WSMO provides support for modeling a goal, but it does not provide the technique for creating such a goal. An effort made towards this technique is presented in [14] . In this paper Stollberg has presented two forms of goals namely Goal templates and Goal Instance. He makes further classification in Goal templates, which are basic type and composed type. Our work is some what along the same lines. Here we currently only consider goals of basic type. Goal will be modeled using the goal modeling technique presented in the previous section. The goal evolves for an accurate discovery of service. As defined in the previous section a goal template contains precondition from the generic type which belong to all the web service of the same type. A user requests for a web service goal template using key words. The matching process retrieves the goal templates which match his request. User input is required for all the precondition variables. The precondition is used to create a user profile which is sent with the goal in a form of instance of the concept. Evolution of goal takes place during the web service discovery process. Each partial input is matched with a complete description of web service. Incomplete inputs become a part of precondition and are requested in the next step. The process can be represented as follows: Let initial partial goal created from goal template be

$$GoalTemplate = G'\{G\rho, G\rho'\}$$
$$G\rho = \alpha\{v1/t1\}$$

Here v's are free variables. These variables are replaced by the t input given by the user.

$$\text{User Data } \{\delta\} \subset \alpha\{v1/t1\}$$

This precondition results into creation of user data as the concept of a profile in an ontology. This concept satisfies the precondition of the goal template.

From a goal template a goal is created having only the postcondition of the goal template. Input for discovery is $\rho', O(\delta)$ goal with postcondition and ontology containing user data profile concept. Through the discovery process user profile is refined. The precondition not matching is returned from the discovery component. Just as the case with goal template this precondition is used to take input from user to extend the user profile. Next the precondition with this extended data is sent again to discovery component. This process continuous until all the precondition of the service is satisfied. The following relation must hold:

$$G\rho \subset W\rho$$

Since

$$G\rho \subset \alpha\{v1/t1, ..., vn/tn\}$$

And

$$\delta \subset \alpha$$

Then

$$\delta \subset W\rho$$

This relation explains that the user data should hold for the precondition of the web service. The postcondition of the goal must also hold for the web service postcondition. Following is the relation for postcondition.

$$G\rho' \subset W\rho'$$

The process of discovery first matches postconditions. Web services which have matching postconditions are then taken for matching the preconditions of the service. The output from the discovery component is list of web service along with precondition which need to be satisfied. If the web service has no more preconditions to be matched then the second attribute is null. From the list the user selects which web service fulfils his need. On selecting a service with un-fulfilled precondition, then the user has to provide input.

Here the deviation from the traditional approach is taken, where the following relation must hold:

$$G\rho \subset W\rho$$
$$G\rho' \subset W\rho'$$

Creating an instance of a concept from the input provided by the user is simpler. This would save the user from writing complex logical expressions and for component to manipulate with these expressions, without complete knowledge of the domain. This instance data will allow creating simple queries from the web service description to verify if the instance holds.

4.2 Storage Requirement

In this section we present the storage architecture of our discovery approach. The underlying storage architecture is based on peer to peer architecture as presented in [15]. Service providers / agency providing the web service description acts as a peer and becomes a part of the semSet which is of the same domain. There are few changes made in the overlay network, to cope with the requirement of the e-gov domain. The domains of the service are clearly defined. The peer can belong to multiple domains. Another e-gov domain specific restriction is the privacy of the member state i.e to keep data of one member state unaccessible to the other member state. There is a communal gateway which provides mediation between ontology. Semantic query (WSMO goal) requiring interaction with other member state passes through the communal gateway. More detail regarding the communal gateway can be found in [16]. The mediation approach used can be found in [17], which is a part of WSMX architecture [18]. WSMX (*web service execution environment*) is running on all nodes. The discovery and storage components are part of WSMX architecture. Each member state has its own coSet. From the member state coSet one of them becomes the member of inter-member state level coSet. Inter-state querying takes place through these peers. For details about the construction and membership algorithm of the network refer to [15]. In figure 1, the doted line ring

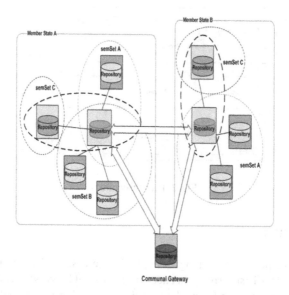

Fig. 1. Peer-to-Peer Architecture for discovery

represent the semSet. Where there is only one peer in the semSet, that peer is a member of the member state coSet. The dashed black line represents the member state coSet.

5   Implementation

The discovery component provides the functionality of discovery of semantic web services which are most suitable for the user. Figure 2, shows structure of each peer. Discovery component performs matchmaking between WSMO goal and profile provided as an instance of citizen concept with the semantic service descriptions. Personalization component handles the ordering of personalization rules in the preconditions needed to be verified by the discovery component, and returns the formatted output to the external component. The Repository holds the semantic data and communication engine handles the peer-to-peer communication. The implementation has been done in Java 1.5. We have used the WSML2Reasoner framework [19], and KOAN2 reasoner for evaluation of logical expressions defined in the semantic descriptions of the services. The underlying communication between the peers is handled by JXTA [20]. The semantic repository used is ORDI [21].

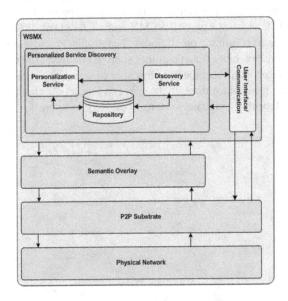

Fig. 2. Peer Structure

6   Run through

In this section we present a running example for the case study. The requirement is that the user needs a Irish driving licence. In this example we will consider that the ontology being used is same for goal and web service. Non-Functional property(nfp) includes the domain and member state the entity belongs to. These nfps are used for

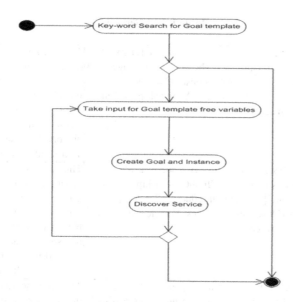

Fig. 3. Discovery Process

routing purpose between the peers. Table 1 and Table 2 shows how the web service, goal template and goal are described. Figure 3, shows how the goal evolves and discovery takes place. Initially the user is provided with a set of keyword, which allows him to select what his need is. Using these keywords goal templates are matched. From the list of goal templates the user selects one. The goal template as defined in the modeling section has precondition with free variables. Input is taken from the user for these free variables. These input result in the creation of instance of the person concept defined in the ontology. This instance along with the goal having the postcondition only is sent to the discovery component. The discovery component performs matchmaking and as a result returns a web service / set of web services, along with free variable which require more user input. If the service has no corresponding free variable it is considered to be discovered. As the user selects a goal template from the list of goal template, here again the user has to select a web service from the list of web services, which serves in the same way as goal template. This activity continuous until no more free variable are available along with the service, or the user is satisfied with the discovered service.

In this case study, there are services which provide different type of driving licences. Here just for simplicity and to present our point we consider only one type of licence. The concentration in this example is to present how the goal evolves and how precondition of the web service plays its part in the discovery processes. The keyword based approach to select the goal template is used. This goal template asks for user to fill the nationality, age and if the user has any physical disability. This resulting in the creation of a goal without precondition and instance data. Next this goal is sent for discovery. The discovery component returns "Web service A" that matches the goal and instance data, which is if the user has the Irish Id. This precondition like the goal template is used to take input from the user and to update the instance data. This final goal and

Table 1. Web Services

webService _"webServiceA.wsml" $W\rho = \alpha\{\nu1, \nu2\}$, $W\rho'$ $= \{\beta\}$ $\nu1 = $?req{Nationality ="IrishCitizenship" $\wedge$ age ≥ 18 $\wedge$ disable = "false"} memberOf request. $\nu2 = $?req{IrishId = "true"} memberOf request. $\beta = $?res{VehicleType = "car" } memberOf drivingLicence.	This web service provides a driving licence of Ireland for a car. The generic precondition for this service is that the person is an Irish citizen and has no disability. For specialized precondition the citizen holds an Irish id as well.
webService _"webServiceB.wsml" $W\rho = \alpha\{\nu1, \nu2\}$, $W\rho'$ $= \{\beta\}$ $\nu1 = $?req{Nationality ="IrishCitizenship" $\wedge$ age $\geq$ 18 $\wedge$ disable = "true"} memberOf request. $\nu2 = $?req{IrishId = "true"} memberOf request. $\beta = $?res{VehicleType = "car" } memberOf drivingLicence.	This web service provides a driving licence of Ireland for a car. The generic precondition for this service is that the person is an Irish citizen and has some disability. For specialized precondition the citizen holds an Irish id as well.
webService _"webServiceC.wsml" $W\rho = \alpha\{\nu1, \nu2\}$, $W\rho'$ $= \{\beta\}$ $\nu1 = $?req{Nationality ="EU" $\wedge$ age ≥ 18 $\wedge$ disable = "false"} memberOf request. $\nu2 = $?req{EUId = "true"} memberOf request. $\beta = $?res{VehicleType = "car" } memberOf drivingLicence.	This web service provides a driving licence of Ireland for a car. The generic precondition for this service is that the person is an EU citizen and has no disability. For specialized precondition the citizen holds and EU member state id as well.

instance data is sent for discovery which finally only returns "Web service A" with null for further input requirement. The routing of the goal takes place using the nfps. Once the peer receives a request for discovery, it uses the nfps to check to which peers to route the query to. Peer receiving the request has in its routing table peers who belong to that domain and member state, it forwards the goal to those peers. In case the peer holds no information for that domain or member state, it forwards the request to the coordinator peer. This forwarding of request continues until the inter-member state coordinator is reached. The coordinator forwards the request to the member state to which the query belongs to. The result is returned along the same path taken to reach the node.

7   Related Work

There has been a lot of work done for web service discovery. Most of the work concentrates on the simple web service discovery without considering the context or the personalized view of the user.

The two phase discovery presented in [13], which we extend to create goal for discovery, provides a way to model the goal for discovery and discover web service, but does not take into consideration about the possible use of precondition for providing accurate web services.

Table 2. Goal evolution

goal _." goalTemplate.wsml" $G\rho = \alpha\{\nu1\}$, $G\rho' = \{\beta\}$ $\nu1 = $?req { Nationality = ?nat $\wedge$ age = ?age $\wedge$ disable = ?dis} memberOf request. $\beta = $?res{VehicleType = "car" } memberOf drivingLicence.	This goal template provides a starting point to discover a service which provides a deriving licence of Ireland for a car. The precondition provide what information is required from the user. The free variables are used to taking input. The postcondition defines that the user is looking for a web service which provides car driving licence. This goal template is created at design time by the service provider.
goal _." goalInit.wsml" $G\rho'$ ={β}, O = {δ}, $\beta = $?res{VehicleType = "car"} memberOf drivingLicence. $\delta = $?data{Nationality ="IrishCitizenship" $\wedge$ disable = "false" $\wedge$ age = 20 } memberOf Citizen.	This goal is created after the user's input for the free variables. The instance created has all the data which is needed for discovery
goal _." goalFinal.wsml" $G\rho'$ ={β}, O = {δ}, $\beta = $?res{VehicleType = "car"} memberOf drivingLicence. $\delta = $?data{Nationality ="IrishCitizenship" $\wedge$ age = 20 $\wedge$ disable = "false" $\wedge$ IrishId = "true"} memberOf Citizen.	This is the second level of the goal, where after the first iteration web service discovered, i.e. "web service A" requires further input for precondition. To check if the person holds an Irish Id card.

Wolf-Tilo presents a personalized selection of web services approach in [22]. The methodology presented there handles the task of personalization at selection time. The discovery approach used in keyword based. Ther discovery proposal lacks expressiveness of the query and the service. They use simple SQL query to select the services that meet the user's requirement.

[6], gives a very comprehensive view for modeling the personalization aspect for web service discovery. They present a discovery methodology which requires interaction with the web services and the resource where the web service has to be executed. They consider three aspects when considering about the personalization, which are User context, web service context and resource context. User context considers user's preferences, including where and when the service is needed to be executed. The web service context considers the constraints on the web service to execute in a specific environment and lastly the resource context is the time and load constraint on the resource. Their approach is quite similar to our in terms user's view, but not much detail is presented regarding the modeling language of the service and query from the user.

8   Conclusions and Future Work

In this paper an approach for discovering web services has been presented. This papers considers discovery from users perspective. Creation of refined goal from a generic one is provided to make an accurate service discovery. Modelling of web services and goal has been provided using WSMO. WSMO allows to model a profile of the user as ontology concept. We have presented how the use of precondition of the WSMO web service description can be done, which earlier has not been used. A distributed architecture has been presented, which handles distributed querying. This has resulted in efficient discovery of services as the load on the discovery component has been distributed. The inferencing time required for discovery is reduced.

This architecture has been implemented in the EU funded SemanticGov, and has result in very accurate service discovery during its testing. More work needs to be done for handling composed goals. Creating sub-goals and handle discovery and aggregating results. This has been left for the future work.

Acknowledgements. This material is based upon works supported by the EU funding under the projects TripCom (FP6-IST-4-027324-STP), SemanticGov (FP6-IST-4-027517) and by the Science Foundation Ireland under Grant No. SFI/02/CE1/I131.

References

1. Clement, L., Hately, A., Riegen, C., Rogers, T.: Uddi version (3.0.2), uddi spec technical committee draft. Technical report (October 2004),
   http://www.w3.org/TR/2004/REC-owl-features-20040210/
2. Paolucci, M., Kawamura, T., Payne, T., Sycara, K.: Semantic matching of web service capabilities. In: Horrocks, I., Hendler, J. (eds.) ISWC 2002. LNCS, vol. 2342, pp. 333–347. Springer, Heidelberg (2002)
3. Srinivasan, N., Paolucci, M., Sycara, K.: Adding owl-s to uddi, implementation and throughput. In: Proc. of 1st International Workshop on Semantic Web Services and Web Process Composition (SWSWPC) (2004)
4. Keller, U., Lara, R., Polleres, A., Toma, I., Kifer, M., Fensel, D.: D5.1 v0.1 WSMO Web Service Discovery WSML Working Draft (November 2004)
5. Hai, L., Qing, L., Naijie, G.: Quantifying contexts for user-centered web service discovery. In: Proc. of 10th IEEE International Enterprise Distributed Object Computing Conference, pp. 399–404 (2005)
6. Maamar, Z., Mostefaoui, S., Mahmoud, Q.: Context for personalized web services. In: Proc. of 38th Hawaii International Conference on System Sciences (2006)
7. Vu, L., Hauswirth, M., Aberer, K.: Towards p2p-based semantic web service discovery with qos support. In: Bussler, C.J., Haller, A. (eds.) BPM 2005. LNCS, vol. 3812, pp. 18–31. Springer, Heidelberg (2006)
8. Makripoulias, Y., Makris, C., Panagis, Y., Sakkopoulos, E., Adamopouloua, P., Tsakalidis, A.: Web service discovery based on quality of service. In: Proc. of 4th ACS/IEEE International Conference on Computer Systems and Applications, pp. 196–199 (2006)
9. Toma, I. (ed.): The Web Service Modeling Language (WSML). WSMO Working Group (September 2007)
10. Roman, D., Lausen, H., Keller, U. (eds.): The Web Service Modeling Ontology (WSMO). WSMO Working Group (February 2007)

11. Amato, G., Straccia, U.: User profile modeling and applications to digital libraries. In: Abiteboul, S., Vercoustre, A.-M. (eds.) ECDL 1999. LNCS, vol. 1696, p. 184. Springer, Heidelberg (1999)
12. Garrigos, I., Gomez, J., Barna, P., Houben, G.: A reusable personalization model in web application design. In: Proc. of Workshop on Web Information Systems Modelling, pp. 40–49 (2005)
13. Stollberg, M., Keller, U., Lausen, H., Heymans, S.: Two-phase web service discovery based on rich functional descriptions. In: Franconi, E., Kifer, M., May, W. (eds.) ESWC 2007. LNCS, vol. 4519, pp. 99–113. Springer, Heidelberg (2007)
14. Stollberg, M., Norton, B.: A refined goal model for semantic web services. In: Proc. of 2nd International Conference on Internet and Web Applications and Services, pp. 17–22 (2007)
15. Sapkota, B., Nazir, S., Vitvar, T., Toma, I., Vasiliu, L., Hauswirth, M.: Semantic overlay for scalable service discovery. In: Proc. of 3rd International Conference on Collaborative Computing: Networking, Applications and Worksharing (2007)
16. Vitvar, T., Kerrigan, M., Overeem, A., Peristeras, V., Tarabanis, K.: Infrastructure for the semantic pan-european e-government services. In: Proc. of AAAI Spring Symposium on The Semantic Web meets eGovernment (SWEG) (2006)
17. Mocan, A. (ed.): WSMX Data Mediation. WSMO Working Group (October 2005)
18. Zaremba, M., Moran, M. (eds.): WSMX Architecture. WSMO Working Group (October 2005)
19. Motik, B., Nagypal, G., Grimm, S.: Wsml reasoner. Technical report (June 2005)
20. Li, S.: Jxta 2: A high-performance, massively scalable p2p network. Technical report (November 2003)
21. Ognyanov, D., Kiryakov, A.: Ontology representation and data integration (ordi.) framework. Technical report (June 2005)
22. Balke, W., Wagner, M.: Towards personalized selection of web services. In: Proc. of 12th World Wide Web Conference (2003)

New Quality Metrics for Web Search Results

Panagiotis Takis Metaxas*, Lilia Ivanova, and Eni Mustafaraj

Wellesley College, Wellesley, MA 02481, U.S.A.
pmetaxas@wellesley.edu
http://cs.wellesley.edu/~pmetaxas/

Abstract. Web search results enjoy an increasing importance in our daily lives. But what can be said about their quality, especially when querying a controversial issue? The traditional information retrieval metrics of *precision* and *recall* do not provide much insight in the case of web information retrieval. In this paper we examine new ways of evaluating quality in search results: *coverage* and *independence*. We give examples on how these new metrics can be calculated and what their values reveal regarding the two major search engines, Google and Yahoo. We have found evidence of low coverage for commercial and medical controversial queries, and high coverage for a political query that is highly contested. Given the fact that search engines are unwilling to tune their search results manually, except in a few cases that have become the source of bad publicity, low coverage and independence reveal the efforts of dedicated groups to manipulate the search results.

Keywords: Web search, Quality metrics, Precision, Recall coverage, Independence, Adversarial information retrieval, Web spam.

1 Introduction

The web has changed the way millions of people are being informed and make decisions. Most of them use search engines to access web information. Since people use search engines daily to make all kinds of financial, medical, political or religious decisions, quality of search results is of great importance. In the last ten years the two major search engines, Google and Yahoo, have gained the lion's share in the search market [9].

But does higher market share implies higher search quality? Performance of information retrieval methods is traditionally measured in terms of precision (fraction of results that are relevant to a query) and recall (fraction of relevant items included in the results) [7]. It is well known, however, that web searchers rarely look past the top-10 results [11]. The web has enormous size. More that 50 billion pages are reportedly indexed by search engines, and this represents just a portion of the static web. At the same time, search results on important issues are being heavily spammed [6,8]. Therefore, high precision is easy to achieve but does not convey useful information, while recall cannot be computed accurately because of the enormous size of the web.

The problem of measuring the quality of search results becomes more interesting when searching for controversial issues. A controversial issue is one that has several

---

* Corresponding author. Part of this work was supported by a Brachman-Hoffman grant.

J. Cordeiro et al. (Eds.): WEBIST 2008, LNBIP 18, pp. 278–292, 2009.
© Springer-Verlag Berlin Heidelberg 2009

possible relevant "answers", depending on one's point of view. Are the results users receive characterized by a reasonably comprehensive *coverage*? In other words, are the various opinions equally represented in the search results?

While search engines are trying to provide unbiased results, Search Engine Optimization (SEO) companies and web spammers are actively trying to force a search engine to list their own sites high on its search results. They do so using a variety of techniques, such as creating "link farms" [6,9]. How *independent* are the top-10 results? For example, is it possible for a successful group of spammers to claim, not only the top spot in the top-10 search results, but a large group of them?

In this paper we take on the problem of defining coverage and independence of web search results. As far as we know, even though several papers have tried to define search quality (e.g., [1]) the metrics we introduce have never been addressed in the past. In the process we study the structure and density of the web neighborhood that supports each of the web search results according to each search engine, and we observe some interesting characteristics of these neighborhoods and of the way the search engines operate.

2   Web Search Results of Controversial Issues

To address these questions we decided to do a sequence of web searches on highly contested issues using the two most popular search engines, Google and Yahoo. A controversial (and thus, contested) issue is one that has several possible relevant "answers", depending on one's point of view. The subjectivity of the answers is what separates a controversial issue from a simple ambiguity, which is a separate, well defined search problem. Searching for "jaguar", for example, one expects fo find results that stem from the ambiguous use of the term (a car, an operating system, an animal, etc.) We are interested in queries that are not ambiguous, but have subjective answers. For each of the queries we selected, one can expect that there are at least three possible answers: a "pro", a "con" and a "bal" (short, for "balanced") answer.

2.1   Coverage

We argue that for a controversial issue, equal and comprehensive coverage in the top-N results is to have an equal number of pro, con and bal results. We will simply refer to this quality as "coverage" and we will define it below. For example, in the top-10 search results that search engines are giving back by default, equal and comprehensive coverage would be to have 3-4 results (or, on average, 3.3 results) from each category.

Let's assume we have k different categories for a complete coverage (above we have $k = 3$) and we have N results in the top-N slots. Let's further assume that category i received r_i results. We define as *coverage bias* the following quantity B:

$$B = \sum_{1 \le i \le k} |r_i - \frac{N}{k}| \tag{1}$$

In other words, B is the distance of r_i from the expected number of results N/k. We note that bias B is bounded by:

$$B_{min} = 0 \le B \le N + (k-2)N/k = B_{max}$$

Specifically for top-10 search results, when we have equal number of results from each category, we have minimum bias $B_{min} = 0$. At the other end, when one category takes all top-10 spots, the bias is maximized at $B_{max} = 13.3$.

The further bias B is from 0, the worst the coverage is. Therefore we can define as **coverage** C, the lack of bias, that is,

$$C = \frac{B_{max} - B}{B_{max}} \qquad (2)$$

Coverage C, therefore, has a value between 0 (one-sided coverage) and 1 (equal and comprehensive coverage). When coverage is in the bottom third of this range, we call it *low coverage*, in the middle third *medium coverage*, and on the top third *high coverage*. For example, if the three categories receive 4, 3 and 3 (respectively) of the top-10 results, then bias is small, $B = 0.66 + 0.33 + 0.33 = 1.3$, and coverage is high: $C = \frac{13.3 - 1.3}{13.3} = 0.9$.

2.2 Independence

The second metric we introduce is *independence* in search results. To define independence we need first to examine the various ways in which search results can be dependent. We see four kinds of dependent results:

- *URL dependency* is the situation when multiple entries in the top-N results are actually coming from the same site URL, e.g., they correspond to different pages of the very same site, as it is defined by the domain URL. For example, in Table 5, results numbered 5 and 6 have URL dependency. In the Tables of this paper we mark one of the two URL dependencies with a (u).
- *Redirection dependency* is the situation when two different site URLs resolve onto the very same location. Redirection is often used by web spammers who try to increase the visibility of a target site by creating many other sites that will point to the target site [6]. For example, in Table 5, results numbered 3 and 4 have redirection dependency. In the Tables we mark one of the two redirection dependencies with an (r).
- *Content dependency* is the situation when the contents of two or more pages included in the search results are essentially the same. The contents may be surrounded by images and menus that are different and are stored on different web sites. This is also a trick used by spammers who try to increase visibility to a target site by creating entries in blogs or "news" sites that lack their own content [6]. For example, in Table 11, results numbered 4 and 8 have content dependency. In the Tables we mark one of the two content dependencies with a (c).
- *Link dependency* is the situation when the supporting link structure in the web graph is substantially similar in two or more sites. Link dependency reveals "link farms' of spammers [6]. This type of dependency has been studied extensively in the literature, and it is considered a major tool that the Search Engine Optimization industry is using to acquire high PageRank [3]. In this paper we will focus on the most basic similarity structure, namely the *circular link dependency* between two or more sites. For example, in Table 11, results numbered 3 and 10 have circular

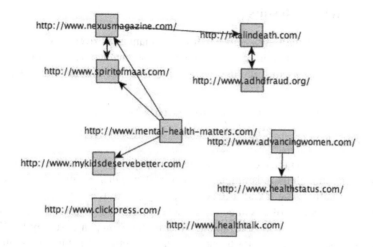

Fig. 1. Link dependencies between the top-10 sites of Table 11. The backGraph algorithm reveals that there is considerable linking between 8 of these sites, effectively influencing the search results. In particular, the pairs of sites in the upper part have circular link dependencies. These four sites occupy locations 1 and 6 in Google's results and 3, 6, 7, 10 in Yahoo's results.

link dependency, as do results numbered 6 and 7. See Figure 1. In the Tables we mark one of the two link dependencies with an (l).

Let's consider the search results of some controversial query. Let's assume that out of the top-N results, u results are URL dependent, r results are redirection dependent, c results are content dependent, and l results are link dependent. We define as **independence** of the search results the ratio of the non-dependent sites over N, or

$$I = \frac{N - (u + r + c + l)}{N} \tag{3}$$

Independence essentially measures the percentage of independent results in a collection of top-N search results. Note that in the formula above we penalize URL dependencies for all but one (their "representative") of the identical URLs. We do the same for all other types of dependencies. Of course, we do not penalize results having multiple dependencies more than once.

Like coverage, independence is also a number between 0 (lack of independence) and 1 (all independent results). As with coverage, the higher the independence, the higher the quality of search results.

We should clarify that, even though it is a very important issue, we are not examining here the correctness or factual accuracy of search results. It is known that misinformation is a serious problem on the internet [12,2,5]. But evaluating correctness or accuracy requires significant amounts of time by qualified experts and there is no easy way to be done automatically by computer. We are mainly interested in exploring quality measures that can be computed using automatic or semi-automatic algorithms that will help search engines increase the quality of their search results.

3   Experimental Results

An examination of a daily newspaper will reveal many controversial issues for which web users may search, and our colleagues have recommended many others. We chose to follow search results to three queries coming from the commercial, medical and political arena:

- Q1 (commercial): *Human growth hormone (HGH) benefits*
- Q2 (medical): *Is ADHD a real disease?*
- Q3 (political): *Morality of abortions*

Q1 aims at information related to one of the more popular steroids, the human growth hormone. Even though there is ample medical evidence that not only does it not help but may even harm those taking it (see, e.g., [14]), there is a strong industry that is promising (unsupported of any medical evidence) miracles: to reverse aging, reduce body fat, and increase lean muscle, among other things. Companies selling HGH products have strong financial reasons to increase their coverage in the top-10 results, and consequently decrease the coverage of the information that discredits them. For most people, this is not a high visibility issue, however, and it is unlikely that the average web user would know of this controversy.

Q2 aims at information related to a psychiatric condition, Attention-Deficit Hyperactivity Disorder (ADHD - as it is known in the USA) or Hyperkinetic Disorder (as it is known in Europe). While the vast majority of medical doctors accept ADHD as a real disease, there is a small but active vocal opposition by a few parents, doctors and religious organizations (e.g., the Church of Scientology), that dispute it. For many people unfamiliar with the condition, this is also not a high visibility issue.

On the other hand, Q3 is a high-visibility and controversial issue that is gaining extra attention in the USA during election periods. There are strong and vocal groups both favoring and condemning abortion, and every candidate for political office has to take a position on the issue. It is expected, therefore that it is one of the issues that will generate a lot of battles for placement in the top-10 search results.

We note that, while we did not choose the queries based on Wikipedia articles, we observed that all three queries have disputed entries or heated discussions in Wikipedia, an evidence of these battles being carried out in the social networks sphere. See [15,16,17].

The question we wanted to address is: Do we get good coverage and independent responses when searching on these controversial issues using the two major search engines, Google and Yahoo?

To evaluate our research question we first conducted the three searches using the Google and Yahoo search APIs in August and September, 2007. We analyzed the search results and computed the coverage and independence of each search.

3.1   The Supporting Web Graph

It has been shown [10] that the link structure of pages is evolving at a very fast pace, faster than the pace of change in page contents. We wanted to check this observation with regards to the web site back links. Do they also change fast? To do that, we followed the link structure of the supporting web graph twice, in August and September 2007, with our results reported here.

We examined several questions regarding the comparison of the results between the two search engines. The results of our work appear in the subsections below. First, we explain how we computed the supporting web graphs of each search result.

We define as the *supporting web subgraph G* of depth d for some URL U according to search engine S the graph that is computed using S's back links for d iterations.

To compute the supporting web subgraphs of each search result, we created a java program, `backGraph`, that, given a particular URL U as input, it first collects the set of links $L(U)$ of sites pointing to U according to search engine S. Since we cannot search the whole web from scratch to determine these links, we used the Search APIs provided by Yahoo [13] and Google [4]. This collection, $L(U)$, corresponds to back link depth $d = 1$. In graph theoretic terms, $L(U)$ is expected to be a star of nodes (URLs) with edges corresponding to hyperlinks from other documents pointing to U, the center of the star.

We continued computing the sets $L^2(U) = L(L(U))$ for depth $d = 2$ and $L^3(U)$ for depth $d = 3$ using each of the two APIs. We stop at depth $d = 3$ following [8] that shows is to be sufficient for revealing the structure of the supporting web graph. Going further would strengthen our results but would also require significantly larger computational time.

More formally, the algorithm and the parameters we used are as follows:

Supporting Web Graph Algorithm

```
Input:
   s[i] = each of top-10 results' URL
   d = Depth of back link search (d=3)
   B = Number of backlinks to record (B=100)
   SE = {YahooAPI, GoogleAPI}

Algorithm:
   S = {s[i]}
   Using depth-first-search for depth d do:
     Find the set U of sites linking to sites in S
       using the SE for up to B backlinks/site
     S = S + U

Output:
   Graph recorded in S for each API
```

One may expect that $L(L(L(U)))$ would create a tree of sites pointing to U in no more than 3 links. It turns out that the graph created is not a tree but a directed graph G with a bi-connected core (called BCC in [8]). It has been shown that this graph reveals the deliberate link support that activists and spammers are using to promote a particular web page so that this page scores high on a search engine's query results. We then evaluated the size of each graph $|G|$ by calculating the number of nodes (sites) $|V|$ and edges (links) $|E|$ as well as the size of its BCC. In this paper, we do not discuss the BCC data.

Table 1. Results for coverage and independence metrics. $C(G)$ and $C(Y)$ are the coverage scores in the Google and the Yahoo results, respectively. $I(G)$ and $I(Y)$ are the independence scores for the Google and Yahoo results, respectively.

Query	bal	pro	con	$C(G)$	bal	pro	con	$C(Y)$	$I(G)$	$I(Y)$
Q1: HGH benefits	0	10	0	0.0	0	10	0	0.0	0.8	0.7
Q2: ADHD real disease	0	1	9	0.1	0	1	9	0.1	0.7	0.7
Q3: Morality of Abortion	5	3	1	0.7	3	2	4	0.8	0.9	0.9

3.2 Overall Results

Table 1 shows the coverage and independence results of the three queries. We observe that in the commercially important Q1 and the medically important Q2, coverage from both search engines is very low. Recall that Q1 and Q2 have low visibility. Results from both search engines show medium to high independence for these queries. On the other hand, for the highly visible and politically important Q3, coverage is medium-to-high and independence is high for both search engines, with Yahoo scoring higher in coverage than Google.

In the late 1990's search engine algorithms used to differ significantly. It has been argued that these days, most search engines use very similar search algorithms. Our results provide some evidence for this.

The size of the support web subgraph is one area where the search results differ significantly between the search engines. Yahoo's supporting web graph size is significantly larger than Google's. Given the popularity and reputation of Google, one might have guessed the opposite.

It has been reported that the search engines APIs do not faithfully report their back links. We found evidence that the reported sizes of the supporting web graphs by Google are affected by some filtering of the back links. This is strongly evidenced by the fact that several supporting web graphs for Google have trivial sizes (e.g., result 7 in Q1 and result 9 in Q2), and this can be explained with the existence of result filtering or some kind of PageRank manipulation.

Another question we addressed is, how much did the top-10 results changed for each search engine in the period of the study. To answer this question we evaluated three similarity measurements between the top-10 search results for each query and for each search engine in the two time periods we retrieved our data (August and September, 2007). We did the same for each query and each time period for the search results by each search engine. As similarity measures we used the *percent of overlap*, the *G-measure* and the *M-measure*.

The first measure is the percent of overlap, O, (which we will simply call *overlap*) between two ordered lists. The greater the overlap, the more items two lists have in common. Overlap varies between 0.0 (no common pages) and 1.0 (permutation of the same pages). Note that the overlap ignores any difference in the ordering of the items in the lists, and it just looks for common presence.

The second measure is the *G-measure* G [18] which tries to address the similarity of item location in two lists. It looks at the absolute difference between the locations of an item appearing in the two lists. For the same overlap, the larger the G-measure, the

Table 2. Intra-SE comparison: Persistence of top-10 search results between August and September, 2007, for each search engine

Search Eng.	Query	O	G	M	Analysis
Google	Q1: (HGH)	0.7	0.82	0.91	Largely unchanged top & mid entries
	Q2: (ADHD)	0.5	0.53	0.41	Medium overlap in lower entries
	Q3: (Abortion)	0.7	0.65	0.68	Mostly unchanged top & mid entries
Yahoo	Q1: (HGH)	0.6	0.60	0.77	Largely unchanged top & mid entries
	Q2: (ADHD)	0.3	0.33	0.51	Small overlap in top positions
	Q3: (Abortion)	0.5	0.55	0.63	Mostly unchanged top/mid entries

Table 3. Inter-SE comparison: Google vs Yahoo result similarity of top-10 search results per observation period

Query	Time Period	O	G	M	Analysis
Q1: (HGH)	Aug. 2007	0.2	0.20	0.21	Little overlap, but in higher position
	Sept. 2007	0.1	0.16	0.20	no convergence over time
Q2: (ADHD)	Aug. 2007	0.4	0.27	0.10	Medium O. b/w top/low positions,
	Sept. 2007	0.3	0.27	0.18	increased convergence over time
Q3: (Abortion)	Aug. 2007	0.3	0.33	0.50	Small overlap in high positions,
	Sept. 2007	0.3	0.38	0.55	significant convergence over time

more nearby positions the items occupy. Like overlap, it ranges betwen 0.0 (no item in common) and 1.0 (identically ordered lists).

Even though G gives a good measurement of ranking similarity, it is not meaningful when the overlap between the top-10 results is very small, because the non-overlapping elements have a major effect it. Also, having two items occupying the last two location in the top-10 will give the same G when the two items are occupying the top two locations. In [19] a new measure, the *M-measure* M, was proposed to capture the intuition that identical or near identical rankings among the top documents is more valuable to the user than are rankings among the lower placed documents. For the same overlap, the greater the M, the smaller the distance of common items near the top. Like the other two measurements, it ranges betwen 0.0 (no item in common) and 1.0 (identically ordered lists).

Since the three measures, O, G and M provide complementary information about the similarity of two lists, we used all three in the analysis below. We present our results for overlap, the G-measure and the M-measure in tables 2 and 3. In the last column we note our observations based on their values.

In terms of intra-SE comparison, we observe the following:

- Google's results were largely persistent over the time period studied; Yahoo showed more change in its results than Google.
- For both search engines, Q2 (on ADHD) was the query that had the greater change, especially in Yahoo's results.

In terms of inter-SE comparison:

- The results showed low to very-low agreement for queries Q1 and Q2, but significant agreement in Q3 (on abortion).

Next, we discuss results for each query in some detail.

Table 4. Top-10 results of the Google search engine when given the query Q1 = *HGH benefits* on August, 2007. See also Table 5.

#	Google top-10 results on August, 2007
1	http://www.i-care.net/hgh-benefits.html
2	http://www.alwaysyoung.com/hgh/benefits/benefits.html
3	http://www.ghsales.com/ghsales2/hgh_growth_hormone_benefits.html
4	http://www.humangrowthhormonesales.com/ghsales2/index.html
5	http://www.hgh-human-growth-hormone.org/
6	http://www.hgh-human-growth-hormone.org/benefits-of-hgh.htm
7	http://www.csmngt.com/human_growth_hormone.htm
8	http://www.associatedcontent.com/article/38893/human_growth_hormone_hgh_benefits_risks.html
9	http://www.hgharticles.com/
10	http://www.godswaynutrition.com/products/growthhormone.html

Table 5. Supporting web graph sizes, as reported by backGraph, for each site in the top-10 results of the Google API for query Q1 (see Table 4). The two columns correspond to backGraph sizes measured in August, 2007 and September, 2007. For each entry we have calculated the size of the backGraph as $(|V|, |E|)$ revealed by the Google API and the change between these two dates. In 4 cases we see significant difference (above 20%) in their sizes over time.

#	August, 2007	September, 2007	Change (%)	Notes
1	(415,426)	(346,353)	-16.6	G1=Y8 (r)
2	(161,167)	(133,137)	-17.4	G2=Y1
3	(1245,1314)	(981,1027)	-21.2	G3=G4 (r)
4	(1245,1314)	(981,1027)	-21.2	G4=G3 (r)
5	(71,77)	(71,77)	0.0	G5=G6 (u)
6	(71,77)	(71,77)	0.0	G6=G5 (u)
7	(1,0)	(1,0)	0.0	filtered
8	(1749,2086)	(2905,3386)	+66.1	
9	(1388, 1585)	(463, 506)	-66.7	G9=Y2
10	(502 ,506)	(419 ,423)	-16.6	

Specific Observations for Q1 Results. The size of support web subgraphs reported by Yahoo is 7 times greater than that reported by Google (total of 49886 nodes vs 6848 nodes). In the period of the two months we monitored the sizes of the supporting web subgraphs, we saw small-to-medium percentage variation in the size of the Google graphs and wide range for the Yahoo graphs. Despite that, they seem to almost agree on the top result (G2 = Y1) as well as in other results (e.g., G1=Y8, G9=Y2).

All of the top-10 results for both Google and Yahoo seem to be coming from companies that sell steroids online (the "pro" case). There are no results from medical authorities or research articles that refer to the medical or legal problems from the use of steroids (the "con" case). There are also no "balanced" views represented in the top-10 results. Coverage, therefore, is very low. We believe that these results reveal the work of very successful commercial SEOs who have dedicated lots of resources to gain from the lucrative HGH industry.

Specific Observations for Q2 Results. As we mentioned, Q2 coverage results are largely similar to Q1 results for both search engines. The size of support web subgraphs reported by Yahoo is, again, far greater than that reported by Google (total of 88737 nodes vs 19901 nodes, or 4 times greater).

Table 6. Top-10 results of the Yahoo search engine when given the query Q1 = *HGH benefits* on August, 2007. See also Table 7.

#	Yahoo results
1	http://www.alwaysyoung.com/hgh/benefits/benefits.html
2	http://www.hgharticles.com/hgh_benefits.html
3	http://www.hgh-pro.com/pro-blenhgh.html
4	http://www.hghhomeopathic.com/HGH.html
5	http://www.hgharticles.com/
6	http://www.hghnstuff.com/faq-benefits-hgh.htm
7	http://linkspiders.com/HGH/benefits%20of%20hgh.htm
8	http://eyecare.freeyellow.com/hgh-benefits.html
9	http://www.hgh-pro.com/homeopathichgh.html
10	http://www.hgh.com/Descriptions/sec.aspx

Table 7. Supporting web graph sizes, as reported by backGraph, for each site in the top-10 results of the Yahoo API for query Q1 (see Table 6). The two columns correspond to backGraph sizes measured in August, 2007 and September, 2007. For each entry we have calculated the size of the backGraph as $(|V|, |E|)$ revealed by the Yahoo API and the change between these two dates. In 7 cases we see significant difference (above 20%) in their sizes over time.

#	August, 2007	September, 2007	Change (%)	Notes
1	(13151,16690)	(7829,9294)	-40.5	Y1=G2
2	(2933,3871)	(3380,4634)	+15.2	Y2=G9
3	(9587,11741)	(6376,7727)	-33.5	Y3=Y9 (u)
4	(2137,2402)	(3125,3551)	+46.2	
5	(2933,3871)	(3380, 4634)	+15.2	Y5 = Y2 (u)
6	(3063, 3444)	(5575, 6877)	+82.0	
7	(3194, 3665)	(491, 495)	-84.6	
8	(1041, 1204)	(1990, 2295)	+91.2	Y8=G1 (r)
9	(6376,7727)	(6376,7727)	0.0	Y9=Y3 (u)
10	(5471, 6460)	(7418, 9114)	+35.6	

Table 8. Top-10 results of the Google search engine when given the query Q2 = *Is ADHD a real disease*, on August, 2007. See also Table 9.

#	Google results
1	http://www.spiritofmaat.com/archive/oct1/drfred.htm
2	http://www.clickpress.com/releases/Detailed/2728005cp.shtml
3	http://www.wildestcolts.com/mentalhealth/stimulants.html
4	http://www.wildestcolts.com/safeEducation/real.html
5	http://web4health.info/en/answers/adhd-real-disorder.htm
6	http://www.adhdfraud.org/
7	http://www.adhdfraud.org/commentary/5-27-01-1.htm
8	http://www.mykidsdeservebetter.com/adhd/disease.asp
9	http://www.virtualvienna.net/community/modules.php?name=News &file=article&sid=295
10	http://www.escolar.com/Escolar-Parenting_Articles/Escolar-is-adhd-a-real-disease.php

These results reveal low coverage, with only one of the top-10 entries differing from the overall "con" direction of the results. There are no "balanced" results included. Interestingly, for both search engines, the "pro" result occupies position 5! The results for Yahoo reveal low link independence as four of the top-10 results are forming two circular link farms (Figure 1).

We believe that when a controversial issue is below the horizon of current news awareness, such as the ADHD issue at the time of the search, those that care about an

Table 9. Supporting web graph sizes, as reported by backGraph, for each site in the top-10 results of the Google API for query Q2 (see Table 8). The two columns correspond to backGraph sizes measured in August, 2007 and September, 2007. For each entry we have calculated the size of the backGraph as $(|V|, |E|)$ revealed by the Google API and the change between these two dates. In 7 cases we see significant difference (above 20%) in their sizes over time.

#	August, 2007	September, 2007	Change (%)	Notes
1	(1928,2135)	(1423,1614)	-25.2	G1=Y6
2	(1223,1297)	(912,991)	-25.4	G2=Y9
3	(496,515)	(873,925)	+76.0	G3=G4 (u)
4	(496,515)	(873,925)	+76.0	G4=G3 (u)
5	(2545,2759)	(1688,1790)	-33.7	pro
6	(3280,3912)	(3955,4791)	+20.58	G6=Y3
7	(3280,3912)	(3955,4791)	+20.58	G7 = G6 (u)
8	(1590,1708)	(1557,1848)	-2.1	G8 = Y2
9	(1,0)	(1,0)	0.0	filtered (c)
10	(5062,5764)	(incomplete)	N/C	(c)

Table 10. Top-10 results of the Yahoo search engine when given the query Q2 = *Is ADHD a real disease*, on August, 2007. See also Table 11.

#	Yahoo results
1	http://www.mental-health-matters.com/articles/article.php?artID=849
2	http://www.mykidsdeservebetter.com/adhd/disease.asp
3	http://www.adhdfraud.org/
4	http://www.healthstatus.com/articles/Is_ADHD_A_Real_Disease.html
5	http://www.healthtalk.com/adhd/diseasebasics.cfm
6	http://www.spiritofmaat.com/archive/oct1/drfred.htm
7	http://www.nexusmagazine.com/articles/ADHDisbogus.html
8	http://www.advancingwomen.com/diabetes/is_adhd_a_real_disease.php
9	http://www.clickpress.com/releases/Detailed/2728005cp.shtml
10	http://ritalindeath.com/Against-ADHD-Diagnosis.htm

Table 11. Supporting web graph sizes, as reported by backGraph, for each site in the top-10 results of the Yahoo API for query Q2 (see Table 10). The two columns correspond to backGraph sizes measured in August, 2007 and September, 2007. For each entry we have calculated the size of the backGraph as $(|V|, |E|)$ revealed by the Yahoo API and the change between these two dates. In 4 cases we see significant difference (above 20%) in their sizes over time.

#	August, 2007	September, 2007	Change (%)	Notes
1	(10263,13422)	(12321,16184)	-16.7	
2	(7610,9556)	(5208,6202)	+46.12	Y2=G8
3	(7567,9093)	(9791,12232)	-22.7	Y3=G6 (l)
4	(13631,17032)	(12590,15645)	+8.3	
5	(7011,8488)	(6704,7993)	+4.6	pro
6	(6425,8651)	(4242,5148)	+51.5	Y6=G1 (l)
7	(8424,10808)	(8266,10184)	+2.0	(l)
8	(19291,25469)	(21150,27145)	-8.8	(c)
9	(5675,6644)	(4920,5775)	+15.37	Y9=G2
10	(2840,3440)	(2359,2604)	+20.4	(l)

issue can be successful in getting the top spots in the relevant queries. The situation seems to be a bit different for issues that have enormous visibility and equally determined groups of supporters, such as the next query.

Table 12. Top-10 results of the Google search engine when given the query Q3 = *Morality of abortion*, on August, 2007. See also Table 13.

#	Google results
1	http://www.efn.org/ bsharvy/abortion.html
2	http://atheism.about.com/od/abortioncontraception/p/Religions.htm
3	http://atheism.about.com/od/abortioncontraception/p/AtheistsAbort.htm
4	http://ethics.sandiego.edu/Applied/Abortion/index.asp
5	http://rwor.org/a/038/morality-right-to-abortion.htm
6	http://www.answers.com/topic/abortion-debate
7	http://ocw.mit.edu/NR/rdonlyres/054E18A6-DC9A-460E-826E-9EEC31A573E1/0/abortion.pdf
8	http://www.nrlc.org/news/2002/NRL06/pres.html
9	http://www.manitowoc.uwc.edu/staff/awhite/mark_b97.htm
10	http://www.keele.ac.uk/depts/la/ documents/rfletcherFlagsubamd.pdf

Table 13. Supporting web graph sizes, as reported by backGraph, for each site in the top-10 results of the Google API for query Q3 (see Table 12). The two columns correspond to backGraph sizes measured in August, 2007 and September, 2007. For each entry we have calculated the size of the backGraph as $(|V|, |E|)$ revealed by the Google API and the change between these two dates. In 3 cases we see significant difference (above 20%) in their sizes over time.

#	August, 2007	September, 2007	Change (%)	Notes
1	(5942,6710)	(5597,6350)	-5.9	G1=Y1
2	(3922,4610)	(3429,4138)	-12.6	G2=G3 (u)
3	(3922,4610)	(3429,4138)	-12.6	G3=G2 (u)
4	(12045,14659)	(10433,13102)	-13.38	G4=Y8
5	(1667,2095)	(2687,3213)	+61.19	
6	(7440,8657)	(5187,6276)	-30.28	G2=Y6
7	(3006,3373)	(2902,3211)	-3.5	
8	(6422,8119)	(5810,7295)	-9.5	
9	(2079,2353)	(1331,1560)	-36.0	
10	(incomplete)	(incomplete)	N/C	

Specific Observations for Q3 Results. Yahoo's sizes of support web subgraphs is roughly equal to Google's, (total of 125376 nodes vs 113463 nodes for the first nine results) in big contrast with the results in Q1 and Q2. Interestingly, both engines also agree on the top spot (G1=Y1), which represents a "balanced" opinion of the query. They both include "pro-choice" and "pro-life" results, while devoting the remaining top-10 entries on opinion gatherers (such as about.com and wikipedia.org).

Over the two month period we observe much smaller variation of the sizes of the supporting web graph, especially for Yahoo. It is not the case that this was due to lack of interest, because the abortion issue has always been at the top of political agendas in the USA. We conjecture that for such highly sensitive issues, the search engines "tune" their results so that they will present wider coverage of opinions. We have seen this happening in the past in a variety of well publicized queries (such as "miserable failure" [21]).

3.3 Supporting Web Graph Overlaps

Another question we studied is how much overlap exists in the backGraphs produced by the two search engines on the same result. Given that Yahoo reports far more links than Google, one might expect that there is a major overlap between their backlink graphs.

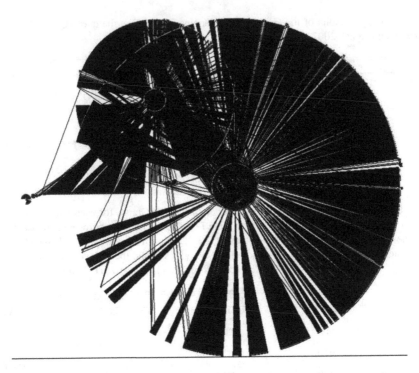

Fig. 2. The graph induced by the backlinks of Google's 1st result and Yahoo's 1st result for Q3 (G1=Y1). The graph has been drawn to emphasize the two BCCs. The upper left group is composed by the majority of Google's 5942 sites, the center right large group is composed by most of Yahoo's 17224 sites, while the group in the middle left side (appears as a horizontal line) is mostly composed of 470 sites in the intersection of the two groups.

Table 14. Top-10 results of the Yahoo search engine when given the query Q3 = *Morality of abortion*, on August, 2007. See also Table 15.

#	Yahoo results
1	http://www.efn.org/ bsharvy/abortion.html
2	http://jbe.gold.ac.uk/5/barnh981.htm
3	http://www.rit.org/editorials/abortion/moralwar.html
4	http://en.wikipedia.org/wiki/Morality_and_legality_of_abortion
5	http://www.abort73.com/HTML/I-H-2-morality.html
6	http://atheism.about.com/od/abortioncontraception/p/Religions.htm
7	http://www.ashby2004.com/abortion.html
8	http://ethics.sandiego.edu/Applied/Abortion/
9	http://www.rit.org/editorials/abortion/morality.html
10	http://gospelway.com/morality/index.php

We have found this not to be the case. See Figure 2 for a graphical representation of a typical example. The two search engines seem to report a largely different set of links in their results: Between G1's 5942 sites and Y1's 17224 sites, there is a mere overlap of 470 sites!

Table 15. Supporting web graph sizes, as reported by backGraph, for each site in the top-10 results of the Yahoo API for query Q3 (see Table 14). The two columns correspond to backGraph sizes measured in August, 2007 and September, 2007. For each entry we have calculated the size of the backGraph as $(|V|, |E|)$ revealed by the Yahoo API and the change between these two dates. In no cases we see significant difference (above 20%) in their sizes over time.

#	August, 2007	September, 2007	Change (%)	Notes
1	(17224,21732)	(15367,19843)	-10.8	Y1=G1
2	(17491,22553)	(16137,21632)	-7.74	
3	(13434,17522)	(13752,17656)	+2.37	Y3=Y9 (u)
4	(25672,35167)	(25672,35167)	0.0	
5	(10282,14156)	(12243,16284)	+19.1	
6	(6274, 8169)	(6274, 8169)	0.0	Y6=G2
7	(7370,9919)	(7370,9919)	0.0	
8	(13877,18248)	(13877,18248)	0.0	
9	(13752,17656)	(13752,17656)	0.0	Y9=Y3 (u)
10	(2195,2721)	(incomplete)	N/C	

4 Conclusions and Open Problems

With this paper, which is the extended and augmented version of [20], we have started an effort to evaluate quality of web search results in terms of two important metrics, coverage and independence. We have found that when searching controversial issues, both of these quality metrics can be low. Given the fact that search engines are unwilling to tune their search results manually, except in a few cases that have become the source of bad publicity [21], low coverage and independence reveal the efforts of dedicated groups to manipulate the search results. Automatizing this computation would be a challenging but rewarding step towards quality analysis of search results.

We also found that Yahoo's API reports a much greater number of back links than Google's API. We do not believe that this means that Google indexes a smaller portion of the web, but that, as others have suggested [22], Google limits the size of its reported backlinks.

On the other hand, between search engines there is a non-trivial degree of overlapping results in the top-10 results for all the queries, selected (reportedly) among millions of qualifying results. This suggests the employment of similar algorithms and heuristics by the two search engines. More research is needed to measure the effect of this conclusion.

Queries on controversial issues will continue to play an important role in web search. Search engines need tools to help them provide high quality results that include high coverage and high independence between results. Evolution of search results of controversial and highly contested queries over time is also needed, as it may reveal information about the part of the web that is being manipulated by spammers, activists and SEOs. Future research will hopefully shed some light on the extend of this manipulation.

Acknowledgements. Part of this work was supported by a Brachman-Hoffman grant. We would like to thank Sociology Professor Rosanna Hertz for providing expert evaluation on the coverage of query Q3's results.

References

1. Amento, B., Terveen, L., Hill, W.: Does authority mean quality? Predicting expert quality ratings of web documents. In: Proceedings of the Twenty-Third Annual International ACM SIGIR Conference on Research and Development in Information Retrieval. ACM, New York (2000)
2. Berenson, A.: On hair-trigger wall street, a stock plunges on fake news. New York Times (2000)
3. Brin, S., Page, L.: The anatomy of a large-scale hypertextual Web search engine. Computer Networks and ISDN Systems 30(1–7), 107–117 (1998)
4. Google. The Google API, google, inc. (2003), http://code.google.com/apis/
5. Graham, L., Metaxas, P.T.: "Of course it's true; i saw it on the internet!": Critical thinking in the internet era. Commun. ACM 46(5), 70–75 (2003)
6. Gyuongyi, Z., Garcia-Molina, H.: Web spam taxonomy. In: Proceedings of the First International Workshop on Adversarial Information Retrieval on the Web, Chiba, Japan (2005)
7. Manning, C., Raghavan, P., Schultze, H.: Introduction to Information Retrieval, forthcoming edn. Cambridge Press, Cambridge (2008)
8. Metaxas, P.T., Destefano, J.: Web spam, propaganda and trust. In: Proceedings of the First International Workshop on Adversarial Information Retrieval on the Web, Chiba, Japan (2005)
9. Moran, M., Hunt, B.: Search Engine Marketing. IBM Press, New Jersey (2006)
10. Ntoulas, A., Cho, J., Olston, C.: What's new on the web? the evolution of the web from a search engine perspective. In: Proceedings of the WWW 2004 Conference, New York, NY (2004)
11. Silverstein, C., Marais, H., Henzinger, M., Moricz, M.: Analysis of a very large web search engine query log. SIGIR Forum 33(1), 6–12 (1999)
12. Vedder, A.: Misinformation through the internet: Epistemology and ethics. Intersentia, Antwerpen, Gronigen, Oxford (2001)
13. Yahoo, The Yahoo search API, Yahoo, inc. (2006), http://developer.yahoo.com/search/
14. Wellness letter, UC Berkeley (June 2003), http://www.berkeleywellness.com/html/ds/dsGrowthHormone.php (retrieved October 10, 2008)
15. Wikipedia entry on Growth hormone, http://en.wikipedia.org/wiki/Hgh (retrieved October 10, 2008)
16. Wikipedia entry on ADHD, http://en.wikipedia.org/wiki/Hyperkinetic_conduct_disorder (retrieved October 10, 2008)
17. Wikipedia entry on Morality and Legality of Abortion, http://en.wikipedia.org/wiki/Morality_legality_of_abortion (retrieved October 10, 2008)
18. Fagin, R., Kumar, R., Sivakumar, D.: Comparing top k lists. SIAM J. on Discrete Math. 17(1), 134–160 (2003)
19. Bar-Ilan, J., Mat-Hassan, M., Levene, M.: Methods for comparing rankings of search engine results. Computer Networks 50(10), 1448–1463 (2006)
20. Metaxas, P.T., and Ivanova, L.: Coverage and Independence - Defining Quality in Web Search Results. In: Proceedings of the International Conference on Web Information Systems and Technologies (WEBIST), Madeira, Portugal (2008)
21. Online article entitled Google Kills Bushs Miserable Failure Search & Other Google Bombs, http://searchengineland.com/google-kills-bushs-miserable-failure-search-other-google-bombs-10363.php (retrieved October 10, 2008)
22. McCown, F., Nelson, M.L.: Agreeing to Disagreeing: Search Engines and their Public Interfaces. In: The Proc. of ACM JCDL 2007, Vancouver, Canada (2007)

Part III

Society, e-Business and e-Government

User Acceptance of Internet Banking Service in Malaysia

Yee YenYuen and P. H. P. Yeow

Faculty of Business and Law, Multimedia University
Jalan Ayer Keroh Lama, 75450 Melaka, Malaysia
{YeeYenYuen,P.H.P.Yeow,hpyeow@mmu.edu.my}

Abstract. The study is the first research in Malaysia that investigates user acceptance of Internet banking service (IBS) based on Unified Theory of Acceptance and Use of Technology model (Venkatesh, Morris, Davis and Davis, 2003). Two hundred and eighty questionnaires were distributed and collected from two major cities, Kuala Lumpur and Melaka. Descriptive statistics was used to analyse the data. The results show that Malaysians have intentions of using IBS (mean rating of close to 4.00). Moreover, Malaysians recognize the benefits of IBS by giving a high mean rating (close to 4.00) to performance expectancy. However, they give relative low mean ratings (close to 3.00) on other indicators of Behavioural Intention to Use IBS such as effort expectancy, social influence, facilitating conditions and perceived credibility. Recommendations were given to promote a safe, efficient and conducive environment for user adoption of Internet banking.

Keywords: User acceptance, Internet banking, performance expectancy, perceived credibility.

1 Introduction

Internet banking service [IBS] was introduced in Malaysia about six years ago (The Star, 2005). Although it is new, it has become one of the most popular services in Malaysia with 51% out of the total respondent base of 8,000 using Internet banking service (IBS) once a month (The Star, 2005). With 12 domestic banks offering IBS to 4.5 million subscribers currently (Bank Negara Malaysia, 2007), IBS is an alternative (to physical banking) and new medium to reach more potential customers as it allows bankers to deliver banking products and services to a wider segment of customers through electronic and interactive communication channels, particularly the Internet (Goi, 2005). However, if a bank offers IBS without a clear understanding of factors affecting customer adoption, the investment may be wasted due to the absence of vital business understanding to support customer adoption (Goi, 2005; Pires and Aisbett, 2002). Domestic banking institutions must therefore seek to better understand their customers in this area to prevent loss and maintain competitive advantage (Goi, 2005). Thus, the aim of the present study is to conduct a thorough research on the user acceptance and discover the factors that encourage and discourage the adoption of IBS. To our knowledge, this research is the first in Malaysia, which applied

J. Cordeiro et al. (Eds.): WEBIST 2008, LNBIP 18, pp. 295–306, 2009.

Unified Theory of Acceptance and Use of Technology (UTAUT) model, a new, robust and powerful model, to measure the consumer adoption of IBS. Although numerous studies such as AlAwadhi and Morris (2008), Chen, Wu, and Yang (2008), Michael and Uzoka (2008) and Siracuse, Sowell, and Musselman (2006) have applied UTAUT model in predicting individual adoption of e-government services, Weblogs, E-commerce, and Personal Digital Assistants (PDA) in daily life, none has examined the IBS adoption in Malaysia.

This research will provide domestic bankers with an improved understanding of end-users' concerns and thus assist them in their efforts to offer better IBS that provides a more satisfactory response to consumers' needs. It also helps the government and Bank Negara Malaysia (central bank) to create a conducive and user-friendly environment that will promote full adoption of IBS.

1.1 Selection of UTAUT Model

Nowadays, researchers are confronted with a choice among a multitude of models to examine the user acceptance of a new technology where they always have to choose a "favoured model" and largely ignore the contributions from alternative models. The UTAUT model captures the essential elements of eight previously established models (i.e. Theory of Reasoned Action (TRA), Theory of Acceptance Model (TAM/TAM2), Theory of Planned Behaviour (TPB), Innovation Diffusion Theory (IDT), Motivational Model (MM), Model of Personal Computer Utilization (MPCU), Technology Acceptance Model (CTAM), Theory of Planned Behaviour (TPB) and Social Cognitive Theory (SCT)) (Venkatesh, Morris, Davis and Davis, 2003). The UTAUT model has been tested, cross-validated and confirmed to outperform the eight abovementioned theoretical frameworks (which can only explain 17% to 53% of the variance in user acceptance) by being able to account up to 70% of the variance (adjusted R^2) in technology acceptance. This is a substantial improvement over the original eight models. By encompassing the combined explanatory power of the many abovementioned models, the UTAUT model advances cumulative theory while retaining a

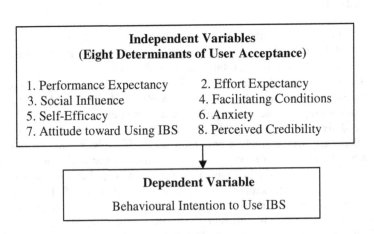

Fig. 1. Research Framework

parsimonious structure. The model encompasses constructs such as performance expectancy, effort expectancy, social influence and facilitating conditions (Venkatesh, et al., 2003). Four additional factors i.e. perceived credibility, self-efficacy, attitude toward using technology, and anxiety are added to this model to measure issues such as security and privacy, confidence, enjoyment and fear during user interaction with IBS, as these factors are highlighted in many IBS literature. The research model of this study is comprehensive and definitive. It redresses the limitations of existing user acceptance models (e.g. TAM/TAM2) by including barriers that would prevent an individual from using IBS (e.g. lack of expertise, and time or money constraint) into the study.

Figure 1 shows the research framework of the study. There are 8 independent variables and one dependent variable.

1.1.1 Dependent Variable

User acceptance is defined as a person's psychological state with regard to his or her voluntary use and intention to use a technology (Dillon and Morris, 1996). It was discovered that some prior studies used attitude while others used behavioural intention or actual usage as the indicators of user acceptance (Sun and Zhang, 2004; Sun and Xiao, 2006). However, behavioural intention is confirmed to be a highly valid indicator of actual usage (Sun, 2003). Therefore, user acceptance is examined by intention to use (equivalent to behavioural intention) in the present study. The dependent variable in the present study is Behavioural Intention to Use IBS which is measured by three items adapted from Venkatesh, et al. (2003) (refer to Table 2: nos. 9-9.3).

Sustained usage of a new technology could be directly hindered or fostered by the accessibility of vital resources and opportunities (Venkatesh, et. al., 2003). The following independent variables are used to measure factors that will encourage and discourage Behavioural Intention to Use IBS.

1.1.2 Independent Variables

The first independent variable is Performance Expectancy. Better Performance Expectancy will lead to greater intention to use a technology (Agarwal and Prasad, 1998; Davis, 1989; Venkatesh and Davis, 2000; Venkatesh, et. al., 2003). Performance expectancy is defined as the degree to which an individual believes that using a service will help him or her to attain gains in job performance (Venkatesh, et. al., 2003). Being one of the strongest predictor of intention, usefulness and job-fit (Thompson, Higgins and Howard, 1991) are key attributes to measure Performance Expectancy.

Another important indicator for Behavioural Intention to use IBS is Effort Expectancy, which is defined as the degree of ease associated with the use of a technology (Venkatesh and Davis, 2000; Venkatesh and Morris, 2000; Venkatesh, et. al., 2003). This factor is significant only during the early adoption of a technology (e.g. first 3 months of service subscription). Perceived ease of use and complexity are crucial attributes to measure Effort Expectancy (Agarwal and Prasad, 1998; Davis, 1989; Thompson, Higgins and Howard, 1991).

The third indicator, Social Influence, is defined as the degree to which an individual perceives others' belief that they should use a new service (Venkatesh, et. al., 2003).

This factor appears to be important only in the early stages (e.g. during service subscription) of individual experience with the technology. Its influence erodes over time, becomes insignificant during sustained usage (Venkatesh and Morris, 2000; Venkatesh, et. al., 2003). Social Influence alters an individual's belief structure, causing him or her to respond to potential social status gains (e.g. prestige) or potential social pressure (e.g. peer or family pressure) in the adoption of a new technology (Venkatesh, et. al., 2003).

The next indicator which has direct influence on Behavioural Intentions is Facilitating Conditions. It is defined as the degree to which an individual believes that a technical infrastructure exists to support the use of a service (Taylor and Todd, 1995, Venkatesh, et. al., 2003). Perceived behavioural control (perceptions of technical and manpower resource constraints on behaviour), and compatibility (the degree to which an innovation is perceived as being consistent with existing values, needs, and experiences of potential adopters) are among the attributes of Facilitating Conditions (Venkatesh, et. al., 2003).

Forming trust or perceived credibility prior to service subscription has a significant impact on customer acceptance since customers generally stay away from a service provider whom they do not trust (Gefen and Silver, 1999; Reichheld and Schefter, 2000). Perceived Credibility is "the belief that the promise of another can be relied upon even under unforeseen circumstances" (Suh and Han, 2002). Distrust (low perceived credibility) of service providers make consumers afraid of providing sensitive information such as financial details on the Internet (Suh and Han 2002).

The following variables, i.e. Attitude toward Using Technology, Self-Efficacy and Anxiety, are other vital determinants of user acceptance in UTAUT model (Venkatesh, et. al., 2003). Attitude toward Using Technology is defined as an individual's overall affective reaction (liking, enjoyment, joy, and pleasure) to using a technology (Davis, 1989; Taylor and Todd, 1995; Thompson, Higgins and Howard, 1991). An individual's positive or negative feelings (e.g. it is good/bad to use a service) and feelings of joy or displeasure (e.g. the innovation makes tasks more interesting / difficult) significantly affect his / her tendency to adopt a new technology in the near future (Venkatesh, et. al., 2003). Self-Efficacy is the judgment of one's ability to use a technology (e.g. computer) to accomplish particular jobs or tasks (Compueau and Higgins, 1995). Since new innovations are often viewed as complex by inexperienced users, confidence in one's ability to handle them can exert an important influence on consumer acceptance (Venkatesh, et. al., 2003). Anxiety is "evoking anxiety or emotional reactions when it comes to using a new technology" (Taylor and Todd, 1995). Unpleasant, strong and negative emotional states (e.g. frustration, confusion, anger) which arise during interaction with a new technology may affect productivity, learning, social relationships, and overall well-being (Compueau and Higgins, 1995; Taylor and Todd, 1995; Venkatesh and Morris, 2000).

2 Methodology

A survey questionnaire was distributed to a sample of 300 IBS users with Information-Technology and business background from two major cities in Malaysia, i.e. Malacca and Kuala Lumpur by using intercepts and snowball sampling methods. Since IBS is new (about six years in operation), it would be apt to first focus on urban areas before rural areas. Therefore, cities were selected in this research on the prospect that there would be more IBS users in urban areas. The response rate was 93.33% (280 respondents). All respondents managed to answer the questionnaire within 30 minutes. They expressed high enthusiasm in commenting on the attributes which deserve modification, clarification or removal. They were also willing to recommend other IBS users to answer the questionnaire. Results of the pilot study were analysed and presented in this paper. The measurement instrument comprised 58 questions on the eight determinants of user acceptance. Of these, 12 questions examined Performance Expectancy, 12 questions related to Effort Expectancy, six questions related to Social Influence, four questions related to Facilitating Conditions, nine questions related to Perceived Credibility, seven questions related to Anxiety, four questions related to Self-Efficacy, and four questions related to Attitude toward Using IBS. In addition, three questions on Behavioural Intention to Use IBS were also included in this measurement instrument. All the questions were rated using a 5-point Likert's scale anchored by 1- Strongly Disagree, 2 – Disagree, 3 – Neutral/Unsure, 4 – Agree, 5 – Strongly Agree. The research data was analysed using descriptive statistics.

About half of the respondents in the present study are male (51.8%) while the remaining (48.2%) are female as indicated in Table 1. Among the respondents, 10.4% are Malays, 77.9% are Chinese and 11.8% are Indians. Sixty-two per cent of the respondents are in the 20 to 29 age-bracket while 31.1% of the respondents are 30 years of age and above. Nearly half of the respondents (48.2%) have 1 to 5 years' experience in using IBS.

Table 1. Respondents' Profile

		Number of cases	%
Gender	Male	145	51.8
	Female	135	48.2
Race	Malay	29	10.4
	Chinese	218	77.9
	Indian	33	11.8
Age	Below 20	19	6.8
	20-29	174	62.1
	30 and above	87	31.1
Number of Years of IBS Use	<1 year	119	42.5
	1-<5 years	135	48.2
	5 years and above	26	9.3

3   Results

Mean and Standard Deviation for attributes measuring each independent and dependent variable in this study are shown in Table 2.

Table 2. Mean and Standard Deviation

Variables	Mean	Standard Deviation
1. Performance Expectancy	**3.81**	**0.981**
1.1 I can manage my money Internet at anytime	3.83	1.057
1.2 I can keep a record of my finances	3.83	0.946
1.3 I need not visit traditional banks regularly	3.89	1.013
1.4 I can transfer money anytime and anywhere	3.94	0.886
1.5 I can save time paying essential bills at the post office	3.95	0.977
1.6 IBS is convenient and easy to access	3.86	1.044
1.7 IBS is efficient	3.87	0.928
1.8 IBS is effective	3.75	0.948
1.9 IBS improves productivity	3.76	1.063
1.10 IBS increases quality of output	3.64	0.959
1.11 IBS is useful	3.90	0.986
1.12 IBS fits into my lifestyle	3.55	0.964
2. Effort Expectancy	**3.41**	**0.896**
2.1 IBS is easy to learn	3.66	1.010
2.2 It is easy to do what I want to do by using IBS	3.50	0.950
2.3 IBS is easy to use	3.61	0.864
2.4 It is easy to become skilful in using IBS	3.55	0.866
2.5 Using IBS does not take too much time	3.61	0.893
2.6 Authentication code is easy to use	3.36	0.905
2.7 There is sufficient time for information entry	3.39	0.905
2.8 Fast information download	3.32	0.897
2.9 Easy web navigation	3.45	0.854
2.10 Detailed answers referring to Frequently Asked Questions (FAQs)	3.16	0.864
2.11 Comprehensive site map	3.16	0.845
2.12 Useful search engine	3.17	0.898
3. Social Influence	**3.13**	**0.923**
3.1 People who influence my behavior use IBS	3.01	0.900
3.2 Coworkers/classmates use IBS	3.40	0.990
3.3 Friends use IBS	3.14	1.031
3.4 People using IBS have high profile	3.15	0.825
3.5 People using IBS have more prestige	3.14	0.848
3.6 Most Malaysians like to use IBS	2.92	0.941
4. Facilitating Conditions	**3.46**	**0.898**
4.1 Basic system requirements for using IBS are met	3.60	0.967
4.2 All contents of IBS are easy to read and understand	3.38	0.872

Table 2. *(continued)*

4.3 Specific person (or group) is always available for assistance	3.38	0.879
4.4 The language in which the document is written is easily understood	3.46	0.875
5. Perceived Credibility	**3.27**	**0.958**
5.1 I trust in the ability of an Internet bank to protect my privacy and personal information	3.27	1.032
5.2 I believe no money will be lost in unauthorized electronic fund transfers	3.27	.942
5.3 I believe Internet bank would not sell my personal information to third parties	3.37	.949
5.4 Other people cannot view my bank account information	3.44	1.004
5.5 Internet bank has enough specialists to detect fraud and information theft	3.27	.960
5.6 I am not worried about being deceived into a fake website	2.90	1.029
5.7 Current password generation is secure	3.17	.910
5.8 Sufficient guidance on password selection	3.23	.930
5.9 Customers are automatically locked out after failed login attempts	3.52	.867
6. Anxiety	**3.13**	**1.048**
6.1 I am afraid of high Internet connection cost	3.57	0.932
6.2 I am afraid of being charged for IBS	3.09	1.097
6.3 I am worried about the inaccessibility of IBS web pages	2.80	1.078
6.4 I don't know how to use IBS	3.40	1.032
6.5 I am afraid of losing information by hitting the wrong key	3.03	1.064
6.6 I am afraid of making mistakes that I cannot correct	2.81	1.152
6.7 IBS is intimidating to me	3.23	0.984
7. Self-Efficacy	**2.98**	**1.033**
7.1 I use IBS only if there is no one around me	3.00	1.137
7.2 I use IBS only if there is built-in help facility for assistance	2.99	0.939
7.3 I use IBS only if I could call someone for help	2.89	0.951
7.4 I use IBS only if I have a lot of time to learn and deal with the service	3.05	1.105
8. Attitude toward Using IBS	**3.50**	**0.879**
8.1 IBS makes banking tasks more interesting	3.50	0.855
8.2 I like working with IBS	3.44	0.857
8.3 It is a good idea to use IBS in daily life	3.64	0.878
8.4 IBS is enjoyable	3.40	0.926
9. Behavioural Intention to Use IBS	**3.83**	**0.893**
9.1 I intend to use IBS in the near future	3.83	.919
9.2 I predict I would use IBS in the near future	3.81	.882
9.3 I plan to use IBS in the near future	3.84	.877

4 Discussion and Recommendations

Malaysians have high expectations on the performance of IBS (Table 2: No. 1) as shown by the average of 3.81 (close to 4.0). This finding is in line with earlier literature worldwide (Chau, 1996; Hsu and Chiu, 2004; Lederer, Maupin, Sena, and Zhuang, 2000), which revealed that the most important criterion in adopting IBS is the ability to enhance job performance without the inconvenience of having to travel, wait and worry about their personal safety while transacting money. Performance expectancy of IBS can be improved by offering more new and unique online banking products and services to tailor the needs of Malaysian communities. For instance, besides allowing customers to check account balances, transfer funds and make online bill payments, domestic banks, in collaboration with other government agencies, could consider allowing consumers to renew car road taxes, settle study loans, and pay for car summons via the Internet. These will help banks to attract new customers, retain old customers and increase profits from online payment and collection of loans.

Standard deviation for the attribute "I need not visit traditional banks regularly" is higher than 1. This indicates that while some respondents think that IBS saves their troubles of visiting physical banks, others still prefer to visit the banks routinely. Perhaps security concerns discourage them from fully relying on IBS to transfer money and pay bills. As indicated by the attributes measuring Perceived Credibility in Table 2, some respondents think that Internet banks cannot protect their privacy and personal information from being stolen by hackers (No. 5.1: standard deviation $=1.032 > 1.0$). Some even suspect that unauthorized persons may be able to access and view their bank account information (No. 5.4: standard deviation $=1.004 > 1.0$). Inadequate knowledge of Internet banking security will probably reduce their intentions to use the technology and drive them to either visit traditional banks or maintain low amounts in Internet accounts. One of the main causes of consumers' unfamiliarity with Internet banking security measures is possibly due to the incomprehensible and lengthy security and privacy policies in the official websites of domestic banks. Customers may not have the time, patience and computer literacy to read and understand the policies. They may not understand some of the technical terms in the security policies, such as, firewalls, secure socket level, encryption, P3P policy, etc. Fake IBS website concern is another reason that deters some respondents from fully adopting IBS (No. 5.6: mean $=2.90$, standard deviation $=1.029 > 1.0$). Wide news coverage on the particular issue may have raised their awareness and sensitivity toward the authenticity of an IBS website. Therefore, domestic bankers should conduct consumer education programmes (e.g. seminars, exhibitions, etc.) to reveal their security policies to customers in layman's terms and educate them about ways to identify a fake website. The effectiveness of these consumer education programmes should be periodically evaluated. Instead of solely relying on banks to tackle phishing, fraudulent websites, and identity theft, consumers should be encouraged to report on fraudulent attempts to obtain their authentication credentials (e.g., attempts to steal username, password, etc.). As revealed by Unisys (2007), Malaysians have nominated Internet identity theft as one of the top three security concerns, similar to those in developed countries such as Australia. Ninety-two per cent of them look forward to having extra security techniques to protect their identity while using IBS (Unisys, 2007). Therefore, Bank Negara Malaysia (central bank) should develop industry-wide best security standards such as two-factor authentication technique which uses transaction authorization code (TAC), digital certificate, smart card or fingerprints in authentication besides username and passwords. Regular report supervision and on-site examinations should be in place to make it mandatory for all domestic banks to comply with the standards issued. In addition, new law such as the Privacy Act or Freedom of Information Act should be enacted to protect consumers' personal information from being misused by unauthorized parties. One important point to consider is security is inversely related to effort expectancy (Lawson, 1998). There should be a balance between these two factors, i.e. the security features implemented should not make IBS too difficult for the users, thus discouraging them from using it.

One of the attributes measuring Effort Expectancy, i.e. "IBS is easy to learn", in Table 2 (No. 2.1) has high standard deviation (>1.0), indicating that while some respondents enjoy learning IBS, others find it difficult to become skilled at using IBS. Similar result is observed in the rating of an attribute measuring Anxiety, i.e. "I am worried about the inaccessibility of IBS web pages" (No. 6.3: standard deviation = 1.078 > 1.0). The difference in perceptions may arise from different personal experience in using the service. This study consists of 42.5% of respondents with less than 1 year experience in using IBS (Table 1), who may perceive IBS as difficult to learn and access due to the lack of personal experience in dealing with the new service. As discovered by Davis (1989)'s study, the more a service is perceived as easy to learn and access, the more likely the service is used extensively. Therefore, to promote the ease of learning and accessing IBS, domestic banks should consider giving free demonstrations and trials to the public at schools or shopping complexes.

Respondents are unsure about the IBS adoption among their coworkers/ classmates and people who influence their behaviours (Table 2; No. 3; mean = 3.13; standard deviation =0.923). In other words, social circles do not have a strong influence on a person's IBS adoption. This contradicts with Venkatesh and Davis's (2000) research in the United States which claimed that social influence is particularly important in the early stages of technology adoption. Perhaps numerous IBS advertisements in mass media have an influence on consumers' adoptions. Malaysians may be attracted to using IBS by its efficiency and effectiveness as widely advertised. This can be seen in Table 2 where efficiency (No. 1.7) and effectiveness (No. 1.8) have high mean ratings of close to 4.0.

High standard deviations (> 1.0) for most attributes measuring Anxiety factor in Table 2 (Nos. 6.2–6.6) indicate that while some respondents take pleasure in using IBS, others are afraid to use IBS due to cost concern, poor Internet connection, knowledge deficiency, and the apprehension of losing important information by hitting the wrong key and making mistakes that they cannot correct. An IBS acceptance study in Australia (Lichtenstein and Williamson, 2006) highlighted similar consumer anxieties. However, these anxieties could be alleviated by improving the quality of the Internet service, standardizing IBS cost structure and intensifying nationwide education programmes.

Respondents are unsure about the availability of technical infrastructure and comprehensible contents to support the use of IBS (Facilitating Conditions; Nos. 4.2, 4.3 and 4.4). In contrast with Taiwanese who are confident in their capability to use IBS (Hsu and Chiu, 2004), Malaysians are unsure of the existence of a call centre that can assist them with IBS (Nos. 4.3). This concern may lower their interest to use IBS (note: the attribute "IBS is enjoyable" has a low mean rating of 3.40; see No. 8.4) and hinder them from fully utilizing the benefits and convenience of IBS. Hence, it is recommended that adequate resources (written instructions, specific person (or group) for assistance) should always be ready to support the use of IBS. Domestic banks should guarantee customers with intensive customer service through call centers where customers can easily seek assistance and guidance when in doubt. The government and Bank Negara Malaysia need to closely review business policies and operating practices of domestic banks and ensure the availability of adequate technical support and secure technologies (e.g. firewalls, two-factor authentications, secure socket level, etc.) before approving the launch of a new IBS.

Despite the above-mentioned worries, respondents show high intention of using IBS (Table 2: No. 9). This ascertains Goi (2005) and Nielsen (2005)'s findings that Internet banking industry has high opportunity for growth and user acceptance is the key determinant for the growth. To increase user acceptance, domestic banking institutions should emphasise on providing high level service. To do so, they need to reassess their business practices to be consistent with the needs and demands of consumers. The above-mentioned recommendations are derived from consumers' demands on IBS; thus, if they are implemented, a very conducive environment will be created to provide high level IBS.

5 Limitations and Future Studies

Preliminary results of factor analysis of independent factors and dependent factors show a high construct validity of 60.71% and 78.93%, respectively. In addition, the Cronbach's Alpha coefficients indicate high internal consistency in the respondents' answers (with Alpha coefficients greater than 0.60). Multiple linear regression showed that Performance Expectancy is one of the most important predictors of Behaviour Intention to Use IBS, which concurs with the descriptive statistics results above. Due to the constraint on the length of paper, the full results of the factor analysis, multiple linear regression and the effects of moderating variables such as education level, income, age, etc. will be examined and presented in our future papers. The results of this study are only applicable to Malaysia where all the subjects are from. However, the study can be replicated in other countries using the same model and instrument to identify factors that encourage and discourage the adoption of IBS in those countries.

Acknowledgements. The authors thank Multimedia University for providing the research grant for this study. The authors also thank the participants of this research. Last but not least, the authors thank Ms Christina H.P. Tong for editing the paper.

References

1. Agarwal, R., Prasad, J.A.: Conceptual and operational Definition of Personal Innovativeness in the Domain of Information Technology. Information Systems Research 9, 204–215 (1998)
2. AlAwadhi, S., Morris, A.: The Use of the UTAUT Model in the Adoption of E-government Services in Kuwait. In: Proceedings of the 41st Hawaii International Conference on System Sciences, Waikoloa, HI, January 7-10, 2008, pp. 209–219 (2008)

3. Bank Negara Malaysia (2007),
   http://www.bnm.gov.my/files/publication/fsps/en/2007/
   zcp07_table_A.34.pdf
4. Chau, P.Y.K.: An Empirical Assessment of a Modified Technology Acceptance Model. Journal of Management Information Systems 13, 185–204 (1996)
5. Chen, C., Wu, J., Yang, S.: Accelerating the Use of Weblogs as an Alternative Method to Deliver Case-Based Learning. International Journal on E-Learning 7, 331–349 (2008)
6. Compueau, D.R., Higgins, C.A.: Computer Self Efficacy: Development of a Measure and Initial Test. MIS Quarterly 19, 189–211 (1995)
7. Davis, F.D.: Perceived Usefulness, Perceived Ease of Use, and User Acceptance of Information Technology. MIS Quarterly 13, 319–339 (1989)
8. Dillon, A., Morris, M.: User Acceptance of New Information Technology: Theories and Models. In: Williams, M. (ed.) Annual Review of Information Science and Technology, ch. 31, pp. 3–32. Information Today, Medford NJ (1996)
9. Gefen, D., Silver, M.: Lessons Learned from the Successful Adoption of An ERP System. In: Proceedings of the 5th international Conference of the Decision Sciences Institute (DSI), Athens, Greece, pp. 1054–1057 (1999)
10. Goi, C.L.: E-Banking in Malaysia: Opportunity and Challenges. Journal of Internet Banking and Commerce (December 10, 2005)
11. Hsu, M.H., Chiu, C.M.: Internet Self Efficacy and Electronic Service Acceptance. Decision Support Systems 38, 369–381 (2004)
12. Lawson, J.: http://www.llrx.com/extras/security.htm
13. Lederer, A.L., Maupin, D.J., Sena, M.P., Zhuang, Y.: The Technology Acceptance Model and the World Wide Web. Decision Support Systems 29, 269–282 (2000)
14. Lichtenstein, S., Williamson, K.: Consumer Adoption of Internet banking. Journal of Electronic Commerce Research 7, 50–66 (2006)
15. Michael, F., Uzoka, E.: Organisational Influences on E-Commerce Adoption in a Developing Country Context using UTAUT. International Journal of Business Information Systems 3, 300–316 (2008)
16. Metzger, M.J., Flanagin, A.J., Zwarun, L.: College Student Web Use, Perceptions of Information Credibility, and Verification Behaviour. Computers and Education 41, 271–290 (2003)
17. Nielsen, A.C.: http://www.acnielsen.com.au/news.asp?newsID=301
18. Reichheld, F., Schefter, P.: E-Loyalty-Your Secret Weapon on the Web. Harvard Business Review, 105–113 (July-August 2003)
19. Siracuse, M.V., Sowell, J.G., Musselman, N.: Behavioral Intentions and Attitudes Towards the use of Personal Digital Assistants (PDAs). The Annual Meeting of the American Association of Colleges of Pharmacy, Sheraton San Diego Hotel & Marina, San Diego, California, USA (2006)
20. Suh, B., Han, I.: Effect of Trust on Customer Acceptance of Internet Banking. Electronic Commerce Research and Applications 1, 247–263 (2002)
21. Sun, H.: An integrative analysis of TAM: Toward a deeper understanding of technology acceptance model. In: Proceedings of the 9th American Conference on Information Systems, Tampa, Florida, p. 2255 (2003)
22. Sun, H., Zhang, P.: A Methodological Analysis of User Technology Acceptance. In: Proceeding of the 37th Hawaii International Conference of System Science, Big Island, Hawaii (2004)
23. Sun, H., Xiao, X.: http://web.syr.edu/~hesun/papers/encyclopedia.pdf

24. Taylor, S., Todd, P.A.: Understanding Information Technology Usage: A Test of Competing Models. Information System Research 6, 144–176 (1995)
25. The Star, http://star-techcentral.com/tech/story.asp?file=/2005/4/21/itfeature/10680731andsec=itfeature
26. Thompson, R.L., Higgins, C.A., Howell, J.M.: Influence of Experience on Personal Computer Utilization: Testing A Conceptual Model. Journal of Management Information Systems 11, 167–187 (1994)
27. Venkatesh, V., Davis, F.D.: A Theoretical Extension of the Technology Acceptance Model: Four Longitudinal Field Studies. Management Science 45, 186–204 (2000)
28. Venkatesh, V., Morris, M.G.: Why Don't Men Ever Stop To Ask For Directions? Gender, Social Influence, and Their Role in Technology Acceptance and User Behaviour. MIS Quarterly 24, 115–139 (2000)
29. Venkatesh, V., Morris, M.G., Davis, G.B., Davis, F.D.: User Acceptance of Information Technology: Toward A Unified View. MIS Quarterly 27, 425–478 (2003)
30. Wang, Y.S., Wang, Y.M., Lin, H.H., Tang, T.I.: Determinants of user acceptance of internet banking: an empirical study. International Journal of Service Industry Management 14, 501–519 (2003)
31. Warrington, T.B., Abgrab, N.J., Caldwell, H.M.: Building Trust to Develop Competitive Advantage in E-Business Relationships. Competitive Review 10, 160–168 (2000)
32. UniSys., Malaysian Unisys, http://www.unisys.com.sg/about__unisys/news_a_events/20070805_1.htm

Convergence of Internet and TV: The Commercial Viability of P2P Content Delivery

Jorn De Boever

Centre for UX Research, IBBT/ K.U.Leuven, Parkstraat 45(b 3605),
3000 Leuven, Belgium
jorn.deboever@soc.kuleuven.be

Abstract. The popularity of (illegal) P2P (peer-to-peer) file sharing has a disruptive impact on Internet traffic and business models of content providers. In addition, several studies have found an increasing demand for bandwidth consuming content, such as video, on the Internet. Although P2P systems have been put forward as a scalable and inexpensive model to deliver such content, there has been relatively little economic analysis of the potentials and obstacles of P2P systems as a legal and commercial content distribution model. Many content providers encounter uncertainties regarding the adoption or rejection of P2P networks to spread content over the Internet. The recent launch of several commercial, legal P2P content distribution platforms increases the importance of an integrated analysis of the Strengths, Weaknesses, Opportunities and Threats (SWOT).

1 Introduction

Although P2P systems have been associated with illegal file sharing since the introduction of Napster in 1999 [1], this negative image has shifted because of the arrival of innovative P2P systems – e.g. Kontiki, Babelgum, Zattoo – that demonstrate the potential for legal content distribution. In addition, the convergence of Internet and TV – i.e. over-the-top TV – results in new challenges for the content industry which is forced to consider new content distribution models in their multi-channel strategies. In this context, the question arises which opportunities and challenges P2P systems offer for legal and commercial content distribution.

Several technical aspects of P2P networks – e.g. performance, information retrieval, and self organization – have been extensively studied in recent years. However, there has been relatively little analysis of the economics of P2P systems. Consequently, we consider it to be important to have a broader more business oriented approach toward P2P platforms as a content distribution model.

The introduction of innovations causes a certain level of uncertainty for the industry, which must decide whether or not to adopt it [2]. The industry will try to limit this degree of uncertainty by exploring the different aspects of an innovation or by mimicking other companies' decisions. Moreover, the viability of innovations depends on whether companies and the target audience will adopt it. Therefore, it is important to grasp why companies would (not) adopt P2P systems and with which uncertainties

J. Cordeiro et al. (Eds.): WEBIST 2008, LNBIP 18, pp. 307–320, 2009.

the industry still struggles. Therefore, we conducted an extensive SWOT analysis by means of interviews and literature review. Accordingly, the aim of the present chapter is to briefly explore the obstacles and potentials of P2P technology to distribute commercial content, which will allow us to evaluate the current business viability of P2P technology. The results of this analysis should enable us to understand how P2P networks might be positioned strategically in order to raise the chances for a successful commercial application for legally exchanging media content.

This chapter starts by reviewing some relevant literature in the area of economics and P2P systems, followed by the elaboration of the methods. The subsequent section presents the results of the SWOT analysis by enumerating these aspects. The final section will confront and link the internal and external elements so as to put meaning and interpretation to these results.

We have to notice that we will use the terms 'user' and 'peer' alternately as they mean the same thing in the context of this chapter.

2 Literature

However substantial research effort has been devoted to the technical aspects of P2P technology – which resulted in an extended body of literature about for instance architectures [e.g. 3], availability [e.g. 4], security [e.g. 5] – this chapter will elaborate on the economics of P2P technology. One of the most characteristic aspects of P2P systems is that, to a large extent, value is being created by the end users since they have to cooperate in distributing the content [6]. MacInnes and Hwang [7] analyzed four cases – KaZaA, Kontiki, SETI and Groove – of P2P business models. According to these authors, the primary challenges for these business models were the revenue model, security and user behavior. Another study, conducted by Rupp and Estier [8], compared different actors in the music industry on how they were challenged by new technologies such as P2P networks. Other researchers explored the revenue models of several P2P systems [9], [10]. The results demonstrated that the revenue models of the most popular file sharing applications failed on efficient allocation, which implies that the revenues do not always end up with the rightful claimants. It is obvious that these studies already identified several of the issues that lead to uncertainty about the viability of P2P networks as content distribution models.

We will endeavor to build our findings on the studies that are mentioned below (infra). The papers that will be integrated in our SWOT analysis are: Smith, Clippinger and Konsynski [11], Hughes, Lang and Vragov [12], Kwok, Lang and Tam [13], Sigurdsson, Halldorsson and Hasslinger [14] and Rodriguez, Tan and Gkantsidis [15]. Although we value the results of the five selected studies, we argue that these papers suffer from some flaws which add to the significance of our contribution. For that reason, the drawbacks of these studies require further examination of the internal and external potentials and obstacles. We will briefly contend why these studies are deficient to a certain extent.

The study of Smith et al. [11] mainly examined the use of P2P technology within organizations (internally), whereas our analysis considers P2P technology in a commercial B2C (Business to Consumer) environment. Another limitation of their study comprises the fact that these authors only held discussions with CIOs, which resulted in a rather narrow focus. In contrast, we have tried to recruit respondents with different backgrounds.

The research of Hughes et al. [12] provided more of a theoretical, analytic framework for market design of P2P networks than it offered empirical results. We have integrated some elements of this framework in our study so as to corroborate our results. Another limitation of this study is that they primarily focused on the constraints while not paying attention to the strengths and opportunities.

Although Kwok et al. [13] use the words "risks and opportunities" in the title of their article, they limited their examination to the free riding problem, the related motivations for cooperation and piracy. In addition, the analysis of these authors contained merely a theoretical perspective and they did not pay a lot of attention to the opportunities.

Sigurdsson et al. [14] provided an analysis that primarily focused on technical and financial aspects while ignoring e.g. user-related aspects. Furthermore, we argue that these authors have failed to make the different concepts of a SWOT analysis operational, which resulted in confusion about the terms.

Finally, Rodriguez et al. [15] described the results of a workshop regarding the issues of legal P2P content distribution. This paper offers a list of items that stresses the weaknesses and threats, while paying little attention to the strengths and opportunities.

In this chapter, we will integrate the results of these five studies, while addressing the flaws of former research in our own analysis.

3 Methods

Our approach consisted of three levels: a literature review, expert interviews and the data of the former two levels were used in a SWOT analysis. The first phase of our methodology comprised a detailed literature review. From this literature review, we selected five papers to elaborate and integrate in our SWOT analysis. We only selected studies that covered a broad range of issues involved in P2P research and excluded others that only focused on one or a limited number of topics so as to avoid overrepresentation of some topics.

In the second phase, we conducted 15 in-depth interviews with people from the industry and with some academics. We interviewed people with different backgrounds to obtain as accurate and as objective results as possible. Therefore, participants, with different backgrounds (social – 3, economic – 3, technical – 8, and law – 1), were selected for these interviews. These respondents were working for broadcasters (4), content providers (4), ISPs (2), research community (4) and copyright lobby organizations (1). Two researchers were working on projects in which a P2P application was being developed. We argue that the results of these interviews allowed us to accomplish a significant contribution to the existing literature.

The findings of the former two phases resulted in the data for the SWOT analysis. First, we clearly defined what was meant by the concepts strengths, weaknesses, opportunities and threats so as to avoid confusion. Second, we scored the different topics that were mentioned in the results section of the papers and in the interviews for our analysis. Based on the defined concepts, we decided, by means of qualitative interpretation, for each item to which category it belonged. Third, founded on literature review and the results of the in-depth interviews, we examined why the mentioned items were issues. Finally, we tried to confront or relate the items of the four categories by analyzing e.g. which strengths might be used to address some weaknesses or to take advantage of certain opportunities; which weaknesses might be mended by further research; which threats must be avoided.

Although SWOT analyses are mainly used within organizations [16], [17], we argue that it is an effective tool as well to grasp the major positive and negative issues of applications and technologies. While studying technologies or information systems, researchers run the risk of considering the technology or the adoption of it as a positive fact. This has also been termed as the pro-innovation bias [2]. The danger of the pro-innovation bias is that it becomes difficult to have a neutral and objective perspective. The advantage of a SWOT analysis is that the researcher is forced to analyze the weaknesses and threats as well.

P2P applications to share files or distribute content in a legal way are not widespread yet. The SWOT analysis will reveal several internal strengths / weaknesses and external opportunities / threats of P2P systems as a commercial application for the legal exchange of media content.

4   Results

In this section, we will define and explore the internal strengths / weaknesses and external opportunities / threats.

4.1   Internal Strengths

The strengths encompass the internal aspects that offer P2P systems for instance possibilities to take advantage of certain factors in the environment. These are the strengths that are characteristic of P2P systems.

Cost Savings. P2P is a technology that is capable of reducing the costs for content distribution because it utilizes fewer resources such as bandwidth [18], [11]. In addition, the avoidance of centralized servers limits the costs in terms of investment and upkeep [14]. Lower costs allow the content industry to distribute high quality video content to a larger audience. Moreover, the implementation of techniques such as 'swarming' – which allows peers to simultaneously download different parts of the same file from different sources – makes it possible for end users to more efficiently retrieve larger content. Finally, it is also an inexpensive solution for the worldwide distribution of content as there is no need for adaptations on the network level, which reduces costs as well. All these aspects result from the fact that P2P systems utilize the available resources that are available for instance on the end users' personal computers. Norton [18] examined and compared several content distribution models based on a cost analysis. This author found that P2P systems were the most inexpensive content distribution models in comparison with e.g. transit models and CDNs (Content Delivery Networks).

Scalability. P2P systems scale with the amount of use as each peer provides resources, e.g. bandwidth, to the network, which results in limited marginal costs [19],

[20], [14]. P2P systems exhibit positive network externalities as each additional consumer in theory also implies additional resources which make these systems very scalable. Some P2P networks are even able to cope with 'flash crowds' (i.e. a sudden and extremely increase of the number of users that consume the same service or content which might overload a system). P2P technology might be utilized to develop overlay networks so as to distribute content around the globe. Furthermore, these overlay networks are cost-efficient as the costs for implementation and maintenance are limited [14].

Easy Implementation. From the position of content providers, P2P systems are easy and inexpensive to implement because it operates more on the application layer. To distribute content on a worldwide scale, there is little need for large investments in infrastructure and control. By contrast, some P2P providers argue that it is more complicated to start a P2P system in comparison with installing a central server.

Fault Tolerance. P2P systems are fault tolerant because there are limited centralized components in the network that are potential bottlenecks or single points of failure [14]. Because of the distributed nature of P2P networks and the redundancy of nodes, the disappearance of one or several nodes has mostly only marginal impact on the overall performance.

Availability. Some respondents consider P2P systems to be more efficient as these systems utilize the idle resources that are available on the edges of the Internet, resulting in an increased availability of resources such as bandwidth and content.

4.2 Internal Weaknesses

The internal weaknesses contain the distinctive characteristics of P2P networks that are disadvantageous. These are the direct constraints of these systems.

Quality of Service (QoS). The reliability of P2P systems in terms of QoS is a major issue for the commercial viability of these systems [21], [14], [12], [15]. QoS in this context relates to the performance of the network for instance on the level of delays, content availability, distribution speed and scalability. The end users' personal computers operate as nodes in the network, which makes it hard to guarantee QoS because of the transient connectivity of nodes. Furthermore, there are still end users with low bandwidth connections. Services might be interrupted if nodes suddenly leave the network, which might result in delays and high buffer times. This appears to be especially problematic for large content that requires more time and resources to download. In this sense, P2P content distribution is a best effort model with low guarantees of QoS. The uncertain QoS is probably the most important obstacle for content providers to adopt P2P systems for content distribution. In summary, it seems difficult to guarantee a certain performance level and it is therefore hard to formulate reliable service level agreements.

Inefficient Use of Resources. Most P2P systems handle the available resources – e.g. bandwidth – in an inefficient way. This results from the fact that there are mostly no centralized components in the system that manages the use of these resources because P2P networks are, to a large extent, self organizing systems. This self organization requires much traffic to maintain the operability of the system. We have to notice that the new legal P2P systems mostly have a centralized component to manage the available resources.

Security and Privacy. Security is still worrisome as for instance other peers can access your computer to retrieve certain data [20], [11]. This makes it easy for malicious nodes to enter your computer and cause damage. This danger for malicious attacks has social implications as well, related to trust [15]. In most P2P systems, users encounter unknown anonymous peers they should trust if they want to exchange data. Inflicting damage in this trust relation might cause users to abandon P2P systems. The 'older' generations of P2P systems are mainly anonymous without actual social interaction, which limits the trust relation among peers. In addition, the lack of centralized monitoring facilities causes difficulties in guaranteeing security [14]. By using P2P networks, users expose private data such as IP address and the downloaded content. This can inflict damage to the users' privacy [15].

Usability and Adoption. These are two issues that received little attention in P2P research and it proved to be a concern for some of the respondents. Most P2P file sharing applications have complex interfaces that are little intuitive. Several terms (e.g. seeders and trackers) might confuse some users. Good and Krekelberg [22] have conducted usability research on the KaZaA user interface. They came to the disquieting result that many users were not able to locate their shared folder, so they did not know which content they were actually sharing. Today, P2P systems are mainly used by computer skilled persons who probably know how P2P networks function. If one wants to develop P2P applications to be consumed by a wide audience, the user interface needs to be more accessible, usable and learnable for users who are less familiar with P2P systems. For instance, the fact that users have to download and install a separate client might be a threshold to adopt these systems. Furthermore, file sharing might frustrate users as they have to wait until the entire file has been downloaded before consuming it [15].

Costs to Users. P2P systems utilize resources that are available on the end users' personal computers. The users' resources – e.g. storage capacity, bandwidth, electricity – are being used for the distribution of content, which entails costs for these users. It remains an open question whether the average user will accept that a content provider utilizes the user's resources to distribute content.

Business Modeling. P2P systems are being confronted with constrains regarding several elements of business models. There is still no proof of concept of a comprehensive business model that integrates P2P systems and where there is a fit between the several business model components. The main bottlenecks in this area, according to most respondents, are related to a lack of control over large parts of the content distribution flow. In addition, there are often no means to measure the consumption of the peers, which makes it difficult to attract advertisers. There exists no proof of concept of P2P systems that integrates an advertising or payment model for revenues. P2P systems therefore need a centralized component which monitors the consumption of the peers in order to be able to implement a revenue model.

4.3 External Opportunities

The opportunities consist of the aspects in the environment that might have a positive effect on the adoption and use of legal, commercial P2P systems.

Costs Centralized Models. In a client/server model, an increasing popularity of bandwidth consuming content, such as video and games, implies increasing costs to distribute this content. Furthermore, the risk of a bottleneck and single point of failure increases as well. Researchers have found an increasing use of and demand for bandwidth consuming content such as video [23]. Some experts predict that video content will have a share of about 80% of Internet traffic in the near future [18]. For centralized distribution models, this implies considerable expenses on the level of e.g.: distribution capacity, storage capacity, bandwidth, servers and control.

Disadvantages of Other Distribution Models. We will demonstrate some opportunities for P2P systems by addressing some flaws of three other distribution models: unicasting, multicasting and CDNs. First, unicasting is a centralized streaming method that has the same drawbacks as client/server models: it is not scalable, it runs the risk of a bottleneck and the costs rise as content is consumed more often. Therefore, most content providers that utilize a unicasting model, limit the quality of the content to confine the costs when popularity increases. Second, multicasting is a more decentralized streaming method, but this technique has some drawbacks as well as it requires adaptations in the network infrastructure and many networks are not multicast enabled. In addition, multicasting is mainly interesting for live content distribution and less for on demand content. A third example of a distribution model comprises CDNs. An elaborated analysis of CDNs can be found in the text of Pallis and Vakali [24]. When content providers decide to utilize a CDN, they first make strategic decisions about the necessary performance and QoS and include these requirements in a service level agreement. But, it is often difficult to predict the popularity of services or content which might influence the service quality.

Increasing Capacity on End Users' Equipment. The end users possess an expanding amount of resources – such as bandwidth, storage and processing capacity – that can be exploited by P2P networks [14]. This also means that there are more idle resources available on the edge of the Internet that might be used by P2P systems. Users have become more than purely consumers in the value chain as they add value by replicating and distributing resources in P2P systems.

Symmetric Networks. The Internet today is still organized in an asymmetric way, i.e. it expects users more to download and less to upload content. This is why users have more download capacity in comparison with their upload capacity. But this trend is shifting because of developments such as P2P networks, telework and user generated content. Several respondents expected the Internet to become more symmetrically organized in the future so that the down-/upload ratio will gradually equals one. This might be an opportunity for systems such as P2P networks that require users to utilize their upload capacity to serve content.

User Orientation. In P2P file sharing systems, a social filtering process occurs in which the community of peers decides which content might remain available and which content not. Content that does not fit the users' needs, or that becomes less relevant, will slowly disappear from the system. In other words, P2P systems offer the opportunity to involve the end users more closely in the value chain.

4.4 External Threats

The threats are factors in the external environment that can interrupt or threaten the success of commercial and legal P2P systems.

Bandwidth Caps. ISPs still maintain bandwidth caps in a few countries as a part of their business model and to be able to guarantee a certain performance level. If a content provider wants to distribute large content such as video files, end users will soon attain their bandwidth cap. This is problematic since more content providers want to distribute high quality video over the Internet.

Asymmetric Networks. The commercial Internet has been build from a top down perspective. The content owners distribute content, and the users download this content. In other words it focuses more on the download link, which resulted in an asymmetric network architecture, e.g. ADSL. This asymmetric architecture causes low upstream rates [14]. For the efficient operation of P2P systems, it would have been better to have a more symmetrical up-/download ratio because P2P systems emphasize uploading as well which results in different usage patterns in comparison with the 'traditional' Internet. In the current asymmetric organization of the Internet, there is a risk that the upstream bandwidth capacity will not be sufficient to compensate the downstream bandwidth capacity in a situation of widespread P2P traffic [18].

Measurability and Control. In server oriented models, it is easier to keep track of the different flows of data in the system which is a prerequisite for advertisers and content owners [11], [14]. This measurability is important to the revenue model within a business model. This measurability of other distribution models is a threat to P2P networks and it is an internal weakness as well.

Competing Distribution Models. By means of some examples, namely multicasting and CDNs, we will demonstrate that P2P systems are being threatened by some characteristics that other models display. Multicasting, for instance, is a streaming model that offers some answers to the flaws of the unicasting model, particularly in the area of live streaming. In addition, multicasting is a system that reinforces itself so that it is very scalable. Furthermore, multicasting can offer better QoS compared to P2P streaming. In this sense, multicasting can be considered as a more reliable model that is mainly suitable for popular live events. A second example of content distribution models contains CDNs. In contrast with P2P systems, CDNs offer high guarantees on the level of QoS which makes it possible to draw up reliable service level agreements, and they are considered to be able to address several security issues.

Position of ISPs. We will now explain why ISPs might not sympathize with P2P content distribution models [15]. Content providers, that implement P2P technology for content distribution, avoid bandwidth expenses by passing the costs on the users. The result of the adoption of P2P technology is an increasing traffic volume on the network infrastructure of ISPs, while these ISPs receive less revenue. Measurement studies have demonstrated that more than 50% of Internet traffic is emanating from P2P systems [25]. The increasing traffic volume, caused by P2P systems, originates from the fact that P2P technology allows exchanging large files and because there is much message overhead required to self organize these systems. In addition, many P2P applications lack locality awareness which implies that a lot of traffic crosses several ISP networks whereas the content might be available on a node of the local ISP [15]. In other words, the current revenue model of ISPs does not fit a situation in which the use of P2P networks is pervasive because the traffic volume might not be proportionate to the revenues. If large traffic volumes are congesting the network, ISPs might decide to squeeze or even block P2P traffic: "Network capacity has a cost. If video Peer-to-Peer imposes costs on network operators, they will have incentives to limit it, especially if they do not receive a commensurate benefit from the activity" [26]. Another consequence might be that many ISPs change their price policy from e.g. flat rates into a system of usage-based pricing [15].

Legal Issues and Image. P2P technology has to cope with an image problem as there is still a connotation of piracy. This is why some authors [e.g. 15] argue that legal uses of P2P content distribution should be promoted. The MP3 encoding format, combined with the decentralized nature of P2P file sharing, have led to a situation in which illegal file sharing has become an omnipresent practice that likely won't disappear [13], [11], [14]. Therefore, content owners are not eager to offer downloadable content, because they fear copyright infringements. If users are able to store content on their hard drives, the chances increase that files are being copied and spread in an illegal way. Control over the rights remains an important issue. However, several respondents argued that control of copyrights was not their major concern. They emphasized the importance of control of their business model. These respondents accept for instance that content is being copied and distributed by the end users, as long as they are able to capture the 'eyeballs' for advertising purposes. In addition, most of the interviewees hold an opinion that solutions such as DRM are not suitable for fighting piracy because (1) every version will be compromised sooner or later and (2) it does not fit the consumers' needs. In addition P2P providers have to cope with different legislations in different countries. For instance, the USA has developed the fair use doctrine, whereas European jurisdiction utilizes an exception list. For a more in-depth analysis of jurisdiction concerning illegal file sharing in different countries, we refer to [27].

Critical Mass. The operation and viability of P2P systems require a critical mass of cooperating users that make sufficient resources available [15], [13]. In client/server systems, it does not matter that content is consumed by little people as long as the server stays available. In contrast, a P2P application must generate sufficient mass so content would be sufficiently available. But, as is the case in many virtual communities, P2P networks are being threatened by the free riding phenomenon [28], [29]. Free riders are users that consume resources from the network while not contributing anything in return. In a situation without critical mass and a large amount of free riders, content will often be unavailable, which will cause users to leave the system with the result that the P2P network would no longer be viable. Consequently, P2P technology is mainly interesting for the distribution of popular content because it is easier to attain a critical mass of cooperating peers.

Content Aggregation. Several P2P platforms – e.g. Joost – operate as content aggregators as well. P2P platforms try to acquire popular content to increase the popularity of their service. A part of the revenue model of several P2P platforms is based on advertising and revenue sharing [e.g. 30]. There are several competing P2P companies trying to gather the same content providers. As more P2P systems will start up, it will become more difficult to aggregate popular content providers and, as a result, to reach a critical mass. This threat of content aggregation is linked to the issues of competing distribution models and the acquisition of a critical mass.

Decreasing Bandwidth Prices and Network Address Translation (NAT). The first issue concerns the relevance of P2P content distribution if the bandwidth prices would decrease significantly. P2P content distribution is mainly regarded as a technology to save on bandwidth costs. As bandwidth capacity might become cheaper, the question arises whether a content provider would still adopt a distribution model that performs badly in terms of QoS. The second issue, NATs, involves mainly a technical burden that needs to be solved [15]. NATs allow several hosts within a private network to use only one IP address to access the Internet. The exchange with nodes that operate behind a NAT router generates a technical issue, by limiting end-to-end connectivity, which needs to be addressed.

5 Confrontation

Some people criticize SWOT analyses for being just an enumeration of several points without any reflection [16]. Therefore, we will try to discover links between the internal and external aspects that have an impact on P2P systems. P2P systems can take advantage of some external opportunities by deploying the internal strengths. Research and experiments might be necessary to address the internal weaknesses, while P2P providers are often unable to change the external threats.

The results of the SWOT analysis indicate that the identified limitations of P2P technology still entail major issues on the way to a legal and commercial content distribution model. The relation between the strengths and opportunities is certainly existent. Particularly, P2P networks can be perceived as inexpensive, fault tolerant and scalable content distribution models. These internal assets can be used to address some external opportunities. For instance, P2P technology provides solutions for some of the flaws of other content distribution models, such as the client/server model (e.g. bottleneck, not scalable), unicasting (e.g. bottleneck, not scalable), multicasting (e.g. network adaptations). The costs of several current distribution models will increase as demand for popular bandwidth consuming content grows. P2P technology distributes content in a cost efficient manner that requires less limiting the quality of content by compression techniques. In addition, the possible evolution toward symmetric networks might create opportunities for P2P systems to utilize the users' uplink even more.

On the one hand, there are several weaknesses, for instance on the level of usability and business modeling, that still can be mended. These are elements that require further research, but these are not insurmountable problems. On the other hand, other weaknesses (e.g. QoS and security) and threats (e.g. legal issues, control) require the integration of a centralized component in the P2P architecture. Moreover, a business model requires companies to be able to monitor and measure users' consumption to support for instance an advertising model. To pursue these goals, a centralized component is necessary in the architecture. Finally, to improve the QoS of P2P systems, it might be an option to close agreements with ISPs to equip its infrastructure so traffic becomes more manageable. In this way, ISPs might be able to generate revenue from the additional load on their infrastructure, caused by traffic of P2P networks. For instance, BitTorrent has closed a service level agreement with GNi, a company that offers data networking solutions, so as to be able to offer better user experiences [31].

Most of the external threats and opportunities are beyond manipulation of P2P providers. P2P providers can only take advantage of the opportunities by promoting the criticalities of these aspects (e.g. demand for bandwidth consuming content, costs of centralized models, etc.). On the level of threats, a strategy might include avoiding these elements, although this seems to be impossible. P2P providers cannot ignore issues such as asymmetric networks and the control of ISPs. Every P2P provider, that offers solutions for the distribution of popular bandwidth consuming content, is being confronted with these threats.

We will now describe a worst case scenario, in which P2P content distribution is massively used for legal content distribution and in which the threats have not been addressed. In a situation in which P2P systems would be used by average Internet users, and not only by young more computer literate users, the positive network externalities of P2P networks might fall into negative network externalities. The network infrastructure of the ISPs might be overloaded which would result in insufficient QoS, which would reveal itself in for instance delays. To retain control of the traffic, ISPs might decide to squeeze or block P2P traffic which would decrease user experiences. Because of these inadequate user experiences, users might decide to stop using the P2P system with the result that content would be less replicated throughout the network. This unstable availability of content would cause additional loss of users, which would again result in less available resources. In other words, this vicious circle would prevent P2P systems to attain a critical mass resulting in the extinction of P2P systems. This is a worse case scenario that will not likely occur because P2P providers will try to avoid or address these weaknesses and threats.

6 Concluding Remarks

The present study examined the internal/external potentials and obstacles of P2P systems to distribute commercial content in an efficient and legal way. Data gathered from interviews and literature was utilized to conduct an extensive SWOT analysis from a business perspective. Although this study reflects previous research findings, we argue that our research succeeded in addressing several limitations of former research as was discussed in the literature section. Interestingly, by conducting interviews with several respondents with different backgrounds, this SWOT analysis added several new elements to the existing results in a structured way. Whereas most researchers primarily examined the internal weaknesses, this study highlighted the importance of the internal strengths and external opportunities/threats as well. In addition, this examination paid thorough attention to the position of users since users are essential in the value creation within the P2P value chain. On the one hand, users have more resources – e.g. bandwidth or storage capacity – at their disposal, which creates opportunities for P2P systems. On the other hand, the use of P2P systems implies that users experience additional costs because they have to make these resources available for other peers in the system. Furthermore, usability requirements of P2P systems have received little attention. This lack of knowledge might impede the widespread adoption of P2P systems among end users. Finally, a large proportion of users, in a great deal of P2P networks, are free riding on the contributions of others, which necessitates the need for incentives to increase cooperation so as to ensure network performance. Beside users, we focused on another often forgotten actor as well, namely the ISPs. P2P systems cause an increased load on the network infrastructure of ISPs, while the ISPs are less remunerated. This causes a negative attitude of ISPs toward P2P systems, which might motivate the ISPs to hinder P2P traffic.

In comparison with the five selected papers, our research added the following topics: strengths (easy implementation, availability), weaknesses (usability and adoption, costs to users, business models), opportunities (disadvantages of other distribution models, evolution toward symmetric networks, user orientation) and threats (data limits, competing distribution models, content aggregation, decreasing bandwidth prices, abandonment open source).

In contrast with former studies, this examination went beyond a mere enumeration of aspects by confronting and linking the internal and external elements. Several external developments offer opportunities for P2P technology. In this sense, P2P content distribution can be envisaged as an inexpensive, fault tolerant and scalable model for content distribution that offers some advantages in comparison with other content distribution models. Some of the internal weaknesses can be addressed by further examination, for instance on the level of usability and business modeling. The QoS, P2P systems produce, remains the major obstacle for a widespread adoption of P2P technology among content providers. Most of the external threats and opportunities are beyond control of P2P providers as e.g. P2P providers cannot avoid issues – such as asymmetric networks – which threaten their services.

Despite the above mentioned positive qualities of this analysis, we have to address the limitations of this study as well. The reliability of this examination might be threatened by the underrepresentation of some actors in the interviews. We only conducted a limited amount of interviews with copyright lobbyists (1) and ISPs (2). However, we did not manage in recruiting P2P providers for this analysis which might have affected the results. In this sense our results might primarily represent the issues identified by content providers. In addition, many issues have been raised involving users whereas this research did not gather data from end users. Indeed, a promising line of study would be to interview P2P providers and end users so as to improve the reliability of the results.

Although P2P technology offers some opportunities for commercial and legal content distribution, the findings of this study indicate that several issues still need to be addressed. Centralizing some elements of the architecture might be necessary to address the weaknesses – e.g. security, QoS – of this content distribution model. The recent launch of several legal, commercial P2P systems – e.g. LiveStation, RawFlow, Joost, Vuze – have demonstrated the feasibility of these models. Therefore, we expect that the convergence of Internet and TV will force several content providers to adopt P2P systems to distribute video content in order to limit bandwidth costs.

Acknowledgements. FLEET (an interdisciplinary research project on FLEmish E-publishing Trends) is an IWT SBO project, with research partners IBBT SMIT, Cemeso, LSTS, MOFI, ICRI, CUO, MICT, EC/DC and TNO.

References

1. Shirky, C.: Listening to Napster. In: Oram, A. (ed.) Peer-to-Peer: Harnessing the Power of Disruptive Technologies, pp. 21–37. O'Reilly & Associates, Inc., Sebastopol (2001)
2. Rogers, E.M.: Diffusion of Innovations. Free Press, New York (2003)
3. Androutsellis-Theotokis, S., Spinellis, D.: A Survey of Peer-to-Peer Content Distribution Technologies. ACM Computing Surveys 36(4), 335–371 (2004)
4. Bhagwan, R., Savage, S., Voelker, G.M.: Understanding Availability. In: The 2nd International Workshop on Peer-to-Peer Systems, Berkeley, USA (2003)
5. Divac-Krnic, L., Ackerman, R.: Security-Related Issues in Peer-to-Peer Networks. In: Steinmetz, R., Wehrle, K. (eds.) Peer-to-Peer Systems and Applications. LNCS, vol. 3485, pp. 529–545. Springer, Heidelberg (2005)
6. Lechner, U., Hummel, J.: Business Models and System Architectures of Virtual Communities: From a Sociological Phenomenon to Peer-to-Peer Architectures. International Journal of Electronic Commerce 6(3), 41–53 (2002)
7. MacInnes, I., Hwang, J.: Business Models for Peer to Peer Initiatives. In: The 16th Bled Electronic Commerce Conference, Bled, Slovenia (2003)
8. Rupp, P., Estier, T.: A Model for a Better Understanding of the Digital Distribution of Music in a Peer-to-Peer Environment. In: Proceedings of the 36th Hawaii International Conference on System Sciences. IEEE Press, Island of Hawaii (2003)
9. Hummel, T., Muhle, S., Schoder, D.: Business Applications and Revenue Models. In: Steinmetz, R., Wehrle, K. (eds.) Peer-to-Peer Systems and Applications. LNCS, vol. 3485, pp. 473–489. Springer, Heidelberg (2005)
10. Hummel, T., Strømme, Ø., La Salle, R.M.: Earning a Living among Peers – the Quest for Viable P2P Revenue Models. In: Proceedings of the 36th Hawaii International Conference on System Sciences. IEEE Press, Island of Hawaii (2003)
11. Smith, H.A., Clippinger, J., Konsynski, B.: Riding the Wave: Discovering the Value of P2P Technologies. Communications of the Association for Information Systems 11(4), 94–107 (2003)
12. Hughes, J., Lang, K.R., Vragov, R.: Electronic Market Design Principles in the Context of Peer-to-Peer Filesharing Systems. In: PACIS 2005 Proceedings, Bangkok, Thailand, pp. 852–865 (2005)
13. Kwok, S.H., Lang, R.L., Tam, K.Y.: Peer-to-Peer Technology Business and Service Models: Risks and Opportunities. Electronic Markets 12(3), 175–183 (2002)
14. Sigurdsson, H.M., Halldorsson, U.R., Hasslinger, G.: Potentials and Challenges of Peer-to-Peer Based Content Distribution. In: The 2nd International CICT Conference: Next Generation Broadband - Content and User Perspectives, Lyngby, Denmark (2005)
15. Rodriguez, P., Tan, S.-M., Gkantsidis, C.: On the Feasability of Commercial, Legal P2P Content Distribution. ACM SIGCOMM Computer Communication Review 36(1), 75–78
16. Vermeylen, S.: Werken met SWOT-analyse. Uitgeverij Politeia, Brussels (2004)
17. Sabbaghi, A., Vaidyanathan, G.: SWOT Analysis and Theory of Constraint in Information Technology Projects. Information Systems Education Journal 2(23), 3–19 (2004)
18. Norton, W.B.: Video Internet: The Next Wave of Massive Disruption to the U.S. Peering Ecosystem. In: The Stanford Networking Seminar, Stanford, USA (2007)

19. Ding, C.H., Nutanong, S., Buyya, R.: Peer-to-Peer Networks for Content Sharing. In: Subramanian, R., Goodman, B.D. (eds.) Peer-to-Peer Computing: the Evolution of a Disruptive Technology, pp. 28–65. Idea Group Publishing, London (2005)
20. Taylor, I.J.: From P2P to Web Services and Grids: Peers in a Client/Server World. Springer, London (2004)
21. Parameswaran, M., Susarla, A., Whinston, A.B.: P2P Networking: An Information-Sharing Alternative. IEEE Distributed Systems Online 34(7), 1–8 (2001)
22. Good, N.S., Krekelberg, A.: Usability and privacy: a study of KaZaA P2P file-sharing. In: Cranor, L.F., Garfinkel, S. (eds.) Security and Usability: Designing Secure Systems That People Can Use, pp. 651–668. O'Reilly, Cambridge (2005)
23. IDC: The Expanding Digital Universe: A Forecast of Worldwide Information Growth Through 2010. EMC (2007), http://www.emc.com/about/desti-nation/digital_universe/pdf/Expanding_Digital_Universe_Executive_Summary_022507.pdf (retrieved April 4, 2007)
24. Pallis, G., Vakali, A.: Insight and Perspectives for Content Delivery Networks. Communications of the ACM 49(1), 101–106 (2006)
25. Haßlinger, G.: ISP Platforms Under a Heavy Peer-to-Peer Workload. In: Steinmetz, R., Wehrle, K. (eds.) Peer-to-Peer Systems and Applications. LNCS, vol. 3485, pp. 369–381. Springer, Heidelberg (2005)
26. Werbach, K.: The Implications of Video Peer-to-Peer on Network Usage. In: Noam, E.M., Pupillo, L.M. (eds.) Peer-to-Peer Video: The Economics, Policy, and Culture of Today's New Mass Medium, pp. 95–127. Springer, New York (2008)
27. Dogan, S.L.: Peer-to-Peer Technology and the Copyright Crossroads. In: Subramanian, R., Goodman, B.D. (eds.) Peer-to-Peer Computing: the Evolution of a Disruptive Technology, pp. 166–193. Idea Group Publishing, London (2005)
28. Adar, E., Huberman, B.A.: Free Riding on Gnutella. First Monday 5(10) (2000), http://www.firstmonday.dk/issues/issue5_10/adar/ (retrieved March 8, 2006)
29. Hughes, D., Coulson, G., Walkerdine, J.: Free Riding on Gnutella. IEEE Distributed Systems Online 6(6) (2005)
30. Warner Music Group: Warner Music Group and Joost announce agreement to offer WMG video content on new Internet television platform. WMG, http://www.wmg.com/news/article/?id=8a0af81211b8cea50111d683c13e0f66 (09.04.2007) (retrieved September 26, 2007)
31. Del Conte, N.T.: BitTorrent pays for direct delivery. PC Magazine, http://www.pcmag.com/article2/0,1895,1983053,00.asp (28.06.2006) (retrieved September 26, 2007)

Website Service Quality in Ireland: An Empirical Study

Regina Connolly

Dublin City University, Dublin 9, Ireland
regina.connolly@dcu.ie

Abstract. Despite the fact that service quality is a critical determinant of website success, studies show that consumers frequently view the service quality delivered through websites as unsatisfactory. This paper outlines a study that investigated the dimensions of website service excellence valued by Irish customers of a small-to-medium enterprise specialising in gifts. The E-S-QUAL measurement instrument was applied to the customers who purchase products online from this retailer, in order to determine their purchasing patterns and the dimensions of e-service quality that they value. The results of this study indicate the effectiveness of the instrument in determining gaps in e-service quality. The findings will be of benefit both to practitioners and researchers seeking to improve their understanding of the factors that contribute towards the creation and maintenance of consumer satisfaction in Irish online transactions.

Keywords: Website service quality, E-S-QUAL, consumer satisfaction.

1 Introduction

In Ireland the need for online vendors to understand the dimensions of website service quality that customers value has an added impetus as Irish consumers continue to resist transacting via the Internet – using it as an information rather than a transaction medium and thus limiting its commercial potential. For example, by the end of 2002, nearly half of the Irish population had Internet access, but only 38% of Irish Internet users had made an online purchase (Amarach Consulting, 2002). Studies in the UK have also found that the percentage of the Internet population who shop online has not increased in line with Internet penetration. Thus, while increases in the sheer size of the Internet population mean that more people have made an online purchase, the proportion of Internet buyers is not increasing. Therefore, in order that the commercial potential of the Internet is to be realized - a potential that is expanding dramatically as a result of advances in consumer wireless technologies and their transaction-facilitating capabilities – understanding the dimensions of service quality that Irish online consumers value is of critical importance.

1.1 Research Objectives

This research extends our understanding of service quality within the setting of online retailing. The study has two objectives. Firstly, it examines the dimensions of website service quality that are valued by customers of a small to medium online company in

J. Cordeiro et al. (Eds.): WEBIST 2008, LNBIP 18, pp. 321–332, 2009.

Ireland. Secondly, by applying the newly operationalised e-S-QUAL measurement instrument, it explores the relevance of this instrument in the evaluation of business to consumer website service quality.

2 Service Quality

The traditional (off-line) service quality construct is one of the most researched topics in the area of services marketing. Although research into the specific dimensions of website service quality that are valued by online consumers is in an embryonic stage, it is an issue of considerable importance. In part, this is due to the fact that as competition for online consumers intensifies, service quality has become a key differentiator for online vendors and thus it has become increasingly important to have an appropriate means by which to measure it. This is particularly true in the business-to-consumer electronic commerce marketplace where web vendors compete for a limited number of consumers and where consumer loyalty has become a key indicator of success.

Service quality has been defined as the difference between customers' expectations for service performance prior to the service encounter and their perceptions of the service received (Asubonteng *et al.,* 1996). When performance does not meet expectations, quality is judged as low and when performance exceeds expectations, the evaluation of that quality increases. Thus, in any evaluation of service quality, customers' expectations are key to that evaluation. Moreover, Asubonteng *et al.,* (1996) suggest that as service quality increases, satisfaction with the service and intentions to reuse the service (i.e. loyalty intentions) increase.

To meet customer service requirements is both a performance issue (whether the service satisfies the customers requirements) and an issue of conformity to measurable standards. For example, Swartz and Brown (1989) distinguish between the consumer's post-performance evaluation of 'what' the service delivers and the consumer's evaluation of the service during delivery. The former evaluation has been termed 'outcome quality' (Parasuraman *et al.,* 1985), 'technical quality' (Gronröos (1983) and 'physical quality' (Lehtinen and Lehtinen, 1982). The latter evaluation has been termed 'process quality' by Parasuraman *et al.,* (1985), 'functional quality' by Gronröos (1983) and 'interaction quality' by Lehtinen and Lehtinen (1982).

The most frequently cited measure of service quality is SERVQUAL, an instrument developed by Parasuraman *et al.,* (1985; 1988). It has been widely cited in the literature and has been used to measure service quality in a variety of settings e.g. health care (Babakus and Mangold, 1992; Bebko and Garg, 1995, Bowers *et al.,* 1994), large retail chains (Teas, 1993; Finn and Lamb 1991), fast food restaurants (Cronin and Taylor 1992), a dental clinic, a tyre store and a hospital (Carman 1990). Designed to measure service quality from a customer perspective, it consists of five basic dimensions that represent the service attributes that consumers use to evaluate service quality. The five dimensions are tangibles, reliability, responsiveness, assurance and empathy. In their model, Parasuraman *et al.,* (1985; 1988) suggest that it is the gap between consumer expectations with actual service performance that informs service quality perceptions. To the degree that service performance exceeds expectations, the consumer's perception of service quality increases. To the degree that performance decreases relative to expectations, the consumer's perception of service quality decreases. Thus, this performance-to-expectations gap forms the theoretical basis of SERVQUAL. However, Parasuraman *et al.,* also note that the evaluation of service quality is not based solely on the service outcome but also involves evaluations of the process of service delivery.

Despite its popularity, a number of issues related to the use of SERVQUAL remain contentious, such as the proposed causal link between service quality and satisfaction (eg Woodside *et al.,* 1989; Bitner 1990), and the question as to whether one scale can be universally applicable in measuring service quality regardless of the industry or environment (Asubonteng *et al.,* 1996; Cronin and Taylor 1992; 1994; Teas, 1993; Carman, 1990; Finn and Lamb, 1991). Moreover, although it remains the dominant model for both researchers and managers, its proposed universality and applicability is made more questionable by viewing the numerous modifications that are evident in many studies that purport to use this model (Paulin and Perrien, 1996).

2.1   e-Service Quality

Website service quality, frequently termed e-service quality, has been defined as "consumers overall evaluation and judgement of the excellence and quality of e-service offerings in the virtual marketplace (Santos, 2003) and "as the extent to which a website facilitates efficient and effective shopping, purchasing and delivery" (Zeithaml 2002). E-service quality is constantly evolving due to the pace of competition and the ease of duplicating service features in the online world (Trabold et al., 2006). Notwithstanding evidence of continuing consumer dissatisfaction with service delivered through the Internet (Gaudin 2003; Ahmad 2002) studies of e-service quality remain limited and frequently employ instruments that were developed for use in a traditional environment such as the SERVQUAL survey instrument. For example, researchers (Van Iwaarden *et al.,* 2004) have used SERVQUAL to examine the quality factors perceived as important in relation to the use of websites, despite the fact that it was not designed to measure perceived service quality in an online environment and its applicability is therefore unlikely to extend to that context. While it is true that past conceptualisations can be useful platforms for describing e-services (Van Riel, 2001), there is an increasing awareness (Cai and Jun, 2003; Lie et al., 2003) that the SERVQUAL instrument is limited in terms of its ability to measure e-service quality particularly as there are dimensions of service quality that are unique to the electronic context. For example, Cox and Dale (2001) argue that dimensions of service quality specific to a traditional environment such as competence, courtesy, cleanliness, comfort, and friendliness, are not salient in the electronic retail environment while such dimensions as accessibility, communication, credibility, and appearance, are of critical importance in an online environment. Support for inclusion of specific dimensions unique to the on-line retail environment is also provided by Long and McMellon (2004) who argue that factors such as geographic distance and facelessness of the experience form part of the online service experience and therefore should be part of any e-service quality measurement instrument.

However, although several researchers have proposed scales to evaluate websites, many of these scales do not provide a comprehensive evaluation of the service quality of the website. For example, the focus of the WebQual scale (Loiacono *et al.,* 2000) is to provide website designers with information regarding the website (e.g. informational fit to task) rather than to provide specific service quality measures from a customer perspective. Other scales such as WebQual (Barnes and Vidgen, 2002) provide a transaction-specific assessment rather than a detailed service quality assessment of a website. The SITEQUAL (Yoo and Donthu, 2001) scale excludes dimensions central to the evaluation of website service quality as does Szymanski and Hise's (2000) study, while researchers (Parasuraman *et al*, 2005) have expressed caution regarding the consistency and appropriateness of dimensions used in the eTailQ scale proposed by Wolfinbarger and Gilly (2003).

Recently however, many of these concerns have been addressed by the original authors of the SERVQUAL instrument through the development and operationalisation of a multi-item scale for examining website service quality (Parasuraman, Zeithaml and Malhotra, 2005). This scale, termed E-S-QUAL, is a four-dimensional, 22-item scale that captures the critical dimensions of service quality outlined in the extant literature. The dimensions are efficiency, fulfilment, system availability, and privacy. The scale has an accompanying subscale called E-RecS-Qual which contains items focused on handling service problems and is relevant to customers who have had nonroutine recovery service encounters with the website. E-RecS-Qual consists of a three-dimensional, 11 item scale. These three dimensions comprise responsiveness, compensation, and contact. Both scales, whose specific purpose is the measurement of website service quality, have been subjected to reliability and validity tests and demonstrate good psychometric properties. As E-S-QUAL is a relatively new measure it has therefore not been used extensively in online service quality research. A recent study that has utilised the measure (Kim *et al.*, 2006) found that online apparel retailers are failing on specific service dimensions leading to dissatisfaction on the part of their consumers. Such insights provide critical insights and have the potential to assist apparel retailers in improving their service and thus increase their success in the commercial arena.

In this study the E-S-QUAL instrument will be applied to a narrowly focused business context as has been done by other researchers who have sought to identify the key dimensions of service quality in contexts such as online banks, or travel agencies (e.g. Jun and Cai, 2001; Van Riel et al, 2001). That context is an online gift store in Ireland with a 5000 strong customer base.

The final survey utilized was based on the Parusaman *et al.*, (2005) questionnaire and was divided into two sections. In section 1 of the survey a varying number of questions were asked regarding the dimensions of online service quality as outlined in the E-S-QUAL instrument. The owners of the online gift website requested that all questions relating to the compensation dimension of the survey be omitted from the final questionnaire as they viewed these questions as introducing a negative view of interactions with the website. The dimensions and number of questions relating to each website service quality dimension are indicated in table 1. Section 2 of the survey collected demographic information on the respondents. The survey was set up in a web-based format and a URL link to the survey web site was listed in the company email newsletter which was then sent to the 5,000 registered customers. The data obtained from the questionnaire was converted into Excel and analysed using SPSS (Statistical Package for the Social Sciences), a widely used programme for statistical analysis.

Table 1. eService Quality Dimensions

eService Quality Dimension	Number of Questions
Efficiency	8
System availability	4
Fulfilment	7
Privacy	3
Responsiveness	5
Efficiency	8
Compensation*	3
Contact	3
Perceived value	4
Loyalty intentions	5

* Dimension omitted on request of online vendor

3 Results

3.1 Response Rates

84 respondents completed the questionnaire within 1 week of the initial notification. This represents 1.68% of the sample. A second notification was sent by email 3 weeks later, which increased the number of respondents to 119. This represents an increase of 43% to a total sample response rate of 2.38%. One possible explanation for the low response rate is the difficulty in checking the validity and continued operation of the email addresses. This response rate is despite the incentive of entry into a draw for a free prize. The second mailing succeeded in increasing the response rate from 1.68% to 2.38%. Within the responses received 25% completed section 1 in full, and all 119 completed section 2. This gives the figure 0.6% as the percentage of the total sample that returned a fully completed questionnaire for section 1, and 2.38% for section 2.

3.2 Reliability Analysis

The independent variables in this study are: Efficiency, System Availability, Fulfilment, Privacy, Responsiveness and Contact. The dependent variables are Perceived Value and Loyalty Intentions. Table 2 shows the Cronbach's alpha values for each of the constructs. All of the constructs worked well with this sample with the four constructs 'Efficiency', 'Fulfilment', 'Responsiveness' and the 'Loyalty Intentions' providing particularly strong internal reliability measures.

Having secured reliability measures for the variables the measure of association between pairs of variables was now examined using correlation techniques. Correlation is a statistical technique that provides a measure of the association between two variables i.e. how strongly the variables are related, or change, with each other. In order to test the data a simple average for each of the related questions was calculated for each construct and the relationship between the variables then considered. The correlation coefficient results are displayed in appendix 1.

The website service quality constructs showing the strongest inter-relationships are system availability with privacy (0.84), and efficiency with system availability (0.80).

Table 2. Reliability Analysis – Scale (Alpha)

Construct	Number of Items	Cronbach's Alpha
Efficiency	8	0.95
System Availability	4	0.86
Fulfilment	7	0.94
Privacy	3	0.88
Responsiveness	5	0.95
Contact	4	0.85
Perceived Value	4	0.87
Loyalty Intentions	5	0.96

The weakest inter-relationships are those of fulfillment with contact (0.39) and privacy with contact (0.53).

The relationships between the website service quality constructs and the dependent variables were then examined. In relation to the dependent variable 'perceived value', the strongest result is provided by the responsiveness construct (0.87), followed by the system availability construct (0.81). The weakest relationship is that between contact and perceived value (at 0.72). In relation to the dependent variable 'loyalty intentions', the results again show a positive relationship between the dependent and independent variables. However, the website service quality dimensions show a slightly weaker relationship with customer loyalty than with perceived value. Efficiency has the strongest influence on customer loyalty at 0.76. Interestingly, fulfillment and privacy were the website service quality variables showing the weakest relationships with loyalty intentions at 0.62 each.

3.3 Regression Analysis

Multiple regression techniques were used in this study to establish whether the set of independent variables could explain a proportion of the variation in the dependent variables at a significant level, and to establish the relative predictive importance of the independent variables. The results, outlined in tables 3 and 4 show that these independent website service quality variables explain 88% of the variation in perceived value and 69% of the variation in loyalty intentions respectively.

Table 3. Model Summary: Perceived Value

R	R Square	Adjusted R Square	Std. Error of Estimate
.936(a)	.876	.844	.28194

Independent variables: Efficiency, System Availability, Fulfillment, Privacy, Responsiveness, Contact. Dependent variable: Perceived Value

Table 4. Model Summary: Loyalty Intentions

R	R Square	Adjusted R Square	Std. Error of the Estimate
.829(a)	.687	.605	.51010

Independent variables: Efficiency, System Availability, Fulfillment, Privacy, Responsiveness, Contact. Dependent variable: Loyalty Intentions

The F-statistics for each of the relationships reported above indicate that with 99.9% confidence, we can assert that there is a systematic relationship between the dependent variables and the set of independent variables. Thus, at least one of the independent variables is explaining changes in the dependent variable.

Predictive Importance of Independent Variables. Perceived Value: The coefficient results indicate that two of the independent variables – system availability (coefficient beta weight 0.390) and responsiveness (coefficient beta weight 0.371) - exert the strongest effect on the dependent variable perceived value. Fulfilment and contact are significant independent variables – but to a lesser degree. Each of these variables is positively related to the dependent variable.

Loyalty Intentions: The coefficient results indicate that two of the independent variables - fulfilment (coefficient beta weight 0.355) and contact (coefficient beta weight 0.329) - exert the strongest effect on the dependent variable Loyalty Intentions. However, none of the independent variables are statistically significant. This result contradicts the results of the F-test that indicated with 99.9% confidence that there was a systematic relationship in this case. This contradiction is a typical outcome where independent variables are highly correlated with one another – where multicollinearity is present. The coefficient results for both dependent variables are shown in appendix 1.

4 Discussion

The study findings provide evidence of a strong relationship between the system availability and privacy dimensions of website service quality. This indicates that consumers' evaluation of a website as reliable (in terms of availability for business) appears to result in a parallel evaluation of the vendor as likely to take adequate measures to protect their personal information. The findings also confirm a strong inter-relationship between efficiency and system availability confirming the close association between these dimensions of website service quality in the mind of the consumer.

An interesting distinction emerged in terms of the difference between contact and responsiveness. For example, the results show that consumers' perception of value is positively influenced by vendor responsiveness but less positively influenced by contact. This indicates that while consumers perceive aspects of responsiveness such as the ability to take care of consumer problems, to handle product returns well, and to tell the consumer what to do if a transaction is not processed as adding value to their service interaction with the vendor, all contact must be initiated by the consumer as non-solicited contact (e.g. as with event notification emails) is perceived as an infringement of privacy.

The service quality variable with the strongest ability to influence consumers' perception of value is efficiency, followed by system availability, again confirming the inter-relationship between these two variables. Similarly, in relation to consumers' loyalty intentions, the dimensions of website service quality that provide the strongest explanatory power are efficiency and system availability respectively. These results indicate that technical website attributes such as ease of use and reliability have strong potential to influence perceived value and customer loyalty and outweigh consumers' fulfillment and privacy concerns. Vendors seeking to increase consumer's perception of value and intention to re-purchase from the website should therefore focus on the ease of use of the website customer interface and the reliability of their websites.

While previous research has argued that privacy of websites may not be critical for more frequent users (Wolfinbarger and Gilly, 2003), the results of this study indicate otherwise. For example, the majority of respondents in this study were reasonably frequent purchasers from this gift website (29% purchased on a monthly basis and 33% purchased every 2-3 months) spending an average of €50-€149 per transaction. While experience may mitigate concerns about website security, it clearly does not mitigate the influence of privacy concerns on the online consumers' trust response.

Finally, the use of the E-S-QUAL measurement instrument in an Irish context provided interesting insights into the critical facets of website service quality valued by Irish consumers. The authors of the E-S-QUAL instrument developed it in the United States. Based on their results they concluded that the most critical E-S-QUAL dimensions were the efficiency and fulfillment dimensions and that customers' assessment of a website on these two dimensions would have the strongest influence on their perceptions of value and on their loyalty intentions. In this study the full measurement instrument (comprising E-S-QUAL and E-RecS-QUAL) was applied in a European context and the results obtained differ considerably from those of the instrument's authors. For example, based on an Irish sample of respondents, system availability and responsiveness respectively were the dimensions of website service quality shown to exert the strongest effect on perceived value, while in relation to loyalty intentions, the variables fulfilment and contact exert the strongest effect on the dependent variable. While system availability emerged as a significant independent variable, it was to a lesser degree. However, due to the study limitations relating to sample size, further research is necessary to establish whether or not the E-S-QUAL model can be described as culture independent. t present, all that can be concluded is that this study has provided results that indicate that online consumers in Ireland differ from US online consumers in terms of the facets of website service quality that most influence their perceptions of value and their loyalty intentions.

5 Conclusions

One of the limitations of this study relates to the sample size, a fact that was beyond the control of the authors. Secondly, the company used in the study was an online gift store. The fact that those purchasing from this website are purchasing products that they will not be consuming themselves may lead to a different emphasis on certain facets of service quality. In order to ascertain whether this could indeed be the case, it is necessary to conduct further website service quality studies of websites where the consumer is purchasing the product for their own use. Thirdly, the online vendor in this study requested that the items on compensation should not be included in the questionnaire, as the company did not provide product compensation assurances. This resulted in one of the E-RecS-Qual sub dimensions being omitted from the study.

This is the first time that the E-S-QUAL instrument has been applied in a European context and thus this study contributes to the small but growing body of work that exists on website service quality. The insights provided by this study will be of interest to website service quality researchers in their efforts to increase understanding of an issue has received comparably little attention to date. However, it is anticipated that the insights will also be of benefit to practitioners in their efforts to compete for and retain customers in the competitive electronic commerce marketplace.

References

1. Ahmad, S.: Service Failures and Customer Defection: A Closer Look at On-line Shopping Experiences. Managing Service Quality 12(1), 19–29 (2002)
2. Amarach Consulting TrendWatch Technology Report, Quarter 2 (2002), http://www.amarach.com/news/press.htm
3. Asubonteng, P., McCleary, K.J., Swan, J.: Servqual revisited: a critical review of service quality. Journal of Services Marketing 10(6), 62–81 (1996)
4. Babakus, E., Boller, G.W.: An empirical assessment of the SERVQUAL scale. Journal of Business Research 24(3), 253–268 (1992)
5. Babakus, E., Mangold, G.W.: Adapting the SERVQUAL scale to hospital services: an empirical investigation. Hospital Services Research 26(6), 767–786 (1989)
6. Barnes, S.J., Vidgen, R.T.: An Integrative Approach to the Assessment of E-Commerce Quality. Journal of Electronic Commerce Research 3(3), 114–127 (2002)
7. Bebko, C.P., Garg, R.K.: Perceptions of responsiveness in service delivery. Journal of Hospital Marketing 9(2), 35–45 (1995)
8. Bitner, M.J.: Evaluating service encounters: the effects of physical surroundings and employee responses. Journal of Marketing 54(2), 69–82 (1990)
9. Bowers, M.R., Swan, J.E., Koehler, W.F.: What attributes determine quality and satisfaction with health care delivery? Health Care Management Review 19(4), 49–55 (1994)
10. Cai, S., Jun, M.: Internet Users Perceptions of On-line Service Quality: A Comparison of On-line Buyers and Information Searchers. Managing Service Quality 13(6), 504–519 (2003)
11. Carman, J.M.: Consumer perceptions of service quality: an assessment of the SERVQUAL dimensions. Journal of Retailing 66(1), 33–55 (1990)
12. Cox, J., Dale, B.G.: Service Quality and e-Commerce: An Exploratory Analysis. Managing Service Quality 1(2), 121–131 (2001)
13. Cronin, J.J., Taylor, S.A.: SERVPERF versus SERVQUAL: reconciling performance-based and perception-minus-expectations measurement of service quality. Journal of Marketing 58(1), 125–131 (1994)

14. Cronin, J., Taylor, S.A.: Measuring service quality: a reexamination and extension. Journal of Marketing 56, 55–68 (1992)
15. Doney, P.M., Cannon, J.P., Mullen, M.R.: Understanding the Influence of National Culture on the Development of Trust. Academy of Management Review 23(3), 601–620 (1998)
16. Finn, D., Lamb, C.: An evaluation of the SERVQUAL scale in a retailing setting. Advances in Consumer Research 18, 483–490 (1991)
17. Fukuyama, F.: Trust: The Social Virtues and the Creation of Prosperity. Free Press, New York (1995)
18. Gaudin, S.: Companies Failing at On-line Customer Service (retrieved, 2003), http://itmanagement.earthweb.com/erp/article.php/1588171
19. Gefen, D., Heart, T.: On the Need to Include National Culture as a Central Issue in E-Commerce Trust. Journal of Global Information Management 14(4), 1–30 (2006)
20. Grönroos, C.: Strategic Management and Marketing in the Service Sector. Marketing Science Institute, Cambridge (1983)
21. Hofstede, G.H.: Culture's Consequences: International Differences in Work-Related Values. Sage Publications, Beverly Hills (1984)
22. Lehtinen, J.R., Lehtinen, U.: Service quality: a study of quality dimensions, Unpublished working paper, Service Management Institute, Helsinki (1982)
23. Loiacono, E., Watson, R.T., Goodhue, D.: WebQual: A Web Site Quality Instrument, Working paper, Worcester Polytechnic Institute (2000)
24. Long, M., McMellon, C.: Exploring the determinants of retail service quality on the Internet. Journal of Services Marketing 18(1), 78–90 (2004)
25. Parasuraman, A., Zeithaml, V.A., Malhotra, A.: E-S-Qual: A Multiple Item Scale for Measuring Electronic Service Quality. Journal of Service Research 7(3), 213–233 (2005)
26. Parasuraman, A., Zeithaml, V.A., Berry, L.L.: SERVQUAL: a multiple item scale for measuring customer perceptions of service quality. Journal of Retailing 64(1), 12–40 (1988)
27. Parasuraman, A., Zeithaml, V.A., Berry, L.: A conceptual model of service quality and its implications for future research. Journal of Marketing 49, 41–50 (Fall 1985)
28. Paulin, M., Perrien, J.: Measurement of Service Quality: The Effect of Contextuality. In: Kunst, Lemminck (eds.) Managing Service Quality, London. Chapman, Boca Raton (1996)
29. Santos, J.: E-service quality: a model of virtual service quality dimensions. Managing Service Quality 13(3), 233–246 (2003)
30. Shaffer, T.R., O'Hara, B.S.: The Effects of Country of Origin on Trust and Ethical Perceptions. The Service Industries Journal 15, 162–179 (1995)
31. Swartz, T.A., Brown, S.W.: Consumer and provider expectations and experience in evaluating professional service quality. Journal of the Academy of Marketing Science 17, 189–195 (1989)
32. Szymanski, D.M., Hise, R.: T. e-Satisfaction: An Initial Examination. Journal of Retailing 76(3), 309–322 (2000)
33. Teas, K.R.: Consumer Expectations and the Measurement of Perceived Service quality. Journal of Professional Services Marketing 8(2), 33–53 (1993)
34. Trabold, L.M., Heim, G., Field, J.: Comparing e-service performance across industry sectors: Drivers of overall satisfaction in online retailing. International Journal of Retail & Distribution Management 34(4/5), 240–257 (2006)

35. Van Iwaarden, J., Van der Wiele, T., Ball, L., Millen, R.: Perceptions about the Quality of Websites: A survey amongst students and Northeastern University and Erasmus University. Information and Management 41(8), 947–959 (2004)
36. Van Riel, A., Liljander, V., Jurriëns, P.: Exploring Consumer Evaluations of E-Services: A Portal Site. International Journal of Service Industry Management 12(4), 359–377 (2001)
37. Wolfinbarger, M., Gilly, M.C.: eTailQ: Dimensionalizing, Measuring, and Predicting etail Quality. Journal of Retailing 79(3), 183–198 (2003)
38. Woodside, A.G., Frey, L.L., Daly, R.T.: Linking service quality, customer satisfaction, and behavioral intention. Journal of Health Care Marketing 9(4), 5–17 (1989)
39. Yoo, B., Donthu, N.: Developing a Scale to Measure the Perceived Quality of an Internet Shopping Site (Sitequal). Quarterly Journal of Electronic Commerce 2(1), 31–46 (2001)
40. Zeithaml, V.: Service quality in e-channels. Managing Service Quality 12(3), 135–138 (2002)
41. Zucker, L.G.: Production of Trust: Institutional Sources of Economic Structure, 1840 – 1920. In: Staw, B.M., Cummings, L.L. (eds.) Research in Organizational Behavior, vol. 8, pp. 53–111. JAI Press, Greenwich (1986)

Appendix

Correlation Coefficient Results

Correlation	1	2	3	4	5	6	7	8
Efficiency (1)	1.0	0.80	0.56	0.67	0.82	0.71	0.79	0.76
System Availability (2)		1.00	0.60	0.84	0.73	0.53	0.81	0.68
Fulfillment (3)			1.00	0.78	0.63	0.39	0.73	0.62
Privacy (4)				1.00	0.75	0.53	0.80	0.62
Responsive (5)					1.00	0.71	0.87	0.72
Contact (6)						1.00	0.72	0.69
Perceived Value (7)							1.00	0.72
Loyalty Intentions (8)								1.00

Regression Coefficient Results: Perceived Value

		Unstandardized Coefficients		Standardized Coefficients	t	Sig.
		B	Std. Error	Beta		
1	(Constant)	-.790	.441		-1.794	.086
	Efficiency	-.099	.177	-.093	-.560	.581
	System Av	.425	.192	.390	2.212	.037
	Fulfillment	.335	.140	.295	2.389	.025
	Privacy	-.100	.183	-.102	-.548	.589
	Responsiveness	.356	.147	.371	2.423	.024
	Contact	.247	.112	.249	2.197	.038

Regression Coefficient Results: Loyalty Intentions

Model		Unstandardized Coefficients		Standardized Coefficients	t	Sig.
		B	Std. Error	Beta		
1	(Constant)	-.863	.797		-1.083	.290
	Efficiency	.284	.320	.235	.886	.385
	System Av	.326	.347	.263	.938	.358
	Fulfillment	.460	.254	.355	1.810	.083
	Privacy	-.281	.330	-.253	-.852	.403
	Responsiveness	.068	.266	.062	.255	.801
	Contact	.371	.203	.329	1.826	.081

Comparison of Social Classification Systems in a Heterogeneous Environment

Steffen Oldenburg

University of Rostock, Department of Computer Science
Albert-Einstein-Str. 21, D-18059 Rostock, Germany
`stol@informatik.uni-rostock.de`

Abstract. This paper presents the results of practical studies comparing five well established social classification services for tagging of bookmarks (del.icio.us, BibSonomy bookmarks) and publications (BibSonomy publications, CiteULike, Connotea) in the context of service interoperability and integration. Contrary to most of current research we exclusively focus on the usage of RSS feeds for retrieval of tag-related data. Here we exploit „recent" feeds, as this method of data retrieval corresponds directly to the way users can retrieve data from these services, e.g. for tag suggestions. We motivate the preferred usage of feeds compared to full site grabbing, and present analysis results of feed data from the same period of one month concerning feature distribution, growth, stability and convergence aspects. Furthermore we compare tag spaces and their intersections for potential interoperability and integration of these services, and reveal that tags in practice are not really as freely chosen as often promised.

Keywords: Social Classification, Heterogeneous Tag Spaces, Efficient Personal and Collaborative Tagging, Tag Space Comparison and Integration.

1 Introduction

Recent years have seen a strong trend of people coming together at online platforms and services in order to share all imaginable types of web-addressable resources, e.g. *del.icio.us* for spare time bookmarking, *BibSonomy* for professional and scientific bookmarks, *CiteULike* for collecting scientific publications, *technorati* for blogs, or *flickr* for sharing recent holiday photos. Users attach descriptive keywords - so-called tags - in order to allow for easy resource retrieval, primarily for their own usage. Implicitly they generate benefit for the whole user community as users explore tagged resources based on their own tags as well as those of other users.

Tagging services can assist users with tag suggestions for a resource of interest. In order to select tags users can exploit these tag suggestions - provided by a service web site or indirectly via tools like browser plugins. Assigning tags to resources interactively users select a subset of suggested tags, reject others, or assign new ones. Thus, the categorization vocabulary in folksonomies converges to a quite stable state with a tag subset comprising frequently used tags (broad categories or thematic clusters).

This emerging trend to collaboratively attach any - theoretically - unrestricted, free-form key words to content - called tagging - has produced a tremendously rising number of isolated, non-integrated heterogeneous tag spaces, and tagged resources. Recent

J. Cordeiro et al. (Eds.): WEBIST 2008, LNBIP 18, pp. 333–346, 2009.

quantitative research of this development raises concern that the growth trend compli- cates for individual users to efficiently benefit from resource discovery and to contribute to resource annotation over time.

In order to assign well matching tags to resources, users need to get operational with tagging services (tag spaces). They can start tagging at zero (empty tag space) which is time consuming, or incorporate existing tags from one or more tag space(s) which we denote as bootstrapping or cold start. An established tag space dynamically evolves over time due to the addition of new, or a reinforcement of existing tags and co-occurring tags (co-tags).

Nowadays users can interact with more than one tagging service in parallel. As these services typically provide non-interoperable tagging features, users cannot be sure to apply the same tagging behavior in all services. For instance they have to maintain separate tag spaces, and are subject to different character sets to assemble tag words from. However, major properties of different systems are similar, and major common portions of tags are applied in all (e.g. English vocabulary), or similar tagging contexts (e.g. IT, natural sciences) while their semantics represented by tag-tag relations (co- tags) differ significantly.

1.1 Issues of Isolated Tag Spaces

In the following discussion we summarize selected issues we see in current non- integrated social classification systems.

Current growth of flat, unstructured and not inter-related tag spaces will render tag- ging to be more and more inefficient for the individual user over time [6]. Heteroge- neous environments with different target groups, classification purposes, and supported resource types on one hand, and the rising number of such growing systems on the other one let arise the question: Can one classification service satisfy the majority of needs of different classification purposes in a heterogeneous environment?

Does one large service - in our test *del.icio.us* - cover the majority of relevant tags, that it can be predominantly used as the number one source for storage of social book- marks as well as tag suggestions?

In the context of heterogeneous tag spaces we expect a major improvement from an exploitation of cross-space similarities and inter-relations between different tag spaces. Our idea is that users can benefit from a virtual uniform tag space transparently mapping user tags on the various services in background, hence supporting a uniform tagging behavior independent from the services being actually used.

In order to decide these issues existing research approaches introduce several metrics and measures to identify helpful tag space properties, e.g. similarity, growth, stability, and efficiency figures. They apply them on basically comparable data sets - mostly the popular broad folksonomy *del.icio.us*, in some cases the less frequently used services *CiteULike* or *BibSonomy*.

However, results from these different approaches cannot be effectively compared due to different time scopes, evaluation targets, amounts of data, data retrieval concepts, and a missing comprehensive analysis architecture following an integrative approach. Thus, chances to evaluate and compare tag or resource spaces, e.g. for efficient tag sugges- tions, and to deduce conclusions to optimize tagging processes are hard to identify.

Thus, there is need for an evaluation approach on comparable actual data sets from the same time span, based on a uniform data retrieval.

1.2 Contribution

The lack of such comprehensive folksonomy approaches to compare, evaluate, and correlate tagsonomies, prevents from identifying or establishing links between various tag spaces. Such an integrated view on tagging requires to gain insight into similar and different properties of the tag spaces involved in order to exploit associations between different tagging services. Focusing on isolated folksonomies and their tag / co-tag spaces as not being inter-related so far, only little research has been done on comparison and integration.

This paper presents work in progress of a PhD thesis in the context of integrated social classification systems. Overview and analysis of comparable key figures to motivate an integrative tagging approach unifying the operation with different tag spaces is the major target of this work. Here, we present results of comparative studies with selected, well established classification services over the same time span of one month (Aug 01 - Sept 01, 2007), exclusively based on RSS[1] recent feeds.

2 Related Works

For a recent overview and motivation of tagging refer to [1], and [22]. Zhang et al. [21] compare the motivations, advantages and drawbacks of traditional top-down and emerging bottom-up semantics concerning web resources and present results from del.icio.us analysis. The BibSonomy service and formal considerations of folksonomies are presented in [11]. For an overview of tag suggestions and a comparison of established tag suggestion algorithms read [15].

Comparison, Integration and Interoperability Studies. Gruber [8] proposes an approach for defining an ontology to enable the exchange of tag data and the construction of tagging systems that can compositionally interact with other systems. The author also promotes a promising follow-up initiative for tag interchange: TagCommons [9]. Veres [20] evaluates semantic intersections and interoperable features between different tagging services (here: flickr, del.icio.us), but lacks profound quantitative evaluation. The relation between texts from blog posts and assigned tags are analyzed in [3]. Inter-relations between different tag spaces are not considered. Bhagat et al. [4] analyze how different information networks (e.g. blogs, web, messenger, chat) interact with each other following a cross network approach. Schmitz et al. [17] analyze and compare co-occurrence network properties of del.icio.us data (actual as of 2004-2005) and BibSonomy data (as of July 2006). Finally, Szomszor et al. [19] correlate user profiles from multiple folksonomies in order to identify user related tag space similarities based on intersections.

Distribution, Growth, and Stability. Feed based analysis using del.icio.us data is exploited in [18] and [2]. The *deli.ckoma*[2] web site derives actual statistics from recent

---

[1] Really Simple Syndication: http://www.rssboard.org/rss-specification

[2] http://deli.ckoma.net/stats

RSS feeds, and evaluates data retrieval coverage and error probability. Additionally read [13]. Halpin et al. [10] analyze whether coherent and stable categorization schemes can emerge from unsupervised tagging, and they evaluate its dynamics over time, including corresponding power-laws in del.icio.us tag distributions.

Tag Space Navigability and Efficiency. Chi and Mytkowicz [6] analyze early data (actual as of 2004-2005) from large-scale del.icio.us with (conditional) entropy concerning efficient navigability, and reveal that efficiency is decreasing over time. Efficiency analysis using entropy measure is also used in [21] and [12]. Santos-Neto et al. [16] analyze the smaller scale services CiteULike and BibSonomy whether usage patterns can be exploited to improve the navigability in a growing tagsonomy. Brooks and Montanez [5] analyze the effectiveness of resource-related tags (TF-IDF) to describe blog contents in *technorati*.

3   Feeds as Exclusive Source for Tag Space Analysis

RSS feeds are offered by many leading social classification services, at least for recently tagged data (recent feeds), in general also for searching for specific tags, users, and resources. This promises a more consistent retrieval of heterogeneous tag data than site-depending methods, e.g. full or random site grabs using web spiders like `wget`.

Past research either fully relied on site grabs or at least initial grabs with further incremental updates using feeds. Grabs are subject to changes in HTML structure, and its dynamical generation, hence need to regard current site properties. While full grabs are not well accepted by many services, full dumps - covering long-term collected data - are rarely available, e.g. in our test from CiteULike and BibSonomy only.

Contrarily, feeds from different services bear a very similar content structure due to XML markup. There are still minor differences in XML tags or in the availability of specific properties of feed items. An example item is given in Listing 1. Selective feed retrieval generates less load on service sites. Feed-based growth in tags, users, and resources promises statistically relevant data amounts in a relatively short time as our analysis will reveal. We can operate without storing long service histories as we are primarily interested in supporting users with actual tag data, and sites dynamically evolve including interest shifts. Furthermore tagging sites growth has produced such a tremendous amount of data, that cannot be efficiently handled anymore for popular sites, e.g. refer to del.icio.us in Table 2. As we want to support users in uniform tagging with heterogeneous tagging services we need to exploit the same data users have access to. Users do not require to download full dumps or grab histories. Using RSS we benefit from a widely uniform format based on RDF / XML, and thus can seamlessly integrate new services complying to this format.

After profound reading of publications emerged in the context of quantitative analysis of tagging services during the last two years we have to pose the question: Do we need complete history-scale dumps of tag spaces, or is it sufficient, and more efficient just to evaluate current and future data with less scale, but similar properties concerning distribution, convergence and stability of tag spaces - over some short time - to get and stay operational? Interestingly, feeds offer richer semantics in tag data than service backends (read Section 4.5).

```
<item rdf:about="http://code.google.com/">
    <title>Google Code – Developer Network</title>
    <link>http://code.google.com/</link>
    <description></description>
    <dc:creator>lhc1111</dc:creator>
    <dc:date>2007–08–31T22:02:16Z</dc:date>
    <dc:subject>API Code Google ajax</dc:subject>
    <taxo:topics><rdf:Bag>
        <rdf:li resource="http://del.icio.us/tag/Google"/>
        <rdf:li resource="http://del.icio.us/tag/Code"/>
        <rdf:li resource="http://del.icio.us/tag/API"/>
        <rdf:li resource="http://del.icio.us/tag/ajax"/>
    </rdf:Bag></taxo:topics>
</item>
```

Listing 1. Example of an RSS feed item

4   Analysis and Evaluation

In the following section we provide insight into our formalism, test environment, and relevant evaluations.

4.1   Formal and Test Environment

For our analysis we selected the highly popular site del.icio.us (fast item updates), the popular sites CiteULike and Connotea (less items per feed), and the less popular site BibSonomy, distinguishing between feeds for bookmarks and publications. Refer to Tables 1 and 2, from now on we will address the services with the given IDs.

Table 1. Service URLs for recent RSS feeds, availability of public dumps for research purposes, and manually adjusted feed retrieval intervals

Service	URL (http://)	ID	Dump	Retrieval interval
BibSonomy	www.bibsonomy.org/rss	Bib1	yes	10 min
	www.bibsonomy.org/publrss	Bib2	yes	10 min
CiteULike	www.citeulike.org/rss	Cit	yes	10 min
Connotea	www.connotea.org/rss	Con	no	3 min
del.icio.us	del.icio.us/rss	Del	no	10 sec

We requested recent RSS feeds using service specific manually adjusted request intervals (see Table 1). Depending on the interval chosen we receive 144 (10 min interval) up to 8640 (10 sec) XML files (feeds) per day, being archived on a daily basis. Item features, e.g. resources and tags, are extracted from archived feeds into CSV tuples using regular expressions. Finally they are propagated to the appropriate database schema. For details refer to Tables 2 and 5.

Table 2. Sizes of tags (T), users (U), resources (R), tag assignments (TAS), co-tags / edges (E), co-tag assignments (CAS), and items (I)

	Bib1	Bib2	Cit	Con	Del
T	8716	1664	14282	12215	238047
U	1433	135	1683	2352	213190
R	4726	1529	17912	17032	823411
TAS	24424	5554	67395	71325	5485163
E	68163	7953	160474	131400	2661505
CAS	114347	12251	3918460	299393	10786194
I	5285	1570	18221	17440	1822456

Tags $t \in T = \{t_1, t_2, ..., t_k\}$, users $u \in U = \{u_1, u_2, ..., u_l\}$, and resources $r \in R = \{r_1, r_2, ..., r_m\}$ are stored with time stamps, and tag assignment counters (*tas_count*) in separate tables and associated to each other in a tag assignments table (TAS) as quadruples $tas = (t, u, r, ts) \in TAS \subseteq T \times U \times R \times TS$ with a time stamp $ts \in TS = TS_{ISO8601} = \{ts_0 \leq ts \leq ts_n\}$ with $ts_0 = $ 01.08.07T16:00:00, and $ts_n = $01.09.07T23:59:59. Triples (t, u, r) are unique.

Feed items (posts) are defined as $i \in I \subseteq U \times R \times TS \times T^*$ - we only process non-empty items (T^+). To preserve a maximum of comparability the extraction restricts to use non-empty items (at least one tag), containing only unreserved characters according to RFC 3986, among these at least one character from [a-zA-Z0-9]. Space separated word groups are split, tags are unescaped (HTML). We decode UTF-8 %-encoding, and remove [, ; " \].

The co-tags table stores edges $e = (t_i, t_j) \in E \subseteq T \times T$ with $t_i \leq_{alpha-numeric} t_j$ and $t_i \neq t_j$ of the tag co-occurrence network with usage counters (*co_count*) as weights. For each RSS item we sort the local tag list and combine each tag with all its successors (filtering self-co-occurrences), resulting in a local fully connected undirected graph with $n_i * (n_i - 1)/2$ tags (clique) for item i with n tags. Each co-tag assignment $cas \in CAS \subseteq E \times TS$ is stored in a co-tag assignments (CAS) table. The integrity conditions $\sum_{t \in T} tas\_count = \sum_{u \in U} tas\_count = \sum_{r \in R} tas\_count = |TAS|$, and $\sum_{e \in E} co\_count = |CAS|$ are satisfied.

4.2 Power-Law Analysis

Does RSS feed extracted data reveal typical distribution features? In order to determine whether our data is representative for a folksonomy we need to show that typical distributions comply to a power-law.

Here we present the distribution of tags (see Figure 1) over tag assignments. Table 3 presents the power regression parameters using the linear function $log(y) = log(f(x)) = k*log(x) + log(a)$ for the power-law formula $y = f(x) = a*x^k$. A mathematically more precise, but by magnitudes slower computation method is introduced in [7]. For faster approximations we propose power regression based on logarithmic intervals (top 10, 100, 1000 ...).

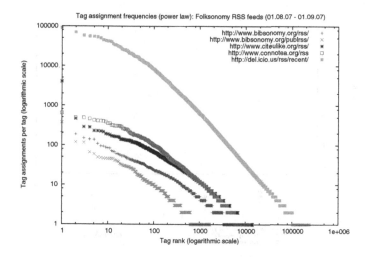

Fig. 1. Tag assignments per tag (power-law)

Table 3. Overall power-law characteristics for tags (T) concerning assignment rank (AR) using power regression with slope k, and intercept $log(a)$. Standard errors are ≤ 0.005

Top	Param	Bib1	Bib2	Cit	Con	Del
AR_T	k	-0,777	-0,847	-0,959	-1,045	-1,179
	log(a)	6,768	5,973	8,938	9,551	14,168

The plots reveal typical power-law behavior (nearly linear in log-log scale) with small head and big tail at different scales. Del.icio.us represents the most popular folksonomy in test, BibSonomy publications the least frequented one, followed by BibSonomy bookmarks. Connotea and CiteULike reveal very similar properties which is not only visible in these plots. The plots indicate that RSS feeds are an absolutely satisfying data source, as feed data very rapidly establish typical power-law distributions. Subsequently, feeds are satisfactory resources for tag analysis and tag suggestions. We do not have to favor tagging history, but can focus on recent tag related information. Less data produces less load on the tagging service, and can be analyzed more efficiently. A major drawback is, that we do not retrieve the same number of tail level tags as with site grabs, the part of the distribution bearing most spam, but also less frequently used specific tags. For a profound quantitative study including tags and co-tags refer to [14].

4.3 Growth and Convergence Analysis

A further question is whether tag related distributions retrieved from RSS feed data converge quickly enough to get stable after short time, and how long feeds need to be requested to achieve that stability. We provide a general overview about per-day growth and cumulative growth - here tags only - in Figures 2 and 3. Both plots are

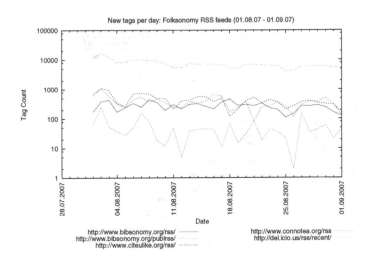

Fig. 2. Per day tag growth over time, log-normal scale

in log-normal scale to reveal scale (popularity) differences between the services. Per-day tag (resource, user) growth reveals falling trends for del.icio.us, CiteULike, and Connotea, indicating that the longer the studies go the more of the most frequently used tags (actual resources, active users) have been retrieved. Normal-normal scale is nearly linear for cumulative growth. The corresponding distribution of tags concerning number of tags per feed item is presented in Figure 4. This distribution reveals the number of tags users typically apply in tagging services, it is relevant for restricting the number of tags in tag suggestions.

In order to assess convergence and stability of tag related data over time, we retrieved top ranking (here: top 1000) tags, users and resources based on tag assignments, and computed pairwise similarity between subsequent top sets. For space reasons we only present top 1000 tags for CiteULike service (Figure 5) being representative for convergence of all top distributions other than del.icio.us. Del.icio.us distributions converge smoothly and stabilize very quickly (90% similarity threshold after two days), the other services need about four days to reach 80% similarity. We use the Jaccard measure for basic set similarity (containment, no regard of rank): $j = sim_{Jaccard}(X, Y) = |X \cap Y|/|X \cup Y|$.

Element rank correlation need to be applied. Kendall τ for instance counts the number of pairwise disagreements between two lists (discordant pairs). This method only applies to lists with the same elements just bearing different order. It does not regard lists with deletion or insertion in order to transform a list X into a list Y.

For a simple joint consideration of element ranks with insertion and deletion we introduce a symmetric look-ahead shift distance measure to assess the number of position shifts of elements. For two sets X and Y with $n = (size(X) <= size(Y))$? $size(X)$: $size(Y)$ in order to transform X into Y for all elements e we calculate shift costs $c_{shift}(X, Y) = \sum_{e \in X \wedge e \in Y} |r_X(e) - r_Y(e)|$, insert costs $c_{ins}(X, Y) = \sum_{e \notin X \wedge e \in Y} |n - r_Y(e) + 1|$ (shift into set), delete costs $c_{del}(X, Y) = \sum_{e \in X \wedge e \notin Y} |n -$

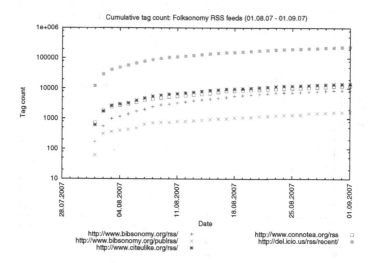

Fig. 3. Cumulative tag growth (tags per day) over time, log-normal scale for better visibility due to the domination of del.icio.us

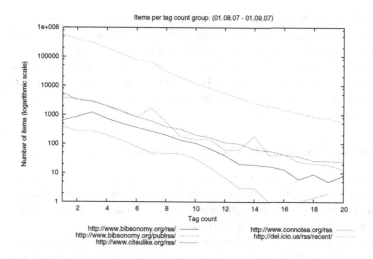

Fig. 4. Tagged items grouped according to the number of used tags, log-normal scale

$r_X(e) + 1|$ (shift out of set) with rank $r(e) : 1 \leq r(e) \leq n$, and summarize $c_{abs-shifts}(X,Y) = c_{del}(X,Y) + c_{ins}(X,Y) + c_{shift}(X,Y)$. The shift weight s then reads $s = c_{abs-shifts}/c_{max-shifts}$ normalizing with $c_{max-shifts} = n * (n+1)$. Applied on j the formula reads: $sim_{Jaccard,weighted} = j * (1-s)$. $c_{max-shifts}$ occurs for two disjoint sets with $n * (n+1)/2$ delete as well as insert shifts, e.g. e_1 shifts down (up) by n positions, e_n by 1 to leave (claim) positions in X (Y).

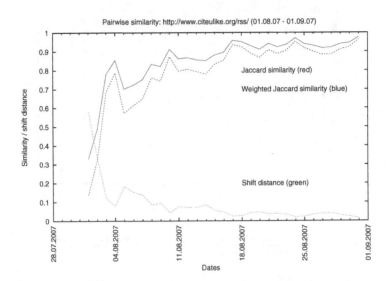

Fig. 5. Pairwise similarity of top 1000 tags, CiteULike

Assumption 1 is that the sets are equal-sized, otherwise we choose the lower size as reference. Assumption 2 is that only insertion is allowed, assuming only equal-sized or growing sets, which is true for our feed-based folksonomy data in test. Hence, between subsequent sets X_i, X_{i+1} holds: $\forall i : |X_i| \leq |X_{i+1}|$. Our shift distance does not perform any reordering, it only looks ahead to assume a measure on it, not taking into account any improved item order after some reordering step. Here, we penalize the initial state of disorder.

4.4 Intersections and Overlaps between Tag Spaces

Before covering interoperability or integration issues of tag spaces from different folksonomies we have to analyze whether there is a fundamental need. This need arises if tag spaces reveal significantly different thematic focuses with relevant portions of unique tags not being contained in pairwise intersections.

We compute pairwise intersections (asymmetric overlaps) between the tag spaces in test bed as well as publicly available dumps (refer to Table 1). The dumps are actual as of Dec. 31, 2007, we regard all tags assigned until the end of our analysis scope (Sept. 01, 2007) from service startup on. The dumps cover the whole tagging history, hence represent the evolution of tags over time.

Thus, we explore common parts of tag spaces using pairwise overlaps based on tag string equality (see Table 4). It is obvious and it was expected that del.icio.us has the highest coverage of common language words or typical top tags (column Del) used in other tag spaces. However, there are differences in usage of tag assignments for common tags as well as a significant portion of tags not being contained in the intersection (difference between 100% and value given in table). For example the intersection of del.icio.us and Connotea makes up to 67% of Connotea tag space (row Con, column

Table 4. Asymmetric ratios of pairwise overlaps between feed and dump tag spaces (row T_i, column T_j): $Ratio[T_i, T_j]$ = $|T_i \cap T_j|/|T_i|$, with T_i, T_j ∈ {$Bib1, Bib2, Bib1 - D, Bib2 - D, Cit, Cit - D, Con, Del$}, D denotes a dump. Bib1-D has 33719, Bib2-D 13893, and Cit-D 197463 tags.

	Bib1	Bib2	Bib1-D	Bib2-D	Cit	Cit-D	Con	Del
Bib1	1,00	0,06	0,51	0,23	0,19	0,75	0,33	0,68
Bib2	0,34	1,00	0,61	0,95	0,46	0,74	0,38	0,68
Bib1-D	0,13	0,03	1,00	0,16	0,12	0,44	0,15	0,56
Bib2-D	0,14	0,11	0,38	1,00	0,27	0,66	0,21	0,49
Cit	0,11	0,05	0,29	0,26	1,00	0,98	0,22	0,44
Cit-D	0,03	0,01	0,08	0,05	0,07	1,00	0,05	0,20
Con	0,24	0,05	0,41	0,24	0,26	0,74	1,00	0,63
Del	0,02	0,00	0,08	0,03	0,03	0,17	0,03	1,00

Del) and 3% of del.icio.us tag space (row Del, column Con). This initially motivates a preferred usage of del.icio.us for tagging or tag suggestion retrieval. However, there is a 33% portion of tags in Connotea not being contained in del.icio.us, motivating a preferred usage of Connotea for topics exclusively covered by these tags, e.g. Connotea and CiteULike have a thematic focus on natural sciences.

We additionally calculated pairwise intersection ratios between tag spaces from full dumps (full long-time data sets) and / or feeds (short time). Here we use dumps from CiteULike and BibSonomy. Dump-only intersections more clearly reveal different thematic focuses than feed-only intersections.

For a more profound analysis of intersections of tags, co-tags, their top ranking portions as well as the inherent dynamics over time read our work in [14].

4.5   Fairy Tale of Freely Chosen Tags

Why is it useful to analyze and compare tag creation and storage? During our analysis we stumbled upon many slang and spam tags as well as tags with a high portion of non-alphanumeric characters. We selected some of these tags and checked, whether these tags retrieve a search result at all, and whether these search results are specific or coincide with those retrieved using normalized tags. All services in test provide a web interface to search for a specific tag as well as a feed interface to request the corresponding recently tagged items.

The idea is also motivated having a look into CiteULike and BibSonomy dumps, revealing that the effective, normalized tags (stored in the service backend) are not equal to those applied in feeds (user intended tags), neither in semantic richness nor (probably) in number. Applying non-normalized tags from feeds either gains no or different search results (exact queries), or the same search result using normalized tags (similarity query, like query). For instance del.icio.us allows usage of unreserved characters (RFC 3986) for tag creation, e.g. @, !, #, +. They are used for tags in feeds, but queries skip them using like-queries. They are not used to enforce specific semantics, e.g. query("c++") = query("c") = query("c#") or query(".net") = query("net").

Table 5. Effective tag spaces and queries: F denotes tag feeds, D: tag dumps, e: exact query (q), l: like q., w: wildcard q., b: boolean q., c: in-collection q., r: ranked order. Unreserved (a-zA-Z0-9_-.~), reserved characters, and URL per-cent encoding refer to RFC 3986.

	Bib1	Bib2	Cit	Con	Del
Method	F/D	F/D	F/D	F	F
Query	e/r	e/r	b/e/w	c/e	e/l
Case-sensitive	no	no	no	yes	no
Unreserved	yes	yes	yes	yes	yes
Reserved	yes	yes	no	no	yes
	yes	yes	no	yes	yes
%-Encoding	no	no	no	no	yes

The result feeds contain combinations of tags "c", "c++", "c#" or respectively ".net" and "net", not only the tag being searched for. Finally this observation contradicts the widely used tagging promise that any freely chosen keyword can be used as a tag. We notice a loss of user specific semantics from feed to backend as well as a much smaller character space to assemble tag words from. Another aspect is that tags are mostly provided in context with other tags (co-occurrences). Even full chapter titles, word groups or sentences are used as tags according to CiteULike and Connotea feeds. In the backend the context between tags is lost due to splitting of word groups, normalizing words in, or eliminating words from them.

This information is not provided by the services, e.g. del.icio.us FAQ says that users are allowed to use character "*" in tags to express emotions or ranking. However, these characters have no effect. Either they get removed from a tag or the tag is not stored in backend. This cannot be reliably determined using feeds without a dump to compare to. BibSonomy FAQ states that feeds are periodically propagated into the backend database, hence does not exclude that effective tags might differ from those applied by users. Users have to know about restrictions in order to adapt their tag spelling and semantic mapping accordingly. Hence, there is a motivation for deeper analysis of intended and effective semantics to evaluate the extent to which different tagsonomies can be compared to and integrated into each other or a separate unified tagsonomy (user based, group based) to support efficient context-based tag suggestions / (semi) automatic classification. For bootstrapping and dynamic evolution (e.g. merging, import, export) of tag spaces it is necessary to know differences and commonalities as well as mutual interpretation of tags and tag properties. Here we provide a brief overview of our observations in Table 5.

5   Conclusions and Perspectives

We presented comparison results from feed-only analysis of 5 leading social classification services. Our analysis reveals that feed-only data satisfy typical distributions well, stabilize very rapidly concerning top-ranked data, and bear significant pair-wise intersections and thematic differences. Thus, they serve as a promising source for comparative and integrative social network investigations.

We expect promising results from exploiting co-tag networks established by the tags in an intersection (same tags, but different graphs). Additionally we plan to exploit similarity and convergence aspects of cross-space tag hierarchies, co-occurrence graphs and graph partitions. Beyond the obvious tag-tag relationships other correlation graphs can be constructed, e.g. for similar users (common tags or resources between any two users), and resources (common tags or users between any two resources).

A further comparative study is scheduled to correlate tag spaces and tagged content using Vector Space Model (VSM) and TF-IDF methods, e.g. in order to bootstrap tags for untagged content. We also intend to compare the (co-)tag spaces and associated semantics resulting from different tag normalization methods. Finally, there is further need for an analysis of loss in semantics from feed data to backend data in order to assess and optimize tag space usage.

Finally, we plan to extend our initial study evaluating different types of tag suggestion algorithms resulting in the motivation of combined tag suggestions [15].

References

1. Ames, M., Naaman, M.: Why We Tag: Motivations for Annotation in Mobile and Online Media. In: Proceedings of Computer/ Human Interaction Conference, CHI 2007 (2007)
2. Begelman, G., Keller, P., Smadja, F.: Automated Tag Clustering: Improving search and exploration in the tag space. In: WWW 2006: Proceedings of the 15th international conference on World Wide Web (2006)
3. Berendt, B., Hanser, C.: Tags are not metadata, but "just more content" - to some people. In: International Conference on Weblogs and Social Media (ICWSM 2007) (March 2007)
4. Bhagat, S., Rozenbaum, I., Cormode, G., Muthukrishnan, S., Xue, H.: No Blog is an Island - Analyzing Connections Across Information Networks. In: ICWSM 2007: International Conference on Weblogs and Social Media, Boulder, Colorado, USA (2007)
5. Brooks, C.H., Montanez, N.: An Analysis of the Effectiveness of Tagging in Blogs. In: AAAI Spring Symposium on Computational Approaches to Analyzing Weblogs (2006)
6. Chi, E.H., Mytkowicz, T.: Understanding Navigability of Social Tagging Systems. In: Proceedings of Computer Human Interaction, CHI 2007 (2007)
7. Clauset, A., Shalizi, C.R., Newman, M.E.J.: Power-law distributions in empirical data (2007)
8. Gruber, T.: TagOntology - A way to agree on the semantics of tagging data. Presentation to Tag Camp, Palo Alto, CA (October 2005),
   http://www.tomgruber.org/writing/tagontology.htm
9. Gruber, T.: Ontologies Vs. Formats Vs. Schema Vs. APIs (March 2007),
   http://tagcommons.org
10. Halpin, H., Robu, V., Shepherd, H.: The Complex Dynamics of Collaborative Tagging. In: WWW 2007: Proceedings of the 16th international conference on World Wide Web (2007); Track E* Applications
11. Hotho, A., Jschke, R., Schmitz, C., Stumme, G.: BibSonomy: A Social Bookmark and Publication Sharing System. In: de Moor, A., Polovina, S., Delugach, H. (eds.) Proceedings of the Conceptual Structures Tool Interoperability Workshop at the 14th International Conference on Conceptual Structures, July 2006. Aalborg University Press, Aalborg (2006)
12. Li, R., Bao, S., Fei, B., Su, Z., Yu, Y.: Towards Effective Browsing of Large Scale Social Annotations. In: WWW 2007: Proceedings of the 16th international conference on World Wide Web, 2007. Track: Web Engineering, Session: End-User Perspectives and measurement in Web Engineering (2007)

13. Oldenburg, S.: Comparative Studies of Social Classification Systems using RSS Feeds. In: 4th International Conference on Web Information Systems and Technologies (WEBIST 2008), Funchal, Madeira, Portugal, May 4-7, 2008, pp. 394–403 (2008) ISBN 978-989-8111-27-2, Best student paper award.
14. Oldenburg, S., Garbe, M., Cap, C.: Similarity Cross-Analysis of Tag / Co-Tag Spaces in Social Classification Systems. In: CIKM 2008: ACM 17th Conference on Information and Knowledge Management, Workshop on Search in Social Media (SSM), Napa Valley, California, USA, October 26-30 (2008)
15. Oldenburg, S., Zielinski, L., Garbe, M., Cap, C.: Comparative Analysis of Tag Suggestion Algorithms. In: KDD 2008: 13th ACM SIGKDD International Conference on Knowledge Discovery and Data Mining, 2nd ACM Workshop on Social Network Mining and Analysis (SNA-KDD), Las Vegas, Nevada, USA, August 24-27 (2008)
16. Santos-Neto, E., Ripeanu, M., Iamnitchi, A.: Tracking User Attention in Collaborative Tagging Communities. In: Proceedings of International ACM/IEEE Workshop on Contextualized Attention Metadata: personalized access to digital resources (2007)
17. Schmitz, C., Grahl, M., Hotho, A., Stumme, G., Cattuto, C., Baldassarri, A., Loreto, V., Servedio, V.D.P.: Network Properties of Folksonomies. In: WWW 2007: Proceedings of the 16th international conference on World Wide Web, 2007. Workshop on Tagging and Metadata for Social Information Organization (2007)
18. Shaw, B.: Utilizing Folksonomy: Similarity Metadata from the Delicious System (December 2005), http://www.metablake.com/webfolk/webproject.pdf
19. Szomszor, M.N., Cantador, I., Alani, H.: Correlating user profiles from multiple folksonomies. In: HT 2008: Proceedings of the nineteenth ACM conference on Hypertext and hypermedia, pp. 33–42. ACM, New York (2008)
20. Veres, C.: Concept Modeling by the Masses: Folksonomy Structure and Interoperability. In: Embley, D.W., Olivé, A., Ram, S. (eds.) ER 2006. LNCS, vol. 4215, pp. 325–338. Springer, Heidelberg (2006)
21. Zhang, L., Wu, X., Yu, Y.: Emergent Semantics from Folksonomies: A Quantitative Study. In: Spaccapietra, S., Aberer, K., Cudré-Mauroux, P. (eds.) Journal on Data Semantics VI. LNCS, vol. 4090, pp. 168–186. Springer, Heidelberg (2006)
22. Zollers, A.: Emerging Motivations for Tagging: Expression, Performance, and Activism. In: WWW 2007: Proceedings of the 16th international conference on World Wide Web (2007)

Part IV

e-Learning

Web-Based 3D and Haptic Interactive Environments for e-Learning, Simulation, and Training

Felix G. Hamza-Lup and Ivan Sopin

Computer Science Armstrong Atlantic State University
11935 Abercorn St., Savannah, GA 31419, U.S.A.
Felix.Hamza-Lup@armstrong.edu

Abstract. Knowledge creation occurs in the process of social interaction. As our service-based society is evolving into a knowledge-based society, there is an acute need for more effective collaboration and knowledge-sharing systems to be used by geographically scattered people. We present the use of 3D components and standards, such as Web3D, in combination with the haptic paradigm, for e-Learning and simulation.

Keywords: Haptics, H3D, X3D, 3D Graphics.

1 Introduction

Web-based knowledge transfer is becoming a field of research worthy of attention from the research community, regardless of their domain of expertise, due to the potential of advanced technologies, such as Web3D and haptics.

In the context of global communication, these technologies are becoming more stimulating, by enabling the creation of collaborative spaces for e-Learning and simulation.

We present several advanced features of Web3D in conjunction with three successful projects that effectively employ those features. In section 2 we provide a brief introduction to the e-Learning concept. In section 3 we discuss the details of different modalities to enrich user interaction with Web3D content and haptics. In section 4 we introduce three case studies demonstrating the potential of X3D in simulation and training: 3DRTT, a radiation therapy medical simulator; chemistry and physics concepts interactive simulations project; and HaptEK16, an e-Learning module which provides interaction through haptic feedback for teaching high-school physics concepts. We conclude in section 5 with a set of remarks from our research and development experience.

2 Background and Related Work

Let us take a look at the notion of e-Learning. According to [1], the concept of Internet-based learning is broader than Web-based learning, as illustrated in fig. 1. The Web is only one of the Internet services that is based on the HTTP protocol and uses a unified document language, HTML, Unified Resource Locator (URL), and browsers.

J. Cordeiro et al. (Eds.): WEBIST 2008, LNBIP 18, pp. 349–360, 2009.

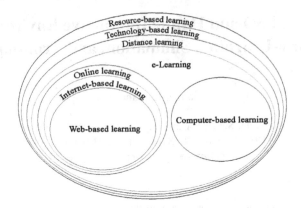

Fig. 1. Subsets relationships among the group of terms

As the largest network in the world, the Internet offers several other services besides Web: e-mail, file transfer facilities, etc. Hence, learning can be acquired beyond Web only; correspondence via e-mail makes a good example. Furthermore, the Internet employs a multitude of proprietary protocols along with HTTP.

Due to the advances in 3D technology, it is now possible to develop and deploy on the Web 3D interfaces and environments that enhance the learning process. An example is Extensible 3D (X3D), an ISO standard for real-time 3D computer graphics and the successor of Virtual Reality Modeling Language (VRML). X3D combines both 3D geometry and runtime behavior descriptions into a single file, with the ability to embed additional scene modules from other sources. X3D files are encoded in either classic VRML or Extensible Markup Language (XML) format. The standard provides means of assigning specific behaviors to 3D objects, enabling users' interaction with them.

On the other hand, advanced interfaces are undergoing a shift towards the incorporation of a new paradigm, haptics. Interfaces combining 3D graphics and haptics have the potential to facilitate our understanding of various concepts and phenomena, as well as to promote new methods for teaching and learning.

Haptic technologies offer new ways of creating and manipulating 3D objects. For instance, in Interactive Molecular Dynamics [2] the users manipulate molecule with real-time force feedback and a 3D graphical display. Another example, SCIRun [3], is a problem-solving environment for scientific computation, which is used to display flow and vector fields, such as fluid flow models for airplane wings.

Initial pilot demonstrations with biology students using augmented graphical models and haptic feedback support the hypothesis that this method provides an intuitive and natural way of understanding difficult concepts and phenomena [4]. Another research group, at the University of Patras, Greece, is involved in designing simulations to aid children comprehend several subject areas of science, such as Newtonian Laws, Space Phenomena, and Mechanics Assembly [5]. Tests show that haptic technology improves the level of human perception due to the deeper immersion provided.

Other fields, such as mathematics and especially geometry, also benefit from haptic interaction. Recently, a system was proposed to allow a haptic 3D-based construction of a geometric problem along with the representation of the problem's solution [6]. Initial performance evaluation indicates the system's elevated user-friendliness and higher efficiency compared to the traditional learning approach.

National Aeronautics Space Administration (NASA) has shown interest in introducing haptics in educational technology. The Learning Technologies Project at the Langley Research Center is concerned with innovative approaches for supporting K-16 education. Pilot study results from the use of simple haptics-augmented machines have yielded positive feedback with 83% of the elementary school and 97% of the college students, rating the software from "Somewhat Effective" to "Very effective" [7] and [8].

3 User Interaction

User interaction can be enriched through 3D content and haptics. In what follows we explore in detail the potential of combining X3D with additional Web-enabled instruments, such as HTML and JavaScript, to provide control over a 3D world. We also explain and explore the haptic paradigm and its potential applications in a Web-based environment.

3.1 X3D Graphics Visualization

To visualize the graphical content of X3D online, a Web browser needs a special plug-in. Most X3D plug-ins are free for public use and apply a small license fee for commercial use. One example is the BitManagement Contact Player which is both a browser plug-in and a standalone X3D player.

Usually, X3D plug-ins are equipped with a set of basic controls for customizing the user interface and specifying the properties of user interaction: navigational tools, graphics modes, and rendering settings. Being handy, these features only facilitate a user in exploring the visual content, but do not provide any means of altering it. It is the X3D standard itself that allows users to dynamically modify and interact with the 3D graphical scene. There are several alternative ways to implement such systems. In the following subsections we discuss the advantages and drawbacks of a stand-alone X3D-based simulation versus the simulation functionally enriched with JavaScript procedures and HTML versus the haptic-enabled simulation.

3.2 X3D-Based Simulation

A stand-alone X3D-based environment has all its functionality and graphical user interface (GUI) stored in an X3D file. When a user interacts with the scene, it only responds to the changes specified in the file.

When significant changes in the graphics of the application are required, the code of the file with the graphical content has to be altered. This entails the necessity to provide an updated version of the file and to also manually refresh the X3D scene. Such organization, in general, corresponds to the common client/server interaction on the Web: when an HTML form is populated with data, the user has to press the "Submit" button to request the server's response.

However, the three-dimensional scope introduced by X3D brings into play new aspects of GUI/user interaction. For instance, volumetric controls, easily implemented in X3D, can better mimic the behavior of the controlled objects. Parts of a 3D world can also be manipulated through a system of specifically designated sensors which respond to clicking, dragging, rotating, and other user gestures. The scripting capabilities of X3D can enrich the GUI interactivity as developers have new means to create efficient customized control panels that meet the project-specific tasks.

3.3 X3D Simulation with HTML and JavaScript Support

A different approach to improving the GUI interactivity is involving external tools that could effectively communicate with the 3D graphical scene. Good examples of such tools are HTML and JavaScript, most commonly used to build Web pages.

In a GUI with HTML and JavaScript support, JavaScript can be the driving force of most features while HTML only serves as its operating environment. However, HTML makes it difficult to encode unconventional GUI components needed to closer represent the dynamics of the virtual objects in the 3D scene. The HTML standard provides a limited set of traditional input elements, such as checkboxes, buttons, and radio buttons, that are not easily customizable. As a result, the creation of powerful and flexible task-oriented GUI components combines inputs with other traditional HTML objects (layers, images, etc.), backed up with extensive JavaScript code.

With the interface functionality programmed as JavaScript functions, the 3D scene still derives its maneuverability from the methods implemented in the X3D scripting nodes. The browser and X3D environment communicate through mutual function calls. The browser refers to the virtual scene as to an HTML document's object with a number of public functions. Different X3D plug-in developers provide their own sets of such functions. X3D feedback is composed of dynamic injections of JavaScript code. Because both visual content and GUI, are synchronized automatically, no manual page updates are necessary. However, synchronization between HTML and X3D can be an issue in such implementation because it involves continuous calls between the two media and may consume considerable processing power, making webpage rendering slow at the client side.

New client/server communication techniques are also feasible for the development of various dynamic environments. For instance, Asynchronous JavaScript and XML (AJAX) is used in our HTML/JavaScript-based GUI (details in section 4.1) to obtain the listing of external X3D components that could be loaded into the scene. Therefore, without refreshing a page, the user is able to visualize external 3D objects and manipulate them as if they were initially part of the 3D scene.

3.4 Multimodal, Haptic-Based GUI

Besides traditional GUIs, a novel paradigm, haptic feedback (from the Greek *haptesthai*, meaning "contact" or "touch") may improve the interface usability and interactivity. The tactile sense is the most sophisticated of all our senses as it incorporates pressure, heat, texture, hardness, weight, and the form of objects.

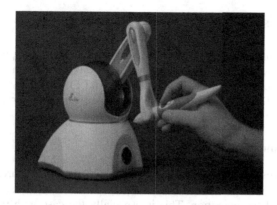

Fig. 2. Phantom® Omni™ device

The summarized four basic procedures for haptic exploration, according to [9], each have descriptive object characteristics:

- *Lateral motion* (stroking) provides information about the surface texture of the object.
- *Pressure* gives information about how firm the material is.
- *Contour following* elicits information on the form of the object.
- *Enclosure* reflects the volume of the object.

Current haptic technologies are capable of delivering realistic sensory stimuli at a reasonable cost, opening new opportunities for academic research and commercial developments [10]. Devices that implement such technologies have a distinct set of performance measures [11]:

- *Degrees of freedom* (DOF) are the set of independent displacements that completely specify the position of a body or a system.
- *Workspace* is the volume within which the joints of the device will permit operation.
- *Position resolution* is the minimum detectable change in position within the workspace.
- *Maximum force/torque* is the maximum possible output of the device, determined by such factors as the power of the actuators and efficiency of the gearing systems.
- *Maximum stiffness* is the absolute rigidity of virtual surfaces that can be presented on the device. It depends on the maximum force/torque, but it is also related to the dynamic behavior of the device, sensor resolution, and the sampling period of the controlling processor.

The presence of haptic feedback enables users to feel the virtual objects they manipulate. We have experimented with the PHANTOM® Omni™ device, developed by SensAble Technologies (fig. 2). The Omni™ became one of our choices due to its low cost and force-feedback qualities. It is also backed up by an open source Application Programming Interface (API).

4 Case Studies

To illustrate the concepts discussed so far, we will describe three projects developed at our research laboratory (www.cs.armstrong.edu/felix/news) using X3D and haptic technologies: a Web-based medical simulator (3DRTT), chemistry and physics concepts interactive 3D simulations, and a haptic-based module for teaching physics (HaptEK16).

4.1 Medical Simulator – 3DRTT

In medicine, success of an operation relies upon practical procedures and the physician's (or surgeon's) experience. Many complex treatment processes are preplanned well in advance of the operation. This is especially the case with radiation therapy. Medical personnel concerned with the planning part (e.g., correct radiation dosages and appropriate patient setup) are sometimes frustrated by the fact that a theoretically sound plan proves inconsistent with the current hardware and patient constraints (i.e., collisions with the patient and treatment hardware may occur). This issue can be addressed by complementing clinical setups with effective visual simulations.

3D Radiation Therapy Training (3DRTT) is a Web-based 3D graphical simulator for radiation therapy procedures. 3DRTT simulates linear accelerators (linacs) that are used to operate patients with cancer by delivering radiation doses to an internal tumor. The project focuses on improving the efficiency and reliability of the radiation treatment planning and delivery by providing accurate visualization of the linacs hardware components as well as careful imaging of their interactive motion.

The virtual representation of the treatment settings (fig. 3) provides patients and therapists with a clear understanding of the procedure. Equipped with the patient Computer Aided Tomography (CAT) scan data, the treatment planner can simulate a series of patient-specific setups and detect unforeseen collision scenarios for complex beam arrangements. Hence, the necessary adjustments to the treatment plan can be made and validated beforehand.

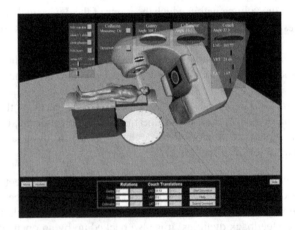

Fig. 3. 3DRTT simulator with X3D-based GUI

Another important application of 3DRTT is improving the current level of radiation therapy education, training, and safety. With such a Web-based 3D simulation tool at the disposal of the radiation therapy staff, there is plenty of room for exploring various treatment procedures (linac components, motion limitations, associated accessories, etc.) and gaining experience for future operations. Moreover, exposure of trainees to harmful radiation and accidents is avoided.

Currently, two versions of the simulator, with X3D and HTML/JavaScript-based GUIs (refer to sections 3.2 and 3.3), are available on the project's website (www.3drtt.org). The X3D-based version provides tools for controlling the angles and locations of the linac parts. The GUI is composed of several semitransparent panels containing various volumetric controls. The controls are designed to logically correspond to the assigned operations (specifically, scrolls for rotations, sliders for translations, and buttons for switching among different simulation modes) and therefore improve the interface usability [12]. GUI components can be rearranged dynamically to avoid occlusions of important parts of the scene.

The HTML/JavaScript-based GUI alternative supports the same functionality and provides additional features (fig. 4). Instead of floating X3D menus, the simulator controls are shifted to the scope of the HTML page. The set of GUI elements includes sliders, buttons, and displays that enhance the interface learnability. For the convenience of navigation in the virtual space, the control panel can be hidden and brought back at the user's request.

Current Web technologies, such as AJAX, introduce new methods of accessing and dynamically processing external modules. For instance, the user may load various hardware attachments for the linacs directly in the virtual world. The source X3D file for the simulator does not "know" how many attachments are available at the moment and what their names are. However, upon user's request, an AJAX function makes a call to a scriptlet stored on the server and receives the listing of available files as a response. This listing is transmitted to the X3D script that handles the loading and embedding of the specified files into the virtual environment. Therefore, no alterations of the X3D source code are necessary when new attachments are uploaded to the server because they become immediately accessible. This dynamic behavior enhances the interactivity of simulation as users can have access to external modules without the need to manually search for them or modify the scene configuration.

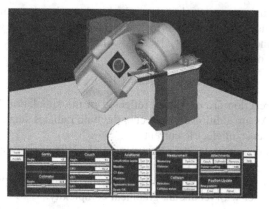

Fig. 4. 3DRTT Simulator with HTML/JavaScript-based GUI

4.2 Chemistry and Physics Concepts Interactive 3D Simulations

The first module of this project is a virtual demonstration of the electrolysis concept. Electrolysis is the technique of separating compound chemical elements into simpler elements with opposite charges by applying an electric current. Our simulation offers an intuitive and effective visualization of the process by replicating the behavior of the decomposed molecules. The interface (fig. 5) includes a 3D tank model with experimental solution (H_2O and NaCl), a cathode and anode dipped into the solution, a cord connecting the cathode and anode to a bulb, and colored spheres representing the atoms of sodium and chlorine. There interface also has a floating menu with a legend explaining the appearance of the atoms, molecules, and ions at different stages, and a slider to control the speed of simulation.

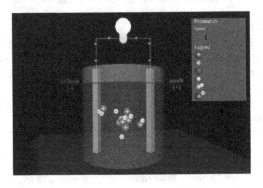

Fig. 5. NaCl electrolysis simulation

The graphical scene is embedded into an HTML page which contains *Start* and *Reset* buttons and provides a textual explanation of the phenomenon. Once the simulation begins, the molecules of NaCl break into positively charged ions of sodium and negatively charged ions of chlorine:

$$NaCl = Na^+ + Cl^- . \tag{1}$$

Then ions of sodium are attracted to the cathode where they lose an electron and become neutral atoms; and ions of chlorine are attracted to the anode where they obtain an electron, become neutrally charged atoms which form molecules of Cl_2 and evaporate based on the formula:

$$2NaCl \rightarrow 2Na + Cl_2\uparrow . \tag{2}$$

All steps of the reaction are explicitly reflected in the simulation by the motion of reagents' atoms. As an additional visual cue, the bulb radiates small portions of light, indicating the presence of electric current.

The simulation demonstrates the effectiveness of a Web3D interface employed as a part of Web page multi-media content. In addition, the animated X3D scene introduces a fair level of abstraction that helps convey the nature of the phenomenon without confusing the user with redundant graphical complexity.

4.3 Haptic e-Learning -- HaptEK16

HaptEK16 [13] is designed to assist students in understanding Pascal's principle and other difficult concepts of hydraulics. The simulator includes three modules: pressure measurement, hydraulic machine, and hydraulic lifting simulation. Students can interact with the 3D scene using a haptic device, as illustrated in fig. 6. The functionality of the simulator is implemented using Python, X3D, and the Sense Graphics' H3D API (www.sensegraphics.com), discussed further.

Python is an object-oriented scripting language that offers strong support for integration with other toolkits and APIs. According to InfoWorld [14], Python's user base nearly doubled in 2004 and currently includes about 14% of all programmers. Python is available for most operating systems, including Windows, UNIX, Linux, and Mac.

Some of the Python's strengths which were considered when selecting a language to implement the system functionality include

- *Low Complexity*: wxPython (an auxiliary library for GUI) was selected because of its ease of use and reduced complexity compared with Java/Swing;
- *Prototyping*: Prototyping in Python is quick and simple and often leads to a quick prototype that can be adapted for the development of the final system;
- *Maintainability*: The code in Python is easy to modify and/or refactor. Less time is spent understanding and rewriting code which leads to efficient integration of new features.

H3D is an open X3D-based haptic API. It is written entirely in C++ and uses OpenGL for graphics rendering and OpenHaptics (de-facto industry standard haptic library) for haptic rendering. With its haptic extensions to X3D, the H3D API is an excellent tool for writing haptic-visual applications that combine the sense of touch and 3D graphics. The main advantage of H3D to OpenHaptics users is that, being a unified scene graph API, it facilitates the management of both graphics and haptics rendering.

Fig. 6. Students using the HaptEK16 hydraulics demo

The scene graph concept facilitates application development, but it can still be time-consuming. SenseGraphics extended their API with scripting modules in order to empower the user with the ability of rapid prototyping. The design approach used in HaptEK16 was the one recommended by SenseGraphics; i.e., geometry and scene-graph structure for a particular application were defined using X3D, and application and user interface behaviors were described using Python and wxPython.

Programming the sense of touch for a virtual object involves two steps. First, the programmer must specify the haptic device to use; second, a set of haptic properties must be defined for each "touchable" object. To specify the haptic device, an instance of the *DeviceInfo* node is created, and the haptic device is added to it. *HLHapticsDevice* is the node used to manipulate a Phantom device. The graphical representation of the device (in case of HaptEK16, a sphere) is also specified in the *containerField* group, as illustrated next.

Example of specifying the haptic device in an X3D file

```
<DeviceInfo>
  <HLHapticsDevice positionCalibration="
        1e-3 0 0 -.15
        0 2e-3 0 .05
        0 0 1e-3 0
        0 0 0 1">
    <Group containerField="stylus">
      <Shape>
        <Appearance>
          <Material />
        </Appearance>
        <Sphere radius="0.0025" />
      </Shape>
      <Transform translation="0 0 0.08"
                 rotation="1 0 0 1.570796">
        <Shape>
          <Appearance>
            <Material />
          </Appearance>
          <Cylinder  radius="0.005"
                    height="0.1" />
        </Shape>
      </Transform>
    </Group>
  </HLHapticsDevice>
</DeviceInfo>
```

To implement the tactile sensation for a generic shape, one must add a surface node with haptic properties to the shape's *Appearance* node. In HaptEK16 this is accomplished with a frictional surface node added to the cylinder's *Appearance* node. The *DynamicTransform* node is added to define properties for rigid body motion.

Example of implementing haptic properties in an X3D file

```
<DynamicTransform DEF="DYN1"
  mass=".05"
  inertiaTensor=".1 0 0 .1 0 0 0 .1">
  <Shape>
    <Appearance>
      <Material diffuseColor="0 .8 .8" />
      <FrictionalSurface dynamicFriction=".6"
                        staticFriction=".2" />
    </Appearance>
```

```
<Cylinder DEF="LEFTCYL"  height=".085"
                         radius=".045" />
</Shape>
</DynamicTransform>
```

The X3D file format is used by H3D as an easy way to define geometry and arrange scene-graph elements, such as user interfaces. A screenshot of the HaptEK16 e-Learning module is illustrated in fig. 7.

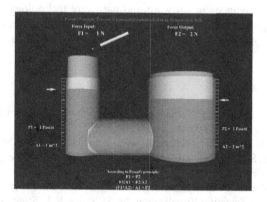

Fig. 7. HaptEK16 screenshot and corresponding Phantom® Omni™ Device

A set of test questionnaires were designed and implemented for the assessment of the e-Learning module. The results from the assessment tests proved that the student group exposed to the HaptEK16 simulator scored better (13% higher total scores) than the group that was not. Such results indicate the potential of using X3D and haptics to develop novel simulation and training environments.

5 Conclusions

3DRTT serves as an example of a Web-based system extensively taking advantage of X3D to improve the efficiency of the user-interface interaction as well as to provide powerful means of professional education and training. Naturally, complex concepts and settings are better understood when delivered with visual support, especially in complicated scenarios. Easy online access, simple control, and advanced capabilities of 3D visualization of radiation therapy treatment scenarios proved to be of great value to the radiation therapists using our system. Currently, 3DRTT has over a hundred registered users and keeps attracting the attention of other professionals working in the radiation therapy field.

Another project, chemistry and physics concepts interactive 3D simulations, proves the effectiveness of X3D interactive models embedded in a Web page content to support the description of the presented phenomenon. X3D scene visually depicts the concept that the user reads about on the very same page. Therefore, Web3D significantly deepens the level of learner's comprehension.

The other development, the haptic e-Learning module (HapteK16) facilitates students' understanding of difficult concepts (e.g., in science) and has the potential to augment or replace traditional laboratory instruction with an interactive and cost-effective interface offering enhanced motivation, retention, and intellectual stimulation. HaptEK16's haptics-augmented activities allow students to interact and feel the effects of forces in the experiment. We believe that force feedback will lead to more effective learning and that HaptEK16 and similar projects have substantial and still unexplored educational capacities.

Considering the advances in software and hardware technology, we foresee many applications of haptics and 3D graphics in the near future, broadening the communication channels among people and narrowing the knowledge gap among us.

References

1. Anohina, A.: Analysis of the Terminology Used in the Field of Virtual Learning. J. Ed. Tech. Soc. 8(3), 91–102 (2005)
2. Stone, J.E., Gullingsrud, J., Schulten, K.: A System for Interactive Molecular Dynamics. In: Hughes, J.F., Sequin, C.H. (eds.) Symposium on Interactive 3D Graphics, pp. 191–194. ACM SIGGRAPH (2001)
3. Durbeck, L., Macias, N.J., Weinstein, D.M., Johnson, C.R., Hollerbach, J.M.: SCIRun Haptic Display for Scientific Visualization. In: Salisbury, K.J., Srinivasan, M.A. (eds.) 3rd Phantom User's Group Workshop, Massachusetts Institute of Technology (1998)
4. Sankaranarayanan, G., Weghorst, S., Sanner, M., Gillet, A., Olson, A.: Role of Haptics in Teaching Structural Molecular Biology. In: 11th Symposium on Haptic Interfaces for Virtual Environment and Teleoperator Systems, pp. 363–366 (2003)
5. Pantelios, M., Tsiknas, L., Christodoulou, S., Papatheodorou, T.: Haptics Technology in Educational Applications, a Case Study. J. Dig. Inf. Mngm. 2(4), 171–179 (2004)
6. Kaufmann, H., Schmalstieg, D., Wagner, M.: Construct3D: A Virtual Reality Application for Mathematics and Geometry Education. J. Ed. Inf. Tech. 5(4), 263–276 (2000)
7. Williams II, R.L., Chen, M.-Y., Seaton, J.M.: Haptics-augmented High School Physics Tutorials. Intl. J. Vir. Real. 5(1) (2001)
8. Williams II, R.L., Chen, M.-Y., Seaton, J.M.: Haptics-augmented Simple Machines Educational Tools. J. Sc. Ed. Tech. 12(1), 16–27 (2003)
9. Klatzky, R.L., Lederman, S.J., Metzger, V.A.: Identifying Objects by Touch: An "Expert System". Perc. Psyc. 37(4), 299–302 (1985)
10. Stone, R.J.: Haptic Feedback: A Brief History from Telepresence to Virtual Reality. In: Murray-Smith, R. (ed.) Haptic HCI 2000. LNCS, vol. 2058, pp. 1–16. Springer, Heidelberg (2001)
11. Wall, S.: An Investigation of Temporal and Spatial Limitations of Haptic Interfaces. Ph.D. Thesis, Department of Cybernetics, University of Reading (2004)
12. Hamza-Lup, F.G., Sopin, I., Lipsa, D., Zeidan, O.: X3D in Radiation Therapy Procedure Planning. In: International Conference on Web Information Systems and Technologies, pp. 359–364 (2007)
13. Hamza-Lup, F.G.: Adams M.: Feel the Pressure: e-Learning System with Haptic Feedback. In: 16th IEEE Symposium on Haptic Interfaces for Virtual Environments and Teleoperator Systems, pp. 445–450 (2008)
14. McAllister, N.: What Do Developers Want?
http://www.infoworld.com/article/04/09/24/39FErrdev_1.html

A Parameterizable Framework for Replicated Experiments in Virtual 3D Environments

Daniel Biella and Wolfram Luther

Institute of Informatics and Cognitive Sciences, University of Duisburg-Essen
Forsthausweg 2, 47057 Duisburg, Germany
daniel.biella@uni-due.de, luther@inf.uni-due.de

Abstract. This paper reports on a parameterizable 3D framework that provides 3D content developers with an initial spatial starting configuration, metaphorical connectors for accessing exhibits or interactive 3D learning objects or experiments, and other optional 3D extensions, such as a multimedia room, a gallery, username identification tools and an avatar selection room. The framework is implemented in X3D and uses a Web-based content management system. It has been successfully used for an interactive virtual museum for key historical experiments and in two additional interactive e-learning implementations: an African arts museum and a virtual science centre. It can be shown that, by reusing the framework, the production costs for the latter two implementations can be significantly reduced and content designers can focus on developing educational content instead of producing cost-intensive out-of-focus 3D objects.

Keywords: Modeling of virtual 3D environments, Code reusability, Parameterizable framework, Automated code generation, Metadata standards, Metadata editing.

1 Introduction

Web-based 3D applications are very popular in the learning, commercial and entertainment sector. Despite the success of these products, the cost of designing and producing content-rich 3D learning environments is still a major issue, especially if realistic models, non-deterministic simulations and special user interaction are required.

Our work focuses on the production of learning content with a high degree of interactivity, photo-realism, reversibility and non-deterministic simulation models, which allows learners to understand the design and methodology of an experiment through an individualized, interactive, Web-based application [1].

In a recent interdisciplinary project concerned with the historical replication of interactive key experiments in psychology and education, 2D and 3D implementations of B.F. Skinner's historical experiment on operant conditioning were implemented, tested and evaluated by students [2]. Results showed that

- the 3D version effected a higher degree of spatial and cognitive immersion,
- the 3D visualization of the experimental setup was more realistic in terms of graphical quality,

J. Cordeiro et al. (Eds.): WEBIST 2008, LNBIP 18, pp. 361–374, 2009.
© Springer-Verlag Berlin Heidelberg 2009

- users tend to accept mixed (2D and 3D) content despite media discontinuities in favor of knowledge creation,
- the experiment was easier to comprehend in 3D.

The question of whether to use 3D or 2D depends on the design requirements, the target user group and the model data to be presented. Design considerations are listed in the section "Modeling pipeline" and discussed in the section "Discussion".

This paper reports on a parameterizable 3D framework for Web-based experiments and identifies reusability options. It highlights three case studies that prove the feasibility of the concept and its cost efficiency, and gives an overview of recent work to enhance the framework.

2   Modeling Pipeline

The modeling pipeline for replicated experiments in virtual 3D environments presented by Biella [2] includes a general framework and several workflow components that are suited for reusability (Figure 1).

Initially, a real-world experiment is analyzed from an authentic setting or from primary and/or secondary sources with a focus on the 3D geometrical model of both the experimental assets and the historical surrounding, an animation model, an interaction model, and a simulation model.

The input/output hardware interfaces and drivers, the rendering software, the modeling languages and tools, and, optionally, a framework development for the integration of multiple experiments are determined by specifying conceptional design requirements that depend on the target user group and the complexity of the geometrical, interaction and simulation models.

The formal model description describes the process of defining the animation, interaction and simulation models in abstract notions, such as mathematical functions, statistical models or state machines. These models are digitized by using suitable model description languages, such as unified modeling language (UML). The implementation of these models (Interaction/Simulation logic) depends on the programming and scripting languages determined as a result of the conceptional design requirements.

The following design considerations have been formulated in [2] with regard to Web-based museums for replicated experiments.

- Historical context representation: Although 2D visualizations may suffice for the presentation of an abstract theoretical model, the visualization of a historical laboratory environment is challenging. In a 2D visualization, such information has to be provided separately through additional sources, such as a sequence of photographs or text descriptions. A 3D model allows the designer to integrate contextual information in the space surrounding the experimental setup.
- Impact of occluded surfaces: Surface occlusion of objects with crucial functionalities within an experimental setup can disturb the knowledge transfer. In this case, 3D implementation must offer sufficient viewpoints or other techniques (for example, surface transparency).

- Implicit 3D experiments: Experiments that involve implicit 3D setups are best suited for implementation based on geometrical modeling and free real-time user navigation.
- Model complexity: Animation, interaction and simulation models vary in their degree of complexity and may require high-level programming languages instead of common Web-based scripting languages.
- I/O Interfaces: Input/output interface requirements must be defined according to user's perception channels.
- Data format consistency: A set of multiple 3D worlds should be implemented in a consistent data format.

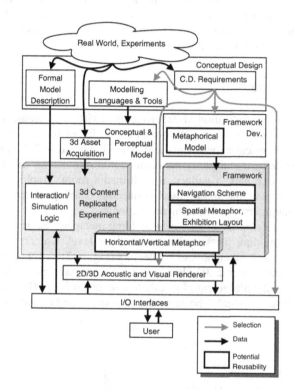

Fig. 1. Reusability options of the framework within the modeling pipeline

3D model asset acquisition describes the process of gathering 3D raw data usually by 3D scanning or 3D reconstruction. The post-production of 3D data implies storage of high-definition 3D data in a flexible file format (e.g.: X3D, XML), polygon and texture size reduction and export in a Web-based data format, as defined in the conceptional design requirements. Both Web-compatible logic and the 3D model represent a single replicated experiment (3D content).

The presentation of multiple experiments requires the development of a metaphorical model, which defines a navigation scheme, spatial metaphors, and an exhibition layout. With regard to a (real world) building metaphor, experiments are connected through vertical and horizontal metaphors that represent thematic and temporal selections of experiments and allow the user to navigate between them.

Cost-efficiency aspects with regard to the creation of particular 3D exhibits suited for learning have already been presented [1].

The virtual laboratory realization presented here underlines the feasibility of the theoretical approach and stipulates that the production cost of 3D content could essentially be reduced by code reusability.

In this paper, we want to focus on reusability aspects of the surrounding museum framework, which is intended to allow 3D content designers to efficiently create several standard 3D museum assets, so they can focus on actual content development, especially for Web-based learning museums and virtual science centers. The modeling pipeline, the framework and reusability options are depicted in Figure 1. They concern the spatial design, including lighting and texturing, interaction logic, navigational schemes and spatial or temporal metaphors.

3   The Framework

The framework for the replication of experiments in virtual environments (referred to below as the Replicave framework) was first developed for an interactive virtual museum for key historical experiments and is implemented in X3D and PHP [2]. It features both pre-defined and partly parameterizable routines for the automated generation of an entrance hall, a gallery, a multimedia room, graphical user interface (GUI) components and metaphor-based connectors leading toward the laboratory rooms in which the interactive experiments are located.

The framework references a real-world building metaphor. Basic framework assets are visualized as building parts at the ground-floor level. Content-related locations can be accessed through metaphorical connectors (Figure 2). A connector's X3D code consists of static and dynamic 3D objects that are combined into a single X3D scene graph. For the dynamic placement of thresholds, seven positions (N1-N3, E1, E2, W1, and W2) are reserved to which laboratory doors, a small media room door or walls are

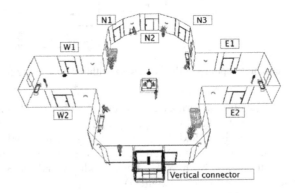

Fig. 2. Conceptional metaphor with maximal number of laboratories (wireframe view including position descriptors)

allocated according to a certain layout matrix. The dynamic generation of the wings is achieved by including static X3D code fragments that define either a wall, which renders the wing's entrance closed, or the full wing layout.

In analogy with the building metaphor, the temporal metaphor is the vertical connector. On each level, the doors of this allocation place form a meta-threshold and give access to meta-paths. The desired path and destination threshold is defined by the user's selection of a different content or experiment on an appropriate navigation panel. The panel is rendered dynamically at runtime and lists all available presents.

3.1 Entrance Hall

As the user's initial starting point in the 3D world, the entrance hall is an obligatory asset. By default, the main hall is cylindrical with a transparent domed ceiling. The design is intended to reproduce the atmosphere of a modern museum building located in an urban environment, which is visualized by a blue sky texture and externally placed building fragments that suggest the urban context (Figure 3).

Fig. 3. Entrance hall (with 3D data progress indicator)

The exit door and the thresholds leading toward the main media room, the gallery, and the vertical connector are exclusively and equidistantly connected to the entrance hall, virtually dividing it into four quarter pie sections. The reception desk, with a receptionist's avatar and a login terminal, is located in the section between the gallery and the metaphorical connector. Dynamically generated information panels listing the available experiments are located at the reception desk and in the elevator. The three other sections are decorated with items that underline the context (research-related images) and 3D furniture objects.

The exit door is an interactive plane that allows the user to leave the system and that can be configured to initialize post-visit routines, such as opening a new browser window for an evaluation.

3.2 Gallery

The mainstream of psychology is presented in the gallery, which is octagonal in shape. This design allows the installation of seven information-related walls and an eighth wall that provides space for a connector to the main hall. The gallery's static 3D model defines outer walls and a transparent roof in accordance with the design of the main hall.

Large colored information boards display the various scientific research fields following the content and color design of an optional 2D-based timeline. 3D information plates are created by dynamic scripts and display short informational texts (for example, a curriculum vitae) and a photograph. Each plate has an interactive event sensor and an individual viewpoint configuration that allow the user to navigate there by simply clicking on them (jump navigation). The text-based content and photographs displayed in the gallery are stored separately from the multimedia content of the laboratories and the media rooms.

3.3 Multimedia Rooms

Replicave uses a two-tier approach: General multimedia content about a given topic or person (image, video, text) can be managed separately from the multimedia data that describes the virtual experiments. Hence, the framework contains pre-defined designs for two multimedia room layouts: a large central multimedia room located on the ground floor and a small layout for topic-related content.

As a result of this approach, learners can access all available 2D multimedia documents in the central multimedia room, which can serve as both a library and an appetizer for a potential 3D implementation. Furthermore, it allows content creators to integrate existing 2D content without the requirement of presenting a 3D experiment. If at least one interactive experiment is present, a small version of the multimedia room is automatically generated in the 3D content section that contains only topic-related documents.

Both room layouts share the same functional elements and visualization metaphors: For each topic or person, there is a book shelf that contains the corresponding multimedia documents represented by interactive 3D icons distinguished by their multimedia document types: book (text based document), film roll (video document) or picture frame with preview (image file).

All multimedia assets can be directly administered via a file-based document management system (DMS). The 3D icons representing the assets are automatically generated at run-time.

The parameterizable layout in the central multimedia room is achieved through an automated shelf creation, which originates in a dedicated corner of the room and is designed as a dynamically sized bulge. For large numbers of shelves (that is, topics presented in the multimedia database), it extends as a corridor of fixed width in a 45-degree angle from the adjacent static walls. This architectural design pattern leads to a library area with convex outer walls, so that the shelf objects are occlusion-free for any user located in front of them (Figure 4).

Fig. 4. Central media room with dynamic 3D architectural design for multimedia content visualization

3.4 GUI Components

Replicave features the following GUI components:

- Five different 3D interactive buttons (exit, context-sensitive help, information on 3D navigation, up, down);
- Single HTML capable overlaid 2D frame.

The GUI components can be reused and individually extended in experiment-related 3D environments.

3.5 Metaphorical Connectors

Connectors allow the user to navigate between the entrance hall and content-related spaces as well as between different experiments. Two connectors are used: The vertical connector (here, an elevator) is used to navigate between the different topics, while the horizontal metaphor (here, a floor) is used to navigate between different 3D experiments on the same topic.

Dynamic content is generated in both connectors. An interactive topic selection panel in the elevator lets the user chose the desired content. The horizontal connector is based on parameterizable 3D model templates. Two templates are available: the building floor (default) and a small-scaled simplified model of the building floor that serves as an interactive 3D map.

The default template's shape depends on the total number of doors that are to be visualized. For a minimal visualization, the centre of the floor, the door leading to the small media room and one laboratory door are displayed. For a complete (maximal) layout, two side wings are added, each of which provides access to two laboratory doors, while three doors (a single media room door and two laboratory doors) are visualized opposite the elevator.

3.6 Other Assets

The framework has been extended by an avatar selection room metaphorically designed as a dressing room and a parameterizable template for experimental rooms [3]. Furthermore, new X3D nodes were created to partly replace external scripting.

3.7 Content and Document Management

In Replicave, we distinguish between two kinds of data: metadata and non-metadata. Non-metadata is always regarded as a hierarchical file archive with a root folder. It is managed by using the open-source document management software Philex[1] for the file and folder administration. The DMS features user administration, Web-based file and folder management with basic operations, editing of text-based files, configurable access restriction regardless of file content and a user interface with tree-based folder visualization. Due to the hierarchical folder structure and multi-user support, content is grouped in dedicated folders and managed via the DMS. At least five administrator or curator roles can be deduced by setting user-specific root folders. Each laboratory or exhibition room is initially loaded by opening a script file. Specific initialization and content files offer a high degree of flexibility. As such, any basic content is represented by a root data folder and rendered according to a positioning algorithm within the metaphor-based templates.

Recent research has focused on museum metadata standards [3]. Various metadata standards were examined and evaluated with regard to their applicability in a 3D museum framework, including DCMI[2], CIDOC[3], VRA[4], and ARCO [4]. Despite its inability to describe metadata about the interaction and simulation logic, the ARCO metadata standard is preferred, primarily due its support for 3D data. In a case study [3], room and object metadata were stored in a separate content database, which then allows exhibition designers to administer and preview content through a web-based interface. Administrative metadata concern the cultural object, the creator or contributors, creation place and date, object metadata additionally the type, material, dimension, acquisition, and the current location. The standard also focuses media objects produced by using 3D modeling systems or VRML editors. Furthermore, objects can be tagged with layout metadata. Given such data, the parameterizable templates can work on data sets derived from database queries, rather than from a fixed list of array elements. However, objects with dynamically changing aspects or user interactions with cultural objects cannot be described within the ARCO Metadata Element Set. Propositions for possible extensions will be subject of a forthcoming paper.

Metadata consistency can easily be accomplished by using a commercial XML editor (Altova) for ARCO-compliant data entry and database upload. Selected variables can later be changed through a web-based interface.

---

[1] http://sourceforge.net/projects/philex/
[2] Dublin Core Metadata Initiative, http://dublincore.org/
[3] The Conceptual Reference Model by the „Comité international pour la documentation (CIDOC)", http://cidoc.ics.forth.gr/
[4] The Visual Resources Association Core 4.0, http://www.vraweb.org/projects/vracore4/

4   Implementation

The Replicave framework is implemented in Extensible 3D (X3D) and the PHP scripting language. Interaction is implemented in ECMAScript. The system requires a PHP5-capable Web server. On the client PC, an X3D browser plug-in is required. The framework has been successfully tested with the BS Contact VRML/X3D plug-in by Bitmanagement Software GmbH and Microsoft Internet Explorer 5. The following case studies work with the BS Contact VRML/X3D plugin, version 6.2 or higher, and Microsoft Internet Explorer 7. Together with DirectX 9.0c or higher, the high-level shading language HLSL is supported and was used for a soap bubble experiment in a virtual science centre [3].

5   Case Studies

The feasibility of the concept presented here has been tested in three case studies. While the Replicave framework has been reused in two implementations, the author of the third implementation decided to create an entirely new framework.

5.1   Virtual Science Center

The virtual science center contains several interactive scientific 3D experiments that refer to various mathematical theories. Users are expected to learn through interaction with virtual installations.

Hiller used the Replicave framework and showed that he could significantly reduce the production time required for framework design and visualization [5]. Decorative 3D-objects, furniture and plants were used or slightly modified for the desk, the wardrobe and the exhibition rooms. With this savings, resources could be spent primarily on the production of learning content, and a total of five new interactive 3D experiments with simulations were developed and implemented.

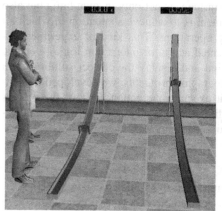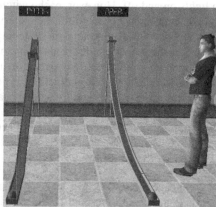

Fig. 5 and Fig. 6. Brachistrochrone – inverted cycloid versus a straight line with the same endpoints; tautochrone – the ball will take a constant time to roll to the end point, regardless of its starting position

First, the experiments were classified with regard to their spatial appearance, simulation model type, interaction logic and manipulation features. This will enable parts of the code to be reused to implement extensions of experiments or similar experiments, such as the brachistochrone and tautochrone problem (Figures 5 and 6).

At first glance, visual representation of the experimental environment enhanced by avatars (Figures 5 and 6) do not deliver the outcome in the form of textual results or functional dependencies among variables written in 2D interface elements. We invite the user to find physical laws behind the experiment by watching and trying out the simulation. However, it may be worthwhile to include additional kinds of text displays or help desks in a future version.

Fig. 7. "Lights on" experiment with initial 2D instruction screen

Figure 7 depicts the "Lights on" experiment, which uses complex action logic. The figure shows a table with seven small lights and individual commutators for switching the lights on and off. However, each switch influences not only its own lamp but also both adjacent lights. The goal of the experiment is to achieve a situation in which all lamps are lit with a minimum of switching operations. This kind of experiment requires a mathematical model or an implemented action or interaction logic to enable the computer to simulate a player and to find and display the correct solution. In a recent project dealing with interactive cryptographic protocols, we developed a methodology to create a Petri state machine that executes the action logic of the players involved [6]. It was shown that Petri net editors and simulation engines, such as Renew[5], support time-efficient modeling of action and interaction logics.

5.2 African Art Museum

The Replicave framework was also successfully used in an implementation of an African arts ("grassland") museum [7], in which the framework's gallery assets were used as a primary exhibition space (Figure 8). Changes could be limited to adapting texture image files in order to comply with an appropriate design for the exhibition context.

---

[5] Available at http://www.renew.de/

Existing interaction facilities allow for manipulating 2D image-based content as well as 3D sculptures. Information panels were updated, and simple new signaling elements were introduced to help users navigate within the adapted room installation. This work could be done by any non-specialist without deep knowledge in 3D modeling languages. Again, it has been shown that resources could be spent on the exhibition content rather than on the framework design surrounding it.

Fig. 8. Gallery room in the grassland museum

5.3 Virtual Art Museum

Unlike the two aforementioned implementations, the virtual art museum created by W. Liu [8] required a specific visual and geometrical framework design (Figure 9). Instead of using the Replicave framework, an individual framework was designed and implemented.

It could be shown that the framework-related work took 50% of the entire content production time, underlining the advantage of reusable framework designs.

Fig. 9. Sculpture room in the virtual art museum

At the same time, the implementation suggested possible extensions of the framework, including the implementation of a graphical editor using drag-and-drop mouse actions to modify the X3D content graph on the fly, encompassing

- spatial design,
- lighting and texturing of walls and furniture, and
- modification of assets.

Such a new framework can be used to create virtual versions of existing museum installations.

6 Discussion

Today, the design of virtual 3D applications is very popular, and there is abundant literature on this topic. However, the realization of virtual laboratories and museums is long and expensive. There are several papers [9] that outline the procedure to follow in the design of a VR application and number important tools for modeling the scene, defining the objects and means of interacting with them. These papers provide a first impression, whereas the inherent complexity of the creational process makes it necessary to consult special purpose literature.

In a recent paper, Hendricks et al. report on virtual African art galleries [10]. In a comparative study, 2D and 3D environments were evaluated. The results of the user study showed that users have a clear preference for 3D environments only if they are not too complex and provide the users with a high level of navigational support, whereas 2D settings are better suited to convey a large amount of information that exists in sequential form.

These results encouraged us to use the Replicave framework in the realization of the grassland museum. An initial evaluation with a small number of participants partly confirmed observations made by Hendricks et al. concerning interaction and 3D navigation.

3D modeling languages, like X3D, use scene graphs to build a 3D spatial design. A notion that is key to reusing code consists in rewriting the scene graph.

Unfortunately, changes in the scene graph intended to bring about a local modification of an object with respect to its geometric shape, texture or position should take into account the context of the relevant node. Reitmayr and Schmalstieg present the idea of adding a context element to the traversal states of a scene graph that allows the scene graph to be parameterized and reused for different purposes [11]. An annotated context-sensitive scene graph improves its own inherent flexibility when acting as a template with parameters set during traversal of the graph. Using the new concepts, a general framework called "Studierstube" is presented, together with a dedicated model server component containing the scene graph of the building model and an interface that allows users to integrate already designed components into their own scene graph realizations.

Automatic generation of user-specific content is addressed in a paper by Chittaro et al. and in further papers cited therein [12]. The authors propose a novel tool that provides automatic code generation for adding personalized guided tours to 3D virtual environments that were developed using frameworks able to dynamically generate X3D content.

7 Conclusions

We have presented a general framework for replicated experiments in virtual 3D environments that is parameterizable and reusable. The framework is embedded in a new generalized modeling pipeline that promotes cost-efficiency by reusing existing design patterns and 3D assets.

The approach was successfully applied in two implementations of interactive Web-based virtual 3D exhibitions: a grassland museum for African art and a virtual science centre. In both cases, designers were freed to focus on content development. A third implementation illustrated the significant amount of additional resources required for individual framework design without using an existing framework library.

8 Outlook

A further extension of the number of parameterizable variables and a complete conversation to XML-based model and content description languages are part of ongoing research. Another focus of our future work concerns the inclusion of conversational agents in analogy to existing solutions for real museums [13].

Acknowledgements. We thank our anonymous reviewers, whose detailed and helpful reports have helped us to improve this paper.

References

1. Biella, D., Luther, W.: Reusability of 2D and 3D Course Content for Replicated Experiments in Virtual 3D Environments. In: Proceedings of the 6th European Conference on e-Learning, ACL Press (2007)
2. Biella, D.: Replication of Classical Psychological Experiments in Virtual Environments, Logos, Berlin (2006)
3. Yapo, M.: Eignung standardisierter Metadatenformate zur Beschreibung virtueller Museen und ihrer Exponate – Datengenerierung und –verwendung aus Sicht verschiedener Usergruppen, Thesis (MA), University of Duisburg-Essen (2008)
4. White, M., Liarokapis, F., Mourkoussis, N.: ARCOLite – an XML based system for building and presenting Virtual Museum Exhibitions using Web3D and Augmented Reality. In: IEEE Proc. Theory and Practice of Computer Graphics 2004, pp. 94–101 (2004)
5. Hiller, A.: Interaktive naturwissenschaftliche Experimente in virtuellen Laboratorien. Entwurf und Implementation in einem Rahmensystem, Thesis (MA). University of Duisburg-Essen (2007)
6. Baloian, N., Breuer, H., Luther, W.: Concept keyboards in the Animation of Standard Algorithms. Journal of Visual Languages and Computing (2007), doi:10.1016/j.jvlc.2007.07.005
7. Mafo, L., Interaktion mit Exponaten in virtuellen Museen anhand von ausgewählten Beispielen. Thesis (MA), University of Duisburg-Essen (2007)
8. Liu, W., 3D-Modellierung virtueller Museen – Interaktion mit geometrischen Objekten, Thesis (MA), University of Duisburg-Essen (2007)

9. Kleinermann, F.: Methods and Tools for Designing VR Applications for The Internet. The European Journal for the Informatics Professional VII(2), 12–16 (2006)

10. Hendricks, Z., Tangkuampien, J., Malan, K.: Virtual galleries: Is 3D better? In: Proceedings of the 2nd International Conference on Computer Graphics, Virtual Reality, Visualization and Interaction in Africa, pp. 17–24. ACM Press, New York (2003)

11. Reitmayr, G., Schmalstieg, D.: Flexible Parameterization of Scene Graphs. In: Proceedings of IEEE Virtual Reality 2005, Bonn, Germany, pp. 51–58 (2005)

12. Chittaro, L., Ieronutti, L., Ranon, R.: Navigating 3D Virtual Environments by Following Embodied Agents: a Proposal and Its Informal Evaluation on a Virtual Museum Application. Psychology Journal 2(1), 24–42 (2004)

13. Kopp, S., Gesellensetter, L., Krämer, N., Wachsmuth, I.: A conversational agent as museum guide – design and evaluation of a real-world application. In: Panayiotopoulos, T., Gratch, J., Aylett, R.S., Ballin, D., Olivier, P., Rist, T. (eds.) IVA 2005. LNCS (LNAI), vol. 3661, pp. 329–343. Springer, Heidelberg (2005)

Web-Based Case Studies for Continuous Professional Development via the ViCoCITY Case Study Support Tool

James A. Redmond, Audrey Stenson, and Alan Mullally

Department of Computer Science, Trinity College, Dublin 2, Ireland
(redmond,audrey.stenson,alan.mullally)@cs.tcd.ie

Abstract. Web-based case studies offer some significant advantages over the traditional paper-based ones. The results from three uses of a Web-supported case study tool giving advantages and disadvantages are discussed from the viewpoints of student, lecturer and administrator with some discussion as to potential future improvements.

Keywords: Case Study, Web-based support tool, e-Learning, Web-based teaching, Distance learning, face to face learning.

1 Introduction

Trinity College has a long tradition of lifelong learning and continuous professional development. In particular, the teaching of Information Systems Management and Information Technology has been actively pursued by the School of Computer Science and Statistics for nearly forty years. Experience in the area led to the development and use of many different formats for presenting the various programmes involved. In particular, the use of case study methods, problem based-learning, simulation exercises and other active learning approaches became key to course and programme delivery. Many of these programmes were part-time programmes with students in employment and seeking up-skilling and development.

A characteristic of these programmes was a close relationship with employers and constant dialogue regarding their educational and training needs. As a consequence of this, there was in addition to the usual pressure to update, adapt and expand curricula, a need to have graduates contribute more effectively, and sooner, to their organisation after graduation. There was also the need to make postgraduates more competent and professional in their approach to work and the workplace. A clear emphasis was needed on the soft skills as opposed to the technical skills. Ideally, for professional students on a continuous, professional development (CPD) course, they should graduate with a real sense of the workplace and the context within which they will operate [1].

Academic faculty associated with these programmes have had considerable industry experience both at technologist and managerial levels. In addition, some had a background in e-Learning methods and technology. ViCoCITY evolved from this mixed background and is an effort to achieve a significant improvement in the way certain professional subjects are taught.

J. Cordeiro et al. (Eds.): WEBIST 2008, LNBIP 18, pp. 375–389, 2009.

2 Professional Practice

The characteristics of the knowledge-based societies of today are an increasing demand for professional specialists and managers in an environment of constantly increasing business competition; high expectations of quality and service from the customers of the professions; unremitting change as a factor in the professions and business in a climate of the regular emergence of powerful new digital technologies.

These characteristics give rise to a growing and changing body of knowledge on an increasingly complex subject matter. They also give rise to a demand for more knowledgeable and skilled graduates, both in technical and managerial terms. There is a perceived requirement to make graduates productive at an earlier stage of their career, and to maintain and improve productivity over the whole of their career [2]. Consequently, there is a need to put more emphasis on acquiring and improving professional practice.

The typical undergraduate degree for a professional discipline usually concentrates on three distinct aspects of education and development of the individual:

- higher level thinking skills
- the understanding of the underpinning theoretical body of knowledge and models for that discipline
- the application of the theory to near 'real-world' problem situations and a reasonable sense of the 'professional practice' involved in addressing them.

'Professional Practice' usually involves:

- Improving relatively unstructured and complex problem situations
- Many of these situations have no 'right' answer so only balanced outcomes and decisions arise
- Rapid evaluation of complex situations as an everyday experience
- The need to take decisions under time, cost and other resource pressures
- Constant need to make judgements and assessments in the absence of detailed or complete facts
- Awareness and understanding of the social dimension within which business and professions actually function
- Facility to handle all aspects of communications and interpersonal skills: written, verbal and presentational
- Ability to think both tactically and strategically
- Understanding of group dynamics including teams, meetings etc.

The academic challenge is to provide a sense of 'real-world' professional practice which addresses the nature of a 'professional's' work. The traditional academic solution to this is the employment of a variety of active learning and experiential formats and coursework assignments e.g. Case Studies, Problem-based learning situations, Simulations, Role plays, Work experience, Projects, Team Projects etc. Games, serious and otherwise, have been used in management learning for decades [3].

A proposed new solution is the ViCoCITY Simulation Centre which was developed with the intention of assisting lecturers to simulate a real world environment. It consists of a set of virtual companies designed to transform coursework and improve the student's sense of 'Professional Practice'.

3 The ViCoCITY Web-Based Case Study Simulation Centre

The Vicocity web-based, case study, simulation centre supports web-based case study learning [4], [5]. ViCoCITY is a research and teaching initiative currently being developed and implemented at Trinity College Dublin. It is also in experimental use in the Oscail Distance Education programme at Dublin City University. The ultimate purpose of ViCoCITY is to improve the quality of educational and training outcomes for certain professionals e.g. Managers, Accountants, IS professionals, Lawyers etc. ViCoCITY is a new innovative concept and support centre designed to transform the nature and purpose of coursework assignments in the teaching of certain professional topics.

The ViCoCITY simulation centre was developed with the intention of assisting lecturers and instructors to simulate a 'real-world' environment for their coursework assignments and so improve their student's sense of understanding and familiarity with actual professional practice likely to be experienced in the real world. It takes the form of a 'City' of companies and institutions, each with their particular culture and identity. Each of these is populated by people, products, services, documents, systems etc. The underpinning rationale and hypothesis for the ViCoCITY initiative is that it should contribute to improving, deepening and expanding the knowledge and practical expertise of the student.

The concept has been influenced by the following authors and methods:

- Kolb [6] with his experiential learning: Problem Based Learning [7], Savin-Baden [8];
- The case based approach in professional higher education [9], the Andragogical Model of adult learning [10] and
- finally, by the development of online, distance learning in the last decade [11].

On the teaching front, lecturers design and implement their own coursework assignments and projects based on the set of simulated companies within ViCoCITY. The companies provide a 'real-world' context within which the student learns. Figure 1 and 2 show the home pages of the EIC brochure website and the Big Ben brochure website. EIC and Big Ben are two of the simulated companies in the ViCoCITY Simulation Centre. Motivation is increased and the student is prepared to address the breadth of complex issues that are encountered within all disciplines. In particular the 'softer' skills can be addressed. The typical unstructured and complex problems without 'right answers' but yet requiring decisions can be simulated. Decisions are required under time and resource pressures just as in the real world. Strategic and tactical decisions and issues can be explored.

While the prototype system is being used on a number of courses within several institutions and has been very well received by academics and students alike, it has not been subjected to rigorous evaluation and research. This paper sets out to stimulate discussion among academics about the concepts involved and highlight the the scope of research topics and questions which can be derived from the initiative.

Fig. 1. M.Sc EIC Home Page

The ViCoCITY web-based case study/ course work tool has most, or all, of the following:

- A population of companies
- Each company has a number of descriptions of key personnel
- Summary accounts for each company
- General information about each company
- Ability to set assignments for a company
- Instructor ability to set a series of assignments over time, with time-released information
- All relevant documentation available online
- Ability for the Administrator to control many companies and assignments
- The ability, for the administrator, to enrich any company
- Assignments can be used as templates for different courses
- Multi-platform
- Multimedia courseware with third-party authoring support
- Results of assignments can be recorded, edited and stored for later playback, instantly creating self-paced content for student review or for instructor training.
- Case studies can be used synchronously or asynchronously or both. A team can access an assignment together synchronously, while at other times team members can access the information asynchronously.

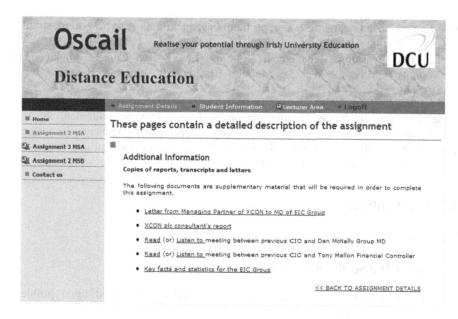

Fig. 2. Big Ben Home Page

Within ViCoCITY virtually any type of assignment or coursework can be set:

- Short coursework assignment
- Individual or group project
- Problem based learning situation assignment
- Case study assignment
- Essay
- Management report or analysis
- Research type project
- Large scale Development Project
- Laboratory or field work type project

The lecturer's imagination is practically the only limiting factor to how ViCoCITY can be effectively used. Lecturers are free to exercise their own individual and particular approach, simply just using the ViCoCITY Simulation Centre for support.

The approach is non-prescriptive and respectful of the academic freedom and professional judgement of the lecturer on the one hand but provides a consistent, 'real-world' experience for the student.

ViCoCITY can support campus-based or distance-based courses.

- Any set of media or media mixes can be used or combined e.g. Paper, audio, video, podcasting, video conferencing, Messaging, Mobile telephony including 3G etc.
- Traditional andragogical approaches e.g. Lectures, classes, seminars, workshops, laboratory sessions, case studies etc.

- More advanced andragogies e.g. problem based learning, active learning, simulations, role plays etc.
- Links to Learning Management Systems (LMSs) and Content Management Systems (CMSs) e.g WebCT, Moodle, Blackboard, Learnlinc, Breeze, Centra, iVocalise etc.

Depending upon the desired learning outcomes of the module or assignment, the academic can choose to use one or multiple organizations and companies in a single assignment, therefore maximizing the use of the virtual environment and simulating problem based learning for the students.

4 Pilot Applications

Three courses were used for testing the ViCoCITY concept.

4.1 The TCD B.Sc. Programme in Information Systems

Project Management is a subject that is most effectively based upon problem situation-based learning.

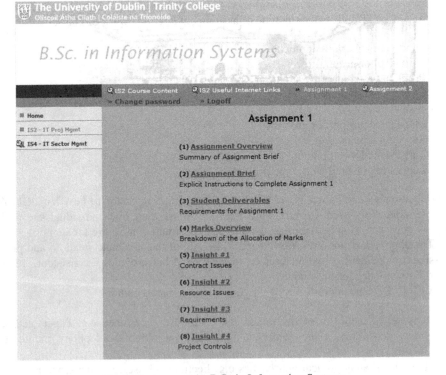

Fig. 3. Assignment 1 - B.Sc in Information Systems

The overall purpose of using ViCoCITY for the project management module was to allow students to face real practical problems that exist in IT project management. While the theory of project management is pertinent, the area of actual application of this knowledge to problems was carried out through examples in class and paper based case studies. The purpose of this module was to explore real-life practical issues through both synchronous and asynchronous learning.

A sample screen for Assignment I for Project Management in the B.Sc. in Information systems is shown in Fig 3. This shows a relatively simple screen layout for an assignment in project management for second year undergraduates. Eight key items for completing the assignment have links on the page.

4.2 The TCD M.Sc. Programme in Management Information Systems

A sample case study scenario used in the first year of the two year M.Sc. Programme in Management Information Systems (about 35 students attended) is shown in Fig. 4.

The case study was essentially a replacement for a paper-based assignment used for a number of years. It still maintained a role-playing aspect by academics on a number of presentation nights. It proved popular with the students. A sample screen for Assignment I Brief for Project Management in the M.Sc. in Management Information Systems is shown in Fig 5. This screen shows details of a Board Presentation that must be done by a team to complete Assignment 1 for the M.Sc in M.I.S. This gives the explicit instructions for a team to give a Board presentation.

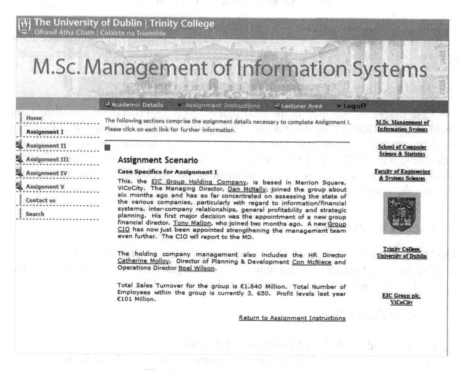

Fig. 4. Assignment 1 - M.Sc in M.I.S

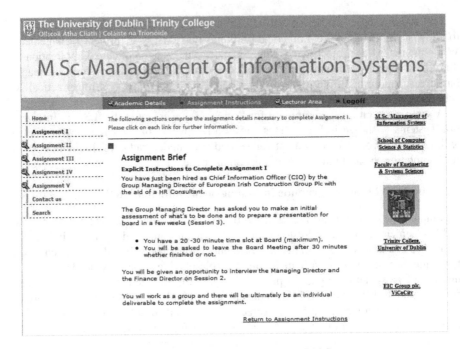

Fig. 5. Assignment Brief - M.Sc in M.I.S

This is a more complex assignment screen than the previous ones, with a less linear layout of links. It also shows the other assignments to be completed in this academic year.

4.3 The DCU B.Sc. Programme in Information Technology

This case study tool was used in the final year of the B.Sc. Programme in Information Technology in Dublin City University. Twenty two students attended this Distance Education course which had no face to face contact with the academic staff. The main differences with the TCD M.Sc. course was that there was no role-playing feature. Other than this, most students were enthusiastic about the course but they also considered that the content needed to be enhanced.

5 Three Perspectives

The key features of Web-based Case Studies are looked at from three perspectives - those of Student, Lecturer and Administrator. These perspectives are informed by the results from the two TCD studies, and the study done in DCU.

5.1 Student Perspective

5.1.1 Simulated Real World Professional Practice
Using ViCoCITY as part of the project management module (TCD B.Sc. in I.S.) with the undergraduate students had a significant disadvantage for the students. ViCoCITY

was being used as part of one subject only and the remainder of the subjects were using other methods for course assignments. As a result the students were exposed to ViCoCITY for a single module rather than across the course. This raised some level of dissatisfaction among the students as they felt that a common platform or integrated projects across some or all subjects would have been more beneficial to their learning and understanding of the subject.

The feedback from the cohort of students consisted mainly of the fact that they would have preferred more information on the company websites and possibly more classroom work, in other words. a combination of synchronous and asynchronous learning.

Anecdotal evidence would suggest that the students preferred the combination of classroom and online delivery. The online delivery proved to be informative and the students could move at their own pace within the set timeframe of the assignment. The classroom environment proved dynamic insofar as teams of students had to resolve a problem quickly and effectively.

5.1.2 Student Reaction

The students also commented on the fact that they would have preferred more information on the 'companies' within ViCoCITY rather than just the brochure information that was available. The main written student reaction was to a small, one question evaluation done in DCU (twelve responses from twenty two B.Sc. in Information Technology students) as follows:

Question: The objective of ViCoCITY was to simulate a more real-life situation where you would have access to both internal and external information on the companies. Have you any comments on this form of assignment? Would you like this type of assignment used more widely?

Responses:

- *This assignment I found very enjoyable as it simulated a real world experience in researching information to produce a report for the boss.*

- *Yes, I thought this was a good idea and was one of the most enjoyable assignments*

- *Yes. I thought it was a good experience.*

- *Challenging assignment but it took up time from other assignments because of the amount of additional effort and research that had to go into it.*

- *Would not like to have this for every subject but worked well for the Management Module*

- *I had no problem with this method*

- *Yes it was good*

- *I did think the virtual company was a good idea. This could be extended to other management modules.*

- *It worked very well*

- *The format as such was excellent. The task was not suitable for undergraduates*
- *Very interesting. Provided a clearer understanding of the role of the CIO in a company*
- *This was an interesting assignment. The format was clever and engaging. As someone who works in the industry I believe that this assignment had good parallels to some of the analytical skills needed in the real world.*

5.2 Lecturer Perspective

The simulated 'real-life' view of ViCoCITY allows the lecturer to focus on competencies and professional development for the student.

ViCoCITY accentuates and illustrates theory covered in the classroom and allows the student to experiment with different approaches to the case studies in a 'safe' environment. Unlike the professional world, ViCoCITY is forgiving of mistakes and is designed specifically so that students can learn from successes and failures. This prevents them from making these mistakes in the real professional world and, more importantly, allows them to build on their successes.

The lecturer needs to plan and design the case studies, perhaps, at least 3 months in advance of using them in the classroom. While this may be an increase in workload at the outset, the workload will decrease as the case studies are completed.

The lecturer also needs to learn how to use the underlying tool, the WebSteps Admission Console, in order to make the changes required. The lecturer must take sole responsibility for this and ensure that they can make changes as quickly and efficiently as possible. The tool itself requires little prior knowledge of development or web design; however the lecturer must be computer literate and be able to use a package like MSWord.

One conclusion from the project management application (TCD B.Sc in I.S.) would suggest that the students gain from a combination of synchronous/ asynchronous learning and traditional learning i.e. a combination of ViCoCITY and the classroom. The anecdotal response of the students would suggest that their understanding of the subject is best when illustrated by practical examples in the classroom environment.

The lecturers in the TCD M.Sc. in M.I.S. application found the web-based case studies were a distinct improvement on the paper-based ones from previous years. They had the advantage that the case studies could be updated and enhanced more easily. The students could also access the material asynchronously. Other media could also be added relatively easily e.g. audio. However, in general, they felt that the content in the companies needed to be enhanced.

The tutors in the DCU B.Sc. in Information Technology were enthusiastic about the use of ViCoCITY and made many suggestions for its improvement.

5.3 Administrator Perspective

There are quite a number of important factors pertinent to the administration of a web-based case study learning system as evidenced by the number of studies discussed above.

Cost of Planning and Preparation. Websteps knowledge, gained through some basic level of training, lasting perhaps two hours, is required to get users set up. Lecturers need to be trained on this in order to maintain their own 'companies' and assignment webpages.

Software Licensing Costs. A modest annual fee for maintenance and hosting of the websites. All hosting is external with no internal costs. ViCoCITY must be set up in advance.

Training Cost. Quite a small amount of training is necessary to run the exercise. Those who will lecture using the synchronous package need a small amount of training, perhaps two hours.

Setup. Little time and effort is necessary to access and run the software.

Staffing Costs. Little expert technical support needs to be available.

Equipment Provision and Upgrading. Conventional PC equipment running on the Internet was used.

The undergraduate project management course (TCD B.Sc. in I.S.) utilized the use of two 'companies' in ViCoCITY that were specifically designed for the coursework. As a result of this small number of websites, the lecturer could also be the administrator. The Administration workload was significantly increased due to the training required on learning how to use the tool to create the websites, designing the case studies so that they were transferable to online learning, and designing the delivery of the coursework so that the students would benefit from this approach. A significant amount of time is required to prepare for the case studies and design the content, delivery and execution of the assignments. The synchronous and asynchronous learning need to be planned separately.

The TCD M.Sc. in M.I.S. application was the pilot course with which to experiment, and develop, ViCoCITY. Quite a number of people were participating and observing (approximately ten) so that the package was enhanced quickly and effectively.

The DCU B.Sc. in Information Technology was essentially a shadow site to the TCD site, to confirm that the experimental changes also worked well elsewhere. However a small evaluation was done on this Distance Education course as already discussed above.

6 Advantages and Disadvantages of ViCoCITY

6.1 Advantages for the Student

ViCoCITY is a simulation centre that allows more intensive engagement with the topic, and according to anecdotal evidence, it is suggested that there is a deeper more permanent understanding of the field because the emphasis is on 'understanding' rather than 'memorising'. This can provide improved motivation to study the necessary material and to digest and engage with the formal lectures or other learning formats employed.

The rich real-world situations and contexts can be provided using a variety of different and appropriate digital media with which deeper learning can be facilitated and enjoyed by the student. In addition to this, implemented as part of a programme over a short period of years, the student can acquire a better sense of organisational culture, management styles, personality types, inter-functional relationships, attitudes to change, institutional pressures etc. ViCoCITY provides a better chance for the student to address 'professional practice' type problems and situations e.g. decision making, problem solving, strategic thinking and collateral issues. This can, in turn, lead to a more effective employee in the workforce.

6.2 Advantages for the Lecturer

Learning to use ViCoCITY is simple and 'non-techie'. It takes about one hour to learn. The Lecturer retains her/his own approach and style of coursework. The readymade set of companies and organisations ease the lecturer workload by providing a choice of contexts within which an exercise or assignment can be situated. The advantages and benefits to the student result in a more satisfied, better motivated learner, and a better quality of teaching is a likely result.

The flexibility to apply any mix of delivery mode, media mix or andragogical model at will, and as appropriate to a given situation, is useful. Documentation is better organised and controlled e.g. version control for descriptions, financials, product details, services, reports, CVs etc. A template to assist in writing an assignment eases that task which is no more difficult than a conventional paper version.

The system is easily interfaced to learning management systems (LMS), content management systems (CMS) and other elearning products and services. The system is easy to use - it's of the same complexity as using Microsoft Word.

Quick changes to content and requirements can be easily made, if necessary. There is also the possibility of customising websites by individual difference such as cognitive style. Through the web, content is accessible world-wide. This suits students who need to travel for their work.

There is potential for evaluating different styles of presentation, perhaps to suit particular needs or individual differences. The tool supports teamwork and also less paper is used.

6.3 Disadvantages for the Student, Lecturer and Administrator

ViCoCITY is not reality, but just a model of reality. One of the current issues with ViCoCITY is the lack of features to allow the student to engage with the online environment. The information that is available on the 'companies' is brochure-like with basic knowledge. As a result, the details are the responsibility of the designer/lecturer to implement as part of the assignment structure, and delivery, to the class.

The ViCoCITY centre itself is not interactive and does not engage the student as a simulation centre in its own right. It requires the back-up of the classroom environment to provide appropriate feedback.

The question of evaluation is a current gap in ViCoCITY, although this is a major problem for most educational/ training tools. While anecdotally we can assume that the centre works sufficiently well, the statistics to enforce this statement are lacking.

For the moment, qualitative analysis has been carried out and anecdotal evidence would suggest that the students can see the benefits of the ViCoCITY approach. The quantitative method of evaluation would seem to fit better at assignment level as opposed to ViCoCITY level, but this method has yet to be defined and subsequently designed.

Specifically for the administrator, there is a small annual cost per annum of about €400 per website. There is a need to maintain sites (not particularly burdensome with the toolset provided) and a need to update the content regularly.

The interaction is not as good as with real, live role-playing "actors" (usually course lecturers). However, in general, real web interactivity can be costly in terms of funds, and resource availability such as fast broadband and webcams. Whether to go for interactivity is a judgement call with economic implications for the Administrator.

e-Learning is here to stay so an important question is how should we use it best. It should not be regarded as just a supposedly cheap way of delivering education and training.

Another question with economic implications is how rich should the model be? For ViCoCITY an important question is how much detail is enough? This probably depends on the course purpose, content and economics.

7 Discussion/ Conclusions

The academic challenge is to provide a sense of a relatively 'real-world' professional practice in a 'safe', simulated and controlled virtual environment. ViCoCITY is a step towards meeting this challenge. The richness of the traditional learning environment is not compromised for the student, but is enhanced, and the delivery method for the lecturer is flexible.

ViCoCITY lacks the interactive dimension with regard to the online experience. Currently the case studies are 'flat' and are emphasized simply through the classroom experience where the students can engage in active discussion and feedback with their peers and the lecturer(s).

Anecdotal evidence would suggest that the ViCoCITY centre is the first step towards providing a 'professional practice' simulated environment for students. The comparison, so far, between the advantages of using paper-based and web-based case studies has been limited to qualitative analysis based upon interviews and discussions with academics and students exposed to the centre. Further quantitative evidence is required to investigate the question of the effectiveness of using web based case studies as opposed to using paper based techniques. To date, qualitative evidence from students, lecturers and administrators supports the hypothesis that ViCoCITY is an effective tool in the learning of professional practice.

Evaluation of ViCoCITY and its effectiveness for the student, lecturer and administrator is a difficult process. At present, there is a lack of information on evaluation of case based techniques and their effectiveness in a learning environment. Case studies are by nature open-ended and do not have one correct answer, so their evaluation can prove difficult and subjective.

Initial trials of the ViCoCITY concept have demonstrated considerable potential and have been generally well received. The next step is to extend the trials to other disciplines, institutions and topics. Systematic research is then needed on the lines outlined above in order to evaluate and hopefully enhance the process further. Although it is somewhat early to judge, there is a significant likelihood that the concept could have significant potential both within academia and business.

8   The Future for ViCoCITY

The ViCoCITY concept is a work in progress. It is in operation at two institutions currently and is planned for implementation at several more. It is being used on seven distinct courses. Upwards of a dozen coursework assignments are currently operating.

So far the reports are very encouraging, both from students and academics. However there are few real research results to support the anecdotal evidence as yet. There are many different questions and issues that need to be addressed.

Immediate issues that spring to mind include: How can the concept best be evaluated? Can it improve the quality of professional education? Is it more suitable to specific disciplines or topics? What are the economic, social and operational implications of using it? What are the advantages for the lecturer, student and institutional administrator? Is it more suitable to certain delivery methods? Is it best used with certain media? Which andragogical strategies does it best support? It is not fully clear what topics are really suitable for ViCoCITY other than topics that are usually covered in paper case studies.

Some other questions are:

- Does the approach improve student motivation, commitment and engagement?
- Is learning actually improved?
- Is 'professional practice' improved?
- Are graduates 'useful' at an earlier stage?
- What mix of media is best suited to any given situation?
- How suitable is the method for different modes of delivery e.g. Distance Education, Campus-based Education, Hybrid/Blended approaches etc.

Is it more suitable for particular types of learning or cognitive styles?

Acknowledgements. We would like to thank George Morgan, Tony Niland, Noel Faughnan, Stuart McLoughlin, Barry Collins and Catherine O'Connor of TCD for their efforts and suggestions. We are also indebted to Séamus Fox, Mairéad McCarthy and Ursula Stapleton of Oscail, Dublin City University. We would like to thank staff and students of the Executive Master of Science Information Systems - Information Technology Management Program of Virginia Commonwealth University, USA for their useful feedback from a presentation of ViCoCITY, in particular, Maureen Carley and others.

References

1. Brennan, J., Shah, T.: Access to what? Opportunities in education and employment. In: Higher education and the lifecourse, pp. 106–121. Open University Press, Buckingham (2003) ISBN 0-335-21377-4 & 978-0-335-21377-1
2. Brennan, J., Little, B., Connor, H., de Weert, E., Delve, S., Harris, J., Josselyn, B., Ratcliffe, N., Scesa, A.: Towards a strategy for workplace learning: Report to Hefce by Cheri and KPMG. Higher Education Funding Council for England, Bristol, UK (2006)
3. Ludlow, R., Wheeler, B.: The use of Business Games in General Management Programmes, in Perspectives in Gaming and Simulation II Gaming and Simulation for Capability. In: Craig, D., Martin, A. (eds.) The proceedings of the 1985 conference of SAGSET, Society of Advancement of Games and Simulations in Education and Training, held at Heriot-Watt University, Edinburgh (1986)
4. Mullally, A., Redmond, J.: A. An Academic Challenge: ViCoCITY - A Virtual City comprising web-based Company Simulations for Improving the Teaching of Professional Disciplines in Elsin XII Exploring Styles: Enhancing the Capacity to Learn? In: Proceedings of the 12th Annual Conference of the European Learning Styles Information Network, Trinity College Dublin, Ireland, June 12-14, pp. 102–107 (2007) ISBN: 978-80-903744-1-6
5. Stenson, A.: Websteps Workshop in Elsin XII Exploring Styles: Enhancing the Capacity to Learn? In: Proceedings of the 12th Annual Conference of the European Learning Styles Information Network, Trinity College Dublin, Ireland, June 12-14, pp. 234–241 (2007) ISBN: 978-80-903744-1-6
6. Kolb, D.A.: Experiential Learning - Experience as the source of learning and development. Prentice Hall, Englewood Cliffs (1984)
7. Glascow, N.A.: New Curriculum for New Times - A Guide to Student centred Problem Based Learning Neal A Glascow. Cowin Press Inc. (1997)
8. Savin-Baden, M.: Facilitating Problem Based Learning - Illuminating Perspectives. SRHE and Open University Press, McGraw-Hill Education, Philadelphia (2003) ISBN 0-335-21054-6
9. Crosling, G., Webb, G.: Supporting Student Learning - Case Studies Experience and Practice from Higher Education. Edited by Glenda Crosling & Graham Webb Kogan Page Ltd. (2002)
10. Knowles, M.S., Holton III, E.F., Swanson, R.A.: The Adult Learner, 6th edn. Elsevier Butterworth Heinemann, California (2005)
11. Wiita, E.L., Lee, C.-Y.: Developing an Online Learning Style Instrument in Encyclopedia of Distance Learning. In: Two Idea Group Reference, Hershey, London, Melbourne, Singapore (2005)

Transforming a Competency Model to Parameterised Questions in Assessment

Onjira Sitthisak, Lester Gilbert, and Hugh C. Davis

Learning Societies Lab, School of Electronics and Computer Science
University of Southampton, Highfield, Southampton, SO17 1BJ, United Kingdom
{os05r,lg3,hcd}@ecs.soton.ac.uk

Abstract. The problem of comparing and matching different learners' knowledge arises when assessment systems use a one-dimensional numerical value to represent "knowledge level". Such assessment systems may measure inconsistently because they estimate this level differently and inadequately. The multi-dimensional competency model called COMpetence-Based learner knowledge for personalized Assessment (COMBA) is being developed to represent a learner's knowledge in a multi-dimensional vector space. The heart of this model is to treat knowledge, not as possession, but as a contextualized space of capability either actual or potential. The paper discusses a system for automatically generating questions from the COMBA competency model as a "guide-on-the–side". The system's novel design and implementation involves an ontological database that represents the intended learning outcome to be assessed across a number of dimensions, including level of cognitive ability and subject matter. The system generates all the questions that are possible from a given learning outcome, which may then be used to test for understanding, and so could determine the degree to which learners actually acquire the desired knowledge.

Keywords: Competency, Assessment, Knowledge level, Ontology.

1 Introduction

In recent years, a variety of tools and learning environments have been created and installed in schools, universities, and organisations to support learning. Mostly these tools have been created to support e-learning content and collaborative learning activities like a virtual classroom [1]. However, e-learning suggests not only new technologies for instruction but also new pedagogical approaches to enhance learning. One new pedagogical approach is machine-processable competency modelling. A competence model is introduced for storing, organizing and sharing learners' performance data in order to seek and interpret evidence for where the learners are in their learning, where they want to go, and how they can get there. Pedagogically effective and informed competency data is vital in any assessment system.

One of the desired outcomes of an assessment system is information about the learners' knowledge, identifying what learners can do by representing their current state of knowledge [2]. This information is collected and updated during the assessment

J. Cordeiro et al. (Eds.): WEBIST 2008, LNBIP 18, pp. 390–403, 2009.

process. Most assessment systems assume that knowledge is something that a learner possesses or fails to possess, and seek to estimate a learner's "knowledge level". As a result, such assessment systems may measure "knowledge level" inconsistently because they estimate this level differently, and inadequately because they use one-dimensional numerical values [3]. The proposed solution is to consider the learners' "learned capability" instead of their "knowledge level", and to consider competencies and learned capabilities as a multidimensional space.

In the context of an adaptive assessment system, an assessment is part of the process of diagnosing the learner's competence. The key idea of an adaptive assessment system is that questions are selected by the computer to individually match the learner's competence [4]. The system's evaluation of the learner's competence is then used to guide the adaptation of the system [5]. The system may skip over what learners have learned and find out what they should learn further. While an adaptive system may be more efficient for summative assessment, a system of adaptive formative assessment is likely to be of greater advantage to learners, since they would receive relevant, personalized feedback. Establishing adaptive formative assessment systems to support lifelong learning is extremely challenging and relies on introducing a competency model to the adaptive assessment. Our intention is not to promote a particular technological platform, but to demonstrate how a competency model can be applied to adaptive assessment.

In this paper, we introduce an advanced competency model named COMpetence-Based learner knowledge for personalized Assessment (COMBA). The COMBA model is represented in a multi-dimensional vector space. We explore the assembly of competencies into a tree structure and then consider the task of adaptively generating assessments from such a competencies structure. Finally, an implementation of COMBA is presented.

2   The Multi-dimensional COMBA Model

Competence-based approaches in the field of e-learning, institutional admissions, learners seeking courses, e-portfolios, job references, human resource management, and job descriptions are becoming more common. They appear to offer the opportunity to develop tools and services for data exchange, discovery, processing, analysis, and visualization to meet needs of learners, tutors, program managers, examination bodies, professional societies, employers, legislators, and so on. We suggest that a complete and coherent model of competencies would support storing, organizing and sharing of achieved, current, and intended performance data relating to all aspects of education and training in a persistent and standard way [3]. We have been developing a competency model, named COMBA, which is proposed for all domains where learning and teaching take place.

In the first stage of developing the model [3], we conceptualised "competency" as involving a capability associated with a given subject matter content, requiring a proficiency level, and associated with evidence, any required tools, and a definition of the situation which contextualizes the competency. In the second stage of developing the model [6], we implemented an exemplar UK Royal College of Nursing competency [7] reflecting relevant features of a learner's behaviour and knowledge that affected their learning and performance. An outcome of this implementation exposed a critical issue involving the expression of ethical practice in the COMBA model. One of the conceptions of competence for a nursing graduate is competence in ethical practice [8] as well as the other characteristics of professional service delivery involving knowledge and psychomotor skill [9]. Hence, attitude, the way in which a learner exhibits their knowledge and skill, is included in the COMBA model, as illustrated in Fig. 1.

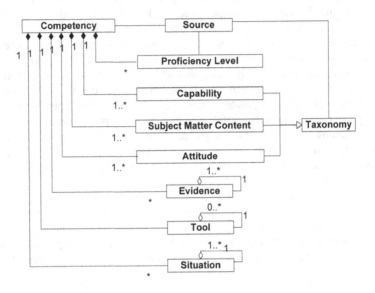

Fig. 1. Competency model including attitude component

The COMBA model considers knowledge in the widest possible sense, and involves the following four major components: subject matter, capability, attitude, and context, along with metadata as illustrated in Fig. 2.

The challenge of capturing and using knowledge starts with the problem of understanding its nature and representation. The failure of previous efforts to 'intelligently process knowledge' (e.g. intelligent tutoring systems) may be due to their pedagogically and cognitively inadequate characterization of this knowledge, and their simplistic assumptions that knowledge is something a learner possesses or fails to possess.

The heart of the COMBA model is to treat knowledge, not as possession, but as a contextualized multidimensional space of capability either actual or potential. Accordingly, the three important components of the COMBA model (capability, subject matter content, and attitude), which are referred from relevant taxonomies or ontologies, may be represented in a vector space as in Fig. 3. The learned capability is the learner's required or observed behaviour, for example using Bloom's taxonomy [10]. The subject matter content in Fig. 3 is based on Merrill's analysis [11], and attitude is based on a version of Krathwohl's taxonomy [12].

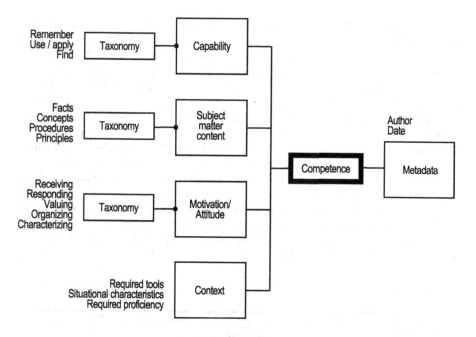

Fig. 2. Individual competence model

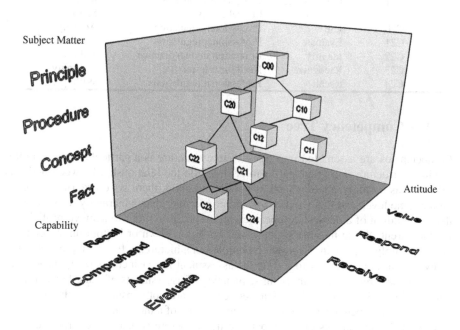

Fig. 3. Multidimensional space of competency model

In this paper, we choose competencies from health care because they are amongst the most sophisticated and challenging to implement [13]. Table 1 represents some nursing competencies based on the multidimensional space of the COMBA model. For example, C00 (students are able to use and value ethical principles) comprises C10 (students are able to actively apply ethical principles) and C20 (students are able to actively use professional regulation). In order to achieve C10, students should be able to demonstrate client confidentiality respectfully (C11), and to identify ethical issues sensitively (C12). In order to achieve C20, students should be able to identify the limitations in their own practice (C22), and to considerately evaluate professional regulation (C21). There is a common competency for C21 and C22 which is C23 (students are able to recognize the need for referral willingly). In order to achieve C21, students should be able to recall relevant professional regulations willingly (C24). This shows that we can map effectively these more complicated competencies into the COMBA model. The subject matter, capability taxonomy, attitude taxonomy, and competence were ontologically represented based on the Simple Knowledge Organisation System (SKOS) [14].

Table 1. Some example nursing competencies represented in the competency model

Competency No.	Capability	Subject Matter Content	Attitude
C00	Use	Ethical principles	Values
C10	Apply	Ethical issues	Actively
C11	Demonstrate	Client confidentiality	Respectfully
C12	Identify	Ethical Issues	Sensitively
C20	Use	Professional regulation	Actively
C21	Evaluate	Professional regulation	Considerately
C22	Identify	Limitation in own practice	Values
C23	Recognize	Need for referral	Willingly
C24	Recall	Professional regulations	Willingly

3   The Competency Tree

Competencies are assembled into trees. A tree structure is a particular way of representing a structure in a graphical form [15]. While the relationship between nodes is modelled as a family relation such as parent and child, there is no ordering of nodes on the same level, and this yields a tree structure rather than a hierarchy. It is assumed that all children of a defined competency are required in order to achieve proficiency for the parent. While the tree structure defines a top-down or bottom-up structure, it does not imply sequencing as might be implied in a hierarchy. For example, a competency tree may specify how to roll up the assessment for each competency throughout a competency tree without implying sequencing of assessments of same level competencies. So the issues of pedagogical sequencings are not considered at this stage by representing competencies as a tree structure instead of a hierarchy.

One of the advantages of a competence tree structure is that a tree structure separates the composition rule in the domain from other structural components. Hence, an application of the competency model, such as in adaptive assessment, may add other rules, perhaps based on pedagogical sequencing, in order to control the adaptation within the competency tree.

More technically, the COMBA model specifies the network of assembled competencies as a directed acyclic graph. In competency terms, Fig. 4 implies that competency *C00* is decomposed into sub-competencies *C10* and *C20*, such that *C10* and *C20* contribute to *C00*. A node may have more than one parent, provided the parent is not a child of the node. Fig. 4 shows a "forest" of two competency trees, where arrows represent parent-child relationships. A competency tree may specify common children for more than one node, or more than one origin node. For example, *C00* and *A* represent different competencies that have certain competencies in common such as *C22*.

It is expected that competency trees will be different for different communities and users. For example, a tree of nursing competencies from the UK Royal College of Nursing would have many points of difference from a similar tree from the Canadian Nursing Association. At a personal level, a student nurse may develop his or her own tree to reflect their own competencies, both achieved and to be attained.

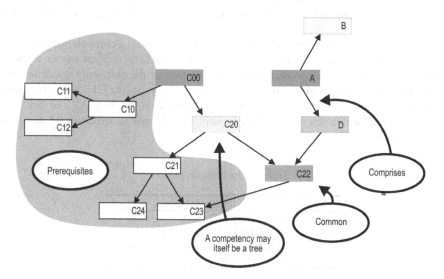

Fig. 4. Competency tree

4 Generating Assessment Items from a Competency Tree

Assessments may be categorized as formative, summative, or diagnostic [16]. Formative assessment provides prescriptive feedback to assist learners in reaching their competences [17]. It is intended to help the learner deal with deficiencies in their understanding, knowledge, or competence. In contrast, summative assessment is generally given at the end of a period of learning to establish what knowledge, skills, and/or attitudes the learner has acquired over a period of time. It helps to establish whether learners have attained the competences required, and is not focussed on supporting learning. Diagnostic assessment is an in-depth assessment related to strengths and weaknesses in each skill area, which identifies priorities and needs [18]. It helps to determine what learners can already do within the goals of the curriculum. This paper focuses on formative and diagnostic assessment.

There are two problems of traditional formative assessment. First, learners are likely to need different kinds of formative assessment at different stages in their 'learning journeys' [19]. Second, formative assessment usually only provides a list of the learner's deficiencies [17] without clearly specifying their boundaries. These problems are relieved by using an assessment tree suggested in this paper.

4.1 Constructing an Assessment Item

We assume an assessment which takes place in the context of the COMBA model. The competency tree might be used to drill down into component competencies for the tested competency, helping to define what to test and how to test it. An assessment for a competency often actually tests component competencies. For example, a paediatric nurse course [20] may test knowledge of professional regulation by testing the learners' ability to demonstrate and evaluate understanding of professional regulation including the demonstration of a variety of specific skills and attitudes, as illustrated in Table 1.

A generic assessment item can be directly formulated from a competence specification by using the parameters of that competence: capability, subject matter content, attitude and other contexts such as tool and situation as the authoring question templates in Table 2. For example, the assessment corresponding to C11 might be something like "What information must be kept confidential in situation A?", or "Identify the information which doesn't need to be kept confidential in situation B", as illustrated in Table3.

Table 2. Question templates

No.	Question Templates
a	[Capability] + [Subject]
b	[Capability] + [Subject] + [Situation]
c	[Capability] + [Subject] + [Attitude]
d	[Subject] + [Situation]

Table 3. Some example questions represented from the competencies

Competency No.	Question No.	Question	Template No
C00	Q1	Identify the outcomes if ethical principles were not valued.	c
	Q2	List ethical principles.	a
	Q3	What ethical principles are involved [in situation X]?	d
C10	Q4	Identify the possible outcomes if ethical issues were not actively applied.	c
	Q5	How would you apply ethical issues [in situation Y]?	b
	Q6	Define the specific ethical issues [in situation Z].	b

A formative assessment may contain items to test finer grained competencies. A competency tree can be used as a guide to assemble the necessary set of test items for assessing each competency. In this process, the competency tree is transformed to an assessment tree. An assessment tree consists of question nodes from Table 3, where each question node corresponds to a competency node, as illustrated in Fig. 5.

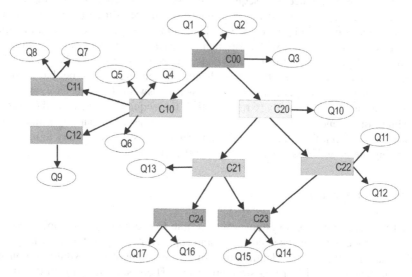

Fig. 5. The group of questions based on a competency tree

Different organizations or communities of practice may have different processes and policies for assessment. By specifying a particular competency tree or sub-tree to be assessed, it is possible to align the assessment needed based on the needs of the organization or community of practice. Hence, the competency tree defines a standard way to specify explicitly the component competencies to be assessed, and provides a "guide on the side", automatically generating a set of general assessment items.

4.2 Navigating Assessment Items on the Competency Tree

There are a number of adaptive assessment methods and technologies that can be used to assess learners' strengths and weaknesses based on item-by-item and learner responses. These allow learners to be tested on materials at a level appropriate to their current understanding. Adaptive assessments change their behaviour and structure depending on the learners' responses and inferred abilities.

There are two major adaptation techniques; presentational adaptation and navigational adaptation [21]. An adaptive system may apply these two techniques with questions. Traversing the competency tree may start at the leaf node or the root node depend on the objective of each application. As a result, a competency tree may be traversed, mapped, extended, visualized, and searched by a variety of applications and tools. For example, a competency tree may be used to specify how to roll up the assessments for each competency in order to personalize the assessment and match assessment items to the individual competences of each learner.

There is a set of possible assessment items associated with each competence node, as illustrated in Fig. 5. Given a pruned competency tree (a tree whose remaining branches and leaves represent competencies not yet attained by a learner), an adaptive assessment system now needs to sequence the assessment items. Sequencing could be based upon pedagogical considerations, and arranged according to the taxonomies of subject matter content [11], of capability [10], and so on. For example, an adaptive assessment system may start with assessment items at the lower level of the capability taxonomy and progress to the higher levels, in order to reach the boundary of the learner's understanding. On the other hand, sequencing could be based on the learner's preferences. Depending on the learner's answers, the next assessment item will be presented. This involves regenerating the sequence based on the learner's unfolding competences. The result of an adaptive assessment partitions the competency tree into "what the student can do" and "what the student is ready to learn" [22] and finding the boundaries of competence for the learner.

5   Implementation

COMBA aims to provide a system which is able to accommodate complicated competencies, link competencies adequately, and support tracking of the knowledge state of the learner. This makes identification of the assessment that would demonstrate successful teaching and learning straightforward. The system focuses on the identification and integration of appropriate subject matter content (represented by a hierarchy of competencies) and cognitive ability (represented by a capability taxonomy). A simplified COMBA system was implemented in this study by omitting the dimension of "attitude".

The system was built upon an ontological database that describes all resources and the relationships between them. The advantage of ontological schemas over database schemas is that ontological schemas define explicit formal specifications and include machine-interpretable definition to share common understanding of the structure of information among people or software agents [23]. Thus, the ontological database is flexible and extensible, allowing the resources in the system to be described on the Semantic Web, interoperability between different systems, and reasoning about the described resources.

COMBA consists of a number of modules (illustrated in Fig. 6): competence navigator, subject matter navigator, capability navigator, question assembler, question to QTI schema converter and sequencing manipulator. The competence navigator is responsible for retrieving the requested competence based on the domain request from the user, and passing the competence to the subject matter and capability navigator modules. The relevant subject matter and capability data received from those modules, together with the authoring question template files, are assembled to generate questions derived from the matrix of competencies crossed with cognitive abilities. Then, the questions are formatted according to the IMS Question and Test Interoperability specification (IMS QTI) standard [24], enabling the sharing of the questions and tests. In order to develop a test, the generated questions are linked together for storing in a test bank. For the delivery of the assessment, the system deploys an assessment delivery service (ASDEL) (http://www.asdel.ecs.soton.ac.uk/) to allow a learner to view a question and answer it. In the next stage of the research, the system will be extended to marking and feedback.

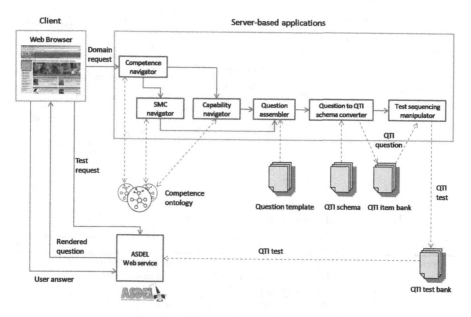

Fig. 6. Architecture for the COMBA system

The following section presents data creation, representation and storage, methods of generating and standardizing questions, and methods of question delivery in the COMBA system.

5.1 Data Creation, Representation and Storage

A domain expert expressed domain content, the capability taxonomy, and competence in an English-like form. A knowledge engineer represented these elements in the form of a semantic network, and then transformed them into an ontology. The ontologies adhered to the criteria of ontology design: clarity, coherence, extendability, minimal encoding bias, and minimal ontological commitment [25]. These ontologies are domain, not structure, ontologies using a controlled vocabulary from SKOS [26]. Sharing and reuse of information are integral aspects of the Semantic Web. In the COMBA system, the ontology was based on Semantic Web technology standards of RDF [27] and OWL [28]. The ontology of the COMBA system is shown in Fig. 7. The definitions of the elements in the competence ontology are shown in Table 4.

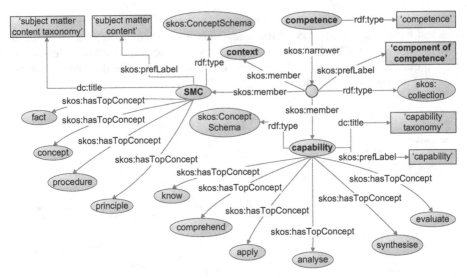

Fig. 7. Ontology of COMBA

Table 4. The definitions of each element in the competence ontology

Class	Definition
Competence	Defines a capability associated with subject matter content, a proficiency level, evidence, any required tools, and definition of the situation which contextualises the competency.
SMC	Defines the subject domain of what the learner can do by the end of the unit of teaching and learning.
Capability	Defines behaviour that can be observed, based on a taxonomy of learning such as Bloom's, Gagné's nine areas of skill, or Merrill's cognitive domain.
Context	Defines the particular context and conditions of the competency, such as tools and situations.
Fact	Defines statements, or factual information which consists of an attribute and a value.
Concept	Defines a group of objects or ideas which are designated by a single word or term. Area concept has a number of attributes which are used to classify or categorise objects according to their values on those attributes.
Procedure	Defines a sequential set of steps to accomplish a task or make a decision.
Principle	Defines cause-effect relationships describing the behaviour of a system. It can usually be expressed as some sort of an equation if the system is in the scientific or engineering domain.
Know	Cognitive domain capabilities according to Bloom
Comprehend	
Apply	
Analyse	
Synthesise	
Evaluate	

5.2 Method of Generating Questions

In the system, when learners submit their domain of interest to the system, the competence navigator module navigates the competency using the competency ontological database based on the request, where relevant subject matter and capability nodes are retrieved. In this stage, both breadth-first and depth-first strategies can be implemented. The authoring question templates as shown in Table 4 are provided from a test instructor. The retrieved subject matter and capability nodes and the templates are assembled in questions. The process of traversing competencies, retrieving the relevant nodes and converting to questions are recursive. The generated questions are standardised for conformance to the QTI specification by a conversion process using the QTI schema. Finally, the QTI questions are sequenced using a desired strategy such as breadth-first or depth-first. The resulting test file is a sequenced set of questions.

5.3 Method of Question Delivery

In this research, ASDEL was deployed as a stand-alone web application in order to deliver the tests to the learners. The test files in the QTI test bank were queried from the ASDEL web service. ASDEL is responsible for allowing a learner to view a question and to answer it. The type of a question currently in the system is the essay type, so a teacher has to provide written criticism rather than relying on ASDEL to provide feedback. A Web service API including marking, giving feedback, and retrieving assessment results, will be extended in the next stage of the research.

6 Conclusions

We have proposed the next generation of a competency model named COMBA to support adaptive assessment. The COMBA model includes "attitude", identified as a critical issue exposed by working with nursing competencies, as well as including subject matter domain knowledge, and learned capabilities. The multi-dimensional COMBA model represents competency in terms of a tree structure.

The benefits of a COMBA-enabled adaptive system are to help learners identify and diagnose their boundaries of their own competencies, understand them, and find out how to progress by comparing them with a given or ideal competency tree. Adaptive assessment involves the dynamic sequencing of assessment items derived from the COMBA competency tree depending on the learner's responses.

Although the system can automatically generate a list of all the questions that are possible at various levels from a competency framework, we face the immediate challenge of representing the subject matter content based on the concept of a hierarchy of knowledge. The hierarchy of knowledge may be classified as fact, concept, procedure, and principle based on Merrill [11]. This needs to use a specialist or subject matter content expert to analyse the domain before a knowledge engineer can process it later, and may be regarded as a problem for the current system.

A major challenge in the construction of a competency ontology is that the existing competencies in the course syllabus are required to be well-defined. This is usually not the case in most existing syllabi.

Acknowledgements. This work was partially funded by The Royal Thai Government.

References

1. Koper, R., Specht, M.: TenCompetence: Lifelong Competence Development and Learning. In: Sicilia, M.-A. (ed.) Competencies in Organizational E-Learning: Concepts and Tools. Idea Group (2007)
2. Shepard, L.A.: The Role of Assessment in a Learning Culture. Journal Information for Educational Researcher 29(7), 4–14 (2000)
3. Sitthisak, O., Gilbert, L., Davis, H.C.: Towards a competency model for adaptive assessment to support lifelong learning. In: TENCompetence Workshop on Service Oriented Approaches and Lifelong Competence Development Infrastructures, Manchester, UK (2007)
4. Way, W.D.: Practical Questions in Introducing Computerized Adaptive Testing for K-12 Assessments (2005)
5. Aroyo, L., Dolog, P., Houben, G.J., Kravcik, M., Nilsson, A.N.a.M., Wild, F.: Interoperability in Personalized Adaptive Learning. Education Technology and Society 9(2), 8–14 (2006)
6. Sitthisak, O., Gilbert, L., Davis, H.C., Gobbi, M.: Adapting health care competencies to a formal competency model. In: The ICALT. IEEE Computer Society Press, Niigata (2007)
7. UK Royal College of Nursing, Competencies,
   http://www.rcn.org.uk/development/communities/specialisms/
   children_and_young_people/resources/
   a-z_of_resources/competencies
8. Ramritu, P.L., Barnard, A.: New nurse graduates' understanding of competence. International nursing review (2001)
9. Defloor, T., Hecke, A.V., Verhaeghe, S., Gobert, M., Darras, E., Grypdonck, M.: The clinical nursing competences and their complexity in Belgian general hospitals. Journal of Advanced Nursing 56(6), 669–678 (2006)
10. Bloom, B.S., Krathwohl, D.R.: Taxonomy of educational objectives: The classification of educational goals by a committee of college and university examiners. In: Domain, H.I.C. (ed.). Longman, New York (1956)
11. Merrill, M.D.: Component Display Theory,
    http://coe.sdsu.edu/eet/articles/cdt/index.htm
12. Krathwohl, D.R., Anderson, L.: A revision of bloom's taxonomy: An overview. Theory into Practice 41(4), 212–218 (2002)
13. Kunzmann, C.: Ontology-based Competence Management for Healthcare Training Planning: A Case Study. In: Proceeding of the International Conference on Knowledge Management, Austria (2006)
14. W3C, SKOS Core Guide, http://www.w3.org/TR/swbp-skos-core-guide/
15. Johnson, B., Shneiderman, B.: Tree-Maps: a space-filling approach to the visualization of hierarchical information structures. In: Proceedings of the 2nd conference on Visualization 1991, San Diego, California. IEEE Computer Society Press, Los Alamitos (1991)
16. McMillan, J.H.: Classroom Assessment: Principles and Practice for Effective Instruction, 4th edn. Pearson Technology Group, London (2006)
17. Rolfe, I., MaPherson, J.: Formative assessment: how am I doing? Lacent 345(8953), 837–839 (1995)
18. Sewell, J.: Diagnostic assessment within the Skills for Life strategy. In: 30th IAEA Conference, Philadelphia (2004)

19. Brown, S.: Using Formative Assessment to promote student learning,
    http://www.ldu.leeds.ac.uk/news/events/documents/
    BrownPowerPoint.pdf
20. Nursing and Midwifery Council,
    http://www.nmc-uk.org/aFrameDisplay.aspx?DocumentID=171
21. Brusilovsky, P.: Adaptive Educational hypermedia, pp. 8–12 (2001)
22. Falmagne, J.-C., Cosyn, E., Doignon, J.-P., Thiery, N.: The Assessment of Knowledge, in
    Theory and in Practice. In: Integration of Knowledge Intensive Multi-Agent Systems
    (2003)
23. Antoniou, G., van Harmelen, F.: A Semantic Web Primer. The MIT Press, Cambridge
    (2004)
24. IMS QTI, IMS Question and Test Interoperability Overview,
    http://www.imsglobal.org/question/qtiv2p1pd2/
    imsqti_oviewv2p1pd2.html
25. Kalfoglou, Y.: Exploring Ontologies. In: Handbook of Software Engineering and Knowl-
    edge Engineering. Fundamentals, vol. 1. World Scientific Publishing, Washington (2001)
26. Jovanovic, J., Gasevic, D., Devedzic, V.: Ontology-Based Automatic Annotation of Learn-
    ing Content. Semantic Web and Information Systems 2(2), 91–119 (2006)
27. W3C, Resource Description Framework (RDF), http://www.w3.org/RDF/
28. W3C, OWL Web Ontology Language (OWL), http://www.w3.org/TR/owl-ref/

A New Concept Map Model for E-Learning Environments

Antonina Dattolo[1,*] and Flaminia L. Luccio[2]

[1] Dipartimento di Matematica e Informatica, Università di Udine
via delle Scienze 206, 33100 Udine, Italy
antonina.dattolo@uniud.it
[2] Dipartimento di Informatica, Università Ca' Foscari Venezia
via Torino 155, 30172 Venezia, Italy
luccio@unive.it

Abstract. Web-based education enables learners and teachers to access a wide quantity of continuously updated educational sources. In order to support the learning process, a system has to provide some fundamental features, such as simple mechanisms for the identification of the collection of "interesting" documents, adequate structures for storing, organizing and visualizing these documents, and appropriate mechanisms for creating personalized adaptive paths and views for learners.

Adaptive Educational Hypermedia seek to apply the personalized possibilities of Adaptive Hypermedia to the domain of education, thereby granting learners a lesson individually tailored to them. A fundamental part of these systems are the concept spaces, i.e., simple and clear visual layouts of concepts and relations among them.

In this paper we propose a new visual layout model in e-learning environments based on the zz-structures, which are graph-centric views capable of representing contextual interconnections among different information. In order to describe the use of these structures, we present their formal analytic description in terms of graph theory, focussing, in particular, on the formal description of two views (H and I views), and on different extensions of these notions to a number $n > 2$ of dimensions. We then apply all these formal descriptions, and some particular properties of zz-structures, to an example in the Web-based education field.

Keywords: Adaptive educational hypermedia, Concept maps, Zzstructures, Graph theory, E-learning.

1 Introduction

In the last decades, a great effort has been devoted to the diffusion of knowledge through the Web. The field of education has evolved towards this new direction, developing the so called Web-based education techniques, which enable teachers and learners to interact and exchange continuously updated educational sources.

---

* A preliminary version of this paper appeared in the Proceedings of Webist 2008 [11]; this work has been partially supported by Miur Project SOFT: Security-Oriented Formal Techniques.

J. Cordeiro et al. (Eds.): WEBIST 2008, LNBIP 18, pp. 404–417, 2009.
© Springer-Verlag Berlin Heidelberg 2009

Web-based education techniques are used in Adaptive Educational Hypermedia (AEH); these last systems apply standard techniques of Adaptive Hypermedia systems [1] to the domain of education: main task of these systems are the creation and diffusion of personalized learning material in order to grant lessons individually tailored to the learners [3]. A fundamental part of an AEH are the concept spaces [7]: they provide an ontology of the subject matter including the concepts and their relationships to one another.

Concept spaces are traditionally visualized using a concept map diagram, a downward-branching, hierarchical tree structure, which, in mathematical terms, can be represented as a directed acyclic graph, a generalization of a tree structure, where certain sub-trees can be shared by different parts of the tree.

Concept maps have got the double advantage of visually representing an information map and linking it to useful material contained in a database. Learners have a referring map to which they can come back to review previous steps, and, mostly, learn how to organize information so "it makes sense" for them. Thus, the main purpose of concept mapping is the representation of visual layouts that clarify concepts and not the production of general maps that only represent at a very high level the relations among them.

Related Works. In the literature different solutions based on traditional concept maps have been proposed [8], and suite very well small collections of information. However, they are inadequate to capture and visualize a very large amount of information. Some work has been done towards this direction with the proposal of more innovative tree visualization techniques which, on the other hand, are not well suited to represent concept maps: for example Shneiderman's Treemaps [22] and Kleiberg's Botanical trees [9] cannot easily differentiate between relationship types; other models (e. g. [5], based on hyperbolic geometry, or [23], based on S-nodes) are not able to dynamically switch from a view to another one. It is often not possible to view the entire concept space on-screen without zooming out so far that the concept and relationship labels are no longer readable. Similarly, the large number of relationships improve the difficulty of understanding the structure of the concept space.

In particular, in the e-learning field, there are many reasons to define opportune structure models for storing and visualizing concept maps:

- They allow the system to be adaptive: current approaches and tools (see WebCT, Moodle, etc.) neither support a comprehensive analysis of users' needs, demands and opportunities, nor they support a semantic analysis of texts, thus they are not adaptive.
- They provide interoperability between different adaptive systems: this feature becomes not only desirable but also necessary, as it enables the re-use of previously created material without the cost of recreating it from scratch [6].
- They simplify the authoring process, in which the user/learner may assume the role of an author (see, e.g., Wikis and Wiki farms).

For all these reasons, in our opinion, it is important to propose new models which better suite the requested requirements. We will thus focus our attention on an innovative structure, proposed in [21], the zz-structure, that constitutes the main part of a ZigZag system [20].

Previous work in this direction has shown how flexible this structure is, and how it can be specialized in different fields. It has been used for the modeling, e.g., of an information manager for mobile phones (zz-phones) [18], of the London underground train lines and stations of bioinformatics workspaces [19], of data grid systems [10], of virtual museum tours [12], of an authoring system for electronic music (Archimedes) [13]. This structure has also been used in Web-based courses [4] in order to establish attribute-based connections among Web documents retrieved by authors using search engines.

Starting from [21] and the other previously mentioned works many informal descriptions of this structure have been provided, and some preliminary formal description has been proposed in [16]. However, in our opinion, a formal and complete description of the structure may be very useful in simplifying the comprehension of the model. Nelson itself writes: "The ZigZag system is very hard to explain, especially since it resembles nothing else in the computer field that we know of, except perhaps a spreadsheet cut into strips and glued into loops ".

Contributions of this Work. The general goal of this work is to propose a formal structure for representing and visualizing a concept space. This model is based both on zz-structures and on graph theory.

Our application field is Web-based education, in which *learners* and *authors* (teachers) have to access a wide quantity of continuously updated educational sources. The learning process of learners, and the course creation/modification/organization process of authors, can be greatly simplified by providing them tools to:

1. identify the collection of "interesting" documents, for example applying semantic filtering algorithms [2], or proximity metrics on the search engine results [4];
2. store the found collection of documents in adequate structures, that are able to organize and visualize concept spaces;
3. create personalized adaptive paths and views for learners.

These three topics are the guidelines of our current research. In this paper, we focus our attention only on point 2. We assume that an author has a collection of available documents on a given topic that have to be organized in concept maps, suitable for different learners. E.g., some users could be could be doing research on a specific research area, others could be preparing a degree thesis, and so on. Thus, authors need adequate tools to organize documents in a concept space, and to create semantic interconnections and personalized maps.

We will show how identifying and defining in an analytic way the graph theoretical structure of zz-structures can both provide interesting insights to educational hypermedia designers (facilitating a deeper understanding of which model might best support the representation and interaction aims of their systems), and to learners (offering them support for Web orientation and navigation).

Summarizing, the novel contributions of this work are:

– a formal analytic graph-based description of zz-structures. Particular attention has been devoted to the formalization of two views (H and I views), present into all ZigZag implementations;

- different extensions of the concept of H and I views from a number 2 towards a number $n > 2$ of dimensions;
- a new concept map model for e-learning environments, based on our model.

The paper is organized as follows: in Section 2, we introduce the reader to zz-structures and we present some basic graph theory definitions; in Section 3, we propose our formal definition of zz-structures, and we use these structures as a reference model for representing concept maps. Finally, in Section 4 we first introduce the definition of the standard H and I views, and then we extend this definition to the non-standard n-dimensions views (with $n > 2$). Conclusion and future works conclude the paper.

2   Zz-Structures and Graph Theory

This section is introduced for consistency. If the reader has a background on the ZigZag model and on basic graph theory, can skip it.

2.1   An Introduction to Zz-Structures

Zz-structures [21] introduce a new, graph-centric system of conventions for data and computing. A zz-structure can be thought of as a space filled with cells. Each cell may have a content (such as integers, text, images, audio, etc.), and it is called *atomic* if it contains only one unit of data of one type [19], or it is called *referential* if it represents a package of different cells. There are also special cells, called *positional*, that do not have content and thus have a positional or topographical function.

Cells are connected together with links of the same color into linear sequences called *dimensions*. A single series of cells connected in the same dimension is called *rank*, i.e., a rank is in a particular dimension. Moreover, a dimension may contain many different ranks. The starting and an ending cell of a rank are called, *headcell* and *tailcell*, respectively, and the direction from the starting (ending) to the ending (starting) cell is called *posward* (respectively, *negward*). For any dimension, a cell can only have one connection in the posward direction, and one in the negward direction. This ensures that all paths are non-branching, and thus embodies the simplest possible mechanism for traversing links. Dimensions are used to project different structures: ordinary lists are viewed in one dimension; spreadsheets and hierarchical directories in many dimensions.

The interesting part is how to view these structures, i.e., there are many different ways to arrange them, choosing different dimensions and different structures in a dimension. A *raster* is a way of selecting the cells from a structure; a *view* is a way of placing the cells on a screen. *Generic views* are designed to be used in a big variety of cases and usually show only few dimensions or few steps in each dimension. Among them the most common are the *two-dimensions rectangular views*: the cells are placed, using different rasters, on a Cartesian plane where the dimensions increase going down and to the right. Obviously some cells will not fit in these two dimensions and will have to be omitted. The simplest raster is the row and column raster, i.e., two rasters which are the same but rotated of 90 degrees from each other. A cell is chosen and placed at the center of the plane (cursor centric view). The chosen cell, called focus, may be changed by moving the cursor horizontally and vertically. In a row view I, a rank is chosen and placed vertically. Then the ranks related to the cells in the vertical rank are placed horizontally. Vice versa, in the column view H, a rank is chosen and placed horizontally and the related ranks are placed vertically. All the cells are denoted by different numbers. Note that in a view the same cell may appear in different positions as it may represent the intersection of different dimensions.

2.2   Basic Graph Theory Definitions

In the following we introduce some standard graph theory notation (see also [15]).

A *graph* G is a pair $G = (V, E)$, where V is a finite non-empty set of elements called *vertices* and E is a finite set of distinct unordered pairs $\{u, v\}$ of distinct elements of V called *edges*.

A *multigraph* is a triple $MG = (V, E, f)$ where V is a finite non-empty set of vertices, E is the set of edges, and $f : E \rightarrow \{\{u, v\} \mid u, v \in V, u \neq v\}$ is a surjective function.

An *edge-colored multigraph* is a triple $ECMG = (MG, C, c)$ where: $MG = (V, E, f)$ is a multigraph, C is a set of colors, $c : E \rightarrow C$ is an assignment of colors to edges of the multigraph.

In a multigraph $MG = (V, E, f)$, edges $e_1, e_2 \in E$ are called *multiple* or *parallel* iff $f(e_1) = f(e_2)$. Thus, a graph as a particular multigraph without parallel edges.

Given an edge $e = \{u, v\} \in E$, we say that e is *incident* to u and v; moreover u and v are *neighboring* vertices. Given a vertex $x \in V$, we denote with $deg(x)$ its degree, i.e., the number of edges incident to x, and with d_{max} the maximum degree of the graph, i.e., $d_{max} = \max_{z \in V}\{deg(z)\}$. In an edge-colored (multi)graph ECMG, where $c_k \in C$, we define $deg_k(x)$ the number of edges of color c_k incident to vertex x. A vertex of degree 0 is called *isolated*, a vertex of degree 1 is called *pendant*.

A *path* $P = \{v_1, v_2, \ldots, v_s\}$ is a sequence of neighboring vertices of G, i.e., $\{v_i, v_{i+1}\} \in E$, $1 \leq i \leq s - 1$. A graph $G = (V, E)$ is *connected* if: $\forall x, y \in V$, $\exists$ a path $P = \{x = v_1, v_2, \ldots, v_s = y\}$, with $\{v_k, v_{k+1}\} \in E, 1 \leq k \leq s - 1$. Two vertices x and y in a connected graph are at *distance* d if the *shortest path* connecting them is composed of exactly d edges.

Finally, a $m \times n$ *mesh* is a graph $M_{m,n} = (V, E)$ with $v_{i,j} \in V$, $0 \leq i \leq m - 1$, $0 \leq j \leq n - 1$, and E contains exactly the edges $(v_{i,j}, v_{i,j+1})$, $j \neq n - 1$, and $(v_{i,j}, v_{i+1,j})$, $i \neq m - 1$.

3   The Formal Model

In this section, we formalize the model presented in [21] in terms of graph theory. In the rest of this paper we describe formal definitions through a simple example in the e-learning field: an author has a collection of different material (e.g., books, articles, etc.) that first wants to link through different semantic paths and then wants to merge into a unique concept space. Books that have been published by the same publisher, or books on a related topic, or books that share one author, are examples of semantic paths, which automatically generate concept maps.

3.1   Zz-Structures

A zz-structure can be viewed as a multigraph where edges are colored, with the restriction that every vertex has at most two incident edges of the same color. Differently from [16], but as mentioned in [10,17], we consider undirected graphs, i.e., edges may be traversed in both directions. A *zz-structure* is formally defined as follows.

Definition 1. (Zz-structure). *A zz-structure is an edge-colored multigraph* $S = (MG, C, c)$, *where* $MG = (V, E, f)$, *and* $\forall x \in V$, $\forall k = 1, 2, ..., |C|$, $deg_k(x) = 0, 1, 2$. *Each vertex of a zz-structure is called* zz-cell *and each edge* zz-link. *The set of isolated vertices is* $V_0 = \{x \in V : deg(x) = 0\}$.

An example of a zz-structure is given in Fig. 1. The structure is a graph, where vertices $v_1, ..., v_{14}$ represent different books, and edges of the same kind represent the same semantic connection. In particular, in this example, thick edges connect a sequence of books published by the same publisher (e.g., Elsevier), dotted edges group books that have at least an author in common, finally, normal lines link books on the same topic (e.g., hypermedia, algorithms, etc.).

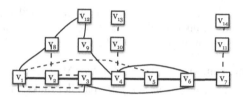

Fig. 1. A zz-structure where thick, normal and dotted lines represent three different colors

3.2   Dimensions

An alternative way of viewing a zz-structure is a union of subgraphs, each of which contains edges of a unique color.

Proposition 1. *Consider a set of colors* $C = \{c_1, c_2, ..., c_{|C|}\}$ *and a family of indirect edge-colored graphs* $\{D^1, D^2, ..., D^{|C|}\}$, *where* $D^k = (V, E^k, f, \{c_k\}, c)$, *with* $k = 1, ..., |C|$, *is a graph such that: 1)* $E^k \neq \emptyset$; *2)* $\forall x \in V$, $deg_k(x) = 0, 1, 2$.

Then, $S = \bigcup_{k=1}^{|C|} D^k$ *is a zz-structure.*

Definition 2. (Dimension). *Given a zz-structure* $S = \bigcup_{k=1}^{|C|} D^k$, *then each graph* D^k, $k = 1, ..., |C|$, *is a distinct* dimension *of S.*

From Fig. 1 we can extrapolate three dimensions, one for each different color (i.e., one for each different semantic connection). As shown in Fig. 2, we associate thick lines to dimension D^{book}, dotted lines to dimension D^{author}, and normal lines to dimension D^{topic}. Each dimension can be composed of isolated vertices (e.g., vertices v_6, v_9, v_{12} in dimension D^{author}), of distinct paths (e.g., the three paths $\{v_8, v_2, v_3, v_1, v_5\}$, $\{v_4, v_{10}, v_{13}\}$ and $\{v_7, v_{11}, v_{14}\}$ in dimension D^{author}), and of distinct cycles (e.g., the unique cycle $\{v_1, v_3, v_6, v_4, v_9, v_{12}, v_8, v_1\}$ in dimension D^{topic}).

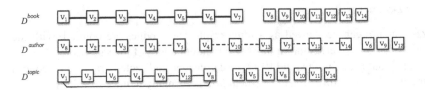

Fig. 2. The three dimensions

3.3   Ranks

Definition 3. (Rank). *Consider a dimension* $D^k = (V, E^k, f, \{c_k\}, c)$, $k = 1, \ldots, |C|$ *of a zz-structure* $S = \cup_{k=1}^{|C|} D^k$. *Then, each of the* l_k *connected components of* D^k *is called a* rank.

Thus, each rank $R_i^k = (V_i^k, E_i^k, f, \{c_k\}, c)$, $i = 1, \ldots, l_k$, is an indirect, connected, edge-colored graph such that: 1) $V_i^k \subseteq V$; 2) $E_i^k \subseteq E^k$; 3) $\forall x \in V_i^k$, $1 \leq deg_k(x) \leq 2$. A *ringrank* is a rank R_i^k, where $\forall x \in V_i^k$, $deg_k(x) = 2$.

Note that the number l_k of ranks differs in each dimension D^k, e.g. in Fig. 2, dimension D^{author} has three ranks ($\{v_8, v_2, v_3, v_1, v_5\}$, $\{v_4, v_{10}, v_{13}\}$ and $\{v_7, v_{11}, v_{14}\}$), and dimension D^{book} has a unique rank ($\{v_1, v_2, v_3, v_4, v_5, v_6, v_7\}$). A ringrank is, e.g., the cycle $\{v_1, v_3, v_6, v_4, v_9, v_{12}, v_8, v_1\}$ of dimension D^{topic}.

Definition 4. (Parallel ranks). *Given a zz-structure* $S = \cup_{k=1}^{|C|} D^k$, m *ranks* $R_j^k = (V_j^k, E_j^k, f, \{c_k\}, c)$, ($j = 1, 2, \ldots, m$, $2 \leq m \leq l_k$) *are* parallel ranks *on the same dimension* D^k, $k \in \{1, \ldots, |C|\}$ *iff* $V_j^k \subseteq V$, $E_j^k \subseteq E^k$, $\forall j = 1, 2, \ldots, m$, *and* $\cap_{j=1}^m V_j^k = \emptyset$.

In Fig. 2 the three ranks of dimension D^{author} are parallel.

3.4   Cells and Their Orientation

A vertex has local orientation on a rank if each of its (1 or 2) incident edges has assigned a distinct label (1 or -1). More formally (see also [14]):

Definition 5. (Local orientation). *Consider a rank* $R_i^k = (V_i^k, E_i^k, f, \{c_k\}, c)$ *of a zz-structure* $S = \cup_{k=1}^{|C|} D^k$. *Then,* $\exists$ *a function* $g_x^i : E_i^k \rightarrow \{-1, 1\}$, *such that,* $\forall x \in V_i^k$, *if* $\exists y, z \in V_i^k : \{x, y\}$, $\{x, z\} \in E_i^k$, *then* $g_x^i(\{x, y\}) \neq g_x^i(\{x, z\})$. *Thus, we say that each vertex* $x \in V_i^k$ *has a* local orientation *in* R_i^k.

Definition 6. (Posward and negward directions). *Given an edge* $\{a, b\} \in E_i^k$, *we say that* $\{a, b\}$ *is in a* posward *direction from a in* R_i^k, *and that b is its* posward cell *iff* $g_a^i(\{a, b\}) = 1$, *else* $\{a, b\}$ *is in a* negward *direction and a is its* negward cell. *Moreover, a path in rank* R_i^k *follows a posward (negward) direction if it is composed of a sequence of edges of value 1 (respectively, -1).*

For simplicity, given a rank R_i^k, the notation $\ldots x^{-2} x^{-1} x x^{+1} x^{+2} \ldots$, where x^{-1} represents the negward cell of x and x^{+1} the posward cell, describes the path composed by a sequence of x's negward cells, by the vertex x and by a sequence of x's posward cells, Thus, x^{-i} (x^{+i}) is a cell at distance i in the negward (posward) direction, and $x^0 = x$.

Definition 7. (**Headcell and tailcell**). *Given a rank* $R_i^k = (V_i^k, E_i^k, f, \{c_k\}, c)$, *a cell x is the* headcell *of* R_i^k *iff* $\exists$ *its posward cell* x^{+1} *and* $\not\exists$ *its negward cell* x^{-1}. *Analogously, a cell x is the* tailcell *of* R_i^k *iff* $\exists$ *its negward cell* x^{-1} *and* $\not\exists$ *its posward cell* x^{+1}.

4 Views

We now formalize the standard notion of H and I views in two dimensions, and we then propose a new definition of H and I-views in n dimensions. We also show some interesting applications of these new higher dimensional views.

In the following, $x \in R_{(x)}^a$ denotes the rank $R_{(x)}^a$ related to vertex x of color c_a.

Two Dimensions Views. Standard two dimensional views may be considered H and I views.

Definition 8. (**H-view**). *Given a zz-structure* $S = \cup_{k=1}^{|C|} D^k$, *where* $D^k = \cup_{i=1}^{l_k}(R_i^k \cup V_0^k)$, *and where* $R_i^k = (V_i^k, E_i^k, f, \{c_k\}, c)$, *the H-view of size* $l = 2m+1$ *and of focus* $x \in V = \cup_{i=0}^{l_k} V_i^k$, *on main vertical dimension* D^a *and secondary horizontal dimension* D^b *($a, b \in \{1, ..., l_k\}$), is defined as a tree whose embedding in the plane is a partially connected colored $l \times l$ mesh in which:*

- *the central node, in position* $((m+1), (m+1))$, *is the focus x;*
- *the horizontal central path (the $m+1$-th row) from left to right, focused in vertex* $x \in R_{(x)}^b$ *is:* $x^{-g} ... x^{-1} x x^{+1} ... x^{+p}$ *where* $x^s \in R_{(x)}^b$, *for* $s = -g, ..., +p$ *($g, p \leq m$).*
- *for each cell x^s, $s = -g, ..., +p$, the related vertical path, from top to bottom, is:* $(x^s)^{-g_s} ... (x^s)^{-1} x^s (x^s)^{+1} ... (x^s)^{+p_s}$, *where* $(x^s)^t \in R_{(x^s)}^a$, *for* $t = -g_s, ..., +p_s$ *($g_s, p_s \leq m$).*

Intuitively, the H-view extracts ranks along the two chosen dimensions. Note that, the name H-view comes from the fact that the columns remind the vertical bars in a capital letter H. Observe also that the cell x^{-g} (in the $m+1$-th row) is the *headcell* of $R_{(x)}^b$ if $g < m$ and the cell x^{+p} (in the same row) is the *tailcell* of $R_{(x)}^b$ if $p < m$. Analogously, the cell x^{-g_s} is the headcell of $R_{(x^s)}^a$ if $g_s < m$ and the cell x^{+p_s} is the tailcell of $R_{(x^s)}^a$ if $p_s < m$. Intuitively, the view is composed of $l \times l$ cells unless some of the displayed ranks have their headcell or tailcell very close (less than m steps) to the chosen focus.

As an example consider Fig. 3 left that refers to the zz-structure of Fig. 1. The main vertical dimension is D^{author} and the secondary horizontal dimension is D^{book}. The view has size $l = 2m+1 = 5$, the focus is v_3, the horizontal central path is $v_3^{-2} v_3^{-1} v_3 v_3^{+1} v_3^{+2} = \{v_1, v_2, v_3, v_4, v_5\}$ ($g, p = 2$). The vertical path related to $v_3^{-1} = v_2$ is $(v_3^{-1})^{-1}(v_3^{-1})(v_3^{-1})^{+1}(v_3^{-1})^{+2} = \{v_8, v_2, v_3, v_1\}$ ($g_s = 1$ and $p_s = 2$), that is $(v_3^{-1})^{-1} = v_8$ is the headcell of the rank as $g_s = 1 < m = 2$.

Analogously to the H-view we can define the I-view.

Definition 9. (**I-view**). *Given a zz-structure* $S = \cup_{k=1}^{|C|} D^k$, *and where* $D^k = \cup_{i=1}^{l_k}(R_i^k \cup V_0^k)$, *and where* $R_i^k = (V_i^k, E_i^k, f, \{c_k\}, c)$, *the I-view of size* $l = 2m+1$ *and of focus* $x \in V = \cup_{i=0}^{l_k} V_i^k$ *on main horizontal dimension* D^a *and secondary vertical dimension* D^b *($a, b \in \{1, ..., l_k\}$), is defined as a partially connected colored $l \times l$ mesh in which:*

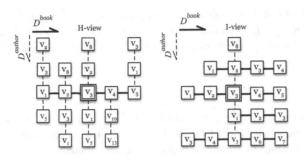

Fig. 3. H-view and I-view, related to Fig. 1.

- *the central node, in position* $((m+1),(m+1))$ *is the focus* x;
- *the vertical central path (the $m+1$-th column) from top to bottom, focused in vertex $x \in R^b_{(x)}$ is:* $x^{-u} \ldots x^{-1}xx^{+1} \ldots x^{+r}$ *where* $x^s \in R^b_{(x)}$, *for* $s = -u, \ldots, +r$ $(u, r \leq m)$.
- *for each cell x^s, $s = -u, \ldots, +r$, the related horizontal path, from left to right, is:* $(x^s)^{-u_s} \ldots (x^s)^{-1}x^s(x^s)^{+1} \ldots (x^s)^{+r_s}$, *where* $(x^s)^t \in R^a_{(x^s)}$, *for* $t = -u_s, \ldots, +r_s$ $(u_s, r_s \leq m)$.

Note that, the name I-view comes from the fact that the rows remind the horizontal serif in a capital letter I. Observe also that the cell x^{-u} (in the $m + 1$-th column) is the *headcell* of $R^b_{(x)}$ if $u < m$ and the x^{+r} (in the same column) is the *tailcell* of $R^b_{(x)}$ if $r < m$. Analogously, the cell x^{-u_s} is the headcell of $R^a_{(x^s)}$ if $u_s < m$ and the x^{+r_s} is the tailcell of $R^a_{(x^s)}$ if $r_s < m$.

As example consider Fig. 3 right. The main horizontal dimension is D^{book} and the secondary vertical dimension is D^{author}. The view has size $l = 2m + 1 = 5$, the focus is v_3, the vertical central path is $v_3^{-2}v_3^{-1}v_3v_3^{+1}v_3^{+2} = \{v_8, v_2, v_3, v_1, v_5\}$ $(u, r = 2)$. The horizontal path related to $v_3^{-1} = v_2$ is $(v_3^{-1})^{-1} \ldots (v_3^{-1})^{+2} = \{v_1, v_2, v_3, v_4\}$ (i.e., $r = 2$), whereas the horizontal path related to $v_3^{+1} = v_1$ is $\{v_1, v_2, v_3\}$ and v_1 is the headcell. Finally, the horizontal path related to $v_3^{+2} = v_5$ is $\{v_3, v_4, v_5, v_6, v_7\}$.

n-Dimensions Views. We can now extend the known definition of H and I views to a number $n > 2$ of dimensions. Intuitively, we will build $n - 1$ different H-views (respectively, I-views), centered in the same focus, with a fixed main dimension and a secondary dimension chosen among the other $n - 1$ dimensions. Formally:

Definition 10. (n-dimensions H-view). *Given a zz-structure* $S = \cup_{k=1}^{|C|}D^k$, *where* $D^k = \cup_{i=1}^{l_k}(R^k_i \cup V^k_0)$, *and where* $R^k_i = (V^k_i, E^k_i, f, \{c_k\}, c)$, *the n-dimensions H-view of size* $l = 2m + 1$ *and of* focus *s* $x \in V = \cup_{i=0}^{l_k}V^k_i$, *on dimensions* $D^1, D^2, \ldots, D^n$ *is composed of $n - 1$ rectangular H-views, of main dimension D^1 and secondary dimensions D^i, $i = 2, \ldots, n$, all centered in the same focus x.*

Analogously, we have the following:

Definition 11. (n-dimensions I-view). *Given a zz-structure* $S = \cup_{k=1}^{|C|}D^k$, *where* $D^k = \cup_{i=1}^{l_k}(R^k_i \cup V^k_0)$, *and where* $R^k_i = (V^k_i, E^k_i, f, \{c_k\}, c)$, *the n-dimensions I-view of size* $l =$

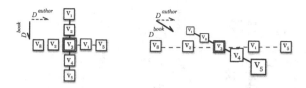

Fig. 4. Two secondary dimensions cross the focus v_3

$2m+1$ and of focus $x \in V = \cup_{i=0}^{l_k} V_i^k$, on dimensions $D^1, D^2, \ldots, D^n$ is composed of $n-1$ *rectangular I-views of main dimension D^1, and secondary dimensions D^i, $i = 2, \ldots, n$, all centered in the same focus x.*

In Fig. 3, we can distinguish only two dimensions (D^{book} and D^{author}).

To display a 3-dimensions H-view we can add a new dimension (let it be D^{topic}). This new H-view has main dimension D^{topic}, and secondary dimensions D^{book} and D^{author}. To construct this view we start from Fig. 1 using v_3 as focus, and we consider the two central paths (Fig. 4 left), related to the two secondary dimensions D^{book} and D^{author}.

The same visualization is shown in Fig. 4 right under a different perspective.

Finally, in Fig. 5 we obtain the 3-dimensions H-view where the vertical paths (on the main dimension D^{topic}) are added.

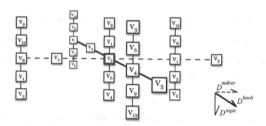

Fig. 5. An example of a 3-dimensions H-view

We can now extend this example to the n-dimensions case. In Fig. 6, we show a 5-dimensions view, considering four secondary dimensions. In our example, we have added other two dimensions ($D^{publisher\ location}$ and $D^{publication\ year}$), representing the location of the publisher and the year of publication of the article. This new view has focus v_3, size $l = 2m+1 = 5$ and main dimension $D^{publication\ year}$.

3-Dimensions Extended Views. In the 3-dimensions case, we can extend the previous definition of a 3-dimensions H (or I) view. Intuitively, we build a standard 2-dimensions H (or I) view and, starting from each of the related cells as focus, we display also the ranks in the third dimension. Formally:

Definition 12. (3-dimensions extended H-view). *Consider a zz-structure $S = \cup_{k=1}^{|C|} D^k$, where $D^k = \cup_{i=1}^{l_k} (R_i^k \cup V_0^k)$, and where $R_i^k = (V_i^k, E_i^k, f, \{c_k\}, c)$. The 3-dimensions extended H-view of size $l = 2m+1$ and of focus $x \in V = \cup_{i=0}^{l_k} V_i^k$, on dimensions D^1, D^2, D^3, is composed as follows:*

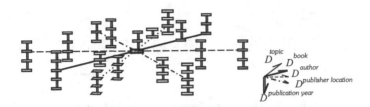

Fig. 6. A 5-dimensions H-view

- *the central path (the $m+1$-th row) from left to right, focused in vertex $x \in R^3_{(x)}$:*
  $x^{-g} \ldots x \ldots x^{+p}$, *where $x^s \in R^3_{(x)}$, for $s = -g, \ldots, +p$, $g, p \leq m$ and $g + p + 1 = l'$;*
- *l' rectangular H-views of same size l and of focuses respectively $x^{-g}, \ldots, x, \ldots, x^{+p}$, on main dimension D^1 and secondary dimension D^2.*

Analogously we can define a 3-dimensions extended I-view.

Definition 13. (3-dimensions extended I-view). *Consider a zz-structure $S = \cup_{k=1}^{|C|} D^k$, where $D^k = \cup_{i=1}^{l_k}(R_i^k \cup V_0^k)$, and where $R_i^k = (V_i^k, E_i^k, f, \{c_k\}, c)$. The 3-dimensions extended I-view of size $l = 2m+1$ and of focus $x \in V = \cup_{i=0}^{l_k} V_i^k$, on dimensions D^1, D^2, D^3, is composed as follows:*

- *the central path (the $m+1$-th column) from top to bottom, focused in vertex $x \in R^3_{(x)}$:*
  $x^{-u} \ldots x \ldots x^{+r}$, *where $x^s \in R^3_{(x)}$, for $s = -u, \ldots, +r$, $u, r \leq m$ and $u + r + 1 = l''$;*
- *l'' rectangular I-views of same size l and of focuses respectively $x^{-u}, \ldots, x, \ldots, x^{+r}$, on main dimension D^1 and secondary dimension D^2.*

As example, we start from Fig. 4 and we consider the related 2-dimensions H-view of size 5 and of focus v_3, on main dimension D^{book} and secondary dimension D^{author}. We obtain the H-view shown in Fig. 7.

Now, we change perspective and, for each cell of this view, we visualize the related ranks in dimension D^{topic} (see Fig. 8).

Star Views. A star view visualizes information related to a focus vertex and a set of n chosen dimensions. We propose a formal definition for two typologies of star views: the *star view* and the *m-extended star view*.

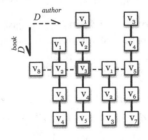

Fig. 7. Standard 2-dimensions H-view

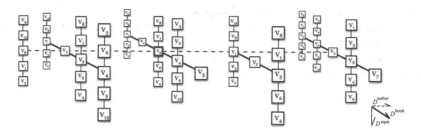

Fig. 8. A 3-dimensions *extended H*-view

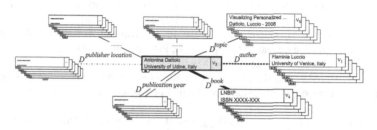

Fig. 9. A 5-extended star view

Definition 14 (Star view). *Given a zz-structure* $S = \bigcup_{k=1}^{|C|} D^k$, *where* $D^k = \bigcup_{i=1}^{l_k} R_i^k \cup V_0^k$, *and where* $R_i^k = (V_i^k, E_i^k, f, \{c_k\}, c)$, *the star view of focus* $x \in V = \bigcup_{i=1}^{l_k} V_i^k$ *and dimensions* $D^1, D^2, \quad \dots, D^n$ *is a star graph* $n+1$-star *on central vertex* x *and neighborhood* $N(x) = \{y \in V : y = x^{+1}, x^{+1} \in R_{(x)}^i, i \in \{1, \dots, |C|\}\}$.

In order to extend the number of documents directly accessible from a view, we introduce the definition of *m-extended star view*; it is based on a star view, but, for each vertex y in the neighborhood $N(x)$, adds the set of the p $(p \leq m)$ posward cells related to the given dimensions.

Definition 15 (m-extended star view). *Given a zz-structure* $S = \bigcup_{k=1}^{|C|} D^k$, *where* $D^k = \bigcup_{i=1}^{l_k} R_i^k \cup V_0^k$, *and where* $R_i^k = (V_i^k, E_i^k, f, \{c_k\}, c)$, *the m-extended star view is a star view of focus* $x \in V = \bigcup_{i=0}^{l_k} V_i^k$, *dimensions* $D^1, D^2, \dots, D^n$, *and extension constituted,* $\forall y \in N(x)$ *and* $\forall i \in \{1, \dots, |C|\}$, *by the paths* $(y^{+1}, \dots, y^{+p}) \subseteq R_{(x)}^i$ $(p \leq m)$.

A schematic example of 5-extended star view is shown in Fig. 9. In this case, the central node v_3 represents a person, and the view shows the connections along seven dimensions ($D^{topic}, D^{author}, D^{book}, D^{publication\ year}, D^{publisher\ location}, \dots$).

5 Conclusions

In this paper we have presented a formal model for the representation and the use of concepts maps in the area of Web-based education. This work is part of a larger project; current advances include:

- automatic semantic filtering methodologies;
- an extension of this model towards an open, distributed and concurrent agent based architecture;
- adaptive navigation and presentation for learners;
- authoring facilities for web-based courses.

References

1. Brusilovsky, P.: Adaptive Hypermedia. User Modelling and User-Adapted Interaction 11, 87–110 (2001)
2. Brodnik, A., Jonsson, H., Rossi, P.G., Tasso, C.: Interoperability and Semantic Filtering. Journal of e-Learning and Knowledge Society 2(2), 165–175 (2006)
3. Cristea, A., Carro, R.M., Garzotto, F.: A3EH: 4th International Workshop on Authoring of Adaptive & Adaptable Educational Hypermedia, Proceedings (2006), http://www.win.tue.nl/~acristea/A3H/
4. Andric, M., Devedzic, V., Hall, W., Carr, L.: Keywords linking method for selecting educational web resources à la ZigZag. Int. Journal of Knowledge and Learning 3(1), 30–45 (2007)
5. Cassidy, K., Walsh, J., Coghlan, B., Dagger, D.: Using Hyperbolic Geometry for Visualisation of Concept Spaces for Adaptive eLearning. In: Proc. of A3H: 1st International Workshop on Authoring of Adaptive & Adaptable Hypermedia, Dublin, Ireland, June 20 (2006)
6. Celik, I., Stewart, C., Ashman, H.: Interoperability as an Aid to Authoring: Accessing User Models in Multiple AEH Systems. In: Proc. of A3EH: 4th International Workshop on Authoring of Adaptive & Adaptable Educational Hypermedia, Dublin, Ireland, June 20 (2006)
7. Dagger, D., Conlan, O., Wade, V.: Fundamental Requirements of Personalised eLearning Development Environments. In: Proc. of E-Learn 2005, World Conference on E- Learning in Corporate, Government, Healthcare & Higher Education, Vancouver, Canada, October, 24-28, pp. 2746–2754 (2005)
8. Freire, M., Rodriguez, P.: Comparing Graphs and Trees for Adaptive Hypermedia Authoring. In: Proc. of A3EH: 3rd International Workshop on Authoring of Adaptive & Adaptable Educational Hypermedia, Amsterdam, Holland, July 19, pp. 6–14 (2005)
9. Kleiberg, E., van de Wetering, H., van Wijk, J.J.: Botanical Visualisation of Huge Hierarchies. In: Proc. IEEE Symposium on Information Visualisation, Austin, TX, October 10-12, pp. 87–94 (2001)
10. Dattolo, A., Luccio, F.L.: A new actor-based structure for distributed systems. In: Proc. of the MIPRO International Conference on Hypermedia and Grid Systems, Opatija, Croatia, May 21-25, 2007, pp. 195–201 (2007)
11. Dattolo, A., Luccio, F.L.: Formalizing a model to represent and visualize concept spaces in e- learning environments. In: Proc. of the 4th International Conference on Web Information Systems and Technologies (WEBIST), Madeira, Portugal, May 4-7, pp. 339–346 (2008)
12. Dattolo, A., Luccio, F.L.: Visualizing Personalized Views in Virtual Museum Tours. In: Proc. of the International Conference on Human System Interaction (HSI), Krakow Poland, May 25-27, pp. 109–114 (2008)
13. Canazza, S., Dattolo, A.: Open, dynamic electronic editions of multidimensional documents. In: Proc. of European Conf. on Internet and Multimedia Systems and Applications, Chamonix, France, March 14-16, pp. 230–235 (2007)
14. Flocchini, P., Mans, B., Santoro, N.: Sense of Direction: Definitions, Properties and Classes. Networks 32(3), 165–180 (1998)
15. Harary, F.: Graph Theory. Addison-Wesley, Reading (1994)

16. McGuffin, M.J.: A Graph-Theoretic Introduction to Ted Nelson's Zzstructures (January 2004), http://www.dgp.toronto.edu/~mjmcguff/research/zigzag/
17. McGuffin, M.J., Schraefel, M.C.: A Comparison of Hyperstructures: Zzstructures, mSpaces, and Polyarchies. In: Proc. of the 15th ACM Conference on Hypertext and Hypermedia (HT 2004), Santa Cruz, California, USA, August 9-13, pp. 153–162 (2004)
18. Moore, A., Brailsford, T.: Unified hyperstructures for bioinformatics: escaping the application prison. Journal of Digital Information 5(1), Article No.254 (2004)
19. Moore, A., Goulding, J., Brailsford, T., Ashman, H.: Practical applitudes: Case studies of applications. In: Proc. of 15th ACM Conf. on Hypertext and Hypermedia (HT 2004), Santa Cruz, California, USA, August 9-13, pp. 143–152 (2004)
20. Nelson, T.H.: Welcome to ZigZag (the ZigZag tutorial) (1999), http://xanadu.com/zigzag/tutorial/ZZwelcome.html
21. Nelson, T.H.: A cosmology for a different computer universe: data model mechanism, virtual machine and visualization infrastructure. Journal of Digital Information 5(1), 298 (2004)
22. Shneiderman, B.: Tree Visualisation with tree-maps: 2-d space filling approach. ACM Transactions on Graphics 11(1), 92–99 (1992)
23. Suksomboon, P., Herin, D., Sala, M.: Pedagogical resources representation in respect in ontology and course section. In: Proc. of the 3rd International Conference on Web Information Systems and Technologies (WEBIST), Barcelona, Spain, March 3-6, pp. 532–535 (2007)

Author Index